THE

Singing

Life

O F

Birds

INCLUDING CD RECORDINGS
OF ALL THE BIRDSONG
SONAGRAMS SHOWN
IN THIS BOOK

T H E

Singing
Life OF
Birds

THE ART AND SCIENCE
OF LISTENING TO BIRDSONG

Donald Kroodsma

DRAWINGS BY NANCY HAVER

HOUGHTON MIFFLIN COMPANY

BOSTON   NEW YORK

2005

For information about permission to reproduce selections from
this book, write to Permissions, Houghton Mifflin Company,
215 Park Avenue South, New York, New York 10003.

Visit our Web site: www.houghtonmifflinbooks.com.

Library of Congress Cataloging-in-Publication Data

Kroodsma, Donald E.
The singing life of birds : the art and science of listening to
birdsong / Donald E. Kroodsma.
p. cm.
Includes bibliographical references and indexes.
ISBN 0-618-40568-2
1. Birdsongs. I. Title.

QL698.5.K76 2005
598.159'4 — dc22   2004065130

Book design by Anne Chalmers
Maps by Nancy Haver and Mary Reilly
Typefaces: Minion, Miller Display, Futura, Futura Condensed

Printed in the United States of America
MP 10 9 8 7 6 5 4 3 2 1

For Melissa

Contents

The earth has music
for those who listen.

—William Shakespeare

Preface

SOMEWHERE, ALWAYS, the sun is rising, and somewhere, always, the birds are singing. As spring and summer oscillate between the Northern and Southern Hemispheres, so, too, does this singing planet pour forth song, like a giant player piano, in the north, then the south, and back again, as it has now for the 150 million years since the first birds appeared.

Ten thousand species strong, their voices and styles are as diverse as they are delightful. Some species learn their songs, just as we humans learn to speak, but others seem to leave nothing to chance, encoding the details of songs in nucleotide sequences in the DNA. Of those that learn, some do so only early in life, some throughout life; some from fathers, some from eventual neighbors after leaving home; some only from their own kind, some mimicking other species as well. Some species sing in dialects, others not. It is mostly he who sings, but she sometimes does, too. Some songs are proclaimed from the treetops, others whispered in the bushes; some ramble for minutes on end, others are offered in just a split second. Some birds have thousands of different songs, some only one, and some even none. Some sing all day, some all night. Some are pleasing to our ears, and some not.

It is this diversity that I celebrate. How the sounds of these species differ from each other is the first step to appreciating them, of course, but those questions quickly give way to "why" questions. Why do some learn and others not? Why do dialects occur in some species and not others? Why is it mainly the male who sings? It is these and similar "why" questions that so intrigue us biologists as we try to understand the individual voices that contribute to the avian chorus.

In writing about our singing planet, I can focus on only a few of its voices. The thirty stories told here are personal journeys, ones that I have traveled over the past thirty years in my quest to understand the singing bird.

Many are based on my own research and are years in the making. Others are based on just several days' experience, or even less, as I seek out birds that illustrate the research of friends and colleagues who share my passions. No matter the source, each story is based on listening and on learning how to hear an individual bird use its sounds, and each story illustrates some of the fundamentals of the science called "avian bioacoustics." Together, I hope these stories and their sounds reveal how to listen, the meaning in the music, and why we should care.

Acknowledgments

SO MANY PEOPLE play a role in putting together a life's passion. I thank my parents, Margaret and Dick Kroodsma, for letting me grow up in the middle of nowhere, the out-of-doors everywhere to explore; Olin Sewall Pettingill, Jr., for first putting a tape recorder, parabola, and headphones into my hands; John Wiens and Peter Marler, graduate and postgraduate advisors, for providing the freedom to play; graduate and undergraduate students who have worked with me at the University of Massachusetts, for fueling a contagious enthusiasm for understanding birds and their songs; and countless other enthusiasts, both professional and amateur, who have shared this passion to know birds and their sounds.

I am indebted to a number of people who helped in various ways with this book. Curt Adkisson, Mike Baker, Russ Balda, the late Luis Baptista, Jon Barlow, Greg Budney, Chris Hill, Steve Hopp, Curtis Marantz, the late Frank McKinney, Gene Morton, Gary Ritchison, and Philip Stoddard all shared their "top ten" lists of North American bird sounds. Tape-recordings from several friends were indispensable in preparing the CD: Mike Baker, Greg Budney, Lang Elliot (www.naturesound.com), Hernán Fandiño, Will Hershberger, Geoff Keller, Randy Little, Steve Pantle, and a number of others who are acknowledged with the CD. Others offered advice or other kinds of help: Mike Beecher, Bruce Byers, Russ Charif, Cal Cink, Terry Doyle, Peter Elbow, Sylvia Halkin, Chris Hill, Peter Houlihan, Steve Johnson, Carrie Jones-Birch, Geoff LeBaron, Wan-chun Liu, Curtis Marantz, Gene Morton, Jan Ortiz, Bert Pooth, Haleya Priest, Don Stap, Dave Stemple, Scott Surner, Jane Yolen, and Bill Zimmerman. Many others have contributed, too, either directly or indirectly, to the stories told here: I thank the chickadee enthusiasts who stormed Martha's Vineyard with me, for example; those who have helped reveal the bellbirds' secrets; Julio Sánchez, for his love of birds and Costa Rica; and so many others with whom I have shared this birdsong journey (thanks, Judy Wells and Roberta Pickert). I'm particularly grateful to Casey Clark, David Spector, and Mary Alice Wilson for reading and trouble-shooting the entire manuscript. And thank you, Nancy Haver, for your wonderful drawings that illustrate the text.

I especially thank the crew at the Macaulay Library of Natural Sounds at the Cornell Laboratory of Ornithology for their generous and expert help in putting the CD together: Bob Grotke, Steve Pantle, Mary Guthrie, Carol Bloomgarden, Jack Bradbury, and especially Viviana Caro, for her patience and skill in getting it all just right. I owe enormous thanks to Greg Budney, tireless friend and birdsong enthusiast, for making so many good things happen.

For the encouragement to write, and continue writing, I thank Pat Schneider and friends at Amherst Writers and Artists; the guys, meaning Bob, Carl, Deene, Fred, Larry, and Mike; my mother-in-law, Linda Parker; and especially my wife, Melissa, who was a partner in much of the research and worked hard to provide the time to get the writing done.

For seeing the potential in an unpolished manuscript, I thank Russ Galen, and for their guidance and expertise in the polishing, I thank Lisa White and Anne Chalmers at Houghton Mifflin.

Not least, for just being there and singing, I thank the birds themselves.

THE

Singing

Life

OF

Birds

1

Beginnings

GETTING STARTED is always a challenge, not only for the research scientist but also for anyone who would simply listen to birdsongs. In the first section of this chapter, I share my secret for listening: It's all in the eyes. Seeing bird sounds as we hear them greatly helps us appreciate the details in the sounds and the differences among them.

In the second section, I share my personal beginnings as a scientist, as I tell of my quest for understanding how a young male songbird, a Bewick's wren, gets his song. After two years of hard work and good fortune, I found not only the answer to my simple question but also a lifelong passion. In the process, I also learned how to listen.

Next, for those who wish to learn how to listen, the American robin in the backyard provides ample opportunity. Anyone truly listening to a robin will begin to hear details once thought impossible. Listening to robins also prepares one for other adventures, such as identifying all of those "robin sound-alikes," hearing the details in how all birds sing, and asking and answering questions of all kinds (that is, "doing science") by oneself.

In the fourth section of this chapter I show how careful listening to a robin evokes the kinds of questions that are addressed throughout this book. How a bird acquires its songs, what they're good for during daily activities, how they've evolved over millions of years, and how they're controlled in the brain and in the dual voice boxes is what this book is all about. These topics may be the focus of a major section in the book, or merely a subplot within an account, but they are always there.

Hearing and Seeing Bird Sounds

"You must have exceptional ears," people often say to me as they lament how tone-deaf their ears must be in comparison. "No," I reply, "they're actually pretty pathetic, and I have no musical ability whatsoever. But, like most of us, I have well-trained eyes, and it is with my eyes that I hear."

Consider my first serious venture into studying birdsong. I tape-recorded the wren in my backyard and struggled with what seemed to be an endless variety of songs that I was hearing. But then I graphed those songs, making sound spectrograms, or sonagrams, which display frequency changes over time, the essence of a musical score. I could then listen to the songs as I followed along with my eyes. I saw the notes rise or fall in frequency and saw the rhythm of the song in how its elements were distributed over time. I sketched each song on a note card and took the note cards to the field to listen there. Soon I could identify each of the 15 to 20 different songs that a male sang and could hear how songs changed from bird to bird over short distances on the wildlife refuge where I worked. Today, some 30 years since I left those Bewick's wrens in Oregon, I can still in my mind both see and hear those song variations.

How do I hear with my eyes? As a bird sings, I see the rudiments of a sonagram form in my mind. The sounds scroll right to left across my mind's eye, sweeping up and down in frequency, with notes repeated rapidly or slowly and with pauses of varying durations; at any given time, I see his last several seconds, with earlier songs dropping out of view on the left and new songs appearing on the right. It's an unavoidable habit developed from years of watching songs display this way on my computer screen. It is the patterns I see that enhance the beauty I hear.

Figure 1. When these three woodpeckers (the sapsucker is also a woodpecker) slam their bill into a tree trunk, they make noisy sounds that cover a wide frequency spectrum. In these sonagrams one can see the differences in their drumming that can be heard on the CD (tracks 1–3). The downy and hairy woodpeckers drum at a steady pace, but the pace of the larger hairy woodpecker is much faster. The sapsucker's drum has a distinctive rhythm, rapid at first, then slow and fairly steady, with a few irregular beats at the end. In this sapsucker sonagram, all but the first three strikes are double hits (as described in the text); in each double strike, the first strike is louder and therefore darker in the sonagram.

Note: See Appendix I, page 366, for a detailed description of the contents of each track.

For each sonagram, the track number and time on the CD where that sound can be heard is indicated at the beginning of the time axis; just after 0 (the start of the sonagram at time zero), a track number is provided together with the starting time on that particular track. For example, "T1, 0:01" indicates that the sound can be heard beginning at time 0:01 on track 1 of the CD. Here I also want to point out that I have used time and frequency scales for sonagrams that best show the singing features of a particular species; as a result, the scales differ from figure to figure, so please check the scales if you compare sonagrams in one figure with those in another.

So, before what you may consider the "good stuff," before you even peek at the following accounts on wrens and robins and our other songsters, I encourage you to consider the sonagram. Put aside any sonagram-a-phobia that you might have built up over the years so that you can now see and hear birdsong in an entirely new way. Trust me—it'll be well worth your effort. (Although I ask you to give the sonagrams a try, I also want to assure you that this book and CD can be enjoyed by anyone who decides that sonagrams aren't any fun. If you so decide, just enjoy the stories and accompanying sounds on the CD and skip over the sonagram figures.)

The elements of a sonagram are pretty simple and straightforward (figures 1–5). The horizontal axis is time, and the sonagram is read from left to right, just as one would expect. On the vertical axis is frequency. A typical scale runs from 0 to 8,000 cycles per second, with "cycles per second" being the number of times per second that air compresses and rarefies to produce the sound that we hear. Keep in mind that middle A on a piano is produced by a string tuned to vibrate 440 times a second; one octave above middle A is a

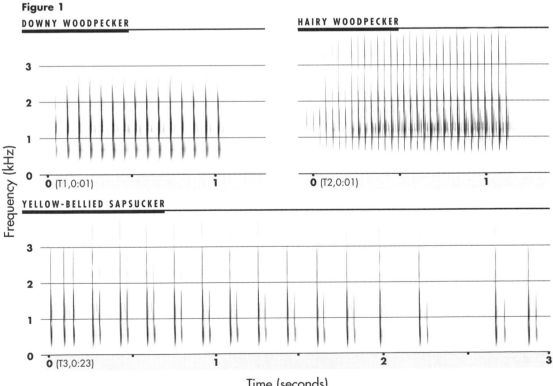

Figure 1

DOWNY WOODPECKER

HAIRY WOODPECKER

YELLOW-BELLIED SAPSUCKER

Frequency (kHz)

Time (seconds)

string tuned to vibrate at 2 × 440, or 880 times a second, and four octaves above middle A is 7,040 vibrations per second (440 × 2 × 2 × 2 × 2). Most bird sounds fall within this human-audible range. For frequency, a couple of abbreviations are standard practice. Instead of *cycles per second* we use *Hz*, short for *hertz*, a unit named for the German physicist H. R. Hertz (1857–1894). And because we usually deal in *thousands of Hz*, we abbreviate *kilohertz* to *kHz*. As a result, *8,000 cycles per second* is more simply written *8 kHz*. A third important feature of sound, in addition to time and pitch, is the relative amplitude of the sounds, which is revealed by how dark the elements are in the sonagram. Loud sounds are darker on sonagrams than softer sounds.

Music buffs will note that the frequency axis routinely used on a sonagram is not "logarithmic" as in musical notations, but rather "linear." On the sonagram, each 1,000 Hz occupies the same amount of space on the vertical axis; in musical notations, however, frequency is expressed in octaves, with each octave spanning a doubling of frequency even though occupying an

Figure 2

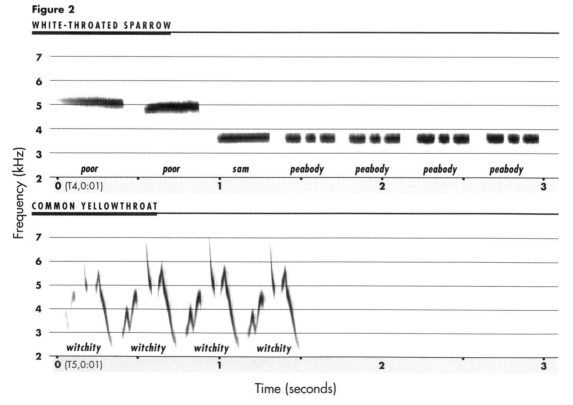

WHITE-THROATED SPARROW

COMMON YELLOWTHROAT

Time (seconds)

The Singing Life of Birds

equal amount of space on the scale. The octave from 440 to 880 Hz, for example, occupies the same vertical space as the octave from 880 to 1,760 Hz, even though the first octave spans 440 Hz and the second one 880 Hz. Using a logarithmic scale makes sense because of how our ears work, since we hear the relative pitch of sounds in a logarithmic scale. For sonagrams of bird sounds, however, the linear scale is preferred because the sonagrams on a logarithmic scale always feel squashed, all of the details squeezed together. And it is the details that we desperately want to see, expanded in a way that we can best appreciate them.

On the sonagram, different sounds have a predictable appearance. A slammed door or a gunshot is a "noisy" sound, consisting of a complex sound spanning many frequencies, and on a sonagram this sound is a brief, vertical mark spanning several thousand hertz. A pure whistle held at 1,000 Hz would be a horizontal line on the sonagram. Slur the whistle down the scale, and the marking on the sonagram slides down, too. One begins to see the possibilities —it's that simple.

Consider what a few bird sounds look like. The noisy drums of woodpeckers are a series of vertical marks on the sonagram, with each pulse the result of the woodpecker slamming its bill into the tree trunk once (figure 1). Species differ in how rapidly they drum and in their rhythm. The downy and hairy woodpeckers (tracks 1, 2; see Appendix I for a detailed description of track contents), for example, hammer the tree at a constant rate, the downy about 15 times a second, the hairy much more rapidly, about 25 times a second.

In contrast, I hear the halting performance of a sapsucker in its uneven spacing of the elements, with three rapid blows followed by slower ones,

Figure 2. Many bird songs consist of pure tones, either held at a constant pitch or rapidly slurred over time. The distinctive rhythm of this white-throated sparrow's *poor-sam-peabody* song (track 4; see page 367 in Appendix I) is clearly revealed in the sonagram, with three longer whistles followed by four series of briefer whistles, the frequency dropping after the first two long whistles. It's actually *poor-poor-sam-peabody-peabody-peabody-peabody* (lower your voice at *sam*). Given the northern range of this sparrow, some prefer *ohhhh-ohhhh-sweet-Canada-Canada-Canada-Canada*. The song of the common yellowthroat (track 5; see page 368 in Appendix I) also consists of pure tones, but they are slurred rapidly up and down, so rapidly it is difficult for our ears to hear the details in this song (but try it at half and quarter speed). This particular song consists of four identical phrases, a song that might be rendered *witchity-witchity-witchity-witchity*. The first *witchity* is not as loud as the others and is therefore lighter in the sonagram. Each *witchity* consists of three identifiable notes: a rising M-shaped note, a simple high note slurred down, and then a descending inverted V.

tapering off at the end (track 3). Studying the sapsucker's sonagram, I was surprised to see that my ears weren't telling me all there is to know about this sapsucker drum: Each of the blows after the first three is actually a double hit, the first hit much louder than the second so that I don't hear the second. When I slow the sounds to quarter speed (easily done with the Raven software described in Appendix II), the double blow is clearly audible, a major blow followed by a mere tap.

The songs of other species are more pleasing to humans because they consist of whistled notes or purer tones. In the *poor sam peabody* song of the white-throated sparrow (figure 2), each whistle is held on a single frequency, with the first three whistles long and the last ones brief and in triplets; both the eye and the ear reveal that the frequency of the first two long whistles is higher than that of the rest of the song (track 4).

Most birdsong consists of whistles that are slurred either up or down in pitch and in a distinctive rhythm. The *witchity-witchity* song of the common yellowthroat (figure 2) appears in a sonagram as a repeated series of three or four notes, each *witchity* phrase clearly evident, the overall rhythm of the song unmistakable. Listen to the rhythm at normal speed, then listen to the song slowed down to half and quarter speed so that you can hear the individual notes (track 5).

Two other sparrows help to coordinate our ears and eyes. Listen to and see the "bouncing ball" day song of the field sparrow (figure 3), how it begins slowly, the slurred whistles coming far more rapidly toward the end of the song (first two songs in track 6); it looks in the sonagram just as it sounds to our ears. The bouncing ball song is the one most commonly heard from a field sparrow, but visit him before sunrise and you'll hear a more complex song,

Figure 3. Songs of field sparrows also consist largely of rapidly slurred, pure tones delivered in distinctive rhythms (track 6). The most familiar song of this sparrow is the "bouncing-ball" daytime song, one that begins slowly and then accelerates toward the end. In the sonagram, see the three longer whistles at the beginning, how the fourth is much briefer, and how successive notes are even briefer and slurred downward, the overall song rising slightly in frequency. The more complex "dawn song" of this field sparrow consists of four distinct sections. The overall effect again is to accelerate, in three ways: during the first phrase, as the first of the five whistles is well out in front; from the first to the second phrase, with the notes in the second phrase delivered more rapidly than those in the first; and then again from the third to the fourth phrase, as the three slowly delivered notes in the third phrase give way to the most rapidly repeated notes in the last phrase. What you see in the sonagram is what you hear on the CD.

Last reminder: From track 6 on, the detailed notes in Appendix I become increasingly important for understanding how to listen to the sounds on the CD.

often consisting of four parts. Watch the lower sonagram in figure 3 as you listen to the third song in track 6; hear the song begin slowly with five boldly slurred whistles, followed by a more rapid trill, then three slowly repeated whistles, finally ending with a rapid trill. Listen to the fourth song on the track and you'll hear the same overall pattern, but the song differs in subtle ways. This time he begins with only three of the bold whistles, for example. (This difference between presunrise and daytime singing occurs in close relatives of the field sparrow, too—see the accounts of chipping sparrows and Brewer's sparrows, pages 313–325.)

The fox sparrow is one of the finest singers in North America (figure 4). Listen to two songs of the "red" fox sparrow (track 7), the form found from Newfoundland across Canada to Alaska; listen to the songs again and again, if necessary, while concentrating on the sonagram, and soon you'll both hear and see the bold whistles in this song. Next try another fox sparrow, the "large-billed" form of the California Sierras. In the first song of this bird on track 7, you'll hear two down-slurred whistles at the outset of the song, but then the

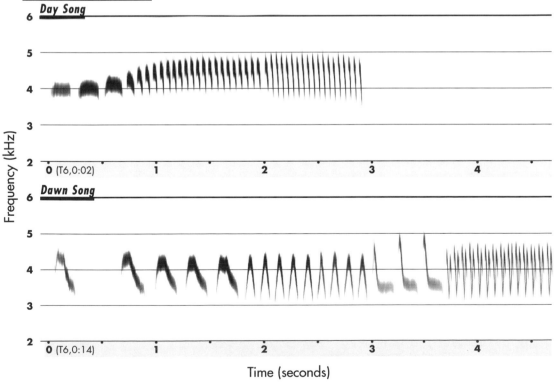

Figure 3: FIELD SPARROW

Day Song

Dawn Song

Frequency (kHz)

Time (seconds)

pace picks up as the following elements are delivered far more rapidly. Hear and see the rhythm in the song, which ends with five rapidly repeated notes. The second song from this male begins with the same two whistles, but then the overall rhythm is strikingly different, and it ends with a brief, down-slurred whistle that sounds a lot like the *klear* call of a flicker. Listen to the third and fourth songs of this male and you'll hear different songs again. (Sorry, I need to digress just once more, as these fox sparrows have such inter-

Figure 4

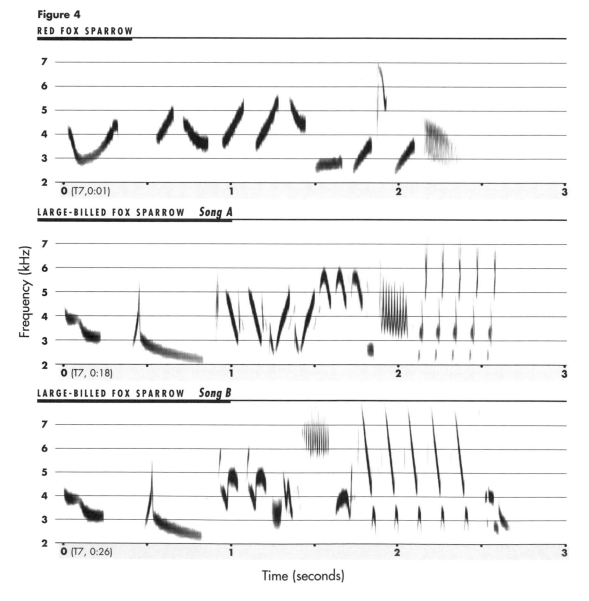

RED FOX SPARROW

LARGE-BILLED FOX SPARROW *Song A*

LARGE-BILLED FOX SPARROW *Song B*

Time (seconds)

The Singing Life of Birds

esting stories to tell. Males of the red fox sparrow variety have just one song apiece, but male large-bills have many more, delivered so that consecutive songs are always different. It's likely that there are actually four different fox sparrow species in North America, a conclusion based in part on differences that can be heard in their singing.)

Just one more example will suffice, the common loon (figure 5). Nearly everyone knows their sounds, as they're in the background of all movies set in the north country (and many movies set elsewhere, too, whenever eerie, haunting sounds are needed—the movie industry has never worried about biologically correct background sounds). Listen to what are called the yodels, the wails, and the tremolos of the loon in track 8 and follow along in figure 5. In the yodel, see and hear the rhythm of the rising and falling frequencies; in the wail, see and hear the sudden frequency shifts, how the two birds in this recording each have a distinctive wail; in the tremolo see and hear the voice waver.

That's basically it. Pretty simple stuff.

Throughout this book I provide sample sounds on the CD and a figure with matching sonagrams. By listening to the CD and watching the sonagrams in the figures, you'll quickly catch on.

If you want more fun with sonagrams right now and can't wait, here's what I recommend. For relatively simple songs, go to the eastern phoebe (figure 18, p. 85), the black-capped chickadee (figure 26, p. 138), the Bachman's sparrow (figure 43, p. 229), the whip-poor-will (figure 54, p. 289), or the eastern wood-pewee (figure 57, p. 306); then find the appropriate track on the CD

Figure 4. More songs of sparrows, this time the elegant fox sparrow. At the top is the song of a male "red" fox sparrow, the form of this sparrow that occurs across Canada from Newfoundland to Alaska (track 7). Most of the song consists of bold whistles slurred up or down in frequency. At the end of the song is a broader-frequency "smudge," a note that will sound buzzy to the ears. The third to the last note is brief and high-pitched, a mere "click" to our ears; listen for it on the CD. The lower two songs (also track 7) are from a male "large-billed" fox sparrow in the California Sierras. Each of the songs begins with two bold, down-slurred whistles, but after that their patterns differ. In song A, notice the overall pattern after the two bold introductory whistles: a pair of falling notes, a pair of rising notes, three higher notes, a brief low whistle, a smudge that will be a brief buzz, and five rapidly repeated notes at the end. In song B, see the pair of notes after the introductory whistles, a lower note, a higher buzz, a brief low whistle before the rapidly repeated series, followed by a couple of low notes at the end of the song (notes that sound to many experienced listeners like the *klear* call of a northern flicker). Seeing these differences in the two songs helps one to hear the differences on the CD.

and feast your eyes and ears on the sights and sounds of these birds. If you're ready, try some of the fantastically complex songs for the following species: northern mockingbird (figures 15, 16, pp. 72, 77), the brown thrasher (figure 37, p. 194), the sage thrasher (figure 39, p. 205), the eastern winter wren (figure 41, p. 218), and the Brewer's sparrow (figure 62, p. 323). Or skim through the text, stopping at any figure with sonagrams that intrigue you, and then find the appropriate track on the CD. Listen while you look, and your ears will soon be the envy of all who accompany you in the field.

Before you know it, you might want to make your own sonagrams, to see the songs that you hear on the CDs in your library or to see the songs that you yourself have recorded. Fortunately, with the modern computers that most of us already have and with free or inexpensive software, anyone can now easily make sonagrams in the comfort of home (or even in the field as you listen to the birds there, if you like). See Appendix II for how to tape-record and how to make your own sonagrams.

Give the seeing a try—it's a small step, but it can open your ears to a whole new world of birdsong.

The Bewick's Wren

JUNE 5, 2000. I cycle among the sea of tents and out of the campground well before dawn, the others to arise and follow later. Just yesterday, the 125 of us had left St. George and bicycled the 43 miles here, to Zion Canyon Campground, the gateway to one of Utah's natural wonders, Zion National Park. We are on "Cycle Utah," an annual event organized by the Adventure Cycling Association, and our goal is to bicycle through Zion and Bryce

Figure 5. Ah, the common loon, the wild and magical and eerie sounds of the north country (track 8). Here are three of the most common sounds made by loons. In the yodel, see and hear how the six sounds actually consist of three pairs, the first sound in each pair distinctly different in shape from the second; both sounds rise, are held at a higher frequency, and then drop, but the second is sustained longer and rises before ending more abruptly. See (and hear, of course) how the wail begins on one frequency, suddenly shifts to a higher frequency, and then abruptly drops down again; two birds exchange wails here, the wail of the first bird longer than that of the second (the smudges after each element of the wail are its echoes). In the tremolo, two birds also call together, one rapidly following the other; for both birds, the sonagram and the sound itself reveal a tremolo that rapidly alternates between two frequencies.

Canyon National Parks, up and over Cedar Breaks National Monument, and back to St. George, 270 miles of bliss over six days.

In the dark I now navigate the narrow bike path, the Virgin River gurgling on my right, western wood-pewees already singing *peer* overhead. Then up onto the deserted highway, and only two miles to the intersection. There I can-

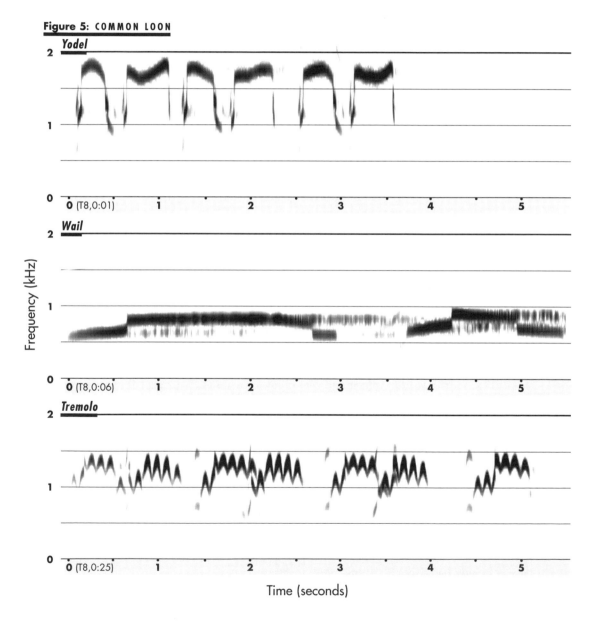

Figure 5: COMMON LOON

Yodel

Wail

Frequency (kHz)

Tremolo

Time (seconds)

not help but pause. At the entrance to Zion Canyon I'm tempted to ride it once more, to hear the world awake among the multicolored sculptures and massive vertical cliffs. But not today. We must move on today, and it is during the dawn chorus that I must experience the steep ascent out of the canyon, the six switchbacks climbing a thousand feet over two miles, and then, I regret, through a mile-long tunnel to another world.

As I now pedal east, looming against the lightening sky behind me are Mount Kinesava, the West Temple, and the Towers of the Virgin, rising the better part of a mile above the canyon floor. A canyon wren song echoes from high on the rock cliff to the right, a hermit thrush flutes his song in the oaks to the left. The oaks are abuzz with black-throated gray warblers, the *your-teeeeeeee* of spotted towhees escorting me up the road.

But now it is only the songs of the Bewick's wrens that I hear. One sings from the left, and another just beyond cascading Pine Creek on the right, each animated, with *see* notes punctuating the silence between songs. They match each other song for song, back and forth, each wren choosing to sing that particular song in his repertoire that best matches what the other is singing (a common practice among songbirds, called "matched countersinging"). Crossing the creek and switching back to the right, I soon listen to both from above—they have now changed their songs to a different tune, no longer matching each other. Soon hairpinning back to the left, I pedal higher still, the wren songs buoying me up from the valley floor below. Midway through my climb I pause to contemplate the glowing, red-rock faces of the mountains basking in dawn's first light, and myself, basking in the songs of the Bewick's wrens.

I realize that my journey began over 30 years ago, when I was just a few months out of college and searching for a research project for my graduate degree. From my home base at Oregon State University I had driven west into the rain forest of the Coast Range and on to the Pacific coast, then back across the Willamette Valley to the east, into the Cascade Mountains and out the other side into the central Oregon desert. I had searched high and low for this project, for any project that involved birds, but found none—until I heard the Bewick's wren singing in my backyard. That was in January 1969, on a brilliantly sunny day after a rare snowfall in Corvallis.

I soon read all I could find about songbirds and their songs and realized that I needed to know the answer to a very simple question, one that no one else had adequately answered: Just how does a singing bird get his song? Does a young wren learn his songs from his father (mothers don't sing), or does he learn from other birds after leaving home, or perhaps both, or neither? This question was important, the center of considerable controversy. I gambled my degree in search of this answer, and just a little over two years later, I stood in the early morning darkness at the nearby wildlife refuge, tape-recording equipment ready, waiting for the payoff.

MARCH 20, 1971. Bird #326 . . . Next to the dark thicket of nutka rose and blackberry, beneath the silhouettes of still-leafless Oregon ash and oak, I wait to learn what he will teach me. He sleeps nearby, perhaps in the thicket, perhaps in a cavity in one of the aging tree trunks, but soon he will awake and sing.

I am ready. Hanging from the strap slung over my left shoulder is my Uher tape recorder, the most affordable reel-to-reel recorder a graduate student can buy. In my right hand I grip the wooden trowel handle I have fashioned onto the back of my dark green, aluminum parabolic reflector. At the focal point of this two-foot dish is the microphone that will capture his songs and convert them to electrical impulses, to be encoded magnetically in the ferric oxide particles on the quarter-inch tape moving at seven and a half inches a second across the recorder's heads. Headphones straddle the stocking cap atop my head, waiting to be slipped down over my ears so I can monitor his every sound. In the daypack slung over my right shoulder are extra tapes, each 900 feet long, each ready to capture 24 minutes of singing from him and his neighbors.

It was just yesterday that I rediscovered him. I walked the bottomland along Muddy Creek that late winter day, stopping to check each of the territorial males. Over the past two years I had caught most of them in my nets and slipped a unique combination of three colored bands on their legs. Now all I needed was a glimpse through the binoculars to see the legs and identify who he was. If he didn't come out to inspect me, I'd get his attention with that old birding trick, a few brief swishing *spishes,* pulsating white noise hissing from my lips. With just a flash of the legs I'd memorize the combination of three bands there and then consult my notebook with its banding records for the past two years. Most of the sightings were expected: the same male on the same territory where he had been last year, and perhaps even the year before, so that I knew his band combination by heart. A few of the males were unbanded, of unknown history. But here finally was a band combination I didn't immediately recognize—a definite newcomer, a yearling, exactly what

I had hoped for. I studied his legs: a single aluminum band on the left and two plastic bands on the right, a dark green band over a red one. Racing through the pages of my notebook, I found him, and instantly realized that my gamble had paid off.

I had last seen him almost a year ago, on June 19, when he was a little over two weeks old. Just out of the nest, where he had spent roughly the first 14 days of his life, he and his two siblings kept low in the shrubbery and the blackberry tangles in the old fence line near the refuge headquarters, persistently calling *sc-i-i-t sc-i-i-t* as they pleaded for food from their parents. Anticipating their direction of movement, I saw the perfect setup. Down the fencerow they would move, coming to a gap in the blackberries beneath the shade of the oak.

To the left of this gap I drove one of my poles into the ground, then stretched the six-meter-long black mist net across the gap to the right, driving my other pole into the ground there. I quickly unfurled the hairnet-like mesh, now stretching from the ground up to five feet, entirely blocking their path with a net that was all but invisible in the oak's shade on this windless day. I next circled around behind the noisy fledglings and gently prodded them down the fencerow. At the gap's edge they perched briefly in the open, *sc-i-i-t sc-i-i-t,* forever hungry, seemingly curious as they inspected me—and unsuspecting, too, as they attempted to flit the short distance across the gap to the next blackberry tangle, falling harmlessly into the pockets of my net.

Birds #324, 325, and 326. I had caught and banded my first wren in early 1969 and had now caught more than 300 birds on Finley National Wildlife Refuge just south of Corvallis. The father of these three fledglings was #94, caught earlier in the year, but their mother had eluded my nets. The father and each of his offspring now had on their legs a unique combination of one aluminum band and two colored bands that would allow me to identify these birds as individuals whenever I encountered them again. Each bird was an individual, part of a family, with its own genealogy. The 100 or so wren pairs who defended territories on this refuge were all related to each other in some way, as parents and their offspring, brothers and sisters, uncles and aunts, grandparents and grandkids, all interwoven into this wren society among the oaks and ashes and tangled undergrowth.

Now, almost a year after I had first caught him, here is 326 again, silver left, dark green over red right, ready to sing me his story. Like the other male wrens on the refuge, I expect that he will have from 13 to 20 different songs in his repertoire. He'll begin singing any minute now, about half an hour before sunrise, though this early in the season and with the temperature in the low 40s, he'll not sing with much enthusiasm. But I am eager to capture whatever he does sing, eager to learn the details of each of his songs.

His neighbors here are an important part of his story, too. To the east is 221, to the north 223, and to the west 229, each on the same territory as last year, each at least two years old. When these neighbors awaken I will tape-record them, too, racing from one bird to the next to capture on tape all the different songs that they sing. By whom will 326 have been most influenced? Whose songs are his most like? The father? One of these neighbors? The evidence will be in the fine details of the songs that they all sing.

I would have loved to follow 326 over the past 10 months, to see how he arrived here. Last June, he entered the world just a little over half a mile to the north. During early July, when only four to five weeks old, he left home in search of his own territory. He undoubtedly wandered some, searching for a home of his own over several weeks, but by early August was most likely already here, perhaps first carving out a small territory in the thicket of black-berries and roses where I now stand. I had found lots of other young birds fighting for their territories last August, but somehow I'd overlooked 326.

Had I been here last August, I would have heard his jingly beginnings. He would have babbled continuously in his scratchy, uncertain voice, some-times for 10 to 20 seconds, mixing his innate *see* call with snippets of songs that he had already learned from the adult wrens during his travels. His early efforts would have been so unlike those of the adult males he was imi-tating; an adult male sings a sharp, crisp two-second song and then pauses for five or six seconds before repeating it precisely, up to 50 times in a row (figures 6, 7). I couldn't help but chuckle at the contrast between the young male and the adults, partly because my 18-month-old daughter back home was also babbling as she practiced all that she knew in a continuous, non-sensical stream of sounds (listen to my daughter and the wrens on tracks 9–11). How similar we are to these songbirds, I muse, as we both learn our adult sounds, with their songs and our speech also showing dialects from place to place.

Bird #326 no doubt started learning his songs while still with his father, who often sang just before feeding him. En route to this location he heard still other males; and then, here, as he established a foothold in the tangles, the res-ident adults harassed him, singing their "go away" threats in his face, giving him ample opportunity to memorize the local songs. In the face of such threats, he retired to the dense underbrush, where he softly babbled, never

Song A

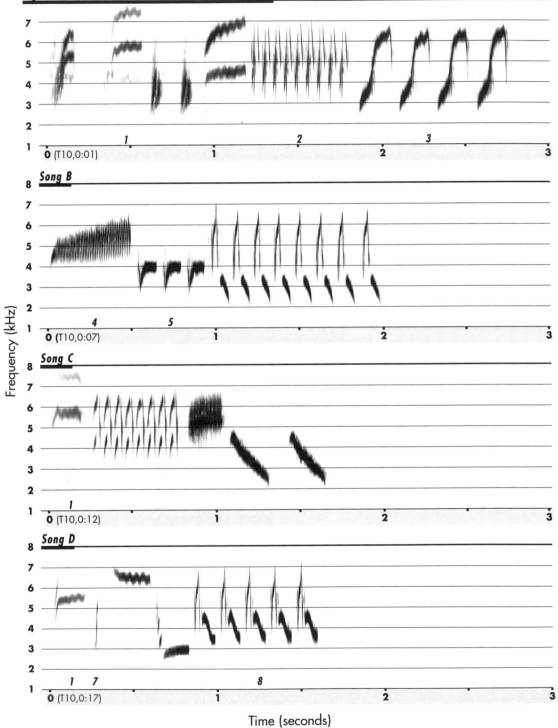

The Singing Life of Birds

singing loudly out in the open like an adult. Through September, October, and into November he sang, gradually improving his efforts; he sang little during the rainy winter, but then revved up again early in the new year, until I found him, just yesterday, waiting to tell me his story.

I stand here, waiting, increasingly amused at how I came to be here in the dark on this late winter morning waiting for this prized wren and his neighbors to sing. Chance and good fortune, not careful planning, were the key elements. It was during the summer of '68 that, by chance, I learned how to tape-record birdsongs at the "bug camp," more formally known as the University of Michigan Biological Station, at Pellston, Michigan. That experience and others in the beginning and advanced courses taught by the famed Olin Sewall Pettingill, Jr., taught me to listen, so that a half year later I was ready to hear that singing wren in my Oregon backyard. By chance, readily available to me then were tape-recording equipment and a machine called a sonagraph, which graphed the songs so that I could see and study them.

As part of a required course project during my first year of graduate school at Oregon State University, I chose to tape-record that wren in my backyard and graph his songs. I listened and looked, and before long I could hear, with the unaided ear, that he'd sing 40 to 50 renditions of one kind, then introduce another, and another, until he had no new songs to reveal. In all, he had 16 different songs, each one easily distinguished from the others. At night he roosted under the eaves of the neighbor's shed, where he fluffed into a ball of feathers protected from the elements.

Just one male, in my backyard, is where it started, "it" being both a research project for a graduate thesis *and* a lifelong journey. As I listened to other wrens sing at the Finley refuge just 10 miles away, I realized that their songs were different. Neighbors had similar songs, but distant males were different. Dialects—these wrens had song dialects. I knew that one of the big unanswered questions about birdsong centered on the importance of these song dialects: Does a young male songbird learn from his father and then set-

Figure 6. Four different songs of an adult Bewick's wren (track 10; a typical male would have at least a dozen more). See how sharp and crisp these sonagrams are, how he has mastered the intricate details of the elements in each song. In song A, for example, see how precisely he repeats the elements in phrases 2 and 3 (selected notes or phrases are identified with numbers beneath the sonagram); see the same precision in other repeated elements of songs B, C, and D. Hear that precision, too, as you listen to these four songs in track 10 and identify each of the phrases as he sings. (Phrases or notes are numbered to identify elements in figure 7 that the young male is learning.)

tle nearby, within the same dialect, so that males of the same dialect consist of close relatives? Or does the young male disperse from home, rejecting whatever he learned from his father, instead learning the songs of the new dialect where he settles? The answers were important, as they would help us understand song dialects, one of the most intriguing consequences of song learning in birds.

Answers to these questions for these wrens now await me in the Finley refuge, just minutes away, when 326 and his neighbors will begin singing . . . *Plit plit.* The first to be heard is 229, to the west, as he leaves his roost. After a few calls of the type these wrens use in their territorial fights, he begins to sing. I swing the parabola his way, turn on the recorder, and begin a marathon recording session as 326 follows soon after, then his neighbors to the north and east. At first each male sings perhaps only 10 renditions of each song before switching to a new one, then 20, 30, and eventually 40. With the sun just peeking over the horizon, I now see 326, singing at the top of an ash tree, a little cloud of his breath forming above his thrown-back head as he exhales his song. For four hours I stay, walking from male to male, recording each, and returning over the following days and weeks, to make sure that I have captured all that each can sing.

Back at the university I use the sonagraph to print a picture, or sonagram, of each of the songs. It's a magical machine, this sonagraph, a gray metal cube two feet on a side with a stainless steel drum perched atop it — magical because it converts sounds to sights, and it is the sight of sound that is so exciting, allowing my eyes to compare the details of songs from one bird to another.

Figure 7. The drunken monologue of the young Bewick's wren (track 11). See how uncertain he is, how he blurts out one sound after another in a continuous, babbling sequence (unlike an adult, who would sing one particular song over and over before switching to another). See how successive elements differ, because he doesn't yet have good control over his voice box (as in phrases 2 and 3 in the top sonagram; see also the last phrases in each of the other rows). Notice also how the young bird is learning the adult songs piece by piece. He blurts out phrases 3 and 2 in rapid succession, for example, but he'll eventually reverse that to sing adult song A (figure 6), which has phrase 2 followed by 3. In the second row, key elements are missing between phrases 7 and 8 (see adult song D in figure 6); he begins singing what appears to be phrase 8, but that quickly transforms into another phrase that he's also practicing, as if he doesn't yet have the two separated in his mind. Other elements are all out of place, too, but the young male will eventually get it right, just as my daughter also got her words all in their correct places, too, and now as a physician can speak either English or Spanish to her patients (track 9).

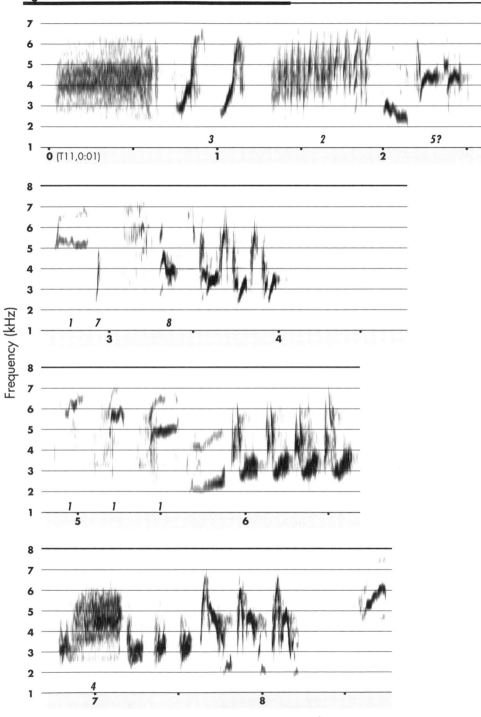

Frequency (kHz)

Time (seconds)

BEWICK'S WREN

Tweaking the dials and adjusting the settings of this sonagraph, I record one song onto the metal surface of a large rotating disc deep inside. Satisfied with the settings, I then place a blank piece of sonagram paper onto the drum and throw the switch to "reproduce," which sets the drum spinning rapidly. Lifting a stylus from the column beside the drum, I gently push it against the spinning sonagram. Gears slowly work the stylus up the column, and as the sonagraph detects sounds at various times and pitches, a spark jumps the gap between the stylus and the metal drum, burning the song's picture into the sonagram paper. Amid a cloud of smoke and the acrid smell of ozone I work quickly, taking as little as five minutes to produce a sonagram of each two-second song. Hours and then days pass, as I need to make dozens of sonagrams for each of the five males involved, to make sure that I know all the songs that each can sing.

Satisfied that I have fully documented the song repertoires of the father, his son, and the son's three neighbors, I lay out the sonagrams on the table tops of one of the undergraduate teaching laboratories. First the songs of 326: I sort his sonagrams and find that he has a repertoire of 15 different songs, each one occurring several times in my extensive sample of his singing efforts. One by one I compare his songs to those of the father and his three immediate neighbors.

Gradually, the answer emerges. Song after song from this young male is almost identical to the songs of his immediate neighbor to the west, bird #229. Next most similar are the songs of 221 to the east, then 223 to the north. A few of the songs in this neighborhood are also shared by the father, about a half mile to the north, but when it matters, when the songs of this new neighborhood differ from those of the father, the yearling always rejects his father's variant and sings the local songs. Just once I caught him reverting to a peculiar phrase sung only by his father. Clearly he had learned his father's songs during the first four or five weeks of his life, but once he left home he was primed to replace dad's songs with songs that would match those of males who would be his neighbors for the rest of his life.

I learn the same lessons from other father-son pairs. Bird #331 dispersed about two miles from his father (202), bird #218 about a mile from his father

(161), and bird #289 less than half a mile from his father (115). Each son acquired songs at his new home and rejected the songs of his father if the father's songs were not also found at the new location. But rejecting dad's songs wouldn't be automatic; one son (43) who settled next to his father (40) would undoubtedly have retained most of his father's songs. Unfortunately, dad disappeared before I could record him, but I would have expected the neighboring father and son to have had almost identical song repertoires.

The seven sons I relocate after they have dispersed from home also help explain why some birds have only 13 songs and others as many as 20. The baby wrens hatching earlier in the summer learned more songs than did those hatching later. Young wrens from late April and early May learned 18 to 20 songs apiece, but those hatching in June learned 15 or fewer. The early birds have a month more to practice before the short days of winter, and the practice seems to pay off. Early-hatching birds probably also get their choice of the best vacant territories, so the number of songs that a male has is probably correlated with the quality of his real estate, too. I can't help but wonder if a female could judge a male, at least in part, by counting the number of different songs he can sing.

Understanding the Bewick's wrens at this Finley refuge isn't enough. I soon visit other places within Oregon's Willamette Valley, up to Sauvie Island in Portland, then to the other side of the Cascade Mountains, to Klamath Falls. Then on to California, visiting Point Reyes and Santa Cruz Island. Then to the renowned birding mecca Madera Canyon in Arizona and to Colorado National Monument in Grand Junction. I needed to hear these wrens elsewhere, to understand who they were across their geographic range. Their differences intrigued me. Oregon males averaged 16 songs apiece, a typical song consisting of three phrases over a second and a half. Colorado males had only about 10 songs apiece, but each was almost three seconds long and more complex, consisting of four phrases. Arizona songs were the simplest, consisting of only two phrases in a second and a half, each male having about 18 different songs.

In the mid 70s my friend Gene Morton and I searched out one of the last remaining populations of this wren in the East, at Dan's Rock in western Maryland. We recorded as many songs as we could, learning that these birds sounded much like the Colorado birds. A century ago these wrens were common backyard birds east of the Mississippi, but the Appalachians are now silent. The best guess of the experts is that the feisty house wrens have killed off the Bewick's wrens, because as the house wrens expanded their range, that of the Bewick's wrens contracted.

When in Bewick's wren country, I now inevitably pause and listen, wondering what is on the mind of these wrens. What's this one singing? Let me feel the rhythm of that song, burning it into my short-term memory, counting how many times he repeats it before switching to another: 10, 20, 30, 40, 50, 60, 70, 71 it was the last time I listened, as I sat on the hillside overlooking the marsh at Coyote Hills Regional Park at the south end of San Francisco Bay. And how fast is he singing? Seventy-one songs in 14 minutes, only 5 songs a minute—about a third of his maximum rate and far slower than the average of 7 to 8 songs a minute. The slower he sings, the more renditions he sings before he introduces a new song. Singing is most vigorous before sunrise early in the season, most sluggish midday late in the season.

And what's his neighbor singing? I always ask. Is it the same song? It seems that they learn the neighbor's songs just to answer each other with identical songs, playing a countersinging game that we humans poorly understand.

As a scientist I am taught to be objective and dispassionate. That's the way I must get answers to my questions. But I have come to realize that the ways to knowing are as diverse as the emerging colors on the glowing West Temple and Towers across the valley as I cycle up out of Zion Canyon.

We have a shared history, these songbirds and I, dating back not just 30 years but to the origins of life itself. We are part of each other's story on this planet. It is no doubt their songs that guided my ancestors' early music, much as their songs now guide me.

I concentrate on one last look before I cycle on. The massive Temple to the west is a reddish glow, the coniferous spires at the top greening in dawn's light and encircling the crowning throne atop this holy place. The Towers of the Virgin to the right whiten as the sun's rays slip across the valley. Up Zion Canyon itself, beyond my view to the right, I know rise the Three Patriarchs —Abraham, Isaac, and Jacob—as well as Cathedral Mountain, Angels Landing, the Temple of Sinawava, the Great White Throne, and the Mountain of the Sun. Towering above me, directly north, is the East Temple. The names of these places echo in my mind. One last listen. The dawn frenzy abates as thrushes and wrens and towhees slow their pace, the warbler having switched to his daytime song (some warblers have different dawn and daytime songs). The dawn wave has passed, replaced by the relative hush of the day.

Were it not for a series of chance events, I would still be back in the campground, just beginning to stir with my friends. It now seems that it was not an hour, but rather 30 years ago that I left them to explore this singing planet. The wrens in the backyard would be joined by robins and sparrows and warblers and blackbirds and flycatchers, to name just a few; the backyard would expand, too, to include all of the Americas, and more distant parts of the globe. Of these birds I would need to know how each acquires its song, what those songs are good for, why the songs change from place to place, why some birds are such extraordinary singers and others not, why females of some species sing, how the brain controls this singing, and so much more.

With the bike still in first gear, I clip my left shoe into the pedal and push off, then swing my right leg over the saddle and secure my right shoe and pedal. Deeply breathing in this rarefied air, one last time I listen and look and feel and smell all that I can. First gear becomes second, then third, picking up speed as I climb the hill.

The American Robin

It was the Bewick's wren who first taught me how to listen, but it is the robin who annually refreshes my memory. That was my resolution for the new millennium, to listen more closely to the robins early in spring.

Yes, the robin, the ultrafamiliar robin in everyone's backyard, unmistakable with its full reddish orange breast and dark gray back, seemingly everywhere and always hopping

AMERICAN ROBIN

along the grass, pausing and cocking its head to look carefully for its earthworm. So familiar is the robin that it is the standard by which we know other birds. The bird in the bush is "a little smaller than a robin" or "about the size of a robin." Learn to recognize the robin's song—a "loud, liquid song, a variable *cheerily cheer-up cheerio*" to some, to Peterson "a clear caroling; short phrases, rising and falling, often prolonged"—and you've got the standard for the songs of other birds, too. Peterson's field guide goes on to describe the scarlet tanager unmistakably as the "hoarse robin . . . suggesting a robin with a sore throat" and the rose-breasted grosbeak as "the robin that has taken voice lessons."

"A clear caroling" says Roger Tory Peterson. My respect for Peterson and his way of getting things right causes me to reflect some on that phrase. I like it that robins "carol," though it might not seem very professional of me. To carol is to "sing joyously" according to my dictionaries. I cannot attribute joy to the robin, but I do know that phrase is entirely accurate if I attribute the singing to the robin and the joy to those of us humans who relish its songs early in the spring. Yes, the robin carols. That word will stick with me.

So familiar is this robin, yet we hardly know him. The expert accounts about robin song, for example, tell us little more than we read in the field guides, and that's such a pity, because robins have much they can teach us. In the robin is a beginning for all those who would like to listen, for those who would hear the nuances of birdsong all around them. Sitting in a lawn chair and listening to robins for a few hours prepares one for sparrows and starlings and wrens and flycatchers and warblers and thrushes and jays and goldfinches and blackbirds—indeed, almost anything that other birds may have to offer. Begin by listening to the robin, and realize then how easily one hears how all the others sing.

❦

FIRST ENCOUNTER

Mid morning, Thursday, April 12, 2001, the first year of the millennium, I stroll down to my neighborhood pond and picnic area. Leafless oaks and maples oversee the lingering snowbanks, and several robins strut about on the lawn. My attention is drawn to one singing in the oak tree just across the road. As I listen, I'm inclined to name him, perhaps Bird 1 or Bird A, to distinguish him from the other robins nearby. But he quickly becomes Rob—though it seems unscientific to name him, I can think of no good reason why he should not be Rob.

Rob sings the way the field guides instruct, with "clear caroling" and "a variable *cheerily cheer-up cheerio*" (figure 8, track 12). Only a few other birds, such as chickadees, titmice, and cardinals, sing this early in the year here in western Massachusetts, and their songs are so different that the robin's refrains are unmistakable.

"Prolonged" singing, says Peterson. Yes, I hear that. The robin is unlike those songbirds that deliver a two-second song, pause for five to ten seconds, and then deliver again. No, this robin often seems to go on for several minutes without such long pauses. But I know to listen more closely, to feel his characteristic tempo — several of those rapidly delivered, liquid phrases every few seconds, the group of them followed by a slight pause, as if he stops to listen ever so briefly before resuming. As I tune my ear, I now count the number of whistled phrases between the slightly longer pauses: 3, 4, 3, 2, 3, 4, 6, 3, 4, 3, 4, and he then stops after about 45 seconds. It's a distinct tempo he has, the robin tempo.

Once I have the rhythm and can pick out each of the brief caroled phrases, I listen more intently to each. Eyes closed, I try to feel each phrase pouring from his open bill, to see the unique pulses of air molecules radiating outward, waves of molecules pushing and shoving, put in motion by vibrating membranes in his two voice boxes. In my mind I slow these patterns down, dissecting and sensing the details of each. One, two, three distinct patterns, as in *cheerily cheer-up cheerio* . . . and then the molecules rest. One, two . . . and rest. For a minute or two I continue, soon chuckling at what now becomes so obvious. Every once in a while, he gets stuck on a particular phrase, repeating it two or three times in a row. *Cheerily cheerily cheerily . . . cheerily cheerily cheerily* he sings. I'd love to know why he does that, singing as if the neurons were simply refiring and couldn't reset, but it seems as if no one has given it much thought. Whatever the reason for his behavior, I take advantage of it, building my confidence in being able to hear how he sings.

As he sings *cheerily cheerily cheerily,* each of the three phrases sounding so identical to my ears, I realize that the robin has already told me a bit about himself. Contrary to what my unpracticed ear might have told me a few minutes before, he's not making up these caroled phrases as he goes. Rather he repeats himself, the repetitions being the first bit of evidence that he has a limited repertoire of these phrases that he sings, in various combinations, during his prolonged performances.

I next detect a slightly more complex pattern of delivery: *cheer-up cheerio cheer-up cheerio.* He alternates two different phrases, a pattern Sibley's guide had advised me of: "often two or three phrases alternately repeated over and over *plurri, kliwi, plurri, kliwi.*" (One person's *cheer-up* is another's *plurri* — such is the difficulty of describing birdsong.) The robin gradually lures me into his singing game, first letting me recognize how he repeats one phrase several times, *cheerily cheerily cheerily,* then how he alternates two, as in *cheer-up cheerio cheer-up cheerio.*

On this first encounter I've already come a long way in listening to this robin, identifying his liquid caroling, feeling the tempo of his delivery, hearing the short-term patterns of repetition. I could be content here and stop for

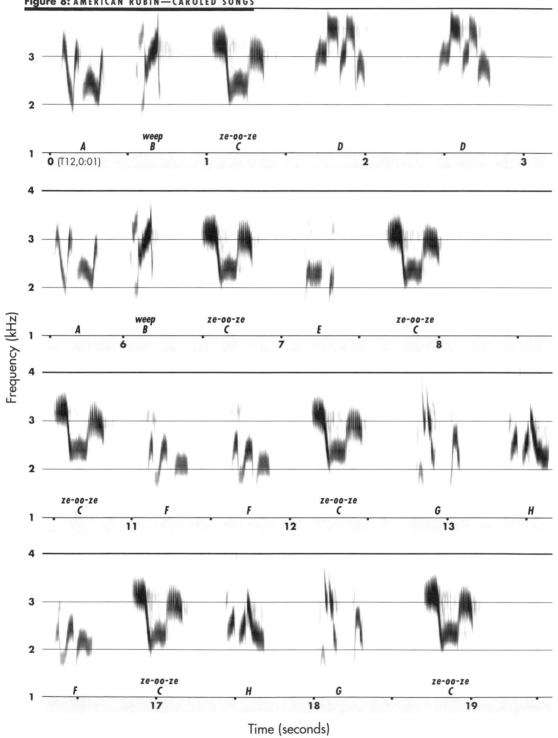

Frequency (kHz)

Time (seconds)

the day. Few bird watchers reach this point, and hardly anyone knows there's so much more to be heard from the robin. Yes, I could stop, but I relish one more challenge: to identify two of this particular robin's caroled phrases so that I'll recognize them whenever I hear them again, whether that be a second, minute, hour, day, or even a year later.

The first distinctive phrase is easy, as I have already heard him sing it many times. It consists of three buzzy notes, the middle one lower-pitched than the other two, a rapid-fire *ze-oo-ze*. For two minutes I listen for the *ze-oo-ze*, starting to count at 1 when I hear it next and writing down when it appears in the sequence . . . 1, 3, 7, 9, 11, 15, 17, 20, 21, 23, 25 . . . 57, 62, 67, 70, 75, 77, 79, 83, 85, 90, 99, 101, 102, 104, 106, 107, 111, 112, 114. This particular phase is clearly one of his favorites. Gradually it all becomes easier, distinguishing this particular sound from all the others and taking notes at the same time (track 12).

While listening for the *ze-oo-ze*, I choose a second distinctive phrase, a phrase I hear as a simple rising *weep*, perhaps his simplest phrase. For another two minutes I count, beginning with the first *weep*: 1, 6 . . . 49, 55, 60 . . . 88, 92, 97. Wow, how differently he uses his *ze-oo-ze* and his *weep*, at least in these two series of songs.

I've listened enough for now, given that the robin isn't singing all that continuously late in the morning, but I want to return this evening, to see and

Figure 8. Here is the essence of robin singing, as illustrated in sonagrams of the "clear caroling" of Rob the American robin (the first 20 seconds from track 12). See (and hear) how this robin sings five phrases over a few seconds and then pauses, then five phrases and pauses, then six phrases more, and so on (note that the time scale is continuous but does not display those longer pauses). Look again at those first five phrases and see the four different phrases, with the fourth phrase repeated: A B C D D. In the next group of five, the robin begins in the same way, with A B C, and then he introduces phrase E, followed by C; note the C E C sequence, because robins often alternate phrases like that. In the third row, phrases F, G, and H are introduced; again, hear and see how he repeats himself (phrase F) and how a phrase recurs within a sequence (phrase C). In the fourth row, he introduces nothing new. To see the bigger picture of robin caroling, step back from the figure a little and see how the bold phrase C recurs throughout these 20 seconds; then listen to track 12 again and notice how phrase C occurs 11 times in the first 31 phrases (the first 32 seconds on track 12) but 0 times in the last 31 phrases (0:32–0:60 on track 12). That's the way a robin sings, emphasizing a particular phrase for some time, then emphasizing others, as he cycles through his song repertoire. During my hours with Rob, I found only one more caroled phrase that he sang (phrase I—see figure 9), for a total repertoire of 9 different caroled phrases.

hear him into his roost. I check my sun "rise and set" Web site, finding that sunset is at 7:29 P.M.

GOING TO ROOST

He's singing when I arrive a little after 7:00 P.M., and as I approach, I hear the liquid caroling, the familiar tempo, and the two familiar phrases I learned earlier in the day. On top of all that, the robin now adds another feature to his singing (figure 9, track 13). Following three or four of those loud, liquid notes featured in the field guides comes something else, a high-pitched punctuation just before the pause, an ethereal whispered note much like the delicate flourish at the end of a hermit thrush song. None of my field guides mentions this sound, but it's described in A. C. Bent's classic Life History series as *hisselly*. For a few seconds I become the robin, whistling three or four of those loud, low-pitched carols, and then whispering *hisselly*.

I wish I could follow the carols and *hisselly*s to their source, peering into his opened bill and deep into his throat. Into the windpipe (or trachea) I'd look, down to where it splits in two, one branch (or bronchus) going to each lung. At the top of each branch I would see a voice box (a syrinx), each consisting of delicate membranes and tiny muscles that are finely coordinated to produce the sounds dictated by the neurons delivering messages from the brain. As my robin sings his pure, whistled carols, just one sound is produced at any given instant, so I know just one voice box, either the left or the right, is operating then; for a more complex caroled phrase, maybe one that alternates rapidly between a higher and lower pitch, perhaps I'd see the two voice boxes rapidly alternate their contributions, first the left and then the right, or vice versa. On the *hisselly*, however, I bet both voice boxes would spring into action; the left and right would operate at once, the tiny muscles tightening and relaxing in a well-practiced pattern to produce the complex of sounds in the *hisselly* flourish.

He continues to sing, and I step back, contemplating his carols and *hisselly*s. I practice trying to capture on paper what this robin is doing. Just four symbols can do the job:

Z   The letter Z for the buzzy *ze-oo-ze* phrase
W   The letter W for the rising *weep*
–   A simple dash for one of the other caroled phrases
+   A plus sign for one of the high-pitched *hisselly* phrases.

So, this sequence in my notebook, Z W – +, means that the bird sang four phrases; the first was the *ze-oo-ze* phrase, the second was the rising *weep*, the third was another one of his low-pitched carols, and the fourth was a high-pitched *hisselly*. Before entering the notations for the next series into my notebook, I leave a little space, so that I preserve on paper the tempo of the robin's efforts.

Each year it comes more easily, but it does take practice, much like the Morse code I once learned. To operate a ham radio I needed to read 15 words of Morse code each minute. At 5 letters per word, that was 75 letters a minute, more than one a second, about the same pace that the robin sings. *Di-dah* was a dot and a dash (• —), an A, *dah-di-di-dit* a B (— • • •), and so on. I remember wanting to master 5 words a minute, then 6, slowly working my way up, but the experienced operators advised otherwise. "Listen from the very beginning at full speed, 75 characters a minute," they said. "At first you'll identify only a few of the letters, but gradually you'll hear more and more of the letters in the stream, until nothing escapes you." It took a few months of dedicated listening, but in the end 75 characters a minute was a breeze.

So it is with the robin. Errors abound during my first attempts each year, and I get frustrated, thinking that perhaps I've "lost it," but that feeling doesn't last long. For now, too, I'm trying to distinguish only two of his many different liquid carols and lumping all of the others into a single category. At least for now. Some who discover how to listen to robins will find this exercise as incomplete as a Morse code operator who learns only two of the letters that stream by. Learning all of a robin's whistled phrases is possible, and I have a hunch that anyone can do it who really loves listening to robins. (Try it with tracks 12 and 13 and you might be surprised how easy it is; but don't try it for the *hisselly* phrases — I'll tell why later.)

As I listen to the robin this evening, I can't help but gain an appreciation for some of the other sounds that he makes. Robins are known for their "complaints and protestations," for the wide variety of notes that they use when we disturb them, or when anything seems slightly awry. One sound is a low, mellow *tut . . . tut . . . tut,* another a sharp, explosive *piik,* often delivered in pairs, *piik piik.* Sounding more urgent is a rapid series of notes, perhaps a bit like *quiquiquiquiquiquiqui,* often seeming to rise and then fall in pitch. These robins are so expressive, taking these and other sounds and uttering them on a variety of pitches and intensities, undoubtedly all the variations of which are meaningful to other robins but which we humans don't begin to understand.

The sun has now set, but the robin continues. A few liquid carols are inevitably followed by a single *hisselly* note now, with an occasional pair of sharp *piik* notes and a *quiquiquiquiquiquiqui* or two. Finally, 29 minutes after the official sunset time, I hear his last comments on the day: *tut . . . tut . . .* And he apparently has gone to roost, in the lower branches of a large white pine that overlooks the pond.

Only now am I ready for the ultimate robin experience. As I've prepared myself, I've heard all that he does, in bits and pieces. I will come back tomorrow morning, an hour before sunrise, and using all that I have learned, hear the robin's world awaken.

THE DAWN CHALLENGE

APRIL 13. Friday. A Good Friday. 5:11 A.M. Sunrise will be an hour later, at 6:12. I open the door to my house and instantly a robin protests from the small hemlocks in the front yard, *quiquiquiquiquiqui,* and off he flies into the darkness, another *quiquiquiquiquiqui* on the wing, fading into the distance. It's heavily overcast and foggy from the rains yesterday—dark, with no sign of daybreak. Walking quietly the short distance to the pond, I hear no more robins, and I station myself about 30 yards from where my robin went to roost last night.

5:15. Dark hemlocks and pines punctuate the southern horizon, and nearby the skeletons of maples and cottonwoods loom above me. A woodcock chirps as he circles overhead, but where he settles to *peent* I do not know— perhaps in the boggy area a quarter mile to the southwest. Is that a robin in the distance, or perhaps spring peepers? It's hard to tell. It could be a robin singing by a streetlight (they start singing up to an hour earlier in heavily lit areas).

Figure 9. Here is the new feature of robin singing, the high-pitched *hisselly* phrases (1–10) contrasted with two caroled phrases (C, I). Listen to track 13 and hear how the robin sings a series of caroled phrases followed by a single *hisselly* phrase (e.g., A B H G H A 1, the first 7 phrases on the track); then match the particular *hisselly* phrases in this figure with those you hear on track 13 (the times on track 13 are indicated below each phrase; phrase 1 occurs at 0:04 and 0:07, phrase 2 at 0:13 and 0:22, and so on). Compared to the caroled phrases (C and I in this figure), see how dainty and intricate these *hisselly* notes appear on the sonagram; see, too, how the *hisselly* phrases tower above the two caroled phrases, the difference in pitch obvious to both eye and ear. On the CD you can hear how the *hisselly* notes are much more softly given, too (although in this figure I have had to darken the *hisselly* phrases so that their details would show). Look again at caroled phrase I (the first phrase in the lower row) and see how it has elements that reach much higher in frequency than do the other caroled phrases. Although my ears can hear much of the variety in the caroled phrases, I need to see the diversity and beauty in these higher-pitched *hisselly* phrases to appreciate them. (The time scale at the bottom of the figure indicates a half-second.)

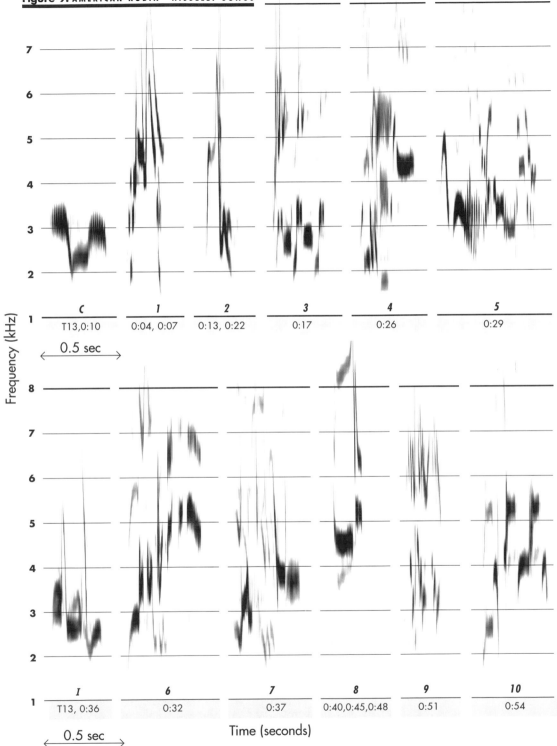

5:24. *Quiquiquiquiquiquiqui* from my robin in the pine, exactly where he went to roost last night. He's awake. I am well hidden from him, but did he see me arrive? Perhaps, but robins often arouse and instantly complain in this way.

5:30. The woodcock circles overhead again, but Rob has been silent for six minutes.

5:31. *Tut . . . tut . . . tut . . .* Another robin heard from, this one up the road —isolated *tut*s, carrying on for 30 seconds, then a few liquid carols, then a more rapid series of *tut*s, and then more song. I mark his position, thinking I'll come back to listen to him later this morning.

5:34. Rob now *tut*s, one to two a second, and a cardinal sounds off down beyond the pond. A few more *tut*s, and Rob then begins to sing. I warm up with him, taking some simple notes. It's only the liquid carols at first, no *hisselly* notes, so I just count the number of phrases between pauses: first 2, then 4, then 2, 1, 3, 3, 3, 2, 4, 3, 2, 1, 2, 2, then *quiquiquiquiquiqui*, 3, 2, all this in just the first minute of singing.

5:36. Another male sounds off to the west, with *piik* and *tut* notes. Rob sings only eight more liquid phrases before he responds in kind. For four minutes these two males square off, at a distance of about 40 yards, *piik-piik-piik-tut-tut-tut-tut-tut,* back and forth, up to five *piik*s followed by up to five *tut*s from each male.

5:40. The western male continues with a series of *quiquiquiquiquiqui*s, and such a variety of them. Some are high-pitched, some low, some fast, some slow, some longer, some shorter, and all combinations. What could they mean? Then *hisselly hisselly hisselly . . .* on and on, about one a second, 71 of those whispered flourishes in a row. Only then, six minutes after I first heard from him, does he begin the dawn routine of several whistled phrases followed by a single *hisselly* (track 13).

5:45. Meanwhile, Rob has resumed his dawn singing, too, and I'm ready for him. Summoning all that I learned about him yesterday, and all of the concentration I can muster, I begin a seven-minute marathon, using the four symbols to represent the songs I can recognize: −, W, Z, and +.

Deep breath, my digital watch reading 58, 59, 00: GO.

Furiously I take notes . . . (see box 1).

I breathe again, my body and my brain starved for oxygen. I glance up to the pine tree where he sings, though I still cannot see him. I look down again at my notebook, eager to explore the record that I've captured. My detailed notes hide the big picture of what he is doing, so I quickly summarize them, tallying all of the whistled notes so that four whistled notes followed by a *hisselly* is written 4+. At the end of each minute I total the number of caroled phrases and, in parentheses, the number of *hisselly*s (box 2).

So much is there. Most series of the low caroled notes end with a single *hisselly,* never two, and then he pauses slightly before the next series. Overall, he sang 398 of the caroled notes and 90 *hisselly* notes, for a total of 488 phrases, about 70 a minute. In Morse code, that's only 14 words a minute. I can handle that.

And how does he use the two phrases that I was listening for? I study my detailed notes again, first for the *ze-oo-ze* (see box 1). I find the letter Z 45 times in my notes, 45 out of the 398, but that's only part of the story. The Zs typically come in bunches of 4 or 5, up to 7 in minute four and 8 in minute seven, revealing that the *ze-oo-ze* phrase falls in and out of favor as he sings. The *weep* phrase is used more often, 55 of the 398 caroled phrases, and the Ws also surge and recede about once a minute over these seven minutes. It's intriguing that the *weep* is now more common than the *ze-oo-ze*, because during the four minutes I listened yesterday he sang 30 *ze-oo-ze*s and only 8 *weep*s. Why? I wonder. What's he thinking?

"Enough of this robin!" I can hear some of my friends say, but I press on, as he has more to teach me. I now focus on the symbols that identify all of the other caroled phrases, all 298 of them. They consist of other phrases used just like the two that I now know so well, and based on my detailed notes I can

MINUTE	SONG SEQUENCE	TOTALS
1	2+ 3 3+ 4+ 4+ 4+ 4+ 3+ 4 3+ 4 3+ 4 3+ 3+ 8	59 (11)
2	5 3+ 4 5+ 4+ 4+ 7 2+ 4 3+ 4 3+ 4+ 4+ 3+ 3+	62 (11)
3	4+ 3+ 5+ 5 4+ 3+ 3 3+ 2+ 1+ 4+ 3+ 4+ 4	48 (11)
4	6 3+ 3+ 3+ 4+ 4+ 3+ 3+ 3+ 3+ 3+ 4 4 3+ 3 4+ 4+	60 (13)
5	4+ 4+ 3+ 2+ 4+ 3+ 3+ 1+ 4+ 3+ 3+ 2+ 4+ 3+ 1 11+	55 (15)
6	6+ 3+ 3+ 6 2+ 5 2+ 3+ 4+ 5+ 3+ 3+ 4+ 4 4+ 3+	60 (13)
7	4+ 3+ 3+ 4+ 3+ 3+ 3+ 5+ 3+ 3 3+ 3+ 3+ 2+ 3+ 3+ 3+	54 (16)
		398 (90)

make an educated guess as to how many different caroled phrases he sings. The *weep* and *ze-oo-ze* occurred a total of 100 times, an average of 50 times apiece. If the two phrases that I chose are fairly typical of how this robin uses his other phrases, then I can simply divide the total number of phrases (398) by the average number of times each is used (50), and in that way estimate how many different caroled phrases this robin used in these seven minutes: $398 \div 50 = 8$. If I wanted to be more accurate in my estimate, I could listen longer than seven minutes, or better yet, I would identify a third recognizable phrase, determine how often that occurred, and then estimate his repertoire again. For now, though, I'm content to know that this particular robin has about 8 commonly used caroled phrases, on the low end of the range of roughly 10 to 20 different caroled phrases for robins. (As revealed in figures 8 and 9, tracks 12 and 13, his total repertoire is 9 different caroled phrases; 8 is a satisfyingly accurate estimate, especially since one of his phrases, I, is used so rarely.)

I now stare at all of those *hisselly* symbols. I know enough about robins to know that I must just enjoy these *hisselly*s as a group and not try to distinguish them from each other. Painstaking computer-assisted analyses have shown that each male has many different *hisselly* phrases, from 75 to 100, but they're different from each other in the smallest of details, inseparable by the best of human ears. I can hear that there is a great variety of them, and I can hear him repeat a particular *hisselly* on occasion (figure 9, track 13), but that's about it. Why does the robin have so many of these whispered *hisselly* phrases and relatively few of those caroled phrases? If he has such a large *hisselly* repertoire, why doesn't he use and flaunt it more? And why does he use those *hisselly*s mostly at dawn and dusk? The robin is slow to yield his secrets to us.

EACH ROBIN AN INDIVIDUAL

Up the road the robin I heard earlier is singing, Rob's neighbor to the east. Slowly I walk toward him, scanning the trees until I see him camouflaged in the red oak tree among some of last year's dead leaves, about 15 yards above the pavement. To get to know him, I start tape-recording him and taking notes, just keeping track of how many caroled and *hisselly* phrases he sings. Using *q* for a *qui* note, *p* for a *piik*, and *t* for *tut*, I begin (see box 3).

Fifty seconds into minute 6 a mourning dove explodes from a perch over my head, its wings whistling it off to the north; the robin stops singing and utters three high-pitched *seee* notes, so high my aging ears can barely hear them. Here is the infamous "hawk alarm," a warning note shared by so many songbirds. So high-pitched is this *seee* that a hawk might not be able to hear it at all. It's ventriloquial, too, the *seee* a high, thin whistle, beginning and ending gradually, thereby making it difficult to locate. In minute 7, 17 more *seee* notes. But where is the hawk? Is this a false alarm, the robin not knowing a

---

BOX 3

MINUTE	SONG SEQUENCE
1	6+ 3+ 3 5+ 6+ 7+ 4 p 5+ 4+ 3 qqq p 6 pp 4+ pp 4+ 3
2	p 4+ 4 3+ 12+ 5+ 12+ 5+ 5+ 5+ 7 3+ 7+
3	6+ 5 7 ppp+ 17+ 10 4+ 7 t qqqq 14+
4	qqqqq 8 p 6+ 7 14 10+ p +++ p 5+ p 10
5	p 5 8 p 5+ p 8+ p 8 4 4 qqqqqqqq 5 qqqqqqqqqqq 3 3 2+ 4 4+
6	4+ 4+ 4+ 4+ 4+ 4 3+ 4+ 3+ 6 6+ 4 seee seee seee
7	seee seee seee seee seee seee seee seee seee seee seee seee seee seee seee seee seee

dove from a hawk? Or perhaps the robin acknowledges with his *seee* the danger that the dove first saw? I freeze, watching the robin, waiting . . . and from behind me and over my head the hawk makes his pass, only to be foiled by the alert robin, he departing to the southeast, the foiled hawk veering off to the northeast.

Just seven minutes of listening and I've heard so much from this robin. He intersperses his *piik* and *tut* and *quiquiquiqui* calls with his song phrases. He also sings long series of caroled phrases without a *hisselly,* up to 14 in minute 4; one series of caroled phrases in minute 3 reached 17 before he ended it with a *hisselly.* Why, I wonder, does he differ so from how Rob was just singing? What is on his mind that leads him to sing so differently? Perhaps days, perhaps years of listening would help me relate these different singing behaviors to different contexts, so that I could understand the mood of each singer.

What I didn't hear from this second robin is just as intriguing. Not once did I hear the *ze-oo-ze* or the *weep* phrase that his neighbor Rob was using. Nor would I hear those phrases with extended listening, because each male robin has a largely unique repertoire of caroled phrases that I can use to identify him as an individual.

I am now ready to listen to all that birds have to offer. I have sharpened my ears by listening to Rob and his neighbors, and they've taught me well. I've heard each robin as an individual, how each has a distinctive repertoire of whistled phrases and how each uses them with his higher-pitched *hisselly* notes. Although my immediate goal was simply to hear each robin as an individual, I knew I was learning much more in the process. By hearing an individual sing, I was learning about robins in general, learning facts that would never again allow me to confuse the song of a robin from what have been called the "robin sound-alikes," such as the grosbeak or oriole or tanager or vireo. By getting to know an individual robin, I have learned how to distinguish all robins from all other species. I've also prepared myself to hear the details in the songs of the most versatile singers, the bluebirds and other thrushes, the mockingbirds and catbirds and thrashers, the wrens, and more. The robin having sharpened all my senses, I quickly transcend the "What species is that" question to "What's he doing now?" The all-American robin in my backyard has prepared my ear for all that will follow.

Good Listening, Good Questions, This Book

Anyone who listens thoughtfully to robins can't help but bubble with questions about why robins are the way they are. What we do know and do not know about these robins (and other birds) centers around four types of questions, questions that are the focus of the rest of this book.

First, how does a robin acquire its vocabulary of calls and songs? Are the calls, such as the *piik, tut, quiquiquiqui, seee,* and others inborn, as in most birds, all of the necessary instructions somehow encoded in sequences of nucleic acids that make up the DNA? Based on what we know about other songbirds, I have a hunch that the robin is hatched with all of the instructions it needs on how to produce and use this part of its vocabulary (much like the songs of flycatchers—see "Songs That Aren't Learned," p. 79). These simple calls are probably not learned, but inborn.

How about the songs? How does each robin come to have a unique set of songs? Among most songbirds, singers imitate each other (see "Learning Songs: Where, When, and from Whom," p. 42; also "Borrowed Songs: Mimicry," p. 68). As a result, neighbors often have the same songs and answer each other with identical songs (see "Dialects," p. 119). But that doesn't seem to be the case with the robin. My best guess is that each robin makes up his own songs, guided largely by some general instructions encoded in robin DNA. Each bird sings unique songs, because he improvises (like three other nonconformists: sedge wrens, p. 102; brown thrashers, p. 191; and gray catbirds, p. 75).

An alternative explanation must be considered: It's possible that a young male robin imitates his songs from another robin or robins and then moves some distance away from his tutor, so that the tutor and pupil are not neighbors. The effect could be the same, giving an apparent uniqueness to the songs of each male. I could test these ideas by raising some baby robins in my home (with all the necessary federal and state permits, of course). I'd give them an opportunity to learn the songs of the singing robin outside; I'd play them songs over loudspeakers and I'd let them hear each other, too. Under these controlled conditions, would they improvise or imitate—or both? Only by doing the experiment could I know (see "Why Some Species Learn and Others Don't," p. 89).

I feel I need to pause here briefly and consider the words "song" and "call" that I have been using rather glibly. I emphasize "briefly," because lengthy discourses have been written about these words and their meanings. For our purposes, we can say that for the vast majority of species, we know when an individual is "singing." It's usually the male, typically high on a perch, uttering what is often a fairly complex vocalization. It's what a male does especially when he is on a territory by himself and when he is unpaired. These songs are thought to help establish and defend a territory as well as to attract and impress a mate. In contrast, "calls" are usually simpler, and they're given by males and females, both adult and young. Birds often have a dozen or so different calls given in particular contexts, each conveying particular information to listeners; the *seee* call of the American robin might warn of a hawk, for example, and the *tut tut tut* tell of some kind of disturbance. These simple distinctions between songs and calls will suffice for now, but by reading on you'll discover that distinguishing between songs and calls sometimes isn't so clear-cut (see "The Blue Jay," p. 179).

A second set of questions focuses on the functions of all these sounds. The *seee* call seems to warn of a hawk, but exactly whom does the robin warn? And what about the *piik* and *tut* and *quiquiquiqui*, and all of their subtle variations? What do they all mean? Why do robins seem to awake and go to roost with these sounds? It seems to us as if robins protest and complain with those calls, but what is the caller saying and how do other robins interpret those sounds?

And the songs? I have so many questions about the function of those songs. Why have two types of phrases, the caroled and the *hisselly* phrases? Why have a dozen or two of the caroled phrases and a hundred or so of the *hisselly* phrases? Do other robins count how many a male sings, and if so, is having more songs better in any way? Why are the *hisselly*s used mainly at dawn and dusk? Why at dawn are three or four caroled notes followed by a single *hisselly,* and what could it possibly mean to sing 71 *hisselly*s in a row? Are females impressed by any of this singing, and if so, by which features? By how early he starts singing in the morning, by how long he can sing without stopping, or by how loudly he sings? And do males listen to each other? Do they adjust their singing when they hear each other, and if so, how?

There are many fascinating questions for these robins, and no answers, but for other better-studied species we do have some clues. The bulk of this book focuses on these kinds of questions, such as why some males have simple songs, or complex songs, or beautiful songs, or sing so tirelessly (see "Extremes of Male Song," p. 177). Or why do some birds sing not from stationary perches but rather from the air ("Songs on the Wing," p. 276) or sing so vigorously before sunrise ("The Hour Before the Dawn," p. 304). Only the male robin sings, but females of many other species also sing. Why? ("She Also Sings," p. 335). And just when one thinks that all of the questions about song have been asked, one realizes that some species seem to have no song at all ("Songbirds Without a Song," p. 179); one bird species (not a songbird, but a vulture) is even mute, with no voice box.

The third set of questions is about how and why this species of robin has come to be the way it is. If we could trace Rob's lineage back 5 or 10 million years, what would we encounter? What was the ancestral robin like, the ancestor that gave rise to the American robin as well as to 60-some other robin species (all in the genus *Turdus*) that now occur throughout the globe, everywhere, it seems, except Antarctica? They're found from New Zealand and Australia to New Guinea and the Himalayas, throughout Asia and Europe and Africa, and there are 35 species in the New World. Central and South America alone have 34 of them. I know some of them from Costa Rica—the clay-colored and pale-vented and sooty and white-throated and mountain robins, some of them superb singers (such as the white-throated, figure 10, track 14), but one of them (the mountain, track 15) often ridiculed as not worthy of being called a thrush (robins are a type of thrush). I've heard of Lawrence's thrush (also genus *Turdus*), too, a world-renowned mimic from the Amazon.

Hints of why each robin species is the way it is could best be gleaned from a worldwide survey of all these species. In such a survey, we'd search for common features in the songs of all *Turdus* species, inferring that those vocal features are shared because they were retained from the ancestor of them all. If they all have two kinds of songs, much like the whistled carols and *hisselly* notes of our American robin, we'd infer that the ancestor had those features in its songs, too.

We'd be eager to document the differences among the robin species, too, to try to understand why those differences arose. Perhaps songs differ depending on the robin's preferred habitat, because certain song features broadcast better in some environments than in others. It's been shown, for example, that North American songbirds in forests use fewer rapidly repeated notes than do birds in open country; in the forests, rapidly repeated notes are apparently avoided because they would echo off vegetation, thereby blurring the details of one sound with the next. Perhaps the number of songs in different species depends on some feature of that particular species' biology, such as how intensely the male singers compete for females (perhaps more intensely in polygynous mating systems or in habitats where territories are small or in short supply), or whether or not the birds migrate (perhaps migrant birds have less time to acquire a large song repertoire). It is the correlations between various vocal behaviors and life history features that help us best understand why each robin species came to call and sing the way it does. In the end, though, we have to be reminded that we are not guaranteed to find our answers, in part because the clues that reveal evolutionary history are not always preserved, and in part because the reasons for the quirks of each species might lie deep within the inaccessible minds of the birds themselves.

The singing behaviors of robins and all other species are more interesting when considered in the context of evolutionary history. We biologists are trained to think in terms of evolutionary trees that show relationships among species and, ideally, exactly when and where each species arose. On this tree, we plot the various behaviors, such as who learns or mimics and who doesn't. In which species do we find dialects, simple or complex songs, vigorous dawn singing, singing females, no songs, and so on? In our minds we are always plotting these behaviors on evolutionary trees, looking for patterns of similarity or dissimilarity and the forces that cause these patterns, trying to imag-

Figure 10: WHITE-THROATED ROBIN

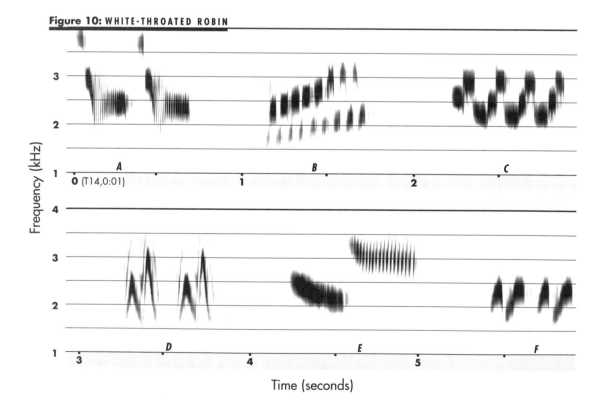

The Singing Life of Birds

ine how species came to be the way they are. Given how pervasive and important evolutionary thinking is, this topic permeates all accounts in this book.

The fourth set of questions is of the "How do things work?" kind. How does the brain control singing? Where among the interconnected groups of neurons in the forebrain are a male's songs stored? How do the neurons coordinate to send the message to the voice box (the syrinx) when it is time to sing? How does the brain choose which song will come next? When the robin whistles, which voice box does he use, his left or his right? Does he use one voice box most of the time, relying on the other only for special effects, as in the *hisselly* phrases? What is different about the female's physiology, such that she doesn't sing? The brain is controlled, to a large extent, by the seasonal hormones, such as testosterone and estrogen, which are in turn controlled by day length, so that more singing occurs during the spring and summer than during the short days of winter.

Answers to this fourth type of question are not available for the American robin, but some of these questions have been asked and answered for other species. Where answers are available, they become a secondary story within my accounts, such as for the northern cardinal (p. 357) and the brown thrasher (p. 191), whose two voice boxes have been studied; or for the flycatchers (p. 79) and marsh wrens (p. 120), whose brains have received some attention.

Figure 10. Sonagrams of the white-throated robin, my favorite *Turdus* species from Costa Rica, showing the first seven seconds from track 14. Listen and follow along here, noticing that this robin, like the American robin, also has low-pitched (A–F illustrated here) and high-pitched phrases, a trait that was no doubt inherited from their common ancestor.

2

How Songs Develop

Introduction

LEARNING SONGS: WHERE, WHEN, AND FROM WHOM

LISTEN TO ANY BIRD SING, and one of the first questions that comes to mind is where he got his song. This is the question that compelled me to study birdsong, and it's the question that has fascinated many others, too, especially for songbirds. To look a songbird in the eye is to see him as an individual, one who has grandparents and parents, one who not that long ago was just an egg and songless. Somewhere, at some time, and from some accomplished singer, the young songbird needed to learn his song(s), in much the same way that we learn our spoken language from adult humans.

This theme of "where, when, and from whom" is an inevitable subplot of a number of species accounts in other chapters of this book and, indeed, of almost every songbird account. From whom does the mockingbird pilfer its songs, for example? Chestnut-sided warblers have two categories of songs, and the answers to "where, when, and from whom" differ for the two types of songs in an intriguing way. A chipping sparrow learns his single song from one adult male with whom he fights for a territory, and this learning process explains why songs vary the way they do among a small community of singers. Because the typical young songbird must learn his songs, the strategy for acquiring the proper songs must include how to learn them at the right place, at the right time, and from the right adults.

How these song-learning decisions play out in the lives of songbirds is the focus of two species accounts in the first section of this chapter. Each male white-crowned sparrow has a single song, and one can walk through the California chaparral, as at the Point Reyes National Seashore, and traverse one dialect after another, with all of the males in one area singing the same dialect. One of the raging controversies of the 1970s and 1980s centered on whether a young male learned the song of his father and settled in his own dialect or whether he could move freely to another dialect and learn the songs there.

Matters are more complex for the song sparrow, as each male has six to ten songs; careful study of the resident birds in Seattle's Discovery Park has revealed a learning strategy that maximizes the probability that neighbors will share the same repertoires, and has also shown why they benefit from sharing.

BORROWED SONGS: MIMICRY

Although most songbirds restrict their learning to songs of their own species, song learning among others is more expansive, and a number of mimics occur in North America. Some are subtle and barely recognizable as mimics, as with the white-eyed vireo, which incorporates brief call notes of other species into its songs. One extraordinary mimic is the European starling, its long though relatively quiet songs containing a wide variety of mimicked sounds. Hands-down, the best-known example in North America is the northern mocking-bird, of course, well-named after its habit of filching the songs and calls of other birds in its neighborhood.

SONGS THAT AREN'T LEARNED

In striking contrast to the song-learning songbirds are their relatives, the New World tyrant flycatchers. A good example is the eastern phoebe, a member of the same order as the songbirds (the birds in this order, Passeriformes, are called passerines, or perching birds). Although true songbirds hatch with some general guidelines about how to learn the appropriate songs, the details of an eastern phoebe's two songs—his *fee-bee* and his *fee-b-be-be*—are inborn, encoded somehow in nucleotide sequences of the DNA. It's the same with the phoebe's close relatives, the alder and willow flycatchers. No imitative learning is required; nothing is left to chance. Songs (and other vocalizations) are routinely believed to be innate not only in these flycatchers but also in most other bird groups, such as loons, ducks and geese, shorebirds, gulls, pigeons and doves, owls, and woodpeckers—indeed, all except the songbirds, parrots, and some hummingbirds (this list, however, may reflect more about our ignorance than reality).

WHY SOME SPECIES LEARN AND OTHERS DON'T

Why some species learn their songs and others don't remains one of the greatest mysteries about birdsong. We humans have a special interest in an answer, too, because our closest living relatives, the nonhuman primates, do not learn their vocalizations, and we'd like to know why we have evolved this ability but our relatives haven't. Perhaps as we study why some birds learn to sing and others don't we can learn more about ourselves, too, and why we are different from the chimpanzees and other great apes.

Hints to an answer for this big question come from two species. One is the three-wattled bellbird, a tropical relative of the flycatchers that has recently acquired an ability to learn. The other is an odd North American wren, the sedge wren, a songbird that has recently (in evolutionary time, perhaps over a few million years) lost its ability to imitate songs. It is in these relatively recent evolutionary events that we have some hope of identifying why imitative learning is important, and some hope of identifying the circumstances under which learning might have originally evolved so long ago in the ancestors of the highly successful songbirds.

Learning Songs: Where, When, and from Whom

The White-crowned Sparrow

It's my favorite kind of dream.

I'm soaring, this time in the mid to late 1970s, high above Marin County in coastal California, just north of San Francisco. It's an hour before sunrise, and soon they'll all be singing. In the dead calm of this predawn hour, rising up to me from the coastal scrub below will be the songs of wrens and wren-tits and towhees and other songbirds, punctuated by the raucous calls of the scrub-jays. But it is the white-crowned sparrows that I'm here for, to soar above the Point Reyes area from Bolinas Lagoon north to Tomales Point, a distance of about 30 miles. I will hear these sparrows sing and will plot with my own eyes and ears this remarkable system of song dialects I've read so much about. More than a thousand singing sparrows I'll hear as I soar the 30 miles of coastline to the north, but only six different songs among them, each of the six confined to its own particular dialect area (figure 11).

Figure 11. A map of the white-crowned sparrow dialect regions in the Point Reyes National Seashore, California, just north of San Francisco. From Bolinas in the south to Tomales Point in the north, six dialect regions can be heard (the names are in bold capitals; dialect boundaries are indicated with dotted lines). Significant features in the area are labeled, including tiny Bass Lake, which lies on the well-studied boundary between the Clear and Buzzy dialects. Habitat unsuitable for white-crowns is stippled, and water is indicated by shading.

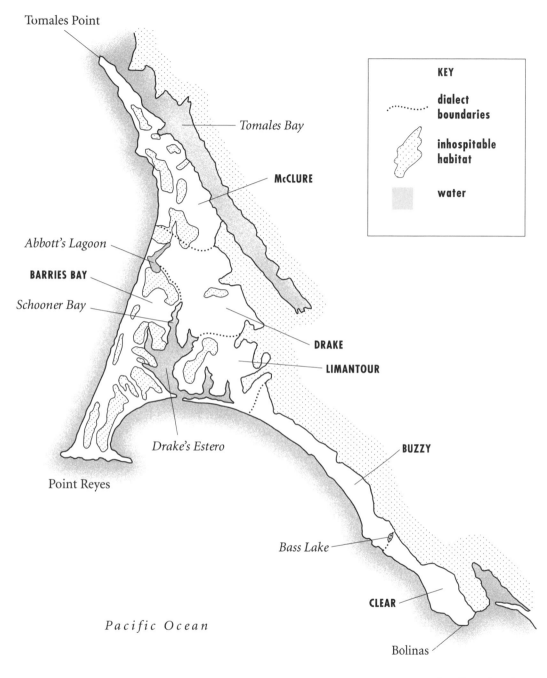

Tomales Point

Tomales Bay

McCLURE

Abbott's Lagoon

BARRIES BAY

Schooner Bay

DRAKE

LIMANTOUR

Drake's Estero

Point Reyes

BUZZY

Bass Lake

CLEAR

Bolinas

Pacific Ocean

San Francisco Bay

KEY

dialect
boundaries

inhospitable
habitat

water

Above the sleeping village of Bolinas I now circle, waiting for them to begin. Just to the east lies Bolinas Lagoon, to the south San Francisco Bay, to the west the wide-open Pacific. The towhees are first to sound off, awaking with their growly *zhreeee* call, then their rapid singing, alternating two or even three of their simple *drink-teeeeeeee* songs. A few wrentits and Bewick's wrens chime in, but soon it is the white-crowns' turn. First one, then another, and then a hundred all seem to sing at once, all with the same song. Each begins with two plaintive whistles, the first lower pitched than the second, and then I know to listen carefully, to feel the pair of relatively complex syllables that follow, each of them only a quarter of a second long. The song then rapidly progresses to a series of simpler whistles slurred rapidly downward, ending with a brief, low whistle trailing off (track 16, figure 12). It's the *Clear* dialect that I've read so much about, so named for that pair of complex syllables consisting of "clear" (that is, "non-buzzy"), slurred whistles. Soaring north along the coast, I crisscross this scrub from east to west and back again, from the shore to a mile inland and back to the shore, the earth a sounding board amplifying all these white-crown songs upward. Two hundred voices, maybe three hundred, yet all one, the Clear dialect.

A little over five miles into my journey I hit an acoustic wall, at tiny Bass Lake and the shallow drainage leading from it to the ocean. The songs begin the same, most of them with the two plaintive whistles, but replacing the pair of clear complex syllables is a pair of raspy, dissonant buzzy notes. I concentrate, extracting this essence of "buzziness" from the half-second following the two introductory whistles. Within another mile, the simpler slurred notes in the next part of the song are completely replaced, too, with brief buzzy notes instead of clear whistles. To the north this buzzy combination continues (track 16). There's no doubt—it's the *Buzzy* dialect, a sharp contrast to the Clear. I can't help but soar back to the south again, savoring this transition zone, amazed at how abrupt is the change from one song form to another, amazed at how all neighbors agree, until one reaches the boundary.

I head north again, hugging the ocean, the Buzzy dialect spanning roughly nine miles along the shore. Hundreds of buzzy songs rise to me, perhaps

Figure 12. Adult white-crowned sparrows learn to sing the local dialect, but unschooled young birds sing nonsensical songs (track 16). Illustrated here are songs of two dialects; the Clear dialect is named for the pure, slurred whistles that occur midsong, the Buzzy dialect for the buzzy elements that occur in the same position. If a young bird never hears an adult song to imitate, he sings the strangest sounds, an example of which is illustrated here.

from 300 or even 400 open bills, but up ahead is another wall. It's the boundary of the *Limantour* dialect, which has no buzzy notes and contrasts sharply with the Buzzy dialect. The simpler notes that follow are unique to this new dialect.

The Limantour dialect now beneath me, I hear to the west, across Drakes Estero and Schooner Bay, yet another dialect. It's the *Barries Bay* dialect, occu-

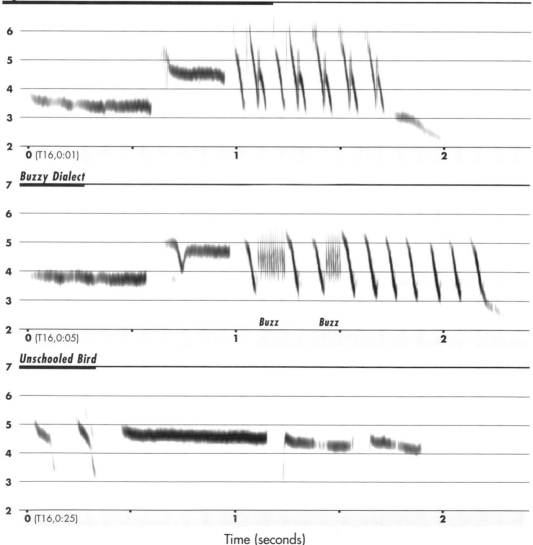

Figure 12: WHITE-CROWNED SPARROW *Clear Dialect*

Buzzy Dialect

Unschooled Bird

Time (seconds)

pying the heart of the Point Reyes National Seashore, south all the way to Point Reyes itself and extending far to the north, perhaps 10 miles to Abbott's Lagoon. With Barries to my left I continue to the north, passing beyond the Limantour dialect and into *Drakes,* and beyond that into *McClures,* in the narrow coastal strip between Tomales Bay and the Pacific, ending at Tomales Point.

In the dawn of my dreams, the sun hangs forever just below the horizon, the birds singing forever, too. I have time to soar over this entire Point Reyes area again, and again, hearing each of these six dialects, all striking in how abruptly they change from one to the next over the coastal scrub of this Point Reyes landscape.

Now a quarter-century later, I reflect on these song dialects and realize that the fascination with them all began with a simple "what if?" When studying the songs of this Nuttall's race of the white-crowned sparrow in California's coastal chaparral, Peter Marler and his colleagues described this system of song dialects. Each male had only one song, and it was always like the songs of his neighbors. A short distance away, however, birds often had a different song, a song of a different dialect. These unique song dialects occurred one after the other all along the coast of northern California, and Marler couldn't help but consider an intriguing possibility: *What if* a young male white-crown learns his song from his father? Wouldn't there then be a "relationship between song 'dialects' and the genetic constitution of populations . . . if young birds . . . are attracted to breed in areas where they hear the song type which they learned in their youth"?

It was a simple speculation of the kind that we biologists engage in all the time, but it was the implications of this one that set a world in motion. At stake was an answer to the big questions of why birds learn songs at all and what the implications of that learning are. For example, of the roughly 10,000 species of birds in the world, why are almost half of them these song-learning songbirds? Has song learning somehow enabled their success? Has it, through the formation of these learned song dialects, somehow hastened the speciation process to give us so many species in such a short time? Finding answers to these questions became a priority for many of us, and certainly for me, as it launched me on my graduate research.

I rethink the details of the process that Marler proposed. Early in life, perhaps during the first 50 days, a young male learns the song of his father. When the youngster becomes independent and can find his own food, he leaves the territory where he hatched in search of a breeding territory for himself. If he encounters a boundary between dialects, perhaps he is repulsed, as he recognizes that he's in unfamiliar territory—his song would be no good in this foreign land. His dispersal trajectory is changed, and he returns, finding a territory closer to home. As a result of this song-learning process, then, relatives nest closer to each other than they would if song played no role. The simple act of learning the father's song helps to isolate one group of sparrows from another, each group identified by a different dialect. And if no young birds cross the boundaries, birds in adjacent dialects will over time diverge genetically, each dialect having the potential to become a separate species. If Marler was right, one consequence of learning the father's song would be a tendency to generate new species at a faster rate, simply because relatively small groups of birds would be isolated from each other.

As I rethink this entire process, I find myself focusing on the one critical issue: From whom does the young male learn his song? If he learns only from his father . . . I need think no further. *If he learns only from his father,* then dialect boundaries MUST inhibit dispersal, which would in turn lead to isolation and rapid speciation. I emphasize "must" simply because dialects do exist and are fairly stable, so that young males CANNOT learn only the songs of fathers and freely disperse across dialect boundaries, or else the integrity of the dialects would rapidly be destroyed. If young birds did learn only the songs of their father and did disperse freely, neighbors would have dissimilar songs, the exact song depending on the geographic origin and lineage of each male. The reasoning then is simple: *If a young male learns only the song of his father, then dialects must inhibit dispersal, and dialects then promote the formation of new species.*

But what if he is not restricted to learning from his father and can instead learn after dispersal? If a young bird can learn his song after dispersing, then he can move freely, without regard to dialect boundaries, learning his final song wherever he chooses to settle. Then song dialects would have little if any role in promoting isolation and speciation.

The central question, then, is this: Just when does the young bird learn his song, before or after dispersal? It's a simple question, but answering it was not so easy, and a variety of approaches was used.

First, to learn more about how young males acquired their songs, baby white-crowns were collected from nests and exposed to all types of conditions in the research laboratory. Two important facts were learned:

1. To sing properly, the young male must hear the songs of an adult, or else he will develop highly abnormal songs. Although the local song dialects in nature had strongly implicated song learning, here was the stronger, more direct evidence (track 16).

2. The ability to learn is greatest between roughly day 10 and day 50. The young birds tutored over loudspeakers learned best during this period, but not so well before or after.

Here was the key evidence, or so it was thought at the time. Field studies had shown that baby white-crowns remain with their parents until about day 50, and the laboratory studies showed that the babies learned best up until day 50. In 1970, Marler summed it this way: "From the learning studies we know that for males . . . [the dialect in which they later breed] is also the dialect of the area where they were born." A few years later, in 1975, another major figure in this controversy, Luis Baptista, concurred: "Song learning in the White-crowned Sparrow terminates before dispersal from the natal area." Dialect boundaries prevent dispersal. It's that simple. End of story.

I remember meeting Luis in the spring of 1971, when I tracked him down at his Berkeley home. He and I were graduate students at the time, I having just finished showing how young Bewick's wrens disperse from home and then learn the songs at whatever distant site they happen to settle. My wrens dispersed freely across dialect boundaries, so I couldn't help but be rather puzzled over these white-crowned sparrows and their proponents, and especially about the notion that the young male learns his song from his father. Frankly, I just didn't believe it, though I tried my best to be courteous. I thought, too, that I shouldn't try to explain the rest of the world based on the one songbird species I had looked at. Perhaps these white-crowns were different. Perhaps these white-crowns had only one song so that they could have sharp dialect boundaries that would then inhibit dispersal. Perhaps. I needed to keep an open mind.

Just a few years later Luis was reconsidering his position. Beginning to have his doubts about these baby sparrows learning only from their fathers, he decided to test the learning ability of young white-crowns under more natural conditions in the laboratory. He found that young birds can learn after 50 days if they are tutored by live birds instead of tape recorders. Although song learning occurs *most readily* before day 50, it can occur later, too, if young birds experience more natural settings. Reinforcing these laboratory results were a few anecdotes from wild birds in which relatively old birds seemed to change their songs from one year to the next, some birds even becoming bilingual.

This emerging picture on song learning didn't settle the matter. It was now known that songs are learned most easily early in life, perhaps before the age at which young birds disperse, but that under the right conditions a young male can learn later, too. But how often do young males learn later, and under what conditions? About all that could be firmly concluded from these laboratory studies was this: White-crowned sparrow males learn their songs, but when and where they learn in nature just might have to be studied there, not in the laboratory.

Although most work was focused on males, because they sing, the females were not entirely forgotten. They play a key role, of course. It was to some extent assumed that a female would behave much like males, in that she would form a preference for a particular song at roughly the same age in life as the male would choose one to sing. She would then use her preference to pick an appropriate male, she being limited in her dispersal, too, by the particular song she came to prefer early in life while still with her singing father. Some evidence supported these ideas, but, again, the only solid conclusion was that females, too, seemed to be somewhat flexible, and that they should be studied in nature, too.

The questions again were simple: Do young females and males form a sufficient preference for the song of their father and the natal dialect so that their dispersal is limited to the geographic area where that song occurs? Do fewer young birds disperse across a dialect boundary than would be expected by chance, because the dialect boundary deflects them? Simple questions, but getting the answers would not be so simple.

Hints at the answer came soon, as it became clear that some young males disperse across dialect boundaries and learn the songs of the new dialect. But that's only a partial answer, because the real question is whether the boundary influences the young birds — that is, whether fewer of them cross than would be expected based on random movements. If for every one bird that crosses a boundary, several are repelled, then song learning early in life could still play an important role in isolating the birds of adjacent dialects.

The needed fieldwork was tackled by Mike Baker and Dick Mewaldt in the chaparral of the Point Reyes National Seashore. Beginning in 1966 and continuing through 1970, Mewaldt banded hundreds of birds along a transect that by chance spanned the boundary between the Clear and Buzzy dialects. Baker realized the potential of this information to address the "dialects limit dispersal" hypothesis, so he continued the effort through 1974. Thousands of birds were handled over the course of the study, 1,768 of which were caught in their hatching year. Attention was then riveted on 371 of those young birds, because they fulfilled two important conditions: they were caught early in the year when they were probably still near their natal site, and they were each recaptured the next year, after dispersal.

The results? Did the dialect boundary between the Clear and Buzzy dialects inhibit dispersal? *Yes,* declared Baker and Mewaldt. They calculated that 26 birds would have been expected to cross the boundary by chance alone, based on where the young bird was first caught and on the average dispersal distance of young birds overall. Only 5 to 15 juveniles actually crossed the boundary, however, far fewer than the number expected by chance. The results were exciting, because the dialect boundary had limited dispersal. Learning a song early in life did influence where the young white-crowns settled, thereby helping to isolate birds in adjacent dialects. This isolation would in turn promote speciation, so it was logical to conclude that song learning and the resulting dialects were one reason that so many species of songbirds existed.

But the rest of the world wasn't quite so sure about these results. Publication of the Baker-Mewaldt story in a prestigious journal led to immediate replies by others, including the doubting Baptista, all of which led to a counterreply by Baker and Mewaldt. Unfortunately, the transect had just barely extended across the Clear-Buzzy dialect boundary, with 85 percent in the Clear dialect and only 15 percent in the Buzzy dialect, so that all of the field effort wasn't focused on the boundary area itself. Of greater concern, however, was that the young birds when caught might have already moved some, already having dispersed from their hatching territory to some distant site, perhaps even across the dialect boundary. One can't accurately determine the age of a young bird caught in a trap, it was argued, and therefore one cannot know its origin or its true dispersal distance.

Still another approach to answering these questions was used, though it was only an indirect one. If dialects limit dispersal, it was argued, then birds in adjacent dialects are somewhat isolated from each other and should therefore be genetically different. These differences would accumulate over time and eventually should be measurable.

Crucial to understanding these possible genetic differences is the idea of how dialects form in the first place. The scrub/chaparral is a "fire climax community," as too many residents of California know, and eventually a chaparral community must burn to renew itself. As pockets of chaparral renew, the white-crowns recolonize, too, perhaps beginning new song dialects in the process. The white-crown populations grow, and as the habitat renews, the dialect area spreads until it comes into contact with another dialect area, at which place a boundary between the two dialects can be heard. Given this probable process of how dialects form, the genetic makeup of those initial founders of the new dialect are important. If by chance those individuals are a little different from other sparrows, then their progeny in that new dialect will also differ genetically from birds in other dialects.

The point, then, is this. Birds in adjacent dialects could differ genetically for two reasons. If dialects limit dispersal, adjacent dialects will differ genetically, simply because isolated groups of birds will, over time, diverge genetically. But dialects can differ genetically even if they don't limit dispersal because of the "founder effect," with genetically different individuals founding each new dialect.

So, after all this, do birds in adjacent dialects differ genetically? *Yes,* according to Baker and his collaborators in the prestigious journal *Evolution. No they don't* declared a response from a pair of scientists two years later. *Yes they do!* echoed Baker and colleagues and yet another pair of scientists in written responses. These were contentious issues, to be sure, and hotly debated.

The beauty of any debate is that one can choose sides. The side I chose was *maybe,* as emphasized in a summary paper I wrote for *Current Ornithology.* Maybe dialects inhibit dispersal, maybe they don't. From how I saw my young Bewick's wrens disperse and learn more than a dozen different songs at their new location, I found it hard to believe that the dialect boundaries would inhibit dispersal in these sparrows. But I keep an open mind to this day, waiting for someone to do the definitive study, waiting for someone to set up a study area on a sharp dialect boundary and then monitor the behavior of young birds as they encounter the boundary. Do they move freely across it? Are they repelled by it? Are they in any way affected by the discontinuity in songs?

The combatants in this debate gradually moved on with their lives, and a relative calm settled on the field . . . until 2001, when a new study of white-crown genetics was published in the journal *Evolution.* Work this time was in the Sierra Nevada mountains of California, with a different race of the white-crown, the mountain white-crowned sparrow. DNA was collected at a total of 18 sites over eight different dialects, and, after lots of laboratory analyses and statistical maneuvering, the authors had their conclusion: Yes, the white-crowns differ genetically among the dialects; dialects do make a difference.

WHITE-
CROWNED
SPARROW

But we're back to considering the two possible explanations of why birds in adjacent dialects might differ genetically. Are these genetic differences among dialects a result of founder effects, or are these differences maintained because song dialects are barriers to dispersal? I also yearn for what we scientists call a "control species," such as another sparrow species that lives in the same areas but has no dialects. Would that species also show genetic differences in the same way as the mountain white-crowns, perhaps just because of how landforms in the area might limit dispersal? I know I ask too much, but that's what scientists do. Any good study raises more questions than answers, and it is answers we want.

I'm still a doubter about song learning early in life limiting dispersal by a young bird. I'm biased by my early studies of the Bewick's wren and by all I've seen since. I'm convinced that the song-learning system in songbirds is flexible enough to adapt to different lifestyles and needs. A chestnut-sided warbler, for example, can learn its "female-attraction" songs at any time and any place and from any adult, but the songs used in male-male interactions must be learned after migration on the territory that he will claim and then return to for life. When a chipping sparrow learns his songs depends on when he hatches: If he hatches in May, he has ample opportunity to learn from singing adults during his hatching summer, but if he hatches in late July after adults have stopped singing for the year, he'll have to postpone his song learning until the following spring, after migration. A sedge wren abandons imitation altogether, improvising instead, most likely because of this species' nomadic habits. Other birds, such as mockingbirds, learn throughout life. If early learning limits dispersal in white-crowned sparrows, it would seem that they might be unusual among songbirds. Unusual cases require strong evidence, and so far adequate evidence is not there.

I wonder what the Point Reyes dialects are like today. I've seen nothing written about them for the past 20 years. Are they the same now as during the 1960s and 1970s? Are there still six dialects, with boundaries between them at the same places? At tiny Bass Lake, will I still find the border between the Clear and the Buzzy dialects?

I must return there, I resolve, to sample them for myself, late next April or early May. I'll bike the roads and hike the trails, taking the old maps with me, replotting for myself how these songs change over space. I'll stop to record, aiming my parabolic reflector and capturing song after song on tape. I'll stop to look, too, to feast on these most handsome sparrows, to reflect on the role that these birds and their songs have played in helping us think about critical issues in where, when, and from whom birds learn their songs. If the Clear-Buzzy boundary is still at Bass Lake, maybe I'll find just the right place to erect a "Point of Interest" sign, much as one sees along the highway at historically important sites.

The Song Sparrow

What I remember most is the intense feeling of guilt. I knew that the only bad birds were the English sparrows and starlings, and Dad often cracked the upstairs window of the house, poked his rifle barrel out, and shot one from the martin house or the garage roof. But now this surprisingly warm body lay in my left hand, just seconds after tumbling from the mulberry tree, the stone from my slingshot having struck its mark. A song sparrow. The one with all the stripes on its front. One of the good ones. Dead.

But no one knew, as I was all alone, out behind the chicken coop. Over to the edge of the corn I walked, grabbing the sparrow's feet in my right hand and flinging it out into the field. It was my secret, the lips of the corn and mulberries sealed, and no one

> ### SONG DIALECTS AND THE WHITE-CROWNED SPARROW
>
> You are standing on the boundary between two dialects of the white-crowned sparrow. Listen carefully to the singing sparrows on your right, and you'll hear a half-second of paired buzzy notes following the two introductory whistles. From the sparrows to your left, you'll hear no buzzes, but instead a pair of syllables that consist only of clear whistles slurred rapidly downward. To your right is the Buzzy dialect, to your left the Clear dialect.
>
> In the 1960s and 1970s, at this very location, ornithologists tried to understand the significance of this kind of song dialect boundary. The question asked was relatively simple: Does this boundary between the Clear and Buzzy dialects inhibit young birds from dispersing freely from one dialect to the other? If the answer is yes, then song learning early in life, from a father or his immediate neighbors, helps to isolate neighboring groups of birds. This isolation would then promote the formation of new species, all of which helps to explain the abundance of song-learning songbirds in your field guides.
>
> Alas, the research generated great scientific debate, but the question was never answered satisfactorily. What do you think, as you stand here? If you were a young sparrow, perhaps two months old and having already memorized your father's song, would you cross this boundary into a foreign land? How easily could you learn the songs of the new dialect? How you respond to this boundary will determine not only your pool of eligible mates and the genetic makeup of your offspring, but also how rapidly your group of sparrows becomes a new species.

would ever know. Except God. And there was the church, back over my shoulder, right next to our house, its steeple a promise of hell to kids gone bad. I worried about that, and prayed. I would be good from now on.

SONG
SPARROW

Years later, in graduate school, as I was seeking models for my own research, I would learn much more about this song sparrow. "Studies in the Life History of the Song Sparrow," by Margaret Morse Nice. Old stuff, done back in the 1930s by a woman in a man's world, in her backyard along the Olentangy River in Ohio. Chapter after chapter I devoured, especially the ones about song, how the males sing, and how they acquire their songs—all this done in her backyard, by simply being among the birds, and being attentive, or obsessed. I could do that, too, I reasoned, and I spent my graduate years living with towhees and vesper sparrows and house wrens and especially Bewick's wrens.

And song sparrows, too. I had learned that a young Bewick's wren or young towhee learns the songs of adults where he settles, so that neighboring territorial males then share many of the same songs in their repertoire. The sparrows were next on my list. They were also resident year-round in western Oregon, so my friend Flash Gibson (no, not Gordon) and I began recording them in March and April of 1972. On the Finley refuge in the Willamette Valley, we'd pick a territory and wait for the resident male to begin singing in the early morning; the pattern of singing was obvious then, as he would sing just a few songs of one kind before he'd switch to another, then another, and we'd quickly learn to recognize his 8 to 10 songs, knowing when he was repeating himself and had no more new songs to tell (figure 13, track 17). After the Finley refuge we drove to the Pacific coast, about 50 miles away, and recorded birds there, too.

These recorded songs were converted to sonagrams, which slowly stacked up in our shared office; and then we sorted the song pictures, confirming the pattern of the wren and the towhee. Neighboring song sparrows shared many songs with each other, but non-neighbors did not, whether those non-neighbors were a fraction of a mile or 50 miles apart. The conclusion for the song sparrow was the same as for the Bewick's wren and the towhee: a young song sparrow, no matter how far away his hatch site, must learn the songs of adults where he settles and where he will spend the rest of his life.

Late during the summer of 1972, my wife, Melissa, and I moved to New York, to join the accumulating group of like-minded scientists under the leadership of Peter Marler at the Rockefeller University Field Research Center. Song sparrows were here, too, but here they were largely migratory, with only a few birds staying throughout the winter. Undeterred, I waited until the following spring, then methodically worked the field center property, and then that of the adjacent Carey Arboretum. I'd find a singing male song sparrow, erect a mist net in his territory, play a song sparrow song from a speaker placed at the base of the net, watch the sparrow helplessly fly into the net as it searched for the intruder, remove the bird from the net, put a unique combination of colored bands on its legs, release the bird, and move on to the next territory.

Within weeks I had more than 100 males banded, a wonderful beginning, but a beginning of what? I tinkered some with these sparrows, asking if territorial males could recognize neighbors by their songs alone (yes) and if males needed to learn their songs (again, yes). I also soon realized that these eastern birds were different from the western birds I had studied in Oregon, because neighboring eastern males shared few songs with each other. I soon became distracted by other species, by swamp sparrows and marsh wrens and sedge wrens and winter wrens and canaries and others, all with questions more appealing than I had found for song sparrows.

In the years that followed, others worked on song sparrows, and much would be learned, but it wasn't until nearly 20 years later, in 1994, that I became truly excited about these birds again. It was the work of Mike Beecher, a friend at the University of Washington, and what he had learned about young western song sparrows in Seattle's Discovery Park that so intrigued me. High on the park's Magnolia Bluff in the northwest part of the city, where old Fort Lawton overlooks Puget Sound, with vistas of the snowcapped Olympics to the west and the Cascades to the east—here, on the better part of a square mile of meadows and thickets, forest and field, sea cliffs and sand dunes, and two miles of secluded beach, live the song sparrows that give us the answers. It is here that we finally learn where and when and from whom a young male learns his songs, and why. Mike had begun catching and banding his song sparrows in 1986, and eight years later he started telling his story.

Much of Mike's story is told by a single illustration (figure 14). In 1990 four male song sparrows held adjacent territories in one part of Discovery Park—they were known as *myrb, myob, brrm,* and *yymr,* the four letters revealing the colors of the four bands on their legs. Bird *myrb,* for example, had a metal over a yellow band on the left and a red over a blue on the right, this bird now recognizable in an instant through the binoculars. Each of these four birds (which we'll simply call Birds 1, 2, 3, and 4) was routinely recorded until his entire song repertoire was documented. Into this neighborhood, then, during the late summer of 1990, a young male carved out a territory of his own (Bird 5). Late during 1990 this young bird practiced his songs, and all five of these birds survived through the winter until the following year, when the young male perfected his songs, confirming for the researchers what he had learned from the other sparrows.

Figure 13. Sonagrams illustrating the entire repertoire of eight different songs from a male song sparrow (track 17). I understand how someone might initially be overwhelmed by all that this sparrow has to say (I was), but looking at his songs one at a time makes the task much easier.

Consider first song A. It begins with three smudges—three bold notes that will sound buzzy because they span a fair amount of vertical space on the sonagram (almost 2 kHz). Next is a prolonged buzzy note, not quite so loud (because it's not so dark on the sonagram) but much "noisier," given that it spans a range of almost 5 kHz. The third part of the song is dominated by five low-pitched whistled notes, and the fourth part is an even lower-pitched soft buzz on the end of the song. Try to "read" the song from left to right over about three seconds and you'll begin to imagine what it might sound like. Now look at the beginnings of the other seven songs. Not one of them begins with bold buzzy notes. Using only the clues of the first three notes, you can readily distinguish song A from all the others.

Let's try song B. It begins with three brief, rapidly delivered notes followed by a broad-spectrum, buzzy hissing sound. Next are five rapidly repeated sounds, each of which will be heard as a brief high note followed by a low one. The fourth part is again a soft, low-pitched buzzy sound. No other song in this repertoire of eight begins with three such brief notes; those notes, together with the prolonged hissy note that follows, give this song away. Two songs down, six to go—recognizing these different songs is far easier than one might have thought initially.

Other songs are equally distinctive. Only song C begins with three bold, high-pitched whistled notes. Look at the whistles that begin song D—they have a high-low high-low pattern, just the opposite of the low-high low-high pattern of song E (though one has to listen carefully to hear those high-pitched notes in E). Look at how song F ends with those bold, high-pitched buzzes. I love the way song G begins: a brief, low whistled note (barely audible) followed by a bolder note slightly higher, that same pattern repeated, then rising to a high whistled note and then back down again. Toward the end of song H is a rapidly delivered series of notes that occurs nowhere else. The more you look at these sonagrams the more you will see, but now look one last time at how each song begins. Each beginning is unique and strikingly different from all the others. With a little practice, one can memorize those introductions and know which particular song he's singing well before hearing the entire song!

Having explored these songs with your eyes, you're now ready to hear what you know is there (track 17).

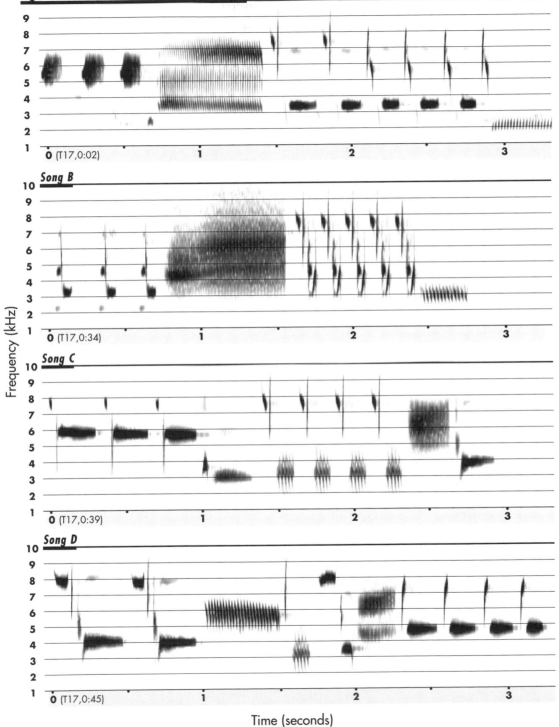

Song B

Song C

Song D

Frequency (kHz)

Time (seconds)

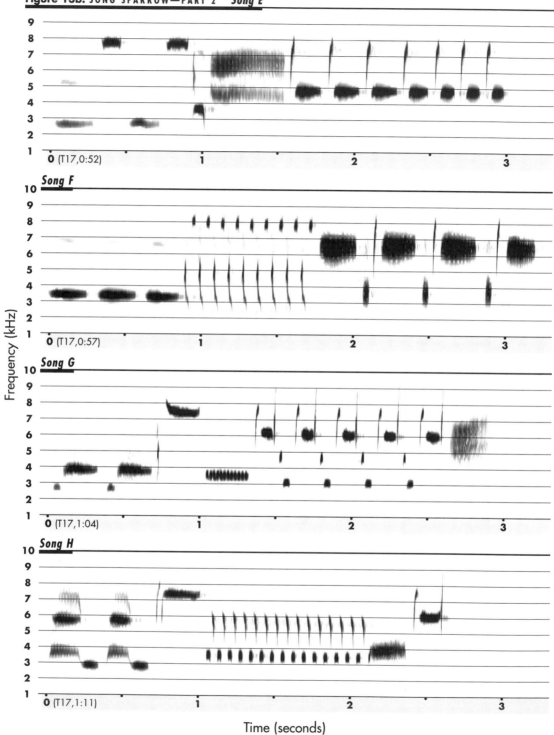

Song F

Song G

Song H

Time (seconds)

The Singing Life of Birds

Exploring the details of figure 14 reveals the essence of the song sparrow story. The repertoire size for the four males ranged from 8 to 11 songs, as revealed by the letters within the circles representing the repertoires of the four males: Birds 1 and 4 each had 9 songs in their repertoires; Bird 2 had 11 songs, Bird 3 only 8. These neighbors also shared many songs with each other, as indicated by the letters placed within the intersection of the circles: Birds 1 and 2 shared seven songs (B, E, F, H, J, K, L), Birds 3 and 4 shared four songs (C, D, I, M), and three of the birds (2, 3, 4) shared two of the songs (D, I). Each

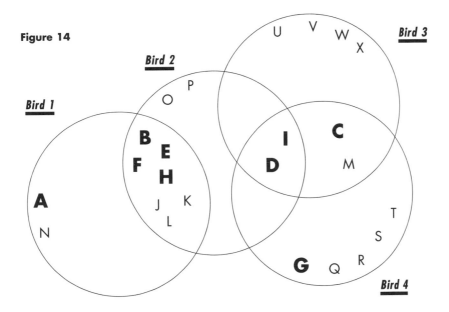

Figure 14. The story of four adult male song sparrows (Birds 1–4) and the young male who settled among them in Seattle's Discovery Park, the story all captured here in a single diagram (see the text for more details). In this group of five sparrows, 24 different songs are used (A through X). The songs used by the four adults (Birds 1–4) are indicated by the letters within each circle; Bird 1 has 9 different songs (A B E F H J K L N), Bird 2 has 11, Bird 3 has 8, and Bird 4 has 9. The songs that neighbors share with each other are represented by the letters within the intersections of the circles (e.g., Birds 1 and 2 share 7 songs, B E F H J K L). The young male (not shown) clearly learned his songs (large, bold letters) from at least two of the adults (Birds 1 and 4), and the community pattern of singing reinforced him to learn songs that were shared among the adults (B C D E F H I) rather than songs that were not shared (A G). I love this figure, as it tells so much about song sparrows, especially about their song repertoires and how they're acquired.

male has two to five songs that are not shared with these neighbors (Bird 1, for example, does not share A or N), though they might be shared with other neighbors who are not part of this group of four birds. Surprisingly, in these neighborhoods of extensive song sharing there can also be neighbors who share no songs, as Bird 1 shares no songs with either Bird 3 or Bird 4; as a consequence, a particular song often exists only in a small neighborhood like this, and males only a short distance away have entirely different song repertoires.

How these four males came to sing the way they do is revealed by how the one young male settled into this neighborhood and acquired the local songs. In figure 14, the songs learned by the young male are indicated by the large bold letters, and they tell so much about how a young male song sparrow hears his world.

First, the young male (Bird 5) imitates the precise details of entire songs from adults that he hears. For example, his song A matches that of Bird 1 precisely, his song G that of Bird 4 precisely. Among the many young song sparrows like this one that have been studied, only rarely is there ever any doubt about which song the young bird copied, and only rarely does the young bird combine parts of one song with parts of another to come up with a "hybrid" song.

Second, the young male learns his songs during his hatching summer. During that summer the fledgling gains his independence and leaves his mother and father when he's about a month old, dispersing a few hundred yards or even a mile to the general area where he will spend the rest of his life. Here he ranges over several territories of established adults, looking for space that he can claim for himself. The adults chase him, singing as they defend their territory, and the youngster fights back, learning their songs in the process. Whatever songs he had learned before dispersal to this place are all different and are therefore no good here; hence, they disappear from his repertoire. It is during this time, perhaps late into the autumn, that he learns his final songs; he may refine them a little the next spring, but by April his repertoire of songs is fixed for life.

Third, during that hatching summer, the young male typically learns not from one adult but from several. The young male in figure 14 learned his songs from at least two birds, Bird 1 and Bird 4, as all of his songs are shared with those two birds, but it's more likely that he was influenced by all four adult singers. Mike's studies have shown that a young male usually learns from three or more tutors, though half of the songs are typically learned from one especially influential adult who often survives past January 1. Early in the new year the birds begin to sing more in preparation for the coming breeding season, and the youngster must then solidify his claim to a territory. As a young bird and the surviving neighbor fight and sing, the youngster selectively retains more of that particular adult's songs in his repertoire. Overall, those adult tutors who survive the winter provide about three songs to young birds; those adults who don't survive the winter provide only one song. The young male can still be selective up to this age, because he has memorized more than the eight or nine songs that he needs, and he now whittles his dozen or more practiced songs to the repertoire of songs that will prove most effective for him.

Fourth, a young male preferentially learns songs that are shared by two or more tutors. This part of the story now jumps out at me as I look at figure 14 again. I count the songs that these four males do not share with neighbors, the 13 songs listed on the outside edge of the circles, and realize that this young male has copied only 2 of them. In contrast, of the 11 songs shared by two or more males, this young bird has copied 7. This example is typical, as a young bird is four times more likely to learn shared songs of tutors than unshared songs of tutors, even though there are often almost twice as many unshared as shared songs.

Fifth, the rare exceptions seem to prove the rules, as illustrated by two conditions under which a young bird learns a "hybrid" song. First, if a young bird acquires parts of a song from two different birds, he does so by blending two slightly different forms of the same song used by those two adult tutors. Alternatively, the youngster might combine two different songs from the same tutor, again showing the importance of learning from individual birds.

As each young male follows these rules, he guarantees that neighboring males will share a large portion of their song repertoires with each other. He imitates his songs rather precisely, preferentially learning the common songs and avoiding the rare ones, and he favors keeping the songs of adults who survive longer. The rules are that simple. By mastering the common songs, the young bird increases his chances of sharing songs with adults who survive in his small community. As an adult, he'll serve as a model for the young birds entering the community, this strategy for learning (and teaching?) guaranteeing a relatively constant level of song sharing with neighbors throughout life. The entire system works, of course, because the birds are sedentary, the adults remaining on essentially their same territory throughout life.

But why? Why is it important to share songs with one's neighbors? If all of the rules are geared toward sharing songs with neighbors, then those shared songs must in some way play a key role in how these sparrows interact with each other.

MAY 31, 2001. Mike Beecher and I are in the front seat, Liz Campbell in the back, as we head out to Discovery Park itself. I will see these sparrows first-hand, breathe the air they breathe, and hear the songs they sing. Over the Ballard Bridge, curving past Fisherman Terminal, over the railroad tracks, and out to Government Way, our entry into the park . . . past the bigleaf maples, the western redcedar, the Douglas-fir, the thickets of blackberry and salmonberry and nettle . . . and here it is, Discovery Park—song sparrow heaven. Through the open windows we hear the songs, from western tanagers, towhees, Bewick's wrens, and, yes, the song sparrows.

We stop near the visitor center, where Liz and Mike identify a singing sparrow. The computer already running, Liz opens the program Syrinx (available free to anyone who requests—see "How to See Birdsongs" in Appendix II), plugs a microphone into the recorder, and captures the next song from the singing sparrow, freezing a sonagram of that song on the screen. For comparison, the file containing the entire repertoire of one of his neighbors is opened and also displayed on the screen, so that a particular song of that neighbor can be chosen to play to the singer. Near the boundary of the singer and his neighbor, Liz quickly deploys a speaker connected by a 15-yard wire to their computer, all of this effort expended to answer a particular question: how does the singer respond when his neighbor sings a shared as opposed to an unshared song? For the birds depicted in figure 14, for example, Mike and Liz would ask Bird 2 if he responds differently to song A (unshared) than to song B (shared). I keep well out of the way, watching the entire setup, in awe of the speed with which they proceed and the sophistication of the question they can ask, amused by the amiable bickering between them about where to put the speaker, which song to play, and whether to throw out the entire effort because the neighbor responded to the songs, too, interfering with the experiment. In the end, following their preestablished guidelines, they abandon this playback, because it becomes too messy to interpret.

Gradually over the years, these kinds of playbacks have revealed how sophisticated these song sparrows are in how they respond to each other. In a first set of such experiments, Beecher and his coworkers showed that a male knows his neighbors well, and knows each of their songs. To show this remarkable ability, the researchers first selected a focal male, and then from just beyond his territory boundary and into a neighbor's territory, they played back a song of that particular neighbor. The focal male preferentially replied with either that same song or with another song shared with that neighbor, not with an unshared song. In figure 14, for example, if any of Bird 1's songs were played to Bird 2, Bird 2 would preferentially respond with a shared song (B, E, F, H, J, K, L) rather than with an unshared song (D, I, O, P). When a stranger's song was played from the same location, however, the male was especially likely to respond with a song not shared with the neighbor who owned that particular location. Clearly a male responds with different sets of songs to the two possible singers.

This was the first time anyone had thought about the two ways in which a male could respond to his neighbor. If he shared the neighbor's song, he could respond with that particular song, but if he didn't share that one, he could still respond with another song shared with that neighbor. In other words, he could either match the exact song the neighbor was singing (a "type match") or he could sing another of the songs that they shared (a "repertoire match"). These choices started to make sense only when the responses to these playback songs were studied throughout the breeding season. Early in the season, when territorial battles are still intense, it was discovered that males respond to each other mostly with identical songs, that is, they type-match. Later in the season, after boundaries are well established, they type-match far less and instead repertoire-match. Never in all of these playback trials did neighbors respond to each other with a song they did not share. NEVER!

Type matching is a stronger threat than repertoire matching, as revealed by further playback experiments. The experiment gets a little complicated to run, so follow along closely here. First Mike and his friends need to know all of the songs of all birds in the population that they want to test, and they need to know which songs are shared with neighbors and which are not. Now, in the field, they wait at a territory boundary between two birds, say, Birds 3 and 4 in figure 14. They want to test Bird 3, so they place their playback speaker on the territory boundary, facing Bird 3, and then wait for him to sing a song shared with Bird 4, either C, D, I, or M. As soon as they hear one of those songs, they respond with a playback over the loudspeaker, as if they were Bird 4. If Bird 3 sang C, for example, they'd respond either with C (type match) or with D, I, or M (repertoire match).

It was found that the singing sparrow was far more likely to escalate the encounter physically when he heard the type match from the boundary. The singer was far less aggressive when the neighbor responded with a repertoire match (in our example, with D, I, or M rather than with C). If the neighbor type-matched, hostilities abated when the singer stopped singing or switched to a different song shared with the neighbor. The results showed that a male addresses his neighbor by choosing a shared song, and the particular song he chooses signals the level of aggression: Responding with the same song type (for example, to C with C) signals greater aggression than responding with a different, but still shared song (for example, responding to C with D, I, or M).

What sophisticated responses these song sparrows are capable of! To neighbors, they always respond with shared songs, and at one of two response levels, perhaps depending on the level of threat. To strangers, foreigners who may be trying to take a territory or a mate, they respond with songs not shared with their neighbor.

It would seem that sharing songs with neighbors is the fundamental reason for the song-learning strategies in these Seattle song sparrows. But why? In some important way, having shared songs must facilitate communication among neighbors, so that territories can be defended more efficiently, or so that responses to particular neighbors can be more efficient. Or perhaps there's some kind of community effect, the males with shared songs somehow codefending their territories against strangers. It's possible, too, that males impress females when they share songs with their neighbors, perhaps by showing that they're part of a stable neighborhood and have lived at that location all of their lives. A male with all the wrong songs for a neighborhood is clearly an immigrant, of unknown history, but a male with local songs reliably shows he's been there since his hatching year, part of the local community. The songs reveal his history, and females might use his songs in this way. Maybe.

In one especially important and intriguing way, sharing songs does seem to matter. Those who share songs live longer, or keep their territory longer. Exactly why those who share songs hold their territories longer is unknown, but there does seem to be a strong relationship between the two.

Perhaps, speculate Beecher and his friends, the advantages of song sharing are so important that an older male actively tutors the young birds that arrive in the neighborhood. What an intriguing idea. I hadn't thought of it that way. I would have assumed that, as the older bird defended his territory and sang, the young bird took advantage of the situation and learned the song directed at him, because it was to the young bird's advantage to learn that local song. Perhaps it is to the older bird's advantage, too, to have the younger bird learn that song, so that his neighbors will be like him. Perhaps there's a lot more going on among these song sparrows than even Beecher and his friends or anyone else could have ever guessed.

So obsessed have I been with understanding these sparrows, I now realize, that never once did two key white-crowned sparrow questions cross my mind. With the white-crowns, it was important to know if a young male learned the song of his father or a distant male after dispersal, and whether he remained in his hatching dialect or dispersed to another. Those are the questions that beg for answers with the white-crowns, but the answers to these questions for song sparrows are so obvious that the questions aren't even asked. Each little neighborhood of song sparrows has its own songs, its own microdialects, and the recruits to these neighborhoods come from some distance, from other song neighborhoods. So of course a young song sparrow does not sing his father's songs, nor does he sing any of the other songs of his natal neighborhood. Those songs would do him no good in his new home.

I flash back nearly 30 years, to my days with the Bewick's wrens, who also sing throughout Discovery Park here in Seattle. Like the Seattle song sparrows, the Bewick's wrens are resident, or nonmigratory; a male learns his songs after dispersal and then stays in his new neighborhood for life. The young wrens enter the song neighborhood in the same way that young song sparrows do, and songs of the father appear to be forgotten (we know that they fall into disuse, but we cannot be sure what the bird retains in memory). I often heard neighbors match each other's songs as they sang. I would bet that if I revisited these wrens with my laptop and an array of playback songs, I could speak to them much as Beecher and friends have spoken with their song sparrows. I would also bet that the wrens and the sparrows are doing exactly the same thing, using their shared songs to type-match or repertoire-match, modulating their responses to each other in remarkably sophisticated ways.

Somewhere east of the Cascade Mountains the song sparrows change to those that we know in the East. Each eastern male sings largely his own tune and shares far fewer songs with his immediate neighbors. Without those microdialects of the western birds, it seems unlikely that the eastern males encode sophisticated responses in type matching or repertoire matching. These west-east differences are probably determined by how stable the singing neighborhood is. Western birds are resident, staying on their adult territories in the same neighborhood for life; natural selection apparently favors shared, learned songs in these circumstances, much as it has in the resident western spotted towhees and marsh wrens and in the resident eastern towhees of Florida. Impose some tough winter weather on these birds and make them migrate, however, and the microdialects break down, as with eastern song sparrows, northeastern towhees, and eastern marsh wrens. The extreme case is the sedge wren, which migrates not only between seasons but also within seasons, so that neighbors know each other only briefly; the sedge wrens' style of song development is also extreme, with males no longer imitating songs but making them up instead (see accounts for all these species later in the book).

How satisfying this story of song sparrows in Seattle, how satisfying to know where, when, and from whom a young male learns, and to begin to understand why he does so. This is how research is supposed to be done. First watch what the birds do in nature, year after year; get to know each bird as an individual, and listen to them, from hatching to death. Then ask questions of them, bird by bird. Speak as a sparrow from a neighbor's territory and see how he responds. Ask another question, and another, each one building on the other, refining the simulated interactions among neighbors. Seek the big picture, but tackle it piece by piece. Last, tell the world about it, and tell it clearly, in a calm voice — "Here is what we see; here is what we think is happening" — in inspiring prose focused on the birds and how they do their thing.

Borrowed Songs: Mimicry

The Northern Mockingbird

I first hear him just after midnight. He is somewhere to the north, somewhere in the distance on the other side of the building where I now stir. Barely conscious, I register songs of wrens and cardinals and titmice and nuthatches and . . . and . . . when I glance again at the clock, it is already almost 3:00 A.M. I had slept, I realize, but he continues, as he no doubt has on and off for the last three hours. I sit up, determined not to doze again, reminding myself that I've been waiting for a night singer for several years now. During my occasional visits to the family condo in Naples, Florida, I have slept on the screened-in porch or in the bedroom with the windows open, just waiting for such a night singer. No, I will not miss this chance.

Dressing slowly as I awake, I eye my gear awaiting me across the room. The binoculars sit beside the tape recorder, which is already wired to the headphones and the parabolic microphone. In the daypack are extra tapes, batteries, a flashlight, and a breakfast bar; my recording cap is there, too, essential for a comfortable fit of the headphones. After loading up, I grab my camp chair and then step outside the screened-in porch.

The mockingbirds who own our condo are quiet, as they have been all night. Perhaps they slumber in the dense bushes against the building, or perhaps high in the cypress or pine or palm now silhouetted overhead against the night sky. They were last heard just after sunset last night, "chucking" harshly before going to roost, just as they will no doubt do when they awake in three and a half hours. I walk to the left, leaving the condo territory, passing the pair of mockingbirds who own the shrubbery on the right; left again, around the northern end of the condo complex and out to the drive and the parking lot, then past the pair of mockingbirds whose real estate includes the mailboxes and the shrubbery surrounding the garbage and recycling bins.

Still to the north, the night singer continues, becoming a little bit louder with each pair of mockingbirds I pass. Between the swimming pool and the tennis courts I walk, and into the territory of yet another pair of mocking-birds; by day they feed several noisy youngsters who scream from the bushes surrounding the tennis courts, but in the night they are all quiet. Onto anoth-er driveway, through a small parking lot and into a grove of long-needled pines, owned by yet another pair of mockingbirds that I know from my day-time walks. They, too, are quiet. But here I pause, beneath a large pine, hidden in the dark shadow of the trunk opposite the streetlight, because I now realize that it is the next territory my night singer owns.

There he sings, well hidden in the fronds of a cabbage palm that stands alone in the fairway just off the third tee at Quail Run Golf Course. I stand, frozen in place, irresistibly trying to identify all that I hear: to my mental list I add the calls of purple martins, the begging calls of a young mockingbird, the calls of a swallow-tailed kite, the *flicka-flicka-flicka* call of the flickers, and many more that sound familiar yet not quite identifiable. Perhaps I am rusty in my sound identification, or perhaps he has altered his pilfered sounds just enough so that I cannot place them. Perhaps it is both.

Dropping my chair into the grass, I now sit, adjusting the seat to get com-fortable. I slip the headphones on, aim the parabola at the palm, and turn on the recorder's amplifier so that his songs now boom into my ears. Now con-centrating better, I try to focus on exactly what he is doing.

Instinctively, I count. How many times does he utter each sound (or phrase) before going on to the next? Here's the purple martin call: three times he sings it over about a second and then he pauses, the pause telling me when one song ends and when another will soon follow. The rousing song of a Carolina wren is next: *tea-kettle, tea-kettle, tea-kettle, tea-kettle,* four times he sings that familiar wren phrase. Immediately following is a different Carolina wren song, this one with three phrases. A song I can't quite place has five phrases, and another unfamiliar one four. A titmouse song with four. A dif-ferent titmouse song with five, and after a second and a half pause, he repeats the same sound five more times, which I write in my notes as "(5, 5)." His next selection has six phrases in a little under a second, and after a brief pause he sings five more phrases of the same kind, then after another pause six more, all written as "(6, 5, 6)." Then just one call of a swallow-tailed kite, followed by the urgency of a blue jay, *jay-jay-jay-jay-jay-jay-jay-jay,* eight times. He tops that by whistling a cardinal phrase nine times, then slows to a six-phrase song of a white-breasted nuthatch, a different three-phrase call of a jay, a four-phrase cardinal song, all these songs written in my notes as 3, 4, 3, 5, 4, 4, (5, 5), (6, 5, 6), 1, 8, 9, 6, 3, 4. On and on he sings, as I continue counting: 4, 3, (3, 3, 3), 4, (3,2), 5, 2, 3, 3, 3, (4, 3), (3, 2), 1, (2, 1), 3, 4, 5, 2, 5, 8 . . . all this in just a few minutes' time. I look at his signature in my notebook, so different from that of his close relatives, the gray catbird who would typically sign 1, 1, 1, 1, 1, 1, 1, the brown thrasher 2, 2, 2, 2, 2, 2, 2, 2.

At this hour his singing seems so deliberate, so measured, at least for a mockingbird. Or is that just my imagination, my sleepy mind deceiving me, the quiet of the night, except for the singing palm, lulling my senses. I must collect more numbers, to better understand how this night bird sings. I check my watch, now marking in my notebook the passing of each minute. Each time he switches to a new sound, I count, tallying 19 songs in the next minute, and then 15, 21, 15, 20, 18, 17, 20, 20, and 21. In just 10 minutes' time, he has sung almost 200 songs. Between most of the songs I count "one thousand one, one thousand," almost two seconds, as if each song must be delivered and briefly mulled over before another can be introduced.

He stops now, and so sensitive is the parabolic microphone that I hear him shifting his position in the dead palm fronds. For the first time, too, I hear the traffic noise in the distance, the traffic at the intersection of Pine Ridge and Airport Roads noisy throughout the night in growing Naples. Across the fairway, on the second floor of another condo complex, a human shadow moves across the grayish television light flickering in the window. Hulking metal behemoths lurk behind me in the parking lot, and the pines tower overhead. Far to the right, perhaps on the fourth fairway, a chuck-will's-widow calls his name.

"Give me another 30 minutes of singing," I find myself saying. So far, I have just been listening, resisting the temptation to capture his concert on tape. Initially I wanted it to be just him and me, just his songs and my memories, but he deserves more, deserves to be preserved on tape for others to hear. He soon resumes, a little after 4:00 A.M., singing again from the heart of the palm.

This time, as I record, I play a different counting game with him. "Just how many different songs can you sing?" I find myself asking him. To estimate his repertoire, I must be able to recognize several of the sounds in his vocabulary. As I was listening before, I became increasingly confident I'd be able to recognize certain songs whenever I heard them again: 1) the *kli-kli-kli* call of the American kestrel, 2) the nasal whistles of the nuthatch song, 3) the cardinal song beginning with two long down-slurred whistles followed by six or more brief up-slurs, 4) the *jeer* call of the Carolina wren, 5) what sounds like the rattle call of the belted kingfisher (though it might be the call of a downy or hairy woodpecker), and 6) the high-pitched begging call of a young mockingbird. I must include a seventh, too, one that sounds unmistakably like machine-gun fire, a burst of six or seven shots followed by a brief whistle, then another burst of fire—a distinctive sound. I had to give up trying to recognize any particular one of the Carolina wren songs that he has mastered, or other cardinal songs, or the titmouse songs—he has just too many versions of songs borrowed from these three species and I can't tell them apart. What kind of performance would a mockingbird muster, I can't help but wonder, if he didn't have 40 *different* songs to pilfer from each Carolina wren, a dozen or so from local cardinals, perhaps half a dozen from the titmice?

I'm now ready. The parabola mounted on a tripod so my hands are free, I record his songs onto the tape (track 18, figure 15), and as I tape-record, I count how many times he switches to a new song during each minute, simultaneously tallying how many of those seven distinctive songs occur. In the first minute I count 17 songs and one mockingbird begging call; 16 songs in the next, one each of the cardinal, the nuthatch, and the machine gun; 19 in the next, and the kestrel and kingfisher chime in; 17 in the next, with one example of the Carolina wren's *jeer* call. In the first four minutes I have already logged one example of each of the songs. I know that the longer I keep at it, the better will be my estimate of his repertoire size, so minute after minute I concentrate.

After 21 minutes I'm grateful for his pause. One, two, three, four minutes go by, the palm silent, my mind recuperating. But he then resumes, continuing through minute 30, until I am jolted by the sound of the tape recorder turning off at the end of the 30-minute tape, the amplified voice in the headphones now silent.

The tallies? In a total of 26 minutes' singing time, he delivers, to the best of my counting ability, 465 songs. That's about 18 songs each minute. And how about each of the seven songs I was listening for? The kestrel sound

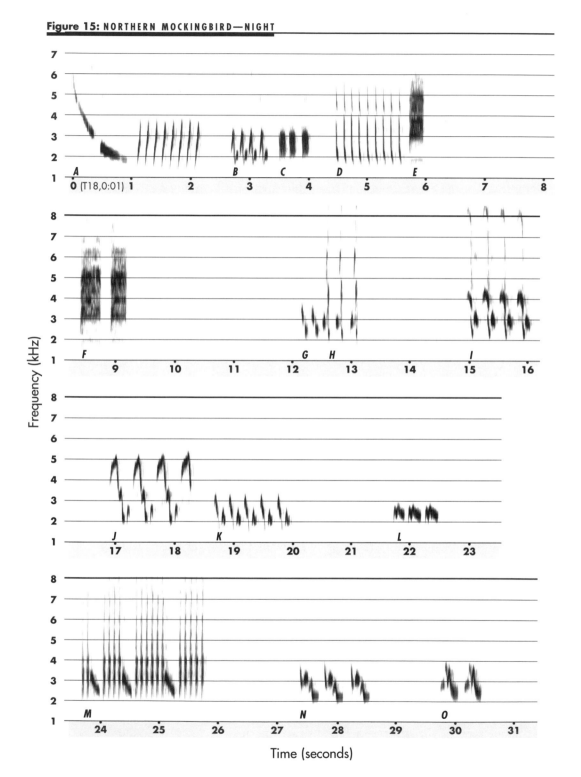

The Singing Life of Birds

occurred on 5 occasions; the nuthatch, 9; cardinal, 5; wren call, 3; kingfisher rattle, 5; mockingbird begging call, 8; machine gun, 2. The seven songs occurred a total of 37 times, or about five times apiece. If I now make a simple assumption, that the sounds I chose to listen for were typical of how this mockingbird used the other sounds in his repertoire, then the other sounds were also used an average of five times apiece during this half hour. By simply dividing 465 by 5, I can then estimate that from this singing palm, during the half hour that I listened, I heard about 93 different songs.

The experts, of course, will note a few problems with this simple approach. For one thing, as many as a quarter of a male's songs seem to never occur more than once, as if he's making some of them up on the spot. Because I had chosen seven familiar songs that I learned to recognize as he *repeated* them, five is clearly an overestimate for the *average* number of times that each of the male's songs occurred. I know, too, that he is far more energetic when he is courting a female, and a larger repertoire might be used then, as if he needs to be more creative, as if he holds some songs in reserve for more exciting occasions than singing in the dead of night. For now, though, I'm happy with what I have heard, happy with my estimate that he has about 100 different songs that he sings.

With a lot more work I could come up with a more accurate estimate, as some mockingbird fanatics have done. In Miami, Florida, for example, Peter Merritt found that males can have as many as 200 different songs. In Kansas, one male sang 194 different songs, and in Florida another male had 134, according to Joyce Wildenthal. Kim Derrickson found that four males in Pennsylvania averaged 148 songs in one year (1980), but the following year their average was 167, because males increase their vocabulary size from one year to the next. The mind of the mocker is dynamic, never completely settled, as he continually changes all that he can say.

In the calm of this 4:00 A.M. hour, each of his songs radiates out, like rip-

Figure 15. Sonagrams for a half-minute of leisurely night singing by the northern mockingbird (the first 30 seconds of track 18). This selection begins with an imitation of a northern cardinal (A) and introduces a total of 15 different sounds (A–O), imitating not only cardinals (A, D) but also what sound like Carolina wrens (J, K, N) and other birds I'm not quite sure of. Phrase M is the "machine gun" for which I listened during his singing. See here the pattern of mockingbird singing in which a sound is repeated several times (A, 8 up-slurred whistles; B, 4; C, 3; D, 9; E, 1; F, 2; G, 2; H, 3; I, 4; J, 3 ½; K, 5; and so on). See also the fairly leisurely pace for this night singing, in which considerable pauses occur between many of the phrases.

ples in a pool where a stone is dropped. Within a half-second all life within 500 feet hears him, the sweep of 1,000 feet completed within a second. In the cool still air, his reach is at least a quarter mile, his sound waves spreading over dozens of mockingbird territories.

How many territories? I find myself asking. Think. A little math. A quarter mile is about 1,300 feet, or 400 meters. I need the metric measure, because I remember one key number from my reading, that mockingbird territories in Florida are about 1.25 hectares, each hectare being equivalent in area to a square plot of land 100 meters on a side (100m × 100m). The mockingbird songs spread out over a circular area with a radius of 400 meters; πr^2 (pi × radius^2) is the formula for area, or 3.14×400^2. I simplify the formula, thinking that it is the same as $3 \times 4 \times 4 \times 100 \times 100$, and $3 \times 4 \times 4$ then gives me the number of hectares: about 64. Could that be? 64 hectares, I say in disbelief. I rethink my logic, then my math. No, that's correct. In those 64 hectares is room for about 50 mockingbird territories, about 100 birds, about 200 mockingbird ears.

Stunned at the number of listening ears, I now feel the social tensions in this mockingbird community. Each bird within earshot knows what I know, that this lone night singer is unpaired, as only a bachelor sings throughout the night. Fifty females know, and each knows she has a choice, to stay with her mate or to leave him and join the bachelor. Each of the males knows, too, that his mate has a choice. This knowledge is carried deep in the genes, in the essence of mockingbird.

I suddenly appreciate how these simple reflections explain patterns of singing among male mockingbirds. An unmated male sings nearly all day and all night, but once he attracts a female and she is committed to him, he sings far less. The singing wanes through the incubation and nestling cycle, only to resume in earnest after the young have left the nest, at the time that the pair considers another nesting cycle. That is the point at which a female might exercise her choice to stay or leave, and that is precisely when he sings the most. Even if she doesn't leave him, during egg-laying she has the option of visiting other males to fertilize her eggs. The singing is no doubt a competition to see who can be most impressive and attractive to her.

And how can a male best impress? Is it by how much of the day he sings, as if singing is a marathon? Or is it a sprint, to see how much he can sing within a much shorter time? Or does she value the quality of his mimicry, or the quantity of it, or his overall repertoire size? Or is it all of these, and more? She no doubt somehow knows that a male adds songs to his repertoire as he ages, so picking a male with a larger repertoire would serve her well, as she'd be choosing the better survivor. By just counting in some crude fashion, she'd avoid the young birds, those with the smaller repertoires, those with little or no breeding experience. Exactly how he impresses, though, is known only by the female mockingbird, and how he now sings is a reflection of the choices that she and her female ancestors have made.

Inevitably, I am led to the question most often asked of these birds: Why does a mockingbird mock? What does he gain by his theft, by singing the songs of other birds? I wish I knew. A friend has speculated that copying the sounds of other birds is an easy way to acquire a large repertoire. That may be true, but the mockingbird's close relatives seem to counter that idea — a gray catbird can have up to 400 different songs, a brown thrasher 2,000, but few of those are mimicked, and most are simply made up, or improvised. If it is the size of the repertoire that is important, then mimicry would seem to inhibit, not enable, developing a large repertoire.

Perhaps he mimics to deceive, it has been suggested. I know I have been fooled by this "many-tongued mimic," which is English for its Latin name, *Mimus polyglottos*. Just last March I heard the first eastern phoebe of the season in western Massachusetts, but within a few seconds' time I knew otherwise. Each *phoebe* seemed perfect, but there was something suspicious about the rhythm of the rapidly repeated *phoebephoebephoebe* that gave him away, and even the best of mockingbirds can hold the ruse for no more than a few seconds. I can't believe that the Carolina wrens and kingfishers and cardinals and jays who heard my night singer were in any way deceived.

Maybe the mimicry shows the mocker's contentious spirit. Sing *tea-kettle, tea-kettle,* and the Carolina wrens are put on notice. Whistle the cardinal's song, and the cardinals know, too, that the ultra-aggressive mockingbird is about. He chases other birds from his favorite feeding trees and perhaps other birds are warned at a distance, warned of an impending attack if they trespass. Perhaps the mocker is able to keep more food to himself that way, by intimidating the other species that would compete for the same foods. But why, then, a kingfisher rattle? Why a washing machine or car siren, as other mockingbirds have been heard to sing? Is the mocker just hedging his bets by imitating broadly, making sure he has a song for all possible comers?

These guesses hardly seem sufficient. My hunch is that the answer lies in the lady mockingbird's "mind," in what many generations of females have preferentially responded to. Neurons there fire when she hears something good, something right, no doubt sending a message of "pleasure" to some

NORTHERN
MOCKINGBIRD

appropriate part of the brain. The pleasure need not register consciously, as it might perhaps in us, but nevertheless something akin to pleasure must be there to make the male mocker sing as he does. In the same sense, I want to believe that he "enjoys" singing, that doing what he does so well satisfies some inner need for performing well.

Deep in the palm he's quiet now, perhaps anticipating the dawn. It's 6:30 A.M., about 45 minutes before sunrise, and I'm poised for action. Any minute I expect him to depart the palm, but how or to where I know not.

There—a shadow gliding down to the left, into the lower bushes just north of the palm. Haltingly he sings, halfheartedly, as if searching for a morsel or two after performing and fasting overnight. A minute passes, then two . . . Is that it, I wonder? Is this the climax to your night's performance, a few wimpy songs from the bushes? I expected more, but then he takes flight, a slow butterfly flight across the fairway, flashing his large white wing-patches with each wing-beat, displaying the brilliant outer white feathers in his fanned tail, all the while singing as he flies, my parabola following him to catch his every song, me running behind to keep up with him.

He flies to one of the larger pines, about halfway up. When I arrive I find him on a large branch low in the canopy, a bare branch with no twigs except at the very end. Roughly midway between the trunk and the twigs is a U-shaped dip, right in the middle of his five-yard runway. Wings outstretched and tail fanned, he runs, or glides, I cannot tell which, to the end of the branch, dipping into the bow of the branch and up the other side, and then back again to the trunk, and beyond the trunk to a similar branch on the other

Figure 16. A half-minute of frenzied dawn singing by the northern mockingbird (the first 32 seconds of track 19). He sings rapidly, filling almost all available time with his ranting, introducing 23 different sounds (A–W) that mimic northern cardinals (A, W), blue-gray gnatcatchers (B), Carolina wrens (E is the *jeer* call, O a song), blue jays (J and V are loud *jay* calls, P the soft *jrrrt* contact calls), northern flickers (L, M, U?), and no doubt more that I don't recognize. Note that the northern cardinal imitation in A is the same rendition that he sang during the night (A in figure 15; the other letters in each figure simply label successive songs and are not meant for comparing sonagrams in the two figures).

The Singing Life of Birds

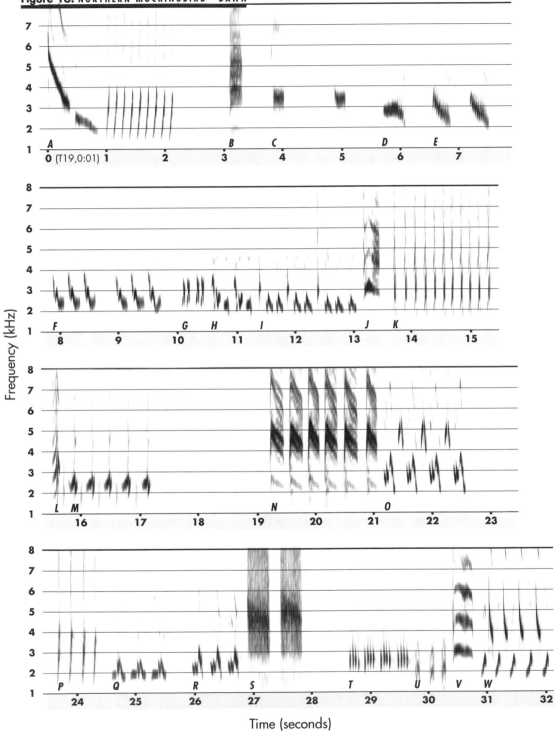

side. Every few minutes he run-glides, occasionally flipping into the air, a somersault, flashing the white in his wings and tail.

All the while he is singing and singing and singing, my parabola now trained on him from just a few yards below, I hearing nothing but him in my headphones (track 19, figure 16). I try to count how many times he switches to a new song within a minute, but I lose track too easily. I next try to concentrate for 20 seconds, registering counts of 13, 11, 16, 11, 12, 11, 14. I multiply those numbers by 3, to get the number of song switches per minute: 39, 33, 48, 33, 36, 33, and 42. Cardinals, wrens, jays, titmice, shrikes, kingfishers, flickers, grackles, nuthatches, and many more, even the machine gun, all delivered at nearly double his nighttime singing rate, with usually only a split second between one sound and the next. Part of the frenzied effect is accomplished, I realize, by how he often seems undecided about how to proceed: he sings a few elements of one song (say, A), then moves on to the next (B), then backtracks to A, alternating the two songs rather than finishing each in turn and moving on.

For 30 minutes he persists, twice flying overhead to a higher singing perch in another pine, but quickly returning to his favorite glide-way, and always singing, pausing never more than a second or two. Roughly 1,000 songs he sings, perhaps repeating each that he knows about 10 times; he seems frantic, presumably delivering an all-out effort to attract a mate. Only as the sun peeks through the trees between the two condo buildings just to the east does he pause, flying down into the shrubbery, now chased by what must be a male from the neighboring territory.

Who is this night singer, I wonder? Why is he unpaired? Why is he the only bachelor, the only one among the 50 territories within earshot? My best guess is that he's a young male, in his first breeding season, and less than a year old. Perhaps he hatched late last summer, maybe even as late as August, putting him at some disadvantage to others who would have hatched earlier in the year, as early as March. So perhaps he's among the youngest of the 20 or so first-year birds that might be expected among 50 males, and he had last choice of territories, taking what was left over after all of the other males had taken what they wanted. His song repertoire seems fairly small, too, as would be expected of a young bird who's just starting out. My best guess is that he's young and inexperienced and therefore less desirable to females; the older females would choose to stay with their partners rather than switch to him, and young females seeking out a breeding partner would bypass him for any available older males, those with better territories and perhaps more impressive song repertoires.

Or maybe there's nothing inferior about him at all. Maybe he's just a lone mockingbird momentarily down on his luck. Perhaps his mate died unexpectedly at the hand of a local cat or hawk, his life and mine coming to intersect this day as he was on the rebound.

As I head back across the third fairway, I find myself wishing him well. I hope he impresses some lady mockingbird and has a long and productive life . . . though I would miss his night singing and his lusty dawn display.

Songs That Aren't Learned

Tyrant Flycatchers: Alder and Willow Flycatchers, Eastern Phoebe

Even if someone had been there to document the event, it would have drawn no special attention. Over a few tens or hundreds of thousands of years, one species gradually became two, as has happened countless times since the first bird appeared some 150 million years ago. Perhaps the two species were at first comparable to our eastern and western wood-pewees, or to the alder and willow flycatchers, the closest of relatives, "sister species" that are virtual lookalikes, reliably distinguished only by their relatively simple songs.

In retrospect, this one event tens of millions of years ago was special, because the descendents of these two new species would become the passerines, or perching birds, by far the most successful group of birds on this singing planet. One branch of this lineage would be the songbirds, now 4,600 species strong throughout the world. These are the song learners, the master singers. Mockingbirds and wrens and thrushes and lyrebirds and all of the world's finest songsters belong here. Their brains are specialized for learning and producing songs, and their voice boxes are highly complex, with multiple pairs of fine muscles controlling dual membranes that enthrall us with their vocal gymnastics.

The other lineage, confined largely to South America, would be the "suboscines," now numbering roughly 1,100 species. Their name identifies them more for what they are not than what they are. The songbirds are technically called "oscines," but this other lineage is "beneath the oscines," or "not the songbirds," implying second-rate status, implying that they are more primitive, perhaps still much like the ancestors of modern songbirds. The voice boxes of these birds are far simpler and their brains seem to lack the sophisticated neural control of songs that the songbirds have. Members of this group are the less accomplished singers and include the ovenbirds (not the warbler

ALDER
FLYCATCHER

of the family Parulidae that breeds in eastern North America, but rather the more than 200 species of "ovenbirds" in the Neotropical family Furnariidae), woodcreepers, antbirds, manakins, and tyrant flycatchers, a few of those flycatchers having extended their ranges into North America.

Could it be true that these suboscines really don't learn their songs? Could this largely South American lineage differ in such a fundamental way from their sister group, the songbirds? If so, it would seem that the ancestor to all songbirds acquired the ability to learn, but that neither the suboscine ancestor nor its descendants ever did.

As I pondered these thoughts in the early 1980s, I realized that the evidence against learning among flycatchers and their relatives was only circumstantial. Songbirds usually have local dialects, an almost inevitable consequence of song learning, but no one had ever documented dialects among suboscines. In fact, if songs differed geographically for a flycatcher species, it was taken as a clue that the birds themselves were different, not just that they had learned different songs. Such was the case with the former Traill's flycatcher. Birds of this species sang either *fitz-bew* or *fee-bee-o* songs (figure 17, tracks 20, 22), and work in the 1960s finally showed that these were actually two different species, even though they were for all practical purposes indistinguishable by looks alone. In 1973, these two were officially recognized among ornithologists as the willow and alder flycatchers.

Increasingly, I realized that I simply needed to know how flycatchers and their relatives acquired their songs. Curiosity loomed large, of course. Knowing which groups learn and which don't is the first step to understanding why learning evolved in the first place. Perhaps we humans have a special fascination with learning and its origin, because the ability to learn a vocal communication system also distinguishes us from our close relatives, the great apes and all other primates. So the mountain was before me and needed to be climbed.

There was a more practical matter, however, of far greater importance. If songs of suboscines were not learned, then the songs could be used to identify species in a way that was not possible for songbirds. Because songbird dialects are learned, they tell us next to nothing about genetic differences among groups. A nonlearned song is different, however, and careful study of, say, *fee-bee-o* songs of alder flycatchers throughout North America could tell us whether or not these flycatchers are a genetically homogeneous group. If two slightly different kinds of *fee-bee-o* songs were found in North America, one from Saskatchewan west and the other from Manitoba east, for example, we would know we have two genetically different groups of alder flycatchers. We would then look a little closer, to see if these two groups warranted species status, much as the songs of the former Traill's flycatcher were used to separate it into the current alder and willow flycatchers.

WILLOW
FLYCATCHER

My thoughts shift to South America, the "bird continent," as it is called, with its 1,100 suboscine species. I see the Amazon forests burning, the Atlantic dry forests just a fraction of their former range — a "developing" continent, with habitats disappearing too fast to catalog. It's a race to just document the existing species, the units of biodiversity, and it is this planet's biodiversity that we fret over. If suboscine songs are not learned, then we have an instant tool for identifying these species, an instant tool for conservation. I must know.

So where do I start? Close to home, of course, for convenience — and why not with the alder and willow flycatchers themselves? Both occur in western Massachusetts, and with a little work I can hope to find their nests. So the search is on for baby flycatchers during the summer of 1981.

Initially, I envision a simple experiment: I'll try to train the offspring of *fitz-bew* singers to sing *fee-bee-o*, and the offspring of *fee-bee-o* singers to sing *fitz-bew*. In one room the baby willow flycatchers will hear alder songs, and in another the alder babies will hear willow songs. Songbirds raised under such circumstances would usually respond in one of two ways: either they'd learn the songs of the other species with which they were tutored, or they'd develop highly abnormal songs, indicating that they had not been exposed to anything they somehow "knew" needed to be learned. Under these mixed-up circumstances, no songbird would be expected to produce flawless, highly stereotyped songs of its own species, songs that contain all of the proper details as visible in a sonagram.

The eight willow babies to be used in the experiment are found fairly easily, from three nests in the towns of Longmeadow and Windsor; each pair of adult willows vigorously chips at us when we approach their nest, giving it away. The alder babies are more difficult. To the town of Windsor, high in the Berkshires, my friend Dave Stemple and I go, day after day. The parents are elusive, more reserved, with personalities quite unlike the feisty willow fly-catchers, giving few clues as to where their nest might be.

Up above Savoy Road I walk slowly among the alders and dogwoods, alert to any sight or sound that might give away a nest. Perhaps it'll be a parent with

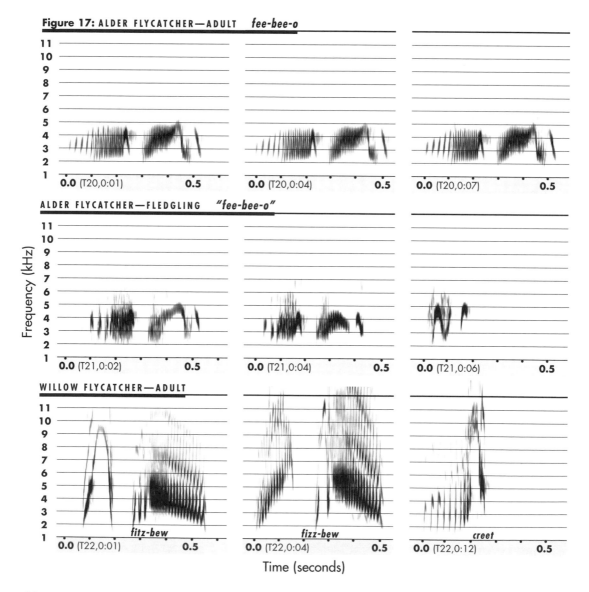

Figure 17: ALDER FLYCATCHER—ADULT *fee-bee-o*

ALDER FLYCATCHER—FLEDGLING *"fee-bee-o"*

WILLOW FLYCATCHER—ADULT

food dangling from its bill, waiting to feed the nestlings nearby; or a parent chipping at me because I've approached too closely to its nest. From the bush beside me flutter three or four birds, olive green blurs as they scatter. Instinctively I pause, waiting, wondering who they are. Then comes a soft, scratchy *fee-bee-o*, first from one bush, then another, until four nearby bushes speak of alder flycatchers (track 21).

This makes no sense, but it takes only a second to see through the possible explanations. Only the territorial male regularly sings, so only one voice, and certainly not four, should be here. And the quality is all wrong, too — the adult male belts it out, a strong, confident, *fee-bee-o*. These are weak voices, wavering, uncertain, as tentative in voice as they seemed in flight. Yes, four babies, just out of the nest, now scattered, calling, perhaps to each other so as to reconvene in the safety of the flock.

Astonished, I run to the car, yelling to Dave on the way — I must get my gear, to tape-record these youngsters, to capture on tape what I have just heard. No songbird does this. No songbird uses what will eventually be its adult song as a contact call just out of the nest. At this tender age a songbird is just beginning to memorize the songs of adults, and it won't be for at least another month, perhaps half a year, before he produces anything as close to the adult song as these baby alder flycatchers are doing. And all four babies are calling their weak *fee-bee-o*s. The chance that all four are males is ½ × ½ × ½ × ½, or only 1 in 16. The female fledglings must also be using *fee-bee-o* as a contact call, even though they won't normally sing as adults. Here, in this chance encounter on the Berkshire hillside, is strong evidence that these flycatchers are fundamentally different from songbirds. To "sing" such a good *fee-bee-o* at so tender an age, these birds almost certainly do not learn their songs.

Figure 17. Top row: Each adult male alder flycatcher has a single song, a harsh, burry *fee-bee-o*, that he repeats with great consistency. Illustrated here are the first three songs from track 20. **Middle row:** The adult song of the alder flycatcher develops from these "contact calls" used by the young bird just after it leaves the nest; see how inconsistently the young bird utters his scratchy *fee-bee-o* as it tries to regain contact with its siblings. The calls here are the first three on track 21. **Bottom row:** An adult willow flycatcher uses three different songs (*fitz-bew*, *fizz-bew*, and *creet*) in his singing performance (track 22). The *fitz-bew* begins with a sharp note that rises and then falls, the song ending with the buzzy *bew*. See the burry nature of both the *fizz* and the *bew* in the *fizz-bew* sonagram, an all-buzzy song. In the *creet*, see the rapidly delivered notes rising and ending sharply on a higher frequency.

The second piece of evidence comes from our collection of alder and willow babies that we eventually convene for our experiment. Despite hearing only the songs of the willow flycatchers, the alder babies develop perfectly good *fee-bee-o* songs when they mature, at about nine months of age after the short days of winter. As babies, too, both male and female alders weakly called *fee-bee-o* when I temporarily moved them from the group and isolated them in the quiet of another room. *Where-are-you?, I-am-here,* they seemed to call in their baby voices.

The willow flycatchers tell the same story. Anyone listening carefully to an adult willow flycatcher will hear him sing three different songs: *fitz-bew, fizz-bew,* and *creet* (see track 22, figure 17). The *fitz-bew* and *fizz-bew* are both two-parted, the *fitz* a little snappier than the *fizz,* the *bew* the same in both songs; the *creet* is a single sound, best imitated by rolling the "r" with an overall rising inflection. The yearling male willows raised in my home sing good renditions of all three songs, despite hearing only the alder's *fee-bee-o* after we took them from their nest. When just out of the nest, the young willows used what would become their *creet* song as a contact call.

EASTERN
PHOEBE

Just two suboscines out of 1,100, but it is a start. But what if those two are oddballs, different from other suboscines? I need another species. The eastern phoebe is abundant in New England, and it becomes the target of the next study (track 23, figure 18). Five nestlings from a single nest are raised in our basement, again overseen by my wife Melissa. From five to six days of age on, just like the alder and willow flycatchers did, they dine on the leanest round steak available, ground up with the other nutritious ingredients of our special diet (hard-boiled eggs without shells, cottage cheese, Gerber's carrots, turkey starter crumbles [a grain mix for baby turkeys], wheat germ, some extra calcium, Brewer's yeast, and, when available, dried mosquito larvae). Every 30 minutes, 15 hours a day, from 6:00 A.M. to 9:00 P.M., we attend to their every need, feeding them from a syringe, cleaning their nests, making them as happy as we can. These youngsters also hear no phoebe songs, only songs of willow flycatchers and marsh wrens, as those birds were housed in the same room.

No matter. As the days lengthen the following spring, the three males in the group sing perfectly normal phoebe songs. So do the two females, just a couple of days after I give them a little hormone boost, some testosterone to bring out the abundant singing that they normally wouldn't do. The details of their normal songs need to be appreciated, too, as there is both the *fee-bee* and the *fee-b-be-be* song. The *fee-bee* is used most frequently, the *fee* a whistled tone rising and falling, the *bee* a raspy note about the same length, the entire song taking less than half a second. The less frequent *fee-b-be-be* begins in the same way, but the second half consists of four or five brief, stuttered notes. All eastern phoebes have these two songs, and it is the detailed instructions for these two songs that each phoebe seems to hatch with.

There's more to this phoebe story, however, again showing that these phoebes "just know" how to sing. When I listen to an adult male phoebe sing during the hour before sunrise, I hear his pattern. For each *fee-bee* I write a "1" in my notebook, and for each *fee-b-be-be* a "2." At 4:30 A.M., 45 minutes before sunrise, he sings the following in a typical minute:

1 2 1 2 1 2 1 2 1 2 1 2 1 2 1 2 1 2 1 1 2 1 2 1 2 1 2 1 1 2 1 2 1 2 1 2 1 2

Half an hour later, still before sunrise, I chart another minute. His singing has slowed, and in my notebook I capture fewer songs, and a different pattern:

1 1 1 2 1 1 2 1 1 1 2 1 1 1 2 1 1 2 1 2 1 1 1 1 2 1 2

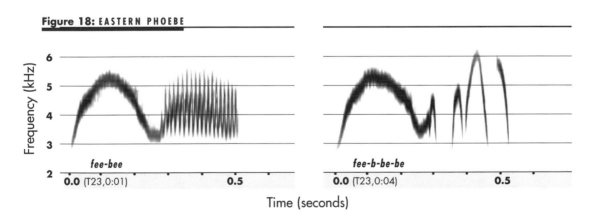

Figure 18: EASTERN PHOEBE

Frequency (kHz)

6
5
4
3
2

fee-bee

0.0 (T23,0:01)   **0.5**

fee-b-be-be

0.0 (T23,0:04)   **0.5**

Time (seconds)

Figure 18. Every eastern phoebe, thanks to its genes, has the same two innate songs, the *fee-bee* and the *fee-b-be-be* (track 23). The *fee* is the same in both songs, a relatively pure tone that rises and then falls. It is the ending that differs for the two songs: the *bee* of the *fee-bee* is harsh or buzzy, the *b-be-be* more of a stuttered sound.

Day after day of recording with many different phoebe males reveals a simple pattern: the faster he sings, the more *fee-b-be-be* songs in his performance, until he alternates his two songs. In the first example above, with a singing rate of 38 songs a minute, essentially every other song is a *fee-b-be-be;* at 25 songs a minute, only 1 in 4 is a *fee-b-be-be.* At only 10 to 20 songs a minute, often no *fee-b-be-be* songs are used at all.

Careful listening reveals even more about how he uses his songs. To preserve his timing, I would more accurately write his 25-song minute as follows:

1 1 12 1 12 1 1 12 1 1 12 1 12 1 1 1 12 12

Each *fee-bee* is evenly spaced, but the *fee-b-be-be* follows quickly the *fee-bee* before it. It's a subtle effect, but measurements from male after male bear out what one hears. From the beginning of one *fee-bee* to the beginning of the next, the males take an average of 1.8 seconds, but it's only 1.6 seconds from the beginning of the *fee-bee* to the *fee-b-be-be* that follows. He then takes a minibreather, the time between the beginning of the *fee-b-be-be* and the following *fee-bee* a whopping 2.1 seconds. After a while the rhythm becomes obvious, even though the time differences are small.

How about those young birds in the laboratory, never having heard this adult singing pattern after the tender age of five or six days, an age at which no songbird has been shown to learn anything? No problem. Not only do they know exactly what to sing, but they also know the rhythm in which to present their *fee-bee* and *fee-b-be-be* songs. Such innate knowledge of what and how to sing is unheard of in songbirds.

I begin to worry that I haven't given these phoebes adequate opportunity to show how they can learn some aspect of how they sing. I need to try one more test. This time I raise baby phoebes in groups, playing the different groups slightly different phoebe songs. If there's any learning, then perhaps the groups will acquire slightly different phoebe songs. Within each group, I also pair birds off, putting their cages side by side, thinking that a social bond might encourage two birds to learn from each other, so that their songs will be more like one another than like any birds in other groups. These are the tricks I know to use when studying songbirds, tricks that routinely reveal how the songbirds learn their songs.

Still nothing. I can detect no evidence in any of my attempts to influence the subtle details of the *fee-bee* or *fee-b-be-be* songs. Nor do siblings have especially similar songs. Each bird just is the way it is, its songs inborn and not influenced by other singing phoebes.

I know where this is headed, and I don't like it. Back in 1981, before I embarked on these flycatcher studies, I had talked with Mark Konishi, an expert on song development at the California Institute of Technology. We had agreed that if I could find no evidence of song learning in my proposed studies, one final step would be needed, a step dictated by how songbirds learn their songs. The young songbird first listens to adults and memorizes a sound; later, the youngster listens to himself practice, babbling until he perfects the match between what he has memorized and what he hears himself sing. It is one factor, listening, that is key in both steps of the song learning process. Prevent a young songbird from hearing an adult singer, and he develops abnormal songs; alternatively, prevent the young bird from hearing himself practice, and no matter what he has memorized, he cannot hear himself and therefore has no access to that memory, and his songs again are highly abnormal.

For all of my studies, one alternative explanation now remains, that the baby alder and willow flycatchers and the eastern phoebes had memorized a song while still in the nest, by six days of age, at an age far earlier than any songbird is known to learn. I now realize, too, that even if I collect eggs from the adult female as she lays them, thus assuring no exposure by the developing embryo to adult song, it would still be possible that the young birds have an "innate knowledge" of their song but still have to "learn" how to sing it by listening to themselves sing. The one final step to eliminating these possible explanations is to prevent the young birds from hearing themselves as they practice. Such a step is not taken lightly, but given the importance of knowing, and having exhausted other possible approaches, Mark and I agree to proceed together.

Four baby phoebes would provide the answer, four being the fewest that we dared use and still obtain results of which we could be confident. With the birds heavily anesthetized, Mark exercises all of his surgical skills in removing the cochlea from the inner ear of each bird. Any songs that these birds now sing cannot be "learned," at least not in any way that we can imagine learning occurring, because an essential part of the ear has been removed.

The results? Months later, these phoebes not only produce perfectly normal songs but also deliver them with the perfectly normal phoebe tempo.

Case closed. The *fee-bee-o* of the alder, the *fitz-bew* and *fizz-bew* and *creet* of the willow, and the *fee-bee* and *fee-b-be-be* of the phoebe are not learned. The details in the songs of these flycatchers are inherited in the genetic material passed from one generation to the next. Evidence reviewed from other suboscines suggests that these results apply to other groups, too, such as the

Central and South American ovenbirds, antbirds, and woodcreepers. The year was 1991, 10 years after my initial flycatcher studies had begun.

Another 10 years pass, and I now reflect on those results. I pull from my shelf the 1997 monograph honoring the memory of Ted Parker, the famed Neotropical ornithologist who, sadly, died in a plane crash in Ecuador in August of 1993. In that monograph I read that the slaty antshrike, a suboscine that occurs from Belize to Brazil, is probably as many as eight species disguised as one. Songs differ substantially from place to place, revealing genetically different groups of birds that have no doubt been isolated from each other over considerable evolutionary time; the authors of that paper cite my flycatcher work as influencing their decision to recognize the additional species. The authors stress, too, the conservation implications of recognizing these eight species, because some will undoubtedly go extinct if we do not protect the rapidly disappearing fragments of dry forest in which they occur.

In North America, too, some populations of the willow flycatcher, especially in the Southwest, are endangered. The songs of those populations differ as well, suggesting that these birds are genetically different from birds elsewhere and as such may warrant protection under the endangered species act.

Several new suboscine and non-songbird species are now described each year, and invariably it is the songs that are used as a key characteristic in distinguishing one species from another. Knowing that the songs are not learned but rather reflect the genes of the birds is crucial for making some of those decisions. In a small but significant way, understanding how my flycatchers developed their songs has helped us catalog the biodiversity of this singing planet.

From my deskside shelf I pull Ridgely and Tudor's Volume II of *The Birds of South America, The Suboscine Passerines,* an entire book devoted to flycatchers and their close relatives. I devour plate after plate, trying to comprehend the diversity of these birds: miners, earthcreepers, cinclodes, horneros, spinetails, thistletails, canasteros, thornbirds, tufted cheeks, treehunters, foliage-gleaners, leaftossers, woodcreepers, antshrikes and antwrens and antthrushes and other antbirds, gnateaters, tapaculos, elaenias and tyrannulets and doraditos and tit-tyrants and tody-tyrants and pygmy-tyrants and chat-tyrants and a host of other flycatchers, manakins, cotingas . . . At the manakins and especially the cotingas I pause, because I have recently verified that males in one small group of cotingas, the bellbirds, do learn their songs.

Most of these suboscines seem to be much like flycatchers in how they sing and acquire their songs, but the facts are few, and among bellbirds is evidence that not all suboscines are equal. I cannot generalize to all 1,100 suboscines what I have learned from only three flycatcher species.

I must spend more time on the "bird continent," studying the variety of suboscines throughout South America. We need to know about them, before they disappear.

Why Some Species Learn and Others Don't

The Three-wattled Bellbird

Departing the Cornell University Lab of Ornithology one late November afternoon, Dave Stemple and I pull out of the parking lot and onto Sapsucker Woods Road, heading home. Our routine for these trips is to leave an hour and a half before sunset, to watch for turkeys and other friends, to drive the twisting state roads in the relative safety of daylight and leave the thruways for the night drive. Once on the thruway, we pull out the CD that Greg Budney has given us; a kind gift from the curator of the Library of Natural Sounds, this CD is one of the latest Lab products that helps us pass the thruway hours.

Our early winter drive takes us by way of the recorded sounds of Costa Rica, the shadows of pines and spruces along the road now palms, the oaks and maples becoming avocados and other tropical delights. From disc 1 we hear tinamous, wood-quails, crakes, macaws, hermits, trogons, jacamars, woodcreepers, and antbirds, rolling past Oneonta, Cooperstown, Cobleskill, now tropical villages all. Rotterdam, disc 2: antpittas, then the cotingas, the umbrellabird, the three-wattled bellbird. Wait. Listen. Did you hear that? What all is he doing? There's that loud *bonk*, and three loud whistles, two more *bonks*, but he's doing something else among the whistles, very quietly. Back up. Turn the volume up. Again. Again.

It is only in hearing the bellbirds that I remember earlier conversations about them. Gary Stiles had told me that their songs vary from place to place in Costa Rica ("Song of male varies with locality," says his field guide to birds of Costa Rica), and such local variation is often the first clue that those songs are learned. Barbara and David Snow had written about them in the 1970s, suggesting that these birds learned their songs. But bellbirds are suboscines, close relatives of flycatchers, and almost certainly don't learn to sing, because it is increasingly common knowledge that suboscines don't learn. I also know that there are lots of other suboscines, however, and my hope has always been to find an example of song learning in this group. My proposals to the National Science Foundation to fund this research were dismissed as fishing expeditions, but I know the value of a good fishing trip.

Julio Sánchez, our Costa Rican friend, is put on notice. We had been working on sedge wrens together for a few years, but on our next visit, in late May and early June of 1998, we need to hear bellbirds, in person. He understands the urgency, and Julio never disappoints.

🐦

MAY 29, 1998, 9:25 A.M. Side by side the four of us stand, Dave to my left, Julio and Bruce Byers (a University of Massachusetts colleague) to my right, each of us with headphones over our ears, each of us with a cassette tape recorder slung over the left shoulder, each of us aiming his parabola over the tree ferns in the foreground and up into the avocado tree. Nearly three hours ago, a good half an hour before sunrise, we had departed our cabin on the flanks of Volcán Barva, scattering over the mountainside, each of us in search of our favorite birds—Dave his antbirds, Bruce his warblers, me my nightingale-thrushes, and Julio whatever good sounds he encountered. In the cloud forest at 2,900 meters, on the edge of Costa Rica's Braulio Carrillo National Park, we had all heard that first *bonk*, about 9:00 A.M. Without a second thought, we had rearranged ourselves on the mountainside like iron filings in a magnetic field, until we came to stand side by side beneath this creature.

Each of us with our left hand on our tape recorder, we instinctively turn the gain down, lest the ear-shattering *bonk* or piercing whistle saturate the tape, distorting the recording. But there is so much more that we hear, the soft swishing sounds almost inaudible when the louder sounds are captured just right (track 24, figure 19). Like photographers, we bracket our exposure, first

Figure 19. Two typical songs of the Monteverde dialect for the three-wattled bellbird (track 24). The top song (A) is dominated by the four loud whistles, with one or three relatively soft sounds consistently preceding each whistle. The lower song (B) begins with an ear-shattering *bonk*, followed by several softer sounds, a loud whistle, and then several soft swishing sounds again (a third type of song, not illustrated, often omits the whistle and a few softer elements just before it). The bellbird of the Monteverde dialect often sings an isolated *bonk*, too. In these sonagrams, I have had to darken the softer elements so that they could be seen; as a result, the relative darkness of the notes does not reflect how loud they are.

high, then low, then in between, hoping one will turn out just right. Then we try one track of our stereo recorders set high, the other low, to capture loud sounds on one track, soft on the other, simultaneously. Never have I encountered such a challenge to tape-record a bird's songs.

His delivery is equally unique. In the subcanopy, on the end of a broken snag he sits, the snag at about a 45-degree angle, rising up to the left. Three black, wormlike wattles, each about three inches long, hang from the base of his bill, one from the left, one the right, and one from the center top, this one flopping to one side and then the other as he jerks his body back and forth. His jet-black bill then opens wide, a cavernous gape sharply outlined against his snow-white head, for a second, maybe more, an eternity it seems. Through our binoculars we can see his chestnut brown body contorting, as if pumping itself up, preparing itself to deliver the *bonk,* exploding onto the mountainside, shattering the midmorning calm, radiating out up to a mile in all directions. The bill closes when he's finished, and he hops into the air, a short flutter-flight, and lands again, facing the opposite direction. Bobbing one way,

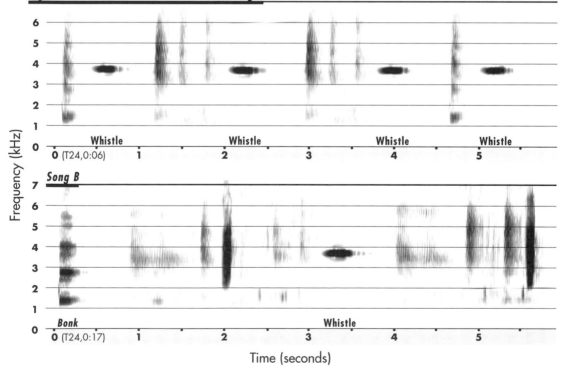

Figure 19: THREE-WATTLED BELLBIRD *Song A*

then the other, his wattles flopping, the bill opens again, the body contorts, and again he *bonk*s. What Dave and I had heard on that CD on a New York thruway last November had poorly prepared us for the charisma of this bird before us.

Besides these isolated *bonk*s, he seems to sing three different songs (track 24, figure 19). Two are almost identical, both beginning with the ear-shattering *bonk,* then a series of swishing sounds; one of these songs has a loud whistle in the middle, the other does not. The third song contains no *bonk,* but a series of four whistles, a single soft *bock* before the first and last, and three soft notes before the second and third.

Breaking for lunch, we run into Debra Hamilton and Pedro Bosques, who are from the Monteverde bellbird research team and are censusing the bellbirds today on Volcán Barva. "Did you hear the other one?" Debra asks. "The one that has more of a *quack* than a *bonk*?" Instantly, I knew. It was the bird off to the side, the one I wished would shut up so that I could get a better recording of *the* bellbird. I hadn't recognized the two singers as being of the same species, so different were their songs.

"Those that *bonk* are what we call the *Monteverde* dialect," Debra explains, "those that *quack* the *Panamanian* dialect." The word "dialect" hits me hard — she uses it so casually, but those of us who study birdsong reserve that special word for consistent geographic differences that arise through learning. A flycatcher couldn't have dialects, for example, because it doesn't learn its songs — if flycatcher songs differ from place to place, the birds differ genetically, too, perhaps enough to be called two different species.

Yes, instantly I know the two possible questions. The first is, Are they two species in disguise? If an individual bellbird acquires his songs like a flycatcher does, then there's no doubt about it — here are two "cryptic" species of three-wattled bellbirds, right under our noses, unknown to science. I recall the recent splits in North America of the Traill's flycatcher into the willow and alder and of the western flycatcher into the Pacific coast and cordilleran, based in large part on differences in their songs.

The other question is even more exciting: Are these true "dialects," regional differences in song that are learned? If so, these bellbirds would be the first example of song learning in a group that is thought not to learn. If they learn, perhaps they will help us understand why, and perhaps even provide an answer to the bigger question, about why song learning has evolved in some species and not others. Yes, I know the questions and the significance of the answers.

Debra having told us where to find a persistent Panamanian singer, we inhale our lunch, then rush downslope to capture a *quack*er on tape. Julio leads the way, at one point pausing to spar with a pair of prong-billed barbets, Julio's whistles provoking the pair into a duetting frenzy in defense of their territory against this intruder. Continuing on the trail through the forest, we hear strange squawking sounds off to the right, high in the canopy. "A parrot," Julio says, even identifying the species, but the quizzical look on his face betrays his uncertainty, and Julio tracks the bird down, stealthily slipping along the forest floor as he stalks the source of these odd sounds.

"A bellbird!" Julio exclaims, his eyes trained through the binoculars on the singer in the canopy. "A young one, all green!" Dave, Bruce, and I quickly gather at Julio's side, spot the bird through the binoculars, and then almost in unison raise our parabolas to listen more closely through our headphones as we capture him on tape. What comically odd sounds, the scratches and shrieks and squawks and squeals shattering the quiet of the forest (track 25).

Quack! Our riveted attention on this young bird is jarred by the sound of what must be the adult Panamanian. Julio is soon gone, working his way closer and closer, searching for this bird, until he whistles to us, the "come here!" whistle that all but we dismiss as just another bird sound within these diverse tropical forests. One by one we snake our way through the forest, lining up at Julio's side, our jaws soon agape. There it is, in the subcanopy, on a broken-off branch that angles up toward us at about a 45-degree angle. He jerks his head to the right, then to the left, flipping his long black wattles over his bill, the coal-blackness of the bill and wattles contrasting sharply with the snow-whiteness of his head. He hops into the air with a flutter, a blur of cinnamon brown topped by a snowball with bill and wattles of coal, then lands, now facing the other direction, his antics electrifying. One by one we raise our parabolas, slip the headphones over our ears, and enter his world (track 26): *quack! quack! swishswishswishswishswish . . . quack! quack! quack! swishswishswish . . . quack! . . . quack! quack! quack!*

The better part of an hour elapses, and we soon start whispering to each other. What do you hear? Yes, three different ear-shattering *quack*s, each consistently different from the others. One is perhaps more of a *bock*? And the swishes? They always end in a trio of rising notes with a distinct rhythm, a more complete series of swishes with an introductory *quack quack* rather than with the *bock! quack quack*. He's consistent, has a limited repertoire, and knows exactly what he is doing, so unlike that young bird.

The two questions reverberate in my head. Are these two different dialects of the same species, these bellbirds learning their songs like songbirds but unlike their flycatcher relatives? Or are these two different bellbird species, their songs encoded in their distinctive DNA strands? Answering these questions is easy, in theory, as the experiment is simple. I must raise a baby bellbird, not letting it hear either a *bonk* or *quack* as it grows. Then, when it is an adult, the bellbird himself will tell me. If he produces a perfect *bonk* or *quack*, the songs are in the genes, and these bellbirds, although identical in appearance, are two different species. But if he produces odd sounds because he's not had the opportunity to learn, or maybe even imitates the song of another species singing nearby, then I'll know that the songs are learned. Simple.

Well, not quite. Debra informs us later that only five nests of these bellbirds have ever been found, and the young birds don't sing well until they reach adulthood, which can take four or more years. They're endangered, too, their numbers declining. No, finding a baby three-wattled bellbird to raise would not only be next to impossible, it would be unethical, too.

Just a few months later, however, I would have a partial answer, thanks to the persistence of a friend in Brazil. Hernán Fandiño tells me that bellbirds of a related species, the bare-throated bellbird, are a popular cage bird in the town near where he lives. The town's name is even Ara*pong*as, which means "bellbird" in Portuguese, "pong" for the bird's loud ringing call, much like that made by a hammer striking an anvil (track 29). Perhaps this bellbird develops its songs in the same way as the three-wattled species. "It's worth a try," I reason with Hernán. "Yes, please, please walk the streets of the town, listening for odd singers . . . If you find a bird without the right songs, that would be exciting, because it would mean that the songs aren't securely encoded in the DNA, but rather that they're learned, and the odd singer hadn't had an opportunity to learn the right song. . . . Yes, I understand how your patient wife might not be too excited about adding this project to your already busy schedule . . . Let's see, what if I buy you both dinner on Sunday, and then you can just take a pleasant walk after dinner? . . . It's a deal." Fair arrangement, I think. I'll buy dinner for two, and Hernán and his wife will walk the streets of the village, listening to bellbirds. I am envious, but the arrangement is far more affordable than my flying to Brazil to enjoy the sleuthing myself.

Initially Hernán finds nothing conclusive, because all birds seem to be singing the right song. But then one odd singer catches his ear. In the courtyard, just over the fence from the bus stop, the caged bellbird utters only the first half of the ear-shattering *pongng* that all the other bellbirds have — like the other bare-throated bellbirds, he strikes the anvil with the hammer, but he lacks the intense ringing that lingers for a split second afterward. In addition, he whistles some odd tunes and has a loud purr. How odd (track 30). Hernán returns with his audio and video recorders to capture the sounds and sights of this strange bird, and when the Brazilian bird experts hear them, they agree that it sounds like a Chopi blackbird (track 31), a distant relative of the red-winged blackbird in North America. But that's impossible, everyone agrees, because bellbirds don't learn their songs.

A detective at heart, Hernán traces the history of this particular bellbird. What he discovers is that the original owner had raised him from a small baby, in the company of, of all things, Chopi blackbirds. When the bellbird grew up singing like a blackbird, the owner was disgusted, because he had wanted a bellbird, not another blackbird. The odd bellbird was booted out of town, coming to reside in the Arapongas courtyard where Hernán discovered him. The conclusive experiment I yearned for had already been done by a cage-bird fancier in a small town in southern Brazil. Bellbirds do learn their songs, I am convinced.

Others caution, It's only one bird, and what can one bird tell you? Maybe he was just a sick bird. But I know that one bird can tell me plenty and that the genes would never permit such a digression from the proper bellbird sounds to these odd blackbirdlike sounds. If songs are inborn, as with the alder flycatcher, I'd expect the young bird to know from hatching exactly what to sing, and there would be no experimenting with other sounds. No, the songs are learned, but the skeptics need better proof. I will get it.

We return to Costa Rica in July 1999, to Monteverde, where Debra assures us that birds of both the Monteverde and Panamanian dialects sing. We want to record as many birds as we can, hoping to describe carefully their differences and, in the process, maybe find additional evidence of the learning. Adults of both singers keep us occupied at Finca las Américas; one group *bonk*s, the other *quack*s, each distinctive, the rhythm of the loud sounds and soft swishes now firmly imprinted on our minds.

It is the young males that we find so captivating. They take six or seven years to reach their immaculate white and chestnut plumage. First-year males are all green with no wattles, just like a female. The wattles gradually lengthen and, by their fourth year, males show some white and chestnut in the feathers. We now know that these young birds take those six or seven years to perfect their songs, too, the young birds squeaking and squawking like parrots, taking an extended babbling period before the young eventually deliver their Monteverde or Panamanian songs. This babbling in itself suggests that the birds learn their songs, just like the babbling (or subsong) of young songbirds or young humans. It's still not conclusive proof of learning, however, as it's possible that complex songs encoded in the genes could take years to perfect, too, and the form of babbling required might be indistinguishable from the form required for learning.

It is one of these youngsters, a fourth-year bird, a mostly greenish bird but with just a hint of chestnut and white, who catches our attention. Dave and I are working together, Dave watching him carefully through his spotting scope, me with tape recorder and parabolic microphone recording and listening carefully through my headphones. Each time the bird opens his bill, Dave signals with his open hand, to make sure that we are recording the bird that we are describing in our notes. Open hand, wait a second or two, and the sounds boom into my ears: *bonk* . . . whistle . . . Closed hand, silent. Open hand: *bonk* . . . whistle . . . Closed hand. Open hand: *bonk* . . . *quack* . . . *quack* . . . (track 27). "Dave, what's going on?" "Same bird," he assures me. In disbelief, we continue, glancing at each other occasionally, for the moment containing our glee and finishing the business at hand, recording for as long as he continues. I now watch through my binoculars with my left hand while holding the parabola with the right, needing to both see and hear him for myself. And he flies. "Same bird," Dave says again, "had my eyes on him all the time, he did everything, the loud sounds of both the Monteverde and the Panamanian dialects, and also all of the soft swishing noises of both dialects."

A bilingual singer. A fourth-year bird practicing songs of both dialects. Here's the proof of learning we are seeking. A young songbird is often bilingual, too, if he lives where he is exposed to the songs of two different dialects, such as a white-crowned sparrow on a dialect boundary in the California chaparral. An adult then usually settles on one song or the other, choosing to sing the song of one dialect the rest of his life. That's exactly what these bellbirds are doing. If these songs were inborn, which would mean that the two "dialects" represent two different species, then a hybrid singer would have intermediate songs, as the hybrid would have half of the genes for each species. Perhaps it'd be a *quank* or a *boack,* but certainly neither a pure *bonk* nor a pure *quack,* and the soft swishes would be all wrong, too, with all the wrong notes and rhythm. But there's nothing intermediate about these songs of this bilingual singer—he has all the songs of both dialects, in pure form. Bellbirds learn.

Not so fast, some of the experts again caution. Maybe these birds have genes for both songs, and only one set of genes wins out in the end. That could explain why some young birds sing both sets of songs and why adults sing only one of the two songs. No, that's not sufficient evidence of song learning, I am told. I think through the reasoning, amused at what seems to me such a far-fetched explanation, one without precedent among all other birds, invoking an unknown genetic mechanism. The logic of my critics seems to be a desperate attempt to keep those upstart bellbirds and other suboscines in their place, or perhaps me in mine. These same observations of a bilingual songbird would have been routinely accepted as evidence of learning. Why the double standard?

I try to step outside of myself and look objectively at this entire situation. It's human nature to take these critiques personally, but as I rise above that, I see myself among my own critics. When something is *big,* I tell myself, when something challenges all that is known, evidence beyond the shadow of any doubt is required. Just as I am critical of the "dialects limit dispersal" story for the white-crowned sparrow, others are critical of my evidence for song learning among these suboscines. If I discover a new species of bird and claim it can fly, for example, no one will question my claim, but if I claim to have found a flying species of mouse, it's a different matter. These bellbirds are important, because they and other cotingas may hold answers to one of the most frequently asked questions among those who study birdsong: Why do some birds learn while others do not? I accept the challenges of my critics and search for further evidence that will leave no doubt.

Our recordings of the Monteverde singers begin to puzzle me. During January of 2000, as I study our July 1999 recordings, something doesn't make sense to me. The adults in my recordings are consistent, each song containing all of the elements of the local dialect. I now reread how Barbara and David Snow described these songs back in the 1970s and look at the sonagrams they published. Something is wrong here. Their whistles are much too high-pitched, and those other notes look different, too. The songs of the 1970s are different from the songs of the late 1990s, in at least a dozen ways that I can readily see.

Two possible explanations come to mind. Perhaps the Snows were sloppy scientists, their equipment faulty, their descriptions and graphs of the songs poorly done. But I know of them, know how highly they are regarded, and I am impressed with the details of their work. No, it has to be the other explanation, that the songs of the '70s are different from the songs we are recording now. That wouldn't be unthinkable among short-lived songbirds, as songs often change at a given location from one generation to the next, the learned dialects in a given area gradually changing over time as one generation replaces the next, with each generation preferentially learning particular songs, as with indigo buntings. These bellbirds live far longer, however, as shown by the banding records of the Monteverde research team, and some birds alive in the '70s would still be alive today. Each of those long-lived males would have had to change his song. Is that possible?

I know what has to be done next. I ask Greg to send me copies of the three-wattled bellbird songs in the Library of Natural Sounds, all years, all locations. Jill Trainer and Dave Nutter agree to send me their Monteverde recordings from the mid '80s. Curtis Marantz has some early '90s recordings. Mario Arguedas, owner of Finca las Américas, had found the songs irresistible back in 1981, and he sends his recordings, too. *Bonks* and *quacks* begin pouring in from all over the globe. The best news is that the Snows had had the foresight to deposit their 1974 recordings in the British National Sound Archives of London; curator Richard Ranft kindly sends copies.

What we find is too good to be true. We at first focus on that loud, pure

Figure 20. The frequency of the loud whistle in the Monteverde dialects (the solid symbols) has dropped dramatically since 1974, when the first recordings were made. Just look at that graph. I've *never* seen anything like it. The whistle has plummeted from 5580 Hz in 1974 to almost 3600 Hz in 2002, a span of 28 years. How might this sound on a musical instrument familiar to us, such as a piano? The highest note on a piano is a C, at 4186 Hz, so the bellbirds' frequency drop ranges from the F above that highest C to the A below (open symbols). I can't play on the piano the range over which these whistles have dropped, but I can transpose their frequency drop down an octave, starting at the highest F on the piano and playing each black or white key down to the next A. That's eight half steps over a 28-year change—that's like visiting the bellbirds every 3 years or so and being able to hear what they've done to their whistle between my visits. It's a striking change. I transpose down another octave, and then another, now ranging over middle C, bringing it into my favored range of hearing just to feel what these birds are doing. Extraordinary! The only (reasonable) explanation is that these bellbirds are continually listening to each other and changing their songs together, confirming not only that they learn their songs but that they continue to relearn their songs throughout life.

whistle of the Monteverde singers, because we can accurately measure its frequency in even the poorest of recordings. In 1974 the pitch averages 5,580 cycles per second (or hertz, abbreviated Hz). By 1984 it is down to 4,740 Hz, by 1991 to 4,405 Hz, and from there it plummets to 3,782 Hz in 1999, an average drop of 72 Hz per year since 1974 (figure 20).

In July 2000 Dave Stemple and I head back to Costa Rica, teaming up with Julio to get more recordings, to see what has happened in a year's time. We discover that the average has dropped to 3,724 Hz, down another 57 Hz from the year before. Here is the clincher, the 1999 and 2000 recordings, because we have used the same carefully calibrated digital tape recorder in those two years, kindly on loan from Greg at the Library of Natural Sounds.

Most satisfying of all is the one banded male with blue over gold bands on the left, gold over blue on the right (known to all of us as *azul-oro, oro-azul*) that we record in both 1999 and 2000. He had been banded as a three-year-old back on August 14, 1994, by Debra and her crew. In 1999 he was eight years old, and his whistle was at 3,771 Hz, remarkably close to the average of 3,782 Hz from all birds combined; in 2000 he is nine years old, and he has lowered his whistle by 75 Hz, down to 3,697 Hz, a little lower than the average for all of the other adults in the population.

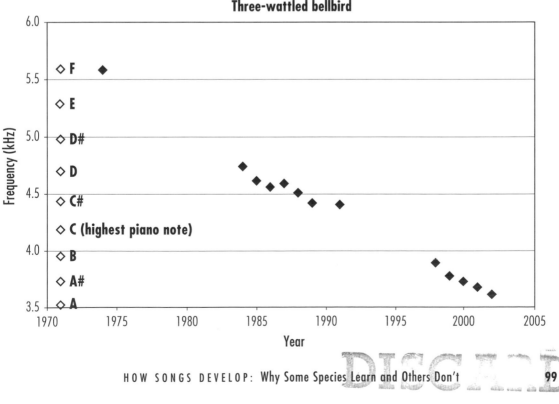

Three-wattled bellbird

There's more. The songs of the Panamanian dialect have changed, too. Gene Morton's recordings from 1966 had been archived at Cornell, and they've changed so much that it's hard to realize it's the same dialect. Bill Hardy's recordings from Nicaragua from the late '60s had also been archived at Cornell, showing yet another dialect to the north, the *Nicaraguan* dialect. In the late 1990s Chris Sharpe visited Selva Negra in the Nicaraguan highlands of Mata Galpa and sent us his recordings. Intrigued, we flew to Managua in July 2001, again finding three-wattled bellbirds singing at Selva Negra; recording them, we were amazed at how different these songs were from the dialects to the south (track 28), and also amazed at how much the songs of this dialect had changed since the 1960s.

Here is the unequivocal evidence. Not only do young birds imitate the songs of the adults, often becoming bilingual in the process, but the adults are constantly listening to each other and *relearning* their songs every year, keeping pace with the changes in the entire dialect. As a result, the pitch of the Monteverde whistle had plummeted from the 1970s to 2000, dropping even farther into 2001 and 2002 (see figure 20). Many other aspects of the Monteverde song have changed, too, including the qualities of the *bonk,* as well as the qualities of the swishes, though it's difficult to extract and measure accurately the fine qualities of those sounds from the earlier recordings.

How well am I doing, the critic in me asks? Am I favoring my "bellbirds learn" hypothesis because I find that explanation most exciting? Am I blind to other possible explanations for my data? I must be objective. If the information we have gathered on these bellbirds is inconsistent with all other explanations and consistent only with the hypothesis that bellbirds learn, then I can accept this rather exciting claim.

The big question, then, is this: Is there any other explanation for the data? My critics focus on the declining frequency of the Monteverde whistle. We know that bellbird populations are declining in numbers, one critic points out, so perhaps their desire to sing is waning, too, and as a result the whistle drops in frequency. Intriguing, but there is no known precedent for such a behavior. Or what about global warming? I'm asked. Perhaps rising temperatures lower song frequency. But no known mechanism exists for any such cause-and-effect relationship, and no other bird species have been affected this way. Or maybe batteries in the tape recorders have been getting weaker over the years, causing the gradual decline in the pitch of the whistle. But that bizarre explanation doesn't explain the other changes in the song, of course, nor how all of the batteries among dozens of field recordists could have conspired over the years to produce the gradual decline. Or what if some unknown bellbird species is hybridizing with the Monteverde "species" at just the right rate to cause the observed song change over time? Or if that young bare-throated bellbird in Brazil was just "sick," then by chance it might have produced blackbirdlike sounds, and it's just a coincidence that it was raised with blackbirds.

Scientists work by a "rule of parsimony," also known as Occam's razor. Take the simplest explanation to accommodate the facts, we are urged. I check the facts, over and over: 1) Young bellbirds babble, just like the song-learning songbirds. 2) Many young birds are bilingual, but adults are not. 3) A captive-reared bellbird sang the songs of a blackbird. 4) Songs differ from Nicaragua to Costa Rica to Panama, like a system of learned dialects. 5) Each male within a dialect changes his songs from one year to the next, keeping pace with changes that other males make in their songs. Based on what I know about how birds acquire their songs, I accept facts 2, 3, and 5 as conclusive evidence for song learning by bellbirds. Facts 1 and 4 are not conclusive by themselves, but they are consistent with the conclusion of song learning. "Bellbirds learn their songs" is not only the simplest explanation but also the *only* explanation that is consistent with all of the facts.

The initial quest is over. Bellbirds learn to sing! Since that November night in 1997 we have collected the data to confirm that these suboscines learn their songs. The help of others was indispensable: those who had recorded and archived their recordings over three decades; George Powell and Debra Hamilton and the nature guides at Monteverde who had become concerned about the plight of these birds and begun to band them, to study their movements, and to fret over their decline; and concerned landowners, who gave generous access to their forests. The *bonk*s and *quack*s from the Costa Rican three-wattled bellbirds are not from two different species, but rather from two different learned dialects, two oral traditions passed on from one generation to the next (and the Nicaraguan dialect is a third). Here is unequivocal evidence of song learning among the suboscine relatives of the song-learning songbirds.

Understanding *why* these bellbirds learn is another matter, of course, and that quest may take another lifetime—but I have a hunch, a working hunch, derived from the social system of these birds. Males display from their broken-off stubs beneath the canopy, but singing and courting is all they do; a female selects the male with whom she'll mate and then flies off to raise the young by herself. Males compete intensely for females, and the "best" males win far more than their share of matings. My hunch is that it is under this kind of intense competition for females that learning evolved. The males are long-lived, too, and all seem to know each other, often visiting each other on their display perches, or else they'd not be able to change their songs together.

I consider some other groups in which song learning has been documented. Among hummingbirds, it seems that learning has been documented only in lekking species, that is, those species in which males congregate and display and compete for females, just like the bellbirds. Or consider the humpback whale—again, males are long-lived, and the mating system is presumably nonmonogamous, with a few males achieving the majority of matings. In both the whale and the bellbird, males apparently compete with their songs and continually relearn them from each other within the "dialect," resulting in marked changes in song over time within each generation.

That's my hunch, that when the stakes are especially high, with just a few of the males being successful, and especially when the birds are long-lived and all know each other, the situation is fertile for song learning to evolve. Young males observe the success of the older birds and try their best to emulate them. The wise old adults change their song from one season to the next, forcing the youngsters to play catchup. That's the way dialects change in humans, too, with a few especially influential people affecting how others speak.

What next? Can I find any support for this idea? It is the other cotingas who may hold some answers, I believe. I would love to see an evolutionary tree of all 69 cotinga species, to know exactly how each is related to the other species. On this tree, I would plot all of the social systems and how all of the species develop their songs. If my hunch is correct, the song learning would occur only among those cotingas in which males compete especially strongly for females, as in the nonmonogamous mating systems of the lekking bellbirds. Given that we know neither how these cotingas are related to each other, nor how they acquire their songs, nor, for many of them, their mating systems, I have my work cut out for me.

The Sedge Wren

Of all biological questions, those about evolution are the toughest to answer. The problem is one of time. For one thing, the events we want to understand happened long ago. No one was there to document why the ancestral songbird learned to sing, why mockingbirds began to mock, or why the jay lost its song. Even if we had been there, though, we couldn't have appreciated the changes taking place, because these events take time, perhaps hundreds of thousands of years, the changes from one generation to the next imperceptible. The eventual results of these slow evolutionary processes are often so remarkable that many people refuse to believe that gradual change could have happened at all, instead choosing to believe what seems a simpler explanation, that birds and other beings were created in their current state.

These frustrations in understanding evolutionary questions were foremost in our minds as Jerry Verner and I contemplated the marsh wrens that he had studied in Washington State. We wanted to know why his male wrens imitated more than 100 songs apiece from each other. Why did the males play games with each other, answering each other with identical songs as they raced through their large repertoires? How did these marsh wrens come to be like this?

We hoped that hints to an answer could be found in the marsh wren's closest relative, the sedge wren. Just a few million years ago, their common ancestor gave rise to these two species (as well as to two others, the Mérida wren, now endemic to the Venezuelan Andes, and the Apolinar's wren, endemic to Colombia). If the marsh and sedge wrens now differ in some fundamental ways, perhaps we can relate their differences in singing behavior to differences in some feature of their life history. We might then learn a bit about how evolution has shaped these two species, and why.

Such was our reasoning as we met at Goose Lake Prairie State Park in Illinois, in mid June, 1974. Jerry's marsh wren work would be published a year later, in Cornell University's *Living Bird,* but we were already looking ahead, taking the next logical step. Little did we realize where these sedge wrens would take us over the next quarter century.

❦

We are late. As we stand on the edge of the prairie, near the relative safety of our camper trailer, lightning bolts dance about the western sky. We know where we wanted to be, a mile's walk out into the prairie, standing among the sedge wrens, waiting for them to awaken and sing, but that would have been well over an hour ago. Here it is, already after sunrise, and we stand, watching, waiting, not wanting to be the high point in the prairie when the next storm cell moves through. The radio had warned of tornadoes in the night and more threatening weather to come, so we stand, tape recorders slung over our shoulders, parabolas and netting gear in hand, other supplies in our loaded packs, waiting . . . slowly convincing ourselves that the storm is heading the other way.

"Let's go," we agree. It is a brisk walk through terrain rendered featureless by my obsession with maintaining a constant compass direction, by my obsession with finding those wrens who have already sung hundreds of songs that I haven't captured on tape this morning. Every few steps I imagine another song missed, as if each wren has just so many to sing and will then stop, leaving our tapes empty, our trip a failure.

Up ahead we hear them, *cut-cut-cut-trrrrrrrrrrrrr*. Approaching, we first see one to the left, clinging to the tip of one of the highest grass stems around, belting out his *cut-cut-cut-trrrrrrrrrrrrrr*, three or four introductory notes followed by a dry, staccato chatter (track 32, figure 21). *Cut-cut-cut-trrrrrrrrrrrrrr,* a song about every four seconds. Laying our netting gear and packs on a tarp, we quickly deploy our tape recorders, Jerry focusing on this first bird, I on his neighbor. Song after song is gathered in by each parabola, these big ears so effective it's as if they reach out and pluck the song from the opened bill of the wren itself. After 24 minutes we put the next 900-foot open-reel tape on our Uher recorders, again and again, filling tape after tape with hundreds of sedge wren songs.

Over the next three days we find other singing wrens at the preserve, too. When we find two males singing near each other, we record in tandem, coordinating our tape recordings with a walkie-talkie. Later, back in the laboratory, I will dissect the exchanges between these birds, discovering exactly which song they use as they respond to each other.

Wanting to make sure who's who, we set about netting a few individuals so we can give each a unique combination of colored leg bands. Between two aluminum poles we string our six-meter-long black mist net, each pole about six feet high, each tiny cell in the net about three-quarters of an inch square. At the base of the net we place a tape recorder broadcasting sedge wren songs, a proven technique to rile any territorial male. We then circle around, knowing that the song will attract the male, but that we'll have to push the wren into a net that is so visible in the open prairie sky. Two of us, slowly moving in, knowing the wren is close to the speaker, then rushing the net, flushing the wren into . . . and through the net! Again we try, and again the bird seems to fly through the net, hardly skipping a beat. These sedge wrens are tiny, just a few grams, perhaps only three-fourths the size of a marsh wren. Chuckling at how easily he eludes us, at how easily he flies through the net that routinely catches his larger cousin the marsh wren, we string a second net with the first, now a double net that the bird will have to fly through. Success.

His tiny head protrudes from between my index and middle fingers, a gentle neck hold, his body secured lightly in my fist. Such a tiny bill, slightly down-curved, so tiny that he was until recently named for it: the "short-billed marsh wren" (the current "marsh wren" having previously been called the "long-billed marsh wren"). Slightly opening my fist, I see the fine black-and-white streaks down the back give way to an orangish buffy rump; delicate bars of white and black and cinnamon grace the short, rounded wings; the tail is short, mottled with black; beneath he's lightest, giving way to buffy sides. Mouse-birds they are, in the secretive way they prowl the grasses, in their soft brown and buff plumage, in their size.

SEDGE WREN

On each leg I now slip a red plastic leg band, forever identifying this particular male as "red-red." I loosen my grip ever so slightly . . . swoosh, and he's gone, fluttering down to the grass, to be identified easily now at a distance through the binoculars.

In all but the first of the four days at the prairie we arise two hours before sunrise, eat a quick breakfast, and hike the distance, waiting where we know they will begin singing. In all we record nine birds from well before sunrise throughout the day.

As we walk out from our field site the last day, our tapes now full, waves of bluestem and Indian grass and switchgrass flow in all directions, and I realize why the settlers called this tall-grass prairie a sea of grass with pretty flowers. Seeing the prairie now for the first time, I puzzle over these sedge wrens. As we recorded neighboring males we heard no countersinging games like Jerry had documented among his Washington marsh wrens; in neither the heat of a dawn battle nor the leisurely singing of midday did we ever hear males answer each other with identical songs. Over the four days my concern had grown that we were failing to capture on tape or in our heads what these wrens were doing. I had expected something different, something more like Jerry's marsh wrens. In my most objective of thoughts, I know that differences between these two wrens would help us understand them better, but I fear that the information we had collected was all wrong and didn't fairly represent the sedge wrens.

It is my job to analyze the tape recordings. Back at the field station of Rockefeller University, where I was based at the time, I play my tapes into the "continuous spectrum analyzer," an exciting new device in which the songs dance on an oscilloscope screen as a camera films continuously. It's a remarkable advance over the old Kay Sonagraph, on which it always seemed to take forever to graph a single song. I soon see those thousands of songs we collect-

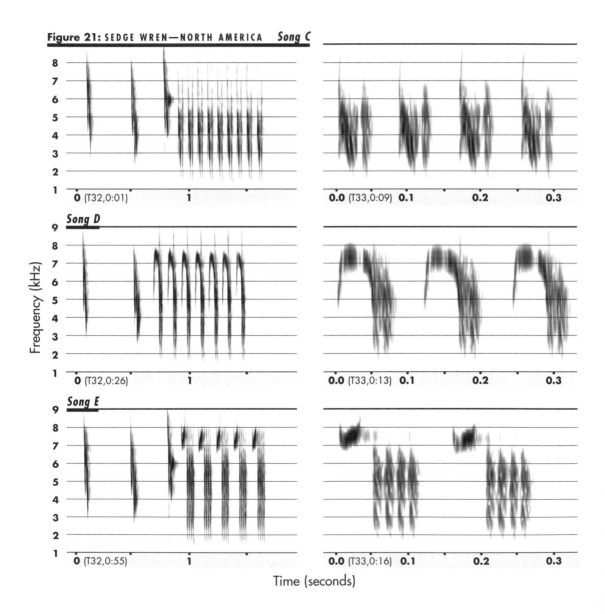

Figure 21: SEDGE WREN—NORTH AMERICA *Song C*

The Singing Life of Birds

ed at Goose Lake Prairie, gradually emerging in the darkroom as the hundreds, then thousands of feet of 35-mm photographic paper are dumped into the big buckets of developer, then stop bath, then fixer. As the paper washes I can't help but dip into the bucket and pull out a loop, admiring how the black images of songs against the white paper reveal the magic in the singing bird.

Hundreds of feet of the photographic paper are hung out to dry on our "clothes lines," then rolled up, and finally stacked on my desk, awaiting study. I take the first roll and scroll through it, clipping out each of the songs, labeling them so that I know who sang them and when. Then the next roll, and the next, until none remain, a small bundle of miniature sonagrams having now accumulated for each male.

In the bundle for Bird 8 I have 1,112 songs, the largest sample for any of our recorded birds, so I begin with him. Each of his songs is of the basic *cut-cut-cut-trrrrrrrrrrrrrrr* form (figure 21). The *cut-cut-cut* is almost always the same, actually four notes rather than three, the pace accelerating as they are delivered, with a third of a second between the first two notes, a quarter of a second between the second and third, and only a tenth of a second between the last two, those last two delivered in such rapid succession that they are heard as one. Then, within an eighth of a second, the trill quickly follows the last introductory note; I find 84 different versions of the *trrrrrrrrrrrrrr*, the staccato trill, each of them precisely repeatable, the details of each rendition consistent from one clipping to the next under my magnifying glass. In the last 400 or so songs, I find only four new *trrrrrrrrrrrrrrr* trills, indicating that he has told me most of what he knows, that I have fairly thoroughly documented all of the songs in his repertoire.

Bird 4 is next. I lay out his 755 songs on the table. His *cut-cut-cut* introductory notes are the same as those from Bird 8, and in these 755 songs I find 141 different staccato trills. My sample seems woefully incomplete, however, as I find almost as many new songs in the last 100 songs recorded as in the first

Figure 21. In the left column are three typical songs of the North American sedge wren, each song with two or three introductory notes and the dry, staccato chatter (track 32). These are the snowflakes of bird song, each male having a unique repertoire of improvised songs. (Songs C, D, and E are part of a longer sequence, as explained for track 32.) The repeated elements of the staccato chatter are difficult to see at this resolution, however, so in the right column I produce two to four of those elements at an expanded time scale; listen to these elements slowed down on track 33 and revel in their details.

100. Maybe he is capable of singing 200 or even 300 different songs. What a difference between these two birds—so unlike the marsh wren, I think, in which Jerry's neighboring males in Washington have almost exactly the same number of songs, just a little over 100.

I'm eager for the next step, to compare the songs of these two neighboring birds. At Goose Lake Prairie I had heard no "matched countersinging," no give-and-take with neighbors answering each other with identical songs. So either these males have identical songs in their repertoires but choose not to reply to each other with these matching songs (as I now know song sparrows do), or they have different songs and are incapable of matching each other. Those are the only two possible explanations I can think of.

I next arrange all 141 of Bird 4's songs on the table, from the slowest to the fastest *trrrrrrrrrrrrrr* trills. At the top left are trills so slow I can easily count the four or five trill phrases as he sings; at the lower right are those trills so fast that they are a blur to my ears, a buzzy rattle. On the next table I arrange all of Bird 8's songs, also from slowest to fastest. Here before me is a window on the mind of each bird, what it knows, what it can sing. Beyond the cold facts on the table, I try to see into the small warm brain, wondering how it got the songs it now knows, wondering how the details of each of these songs could be encoded there.

I pick up the slowest trill for Bird 8 and then search for the identical trill in the repertoire of Bird 4. Scanning the rows and columns of song clippings once, twice, three times . . . I find nothing. No match. If these were marsh wrens, I'd almost certainly find an immediate match. But maybe that first song was an odd one. I pick up the next—again nothing. And the next, and the next. Thousands of comparisons later, I step back from my efforts, flabbergasted at what I now see before me. Very few songs of these two birds match each other. How could this be? Perhaps the recorders or the analyzer were playing tricks on me? I imagine demons at work, somehow transfiguring the true sedge wren songs into the charade before me. No, my trustworthy equipment leaves no room for such trickery. There's only one conclusion possible: Each of these two males has essentially a unique repertoire of songs. I now know why they didn't match each other's songs at Goose Lake—they couldn't.

Maybe either Bird 4 or Bird 8 is an oddball, an imposter, an immigrant from elsewhere bringing new songs to our prairie. I quickly gather the song clippings from the other seven birds that we recorded at Goose Lake. One by one I compare them, first to the songs of Bird 4, then to the songs of Bird 8. Again, I find hardly any matches.

How can neighboring sedge wrens come to have such different songs? I can think of only two ways. One simple possibility is that the sedge wrens improvise their songs and don't imitate at all. Perhaps each bird hatches with general instructions on how to make its songs up, without the drive by many other songbirds, including marsh wrens, to imitate precisely the songs of adults around him. But before I can accept such a wild conclusion, one never before documented among birds, I have to eliminate the second possibility, that sedge wrens imitate just like marsh wrens, but then scramble themselves and their songs all over the continent so that tutor and pupil never live side by side.

In the dead of winter, the sonagrams still on the tables, I know the next step. I must raise some baby sedge wrens. I will try to train those babies to sing particular sedge wren songs and let them hear songs of other species, too. For a critical comparison, in the same room I'll raise some baby marsh wrens. Having these close cousins, these two wrens, raised under identical conditions, hearing all of the same songs, will be the perfect setup to determine if they are truly different from each other in how they acquire their songs. Based on what I already know about these two species, I predict that marsh wrens will imitate the songs they hear, but my hunch is that sedge wrens will not, instead making up most of what they come to sing.

In late June I fly to Grand Rapids, Michigan, visit Mom and Dad in Vriesland, then drive to the Baker Sanctuary in Calhoun County, between Battle Creek and Lansing. It takes me six days to learn the ways of the sedge wren, to out-stealth the female wren as she sneaks to the nest and feeds her nestlings. But I find them, two nests, 10 nestlings, all I need for the critical test. At the airport, Mom and Dad see me off, together with Uncle Bert and Aunt Ede, Uncle Bert and Aunt Jo, all of them worrying about my sneaking through security and onto the plane with these babies in my carryon. Knowing the power of a baby bird, I ask for a hand-inspection of my carryon luggage. "Ahhhh . . . how cute," as the security personnel gather for a peek. I'm home free, the relatives now all smiles behind me.

Back in New York I find the baby marsh wrens I need along the Hudson River, in the marshes of North Bay near Tivoli. All together now, the baby marsh and sedge wrens listen to the songs broadcast from the loudspeaker: marsh wren songs, sedge wren songs, combinations of the two, even some swamp sparrow and Bewick's wren songs thrown in. I try to give them ample opportunity to imitate anything they want; I don't necessarily care what they learn, as it is the difference in how the two wrens approach this developmental task that interests me.

By August the young male wrens babble and babble, practicing their songs. Three sedge wrens are males, as are five marsh wrens; the females are silent, as expected, because they don't sing as adults either. The males fall silent for the winter, and I patiently await my answer the next spring, because what a songbird learns during the hatching year isn't fully mastered until the following spring. Eager to know, in late winter I begin advancing the time clocks that control the room lights, lengthening the days so that spring will come early for my wrens. It is, after all, the light that dictates their yearly schedule, the shortening days shutting them down for the winter, the lengthening days bringing them into song in early spring. With snow still on the ground outside their window, they sing as if it were June; their songs are now sharp and crisp, without the wavering uncertainty of a young bird.

I record and record, filling tape after tape; then I film, song after song, their tiny photographs soon covering every surface in my office. The results leave no doubt. The marsh wrens prove adept at imitating the details of songs from the training tape, learning not only marsh wren songs but a few of those of the other three species as well. Nine out of 10 songs developed by these marsh wrens are imitations of songs on the training tape, only 1 in 10 being sufficiently different that I cannot know its origin. But the sedge wrens are polar opposites. One male has 20 songs, one 60 songs, and one 70 songs; none of these 150 songs are what they heard from the tape. There's some evidence that they might learn a little from each other, but the vast majority of the songs seem to be pulled out of thin air, somehow improvised in the mind of each young bird.

But why? Why the striking difference between these close relatives? Jerry and I reflect on the life history of each, searching for clues. They are similar in many ways: males of each are polygynous, each male trying to attract several females; in their bid for success, males sing rapidly, throughout the day and often even the night; and perhaps because they are polygynous and sing a lot, their song repertoires are large.

In one key life history feature, however, they seem to differ. Sedge wrens live in sedge meadows and are highly unpredictable from year to year, almost seeming to be nomadic. A friend bands 10 adults in Minnesota but finds none of them back the next year. In Michigan, too, birds are opportunistic, taking advantage of good habitat when and where it appears. In Iowa they might arrive to breed in July, August, or even as late as September; in Arkansas babies are in the nest during September. At these times, most other songbirds have long since finished all family activities. In contrast, marsh wrens live in the deep-water marshes and are more typical songbirds: many are resident year-round, and if migratory they typically return to the same places year after year.

The explanation seems simple, almost too simple. Marsh wrens live in stable habitats, the deep-water marshes, and as a result are resident or at least site-faithful. The singing males in a stable community all know each other, and they learn their songs from each other, as seems to happen with most songbirds. These learned songs are then a crucial part of the countersinging games that the males play in their attempts to secure both a territory and mates.

The sedge wrens are different. They move around a lot, seemingly always in search of a better sedge meadow, the quality of which is dependent on rainfall. Conditions may be prime at one site in one month, but the next month the birds may have moved hundreds of miles to breed at a new location. As a result, birds never get to know each other. Because it is an impossible task to learn hundreds of different songs from the new neighbors at each breeding location, perhaps twice each spring and summer, they do the next best thing. They make them up.

It's the snowflake strategy (track 33). It is as if the male has a song generator in his brain, one that knows roughly what the song must be like; when he is a young male, that generator produces song after song, sometimes over 300 of them in a single male's repertoire. Then, in his first breeding season, he flaunts what he has created, using those songs for the rest of his life. Each song is a snowflake, unlike any others, but all are built on the same common sedge wren plan: *cut-cut-cut-trrrrrrrrrrrrrr*, beginning with a couple of distinct introductory notes and ending in a dry, staccato chatter. There seems to be an infinite variety of different chatters, subtly but distinctly different from each other, but each instantly recognizable, so that no matter where in its geographic range he sings or no matter where she listens, each song unmistakably declares "Sedge Wren!"

Case closed. Or is it? Could marsh wrens and sedge wrens really be so closely related yet so different from each other in how they acquire their songs? As I learn more about how extraordinary the marsh wrens are at imitating, I fret over our conclusions for the sedge wrens. What if those Illinois males at Goose Lake with the unique song repertoires were not representative of sedge wrens in general? Maybe the baby sedge wrens from Michigan were dunces. These possibilities, though unlikely, continue to haunt me, and nearly 20 years later, in the mid 1990s, I feel compelled to revisit these wrens. Instead of recording more birds in Illinois, I now record in Nebraska, to see if those sedge wrens might have songs like their neighbors.

Not trusting baby sedge wrens from Michigan, I fly to North Dakota, looking for "smarter" babies who would surely show how well they can imitate. It's midday in late June when I check in at the office of the Clark-Salyer National Wildlife Refuge. From there I drive slowly to the west. Windows down, I listen for my first wren, stopping when I hear him. C*ut-cut-cut-trrrrrrrrrrrrr* from beside the road, perched atop a fence post. Only he sings, no other wrens within earshot. I listen to each song, memorizing its details just long enough to compare it to the next, and quickly realize that he's singing several songs of one kind before switching to another (track 32). I letter the songs, in my notebook writing A A A A A A A B B B B B B B B B C C C . . . The A song has a dry, buzzy chatter, the individual bursts in the *trrrrrrrrrrrrr* delivered so fast that I can't count them; in the B song the bursts in the *trrrrrrrrrrrrr* are sung much more slowly, and each begins with a high whistled note followed by a loud, harsh *chah*. The C song is somewhat like B, the *trrrrrrrrrrrrr* slowly delivered, but the overall pitch is markedly lower. I listen some more, hearing him switch to a new song every minute or so. Five of one kind, 7 of the next, then up to 15. A lone male singing with no others to spur him on, no females evident, and at midday—a clear recipe for an uninspiring performance. He's singing, but slowly, only about 10 songs a minute, once every six seconds, just a notch above stalling.

I drive on to the Grassland Trail, up above the Souris River. The car parked, I walk in toward the dark green meadow in the distance. Approaching, I hear them, *cut-cut-cut-trrrrrrrrrrrrrr*, the entire field effervescing with their chatters. How many—10, 15, maybe 20 within earshot? I walk the trail through them, pacing my steps, passing through territories of 5 singers in 200 yards. A bird every 40 yards, each territory about a third of an acre—tiny, but typical for these birds in the best of meadows.

Across the trail in front of me is one bird to the left, another to the right. On the left he perches atop a swaying sedge. He is among the smallest of songbirds, a mere 10 grams at most, just a third of an ounce, 50 to a pound, while I am almost 10,000 times his bulk. As he swaggers and sings from his perch, I tune in, quickly realizing that successive songs are not the same. The bird to the right of the trail now sings, too, he also singing what seems like an endless variety of songs, though each also conforms to the simple, recognizable *cut-cut-cut-trrrrrrrrrrrrrr* pattern.

I know to listen now more carefully, concentrating on each song, trying to hear how he sings. Yes, as I expected, every other song, or every third song, is the same. I letter the songs and hear A, then B, A B A B C B B C, successive songs rarely (perhaps only 1 in 10 times) the same, and about 3 different songs in every 10 that he sings. The male on the right is doing the same, alternating songs, but never do I hear the two males singing the same songs. With so many birds in this field, here is where I'll find the babies for my learning experiment.

I return early the next morning to hear them at their best, and eventually, I hope, to find the hungry babies in the nest. At 3:00 A.M., in the soft shadows of a waning moon and with dew heavy on the grass, song after song rises above the meadow. How many birds are singing? I choose not to count, but guess that it's about half of those present. Are those the bachelor males who do all the night singing, I can't help but wonder, as it is with mockingbirds? About an hour before sunrise the singing pace picks up. All of the birds now join in, and each sings at a faster clip, up to 20 songs a minute, a song every three seconds. I focus on the nearest male and strain to hear the pattern in his singing, often recognizing 5 or 6 different songs in each 10 that he sings, one sequence being A B A B C D E D E F. At this pace, successive songs are almost never the same, and few songs occur more than twice before he abandons them and hurries on to others. Given the variety of his songs, I cannot keep track of the pattern after more than 10 songs. Had I the mind of a sedge wren, I'd do far better, hearing him start to repeat himself regularly after about 500 songs, perhaps half an hour later.

An hour after sunrise I realize I've been duped. There are no babies in this field. Here it is, almost July, and it seems that the birds have just arrived, that they have only now discovered this best of all possible fields for raising a family over the next month. They're animated in their pursuit of territories, and females are about, too, but none of them with babies in the nest. I am at least three weeks early for this field. I must search elsewhere for the nestlings.

"I remember there were sedge wrens here in the lower part of the refuge, but that was so long ago, perhaps a month," says Todd Grant, refuge biologist, as he shows me the site that had been flooded just a few weeks before. With just an occasional song here from a male sedge wren, I am not hopeful. Another dead end, I fear — perhaps we'll never find those babies we're after. We step off the road and into the drying marsh, but within a minute a female sedge wren chips at us, her beak full of food ready to deliver to her young. A second, then a third and fourth nest, all in rapid succession, all within a hundred yards of each other, an unimagined bonanza. I think back a month, when this field was bubbling with male song, just as the field at the Grassland Trail is now. Just a few miles away and a month apart — different worlds for these opportunistic wrens.

Babies in hand, it's off to the airport, to ditch the rental car, to catch the next flight home. I try to be inconspicuous as I feed these babies, squirting a nutritious mixture of steak and eggs into their open bills every 30 minutes, but they are old and vociferous nestlings, almost ready to leave the nest. From the corner of the waiting area I see other passengers glancing my way. Good fortune and luck and no small amount of pleading see me onto the plane, as I pray none of these birds escapes on the flight home. In turbulence, with the "fasten seat belt" sign lit, I sneak off to the restroom for their feeding, knowing no one will disturb me and wanting a contained room should one escape.

I make it home. We run the babies through their paces that summer, then wait over the winter until the next spring to find out if these birds imitate. In the intervening time we analyze those songs from Nebraska, too, to determine if neighbors there are just as different from each other as were the neighboring birds in Illinois.

The results confirm what we had found almost 20 years earlier. The North Dakota babies from 1996 improvise songs just as the Michigan babies did in 1975. The simple fact that a young male invents his own songs is sufficient to explain why each Illinois male had unique songs back in 1974, just as each Nebraska male did in 1995.

I am still not satisfied, because I know that the sedge wren occurs throughout the New World, down to the tip of South America. I soon fly to Brazil, accompanied there by Jacques Vielliard and Maria Luisa da Silva to Brasilia National Park, to study the sedge wrens there; and then to Costa Rica, working with Dave Stemple and Julio Sánchez; then to the Falkland Islands, with Robin Woods, who wrote the book on birds of the Falklands; and a graduate student, Elijah Goodwin, departs for Mexico, with visions of Ecuador, Bolivia, and other places in South America. I help Fabian Gabelli with his studies in Argentina. Another graduate student, Steve Johnson, leg-bands hundreds of sedge wrens in Michigan and Minnesota and North Dakota, challenging the "common knowledge" that the wrens never come back to the same place year after year like the marsh wrens typically do.

And there are two other wrens in this same genus *Cistothorus*. For the Mérida wren I fly to Caracas, Venezuela, where I am met by Viviana Salas and Roldan Muradian, the three of us quickly heading to the thin air of the high Andes. The Apolinar's wren is endemic to Colombia, and much as I would love to go to Colombia, I choose discretion and instead help support a Colombian, Paula Caycedo, as she studies those wrens in marshes around Bogotá.

The results of our survey are astounding. In all populations, including the sedge wrens in Central and South America, we find abundant evidence that males learn their songs. In Brasilia I record two neighbors countersinging with matching songs, just as Jerry Verner's marsh wrens did in Washington State (track 34, figure 22). Whether in Costa Rica, Brazil, Argentina, or the Falklands, neighboring male sedge wrens share many songs with each other, indicating that they learn them from each other. In Costa Rica, the sedge wrens have dialects, songs differing between two locations only 20 miles apart (track 35). Two islands in the Falklands have different songs, again showing that neighboring male sedge wrens learn their songs there (track 36). Neighboring male Mérida wrens in the Venezuelan Andes have almost identical song repertoires, with males only a few kilometers away having very different songs. The same is true for the Apolinar's wren in Colombia.

So what is different about the North American sedge wrens? Why do they improvise while all of the other sedge wrens and all of the other species in this genus imitate? It seems that all of the other wrens are either resident or highly site-faithful. In those stable populations, in which males come to know each other and sing against each other for as long as each lives, males imitate each other. The North American sedge wren shares an ancestor with these other wrens, and that ancestor was undoubtedly an imitator. The simplest conclusion, one consistent with all of the facts, is that the North American sedge wrens largely lost their ability to imitate, instead favoring improvisation as they adapted to the ephemeral habitats in which they now make a living.

The North American sedge wren is something of a nomad. During the winter these wrens feed in the grassy areas along the Gulf Coast, but come spring they head north and west in search of prime meadow habitat. In late May or early June many birds settle as far north as Saskatchewan, Manitoba, or North Dakota. The particular meadow chosen depends on the moisture conditions at the time, and rarely does a bird return to the same meadow in successive years. (Of more than 300 male sedge wrens banded by Steve Johnson, only one was relocated the following year.) A meadow that is good for the first half of the season might not be good for the second half, so the wrens pick up and move, often flying south, back toward the Gulf Coast, stopping along the way at another prime site. In mid July these wrens arrive in the southern part of their breeding range, in Nebraska or southern Indiana or Kentucky, ready to breed again. Here today, there tomorrow, they remain one of the bird mysteries of the North American continent.

🐦

I still feel the winds and rain that buffeted our camper that first night at Goose Lake Prairie. I feel, too, the anxiety as we watched the lingering storm from the edge of the parking lot, and remember well the hesitation before we took that first step off the graveled parking lot and into the prairie.

We took that first step because of our confidence in what is called the "comparative method." To understand an animal, we look at its closest relatives, comparing one with the other. It is likely that their similarities are retained from their common ancestor, and it is in their differences that we see the process of evolution at work. Among these *Cistothorus* wrens, it seems that the ancestor imitated, because all but one modern lineage of these wrens imitates. The nonconformist is the North American sedge wren; since the time of the ancestral wren some millions of years ago, evolution has played with this lineage, in the end favoring those individuals who improvise rather than those who imitate.

These North American sedge wrens are an evolutionary reversal of sorts. They've not reverted all the way back to the flycatcher strategy, in which the microdetails of each song are encoded in the DNA; it would probably be impossible to encode more than just a few songs that way, and, not surprisingly, flycatchers typically have just one to three songs. Rather, these sedge

Figure 22. Unlike the North American sedge wrens, those in Brazil imitate each other and countersing with matching songs (track 34), much like their distant relatives the marsh wrens in North America. In the sequence of sonagrams in this figure, each song begins with a brief whistle (the dark note on the sonagram) between 3 and 4 kHz, an introductory note that is markedly different from the introductory notes of North American males (see figure 21). Beneath each introductory note I identify the particular song that follows, either A, B, or C. After an opening volley of song A from one of the birds, a quick exchange follows in which the two males overlap each other with song B, then match each other with C, B, A, B, and C again; one of the birds then ends the exchange with a B before the birds stop singing and begin calling and fighting. Follow along in this vocal duel by listening to track 34. (The dark band between 5 and 6 kHz in the sonagram is a chorus of insects; they are easily ignored if one just listens to the track by itself, but they grab the attention of our eyes, encouraging us to go back and actually verify that the insects are there in the recording. Such is the power of selective listening.)

Figure 22: SEDGE WREN—BRAZIL

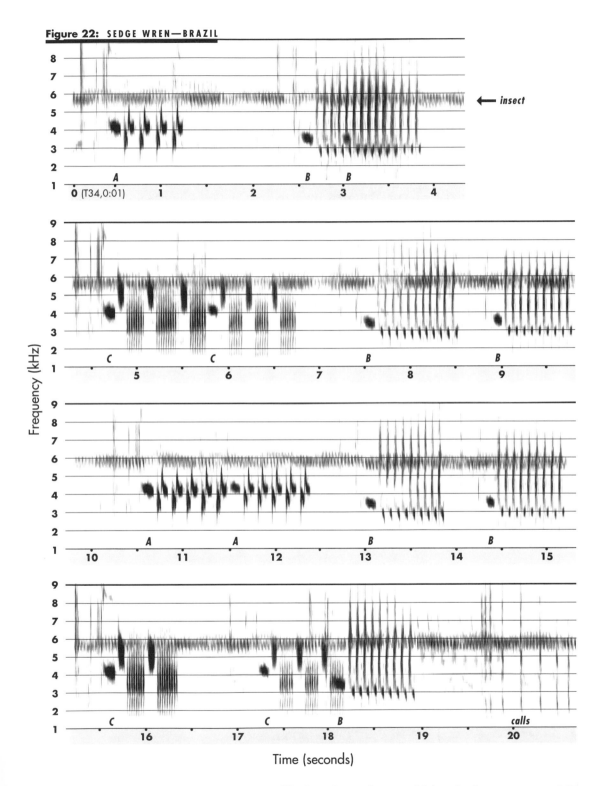

← *insect*

Frequency (kHz)

Time (seconds)

wrens have resorted to a different strategy in which just a few general instructions in the DNA guide the male to generate hundreds of different songs, each song instantly recognizable as that of a sedge wren.

And why improvise? If males were to imitate so that they could play the matched countersinging games of other songbirds, such as marsh wrens or Brazilian sedge wrens, they would have to imitate a repertoire of 200 to 300 songs twice a year, an almost certainly impossible task (some songbirds make relatively minor adjustments in their songs from year to year, but never on this scale). If a lot of effort were put into learning songs at one location, as do resident or site-faithful birds, those songs might not be recognized at another site, the learning effort then largely wasted. So the sedge wren has found a different way. Always singing among strangers, a male improvises a large repertoire of songs that will suffice no matter where he settles and no matter who is listening.

3

Dialects: How and Why Songs Vary from Place to Place

THOSE WHO LISTEN to this singing planet with attentive ears hear how birdsong changes from place to place, on both a local and continental scale. Two neighboring territorial male chipping sparrows might share identical songs, for example, because one male has learned his song from the other; they comprise a "minidialect," with other birds in the area having entirely different songs. In white-crowned sparrows, a few hundred males in a small geographic area may sing the same dialect, all the males singing the same song. The local dialect patterns in these two sparrows can shift in just one to a few generations, but some patterns occur on a continental scale and are far more stable, having arisen over geological time, as with marsh wrens (see below).

How songs vary from place to place has had a special fascination for those who study birdsong. "Song dialects" especially intrigue us because they are similar to the dialects in human speech. Dialects in both songbirds and humans are maintained in much the same way, too, by youngsters acquiring the local dialect and remaining within that dialect for the rest of their lives. There's one key difference, of course. Among humans (at least until recent times), children learn the dialect of their parents and then tend to remain within the broad confines of that dialect. Among birds, however, the young often leave home and then settle in a new dialect before learning their final songs, so that the dialect of a particular singer doesn't always match that of its parents.

Various types of geographic patterns are illustrated in many accounts throughout this book, but in this section I focus on five of them and on why those particular patterns might exist. 1) In the first account, I tell of my quest to understand how marsh wrens vary over the entire continent, discovering a

Great Plains fracture zone that reveals processes set in motion by Pleistocene glaciations. 2) How chickadees maintain their stereotyped *hey-sweetie* song from the Atlantic to the Pacific is a mystery, as is the significance of the variant songs on Martha's Vineyard in the East and in isolated pockets west of the Cascade Mountains in the Northwest. 3) The chestnut-sided warblers tell their story not with the all-purpose songs that most songbirds have, but with two different categories of song, one used primarily for males, the other for females; how these two song categories vary geographically tells us about the functions of song and why songs vary from place to place. 4) Towhees around the continent, from Oregon to Florida to New England, tell how being migratory or resident can influence how one learns to sing and the effect that has on how males sing to their neighbors. 5) The last example is the tufted titmouse, chosen to illustrate how males use their shared songs as they countersing. When songbird males learn a repertoire of songs from each other, they learn to sing the local dialect, and they then have choices about how they sing. One choice is to match the exact song that the neighbor is singing ("matched countersinging"). The singing males match each other song for song as they take turns singing, two males or a community of males all changing to another song in their shared repertoire at about the same time. These interactions are especially frenzied and difficult to track in western marsh wrens, as successive songs are different, and a male must choose which song to sing next 15 to 20 times a minute. These patterns of interaction can be heard more easily among cardinals and titmice. Male titmice (like cardinals) sing one song many times before switching together to another song, neighbors usually echoing the same song.

The Great Marsh Wren Divide

The icecap of Greenland and a few mountain glaciers are all that is left. The rest melted over the last few thousand years, the official death of the Pleistocene epoch declared to be only 10,000 years ago. Massive ice sheets, a mile or more thick, grinding, leveling, polishing, changing the face of North America. Originating in the Arctic, they had pushed south to as far as our Ohio and Missouri Rivers, repeatedly advancing and retreating, waves of ice and its effects sweeping the continent.

Left behind was a transformed continent. Where the ice had scoured the landscape, the land had been bulldozed and rearranged; depressions quickly filled with water, from the tiny prairie potholes to the massive Great Lakes.

The effects were felt well beyond the ice, of course, as northern taiga and bore-al forests and temperate hardwoods were pushed south, subtropical habitats squeezed off the continent. In the wake of all this habitat shifting were left new plants and animals, including, best of all, new birds. The ice ages and the habi-tats they altered had divided continental populations, pushing some to the west, some to the east, and in isolation they slowly transformed. With the ice sheets now fully retreated, the birds have expanded their ranges again, many of those eastern and western forms now meeting in the Great Plains.

Holding a map of North America in my hands, I let my eyes settle on the Great Plains, from Saskatchewan down through the Dakotas, Nebraska, Kansas, Oklahoma, and Texas. I see fracture zones, north to south, separating western and eastern wood-pewees, western and eastern kingbirds, red-shafted and yellow-shafted flickers, lazuli and indigo buntings, black-headed and rose-breasted grosbeaks, spotted and eastern towhees, western and eastern meadowlarks, Bullock's and Baltimore orioles, and many more. In my mind I hear these meeting places, too, the songs of western and eastern taxa distinct-ly different, the differences having arisen over countless years of males and females fussing over which songs are best, the decisions made in the West and the East never the same. Their songs play in my head, buntings and towhees and meadowlarks and more, telling of their ancestors and how they were moved about on the continent.

For all of the attention that this Great Plains evolutionary playground had received from ornithologists by the mid 1980s, however, I knew there had to be yet another fracture zone, another pair of birds that had been overlooked by all those who had looked before. The problem was in the looking—this meeting of West and East would not be seen, but heard, and my ears were primed.

🐦

JUNE 4, 1986. My flight taxies down the runway at Bradley Airport, a quick trip from Springfield/Hartford to Chicago, then on to Sioux Falls, South Dakota. I'll start there, following my ears to the west or east, eager to find where and how the western and eastern marsh wrens meet. Is the change gradual or abrupt? If abrupt, perhaps they even occur together in the same marshes, suggesting that they are two species, not one.

From the seat pocket in front of me I pull the United magazine, opening it to the route map of North America. My eyes range about the continent as I review all that has brought me here, to this flight, on this hunt, a treasure hunt no less, perhaps to document a new species of bird in North America, but more important to me, just to know how the pieces of this singing continent fit together.

HOLLAND, MICHIGAN. May 5, 1968, a little after 7:00 A.M. I realize that it was here, and at this time, that my journey began. Over eighteen years ago, but I still see him as clearly as if he were before me now. There was my future, perched atop that cattail.

Throughout college I had struggled with the Big Decision: Just what would I do with my life? At first I thought chemistry was the answer, and I did well, advancing to the honors section, receiving awards; I was even invited to join a select few for a summer of research in the organic chemistry laboratory. But outside the laboratory windows were the oak trees, the birds flitting about, life itself distracting me from those inanimate molecules of alcohols and amines within my test tubes.

During the second semester of my junior year, I started another major, biology. After an introductory course that surveyed all forms of life, I immersed myself in genetics and embryology and botany and other courses I've long forgotten, all so that I could graduate with a double major. But it wasn't until late in my last semester, during May of 1968, when I knew for sure. As a class project for vertebrate biology, I chose to study the migration of birds through a local marsh, just off the campus of Hope College.

I first saw him just 10 yards off the access road to the windmill, on the left, perched high on one of last year's brown, disintegrating cattails, facing the sunrise. His tail was cocked over his head as he bobbed and swayed, buzzing and chattering, gurgling nonstop with what seemed like an endless variety of sounds (track 37, figure 23). A tiny, animated fluff of brownish feathers, this overnight arrival spoke eloquently of my future, though of course I did not know it at the time, nor did I know I was listening to an eastern, not a western marsh wren, as the field guides told nothing of this distinction that I would later discover.

CORVALLIS, OREGON. April 1970. As a graduate student at Oregon State University, I attended a weekly seminar in the Department of Zoology; this particular presentation was by a Professor Jared Verner, visiting from Central Washington State University in Yakima, just a few hours to the north. Dr. Verner, who would soon become Jerry, told of his Washington State marsh wrens, especially those at Turnbull National Wildlife Refuge in eastern Washington. It's the only seminar I remember from the four years in graduate school.

What he described for his marsh wrens was hard to believe: Each male had more than 100 different songs in his repertoire, and all males in a marsh had the same songs, with the next song from a male often depending on what his neighbor had just sung. He described how he recorded a sequence of songs from a male and then played it back from a speaker hidden in the territory. The resident male, responding to this "intruder," often matched the play-back songs identically, song for song, up to nine times in a row—but the bird anticipated what was coming next from the tape recorder and sang it first. After the recorder played, say, song 50, the bird then sang 51. The tape followed with 51, and the bird jumped ahead to 52. The bird knew the local sequence of songs and refused to follow the intruder, instead leading it through the local dialect. These, I would realize later, were quintessential western marsh wrens (track 38, figure 24; in track 39, hear how different eastern and western songs sound at one-fifth speed).

MARSH
WREN

GOOSE LAKE PRAIRIE, ILLINOIS. June 1974. Just a little over four years later, Jerry and I were in the field together, recording two neighboring male marsh wrens. Our tape recorders coordinated by walkie-talkie, we planned to document how these male wrens answered each other with identical songs, just as his Washington birds did. Disappointed, we found one male had only 30 different songs, the other 36. With small song repertoires of relatively simple songs, these birds engaged in none of the countersinging duels that his Washington birds did. How different these Illinois wrens were from the Washington wrens, how different the eastern from the western.

TIVOLI NORTH BAY, ON THE HUDSON RIVER, NEW YORK. Summer 1975. Throughout the summer I parked along the railroad tracks and slipped the canoe into the river, paddling downstream briefly and then turning left under the railroad bridge. As I floated under the bridge, I prepared myself in the dimmed light to enter another world. Breaking into full daylight again, I would see the cattail marsh extending in all directions. The main channel to the marsh lay directly ahead, my initial escorts the singing swamp sparrows and yellow warblers and eastern kingbirds. These birds were soon just back-ground as the cattails closed in around me, the entire marsh buzzing and chat-tering with marsh wrens, left, right, and up each narrow channel.

Over the next few years babies from this marsh would help me under-

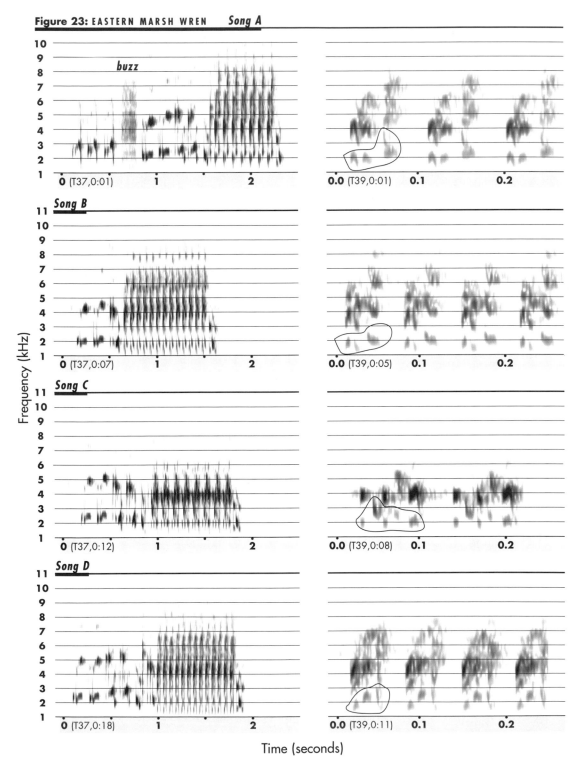

buzz

Frequency (kHz)

Time (seconds)

Song B

Song C

Song D

stand how these eastern wrens learn their songs. They learn most easily during the first two months of life, I discovered, beginning about day 15, just a day or so out of the nest. If a baby hatches in August, however, after adults have stopped singing for the year, he can wait until the following spring to learn his songs. When given a choice, he prefers to learn marsh wren songs over songs of other species. If raised by a house wren, he sings the strangest songs, nothing like anything that I know. Each male learns, at most, about 50 different songs, far fewer than those western wrens, more like the two Illinois wrens.

Eager to understand the countersinging games that Jerry had documented in Washington, I devised a grand scheme for the summer of 1976. Once a week, for the first hour or two of the day, six of us would simultaneously record six neighboring marsh wrens, documenting how males within this group chose their songs. Around midnight, I canoed alone into the marsh, stringing microphone cables and stabilizing stepladders and other platforms, putting three two-channel stereo recorders in place. By 3:00 A.M. car lights shined down the railroad tracks — my five assistants arriving. One by one I ferried them to their recording stations. Week after week throughout the summer season, mile after mile of tape recordings . . . and in the end, it all seemed for naught, as we captured nothing like the intense singing duels of Jerry's western birds. After the Illinois experience I should have known, but it took a full summer to drive home this fundamental east-west difference. The boxes of tapes languish in my cabinets, never having been analyzed.

MOREHEAD CITY, NORTH CAROLINA. June, 1977. Males here sang much like the Illinois and New York birds. One male had 36, another 41 different songs, about a third of what the Washington birds sing.

HOLLAND, MICHIGAN, AGAIN. June 1979. I returned home, to hear again that

Figure 23. Songs of an eastern marsh wren, A–D, the first four songs on track 37. The full song in the left column shows that each song consists of several introductory notes followed by a series of repeated elements, the song often ending with a brief low note. All eastern males have a nasal buzz before at least some of their songs (see song A). At this scale, however, the intricate details of the repeated elements cannot be appreciated. On the right are two to four of those elements from each song at an expanded time scale; listen to them at one-fifth normal speed on track 39 and hear the intricate details of these songs. Look at those dainty notes below roughly 3 kHz that I have circled in the first phrase of each expanded sonagram; it is those notes that are the basis for each repeated element, as all of what happens above these notes seems to involve harmonics of those lower notes. This is quintessential eastern marsh wren singing.

first wren, or, more likely, his descendents. Eleven years and a month after our first meeting, I listened with a more attentive ear to a singing male in the same windmill marsh. How "eastern," I remember thinking.

Each song began with a few low-pitched notes, followed by a distinctive nasal buzz, and then a chatter (figure 23). Some songs also had a couple of brief notes at the end, but it was the second-long chatter that defined each song. Every three to four seconds, 15 to 20 songs a minute, a never-ending variety it seemed, but only to the uninitiated listener. For just a few seconds, I tried to memorize the sound of each chatter as it passed me by. I felt its individual bursts of sound, sometimes only five or so, delivered so slowly I could count them, but other times so fast they sounded like a continuous buzz. Some were high-pitched, some low, some in between. I memorized these details, the best I could, just long enough to compare that chatter to the next, which was almost always different in some easily recognizable way. The memory of the first song now replaced with that of the next, I listened again, and again, to song after song, each different from the one just before.

As he carried on, I was alert for an especially distinctive song, one that I knew I'd be able to remember for a minute or more. Perhaps it would be a slow chatter, or a fast buzzy chatter, but something distinctive. I chose the song and then listened for it to recur. Not the next song, but the next, then two songs of other kinds, and my song occurred again. And then he sang dozens more songs over the next few minutes, but none were my chosen song. (In my notes I wrote such a sequence as A X A X X A X X X X X X X . . . , with A being my chosen song, X being any other song — see track 37.)

I then picked another song and listened for it, discovering much the same pattern. He sang each distinctive song two to four times over a span of about 10 songs, so that every other or every third song was the one I chose to listen for. I next listened continuously, trying to remember each song as long as I could. I heard him alternating two different songs, A B A B A, before introducing another song, A B A B A C B C D, and so on. With no effort I could now routinely hear that pattern, as he alternated two or three different songs in a rolling presentation of all that he knew.

I knew, too, that as I listened in the hour before sunrise, I could estimate for myself how many different songs he sang. As he sang continuously, perhaps what would be 500 songs without stopping, I picked a distinctive song again, one that I would easily recognize when I heard it again. When I heard it, I started counting each song. That first song I numbered 1, the next 2, 3, and so on, writing down the positions where my chosen song occurred: 1, 3,

7 . . . and then I didn't hear it again until song 142, when I stopped counting. I knew not to panic if I lost track. I could just start over, perhaps with a different song. In a span of 141 songs (not counting 142, because that's the beginning of a new series), he used my distinctive song three times. The other 138 were different. If each of his different songs occurred 3 times in the 141 songs, then he used 47 different songs during that brief performance (141 ÷ 3 = 47).

But I knew he might have favorites that he sang more often than others, so I picked another song and listened for that one for several minutes, and then another one, repeating that process until the wren's burst of singing before sunrise was over. I checked my numbers, did my divisions, and had 47, 35, 55, and 40 for the four songs I'd used. An average of those numbers was 44. Based on what I heard from this wren, I could conclude that he had about 44 different songs in his repertoire.

Such is the eastern marsh wren, the one I have come to know from Illinois, Michigan, New York, North Carolina, and all places in between where I have stopped and eagerly sought out the local cattail marshes.

FAIRFIELD, CALIFORNIA, GRIZZLY ISLAND WILDLIFE AREA. June 1982. If Washington birds differed from the eastern birds, I remember thinking, how about California? Rick Canady (then a graduate student at Rockefeller University) and I flew to San Francisco, intent on finding out. We recorded seven males in all, seven males that put even the Washington birds to shame. We would find that these California males averaged 158 songs apiece, one male having more than 200 different songs at his command. The variety of songs was mind-boggling (track 38, figure 24). As in Washington, each song began with a few soft *tik* notes, not the nasal buzz of the eastern males. After the *tik tik*, the song exploded into a harsh rattle or buzz, or even a loud whistle, an invigorating diversity of sounds. A male raced through his large repertoire, too, often doubling songs, singing them back to back as if he couldn't deliver them fast enough. I picked a distinctive song and listened for it again, but it was 5 to 10 minutes and more than 100 songs before I heard it again. He seemed in such a hurry to flaunt all that he could do, even more energetic and animated than his eastern cousin, intent and focused on the activity of singing and impressing his listeners.

Rick and I then began the all-important tests, to determine just how different these western birds were from the eastern birds. We collected 15 babies, flying them cross-continent on the overnight United red-eye. In the bird rooms of Rockefeller University's field research station in Millbrook, New

York, we played 200 different songs to them, 150 from California and 50 from New York. Joining them in the same experiment were babies from the Hudson River marshes in New York, all of them hearing the same 200 different songs. What mindset would the babies of California and New York, the babies of the West and of the East, bring to this learning task? The sound environment experienced by the young birds was now the same. As they sang, it would be their genes on display, the genetic instructions that each young bird had inherited from its parents, instructions that would guide it in how to sing and be successful in acquiring a territory and mates. So just how genetically different were birds of West and East?

Lots. The western babies learned well over 100 songs apiece, the eastern babies only 40-some. Overall, western birds learned about two and a half times more songs than did the eastern birds, about the same difference found between free-living birds in the California and New York marshes. How the young birds used their songs was also strikingly different. As in the wild, the California babies raced through their repertoires, as in A B C D E F G H, while the eastern males sang more leisurely, alternating their songs in the typical A B A B C B C D fashion.

Two species of marsh wren? Perhaps. Perhaps not. The answer depended on what happened between California and Illinois. If marsh wrens gradually changed from one style of singer to the other over this distance, then they'd still be one species. But if I could find an abrupt transition zone, perhaps even birds of the two types in the same marsh, and could show that they didn't mate with each other, I'd have conclusive evidence for two species.

LOWER LATHAM RESERVOIR, WELD COUNTY, EASTERN COLORADO. July 1985. I needed to close the gap between California and Illinois, to get a better fix on where to search for a transition zone. Mike Baker from Colorado State University kindly offered to record a wren for me. Battling the bellows of a mooing cow and her calf, he captured hundreds of songs from a male wren. Western. No doubt. More than 200 different songs from this one male, with

Figure 24. Songs of a western marsh wren, songs A, D, and GH (a double song, each song displayed separately here) from track 38. The full song in the left column shows the typically brief introductory notes, the trill of repeated elements, and the occasional brief concluding note (as in D) or buzz (in H). In the right column are two to five of the repeated elements at an expanded time scale; hear them at this slower pace on track 39. What a contrast these repeated elements are to the dainty notes of the eastern songs; these western songs emphasize harsh, grating sounds and are more diverse, with rattles, buzzes, and whistles, all of which combine to produce a great diversity in the western songs.

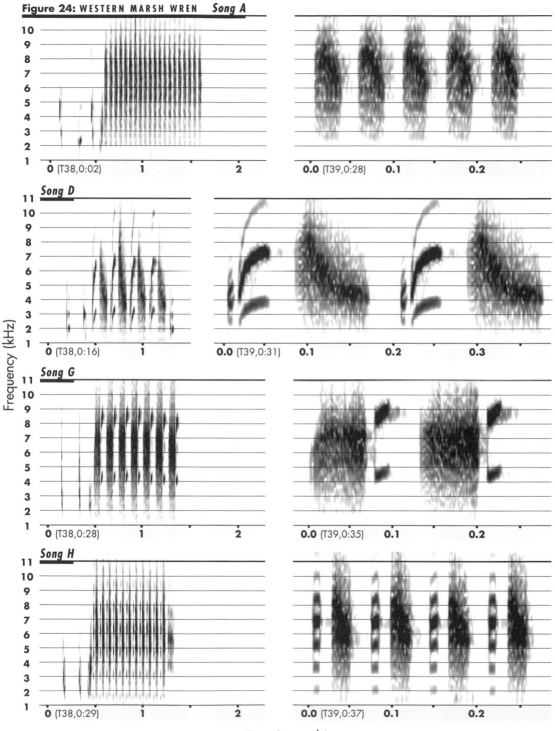

Figure 24: WESTERN MARSH WREN *Song A*

Song D

Song G

Song H

Frequency (kHz)

Time (seconds)

the diversity of rattles and buzzes and whistles typical of California and Washington.

🐦

SIOUX FALLS, SOUTH DAKOTA. 2:00 P.M., Wednesday, June 4, 1986. Touchdown. Clutching my carryon tape-recording gear, collecting my luggage at the carousel, I'm soon met by Gilbert Blankespoor, professor at the local university and brother of Harvey back at my Hope College. Small world, these academic circles. We go directly to two small marshes in Tea, a small town just southwest of Sioux Falls. Windows down, I hear them as we approach. Eastern. The nasal buzzes precede the song, and the chatter is eastern in quality, almost musical, delightful combinations of brief whistled notes given so rapidly that in the distance they sound almost like water tinkling down a small woodland stream. How odd that others should hear these same songs as an old-fashioned sewing machine, an unmusical clatter in the marsh. I return in the morning to record 200 songs apiece from three males, a few dozen from seven others. Later, I want to analyze these recordings, to determine how many different songs these three males have, and to measure the details of each song to determine what makes a song "eastern."

LAKE ANDES NATIONAL WILDLIFE REFUGE, SOUTH DAKOTA. Late Thursday afternoon, almost 100 miles west of Tea, I scout Owens Bay at Lake Andes. Eastern songs again. I find a motel nearby and return the next morning, repeating my routine: beginning the hour before sunrise, I record long sequences from three males, then shorter ones from seven others.

SWAN LAKE, NEBRASKA. 2:00 P.M., Friday. Done at Lake Andes, I have navigated by road the 70 crow-flight miles south-southwest to Swan Lake. It was a bleak trip, across the highlands drained by the Niobrara River, south on Route 281 through O'Neill, then across the Elkhorn River, a right on 95, through Chambers, south on 11 to the town of Swan Lake — no marshes along the way, no wrens. The wind has picked up, too, gusting, buffeting the car. Pulling up beside Swan Lake, I spot the cattails flowing in the wind on the opposite side. Opening the car door, I hear them, two of them, the wind kindly carrying their harsh buzzes and rattles and whistles across the lake to my ears, to my disbelieving ears. It is here — the wind and the song in my face, under the clearest of blue skies, the brightest of sunshine, in the early afternoon on this finest possible of June days — that I know. I have just driven across the Great Marsh Wren Divide, across the wooded highlands drained by the wild and scenic Niobrara. I capture these two western wrens on tape the best I can, the songs of wind and wren in harmony (figure 25).

DOOLITTLE LAKE, NEBRASKA. Friday evening I scout Doolittle Lake, just a few miles west of Swan Lake, getting permission from the farmer to pass through his yard to the lake behind his house. Early the next morning I'm back, before sunrise, the routine now well in hand. I record western wren after western wren seven, eight, but what's this in the distance? An eastern bird among the sea of westerners? Gingerly I work my way out into the marsh, parting cattails, feeling my way, careful to avoid what at times seems the inevitable, a face-first flop into the deepening water, the gear weighting me down, pulling me under. I'm soon near enough, and I fill two tapes, a few hundred songs, enough to document exactly what kind of singer he is. To my ears, he is all eastern, his neighbors all western.

PONY LAKE, NEBRASKA. Saturday afternoon, knowing I cannot linger in this area, I check out Pony Lake, about 15 miles to the northwest. More wrens, all

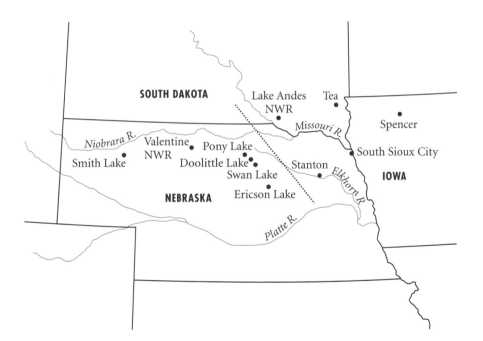

Figure 25. To the east of a line drawn in the Nebraska corn fields, the marsh wrens sing eastern style all the way to the Atlantic; to the west they sing western style all the way to the Pacific. At only two locations (Pony Lake and Doolittle Lake) did I find a single displaced eastern marsh wren, each one singing among a sea of western birds. At those two lakes and far to the north, across Saskatchewan, eastern and western birds coexist in the same marshes. Their voices clearly declare that they are two species, though their looks had fooled us for more than a century into thinking they were only one.

western except one, another pure eastern singer. There's nothing intermediate about his singing that I can detect—not a hybrid, but a pure eastern bird. I record brief samples from 10 birds, a longish sample from the easterner.

VALENTINE NATIONAL WILDLIFE REFUGE, NEBRASKA. Saturday evening I drive the 100-plus miles to the west, to Watts and Hackberry Lakes on the refuge. If the wren songs do change gradually in any way across this Nebraska landscape, I must document it thoroughly. Finding abundant wrens at the refuge, I retire for the day, awakening early, knowing where to go in the dark, then recording wren after wren, all westerners. Not a trace of eastern songs here.

SMITH LAKE, NEBRASKA. Sunday evening finds me another 100 miles to the west, 20 miles south of Rushville. Wrens are everywhere. I return in the morning, recording wrens to the accompaniment of thunder, mostly in the distance. Western, western, western . . . bird after bird.

ERICSON LAKE, NEBRASKA. Monday afternoon I head back east, wanting two more sites straddling the divide. Here is a site with three males, all western. The next morning I return, capturing hundreds of songs from each.

STANTON, NEBRASKA. Tuesday afternoon, on the Elkhorn River just a few miles southwest of Stanton, I stake out my wrens for the next morning. In the 75 miles from Ericson Lake I have again crossed the divide, as these are eastern singers. It's raining in the morning, so I pull the car as close as possible and record them from the open window. Not a trace of western songs.

SOUTH SIOUX CITY, NEBRASKA. Wednesday afternoon I head east, needing to extend my survey east of the divide just as I did to the west. At Crystal Cove State Park, in an old oxbow of the Missouri River, I find them: three birds, all eastern.

SPENCER, IOWA. Thursday evening, June 12, I drive almost 100 miles to the northeast, to Deweys Pasture and Smiths Slough State Game Management Areas. Tomorrow will be my last morning, as I'll catch a plane midday and head back to Amherst, Massachusetts, to analyze the songs on my tapes. Battling what must be food poisoning on this last morning, I force myself out of the car, step by step through the marsh, to sample bird after bird, getting long sequences from two males and shorter ones from three. All eastern. A late breakfast of toast and jelly, trying to hold it down, I dash for the airport, returning to Sioux Falls for the flight home.

The analyses soon confirm what I had heard as I crisscrossed the marsh wren divide. The eastern wrens are as eastern as can be, from those two lone males at Doolittle and Pony Lakes on the western side of the divide all the way to the Atlantic; they have smallish song repertoires (30 to 60) and relatively simple songs. Western birds are typically western, from Swan Lake and Ericson Lake to the Pacific, each male with a diverse array of well over 100 different songs. In my Great Plains survey I find no intermediate or hybrid singers, just pure eastern or western types.

The last piece of the big continental jigsaw puzzle is in place. I can now draw this marsh wren fracture zone on the map, a northwest to southeast line through eastern Nebraska and southern South Dakota, with Stanton and Lake Andes just to the east, Ericson and Pony and Doolittle and Swan Lakes just to the west.

I soon grow restless. To determine if these two wrens are really different species, I need to have them both in the same marsh, and in abundance, not just one or two easterners who have crossed the divide. If they maintain their distinctiveness in the same marsh, then I will know that they are mating "assortatively," east with east and west with west, two good species. I look north on my maps and during August consult with Stuart Houston in Saskatoon. Yes, marsh wrens occur all across southern Saskatchewan, he assures me, especially in the Qu'Appelle River valley. Together we chart on my maps the locations that he knows: Chaplin Lake, Eyebrow Lake, Crane Lake, Nicolle Flats, Last Mountain Lake, and many more.

The next spring I pack the bags again, this time flying into Regina. The first stop is Last Mountain Lake, and it could have been the last stop, too, as here is the answer. Side by side, on adjacent territories, are western and eastern singers. Listening as I walk the marsh edge, I can easily pick out the eastern and western birds, rarely hearing an intermediate song. I catch and band dozens of males, finding that the eastern birds are consistently about 10 percent heavier than the western birds. Their personalities are different, too. As I set up a net near a western male's courting center, I can easily drive him into the net; eastern birds seem far more coy, far more difficult to capture. Returning over the next few years, I crisscross southern Saskatchewan, listening to thousands of birds, tape-recording their songs, and studying them one by one.

First impressions are borne out: Almost every singer is unequivocally western or eastern, distinguishable by the quality of his songs. Here, in my mind, is the conclusive evidence of two species. If western and eastern birds are mating with each other in these marshes, the males would lose their distinctiveness, becoming intermediate songsters, hybrids both in their genes and in their behavior. That isn't happening, so they are indeed two species. This conclusion is further supported by an analysis of DNA taken from the birds. East was East and West was West, with only traces of cross-matings, declared Mike Braun and Darilyn Albright, my friends at the Smithsonian Institution who did the analyses. Two species, beyond any doubt, distinguishable by both their songs and their genes, but not easily by their appearance, as they are essentially impossible to tell apart by sight.

Their names? Perhaps something as simple as eastern marsh wren and western marsh wren will do? They'll be featured in future field guides, I'm sure, as soon as I can get all of the crucial information published and available for the authorities to inspect. It is the authorities of the American Ornithologists' Union checklist committee who will have the last say on species status, of course. No rogue scientist can preempt the committees, but the marsh wren story leaves no doubts, and the conclusion of the experts is a foregone conclusion . . . once I tell my story.

It is the songs of these two wrens that tell their story, telling of the earth's recent history, how it cooled and warmed with glaciers repeatedly advancing and retreating. View this history not at the glacial pace of real time, but speeded up, perhaps a thousand years to the second, a million years every quarter hour, and watch the amoeboid range maps of these western and eastern wrens move about the continent. Currently, one is restricted to the West, the other to the East, pressing against each other during this interglacial period from present-day Saskatchewan down through eastern Nebraska. Trace them back far enough, perhaps just a couple of hours on our hurried trip through evolutionary time, and see these two amoebas separate into refugia to the west and east and then merge, West and East one, the ancestral marsh wren.

Study the range maps in any field guide now and see the effects of earth's history. See the abrupt range boundaries in the Great Plains for the pewees, the buntings, the orioles, the meadowlarks, the flickers . . . and now for the marsh wrens. In Nebraska the boundaries for marsh wrens are abrupt, just a few stragglers crossing the line. Travel across southern Saskatchewan, however, and you hear a different story. There, eastern and western birds mingle over a 200 mile transition zone, from all eastern birds on the Manitoba border to all western on the Alberta border. Midway, at places like Last Mountain Lake, Nicolle Flats, and Eyebrow Lake, the two live side by side. A male defends his territory against all other male wrens, no matter whether he is eastern or western, but a female apparently is selective in whom she chooses as a mate, an eastern female choosing an eastern male, a western female a western male. Her eyes and ears are no doubt far more perceptive than mine, but at least one of the cues she must use is the striking differences in the songs and singing abilities of wrens from the East and from the West.

The Black-capped Chickadee

It snowed last night, on the first official night of winter, just enough that the driveway needs a little cleaning this morning. I smile, knowing what's in store for me, knowing who will greet me and what I'll hear for the first time this season. How do they know? I wonder. How do they know this is the first day with promise, the first day that is longer, if ever so slightly, than the one before, our first day of winter that in reality is their first day of spring?

The fresh snow sparkles in the rays of the rising sun, the hemlocks aglow beside the driveway. It is there that I first hear them, the bustling winter flock in search of an early morning meal, chickadee-sized snow showers exploding from the branch tips where they forage. *Chick-a-dee-dee-dee* they call (track 40), but I know there will be more. I silence the shovel, resting, listening, feasting. A pileated woodpecker calls *kuk kuk keekeekeekeekeekee kuk kuk* down by the pond, the mate quickly answering on a higher pitch. A lone goldfinch commutes overhead, *per-chick-o-ree, per-chick-o-ree*, each cycle of its bounding flight punctuated by yet another call. *Yank yank*, the nasal call of a white-breasted nuthatch traveling with the chickadees . . .

Hey-sweetie! To some he sings *fee-bee*, or *fee-bee-ye*, but I choose to hear *hey-sweetie. Hey-sweetie.* It is the purest of whistles, this promise of spring. Again he sings, and again (track 41, figure 26). I wonder who he is. Perhaps the dominant male of the chickadee flock, the oldest, the strongest? Away from his flock-mates a short distance, he offers a few more songs, as I hang on every syllable. *Hey.* Loud and pure and unwavering, a confident whistle that from my studies I know is slurred down ever so slightly, a little less than half a second from beginning to end.

BLACK-CAPPED
CHICKADEE

A brief pause, then *sweetie,* another delightful whistle about as long, but the pitch is markedly lower than the *Hey,* and it sounds as if he pauses ever so slightly in the middle of the *sweetie.* I know that he never actually stops whistling—instead, he whispers just briefly, lowering the amplitude enough so that my ears register the *sweetie* as two syllabless.

Hey-sweetie. In the calm of this winter morning, I could ask for no better acoustics, as the fresh snow deadens reverberations and all the crisp details of the chickadee's whistles pass directly from his bill to my ear. Not only do I hear the fine points of each song, but I see them as well, each whistle a stick figure emerging from the bird's open bill, the first figure higher than the second, the second with a little notch in it. Eyes closed now, I can't help but feel each song, too, feel the details penetrate me, as I am part of this winter scene.

🐦

Just a single *hey-sweetie* does it to me. I travel to places where I have heard this song before: in Massachusetts, away from my home in Amherst to the Berkshires and to Boston, from the far west to the far east; in greater New England, to Connecticut, Rhode Island, the Green Mountains of Vermont, the Whites of New Hampshire, and the slopes of Mount Katahdin in Maine; traveling west, to the Catskills and Adirondacks of New York, or across Pennsylvania to the south or Ontario to the north; to Michigan, both upper and lower; to Wisconsin, Minnesota, Nebraska, and Iowa; to the Dakotas, Utah, and Montana; to eastern Oregon and Washington, and on to British Columbia on the Pacific Ocean. Everywhere it is the same: *hey-sweetie.*

I hear, too, the scales each male plays (figure 26). First comes a series of *hey-sweetie*s, all identical, all on the same pitch. Then abruptly he switches, either higher or lower, to sing a series of songs on another pitch. And eventually to another, and another, switching every 10 to 25 songs if he's singing intensely at dawn, switching far less frequently later in the day. It's a subtle effect if one is not expecting it, as when I first heard it in May of 1983 and doubted my ears, but it's a striking effect once one is expecting it.

How do they *all* know, across the 3,000 miles of this continent? Millions upon millions of chickadees, each one knowing the proper song, both the *hey* and the *sweetie,* the relative pitches of the two whistles, the appropriate moment to whisper in the *sweetie,* and how to transpose that song over a range of frequencies. It's a mystery because chickadees are songbirds, and songbirds learn their songs. Because songbirds learn, they typically have local song dialects, with birds just a few miles apart often having completely different songs. That's the norm among these imitating songbirds, having local dialects that are local traditions, each maintained because young birds learn a local song and settle to breed within that particular dialect. But not the chickadees.

Why not these chickadees? Is it possible that they don't learn their songs like normal songbirds? What if the details of this *hey-sweetie* song are somehow encoded in the genes, much like the *phoebe* song of the eastern phoebe? Then the uniformity of songs over vast geographic spaces would be no surprise.

I remember those concerns back in the late 1980s, realizing that I needed to address these doubts head-on. So we asked the chickadees directly. Our test subjects were baby chickadees from three nests in western Massachusetts. They were cared for by my wife, children, and other helpers, and we tried to teach them various whistled songs, including the normal *hey-sweetie,* from the laboratory speakers.

The results? Not a single one of our birds sang the proper *hey-sweetie* song. Instead, they sang the strangest assortment of whistled songs, up to four apiece, and the males in different rooms sang different songs (figure 26, track 42).

From this simple experiment we learned a great deal. Clearly, the *hey-sweetie* song is not encoded in the DNA, or else each bird would have acquired a normal song no matter what he heard. These chickadees are "good songbirds" after all, as they must learn their songs. It was also clear that the males learned none of the simple songs we presented to them, but rather learned from each other, so that all males within a group had essentially the same songs. According to these males, there was nothing inherently special about the *hey-sweetie,* as all that seemed important to them was that they conform to whatever songs the group was singing, and as a result each group in a different room had its own dialect.

In spite of what we had learned, the mystery of chickadee singing behavior had only deepened. Why in nature is a male constrained to sing a single song, the *hey-sweetie,* when he clearly has the ability to learn a larger repertoire of diverse whistled songs? And why do all males in nature conform, from the Atlantic to the Pacific, when in our laboratory rooms birds just out of earshot from each other developed distinctly different dialects?

In late 1993, while puzzling over these questions, a most remarkable article was called to my attention. It was in the 1958 magazine of the Massachusetts Audubon Society, and it confirmed a report back in 1891 by noted ornithologist William Brewster: On Martha's Vineyard, just a couple of

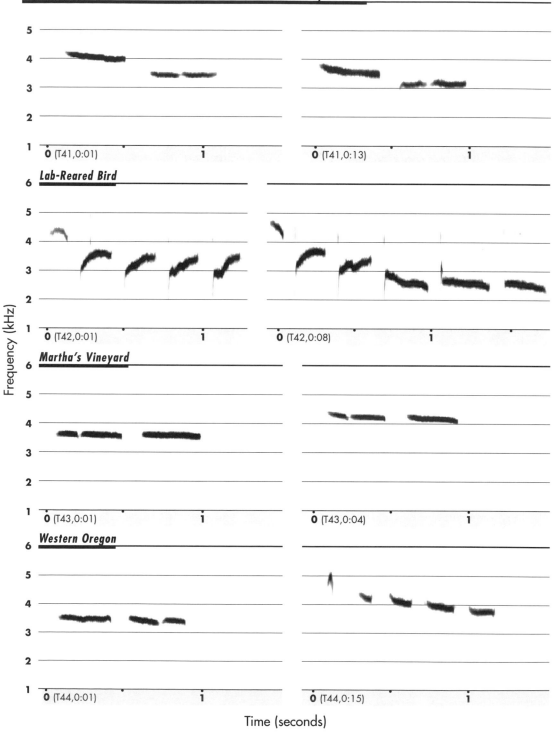

Lab-Reared Bird

Martha's Vineyard

Western Oregon

Time (seconds)

miles off the coast of Massachusetts, chickadees sing monotonal songs. Both whistles on the same pitch? No pitch drop from the *hey* to the *sweetie?*

At the time, I was on sabbatical, spending as much time as possible at Cornell's Library of Natural Sounds. When I mentioned this 1958 article to Greg Budney, curator of the library, he responded, "Oh, yes, and a long-time associate of the Library, Dolly Minis, has recorded them for several years now, and as soon as I can grab the tape from the archives you can hear them." Within minutes the studio was whistling chickadees, but whistling unlike anything I had ever heard before. Yes, the two whistles were on the same pitch, but there was more to it than that: The whispered break was now in the first, not the second whistle. The song was monotonal *and* "backward," a *sweetie-hey!* Over and over, with absolutely no doubt in either his or my mind, this male sang his *sweetie-hey.*

By May 9 I could wait no longer. I set out for the Vineyard, determined to hear these odd songs for myself. After the short ferry ride, we docked in Vineyard Haven and I drove to Gay Head, the far western end of the island, where a friend had offered his house for a base. I scouted briefly before nightfall, finding several chickadees, hearing a few brief songs, verifying that they did indeed sing *sweetie-hey.*

After a short night, I was soon waiting in the predawn darkness where I had last heard them. Almost overhead he began, *sweetie-hey sweetie-hey sweetie-hey sweetie-hey sweetie-hey sweetie-hey sweetie-hey.* Over and over, but now

Figure 26. The magic and the mystery in chickadee songs (tracks 41–44).
Top row: See the North American standard that most chickadees sing; it is the *hey-sweetie,* a two-toned song that starts with a high whistle and ends with a low whistle, the lower whistle having a detectable break in the middle. Males transpose this simple song over a range of pitches, only two of which are shown here. **Second row:** Keep a baby chickadee from hearing the *hey-sweetie* of his parents and other adults and he sings the strangest songs. Here are just two of the odd songs that one such unschooled youngster sang. **Third row:** On Martha's Vineyard, just a few miles off the coast of Massachusetts, the *hey-sweetie* has been lost; now all songs are a monotone, with both whistles on the same frequency. Furthermore, on this tiny island there are dialects of different songs; illustrated here is the dialect at the far western end of the island, at Gay Head, where the standard song is a low-pitched and a high-pitched *sweetie-hey,* with a break in the first whistle instead of the second. **Bottom row:** West of the Cascade Mountains the songs again differ from the North American standard; in the Oregon dialect illustrated here, the male has two songs, one a monotonal *hey-sweetie,* the other a descending series of whistles, with successive whistles increasingly longer.

I heard in disbelief what would prove to be another unique feature of Vineyard singing: this male alternated between a high-pitched and low-pitched version of the *sweetie-hey*. To the best of my hearing ability, I heard nothing in between in the more than 200 songs I recorded before he flew off to a distant part of his territory (track 43, figure 26).

That day I drove the Vineyard, from Gay Head to Edgartown to Vineyard Haven and back to Gay Head, stopping here and there to listen and record. More surprises, as I was astonished at the variety of songs that I heard. Dumbfounded, confused, disbelieving, I knew I needed a more systematic approach to understanding these chickadees and their songs.

By 4:00 the next morning, May 11, I was ready for the tell-all survey. At the airport, at the center of the Vineyard, I parked my car, strapped my recording gear to my body, and mounted my bike, waiting for the first whistles. At 4:46 I got them, my highly directional shotgun microphone capturing the sounds, sending them to my cassette recorder and to my headphones:

sweetie-sweetie   sweetie-sweetie   sweetie-sweetie
sweetie-hey   sweetie-hey   sweetie-hey

Other chickadees nearby were doing the same, alternating a low-pitched *sweetie-hey* with a high-pitched *sweetie-sweetie*, a song with a whispered break in the middle of both whistles. Up and down and up and down he sang, with nothing on intermediate pitches. These birds had two different songs, each one the standard Vineyard monotone, but each recognizably different based on where the whispered break occurred in the whistle.

I rode toward Edgartown, stopping to record each singing chickadee along the way. The low-pitched *sweetie-hey* song soon gave way to a low-pitched *sweetie-sweetie*, then in Edgartown, on the far eastern end of the island, to a *sosweetie-sweetie*, a song with two whisper breaks in the first whistle, one in the second. In Edgartown, the high-pitched songs were also *sosweetie-sweetie* (figure 27).

The sun now rising, I headed northwest, back toward Vineyard Haven. There I turned the corner heading back toward Gay Head again. After being detained briefly by police officers who had been alerted to a mad cyclist terrorizing Vineyard citizens with his big gun, I was soon on my way again, finding that the western *sweetie-hey* on both high and low pitch soon predominated.

Extraordinary! On this small island of Martha's Vineyard, less than 20 miles across, was more variety than I had known across the entire continent of North America. The western dialect at Gay Head consisted of the low- and high-pitched *sweetie-hey.* The eastern dialect, at Edgartown, was the low- and high-pitched *sosweetie-sweetie.* In the central part of the island were the *sweetie-sweetie* songs, intermediate between the eastern and western dialects.

A year later, in 1995, we invaded the island in force. Nine chickadee fanatics, each of us armed with tape recorders and microphones and miles of tape, traveling by foot and by bicycle and by car, each of us determined to understand these birds better. By 4:30 each morning we had deployed to strategic locations all over the island, filling in the sampling holes on our emerging map. After the morning's effort, we'd reconvene back at the Gay Head house, study our recordings, and then decide where to sample the next day. My colleague Bruce Byers and I took the last ferry to neighboring Chappaquiddick

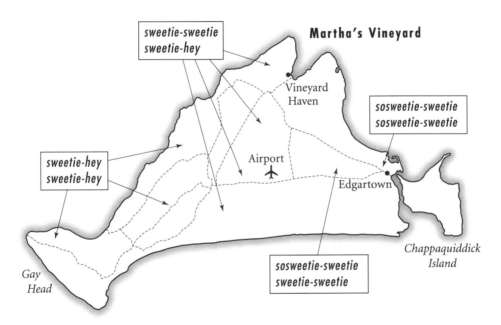

Figure 27. An outline map of Martha's Vineyard, showing the airport at the center and the primary roads (indicated by dashed lines) that we traveled in our quest to understand how songs of the chickadees varied over the island. The low- and high-frequency mnemonics of sonagrams in the boxes point to what one might expect to hear from the chickadees throughout the island. At Gay Head and throughout much of the western end of the island, chickadees sing a low and a high *sweetie-hey.* Much of the center of the island is dominated by birds that sing a low *sweetie-hey* and a high *sweetie-sweetie.* Only near Edgartown can one hear birds that sing a low and high *sosweetie-sweetie.* The low *sweetie-sweetie* is also found primarily on the eastern end of the island. Songs of Chappaquiddick Island are altogether different and not illustrated here.

Island one evening, slept in the car at the southeastern tip of the island, and chased chickadees all morning. No corner of these two islands was left unrecorded.

We couldn't resist returning the next year, in 1996. Two groups revisited Martha's Vineyard and Chappaquiddick, and Bruce and I visited Nantucket, an even more isolated island.

The impressions of my initial survey were largely confirmed. On Martha's Vineyard, these chickadees had song dialects unlike anything that we knew from mainland North America. And as for Chappaquiddick—well, on this tiny island a mere three miles across and a literal stone's throw from the Vineyard was an astonishing variety of songs: predominating songs were monotonal *hey-sweeties, sweetie-sweeties,* and *sosweetie-sweeties,* but four birds sang surprisingly normal two-tone *hey-sweeties* typical of the mainland. A couple of birds had four or more different songs, revealing the potential for individual repertoires in these chickadee whistles. Males in each small neighborhood countered each other with identical songs, but the dialect just a short distance away could be entirely different.

So immersed was I in trying to understand these birds that I had forgotten the black-capped chickadees I had encountered 25 years before, in the Willamette Valley of western Oregon. As a graduate student I had been obsessed with the Bewick's wren, but I now remembered those odd chickadee songs I recorded one day. One was a series of five whistles, all evenly spaced, all on the same pitch. Another was the prettiest I had ever heard from a chickadee: a series of six or seven whistles, starting high and sliding down the scale, with successive whistles getting longer. And both songs were from the same bird.

I now needed to learn more about these western birds. I called Geoff Keller in Oregon and he agreed to record birds there (track 44). Chris Hill tackled the Seattle birds, working Discovery Park morning after morning. Doug Innis got more recordings from British Columbia. What we learned was that chickadees west of the Cascade Mountains in Oregon and Washington were just as strange as the birds on Massachusetts' offshore islands. Males had repertoires of whistled songs, and dialects differed from place to place. We learned, too, that the transition between those "strange" songs and the "normal" *hey-sweetie* songs lay somewhere between Everett, Washington, and Vancouver, British Columbia, though to this day we do not know exactly where the change-over lies.

So many questions, so many unknowns. We want answers, need answers. So we guess, in as educated a fashion as we can muster, and let those guesses (formally called hypotheses) then guide what we do next, to see if what else we learn is consistent with our initial guess.

Why are there song dialects on the Vineyard, for example? My best guess is based on some old pictures I saw of the now heavily forested Vineyard, and on a description back in 1844, when the view from Gay Head was "a level, desolate moor, treeless, shrubless and barren of all vegetation, save coarse grass and weeds, and a profusion of stunted dogroses." As the settlers cleared the island, few trees remained, and it's likely that only a few pockets of chickadee habitat remained on the entire island. Perhaps three such pockets remained, and in those three areas arose, from west to east, the *sweetie-hey,* the *sweetie-sweetie,* and the *sosweetie-sweetie* songs. These dialects were maintained because young dispersing birds either stayed within the home dialect or, if they moved to another forested area, they learned the particular dialect there. Only when the island became reforested did the three dialects come into contact with each other, and then the low-pitched and high-pitched songs "competed" for survival with other songs on the same pitch. Today, the low-pitched *sweetie-hey* seems to be a winner, as it covers most of the western two-thirds of the island, but the three high-pitched songs are about equally successful, with perhaps a slight edge for the *sweetie-sweetie.* Such a scenario is reasonable, I think, based on what we know about other songbirds.

The big, tough question then becomes why there are no dialects in the two-tone, pitch-shifting *hey-sweetie* singers from the Atlantic to the Pacific. No songbird I know comes close to achieving this level of uniformity over such a huge geographic area. To appreciate this feat, we need to think only of how gossip spreads among us, how the story is altered just a little with each transmission, and then how inevitably a learned chickadee song would change from one generation to the next if there were not some way to constantly standardize the singing. How, and why, do they do it?

Here's the logic of my best guess. Because our laboratory birds showed that they must all hear each other to come up with the same songs, there must be enough movement among the mainland populations to keep them in touch with each other so that they can maintain the uniform behavior. Such movements are well known among young chickadees in North America, as they often "irrupt," moving great distances during the fall and winter seasons. It must be this regular, large-scale mixing of populations that enables the uniformity, especially if young birds learn the most common song that they hear, or if they learn an "average" song from among all those heard. (Note that this chickadee uniformity would eventually break down if a young chickadee learned the song of just one particular male, as young chipping sparrows do, just as a gossiped story is altered a little each time one person passes it to the next.)

That's the best guess as to *how* the chickadees might achieve this uniformity, but *why* they would bother to do so remains the greater mystery. Is it to a male's advantage to have a song that is widespread, so that he can impress any female he encounters, regardless of her origin? Does the female somehow enforce this uniformity? She might be assured that a male with the "right song" is "mainstream," and not a risk. Or perhaps females demand that all males sing the same song so that they have a standard by which to compare them. Or perhaps it's crucial that all males have the same song so that they can compete vocally with each other; they can respond to each other with the same song, sometimes alternating, sometimes overlapping, and they play games as they shift from one pitch to another, too, one bird leading the shift, one or more following. A young bird without the right song might be unable to compete, unable to gain a territory and impress a female. The nonconformists would leave no young, and only those who conform would survive in the chickadee population.

Why do they have just *one* song rather than many, when we know that each male is capable of singing several, as we showed in the laboratory? Again, I guess. If there is some need for geographic uniformity, then achieving that uniformity would be much easier with one than with several songs. With more variety in the males' songs, some would become more common than others, geographic distributions of variants would soon differ, and the uniformity of behavior across the continent would soon be lost.

What about those odd singers in Oregon and Washington west of the Cascade Mountains? Based on the above reasoning, I predict that these birds are resident and nonmigratory, and, more importantly, that they are relatively isolated from chickadees on the rest of the continent, not participating in the mass movements that shuffle chickadees elsewhere. That's my best guess.

Such power in a song—power that has moved me for more than a dozen years, power that has mobilized more than a dozen fanatics to join me on the Vineyard and elsewhere in search of answers. Power that can transport me while I shovel snow on the first day of winter, as it has over just the last few minutes, to reflect on the mysteries of the most common songs from one of our most common songbirds.

Wherever and whenever I now hear a chickadee sing, I am instantly riveted to the details, as I need to know how this particular song of this particular bird at this time fits into the larger continental patterns. Whether shoveling snow in New England on the first day of winter or hiking the Rockies in August, I listen to hear the relative pitch of the main whistles in the song, to hear where the "whisper-breaks" are in each whistle, to hear what the next song is like, and to hear what his neighbors are doing. Each song is both magic and mystery. Just how do they know . . . ?

The Chestnut-sided Warbler

Barely visible against the Swan and Cassiopeia are the five high-tension lines humming overhead. Towering above me is pylon #142, the first of a line of huge metal towers that carry power across these Berkshire hills to a still sleeping world to the east. I know that pylon #141 stands in the dark just beyond Busby Trail, two more towers before I will descend to the brook, then three more before the next ridge a half mile away, now capped with an orangish glow from the horizon beyond. To the left and to the right, just 15 yards away, is a still black wall of oak and maple and hemlock and birch, the beginning of the extensive forest that covers these hills.

Behind me, from down in Busby Swamp, I hear an alder flycatcher, no, two of them, *fee-bee-o, fee-bee-o*, over and over, seemingly taking turns in what appears to be some overnight competition. Bullfrogs chug away and the peepers peep, the flycatchers and the frogs providing continuous background now, at 4:00, almost an hour and a half before sunrise. Seven minutes after the hour a swamp sparrow cuts loose with a single song; five minutes later, from the forest beyond the swamp, a *who-cooks-for you-allllll*, a barred owl, most likely the female.

AT 4:18 I hear the first sign of awaking, rather than sleepless, birds: *chewink chewink* calls the eastern towhee just to my right, his waking call that will soon give way to his better-known *drink-your-tea* song. There's a robin, too, now caroling from down in the swamp.

4:19. *Poor sam peabody peabody peabody*. A white-throated sparrow is also waking down below, his pure whistles penetrating the dawn.

4:20. From just inside the forest to the north, an ovenbird launches into the air, his ecstatic flight song bubbling from the canopy. His familiar *teacher teacher teacher* song will soon follow from a perch nearer the ground. Just beyond the ovenbird a hermit thrush announces his presence, his fluty, ethereal song added to the growing chorus.

Overhead the Swan fades, as to the east the narrow band of orange on the distant ridge grows, extending upward, the orange on the horizon giving way to yellow, then green, blue, but soon yielding to the blackness of the night sky.

Still I wait. All of Nova Scotia and Maine are already in song, and this wave of singing warblers approaches, just a few tens of miles to the east now. Over the Berkshires this dawn wave will be channeled through a lattice-work of road edges and, most important to me, the perpetually brushy power-line swath in which I now stand. To the east, I imagine the tension building. From here to the distant ridge are 20 or more male chestnut-sided warblers, all in their night roosts, no doubt stirring, listening, waiting for the right moment, just as I wait for them.

4:31. Behind me. I whirl around, now facing the swamp below, and at eye-level, about halfway up in the trees to the left, he sings. It's a low-pitched warbling song, building to a crescendo, then dropping again. Almost instantly I hear another male off to the right, and then another behind me, to the east.

Figure 28: CHESTNUT-SIDED WARBLER—AGGRESSIVE SONGS

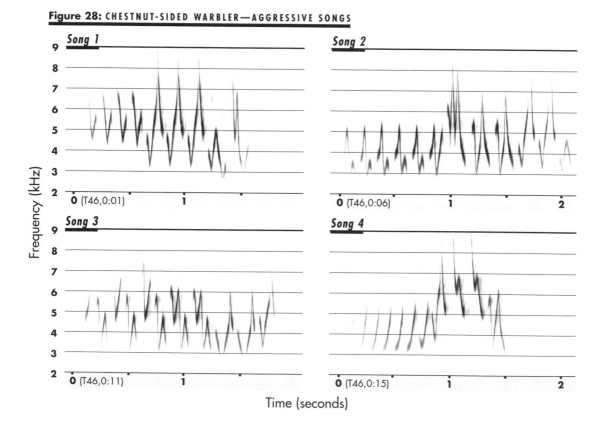

The Singing Life of Birds

The wave has swept over these hills, almost instantaneously, the males contagiously caught up in it.

I focus again on the first bird, to the left, feeling the rhythm of his song, how he begins with six or seven seemingly identical low warbling notes, smooth and mellow, then rising to two or three distinctive notes before dropping again, the song trailing off at the end. I need no words to describe his songs, as I feel them, anticipating each swing in pitch, memorizing the overall effect (for examples of these kinds of songs, see tracks 45, 46; figure 28).

Between songs he now *chips* and *chugs,* bursting with energy, then a song, repeating the cycle every 10 or so seconds. *Chip chip chip chip chip chug-chug-chug,* first the high pitched *chip* notes, then often a staccato, rapid-fire burst of lower-pitched *chug* notes, as if he's clearing his throat, and then another song, yes, the same song as before. I give myself two minutes, perhaps a dozen songs, all the same rhythm, all the same song from this male chestnut-sided warbler somewhere up there in what looks like a birch tree leaning into the power-line swath.

One ear still on him, I now shift the other toward the right, to the male singing just a little nearer to me. He, too, *chip*s and *chug*s, but the song is altogether different. Two soft and simple low-pitched notes are followed by three much louder, complex notes that sweep up the frequency spectrum; he then drops down to what sounds like a single low note, and then rises again to two distinctive notes on the end. Two soft low, three loud high, one low again, and ending with two intermediate. I know how I would write it: $2^3 1\, 2\, \ldots 2^3 1\, 2 \ldots 2^3 1\, 2 \ldots 2^3 1\, 2.$ Over and over again this male sings his song, the pattern and rhythm markedly different from the male to the left, each individual easily recognizable by his song alone.

I now turn, slowly, so that these two singers and the Busby Swamp are at my back, the distant eastern ridge before me. Over the next half hour I will walk this half-mile channel, this river of warblers, listening to each voice in turn, and at the end of my travel sit on the distant ridge top and await the transformation.

Up to the right now, again high in the trees, I listen once more. From behind me the two distinctive signatures continue, each from his singing post within his own territory. I listen to their unique rhythms again, contrasting

Figure 28. The aggressive dawn songs of four chestnut-sided warblers (the first four songs on track 46). See the variety of patterns here, how no two are alike, and match what you see with what you hear on the CD.

them with the third that I now hear. The warbling, mellow quality is the same, as are the energized *chip*s and *chug*s between the songs, but the rhythm is entirely different: three mid-range notes, then alternated low and high notes, ending with two other notes. These three male warblers consistently sing their own song, each unique, each easily recognizable to my ears.

From this ridge top I can hear still another singer. The territories are packed in here, the prime habitat of dense brambles offering some of the best nesting and eating places. The first male I heard sang from the south side of the swath, the next from the north, then south, and this fourth male is up to the north again. It seems that territories are so small that the males must alternate which side of the swath they sing from, lest they sing too close to each other (figure 29).

Focusing on the fourth one, I hear yet another unique song. The overall rhythm feels much like that of the first bird, but this one begins on a higher pitch. Eyes closed, I concentrate, realizing that I have reached my limit. Four birds within earshot, each distinctive. Each weighs in, seemingly in turn,

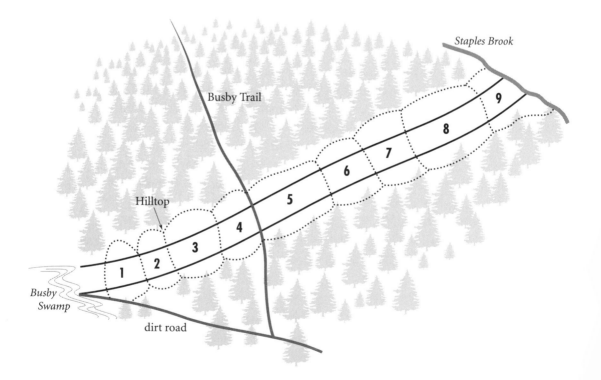

The Singing Life of Birds

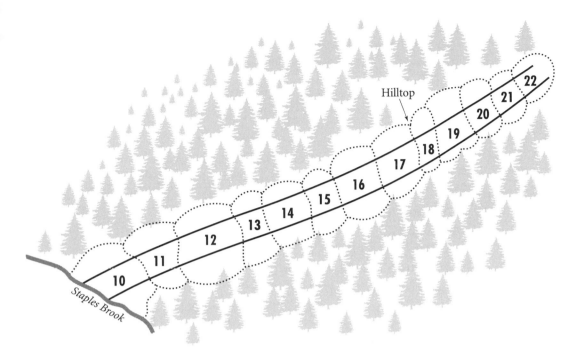

Figure 29. In the predawn darkness, I stood on the western hilltop overlooking Busby Swamp. As the eastern sky brightened, the dawn chorus would begin at the Atlantic and sweep toward me, a river of chestnut-sided warbler song soon to be channeled through this power line swath and over me. When the warblers began to sing, I worked my way to the east, crossing Busby Trail, walking down to Staples Brook and then back up and over the next hilltop about a half mile away, numbering the 22 singing males I encountered along the way.

alternating, sometimes overlapping songs of his neighbors, each with his own signature, each filling the gaps between his songs with his *chip*s and *chug*s.

With a half mile to go before I rest, I must move on. I shift strategies now, concentrating only on the song of the fourth bird. Walking past him, I listen for the next singer, hearing him up ahead just across Busby Trail, by the next utility tower. I now focus on these two birds, listening intently, declaring their songs markedly different, too.

I concentrate on Bird 5 now, walking past him, listening on ahead for the next bird. Low in the azaleas, in the middle of the swath, is number six. I compare the song beside me to that ahead, and again hear the contrast.

Up ahead I hear the seventh bird, then the eighth, and down at the creek bottom is number nine. Following the trail beneath the power lines, I walk among the meadowsweet and steeplebush, the brambles and the arrowwood, the cinnamon and interrupted and bracken ferns abundant on this Berkshire hillside. I listen in turn to each singing warbler, comparing his songs to the bird before and to the one that follows.

In my knee boots I wade the creek, then begin the climb to the ridge, knowing that the next several hundred yards are among the most favored by these warblers. They're close together here, the territories the smallest of anywhere that I know. No longer are they linearly arranged along the swath, but here they often double up, one male holding the south side of the cut, another the north side.

Regardless, the story remains the same. Each *chip*s and *chug*s between songs, and each male has his one song that he uses over and over, and no two neighbors sing the same song.

Just before the ridge top, nearly a half hour into my walk and my mind swimming in these warbling songs, I stop short. Did I hear that? Yes, there it is again. For a minute or more I had been listening to three warblers, each singing from his own perch and well spaced from the others. "Different," I had declared, ready to move on, until the male in the bush to my left changed his tune to a song indistinguishable from what one of his neighbors was singing.

Focusing on that bush, I watch and listen for any evidence of another bird, all the while listening to where those other two songs were coming from. No one is moving, but *chip* and *chug* and sing they do. How much time passes I cannot be sure, perhaps only a minute, but the male in the bush again changes his song, so that again it is different from those of his two neighbors. "Different," I again declare, smiling, as I know what this one male has just told me.

I continue to the crest and 100 yards down the other side—different, different, different. Neighbors warble different songs, 22 unique voices from where I stood earlier on that western hilltop.

Returning to the ridge top, I drop my raincoat into the trail and sit, listening, waiting. Six males within earshot continue their warbling, the time now 5:12 A.M. With sunrise only 15 minutes away, they seem to slow their pace, or is it me, in anticipation?

Pleased-pleased-pleased-to-MEETCHA. Just to the west of where I sit, a new song rises from the power-line swath, a song so different that had I not been prepared for it I would have thought it from a different species. I listen to the second song more carefully, recognizing which particular *meetcha* song this is: *wheedle wheedle wheedle wheedle sweet sweet MEETCHA*. He begins softly with several two-syllable *wheedle* notes, building to two clearly enunciated *sweet* notes over a much wider pitch, ending with the climax, the strongly accented finale—a loud whistle sweeping up *(MEET)* and then down *(CHA)* the scale (for examples of those "accented-ending" songs, see tracks 47 and 48, figure 30).

There's no time to savor it, as the shift in singing mood is as contagious as was the initial burst of singing over half an hour ago. The male to the east now sings *see see see see see MEETMEETCHA*, his neighbor *che che che che che MEETMEETCHA* (track 48, figure 30). The endings consist of two bold upsweeps followed by a single downsweep. The difference between the *che* and *see* is subtle, but some are recognized as different when I hear them back-to-back like this. From graphs of their songs, I know the whistled *see* is a little smoother and bolder, the *che* just a little harsher and more choppy.

Quickly I walk west, down to the stream, then back up to this eastern ridge, as I know my time is limited. I listen to each singing male and compare him to his immediate neighbor: different, same, same, different, same, different. As I listen, each male sings a particular song several times, and within earshot is usually at least one other male who is using the identical song.

Within just a few minutes they are mostly silent, now just an hour since I began on the ridge to the west. Only one male continues, the male who first switched to his *meetcha* songs just a few minutes ago. I choose to sit in his territory, breaking out my traditional six-cereal field breakfast premixed with powdered milk, to which I simply add water. There I feast, reflecting on the morning's journey and on the journey these warblers have taken me on over the past 20 years.

For me, it all began in 1978 when a friend published a paper on the remarkable singing behavior of these chestnut-sided warblers. They had two categories of songs, like several other species of warblers, with one song used mainly when fighting, the other when trying to impress females. Their singing was more complex than that of most warblers, however, because the chestnut-sided warblers had several different songs within each of the two song categories.

I was hooked and needed to know more. Early the next May I was out recording the first chestnut-sided warblers I heard, and I found the blue-winged warblers irresistible, too. In order to understand how songs varied from place to place, I begged for copies of all the recordings for these two species that were archived at Cornell's Library of Natural Sounds and Ohio State's Borror Laboratory of Bioacoustics. We played songs to territorial males, asking them what they thought of this song, or that. My wife and I raised baby warblers, to understand both how they learned their songs and how they knew which songs to sing when.

Others found these warblers enticing, too, and joined us in the fun. Cindy Staicer did her master's degree on the Grace's warbler in Arizona and came to the University of Massachusetts to work on the Caribbean Adelaide's warbler for her doctorate. Tod Highsmith worked on the golden-winged warbler in Minnesota, David Spector on the yellow warbler in Amherst, Peter Houlihan on the prairie warbler in nearby Montague. Jeff Bolsinger went to Texas to work on the endangered golden-cheeked warbler.

For me, 1986 was the year of the chestnut-sided warbler, as I needed to understand them better, to live among them for a summer. I hired Bruce Byers as an undergraduate to work with me, and he in turn got hooked, soon joining us as a graduate student, spending his summers in the late '80s and early '90s in the Berkshire power lines, learning far more about these birds than I thought possible.

We were not alone in our enthusiasm, and we knew well the work of others. In the '60s and '70s there were Bob and Penny Ficken, Doug Morse, Frank Gill, Bud Lanyon, and Ross Lein. Then came the work of Bob Lemon, Gene Morton, Haven Wiley, and others, all warbler enthusiasts.

It is this collective work, seasoned with my personal experiences, that now allows me to sit here in the grass and interpret this morning's activities. Take this male in whose territory I now sit, for example: with every *wheedle wheedle wheedle wheedle sweet sweet MEETCHA* that he continues to sing, he declares that he is a bachelor, eager for a mate. Based on the relative silence of the other males, I know they are paired, busy raising families.

Figure 30. The daytime *meetcha* songs of four chestnut-sided warblers, chosen to illustrate all of the variations in these songs that occur in our Berkshire power-line swath (and, for the most part, everywhere in this warbler's geographic range). See how all songs end emphatically with a single bold down-slurred whistle, the *CHA*. The bold *MEET* of the *wheedle* song is a single upsweep, but the two *MEETMEET* notes of the other three songs are highly similar to each other. Each song variation has a different series of introductory notes, here labeled *wheedle, see, che,* and *swee*. Songs illustrated here are the first, second, fifth, and seventh songs on track 48.

I know this because in the spring, a male sings one of these *meetcha* songs throughout the day until he attracts a female, after which he sings far less frequently. We can show that experimentally, too. A male is a miniature *meetcha* robot with a simple on/off switch, which we can show by simply catching his female and temporarily removing her from the territory, then replacing her an hour or two later. With the female, he's largely silent, the switch "off"; take her away, and he sings six or seven *meetcha* songs a minute ("on"), endlessly, until he is again silenced by her return ("off" again). Many other warbler species behave in the same way, a blue-winged warbler, for example, uttering his *beee-bzzzzzzz* song all day until he attracts a female.

There's so much more to these *meetcha* songs. Careful analysis has shown that only four (maybe five, if you're a splitter) different *meetcha* songs occur here in the Berkshires (figure 30). I heard three of them just this morning. What's even more surprising is that the same four occur everywhere that these warblers do, from New England down the Appalachian chain and west, to

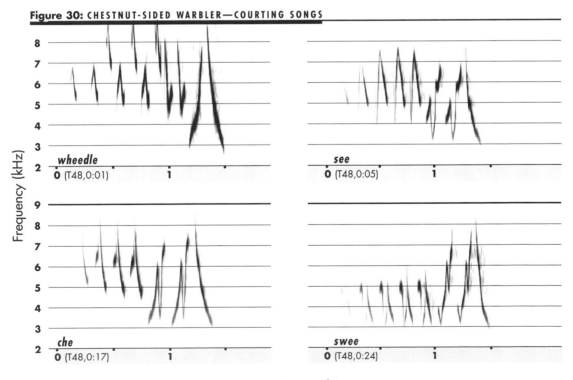

Figure 30: CHESTNUT-SIDED WARBLER—COURTING SONGS

Time (seconds)

Ohio, Wisconsin, and Michigan. They are the same four, with just one exception, a fifth type that we've found only in northern Minnesota and Wisconsin.

How do they do that? I wonder. By default, songbirds have local dialects, and such a widespread distribution of identical, learned songs is extremely rare. How are these songs homogenized throughout the range? This uniformity in the *meetcha* songs would be understandable if all of these warblers practiced together on the wintering grounds in Central America and then migrated north to disperse throughout North America, but they apparently don't sing in the tropics. Perhaps they travel together and study each others' songs during migration, annually standardizing the nuances of each of the *meetcha* songs? How else could songs of the 1950s be the same as those today? How else could the songs be the same throughout the range?

Why? Why the uniformity? What does it accomplish? We can only guess. Here's the best clue: These are the songs a male advertises from the treetops to attract a female, and, when he courts a newly arrived female, these are the songs that he, sometimes literally, whispers in her ear. Because female songbirds tend to move farther from their birthplace than do males, perhaps males are making sure that they have a *meetcha* song that will be recognizable to any female, regardless of her origin. Or perhaps females demand some kind of standard among males so that the males can easily be identified and compared; the nonstandard singers would then have no chance to reproduce. Whatever the reason, because she is the object of these songs, it must be she who somehow controls the uniformity in these songs.

Still another mystery is that, if I sit here and listen to this male long enough, I'll almost certainly hear him deliver another of the *meetcha* song versions, and perhaps a third and a fourth. With another male I had waited patiently for hours, no, days, for him to tell me more of what he knew, only to hear him switch to another song after I was walking away from him, almost out of earshot down the trail. But we've caught others in the act, a single male using two, three, or even four of those ubiquitous *meetcha* songs. Why does each male have a favorite, and why does he choose that particular one? Why does he seem to hide the others, and on what occasions does he bring them out, and for whom?

Equally puzzling are the warbled songs used at dawn. These are also the songs that males use when fighting, especially on territory boundaries, no matter what the time of day. They're used when near other males, in aggressive situations, and in the absence of females. If the *meetcha*s are love songs, then these warbled songs are the battle songs.

The *meetcha* and warbled songs differ in one other fundamental way.

Tape-record a male day after day, week after week, for as many years as he returns to his territory; do the same with his neighbors and others in the power-line swath, too, and a pattern emerges, as Bruce eventually discovered. As with the *meetcha* songs, each male has his favorite warbled song, and he'll sing several others, too, up to a dozen. But what a contrast to the *meetcha* songs in how these warbled songs are distributed over space. Neighboring males have most of the same warbled songs in their repertoires (although the favorite song of one male is rarely used by his neighbor), but the songs just a few territories away are all different. Unlike the four or five *meetcha* songs used throughout the range in North America, there seem to be an infinite number of these warbled songs, each highly localized, each occurring in a minidialect on just a few adjacent territories.

How do these minidialects develop? Unlike the *meetcha* songs, which a young male could learn from any adult singing male wherever and whenever that adult is encountered (in Texas, for example, during migration), these warble songs must be learned at the specific location where the young male establishes his territory. Consider a yearling male returning from Central America in the spring, typically a few days later than the older males; this youngster on his first territory begins singing his *meetcha* song(s) immediately, in the hopes of attracting a female. It is then, it seems, that he must learn the nuances of the warble songs in his particular minidialect. During fights with his neighbors he listens and learns, acquiring the local fighting songs. The next year, if he survives, he'll almost certainly return early to the same territory (as our banded birds routinely have), and he will then be the adult teaching the first-year birds the local songs.

Why this geographic pattern for the warble songs? Why are these songs so local? Because each song is used to counter immediate male neighbors, it would seem that there's no need for a male to have songs that are identical to those of more distant birds. These warble songs are specialized for interacting with males, and it seems that natural selection has refined this form of singing so that neighbors speak the same tongue, each neighborhood effectively isolated from and independent of other such neighborhoods. Only these warblers know what games they play with each other as each chooses his favorite song, and only these warblers know what they are saying to each other when they occasionally use a rare song to match each other. Perhaps they play some of the same games that song sparrows play, each male highly aware of the entire repertoire of each neighbor, each male choosing which song he sings depending on the intensity of the encounter.

Last, what is the intense game being played at dawn? Why the *chip chip*

chip chip chip chug-chug-chug followed by a warble song, over and over, for up to an hour? We have a few hints. Before the females arrive, the males begin singing near sunrise, skipping the predawn effort altogether and beginning the day with their *meetcha* songs. When females begin to arrive, however, the males sing earlier and earlier, beginning their intense warble singing 45 to 50 minutes before sunrise. And it's not just the paired males that play this game, as the bachelors follow suit.

The answer probably lies in Bruce's latest surprise. He caught all the females and males in this power-line swath, taking from them and their babies a small sample of blood. Analyzing the DNA in this blood, Bruce determined that about half of all the babies in each nest were not fathered by the male who owned the territory and who was "socially paired" to the mother. Instead, the fathers were often neighboring males who had mated with the female, leaving their genetic fingerprints in the offspring.

What else could this dawn singing be but a massive competition among neighboring males, to see who can sing most intensely, or the longest, or the fastest, or the earliest, or in some way "the best"? Each female must be listening as males exchange barbs, noting who sings and how, who the aggressor is, and who backs down. In her mind she must have some standard that she uses to compare males, some measure that then guides her mating efforts to enable her to have the healthiest babies possible. If she decides that it's in her best interest, she'll mate not only with her social partner but also with other males nearby. At least that's the best guess as to what she's up to.

CHESTNUT-
SIDED
WARBLER

Nearly two hours after sunrise now, this lone male continues to sing, *wheedle wheedle wheedle wheedle sweet sweet MEETCHA*. A metronome, six songs a minute, from high in the sugar maple overhead, pausing just a few minutes now and then to search out some insect food. I eye him through my binoculars, watching his entire body quiver with each delivery, feasting on his immaculate dress, sweeping my eyes from the tip of the bill to the tip of the tail, the yellow crown, the coal black eye- and throat-lines contrasting sharply with the white throat, the chestnut sides and white belly, the fine greenish and whitish and yellowish and blackish markings on wing and back.

Lowering the binoculars, I close my eyes and take a deep breath, taking deep into my being the sounds and sights of the morning, as I want to take them with me, to make them last. Another breath, and another, the *meetcha*s and warbles and his quivering chestnut sides now firmly fixed within me.

Opening my eyes, I can now leave. I pack up, wishing the singer above me good fortune, and retrace my steps to the west, across the stream and back to the distant ridge, past mostly silent chestnut-sides, then down Busby Trail to the car.

Travels with Towhees, Eastern and Spotted

The towhee range map lies before me, and I can't help but plot where they and I have been together. It was Michigan where we first met, in May of 1968 when I first discovered birds as a college senior. This "rufous-sided towhee," as he was called back then, was an easy one, boldly and distinctly marked, the name itself descriptive. The song was easy, too: *drink-your-te-te-te-te-te-te-te-te*, those *te-te* notes usually delivered so fast it was hard to count them. And he called his name: a *tow-hee*, or *chewink*, rising in pitch, with a raspy or burry quality to it (track 49, figure 31).

That summer, at Pellston's University of Michigan field station at the tip of the mitt in southern Michigan, the towhee's distinctive song was always a welcome sound. With the famed Dr. Olin Sewall Pettingill, Jr., as our leader, we'd load the ornithology bus in the predawn dark and head out for the morning's adventures. We followed along behind him closely, eager to learn from the master, but also eager to hear the next quiz bird, as at any moment he could stop, fall silent, and point his walking stick, wiggling it when a distant bird sang. The warblers were toughest, but the towhee was always a "gimme." *Drink-your-teeeeeeeee.* When asked to identify the towhee song, we knew that behind our professor's intimidating exterior lay a warm heart.

In August, Melissa and I honeymooned across the map to Corvallis, Oregon, where she would teach high school while I attended graduate school at Oregon State. Here was a different towhee. Replacing that solid white mark halfway out on the wings were rows of fine white spots, hence the unofficial name of "spotted towhee" for this western variety. The *chewink* was gone, too, replaced by a harsher, growling *zhreeee*, but still rising in pitch and unmistakably towhee (track 50).

The songs of the following spring were also different. Out was the full, distinct *drink-your-teeeeeeeee*. In were much shorter and simpler songs, without the emphatic *drink-your* at the beginning, and the *teeeeeeee* was often hurried, more of a buzz than a musical trill. A sorry excuse for a song, I recall thinking, compared to what my Michigan towhees sang.

Late that year, in 1969, a paper appeared in the ornithological journal *Condor,* and it was the cautious yet excited disbelief at what I read there that started it all. The author believed that the *teeeeeeee* trills of these Oregon towhees were "of only a few readily distinguishable rates." That's such a simple statement, easily glossed over, but I reflected on the consequences of that claim. If the claim were true, it would mean that the towhees develop songs with certain trill rates, but not others, as if certain trill rates have special significance or meaning; a fairly sophisticated communication system, with specific and discrete messages, could be based on these different categories of trill rates. That was an exciting possibility. But perhaps the author was wrong, there being no natural categories of trill rates at all, but rather trill rates simply varying continuously from slow to fast. Trill rate in a song could still mean something to the towhees, such as faster trill rates indicating greater aggression, but the sophistication of the towhee mind controlling this kind of continuous variation could be far simpler, I reasoned. Distinguishing between these two possibilities was important, as I needed to know which was the real towhee.

By that time I knew just where I would study them. Almost daily that summer I had been visiting the Finley National Wildlife Refuge just south of Corvallis. Arriving an hour before sunrise, I waited for my Bewick's wrens to begin singing, because it was on the wrens that I would focus for my graduate thesis. The towhees always sang first, while it was still pitch black.

In April of the next year, 1970, I was ready for them. That spring I netted and banded the four male towhees near the east entrance to the refuge. Arriving half an hour before my morning schedule of the previous year, I now waited for the towhees to start singing. Using a flashlight to adjust the recorder's controls, I tape-recorded song after song from those four birds. For a comparison I also recorded another 40 birds within a mile of those four, so I could know how the towhee songs varied from place to place. Back in the laboratory I made hundreds of sonagrams of the songs that I had recorded.

EASTERN
TOWHEE

158   *The Singing Life of Birds*

The following winter I also confirmed that the same banded towhees were still on their territories; that was important, because I had the hunch that resident birds would be more likely than migratory birds to imitate each other's songs.

As I recorded the birds that April, I realized what they were doing. At first, they alternated two or even three different songs. After a minute or so, they'd alternate two other songs, so that rather quickly they moved through a repertoire of what sounded like at least a half dozen different songs. Well before sunrise they then switched to their daytime mode of singing in which they repeated one song many times before switching to another. And I was convinced, too, that these neighboring males were answering each other with identical songs, sometimes even matching each other with pairs of alternating songs in the dawn frenzy—at least that's the way it sounded to my ears.

SPOTTED
TOWHEE

After studying my tape recordings in the laboratory, I appreciated better the fundamentals of towhee singing. The song repertoires were fairly large: two of those towhees sang seven different songs, one eight, and one nine. Those four neighbors shared many of the same songs, too, and I confirmed that they did often answer each other with identical songs. Males just a few territories away, though, had different songs.

The variation in trill rates? Continuous. There were no discrete categories, but my initial fascination with this question of trill rates was quickly replaced with my interest in the resident status of these towhees and how their songs changed over space. I needed to understand what these towhees were all about. They were on their territories throughout the year at this Oregon refuge, and most likely they stayed on the same territory for life. Each male knew the singers on the adjacent territories well, and each had the same songs as his neighbors so that he could reply with identical songs. An adult male and female would raise their young, who would then set out to find a territory of their own; a young male would find an opening somewhere, perhaps only a few hundred yards from home, perhaps a mile, and then learn to sing the particular songs of his new neighborhood, thereby perpetuating the local song tradition. It seemed that simple, a conclusion I would come to for the Bewick's wren, too. That had to be how it happened—there was no other reasonable explanation. What I didn't know was why it was important for them to answer each other with identical songs, but I was content to leave that more difficult question for another time. What I had learned was sufficient to warrant a scientific publication, my very first, in the 1971 volume of the *Condor*.

Just how different these "spotted" Oregon birds were from the eastern birds I learned a few months later, in late February 1972. While on my way to

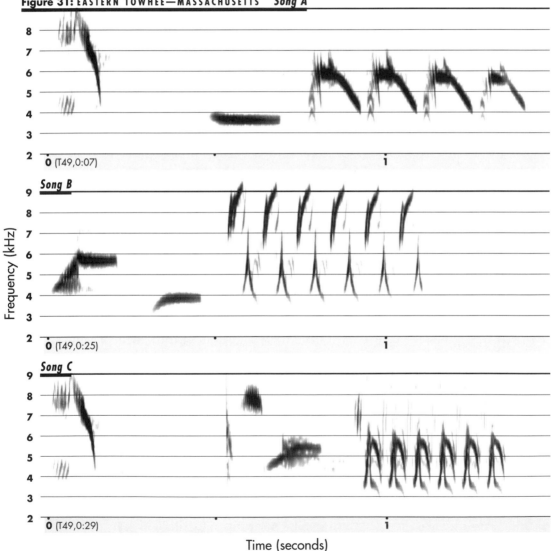

Figure 31: EASTERN TOWHEE—MASSACHUSETTS *Song A*

Song B

Song C

Frequency (kHz)

0 (T49,0:07)

0 (T49,0:25)

0 (T49,0:29)

Time (seconds)

an Organization for Tropical Studies course in Costa Rica, I met Dave Ewert during an all-nighter in the Miami airport. He was doing a similar, though far more thorough, study of the towhee on Long Island, New York. What different birds his were! For one thing, they were migratory, leaving his site for warmer places during the winter. And the repertoire size of an eastern towhee was only half that of a western bird: each male typically had only three or four different songs, with a range of two to five. Even more striking was that neighboring males on Long Island shared few songs, so it would be impossible for them to converse with each other with matching, identical songs.

Just a few months later, in August of 1972, Melissa and I moved to New York, where in the spring of 1973 I listened carefully to Dave's northeastern towhees. A little over an hour before sunrise, he awakens with a few *chewinks,* then settles into at least a half hour of singing. The general form of each song is *drink-your-teeeeeeee,* but at first he alternates two strikingly different songs. Soon he switches to one or two others, then perhaps back to the first two, his pace eventually slowing as he sings strings of just one of the songs. A few sketches in my notebook and I know these three or four songs well enough to recognize them any time. I hear the neighbor, too; his singing style is the same, but the particular songs each male sings are unique.

Why, I can't help but wonder, are the spotted and eastern towhees so different from each other? My best guess is that the difference in repertoire size and sharing with neighbors has to do with whether the birds migrate. Those western communities are stable, with a singing male on his same territory throughout life; a young male disperses just a short distance from home and settles for life into his chosen song neighborhood, learning his songs there. The migratory movements of eastern birds might reduce the stability of song neighborhoods, in one of two ways. Perhaps eastern birds learn their songs just as precisely as do the western males, but after migrating, eastern birds don't settle in the exact place where they learned, so that the songs become more mixed up and neighbors don't sing alike. A second possibility is that eastern birds simply don't imitate songs as precisely—maybe the eastern birds improvise more, in part because there's no need to imitate when migra-

Figure 31. Songs of the eastern towhee from Massachusetts (track 49). *Drink-your-teeeeeeeee* is the standard fare among migratory birds in New England, typically with two introductory notes (*drink-your*) followed by a series of repeated elements (*teeeeeeeee*). These are the three commonly used songs of a single male, each readily distinguished from the others.

tion is more likely to mix the birds up anyway. I also can't help but wonder about those larger repertoires out west—are they perhaps larger because males are on their singing territories throughout their lives, and their singing season each year is longer, so that singing is more important and they have more time to learn their songs from each other?

I eye that map of North America again, realizing that my experiences are all northern, from the North-central to the Northwest to the Northeast. My eyes drop to Florida, where birds must be resident. And they're white-eyed, which means they're genetically different from the more northern red-eyed birds, suggesting that they've had ample time to adapt to a different lifestyle in Florida. Although they are "eastern" birds, their resident lifestyle is more like the Oregon birds. If my reasoning is correct, that a resident bird is more likely to have songs like its neighbor, then I'd predict that the style of singing of the resident Florida birds would be more like towhees in the Northwest than in the Northeast, even though the Florida birds are more closely related to the Northeastern birds.

It wasn't until 1987 that I would devote the time to answering this question. The entire family went to Florida, for a sabbatical, and I spent time recording towhees at Corkscrew Swamp Sanctuary near Fort Myers and at the Archbold Biological Station near Lake Placid. Well before dawn I was in place, waiting for their first songs beneath the stars among the longleaf pines and saw palmettos. A whistled *sweee,* the Florida version of the northwestern *zhreeee* and the northeastern *chewink,* was the first sign that they stirred from their roost, and then they were off and singing at a frenzied pace, alternating two or even three different songs (track 51). For half an hour or so each continued, each on his own territory, but always within earshot of others nearby.

I heard lots of *drink-your-teeeeeeeee* songs, but many were *drink-drink-teeeeeeeee,* others *drink-drink-your-teeeeeeeee.* It didn't take long, though, to realize what they were up to. Especially during the first half hour of singing, when a male raced through his repertoire at the most frenzied pace, I heard an impressive variety of songs from each male, far more than the three or four expected in the Northeast. I often heard them answering each other with identical songs, too, just as the Oregon birds had. Detailed analyses on my computer would later show that eight or nine was a typical repertoire size for these birds, and two neighboring males at Corkscrew Swamp even had identical repertoires of seven different song types apiece. Perhaps one was a yearling, having learned all of the songs in the repertoire of his older neighbor (just as chipping sparrows do).

So there it is, a map quest fulfilled. It is an answer I had hoped for, one that made sense, a correlation between towhee singing style and towhee lifestyle. In Florida and Oregon, from the far Southeast and the far Northwest, birds are resident and remain on the same territory in the same neighborhood throughout their lives. A young male leaves home and establishes his territory in the local population, learning a relatively large repertoire of highly local songs from his parents' generation and tutoring the next generation himself. But in the migratory birds of the Northeast, it is different: repertoires are smaller, and neighbors share few songs with each other.

That's the pattern, but I again fret over the two possible explanations of how it comes to be. Does a young towhee in both Florida and New England imitate his songs equally precisely, only to have the uncertainties of migration scatter the birds and their songs in the Northeast, so that neighbors don't share songs? Or, over evolutionary time, has the uncertainty of migration reduced the premium on precise imitation for the northeastern birds, so that now they improvise more than do the Florida birds?

I know of only one way to answer that question. I must raise some baby birds from Florida and from New England in the same large aviary. I'll get all the right permits, of course, and then play lots of towhee songs over loudspeakers to them; maybe I'll even import some adult towhees to tutor the youngsters properly. I bet that the Florida males will develop larger song repertoires than the New England males because they are naturally skilled at acquiring more songs (just as western marsh wrens are genetically different from eastern wrens and more capable of learning larger song repertoires). But I'm more interested in how well the young towhees from the two locations imitate. It would be exciting if Florida birds imitated more precisely, because that result would be consistent with something I want to believe. I want to believe that different lifestyles favor different kinds of song development, and that natural selection is able to shape song development in different environments to achieve the "best fit." If there are reasons for small patterns in nature, then there's hope for understanding the great diversity of singing behaviors among all birds. One of these years, I'll have to try that aviary experiment.

The map again. My eyes drift across North America to the Great Plains, settling on North and South Dakota. In the western part of these states, the spotted towhee is migratory, as is the eastern towhee in the eastern part. In the Dakotas, the two towhee forms have essentially identical lifestyles, as both are migratory. The eastern birds probably behave just like the New England birds, but how will those migratory spotted towhees sing? Will neighboring males have identical songs, just like the spotted towhees from Oregon? Or will they behave more like the migratory eastern towhees, with less matching among neighbors? If evolutionary heritage is the stronger influence, they will sing like Oregon birds, but if current lifestyle matters more, then they will be more like the New England towhees, each male with a small repertoire unique to himself. It's a simple question, and easily answered. Some day . . .

The map before me is static, the paper permanently colored to show the western and eastern form of this bird. But I know better, that over time range maps are like giant amoebas, expanding and shrinking, arms extending and retracting. My amoeba is colored to show ranges of the white-eye to the southeast and of the two red-eyes to the north, and as I travel back in time, I imagine how glaciers must have transformed this multicolored amoeba on the continent. It was no doubt one giant amoeba at one time, the ancestral towhee, but advancing glaciers fractured it, isolating three fragments. In the West the birds would eventually *zhreeee,* in the Northeast *chewink,* and in the Southeast *sweee.* These nonlearned calls gradually revealed the accumulating genetic differences among the three groups, as did their subtly different looks, such as the color of their eyes or how white was displayed on the wings. As the glaciers receded, the range-amoebas expanded again, pressing against each other in the Southeast and in the Great Plains. In the Dakotas, intermediate birds became common, revealing that some females mated with males of the other type, producing hybrids.

With a little bit of information from where ranges of the three forms meet, biologists play guessing games as to what the consequences of mixed matings will lead to. In the Great Plains, for example, will eastern and western forms interbreed so freely that eventually, many years from now, only one form of the towhee will appear across North America? If so, then we have one towhee, the "rufous-sided towhee." Or will eastern and western birds sort themselves out, the hybrids being at somewhat of a disadvantage, so that North America will retain pure eastern and pure western forms? If so, then we have the "spotted towhee" to the west and the "eastern towhee" to the east, two "good species." The pendulum has swung on the best guess, from two to one and back to two species during the 1900s alone, but as of 1995 the experts proclaim we have two species in North America. (The white-eye is left out of these "species arguments" because it has never been considered different enough from other eastern towhees to be a different species.)

I flip the page in my field guide: more maps. My eyes go to the Southwest, to three almost identical towhees, the California, canyon, and Abert's, each in its own well-confined range, from California across Arizona and New Mexico; I know there's a fourth, too, just across the border in Mexico. Each map is a single, solid color, showing that the birds are permanent residents, nonmigratory. Based on the journeys I have taken with my rufous-sided towhee throughout North America, I predict that neighbors will have identical songs in their repertoires, because they have learned them from one another. I predict that repertoires will be fairly large. I have always wanted to spend more time in the Southwest . . .

The Tufted Titmouse

MAY 10, 4:35 A.M. Sunrise will be an hour from now. Sipping a glass of orange juice, I eye the gear on the kitchen floor, checking items off in my mind one last time. Parabola. In the backpack: stereo recorder and tapes, shotgun mike and cable, headphones. Hand-counter. Two flashlights. Extra batteries, 9 volt and D cells. Umbrella and tarp, just in case the overnight rains return. Binoculars. Tripod. Ropes. Crazy-Creek Camping Chair. Ready.

I'm out the door. Around the front of the house to the left, to the south side where the ladder leans against the house just to the left of the chimney. Hesitating in the dark, I remind myself to concentrate, always three of the four on the ladder at a time, only one moving . . . each hand gripping a different rung, left foot up, then the right to the next rung, move the left hand up, then the right, past the living room windows, then our bedroom windows, finally to the rooftop. Slowly, methodically, thinking about every move, I hold onto the chimney and step around the top of the ladder, keeping low, to the right and over the peak of the roof, kneeling, opening the chair, and sitting down. Leaning back, I tie the safety rope to the ladder, and then to my midsection, and can now breathe more easily.

Quickly the gear is laid out. Parabola to the tripod, pointing northeast. Shotgun mike resting on the chimney, pointing southwest. Mike cables to the recorder, headphones plugged in, atop my head, 90-minute tape in the recorder. I'm ready. At 4:50 the tape rolls.

For years these titmice have been after me to listen to them. They begin anew every January, insisting that I listen, that I take more notice. Always something else has been more important, but not this morning. I am here now, ready, having finally heeded their call. For at least an hour, and for a full 90 minutes, I hope, I will sit here in the treetops, three stories up as I look off to the east, and listen. So that I can relive the experience later, I let the tape roll, but it is the listening, here and now, that is the goal.

4:50, and already the early risers are singing. To the right, down by the pond, is a study in opposites, the catbird and the wood thrush, some of the worst and the finest music, at least by our standards. A robin sings over on Aubinwood Road, perhaps a hundred yards through the woods. *Fee-bee fee-bee fee-b-be-be* announces the phoebe from the neighbor's backyard. The barred owl is about, as he sounded off when I climbed the ladder. One spring peeper, just one, calls from the pond.

As I wait for the titmice, I review what I know about them.

1. "A whistled chant: *peter, peter, peter* or *here, here, here, here*," says Peterson. It's these songs that I want to hear, but it's worth knowing that the other notes are like a chickadee's, though more "nasal, wheezy, and complaining."

2. Each male has not just one of those whistled chants, but as many as 9 or 10, though perhaps only 5 or 6 are commonly used. As he sings, he repeats one of those songs over and over, eventually switching to another song in his repertoire. I've heard this pattern of singing often over the years, a titmouse repeating a particular song over and over, then abruptly jarring me with a new type.

3. Singing seems to be contagious among titmice: when one sings, neighbors often reply, and usually with an identical song. Perhaps as a result, each male's commonly used songs are shared by his neighbors, and throughout the spring, before the leaves are on the trees, I hear this "matched countersinging," as we call it.

4. Occasionally, females sing, too, using the same songs as the males, but they are not regular participants in the dawn chorus. It will be only the males proclaiming themselves from the treetops.

5. I puzzle over some of what I have read. Neighboring titmice tend to use one particular song first in the morning. Why? Is there any special meaning to this first song? Why are some songs favored early in the season, others later; and why are some favored in the center of the territory, others nearer the edge, when males are defending their territories? I wonder . . . do these patterns tell us something special about titmice minds, that the birds use different songs in different contexts as they interact with each other? Or are the patterns just an artifact of commonly used songs being shared with neighbors, and

others not? Perhaps shared songs are used on territory boundaries, nonshared songs more in the center of the territory? I puzzle, and begin to think there might be a lot more going on in the titmouse mind than we appreciate.

6. I remind myself, too, that each male I will hear this morning has a history. Perhaps half of all titmice survive from one year to the next, so roughly every other singer is a first-year bird, having claimed his first territory just this year. Each of these yearlings emerged from the egg in early June of last year, left the cavity nest about two weeks later, and by late July, while still with his parents, was already practicing all of the songs of the parents' neighborhood. At that time I'd know him as a young bird by his looks, with his indistinct crest, paler face, and lack of black on the forehead, but no doubt I'd hear him first, the babbling voice of a youngster being unstable, the whistles wavering in pitch and the tempo of the song so uneven. He perhaps stayed with his parents over the winter, foraging in a small flock, often with chickadees and nuthatches and a downy woodpecker or two, ranging over about 10 acres of woodland in our neighborhood. In March or early April, he left his parents' territory in search of a territory of his own nearby. At that time, singing by the adult titmice became more persistent, and the young bird then had to adjust his songs to match the songs of established adults where he settled. I puzzle again, because if a young male moves to a neighborhood with different songs, does he have to learn not only the songs there but also the proper contexts in which the local males use those songs? . . . Now it's early May, and birds are paired, about to begin nesting.

TUFTED
TITMOUSE

4:59. Titmouse. How long has he been singing? Five seconds? My mind seems drugged, in slow motion, the synapses glacial in delivering the message to the titmouse detection center in my brain, the brain in turn taking its time to process the arriving message. Yes, titmouse, just to the northeast of the house, where I expected him. *Here here here, here here, here here here* . . . pairs or trios of brief downslurred whistles in rapid succession, 10 songs by 5:00 A.M. I'll call it "song A" (track 52, figure 32).

Where will he take me, I wonder? I begin clicking off the songs by the minute, 26 in the first minute, then 26, 27, 22, and then I detect a change. It's a subtle difference, but I feel it in the tempo. The down-slurred whistle feels just a little longer, and he gives just one, one, one, one, then in twos, *heere heere* . . . *heere heere* (song B, track 52).

I continue clicking off song B by the minute, 27, 28, then slip the head-phones on, just to hear him better. Only now do I realize that a second tit-mouse also calls *heere heere* in the distance, the two singing males matching each other by singing the identical song. I realize, too, that cardinals and blue jays and chickadees and chipping sparrows have weighed in. Two robins cop-ulate high in the canopy, directly in front of me . . . 27, 28, 20, 25, 21, 29, 25,

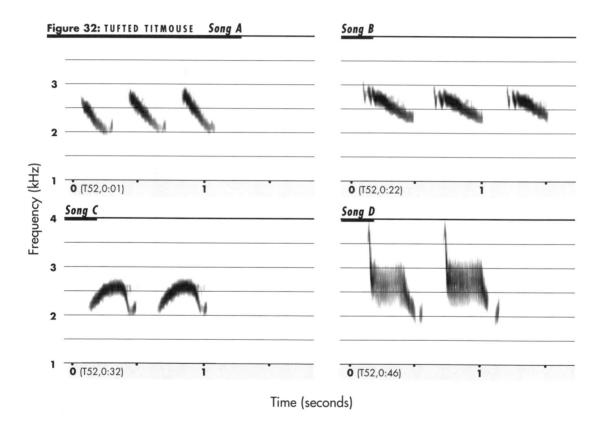

Figure 32. Four songs of the tufted titmice that are commonly used near my home in Amherst, Massachusetts (track 52). These are simple songs, each consisting of a simple element repeated just a few times.

and in the distance I hear his neighbor switch to a new song (C), the simplest of songs, a single note that rapidly rises and falls in pitch, like an upside-down "U" on a sonagram. One, two more C songs from him, and my male switches, too. Just four or five seconds they were out of sync, my male singing B and the distant one C, until my male switched, too, now both of them singing C. My nearby male rounds off the minute with 11 C songs (figure 32).

Now it is song C: 45 in the first minute, then 38, 36, 35, 36, 38, 39, 35 by 5:20 A.M. How many hundreds of songs has he already sung in these 20 minutes? Behind me I hear that the western male has approached, he also unmistakably singing song C. The three birds continue singing, and I continue to count for the male just off the corner of the roof to the northeast: 39, 36, 38, and after 2 more songs I hear the western male switch back to *here here here,* unmistakably the first song of the morning, the A song. My male responds with C, C; an A from the neighbor then overlaps with my male's third C; then another C from my male; and next they simultaneously sing *here here here.* I now hear A from the male in the distance to the east, he having switched, too, the three of them singing *here here here, here here here.*

The A song with its two or three notes is longer than the C song with a single note, and as a result the singing pace slows: 25, 21, 14, 23, 22, 21, 17, now 5:30 A.M. The near and the far bird to the east are trading mostly threes now, taking turns, *here here here* from one, then *here here here* from the other.

On and on they sing, all three birds singing *here here here.* The sun peeks through the trees to the east, sparking a goldfinch's chattering song. Warblers now seem to be everywhere in the canopy, as if a wave of them just dropped out of the sky. I hear parulas and pines and black-throated greens and yellow-rumps, and what are those others, my warbler-ears so rusty at spring's first encounter? At eye level I see these northbound migrants working the tips of the oak branches, refueling on what must be insects among the freshly emerged leaves and flowers. A nuthatch sings, and at 5:42, eight minutes after official sunrise, I hear that the local hairy woodpecker has emerged from his roosting hole. Orioles and jays and crows are about, too.

5:50, THEN 5:55, and the *here here here* continues from the west, the northeast, and the east, all three birds still on song A, over half an hour since they returned to the A song. How many is that? About 20 songs a minute, perhaps only a few minutes not singing—that's at least 500 *here here here*s from my bird in this session alone. Why? Why so many of this song when he has others he could sing?

5:56, and he changes to the slower-tempo version, song B. Curiously, I now hear only this bird, as the other two are either not singing or are out of earshot. But three minutes later I hear the two eastern birds, both singing *heere heere,* song B, above the neighbors' house. What a pity no one sits there to hear these exchanges up close.

AT 6:05, in the distance behind me, I hear a different titmouse song, a raspy *jeer jeer* (song D; figure 32, track 52). He continues, perhaps so distant that he is out of earshot of the two males singing their *heere heere* to the east. For the first time this morning this small community of titmice speaks with more than one voice.

A pack of six jays moves through, they, too, working the oak leaves and flowers, uttering a variety of sounds—bell calls, squeaky hinges of all tonal varieties, and the red-shouldered hawk imitations.

6:18. I hear a new titmouse song from the nearby male, like song C in that it is a single whistle that rises and then falls, but the rise is more gradual, the drop more sudden, as if someone had taken the midpoint of that upside-down "U" on the sonagram and pulled it to the right. Three minutes later I notice that the male to the far east is singing the same song, alternating this new song, song E, with my male.

In the next minute, both males switch back to song B, *heere heere.*

THUD! The 90-minute tape has come to an end, the "play" and "record" levers on the tape recorder abruptly popping up and turning the recorder off. I can ease up now, I tell myself, my 90-minute goal having been reached. I breathe deeply, the session completed, and can't help but notice a larger world that has emerged around me.

The sun is up above the canopy of the most distant trees now, sneaking its rays through a lingering cloud cover. The dampness of the overnight rain lingers, condensing on my parabola and chilling my bones. It's a cool, wet morning, upper 40s, not a bit of wind, and I tense my body, working the muscles, hoping to generate some heat from deep within.

Over the last hour and a half, from the layers of blackness around me have emerged the soft, striking colors of a New England forest in spring dress. Layers of new life lie before me, the maples down below almost fully leafed out, the seeds already hanging from the branch tips. Above them are the dark green of the hemlocks and the lighter greens of the pines in the subcanopy, and then the tiny golden red leaves of the oaks reaching to the sky. Birds of all kinds still cavort in the canopy, so close. It would be but a small leap from the rooftop to them, and for just a moment I see myself there in the canopy, too, plucking delectable morsels from the branch tips and, best of all, singing with them.

The titmice. Just what did they do this morning? What sense do I make of their singing activities? I reflect again on those six points I reviewed earlier:

1. "A whistled chant: *peter, peter, peter* or *here, here, here, here.*" Yes, but I feel cheated, as all of the songs I heard were so simple, just a single syllable, as *here, heere,* or *jeer.* I like those more complex two-syllable songs better, partly because the more complex the songs are, the easier it is for me to tell them apart by ear. I've heard them locally, but not from my birds. These are different titmice dialects that I'm hearing, I realize, with songs varying markedly from one little community to the next.

Figure 33. What better way is there to hear the titmice than to be up among them at dawn, facing the sunrise. I'm safely tied to the ladder, my shotgun microphone on the chimney recording the bird behind me, my parabolic microphone capturing two other birds, the nearby male just off the corner of the house and the more distant bird to the east.

2. Repertoires? Yes, not just one chant, but I heard 4 different songs from the nearby male in the 90 minutes I listened to him, each one repeated many times before switching to another. And how many times they were repeated amazes me. The first A bout contained 111 songs over about 4 minutes, then B for 236 in 8 minutes, then C for 432 in 11½ minutes, and A again for 534 songs over 32 minutes. That's a total of more than 1,300 songs in about 55 minutes.

3. Yes, neighbors did reply to each other with identical songs, switching within seconds of when the other bird switched. Answering each other with identical songs is undoubtedly the reason that the commonly used songs are shared by neighbors. What a contrast this behavior is to that of a western marsh wren, for example, who also matches songs of neighbors but whose next song is always different, so that every minute about 20 choices are made as to how to respond to a neighbor. A marsh wren singing for an hour needs to make about 600 choices as to how to respond to just one neighbor, but a titmouse has only about 4 such choices. Or make it two neighbors, and the marsh wren has 1,200 choices, the titmouse 8. The game of matching a neighbor's song might be the same, but the pace is markedly different.

4. Female song? I didn't hear it, but wouldn't have expected to. I would have had to be following a pair of birds, I think, up close, listening to the male sing and then hearing a few songs from his mate. The overview from my rooftop kept me at too great a distance.

5. Different songs in different contexts? Fascinating. I'm almost hooked, almost convinced to spend much of next year studying these birds, as I'd like to know more about how they use their songs. It would be simple, too, just a matter of making a commitment and spending more time with them. Do my local birds favor the A song as their waking song, for example? I simply need to be out at dawn more often. And what are the characteristics of this particular song? The *here* syllable is the briefest and most rapidly repeated in all songs that I heard this morning, for example. How does that *here* compare to the waking songs of titmice who sing a different dialect? Do those waking songs also consist of brief, rapidly repeated syllables? If the waking songs of different dialects are similar in some consistent way, then I'm on to something, on to some titmouse rule about how they awake. Birds of many species awake with aggressive calls, for example, the mockingbird with its sharp *chat chat*, the wood thrush with its

whit whit whit. Maybe there are characteristics of this waking song that make it more aggressive in some way?

I'd want to ask the same kinds of questions about other songs in the repertoire. Can I confirm that, in a couple of different dialects, certain songs are used near the center or edge of the territory, and some are used early or late in the season? Perhaps songs used in the middle of the territory have common properties, for example—they might be especially short, or harsh, or perhaps simply not shared with immediate neighbors. If songs of different dialects that are used in the middle of the territory consistently have the same properties, then I'd have a small window on the titmouse mind, as I'd begin to understand some of the rules by which these titmice sing to each other.

If, on the other hand, the characteristics of songs and their contexts are not consistent from one dialect to another, then some of these apparently complex rules within a given dialect are probably the consequence of something simpler, such as the need for individuals to match each other's songs in highly aggressive contexts (as in song sparrows). Aggression is stronger at territorial boundaries than at centers, for example, and aggression is relatively high early in the season amid the tensions of establishing territory boundaries. The simple rule of matching the neighbor in highly aggressive contexts then dictates that shared songs will be favored at territory boundaries; if throughout a day a titmouse tries to play no favorites among the songs in his repertoire, then the songs not used in matching contests at the boundary will tend to be used in the center of the territory. As aggression wanes throughout the season, patterns of song use would change, too. What initially seemed like a complex pattern of song usage in different contexts could thus be the result of one simple rule, of matching neighbors in aggressive contexts.

Perhaps there are other rules I might uncover. This morning my male began with 111 songs of one form (A), then 236 of another (B), then 432 (C), and then 534 (A), increasing the number of times he repeated a particular song over the first hour. The average number of songs per minute tended to increase, too, from 28 to 30 to a high of 38, before dropping down to about 17. Does this pattern hold each morning, or in other dialects? If the patterns hold, then they, too, tell me something about the titmouse mind and how it works.

6. I'd love to know more of each male's history, too. I'd probably have to catch them and band them so that I could identify individuals. Maybe I could band babies in the nest and then follow them during their first summer, hearing them practice songs of their parents' neighborhood by the time they're six weeks old. I'd also love to be able to follow those youngsters when they disperse to another neighborhood early the next year. How much would they have to change their songs to fit in there? How do patterns of singing begin in January and intensify as territories are claimed, peaking by nesting time in early May? And what is the fate of the yearling in his new community? My bird tended to switch songs after his neighbors had. Does that make him lower in the local hierarchy, subordinate to what might be older birds on adjacent territories, so that he follows their lead? Or does his matching reveal dominance, because responding in kind to his neighbor's song change is especially intimidating? I'd like to know. I could know, with a little investment of time.

Soon the sun will be rising on other titmouse species, too. Just beyond the Great Plains is a plain gray one, formerly called the plain titmouse, but now divided into two species. The first is the juniper titmouse, in the open juniper and pine woodlands from Colorado and New Mexico through Nevada; farther west is the oak titmouse in the open oak and pine woodlands of the Pacific slope in California. Although the songs of these titmice are different from those in the East, much of their overall behavior is the same. All that is known of them, however, is that males have repertoires of songs that match those of their neighbors. How I would love to know more, to understand not only the tufted titmouse but also its close relatives, to see how patterns of communicating have evolved within this group. Do they all sing by the same rules, or if they differ, how, and why?

I confess that I'm especially drawn to southeastern Arizona, to birding meccas like Madera Canyon, roughly 40 miles south of Tucson. There, among the sycamores in the canyon bottom I'll find the bridled titmouse, so named because of its distinct facial markings. It is this bird's sounds that so intrigue me. I have read that he has only three different songs in his repertoire, not ten or so like the other North American titmice, and he seems to use each of those songs in special circumstances: one is used in close encounters and a second in distant exchanges with other males, and the third in spontaneous singing, perhaps more related to addressing females. Three different songs, each used in a different context.

That's remarkable, and I'm amazed that since these findings were first published in 1983 no one has followed up on this discovery. I seek out that original paper, pulling down reprint #741 from my shelves, and study the details. Each of four males had the same three song types, as determined from sonagrams, and other males in the area had the same songs as well. And those three songs are strikingly different. Instantly, I realize that I need to know how those songs change over distance, and no matter what the outcome, I will learn something exciting.

One possibility is that the songs used in close encounters vary considerably from place to place, but that songs used at a distance change little. Such a system would be much like that used by the chestnut-sided warbler and would suggest that the same rules govern the titmouse and the warbler (and the grasshopper sparrow—but that's another story). To me, that would be truly exciting, because it would mean that two (or three) unrelated birds have independently evolved the same communication system. The reason we do science is to uncover organizing principles, and this titmouse is a perfect opportunity to test whether a general rule now dictates how warblers and this titmouse sing.

Another possibility is that all three songs vary over distance. If so, then I have an opportunity to uncover the rules that govern this titmouse's behavior. I'd study the characteristics of the close encounter songs used in different dialects and contrast those songs with the songs used when males are a greater distance apart. The consistent features within each song category from dialect to dialect would have to be the meaningful features of the songs to the birds. The songs provide the looking glass into the mind of these birds.

Still another possibility is that the songs change relatively little, especially compared to the songs of other species. If there is some highly sophisticated communication system among these titmice, then perhaps the same three songs need to be preserved from place to place, so that each bridled titmouse can know what another is saying.

No matter how these songs change over space, I realize what an opportunity this is. Why has it taken me almost 20 years since I first read this paper to understand the importance of this bridled titmouse?

How he sings at dawn is extraordinary, especially when his mate is fertile and laying eggs, with a combination of all different kinds of vocalizations, including both songs and calls. What a contrast this bridled titmouse is to the others! I must get to know this bird better, to record its songs in a transect radiating out from Madera Canyon to determine how these songs vary over space. Getting to know the bridled titmouse better will almost certainly help me understand the other titmice, too.

Tufted. Juniper. Oak. Bridled. And one more: the black-crested titmouse. It's the closest relative of the tufted, so close that it's currently considered only a subspecies of the tufted. Unlike the normal tufted titmouse, this black-crested form has a pale forehead and, of course, a black crest. Perhaps my quest to find the titmice rules should begin in central Texas before I head farther west.

Now the big dilemma. I have a choice. Do I keep these plans to myself, and not let on how exciting these titmice are? Few people seem to care about them, and apparently no one is currently trying to understand how sophisticated their system of singing might be. One of the hot topics in behavioral biology these days is "cognitive science," or how animals "think." These titmice are a well-kept secret, and perhaps I'd best keep it that way so that I can have all the fun myself. Next chance I get, I'll head to Arizona myself, to explore the titmouse mind myself, to claim all glory for whatever I find *all for myself*.

But maybe I should share the fun and shout it from the rooftop. "TIT-MICE!" It's so easy to get some simple tape recordings, and so easy to identify the different songs that a male sings (see Appendix II). Anyone can do this. Anyone should do this. What better way is there to spend a few hours than tailing a titmouse around his territory, recording a few songs, and then taking them back to the computer to see and hear the mind of a bird at work?

TITMICE! . . . TITMICE! . . . TITMICE! . . . TITMICE! . . .

4

Extremes of Male Song

Introduction

SONGBIRDS WITHOUT A SONG

THOSE WHO DELIGHT in listening to birdsongs soon realize the extraordinary variety among species. Some birds are mute, with no voice boxes at all, such as the turkey vulture that can only hiss. Some songbirds seem to have no song, such as the waxwings, which get by in life with a couple of high, thin *sreee* or *see* notes. Or take the corvids, which include jays and crows and ravens. These species do just fine with an assortment of what seem to be non-song vocalizations. One of these corvids, the blue jay, is the focus of this section.

SONGBIRDS WITH ESPECIALLY COMPLEX SONGS

Songs of some species are exceptionally simple. The Henslow's sparrow "has the simplest and shortest of all our birdsongs," its brief *hic-up* song "one of the poorest of vocal efforts of any bird." Males of many species sing a single song, such as the white-crowned sparrow, the chipping sparrow, the black-capped chickadee, and the whip-poor-will.

At the opposite extreme are males with huge repertoires or with exceptionally long and complex songs, the focus of this section. The brown thrasher epitomizes those birds with large repertoires, a male being able to sing as many as 2,000 different songs; his cousin the sage thrasher is also an accomplished singer. The winter wren's songs are a pinnacle of song complexity among birds.

SONGBIRDS WITH ESPECIALLY BEAUTIFUL SONGS

Songs of some species sound harsh and grating, such as the chatter of a sedge wren or the squawk of a common grackle, but others strike us as beautiful and musical, making us wonder how similar our aesthetic values might be to those of the birds who sing them. In North America, songs of thrushes and of the Bachman's sparrow are especially highly regarded. After three accounts on the finest of singers—the Bachman's sparrow, the wood thrush, and the hermit thrush—I ask what it is about these songs and those of other birds that strikes us as musical, or pleasing to listen to.

SONGS ON THE WING

Most birds we know perch and sing, but others sing from high above the ground. In the dead of night, for example, the ovenbird occasionally launches into the canopy of his woodland territory, singing an ecstatic jumble of notes, giving his species away only at the very last as he offers a few phrases of his normal *teacher-teacher* song.

It is the grassland birds that are more prone to these song flights, however. With no elevated perches, bobolinks and meadowlarks often take to the sky to broadcast their message. Sprague's pipits in the Great Plains jingle their cascade of *ching-a-ring-a-ring-a-ring-a-ring-a-ring-a-ring-a* from high overhead, sometimes staying aloft for more than three hours and singing a thousand or more songs. And in Percy Shelley's skylark is the quintessential song flight: the "blithe Spirit / . . . that from heaven, or near it, / pourest thy full heart / in profuse strains of unpremeditated art / . . . a flood of rapture so divine."

Nowhere are song flights more pervasive than among the shorebirds. Study the range maps of any field guide, and you'll see the diversity of these birds that breed in the treeless Arctic, most likely the ancestral type of environment for this group. Many of these species have extensive song flights, and we focus here on one such species that is common and accessible in eastern North America, the American woodcock.

TIRELESS SINGERS

How tirelessly some of these males sing, their stamina and persistence on display as they bid for success, all in an attempt to win a female from other competing males. Such is the power of the discriminating female as she makes her choices as to which male will be represented in the next generation. Among the most persistent singers are the nightjars, represented here by the whip-poor-will, and the red-eyed vireo, who sings throughout the heat of the day and late into the summer.

The Blue Jay

By their bloodlines, jays (and other corvids) are songbirds, the name given to those 4,600 species whose similar traits, such as complex syringes (voice boxes) and unique sperm and DNA, give away their relationships to each other. But by their behavior, one would never know jays are songbirds. Never does a jay rise to the treetops and "sing." During the dawn chorus, a wren or thrush or other typical songbird may sing nonstop for 30 to 60 minutes, but not a jay. An unpaired male songbird typically broadcasts his song from his territory all day long, sometimes even all night long, in his attempts to attract a female, but not a jay or crow or raven.

BLUE JAY

Instead, from our crows we hear *caw caw,* from blue jays *jay jay,* simple calls that seem to suffice for whatever these birds are up to. But simple these birds are not, as close study shows their vast repertoires of different calls. Widely regarded as some of the most intelligent of birds, they're also extremely hard to study, as it's difficult to trap and mark the members of a group; catch one of a flock of blue jays in a net, my friend Curt Adkisson tells me, and he has to move all of the nets to an entirely new location before he has a chance of catching another individual. Given the diverse repertoire and the difficulties in studying these birds, it's no wonder that for blue jays, despite their abundance, the definitive study on their sounds remains to be done. To my knowledge, blue jay sounds have been studied by three graduate students, one in Michigan, one in Illinois, and one in Oklahoma, and their stories have never been published, as if the jays would not reveal enough of their secrets to warrant a public story.

Having heard the *jay jay* nearly every day of my life, 22 years in Michigan, 4 in Oregon (where the backyard jay is the scrub-jay), 8 in New York, 21 in Massachusetts, I knew their time had come. I needed to know better what it was like to be a songbird without a song. From university archives, I borrowed those three unpublished theses. I studied the *Birds of North America* account, absorbing all I could about my quarry. I was then ready, or as ready as I could be.

APRIL 30, MONDAY. 4:30 A.M. Behind me to the west is the nearly completed nest, just 10 yards off the paved rail-to-trail bike path and 15 feet up in the large white pine—a loose construction of twigs nestled up against the trunk and supported by two large dead limbs. Farther to the west, beyond the nest tree and the other trees in the narrow strip along the path, is an open field, where the bobolinks will soon arrive. To my left the bike path extends to Amherst and on to Northampton, to my right back to the Station Road parking lot where I have just left my car. By the light of the waning quarter-moon overhead I can see the beavers' drowned forest before me, dead snags of pine and oak and maple silhouetted against the eastern sky. A few hummocks of raised ground here and there have spared some trees, the pines fully needled, the oaks and maples still leafless. The ground slopes quickly from the bike path to the water, where a beaver now swims back and forth just a few yards away, eyeing me, this strange creature here at such an odd hour.

It is here, I decided yesterday, that I would learn of jays. With the nest in view, I could monitor the roving bands of jays in the open swamp, trying to understand how the pair with the nest interacted with all the others. The open field to the west would force the jays to me, to where I'd be able to see and hear them as I walked the bike path through their domain.

In the distance to the right, from the depths of Lawrence Swamp, I hear a muffled *who-cooks-for-you, who-cooks-for-you-all,* the familiar call of the resident barred owl. From the higher woodlands to the east, beyond the beaver's playground, come the rhythmic hoots of a great horned owl, a pair of them, her voice higher pitched than his. Songbirds with songs gradually weigh in, robins, chickadees, titmice, and creepers, the dawn chorus now in full swing. A Virginia rail calls *kidick kidick* incessantly in the wet meadow beyond the nest tree.

AT 5:14 I finally hear one, a single bird in the distance, a penetrating *jay jay* to the east. Four minutes later a raspy, nasal *jay jay* from the southeast, and five minutes after that a "squeaky-gate" call to the north, all in the distance, nothing here yet by the nest. They all sound like single jays, as if each is just waking in its separate roost.

Only three jays have weighed in, and only briefly, but already they have told me much. As I listened carefully, each jay repeated its chosen sound several times, so it's clear that the sounds from a jay's bill are not random and unrepeatable—no, they're repeatable, no doubt highly structured, with some order that makes good sense to the jays. Knowing that is an important place to start. And I heard the two major categories into which we humans have lumped their sounds: the *jay* call and the squeaky-gate call (tracks 53, 54, figure 34). The *jay* call is typically harsh, loud, and unmusical, from these saucy birds perhaps sounding more like *jeer jeer*. The squeaky-gate is more musical, consisting of clear whistles, liquid in quality, often beginning at one pitch and dropping abruptly to finish lower, so named because this call sounds a bit like a rusty gate. What these three jays have also told me is that I know nothing of what these calls mean, for I have no idea why a jay awakes with a particular sound, why the first two jays chose a different variant of the *jay* call and why the third jay chose the squeaky-gate.

It's now light enough to see the nest, but the female is not there. She's undoubtedly nearby. The jays, here and in the distance, are quiet. What are they up to?

AT 5:38, eight minutes before sunrise, a flicker sings his lengthy *wick wick wick wick* song, the first sounds from the woodpeckers who have settled here to take advantage of the dead trees produced by the beavers' work. Soon I'll hear the downy and hairy and pileated and red-bellied woodpeckers, too, these late risers of the bird world, waiting almost to have the sun strike their roost trees before they're willing to emerge. The flicker soon flies to his favorite drumming post, a fence post with a loose wire passing through a half-inch opening in the staple. As he drums against the post, the wire vibrates within the staple, adding a musical ring to his drum. These crafty woodpeckers—they're always looking for an edge in their drumming, it seems, sometimes using a metal downspout, sometimes metal garbage cans, here an abandoned fence line.

Two dogs and their master pass, the dogs barking at me and the master barking at the dogs, tempting me to bark at the master to complete the circle.

6:08. The jays have been *so* quiet, without a songbird-like dawn chorus, but now, finally, almost an hour after I heard the first jay, and 22 minutes *after* sunrise, a single jay calls overhead, near the nest. Perhaps it's the male of this pair? It's the squeaky-gate call, a high-low-high-low call, and he bobs comically twice each time he calls. Twenty times he gives the doubled high-low call, twice just a single high-low, and always the same tonal quality, same pitch, same duration—remarkably consistent throughout the 80-second sequence. Why that particular call?

A minute later, they are upon us, as if the resident bird had asked for it, or maybe anticipated it. Swarming in the trees overhead, bobbing up and down, it's a blue jay melee. A loud *jay* call starts it all off, followed by *jrrrt* calls, escalating to a whiny pitch—perhaps that's the local pair. Then long squeaky-gate

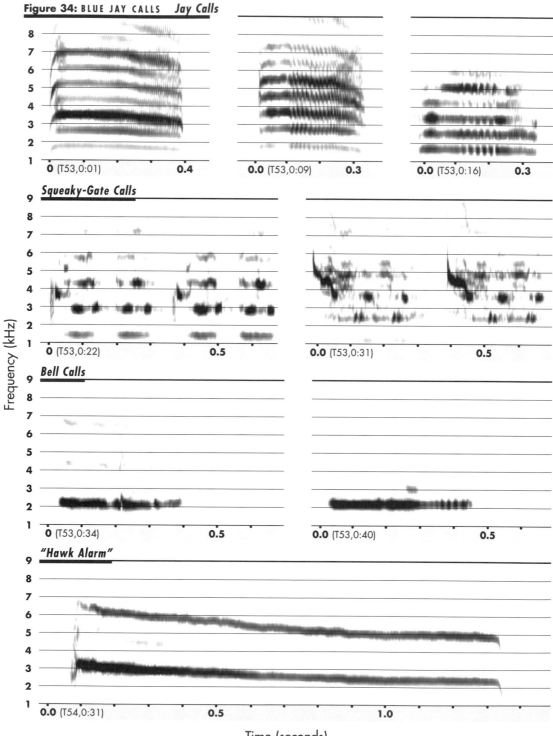

Figure 34: BLUE JAY CALLS   *Jay Calls*

0 (T53,0:01)   0.4

0.0 (T53,0:09)   0.3

0.0 (T53,0:16)   0.3

Squeaky-Gate Calls

0 (T53,0:22)   0.5

0.0 (T53,0:31)   0.5

Bell Calls

0 (T53,0:34)   0.5

0.0 (T53,0:40)   0.5

"Hawk Alarm"

0.0 (T54,0:31)   0.5   1.0

Frequency (kHz)

Time (seconds)

(SG) calls, high-low-high-low-high-low, then a female rattle, more SGs, escalat-ed *jrrrt* calls from what sounds like two birds, another rattle, and at least three birds all giving the same SG call. Another rattle, *jrrrt* sounds, more SGs that I've heard before, then a different SG, almost gurgling, followed by lots of *jay jay* calls.

For five minutes they carry on, bobbing and calling, trading places in the treetops. At least four or five different kinds of *jay* calls, at least two squeaky-gate calls, a particular jay repeating each distinct sound many times, at any moment the jays all seeming to agree on which particular call to use. A female, perhaps the local female with the nest, rattles throughout much of the sequence. At the end, a series of beautiful bell calls, followed by *jrrrt* calls, a female rattle, and four jays depart to the northeast, across the bike path and to the tall pines, screaming *jay jay jay jay.*

Then there are two. These two stay close together, and one eventually goes to the nest, nestling into it, as if shaping it to her body. Only the resident pair remains, she on the nest, he perched nearby.

In this single encounter I have heard much of what those three pioneer-ing graduate students had prepared me for. The jays seem infinitely expressive, capable of transforming the simplest of *jay* sounds into a diverse array. Some *jay* calls are short, some more drawn out; some are loud, some soft; some are distinctly doubled, as in *jay-jay, jay-jay;* inflections vary, with some slurred downward, almost sounding like two distinct parts, *ja-ay;* some are high pitched, some low, some in between. At one extreme the harsh *jay* becomes a single, fine, pure whistle, often with harmonics. Sometimes only one voice box will be engaged, sometimes two, creating special tonal effects. In these few minutes I heard at least five distinctly different *jay* variations, but the possible combinations seem endless.

And what a variety of other calls, too. The jays used two versions of the

Figure 34. What a variety of fantastic sounds these non-singing blue jays make, as illus-trated by selected examples from tracks 53 and 54. **Top row:** The three different *jay* sounds all consist of a low-frequency fundamental note between 1.5 and 2.0 kHz with a stack of harmonics above, but see and hear the different qualities among the calls. **Second row:** The squeaky-gate calls are more complex; they begin with a brief, rela-tively high-pitched tonal note, and then the overall energy in the call drops to a lower frequency, a drop that is more easily heard on the CD than seen in the sonagram. When listening to these calls, I hear a variety of brief tonal notes, but I marvel at the intricacies of these calls all the more as I look at the sonagrams. **Third row:** The bell calls are sim-ple whistles between 2.0 and 2.5 kHz, lacking any appreciable harmonics above the fundamental. **Fourth row:** The hawk alarm is the longest of the calls, a descending "asthmatic squeal" not unlike that of a red-tailed hawk.

squeaky-gate, one consisting of pure whistles, the other more throaty and gurgling. The "bell call" toward the end of the interaction was a third form of squeaky-gate call, given without the pitch inflections, so it's just a double whistle, both whistles on the same pitch, highly musical. This call is often given, I have read, by males as a human approaches the nest tree, as if in alarm. Perhaps it was the male of the local pair who finally gave the bell call, a form of alarm at the other jays intruding near the nest; most likely the reaction was not to me, as I had been standing there for some time.

Amid the raucous *jays* and squeaky-gates and bell calls, it would have been easy to overlook her odd rattle. It's like the purr of a large cat, but faster and sharper, lasting two to three seconds, sometimes broken up into two or three shorter rattles. Listening closely, I could hear a sharp click at the beginning and end of the purr, and the rattle undulates, too, apparently because she bobs as she rattles. It is only she who rattles, I have read, the male and female sharing all other sounds, and she often rattles when other jays intrude near her nest, as happened here.

The other sounds in that sequence were the *jrrrt* calls. They're typically the quiet, conversational tones of two or three jays as they forage together, or as the male and female communicate around the nest. The low-level form is a soft guttural *jrrrt jrrrt*, repeated several times, with the bill closed. Should the bird become a little more excited, as happened here, the sound becomes more nasal and whiny, and even whistlelike under the most extreme conditions. My best guess is that it was the local pair giving these calls, but that's only a guess.

Just minutes later, from 6:24 to 6:29, another five-minute confrontation breaks out. This time it's almost all *jay* calls, all varieties, with just three or four squeaky-gate calls, all of the same kind. The birds are more spread out this time, not displacing each other in the canopy. How many birds are there, and who is involved? I can't see, as they are back in the pines.

6:54. It's been quiet for 25 minutes now, no jays to be heard nearby, and the female retires to the nest. As the male flies off to the south, down the bike path, he utters a squeaky-gate, then some loud *jay jays* when he lands, followed by a few softer *jrrrt* calls. Three different sounds within just a few seconds. Why? What is he saying with each? And to whom?

7:03. The female departs the nest, flies up to the canopy of the oaks over the bike path, gives two bell calls, and flies off to the southeast. She's met midflight by the male, and together they fly to the top of a favorite roosting tree, an old dead oak standing in the beaver pond beside the bike path. A third jay is there, and the male halfheartedly chases it about the top of the tree, as if not really serious about his intentions. The third bird finally flies off, screaming *jay jay* in flight, leaving the two. *Jrrrt jrrrt,* the pair calls.

7:06. Near the nest again, I hear strikingly pure bell sounds, like double whistles on the same pitch; they're followed by an especially shrill squeaky-gate, high-low in form. More bell sounds, followed by a high-low-low-high-low-low squeaky-gate, and loud, double *jay-jay, jay-jay, jay-jay*s as it flies. Wow! One bell sound, two forms of the squeaky-gate, and one *jay* sound—four different sounds within a few seconds of one another, all from the same bird, all in the same situation (track 55, figure 35). Or did the jay see it differently, the context changing as the jay called, each call then carefully chosen to communicate the evolving contexts? What do all of these call variations mean? And just who was this jay? One of the pair that owns the nest?

7:15. The male flies from his nest far to the east, perches at the far edge of the beaver pond, calling *jay jay*. He then departs to the east, over the railroad tracks, and seems to return with two other jays. They all now scream *jay-jay, jay-jay,* the double *jay* call. Within a minute they separate, my male returning to the nest area. There, I realize, is a hint of what has happened overhead when multiple jays have visited this nesting site. For whatever reason, it seems that these jays visit their neighbors, raise a ruckus for a bit, and then depart, heading back to their respective homes.

7:25. She is now on the nest, but her mate is to the east, about 40 yards away, interacting with three other jays. From the treetops there I hear two-noted bell sounds, *jrrrt, jay jay,* some squeaky-gates, and 90 seconds later the three visitors depart for the east, *jay jay jay* en route. My male returns to the nest area, *jrrrt jrrrt,* perching above the bike path near the nest, preening his feathers, adjusting himself after the fracas.

7:41. The male softly calls *jrrrt* continually, working his way to the nest, where she already sits. He dips down, she extends her bill up, and he passes some morsel to her, then flies off, *jrrrt jrrrt,* and he's gone. He'll do more of this in the coming days, feeding her repeatedly while she forms her eggs within her, and he will then be her only source of food as she incubates the 17 to 18 days it'll take to hatch those jaylings.

7:53. His double *jay-jay* overhead seems to start it all off, a double bob accompanying it. In the distance I hear some single *jay* calls, followed by *jrrrt* and loud *jay*s from the local male. Two birds then call side by side overhead, one bobbing with loud *jay* calls, the other bobbing with two-noted bell calls, the second note sounding strained, as if reverberated electronically. Muted, in the background, are two rattles from the female on the nest. She stays put, keeping out of the treetop interaction, but she makes her presence known. Then silence. It must have been only one extra jay who came, *jay*ed, and then left, the local male doing the bell call — though I never saw that extra jay arrive or leave.

Just three and a half hours with the jays, and I have heard so much.

April is a time of transition for these jays. The winter flocks break up, pairs of birds separating out to claim their own nesting areas. Throughout April the jays jockey for position, squabbling over the space needed to raise their families, holding regular and highly vocal dominance contests throughout the flock's home range. Although they don't defend territories like most songbirds do, a pair of jays does try to keep others from nesting nearby, and the jays negotiate for their space as they interact in these groups. A pair gradually secures an area for its nest but still engages the flock of roving birds as it moves through the area, pairs joining and then dropping out of the flock as it moves by them. Just a few days from the first egg in their nest, my pair still engages what is left of the jay flock as it passes, members of the flock that late in the season perhaps consisting mostly of yearlings who are still prospecting for mates and for space. Sometimes just the male confronts the flock, as the female sits on the nest. It's likely, too, that neighboring pairs regularly visit each other before they are too busy nesting, much as my male incited an exchange with what were probably nesting jays to the east.

In my few hours, I never heard the infamous hawk calls that these jays are so good at. It's another mystery, why the jay mimics so many hawks. Just yesterday, when my wife's cat escaped from the house through the open door and bounded off into the woods, *kee-eeee-arrr* screamed the jay, sounding part broad-winged and part red-tailed hawk (track 54, figure 34). It could just as well have been a red-shouldered hawk, and jays are reported to imitate other hawks and predatory birds, too, including the Cooper's hawk, kestrel, screech-owl, and osprey. Just what does the jay accomplish with this blatant mimicry? It's usually an "excited" jay that calls, such as one that is coming to a feeding station, or one whose nest is being approached by a human, or one startled by a cat. Perhaps it's just a "heads up" to other jays within earshot. Perhaps. Why use a hawk's call to do that? No other bird species needs to mimic a hawk to gain attention.

Nor did I hear what is sometimes considered to be a "song" from these jays. Some have heard the jay "sing" as it sits all alone, sometimes in the private quarters of a thick evergreen, as if musing to itself for up to two or three minutes at a time. At first it may sound like a muted gray catbird, or an American robin, giving an assortment of whistles and whines, clicks and chucks, twitters and buzzes, chortles and mews, whirrs and liquid notes. One then realizes that many of the sounds are the jay's own raucous calls, well disguised by the gentle and peaceful delivery. It's as if the jay is its own audience, as typically no other jays are within earshot. Perhaps it is the jay's way of practicing its own sounds, rehearsing all that it must learn, much like young songbirds of other species do as they are practicing their learned songs. Perhaps— we don't really know, as must be confessed about so much concerning this jay.

How little we know about these jays—that's what my brief experience with them has taught me. But I have also come to realize how I would proceed if I wanted to crack the jay code.

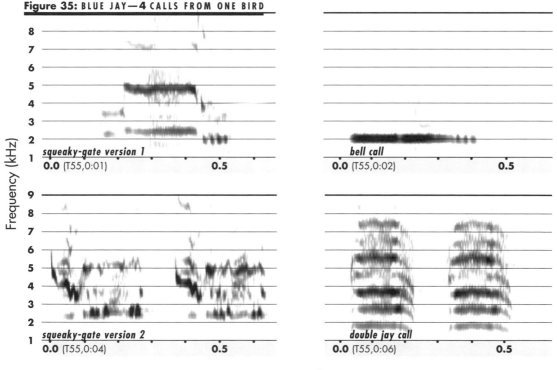

Figure 35: BLUE JAY—4 CALLS FROM ONE BIRD

squeaky-gate version 1
0.0 (T55,0:01)   0.5

bell call
0.0 (T55,0:02)   0.5

squeaky-gate version 2
0.0 (T55,0:04)   0.5

double jay call
0.0 (T55,0:06)   0.5

Frequency (kHz)

Time (seconds)

Figure 35. Four different calls from a blue jay over just a few seconds' time. To hear a blue jay utter these calls is one thing (track 55), but to see the extreme differences in these calls simultaneously makes me wonder all the more what is on this blue jay's mind as he quickly runs through this small portion of his call repertoire.

In late April or early May, I'd pick just three or four blue jay pairs, preferably neighbors, and I'd do my best to get to know them, pair by pair. In just a few hours at a nest, I now know that I can learn much about a male and female. As I watched this first pair, I'd see the female settle into the nest, and see the male attend her, and then I would know who was who. Training my microphone on one bird or the other, I'd record, gradually revealing the vocabulary that each bird used. I'd do the same with the neighboring pairs, and within several days' time I'd have a repertoire of calls used by each of several known individuals. As flocks of jays visited these selected pairs, I'd record them, too, to learn more of how jays call in the local community. It's a simple beginning, easily accomplished by just being attentive at a couple of nests.

I'd next take these field recordings to my computer, graphing out all of the calls used by these birds (see "How to See Bird Sounds" in Appendix II). For each bird I'd then have its vocabulary, which I'd then compare to those of its mate and its neighbors. I'd soon discover the extent to which local females and local males share each other's vocabularies, the first step toward discovering how the birds use them during their interactions.

I know I'd be helpless at this point, obsessed with these jays, eager to go on, and there'd be much more to do. I'd inevitably try to catch the birds, putting unique colored bands on their legs so that I'd know which birds were taking part in these group encounters at the nests I was watching. Perhaps I'd put a radio transmitter on a few birds so that I could follow their movements and plot them on a map of the area, to know how each moves around in its home range. Wow, wouldn't it be great to put a microphone transmitter on a few birds, so that every call the bird made would be sent to my receiver, to be recorded there and analyzed later.

What do I think I'd learn? I would bet that, in this small community of jays, all individuals (or at least all individuals of the same sex) would share the same vocabulary of calls. That's my first impression from my few days in the field: I listened to all the jays in a flock using the same *jay* or squeaky-gate calls, so there are probably a limited number of different calls used in the community. I know these jays are intelligent, too, and I would also bet that they have a sophisticated communication system based on a shared vocabulary. Without shared sounds and shared rules about how to vary those sounds, these jays would communicate no better than did those builders who had to abandon the Tower of Babel in the Bible, when God's displeasure caused each to speak a different language, leaving the workers unable to coordinate their efforts.

Once I knew the categories of calls and understood how they vary, I'd try to relate the different call variants to different contexts in which those variants were used, searching for the meaning in each sound. Exactly when are those bell sounds used, or the squeaky-gates, or the *jay* calls, or the hawk imitations, and why do they vary from context to context? To understand those hawk imitations better, perhaps I could find a falconer to fly a hawk near the jays. To test my conclusions, I'd eventually need to try some "playbacks" of their own sounds to the birds, in which I'd pretend to be a jay and try to influence in a predictable way how the birds respond. Maybe I'd have to raise some baby jays, too, to understand how the young jay becomes competent in using this complex vocabulary. Much could be learned about these jays, and fairly easily. I can hardly wait to get started.

On my mind's to-do list I check the box "all of the above," but there's one thing more. Thanks to a jay who roosted for several nights outside our bedroom window during late April 2003, I'm now hooked on listening to how jays awake in the morning. She (for no explainable reason, I think of her as a female) roosted in the hemlock, the one I had wanted to cut down to let the house breathe, but Melissa had said no—she liked the tree, as did the jay, as I now do.

All that my jay friend had to say from her roost was captured by a microphone extended out to her on the end of a cane pole, the other end of the microphone cable plugged into the recorder beside me in bed, where I lay with headphones on, listening to the jay-world awake. The first morning I recorded her, she carried on for four minutes, giving a total of 66 *jay* calls, all of the same type; in the distant background I could hear another bird giving the identical call, and a third bird giving a squeaky-gate call.

On the second morning she gave 114 *jay* calls in five minutes, all identical to those of the first morning, but I now paid more attention to the background symphony. Perhaps 50 to 100 yards away, two other jays were also waking and calling from their roosts, initially one of them (say, Bird A) matching the less strident *jay* call of my hemlock bird, the other (Bird B) using a squeaky-gate. Within a minute, Bird A switched to a much harsher version of the *jay* call, matching a third bird that I could just barely hear in the distance. For three and a half minutes they all carried on in this way, but by the fifth minute, Birds A and B had both switched to match the call of my hemlock bird. They had come to agree, though on what I don't know, and for a minute they called back and forth, continuing for the better part of another minute after my bird left her hemlock.

It was the third morning that set the hook (track 56, figure 36). For nearly 10 minutes my hemlock bird called from her roost, interacting with other jays throughout the neighborhood. During the first three minutes, all four birds within earshot, including my hemlock bird, used the same call, the very call that my hemlock bird had used the other two mornings. For the next four minutes they diverged, my bird continuing with that same call, as did one neighbor, but from the other two I heard a harsh *jay* and a squeaky-gate call —three different calls among the four birds now. Minute 8 was dramatic, as the background birds now all switched to the harsh *jay* call, two of them invading our yard and calling loudly nearby. For 15 seconds my bird paused, the longest pause of the morning, as if to consider her response, before she replied harshly in kind, *jay . . . jay . . . jay.* After she matched her neighbors 25 times in 90 seconds with this new call, the two neighbors switched back to the less strident *jay* call, and she followed suit, calling 8 more times in 30 seconds before departing her roost.

For three mornings my hemlock bird shared her early mornings with me, inviting me to listen in as she and her neighbors awoke. She then roosted elsewhere, perhaps settling in with a mate and nesting nearby, or so I'd like to think.

Her brief visit left me bubbling with questions, none of them with answers. Who is she (or he), and who are these other birds? Do they all know

Figure 36: BLUE JAY CALL MATCHING

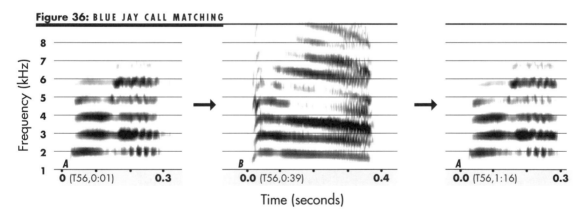

Figure 36. Blue jays often choose to use the same particular call that other jays around them are using (track 56). Here the jay in the hemlock outside my bedroom window begins her morning with a tonal version of the jay call (A) but then switches to a harsher version (B) to match two jays calling nearby. After the nearby jays switch to the tonal version of the *jay* call, the bird in the hemlock does so, too. These jays clearly respond to what others are saying, though the message delivered is unclear.

each other? Perhaps some are even close relatives? What call does each choose to awake with, and who matches whom, and under what conditions, and why? Just what are they saying to each other, and what are they thinking? By using all the same calls, calls that were no doubt learned locally, perhaps they simply affirm that they are part of the local social network, that they belong. But that's like saying that my native English confirms only that I belong to a larger English-speaking network, and that how I use my English is irrelevant. No, I'm sure that there's far more to these jays than I know, that the shared vocabulary of calls must be a means to some end that enables these saucy jays to live and function in a complex jay society.

Yes, I'm hooked on these songbirds without a song. I'm convinced there's something deep and rich here, that spending time studying the pairs at a few nests and listening to these jays awake will provide a window on their minds. It is to understand their minds, after all, that is my goal, as I use their sounds only as a tool to that end.

Then there are all of those other jay species: in North America alone the Steller's and gray and pinyon and scrub-jays, and the special jays such as nutcrackers and magpies . . . and the crows . . . and the ravens . . . all believed to be among the most intelligent and clever of birds. Ah, here are challenges for several lifetimes, but I would like to think that the minds of these birds will be revealed with the same kind of patient, methodical, yet simple approach that I am now committed to with my blue jays.

Songbirds with Especially Complex Songs

The Brown Thrasher

Back in the early 1970s, you would have found a paragraph like the following in general articles on birdsong:

> The number of different songs a male songbird can sing depends on the species. Each male chipping sparrow has just one song, for example, as do white-crowned sparrows and common yellowthroats and a number of other species. A rufous-sided towhee [now called the eastern towhee] may have four or five, song sparrows up to a dozen or so in some San Francisco populations. A Bewick's wren sings 14 to 20, a Carolina wren a couple of dozen different songs, and the largest repertoires are those of northern mockingbirds, who routinely sing 100 to 200 different songs.

The amount of effort behind each of these simple statements would have varied considerably, depending on how "versatile" the singer was. Sit and listen to a male white-crowned sparrow, for example, and you'll hear him sing the same song over and over; return tomorrow, or next week, and it'll be the same. It's rather obvious that he has just one song. To make sure, the research scientist records a song here and there, makes a few sonagrams, and compares them with each other; for the white-crown, or the yellowthroat, or the chipping sparrow, what one can readily hear in the field is confirmed back home in sonagrams.

For the towhee or song sparrow or Bewick's wren, it takes a little more effort, but the procedure is essentially the same. A male typically sings a particular song many times over before switching to another, and these switches are readily heard while listening to the male sing. The scientist records an example or two in each series of songs and eventually hears that the male repeats a song he had delivered earlier. The sonagrams confirm what the ear has heard: each male has a limited number of discrete songs.

It's not quite so simple for a mockingbird. In the field, one can hear the immense variety of songs, and the standard approach to studying mockingbird repertoires has been to graph every one of perhaps 500 songs in a 30-minute continuous recording. After a sonagram is made of each song, each sonagram is compared with all the others, with different renditions of each song type stacked together in one pile on a large table. After all the comparisons are made, one tallies the number of piles on the table and can say, with considerable confidence, that the male mockingbird sang, for example, 127 different songs in this half-hour period. Using some mathematical tricks, one might be able to estimate how many other songs the mockingbird could have sung but didn't in this half hour, and perhaps the estimate of his repertoire would then be revised upward slightly, perhaps to 140. The effort is enormously time-consuming, and as a result few individuals get studied. (See pages 71–73 for a shortcut approach that anyone can use to appreciate and estimate mockingbird repertoire sizes.)

Driving all of this effort, of course, are the questions: Why do these species differ? Why do males of some species have just one song and those of other species have more, some far more? Perhaps if we study more species, we'll begin to see some kind of pattern that provides an answer? Just how large a repertoire can a "bird-brain" achieve? The 100 or more from a mockingbird is pretty impressive, but are mockingbirds the champions?

It was in that context that I eyed the singing brown thrasher during May of 1973. Just the August before, I had finished my graduate degree at Oregon State University and moved across the continent to Rockefeller University in New York, to begin a postdoctoral study with the famed Peter Marler, the one whose papers I had read in total fascination and whose writings heavily influenced me in my thesis research. Marler had studied with William Thorpe in England, and subsequently moved to Berkeley, continuing his studies of birdsong there, especially on white-crowned sparrows. He then moved to the new Rockefeller field station near Millbrook, about 100 miles north of New York City, where he was now gathering a most remarkable group of scientists who cared passionately about birdsong, and I was lucky enough to be among them. What was also exciting was that a new sound analyzer had just been devised, a "continuous spectrum analyzer," that would process and graph songs in "real time," as fast as a bird could sing them.

When I heard of this new analyzer, I knew instantly I would be its champion user. Making sonagrams would be about 100 times faster with this new approach, and projects that I had only dreamed of doing before would now be possible. News of it had reached me in Oregon a few months before I was to move, so a friend and I raced out to record rock wrens at the Malheur National Wildlife Refuge in eastern Oregon, because I knew that I could take the tapes east with me for the analysis (and I would eventually show that a male rock wren can sing well over 100 different songs). Now the thrasher invited me, one singing above us during early May as all the field station residents laid out the new grid for Marler's field sparrow studies. I recorded a few songs then but knew I needed a more intensive effort.

MAY 14, 1973, a little before sunrise, I am poised, standing in the old-field to the east of the field station headquarters. I know his favorite singing perch is to the south, high in the oak overhanging the field. Next to a juniper I stand, as inconspicuous as possible, raising the parabola and starting the tape recorder as he takes the perch. His is the so-familiar silhouette in the very top of the tree, perched erect, graceful tail draping down, body feathers slightly fluffed on the back, bill up (track 57, figure 37). He delivers song after song, each a couplet: *good morning good morning . . . how are you? how are you? . . . singing now singing now . . . listen up listen up . . .* It's the thrasher rhythm, singing in twos, almost one couplet a second when he's at his best. Not as frenetic or emphatic as the mockingbird, who typically sings five or more renditions of a sound before proceeding, but seeming more confident than the

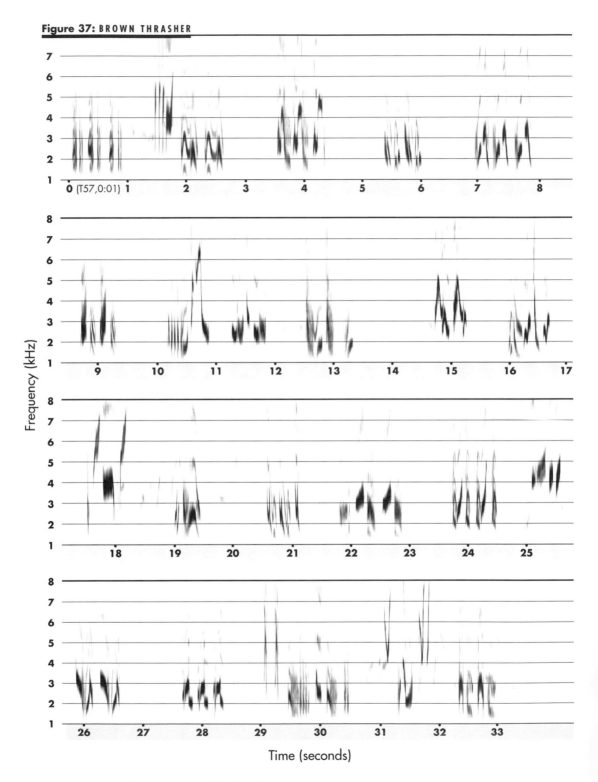

Figure 37: BROWN THRASHER

0 (T57,0:01)

Frequency (kHz)

Time (seconds)

The Singing Life of Birds

catbird, who hastens through his repertoire as if he couldn't repeat anything. For almost two hours I let the tapes roll, capturing thousands of his songs, later counting 4,654 of these couplets on my tape.

That is just the beginning, and certainly the most enjoyable part of the task; now comes the indoor part. Every song is effortlessly graphed on the new analyzer, where they dance across an oscilloscope screen and are then exposed onto 35-mm rolls of photographic paper, taking almost a quarter of a mile of paper to graph all of the songs.

What to do next? If I were to use the standard approach to estimating a repertoire, I would take the first couplet and compare it to the remaining 4,653, looking to see if he repeats that particular couplet. Then I'd take the next couplet, and the next, and so on, comparing each with all of the remaining couplets. I immediately realize that millions upon millions of comparisons would be needed to determine *exactly* how many differ-

BROWN
THRASHER

ent songs occur in this recording, and even if I could make one comparison a second, it would take hundreds and hundreds of hours, a Herculean task that could easily consume me for the better part of a year.

I don't need to know exactly, I reason, so I compromise, devising a simpler approach that will give me a rough estimate of his repertoire size. From the stream of over 4,600 couplets, I cut out every hundredth one, so that I now have 46 of them lying before me on the table. If I simply determine the average number of times these 46 different songs occur in the sample, I can divide that average into 4,654 and know about how many different songs he sang in my recording. It's that simple. If each of his songs occurs, on average, 10 times, then I'll know that about 4,654 ÷ 10 = 465 different songs occur in the sample.

I now know how I must proceed, slugging out the 200,000 or so compar-

Figure 37. A half-minute of singing from a male brown thrasher (track 57). See and hear his measured pace, how each song is about as long as the silent interval before and after, and see how each song tends to be a couplet, a particular sound occurring twice. Shown here are only a few of his thousands of different songs.

isons that will be required. Or will it actually be *I*? Perhaps I can find someone else to invest the several weeks it will take, sitting in a chair, comparing one sonagram with another. I know just the person: my mother-in-law, Linda. It doesn't take much to convince her that this is an exciting project, and after a brief training in how to read these sonagrams, she is hard at work.

What does she find? Do thrashers ever repeat themselves? Or do they make their songs up as they go? The answers: Yes, and probably. I perhaps should have recorded that thrasher for a few more hours and captured thousands more songs, but it's possible even then that we still wouldn't have known for sure exactly what he was doing. We did learn that he was able to repeat many of his song couplets over the course of two hours; 26 of the 46 occurred two to seven times in the sample of 4,654 songs. But 20 of them never occurred again. If we had recorded more songs from this thrasher, would we then have found that he repeated those 20, too? Or no matter how long the recording, would there always be some songs that never recurred, because he was making some of them up on the spot?

We ended with perhaps more questions than we had when we began, but we did know a little more about this thrasher. He retained at least some of his songs in memory long enough to repeat them later during the two-hour session, so he was not improvising each song as he delivered it. That's good to know. We confirmed the obvious, too, that he had an enormous variety of songs. How many? The 46 couplets occurred an average of 2.6 times apiece, so that in these two hours of this singing thrasher's life he probably sang about 1,800 different song couplets (4,654 ÷ 2.6 = about 1,800 different songs). (If instead of the average value of 2.6 I use the median value of 2, meaning that the "typical" song couplet occurred 2 times in the sample, then the repertoire estimate is even larger, 4,654 ÷ 2 = 2,327). This astounding result, a song repertoire numbering in the thousands, was even reported by "Ripley's Believe It or Not!" in newspapers across the land.

About 2,000 different songs . . . but that's an estimate only of what he sang during those two hours. What about the songs that he could have sung but didn't? What is his true repertoire size? In the sample, some songs occurred seven times, some six, some five, and so on, down to one, but how many songs are in the "zero" category, the songs he has in his head but didn't get to in these mere two hours of singing? By some simple math I can estimate that 800 to 900 of the songs in his repertoire occurred only once in the sample, and perhaps there were just as many he could have sung but didn't. Perhaps his repertoire is closer to 3,000 than to 2,000 songs? Or perhaps it's infinite, if he improvises some of his songs as he sings?

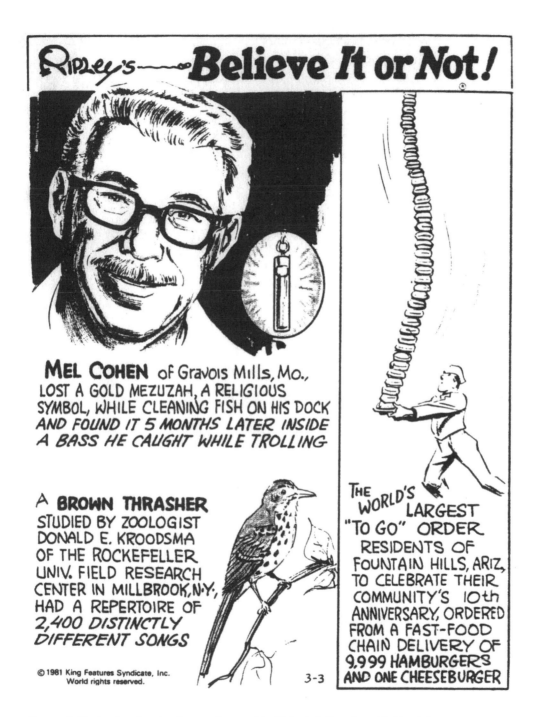

So special is the thrasher that he was featured in *Ripley's Believe It or Not!* back in 1981. Who would have believed that a songbird with its pea-sized brain could have such an immense vocabulary?

I would love to have found that same male again the next year, to record him for another two hours, or the year after that, if he was still alive. And I would love to have recorded the Methuselah of brown thrashers, who is reported to have lived to a record age of 13 years! Just how good is the thrasher's memory of his huge repertoire? Does he remember songs from one year to the next, or does he gradually change his entire repertoire over time? Just how does this thrasher mind sing to the world? I would love to know.

Years later, in 1981, I discovered that I was not alone in my fascination with brown thrashers. Just a year after I recorded my thrasher in New York, Michael Boughey was hard at work a hundred miles to the west, in central Massachusetts. He recorded not one, but two males, and estimated their repertoires the old fashioned way, doggedly printing out each of about 2,000 sonagrams for each bird on the much slower Kay sonagraph machine and then for each male comparing each sonagram with all of the others. With this Herculean effort, and after a few mathematical maneuvers, he estimated that his two males had repertoires of 1,500 to 2,000 songs. He also found that one thrasher could remember at least some of his song types over a 19-day period. Both Michael and we could conclude that a male brown thrasher sings an enormous variety of songs, but we could not know what seemed unknowable, and that was how much of this song variety was fixed in his memory and how much was improvised on the spot.

For me, a partial answer to this conundrum is provided by a single thrasher experience that is burned into my memory. I'm standing in our garden behind our house in upstate New York, among the tomatoes and beans and peas, subconsciously listening to a thrasher singing in the top of the oak tree overhead. One thrasher, singing in twos, just as he is supposed to do. Softly, gently it seems, from somewhere mid-oak, and gradually easing into my subconscious, another thrasher chimes in, singing his twos. I freeze, now aware, listening, challenging myself as to what I am hearing. No. Impossible. Listen more carefully, concentrate. Yes, the thrasher below softly echoes the songs of the male above, matching him song for song. HELLO HELLO *hello hello* IT'S ME IT'S ME *it's me it's me . . .*

How long did it last? 10 seconds? 20 seconds? I don't know, as my mind raced through the possible explanations for what I was hearing. If one thrasher can match the other like this, song after song, it could mean that each has the same large repertoire of songs, and one way that could happen is if they have learned all of their songs from each other. What a huge task that would be, so huge it seems impossible. It seems more likely that the second thrasher is able to copy songs that he hears on the spot, thereby enabling him to match the resident. A friend later told me that he played over a loudspeaker some thrasher song to a territorial male and heard much the same thing, the resident male matching the songs that he heard from the tape recorder. Amazing. Is it possible that the thrasher is so skilled and so versatile that he can hear another male sing and repeat it instantly? I shake my head in disbelief, because I know of no other songbirds with this ability.

But this is a *brown thrasher,* and I begin to believe. I know he has some songs that he retains in memory, at least for a period of 19 days, but I now believe he is highly skilled at acquiring new songs for his performance. Some songs are no doubt improvised at his leisure, as he sings all alone from the treetops, the general form of the song dictated only by the need to conform to thrasher twoness. But other songs are added to the performance on demand, as when he mimics the exact couplet that a neighboring bird has just sung. If only I could listen as another thrasher . . . if only. I'd then know so much more about his memory, about how he plays out his old and new songs, and how long he retains each. A most remarkable songbird, champion among champions I can't help but think, as I know of no other songbird that comes close to his skills. And, oh my, to this frosting add a sugar coating: We now have a glimpse of how the thrasher brain controls the two voice boxes to produce each song, thanks to the ingenuity of a team of researchers at Indiana University. In the two air passages (bronchi) from the lungs, just beneath each of the two voice boxes (syringes), these researchers implant a tiny device that can monitor airflow. Now, when the thrasher sings, we can make a sonagram of the song and know exactly how much air was flowing through the left and right voice box. Remarkably, the contribution by the left and right syringes to a simple song couplet are unmistakable.

Consider just one example, one of thousands of examples that could have been chosen, of course (figure 38). On the sonagram are five different notes, in the sequence *a b* c *d e* c *a b* c *d e*. I underline *a* and *b* as well as *d* and *e*, because it is clear from the sonagram that they occur simultaneously, one above the other; because those pairs of notes are not harmonically related (the frequency of the upper not being a simple multiple of the one below), *a* and *b* must come from different voice boxes, as must *d* and *e*. These note sequences are uttered so fast that our ears hear only that an overall pattern has occurred twice, but the thrasher's song is clearly a precision-guided breath of air. Air flows through the left voice box as he sings notes *a* and *d*, and through the right voice box as he sings notes *b, c,* and *e*. Harnessing the air flow to produce and reproduce the song are up to a dozen tiny muscles, each adjusting tensions of membranes within the voice boxes and gating the air flow, each of the muscles controlled in turn by nerve signals from the brain, roughly half from the left side of the brain and half from the right. With the air flow through each voice box controlled independently, the left tends to produce the lower-frequency sounds, the right the higher sounds, which are often more wavy, or modulated, in pitch. Thousands and thousands of these couplets he sings, each expertly created by coordinating nerve impulses from the left and right brain to the muscles in the two voice boxes, harnessing the air expelled through the two bronchi, producing some of the finest music among songbirds.

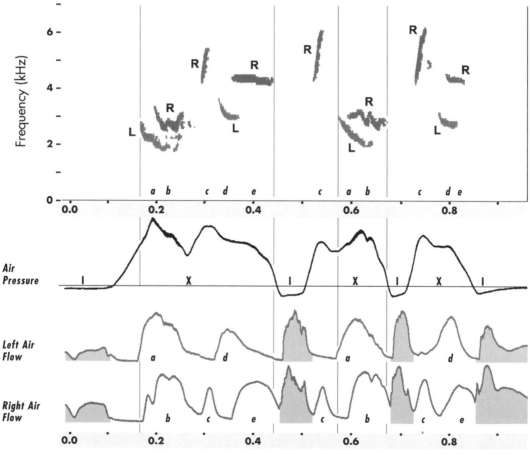

Time (seconds)

The Singing Life of Birds

Why does he have so many songs? I'd love to know for sure. The only clue is that he sings far less once he convinces a female to pair with him. Could she really be that demanding of him? Is she somehow impressed with the great variety? Can she actually count the number of different songs that he sings? Or is the number of songs less important than the overall quality? "Nothing succeeds like success," it is said, so something that the male thrashers are doing is "right" in her ears, because these females, by choosing to mate with some males and not others, have very likely been the creative force behind why males sing the way they do.

I also have to consider the idea that this master of the largest song repertoire known among birds is somehow enjoying himself. It certainly can't be painful to sing like that. It seems plausible to me that some endorphins or other bodily chemicals are released into the blood and synapses that make him "feel good" as he sings.

Next spring, I'll pick an early day in May to sit beneath a newly arrived thrasher. I want to listen to each couplet, clicking it off on my hand-counter,

Figure 38. Secrets of a vocal gymnast revealed, showing how a male brown thrasher coordinates the left and right side of his syrinx as he sings. The sonagram (top) shows the sounds produced, labeled L (left) or R (right) for the side of the syrinx that produced those particular sounds, and labeled a–e along the baseline to identify the five different sounds in this brief song. Evidence of two sound sources operating simultaneously is in the sonagram itself, as the first two sounds (a and b) overlap in time and are not harmonically related (that is, the upper note is different from the lower note and is not at twice the frequency of the lower fundamental note). The sounds produced by the right syrinx tend to be at a higher frequency than those produced by the left syrinx. Look next at Air Pressure, which reveals the thrasher's pattern of breathing as he sings; he first inhales (I), and as he begins to sing notes a and b, he exhales (X), as indicated by the pressure line being below (I) or above (X) the baseline. See how quickly he can inhale, as he takes a minibreath in about a twentieth of a second at two places in the song. Left Air Flow reveals how fast the air is flowing through the left syrinx; see how he is exhaling through the left syrinx as he sings notes a and d (stippled areas indicate when he is inhaling and not vocalizing). Likewise, Right Air Flow shows how notes b, c, and e are produced by the right syrinx as he exhales there. And all this happens in less than a second's time! Notice how precisely his breathing is coordinated in the left and right syringes to produce this song. Note, too, that this sonagram contains two complete renditions of the same series of sounds (a b c d e) and that the gymnast executes the identical moves with the left and right syringes to produce the two renditions. Now that you can appreciate what is involved in producing just one simple song, look again at figure 37—see the songs there with new appreciation and imagine the monumental task this thrasher faces in controlling air flow so precisely for his thousands of different songs.

tallying the songs for an hour or so, contemplating how the air flow through his two voice boxes produces the song, and pretending that I am the one for whom he sings: *sun's up sun's up, yeah yeah, great day great day, listen up listen up, here I am here I am, look ladies look ladies, settle here settle here.* I'll listen for an especially distinctive song, one that I can easily remember, perhaps because it sounds like he's mimicked it from another species; then I'll listen for it again, just to appreciate his enormous repertoire, knowing that there's perhaps only a fifty-fifty chance I'll hear it again, even if I listen for two hours. And I'll hope he pauses at some time, drops to earth, and thrashes about in the leaf litter near me as he forages, and that we get a chance to look into each other's eyes, his large yellow iris and big dark pupil another window on a truly extraordinary mind.

The Sage Thrasher

The "thrasher who is brown," in the previous account, implies that there are other thrashers, and a quick check of the field guides shows a veritable smorgasbord of thrashers west of the Mississippi. The California thrasher of the California chaparral is the largest of them all, a fifth larger than the brown; it is also an extraordinary songster, singing throughout the year on its permanent territories, and females often sing, too. I look to the desert Southwest and discover four more thrashers there, Bendire's, crissal, curve-billed, and LeConte's. And I'm told that the tiny island of St. Lucia, in the Caribbean, has four more thrasher species — four on one little island! Opportunities to go thrashering abound.

My mind darts back to May of 1969 at Cabin Lake, Oregon, where I first met the smallest of them all, the sage thrasher. I still see him in his undulating song flight, his songs stitching sage to heaven as he dipped into the sagebrush and out again, over and over, circling around his territory and singing all the while.

I knew that eventually I'd have to track him down, to hear and see him again. So it is, 32 years later, on June 12, 2001, a Tuesday, at 6:25 A.M., that it happens. I stand in the sage in Sierra Valley in east-central California, minding my own business and that of the Brewer's sparrows (see page 320), when he swoops into the sage next to me and then out again, bounding from sage to sky as he circles his territory, constantly singing. Constantly, as in never ceasing, it seems. On a nearby sagebrush he eventually perches, inviting me to raise my parabola and record.

What I hear is hard to believe (track 58, figure 39). He's in clear view, perched in the dead twigs atop the sage, and I eye him through my binoculars, making sure it is his bill opening and closing as from that sage pour the sounds of nighthawks and meadowlarks and sora rails and California quail and house finches and barn swallows and gulls and snippets of song that remind me of so many other species that I can *almost* identify.

I listen to the tape again in the afternoon, dumbfounded at all this bird can do. The first song is a 25-second outburst, rollicking at breakneck speed through what seems an infinite variety of sounds, but twice he delivers his sora rail rendition, the unmistakable descending whinny, rapid at first, slowing at the end. A four-second rest, and he's singing again, this time for half a minute, ending it all with the sora rail. A few seconds' rest, then another song, and he continues that way for the hour and a half that I chose to stand and absorb it all. Some of the imitations are full and unmistakable, such as the sora's and the quail, but it is those snippets of sound that drive me mad, as he gives me ever so brief a glimpse of a sound I'm sure I've heard before, a sound borrowed from a killdeer, or meadowlark, or lark, or . . . I must get a local expert to listen to this bird, to tell me what I'm missing.

Ninety minutes isn't enough, so back I go the next morning, now awaking at 2:30 A.M., arriving in his sagebrush domain early, suspecting he'll be singing by moonlight. Walking out into the sage at 4:00 I hear him, the first song just three seconds, then perhaps half a minute of silence, then a brief song again. On and off like this he sings for perhaps 15 minutes, but by 4:15 he's singing his heart out again. Entranced for two full hours, I track him from sage to sage as he works his territory, following him with the parabola in his undulating song flight, capturing all that I can. By 6:00 I realize how cold I am, shivering here, frozen in place with the temperatures just above the water-to-ice mark.

That afternoon I listen to the morning's tapes for two full hours, immersing myself in his revelry.

Two sessions, three and a half hours of his sounds captured—it's not enough, and I plan my return. I want to do this right, to be comfortable and to take in all that I can absorb in a four-hour session, from 4:00 to 8:00 A.M.

Up by 2:30, I arrive early again, by 3:45. This time I'm wearing everything: heavy socks and boots; three layers on the legs; three layers of polypropylene on the torso, plus a heavy fleece jacket, plus a rain-shell, all under my heavy three-season lined coat; wool stocking hat; and two pairs of gloves. In my pack are extra tapes and batteries and backup supplies. The tape recorder is slung over my shoulder, headphones are atop my head, and the parabolic microphone is in hand.

3:47, almost two hours before sunrise, I step from the road and into the sage, the Milky Way and the crescent moon to the east lighting the way. Venus is already above the eastern horizon, Jupiter soon to set in the west. A horned lark sings just behind me, hundreds of others all around in the distance; two snipe winnow overhead, their home in the marsh to the east. It's cold, windless, and clear—perfect recording conditions.

Nine minutes later, at 3:56, I first hear him, far to the north. It's just a few seconds, maybe three, and then he's quiet. I work my way closer, my pathway through the sage highlighted in the light sandy soil. A half-minute later, another three-second song, just 30 or so yards in front of me, and at that I start the tape, at 3:57 A.M. Slipping my headphones over my ears, I listen—to the quiet of the night, to the faint larks in the distance and the snipe overhead —when 20 seconds later he explodes into my ears, four seconds of boundless energy, rollicking, frolicking, hints of pilfered barn swallow and house finch, ending as abruptly as he began. Then silence, seemingly forever, a minute and a half, and another four seconds of pent-up energy exploding into the night. Two minutes pass, and then it's a full six seconds that he sings.

He's just warming up now, I sense. Or has he been singing like this all night long, perhaps since early morning, much like his cousin the mockingbird often does? For 20 minutes he continues, a one- to seven-second song

Figure 39. This sage thrasher song (the second one on track 58, from 0:24 to 0:57) begins with a series of soft clucking sounds (darkened here so that they can be seen on the sonagram), and for another half-minute this male makes over 50 decisions about which particular little song unit he will sing next. Take special note where this sage thrasher launches into three renditions of the descending whinny that is so typical of the sora rail. To appreciate how busy this sage thrasher is in his half-minute of singing, compare his singing to that of the brown thrasher (figure 37, track 57) and northern mockingbird (figures 15 and 16, tracks 18 and 19).

Figure 39: SAGE THRASHER

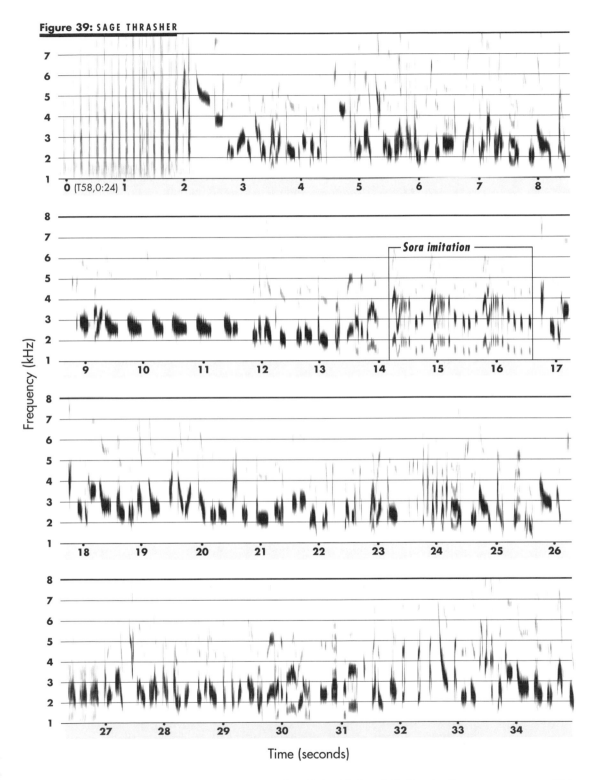

Sora imitation

Frequency (kHz)

0 (T58,0:24)

Time (seconds)

EXTREMES OF MALE SONG: Songbirds with Especially Complex Songs

bursting into the night, a half-minute or more of silence between songs. The pace then seems to quicken. The silence between songs approaches 20 seconds, the songs themselves 10 seconds, so that he's now singing a third of the time. Then a 12-second song, a 15-second song, the next only 2. His heart seems in both worlds now, one the slow, deliberate pace of the night, the other the breakneck pace of the day, and which world will win the next song is in doubt. His intentions are clear, as on he presses, songs soon consistently longer than 10 seconds, some longer than half a minute. Pauses between songs soon feel as long as the songs themselves, he filling half of the night air with his arias.

It's easy to listen in the moment, to absorb each song, but I want to do something to challenge myself to stay alert, to hear what he's up to. I decide to listen for just three of his mimicked sounds that are so easily recognizable: the nighthawk, the gull, and the sora. By paying special attention to how and when he uses them, I reason that I'll understand how he's using what must be his hundreds of other sounds, too. It is these three songs that will give me a handle on his breakneck singing, a window on his singing mind.

4:51. Nighthawk, I call to myself, noting my watch, the first of the nighthawk calls almost an hour after he started singing this morning. Just two notes, a raspy *peent peent,* a bit like a woodcock, though raspier and lower. Unmistakably a nighthawk, my memory having just been refreshed by their calling off to the west as I walked from the car.

4:57. Gull, two clear plaintive calls, one of his favorite sounds from the two previous days, and two seconds later, the sora rail, absolutely no doubt about that descending whinny. I continue listening for all three imitations, hearing the gull 15 more times over the next 15 minutes, the sora just 2 more times in the next 2 minutes.

Then none of these three sounds for 9 minutes, until he gives a single sora; then 13 minutes to a gull; 15 minutes to the next sora; 12 to the next gull; 20 to the next gull, and twice in the same minute.

6:27. Sora, and I start counting: sora, sora, sora, sora . . . about 1 a minute, 16 of them over a 19-minute period, the time now 6:45 A.M. And then he visits the gull again, giving it 7 more times over 7 minutes, interspersed among an enormous variety of other sounds.

Perched in the sage before me I hear a magician juggling what must be 100 different sounds at a time. At any given instant, 99 are in the air, 1 on the bill. One by one he tosses each upward again, catching another with his bill and in a split second sending it off again, quickly retrieving another.

Sometimes once is enough for a sound, but sometimes he plays with a sound repeatedly for a quarter-hour or more before casting it aside, then picking a replacement from his immense repertoire, continuing the act, always juggling an immense variety of different sounds at any given time.

7:06. Nighthawk again. Just 6 of them, over 5 minutes. It had been over two hours since I last heard them, at 4:51.

I expect to hear the nighthawk and sora and gull, as well as the now familiar quail and house finch and barn swallow and meadowlark and killdeer and willet and all of the others that I have heard before, but the song sparrow at 7:07 catches me off guard (track 59). Here it is, into my fourth hour this morning, seven hours of listening and taping over the last three days, and he sings something completely new. It is a song sparrow trill, so distinctive, two of those buzzy notes that I expect at the beginning of a song. I'd know them anywhere, or would I? Am I hearing things? Has all of this listening driven me mad? Please repeat that, I ask. Song after song goes by, a half a minute, 40 seconds, soon I expect it, if at all . . . and there . . . No, wait, it's a song sparrow all right, but now it's a trill from the last half of the song sparrow's song, five rather musical notes, all evenly spaced. Yes, it *is* song sparrow, two completely new sounds here at the beginning of my eighth hour of listening, both song sparrow. I listen for them again . . . nighthawk I log . . . and more song sparrow, 2 more times for those introductory buzzes, 6 more times over the next few minutes for that ending trill (see track 60, figure 40 for examples of mimicry).

7:29. Gull again, juggling 5 of them over the next 8 minutes. He continues to sing, dropping the gull, reintroducing it again at 7:52, singing 9 more in 9 minutes by 8:00, the time I promised myself I'd stop, as the third tape clicks to a halt.

From any ordinary bird, 8 hours and 10 minutes of recordings would be enough, but not for this one. Saturday morning, we're back, this time for the ultimate recording. Greg Budney has been leading the Library of Natural Sounds tape-recording workshop at the nearby field station in the Sierras, and he has heard my tapes as I played them each afternoon. This thrasher is special, he enthuses, and determines to capture this bird as no sage thrasher has ever before been recorded. Now just after sunrise, Greg and his friend Dawn Edberg survey the landscape with thrasher eyes, noting this maestro's favored song perches. From a distance we watch him sing now, and as soon as the thrasher flies from what appears to be his favorite perch, Greg quickly moves in, placing his stereo microphone just a few inches below the perch and running the cable some 30 yards off to the east. We then hunker down in the sage, digital tape recorder poised, waiting for the thrasher to return.

And waiting . . . the thrasher now far off to the north, as if he somehow knew what we were up to. Impatient with the passive approach, I now head off to the east, then north, circling around him, well over 100 yards from the perch where we now beg him to land. Drat the luck. Another thrasher enthusiast, Eric Sorenson, arrives by car, walks casually out into the sage, stands and chats with Greg . . . I wait, politely, though just barely, with the thrasher singing here before me, the opportunity to push him toward Greg rapidly fading, I fear . . . and he drops down into the sage. Please come back, please, up here in the sage, so I can nudge you toward the mike . . . and minutes later he's up again. It's a long shot, I catch myself saying, laughing at myself that we think we know this thrasher so well that we can predict exactly where in his domain he will fly next. I whistle to Greg, catching his attention, and circle my arms, telling him to roll the tape; Greg and Eric drop out of sight into the sage, the recorder now running, I'm sure, waiting for Mr. Thrasher.

Gently, arms outstretched and waving slowly, I approach him, talking to him, begging him to pick our perch far to the south. From the sage before me he launches, bounding up into the air and dipping into the sage, a trampoline flight, circling his territory, and what seems like an eternity later, he lands, on *our* perch, the mike beneath him, his songs no doubt now booming into Greg's ears in a way that no one has ever before heard a sage thrasher sing. And all I can do is stand here and wait, envious, green that I cannot be there sharing the headphones. Ten minutes, 20, 30, . . . 33 minutes he sings, and off he flies. I hustle back, needing to know . . . Did you get it? How much? Everything? And all of my questions are answered at a distance as Greg rises from the sage, his face beaming (see track 58).

The thrasher cooperates for 17 more minutes of recording before we attempt what at the moment seems sacrilegious. We must catch him and hold him in our hands, we reason, so that we can slip a band on his leg. If he returns

Figure 40. Mimicry by the sage thrasher. Although the thrasher proceeds with great haste, he is not without considerable grace and precision, as shown here in his mimicry of a sora rail. Listen to these sounds on track 60 and hear how good a mimic he is. In the top row is the descending whinny of a sora. Next is the thrasher's imitation of the sora, showing how he abbreviates the sora's long whinny to fit his rapid style of singing. In the bottom row is a computer-generated song made by extracting the relevant portions of the sora's whinny to match what the sage thrasher has done.

next year, we want to know it is he, so we can record him some more, to see how he has aged, what new songs he might sing, what old ones he might retain. I know our chances of success are slim: it's already midmorning, the sun bright, the wind blowing gently, and we have no good place to hide our mist net. We make a valiant effort, trying to herd him toward the net placed

Figure 40: SAGE THRASHER IMITATES SORA

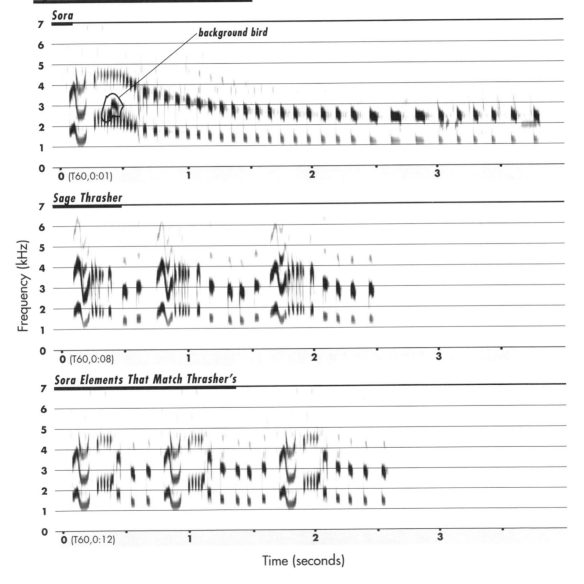

as best we can near one of his singing perches. Again and again he eludes us, at one point seeming to sit by the net and chuckle. I try to look objectively at this scene, Greg and Dawn and Eric and I racing around the sage trying to herd this bird, shouting updates to each other about where he is, the thrasher singing and bounding about, the net so obvious as it ripples in the bright sunshine. It seems only right that this spirit be free, I rationalize; unfettered, the wild stallion who is never caught, comments Dawn; forever free to compose, the Charlie Parker of birds, comments Eric.

But science prevails. Two days after I had departed, in the wee hours of the morning, the team arrived with Mac McCormick in charge, the master bird bander, a professional, as he was quick to point out. In the dead of night the net was set near one of the thrasher's favorite perches. Then it was a matter of waiting. The thrasher sang his brief night songs, just a few seconds long, then paused half a minute or so, the routine continuing, and he became more active a little after 4:00, right on schedule. Then silence, for too long. Approaching the net, Mac and his crew found him there. Gently removed from the net by flashlight, he soon had an official, metal United States Geological Survey band on his left leg, number 15913417. "Should the body be found with band still attached, send a notice to the government," is the implied message. Mac quickly checks him over, using a practiced eye, searching especially for clues to his age. Probably at least two years old, Mac says, based largely on patterns of wear he sees in the wing and tail feathers.

Back home, I got the report a few days later. It is exciting to hear that he now has a band on his leg, because he has so much he can teach us if he returns the next year. Will he have the same songs in his repertoire, or will he have a whole new set next year? Does he mimic sounds he hears over the winter, so we can trace where he has been, as with European marsh warblers that imitate sounds of African birds that they visit during the winter?

It was not to be. Mac eagerly checked the sage the following spring, beginning in March. Other thrashers eventually arrived, but not ours. Perhaps our bird chose to try his luck elsewhere. He had never attracted a female the year before, and it is known from other species that birds are more likely to move and to try a new breeding location when they are unsuccessful. I imagine him still singing somewhere, stitching sky to sage, magically juggling his hundreds or thousands of songs.

Hundreds? Thousands? Just how many different songs does he have? Does he top the repertoire of about 2,000 songs that a brown thrasher can sing? I must know.

Taking advantage of a new software program for my computer, I begin printing out the nine hours of tape recordings so that I can both see and hear them. On each 8½ × 11 sheet of paper I print 20 seconds in five rows, the papers soon stacking up on the overnight printing sessions to seven inches high on my desk. In all, 1,620 sheets of paper, each detailing 20 seconds in the life of this sage thrasher.

I proceed as I did with the brown thrasher. First I find an accomplice in Mike Moriarty, an undergraduate student who wants to immerse himself in this research project. Together we pick out 32 distinctive sounds in the repertoire of this thrasher, sounds that we know we'll be able to identify easily if they are encountered again in his continuous stream of singing. We study how the thrasher uses each of those sounds, to make sure that each of the 32 represents the smallest unit that the thrasher recombines with other such units to produce his songs. Among them are my favorites: the gull, the nighthawk, the sora, and the quail. With copies of those 32 now before him, Mike scours the entire nine-hour record for them, marking where they occur, entering all of his data into a spreadsheet.

We confirm that some of the songs are rarely used in the 540-minute record. The song sparrow trill occurs seven times in minutes 416 through 423, and that's it. Another song that occurs six times in the first 10 minutes on the first day never occurs again. Never, in nine more hours of recording. Another song is found just twice, in minutes 461 and 462.

The thrasher's favorite is the meadowlark song, found 195 times, an average of almost one every three minutes. He doesn't sing in averages, though, as a quick check of Thursday's four-hour session shows. Thirty-four minutes into the session, I first heard the meadowlark. He sang it 33 times over 15 minutes, then not at all for 21 minutes; then 11 times in 20 minutes, then not for 10 minutes; 15 in 13 minutes, then silent for 24; 20 in 15 minutes, and then silent on the meadowlark for over 69 minutes until the end of the recording. He sang the meadowlark song 79 times, but during only four sessions, each session separated from the others by 10 or more minutes.

It's the same way I heard the soras and gulls when I listened as I recorded that Thursday morning. He picks a song and plays with it, sometimes for just a few minutes, sometimes for as many as 20 minutes. During that time he sings it about once a minute, and then eventually discards it for some time, until he thinks of it again. So although the meadowlark song occurred 195 times in the nine hours, he really brought it up for discussion on only 12 separate occasions.

How many different songs has he mastered? I need to think this through. I can't use exactly the same approach as I did with the brown thrasher, because I can't identify the individual songs in this sage thrasher. Because he sings so continuously, not neatly in pairs, I cannot know which are the individual units that he recombines with others to produce his continuous stream. Ah, but I have a method that will work, I am convinced. If I can determine the proportion of the entire singing record occupied by my 32 defined units, then I can estimate how many different units occurred overall. If the 32 units occupy a tenth of the entire record, for example, then I simply multiply 32 by 10, obtaining 320 as my estimate of his repertoire that he used during the nine hours that we listened.

OK, proceed. I first determine the duration of each of the 32 units (by measuring up to 11 examples of each and then taking the average), and then multiply that duration by the number of times that unit occurred in the sample. The song sparrow trill was 0.57 seconds in duration and occurred seven times, for example, so it occupied four seconds of the total sample ($0.57 \times 7 = 4$); each meadowlark song was 0.47 seconds, and with a total of 195 occurrences occupied 92 seconds ($0.47 \times 195 = 92$). I repeat this process for all 32 song units and calculate in the end that the average time that each song unit occupies in the entire record is 20 seconds. There's the essential number I need: if I pull a "song unit" at random out of the nine hours of recording, it will take up, on average, 20 seconds of the total record.

I need one more number before I can calculate his repertoire size. How many seconds during the nine hours was the bird actually singing? If the bird sang every one of the 540 minutes, I could do the math in my head: Every song unit in his repertoire takes up 20 seconds, so 3 song units take up a minute, and with 540 minutes, $3 \times 540 = 1,620$ different songs in this nine-hour record. Already I have learned that he will not beat the world record held by the brown thrasher, as this sage thrasher sings only about half of the time. Because he doesn't sing every second, I must go back to the printouts and determine the duration of each of his singing sessions, then add them all to come up with the total number of seconds that the bird sang during this period. That number, divided by 20, will give me the best estimate I can come up with for the number of different song units he sang during my nine-hour sample.

Hours later, I have it. I measured 1,077 sessions, ranging from 1 second to 120 seconds, for a total of 13,733 seconds of singing in this nine-hour song sample. I divide this number by 20, coming up with an estimate of 687 for his repertoire. About 700 different song units he has in his head; 700 . . . 700 . . . I repeat the number a few times, letting it sink in. A remarkably large number —the red ribbon among songbirds, second only to the repertoire of his cousin the brown thrasher among all songbirds that have been studied.

I cannot know for sure how many different songs he has at his command, because some were used rarely in my sample, and almost certainly some at his command weren't used at all. Perhaps some of those rare ones he makes up on the spot, but certainly not all. There were no song sparrows anywhere near this male's territory, so he pulled those from what must be a vast memory of the sounds he has heard in his life.

My calculations have given me one more number by which to appreciate how I hear this bird: 0.57 seconds. That's the average duration of the song units that he recombines to form his songs. That means that in a typical 60 seconds, a mere minute, he delivers 60 ÷ 0.57 = 105 song units. Each is allowed a split second, and he's on to the next, 7 decisions every 4 seconds, 105 decisions made every minute as to what he will choose to sing next. Never, never have I heard such a maestro, a repertoire of hundreds of different song units, lots of them pilfered from other species, and delivered with a style and speed unmatched by anything I have ever heard in my 30-plus years of listening.

The weeks of effort provide a few numbers that help me better understand this thrasher: a repertoire of about 700 different song units; each minute, over 100 decisions. I add the facts to my lasting images of the setting in the sage, his singing by moonlight and by sunrise, his mimicry, the reckless abandon in each song, the undulating song flights throughout his territory.

I find myself talking to him: Who are you? Why the large repertoire? How are all of those songs stored in your brain? How do you decide what to do next? Why do you mimic? What are you thinking when you pair your two song sparrow trills during those few minutes, and then "forget" them for the other 8 hours and 50 minutes that I am with you? Do you remember that you got them from the same bird, and they should therefore be associated in your singing? Or did you get them from different birds, but you know song sparrows well enough that you now associate those two song units here? And where in your past did you pilfer those song sparrow sounds? It wasn't here in Sierra Valley, as no song sparrows are anywhere around. What other sounds do you remember that you might reveal if I stayed with you another 8 hours, or 16, or more?

And all the other sounds? Where have you traveled, and how have you listened there? Where did you get your quail? Not here. Why the sora? I can understand how you could easily borrow the sagebrush sounds about you, like the meadowlark and nighthawk, but the sora is over in the marsh, well beyond your territory. The sora is one of your favorites, too. Is there something special about that sound that satisfies some inner craving? Why the gull, such an unlikely sound from the sage? Do you also have songs from Mexico, where you perhaps overwintered, songs that I wouldn't recognize?

He is the free spirit, the wild stallion of the sage. The answers to these questions are his secrets, and likely to remain his . . . at least until I return, when he might share a few more with me.

The Winter Wren

Smothering the boulders and rotting logs and uprooted tree stumps all around me is a luxuriant growth of soft, green mosses. The brook bubbles lazily nearby, the boggy forest floor extending in all directions, the air heavy with moisture. Though it is midmorning, the sunshine barely penetrates the hemlock and spruce towering overhead. Here in the cool of my dark New England forests, here is his home.

WINTER
WREN

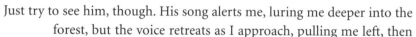

Just try to see him, though. His song alerts me, luring me deeper into the forest, but the voice retreats as I approach, pulling me left, then right, ever farther into this mousebird's haunts. Over here . . . no, there. A glimpse if I'm lucky, and then he's gone. His subtle shades-of-brown-on-shades-of-brown is only a blur. The weight of a few shreds of decaying leaves on the forest floor, he is hardly enough to sway a twig as he darts from shadow to shadow. But I finally catch him in the act, standing alone on a leafless twig, poised, looking, peering, menacingly strutting. Haughty, with stubby tail cocked toward his thrown-back head, bracing himself, bill open, swinging his head from side to side, this tiny wren delivers.

Ka-wa-miti-go-shi-que-na-go-mooch is what the Ojibway called him, in honor of his long song (tracks 61, 63, figure 41). Understaters, these Ojibway, because he sings for longer than it takes me to say the name, with song sometimes extending 10 or

20 seconds or seemingly minutes on end, over and over, and with a vehemence unthinkable for such a small bird, as if he were "trying to burst [his] lungs."

What a song! "Wonderful . . . charming . . . marvelous . . . startling . . . entrancing . . . Copious, rapid, prolonged and penetrating, having a great variety of the sweetest tones, and uttered in a rising and falling or finely undulating melody . . . as if the very atmosphere became resonant . . . [a] gushing melody, which seems at once expressive of the wildest joy and the tenderest sadness"—that's how the naturalist Arthur Cleveland Bent reacted. It's as if this wren started with a long, pure whistle, and as the whistle tumbled through the tangles and down the boulders, it was shattered into dozens of split-second slices, some longer, some shorter, some high and tinkling, some lower and penetrating, an unmistakable tumble of note after note, this tiny wren's signature.

It's late May, but still early in the breeding season for him, so he has much to sing about. I retreat slightly, giving him some space, and then sit down in my camp chair. His song at first seems a random jumble of note after note, all pure whistles, some so rapidly delivered I can't count them, others more slowly tumbling by, some slurred up, some down, some holding a steady tone. Some notes lightly tickle, others penetrate more deeply. I close my eyes and concentrate on this maestro's efforts, feeling the rhythm of his song, letting it linger on all my senses during the few seconds of silence that follow, and then I gather in the next song, and the next, feeling the tumbling whistles cascade over me.

I know there's nothing random about his song, based on several males I have studied thoroughly, and with some careful listening I can hear what he's up to. He has two, at most three, different songs, each a distinctive arrangement of his whistled notes. At this time of day, I expect him to repeat each of his arrangements 20 to 40 times before switching to another.

I now listen to each song, counting out the seconds as he sings, one thousand one, one thousand two, one thousand three, one thousand four, one thousand five, one thousand six, one thousand seven, and he's done. Again, and again, I feel the rhythm over the seven seconds. He begins softly with a jumble of notes, and after two seconds I hear a rapid, high-pitched trill; two seconds later he delivers a low-pitched, much slower trill; and at the end of his song is another high-pitched trill. Over and over, it's the same pattern. I sketch this song in my notebook, showing the location of the three recognizable trills; as crude as the sketch is, it captures the essence of what he does and should serve to distinguish this song from the next.

A.

Ten, twenty, thirty songs . . . they all sound alike to me. Does he have only one song? My mind wanders, to the red squirrel chattering overhead, then to the high-pitched songs of warblers in the canopy, all the while almost sub-consciously tallying each rendition of this now familiar song in my notebook . . . Wait. That one felt different. I listen more carefully to the next. One thousand one, one thousand two, yes, there's the high-pitched trill, but within half a second he's dropped to the low-pitched trill; two seconds later is another high-pitched trill, but it's not at the end of the song. At the end, instead, is a jumble of notes followed by an emphatic high-pitched down-slurred whistle. The overall rhythm is unmistakably different, the high-pitched and low-pitched trills in different places. I sketch the overall pattern, watching him sing it again so consistently, always different from his first song. Forty-two songs later he returns to his first, as I can see from the script in my notes. Like most eastern winter wrens, from Nova Scotia west to Saskatchewan, he probably has only two versions of his spectacular song.

B.

At 3:50 the next morning, 89 minutes before sunrise, I sneak back to my comfortable nook among the logs and boulders. I've done my homework by learning his two songs yesterday, and now I will hear him at dawn. Ten, twenty, thirty . . . 38 minutes later he sings, at 4:28, just beyond where I first heard him yesterday. It's his first song from yesterday, what I'll call his A song. The next is B, then A, then B, back and forth he sings, as if he can't make up his mind. For a full 30 minutes, the sun nowhere in evidence, he sings at most two of a kind before switching to the other: A B A B A B B A B A B A B A A B A B. Gradually he eases toward the pattern I had heard midmorning yesterday, A A B B A A B B A A A B B B B, but 30 minutes past sunrise, just a little before 6:00, he still sings only three or four of each kind before switching to the other. Then, the intensity of the dawn effort past, rather abruptly he shifts to his day-time singing mode, singing 12, then 18, 25, and finally 40 or more renditions of each song before switching back to the other.

The Singing Life of Birds

He is an eastern winter wren, with pure whistled tunes, parts of his songs delivered slowly enough that I can appreciate some of the details. Those details differ from place to place, my ears tell me, as local males learn their songs from each other, so the dialect in my particular western Massachusetts forest is different from those I've heard in the southern Appalachians and in northern Michigan.

Somewhere to the west, somewhere beyond Saskatchewan, perhaps in northern Alberta, perhaps British Columbia, all that changes. In Montana and Idaho, and all along the Pacific coast, from southern California to coastal Alaska, in the magnificent forests of Douglas-firs and giant redwoods, among the tangles of huckleberry vines and huge rotting logs and upturned tree stumps, and from sea level to the limits of trees in the highest mountains—here is an altogether different wren. He sings at breakneck speed and at a much higher pitch. His song is a blur, the notes so brief, so minute, so high that my human ears cannot pick them out, my head spinning as I try, it being challenge enough just to listen and breathe at the same time (tracks 62, 63, figure 42). From my studies in the West, I know that males don't settle for two or three different songs either; rather, they have dozens to hundreds of songs in their arsenal, and successive songs are often different, even at midday, making it impossible to appreciate the nuances of one before hearing the next.

I know how I can try to listen to them, because I have put in my time. I have tape-recorded them for days and graphed thousands of their songs, studying the intimate details of each little whistled note. I am convinced that I can listen to them and hear some of what they do. At least I have a plan, an "I'll give it a try plan" for the next time I go west.

The key to listening will lie in the first half-second of the song. As difficult as it will be, I will, initially at least, ignore the rest of that 5- to 10-second song. I need to focus on the rhythm of those first 10 or so introductory notes, because in all of my efforts studying these birds, I have found that each male has about 10 different half-second introductions, and that he sings many songs in succession with the same particular introduction.

I can't help but think back to the marathon effort required to yield that simple fact. It all began back on April 4, 1970; on that day I awakened well before sunrise so I could be on a wren's territory when he awoke in nearby McDonald Forest, just north of Corvallis, Oregon. I waited patiently in the darkness, anticipating his first song well before I had any hope of seeing him. When I first heard him chatter his usual awaking call, I started my tape-recording session.

Figure 41: EASTERN WINTER WREN *Song A, Part 1*

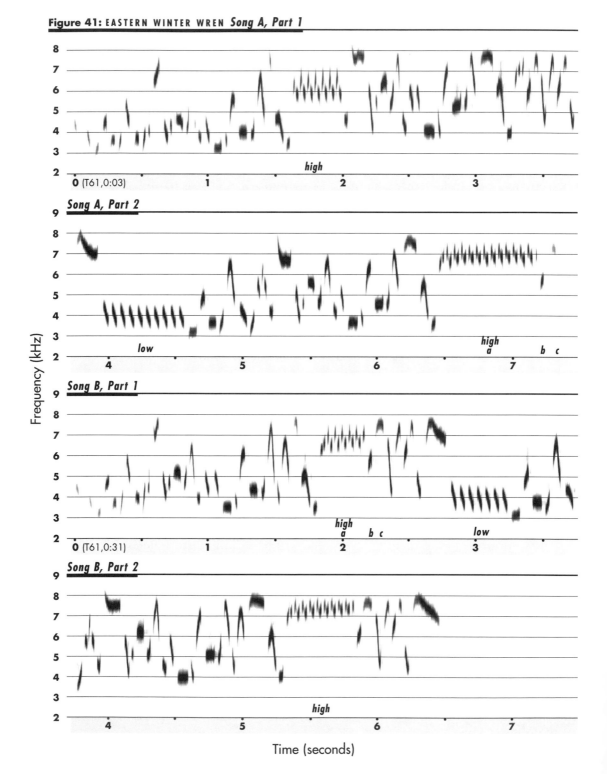

Frequency (kHz)

Time (seconds)

The Singing Life of Birds

Later, after I graphed and studied his songs, I would discover that he first sang 27 songs with the same introductory sequence over about five minutes' time, and then 81 songs with a second introduction. Throughout this early effort, he was high in a Douglas-fir, and I was straining my neck and back to aim my parabolic microphone almost directly overhead. He then descended to the forest floor, singing on and off for another three hours. His first bout in the bushes beside me consisted of 69 songs, all with the same introduction, then 34 songs with another, then 39, 39, 25, 6, 52, 34, 23, and 12, a total of 441 songs in all.

Eager for more, I returned to the same male again the next morning, for another 390 songs. The first series consisted of 39 songs, then 77, 46, 54, 38, 32, 49, 8, 33, and 14, as I would discover after months of analyses. I have never tried listening ultra-attentively to a western wren, but once I had finished the analysis, I would like to think that maybe, if I really applied myself, I'd be able to hear when he switched to a new introductory phrase. There's the challenge for my next trip west.

I know I will be overmatched in the rest of his song, because after that

Figure 41. The song repertoire of an eastern winter wren (track 61). Each of the two songs (A and B) is a series of more than 100 perfectly rendered tiny whistles, the song beginning softly and building to one of the most intense songs imaginable for such a tiny bird. Inspect the first song, extended over the top two rows of this figure. See the high-pitched trill beginning at about 0:01.7, the bold low-pitched trill two seconds later (at 0:04), and the high-pitched trill at the end—those are the landmarks for this particular song. Now inspect the second song in the bottom two rows. The first high-pitched trill is in roughly the same place, but the low-pitched trill follows almost immediately, and the song ends not on the high-pitched trill but on a bold, down-slurred whistle. These landmarks are readily heard in the songs of track 61, even more so when the songs are slowed to one-sixth speed (track 63).

Compare the details of these two songs and you will see the mind of this wren at work. How these two songs share elements is especially evident if you compare these two sonagrams note for note. Go ahead, starting at the very beginning of the two songs, and you'll soon identify major sections of the two songs that are almost (but maybe not quite) identical. What I find amazing is that this wren can sing each of these songs with precision, keeping all of the subtle differences between the songs in mind. Given the similarity of these songs, however, it's not surprising when he makes a slight mistake, confusing one song with the other. For example, look at the end of song A where I've labeled the phrase *a* and then the tiny elements *b* and *c*. Elements *b* and *c* don't normally occur after phrase *a* in song A, but all three elements do routinely occur together in song B. When you listen to song A at one-sixth speed on track 63, you hear these two tiny elements at the end of the song, and you can almost hear the wren saying "Whoops! That's wrong. That's the other song. I need to stop now."

first half-second he unleashes his creative bent. Those tiny whistled notes are then combined in many different ways, creating a seemingly endless variety of songs. Among those 831 songs from April 4 and 5 of 1970 were 67 different variations, an average of almost 7 different song conclusions for each introduction, each variation occurring on average only a dozen times in my two-day sample. My brief sample offered only a glimpse of his creative genius, I am sure, and the more songs I would have recorded, the more of his song repertoire I would have seen. Had I recorded him when he was courting a female, I would have learned much more. He then tacks one song on to another, singing nonstop for what seems an eternity, though it may be only 30 seconds. What an expert breather he must be, because the only way he can sing for so long is by taking minibreaths in the split seconds between those short whistled notes.

I experience the winter wren's performance on yet another level. The wren family (Troglodytidae) originated in the New World, and this wren is the only one that has escaped the New World, now occurring all across Asia and Europe, even into northern Africa. In the Old World, it is "The Wren," as if there were no other.

Literally, then, the sun always rises on this wren, and his song is heard around the world. I like to imagine waiting in the early morning darkness at Cape Spear, the easternmost point of Newfoundland, where dawn first greets North America each day. There, these wrens are among the first to sing, singing their name *ka-wa-miti-go-shi-que-na-go-mooch*. Each wren seems to shout "pass it on," and, half a second into the infectious charge, the male on the next territory to the west responds, and then the next, and the next, each

Figure 42. The songs of a western winter wren are far more complex than are the songs of its eastern cousin. The individual notes are slurred over a much broader frequency spectrum, making the sound more percussive and less tonal. **Top row:** First ~4 seconds of song 1 on track 62. **Second row:** First ~4 seconds of song 2 on track 62. **Lower two rows:** The complete third song from track 62. Beginning on the left, compare the sonagrams of the first two rows and you'll see that they're essentially identical for a little more than two seconds (up to the solid disk just above the baseline), after which the two songs differ. Now compare the introduction for the third song and you'll see that it is completely different. Each male has about ten different song introductions, but he creates hundreds of different songs by varying the song endings. It's a challenge to follow along in the sonagrams as you listen to this song at normal speed (track 62); at one-sixth speed, however, many of the details become accessible (track 63).

The Singing Life of Birds

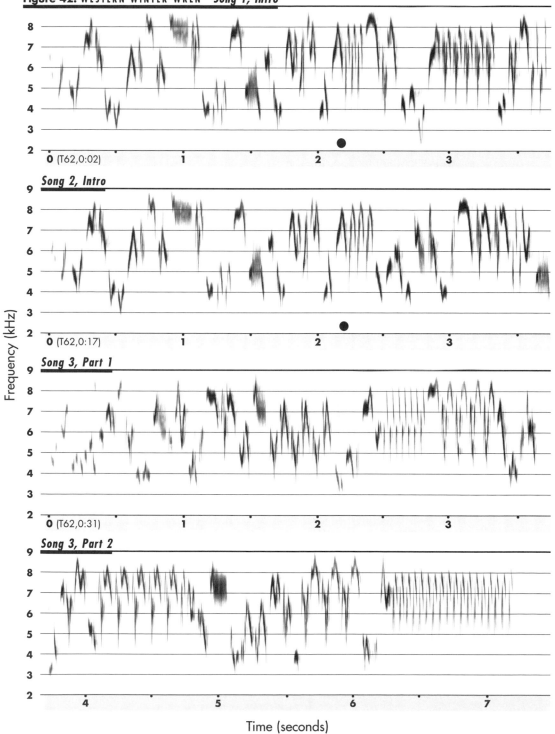

with an intensity as if his own song were to be heard around the world. All along this front where dawn's first light sweeps Newfoundland, "pass it on" radiates from thousands of bills thrown wide, each singer pausing after his first song only after the next hundred wrens to the west have heeded his call.

This dawn-and-wren wave progresses to the west, and I imagine surfing this wave, keeping pace with the light and the song. To the southwest, the wave races down the narrow ribbon of the Appalachian chain to a sudden dead end in northern Georgia, where the wren's hemlocks of the mountaintops give way to the loblolly pines of the warmer lowlands.

In the north the wave continues westward, across a 500-mile swath extending from northern Michigan to Hudson Bay, then across a narrow band of boreal woodlands in central Manitoba, Saskatchewan, widening again in central and northern Alberta. Suddenly, the wave expands to the south, now advancing over a 1,000-mile front through the Rocky Mountains. Contracting only briefly, the wave then expands to a 2,000-mile front, from the southern Sierras in California through western Oregon and Washington to very northern British Columbia and into the Yukon. Here are this wren's finest moments, its dawn effort the strongest and the broadest; from Yosemite to the Yukon, millions of tails are cocked, heads thrown back and bills wide, all hailing each other and the dawn.

This giant wave now narrows and shoots far to the north, riding a narrow coastal ribbon of wrens through southern Alaska, only to be hurled out along the Aleutian chain. "Pass it on," off the end of the Aleutians and across the open Pacific, just a few minutes later arriving at the Kamchatka Peninsula, and then down the Kuril Islands to Japan (track 64). Spanning the Seas of Japan and Okhotsk, the wave continues in Korea and southern Siberia, halfway around the world from Cape Spear.

South through China to northeast Burma, then over three miles high in the Himalayas of northern India and Tibet, and down the other side, continuing through northern Pakistan and Iran. Well north of Iran, about an hour from Moscow, a second front gains strength, creating a double wave that now progresses in the north through Russia and in the south through northern Turkey and the Balkans. There the two waves join, forming one broad front from the Mediterranean to central Scandinavia. Next it passes southern Scandinavia and the rest of Europe, the Alps, the Pyrenees, a bit of northern Liberia and Morocco in Africa, through all of the British Isles, where it is hurled out to sea, to Iceland, a wren bridge poised there in the North Atlantic. "Pass it on."

The New World now awaits, and within an hour the wave will again sweep over Cape Spear. In the span of 24 hours, this wren's dawn signature sweeps the world. It knows no political boundaries, honors no demilitarized zones; around the globe, dawn is continuously celebrated. My knees are weak, my head dizzy from the intoxicating ride.

I feel this wave every day. As I linger in bed on a summer morning, it hits me a little before 5:00. Within an hour it has swept by, leaving me to carry on with my day. But every day part of my spirit rides this wave. By midmorning I am already accelerating up coastal British Columbia. By midafternoon I am in Japan, by 6:00 high in the Himalayas, on top of the world. By midnight I have visions of invigorated wrens and airborne skylarks greeting the new dawn throughout France and England. The 24-hour clock on my wall is marked with locations, not with numbers, so that I may always know where, not when, I am.

I sense some of the details of this wren's dawn signature, too. It occurs in three movements, because wrens in eastern North America, western North America, and Eurasia are probably three different species, each with recognizably different songs. In North America, eastern males have just two songs apiece, consisting of high-pitched tinkling whistles; in contrast, western males have dozens, perhaps hundreds of different songs, higher-pitched than in the East, and consisting of a blistering blur of whistles and trills delivered at breakneck speed. These behavioral differences in North America are no doubt based on important genetic differences between eastern and western birds, just as in marsh wrens, and on that basis I know, in my gut, that they are two different species. Birds throughout Asia and Europe are intermediate, with much the same song quality and singing patterns of the wrens in eastern North America, but with six or seven songs apiece.

This signature changes with the seasons, too. In late summer, dawn is greeted by young wrens practicing the songs that they have already learned from the adults, ensuring that the local tradition will continue, the link between past and future generations guaranteeing the integrity of the wave. In autumn the wave transforms, as wrens move south and to lower altitudes during the winter, dawn then being greeted with a grating chatter, not with song. In the spring the higher latitudes and elevations are again reclaimed, *ka-wa-miti-go-shi-que-na-go-mooch* the renewed dawn clarion, sweeping the globe, continuously, day after day.

I would love to know more about this wren. His songs are so expressive, ranging from the loud and vehement to soft warbles, to whispers of sibilant notes that might be audible only a few inches from the bird. Perhaps only if I were a wren for a day would I know all he is saying and thinking.

Much is unknown, too, about the relationship between the eastern and western birds in North America. Perhaps the ancestors of our two current wrens once spanned the continent, but eastern and western groups were isolated from each other during the ice ages, each then evolving independently. Their looks didn't change that much, but their songs certainly did. Because the songs of eastern North America are similar to those throughout Eurasia, I bet that the eastern wren gave rise to "The Wren" of the Old World after the split with the wrens in western North America. Perhaps the eastern wren made it to Europe by way of Iceland, or to Asia by way of the Bering Straits, and then spread throughout Eurasia and northern Africa. At least I know the direction of movement, from the New World to the Old, because all wrens originated in the New World, in North or Central or South America.

It is not only their songs but also their call notes that give away the history of these wrens. The songs are learned, but the calls are not, and are instead a relatively direct reflection of the genes within the wrens. The calls of eastern birds are richer and lower-pitched, a *churp*, much like the call of a song sparrow; those of western birds are sharp and higher pitched, more of a *chip*, like two rocks hit together, like the sharp call of a Wilson's warbler. These differences in calls tell of two winter wren species, one eastern and one western, each having been isolated for some time from each other.

I'd love to know where eastern and western wrens meet, too, and what they think of each other there. Perhaps it would be somewhere in northern Alberta or British Columbia, or maybe coastal Alaska? Could I hear eastern and western birds at the same location, even on neighboring territories? If they breed true there and don't blend to form an intermediate wren (as eastern and western marsh wrens do not blend in Saskatchewan), I'd have good evidence that they are two species, because the wrens themselves would be declaring their uniqueness. The North American field guides would then have to be changed to show two winter wrens instead of one; all birders who have seen both would automatically add one more tally to their North American list. Perhaps they'd be called the "eastern winter wren" and the "western winter wren"—or perhaps they deserve something more fitting, such as the Whistling Wren and the Whistling Wren On Speed. Some day I will discover the limits of eastern and western wrens, somewhere in the

Northwest, no doubt, unless some intrepid explorer rises to the challenge and beats me to it.

Songbirds with Especially Beautiful Songs

The Bachman's Sparrow

It is the unknowns that have conspired to bring me here, to be standing in the wiregrass and broomsedge among the pines and the palmettos in south Florida. An hour and a half before sunrise on this early April Sunday morning, Orion and Jupiter are long gone. To the south is reddish Mars, between the Archer and the Scorpion; in 10 minutes, Venus will rise in the Fishes, now on the eastern horizon. In that direction, two chuck-will's-widows still call their name, their individually distinct calls enabling me to hear how each moves about in the night. From the west arrives a distant *you-alll* of a barred owl. Frogs call contagiously from the nearby lake, surging and then fading. All else is silent.

Just when will these sparrows begin singing? It's possible that they hold the secret to why birds sing at dawn, at least if my friend Barney Dunning is right. In the "everything you ever wanted to know" account of this species, he says that they rarely start singing in South Carolina until 30 minutes after sunrise. Among songbirds, such a late start to the day is unheard of. Perhaps in this sparrow is the exception that will finally explain the rule, the rule that the most intense singing of the day begins in the dark, during the hour before the sun appears, well before the owls and nightjars have gone to roost.

How many different songs will he sing? I know he has a sizable repertoire, based on two birds recorded by Donald Borror, the pioneer sound recordist who founded what is now the Borror Laboratory of Bioacoustics at Ohio State University; one of his birds in Ohio had 36 different songs, one in Florida 39. Another bird in Texas sang 23 different songs. How complete were those samples? Maybe those recordings weren't long enough to capture all that he could sing. My goal is to record him until I am sure I have recorded all he knows, perhaps until he introduces no new songs in the last 50 recorded.

Just how will he use his repertoire of different songs? In 77 consecutive songs, the Texan sang 23 different ones, repeating each two to four times before switching to another. That's puzzling, as I know of no other bird who sings quite like that. Birds with repertoires typically sing with one of two extreme styles. One is called "immediate variety," with successive songs different. Good examples include the marsh wren, the wood thrush, the hermit thrush, and the red-eyed vireo. A repertoire can also be delivered with "eventual variety," the bird singing many renditions of one type before switching to another. Repeating a song 50 or more times before switching is typical of a Bewick's wren or Carolina wren, a dozen or more times typical of a song sparrow. I know of no bird so squarely in the middle, consistently singing a song just two or three times at a leisurely pace over a half-minute or so before switching to another song. I need to hear him, to try to understand why he might sing like this.

I will eventually take my tape recording back home and graph out every song, determining exactly how many different songs he has, but I also wonder how well I might do here, in the field, just listening. After gaining some familiarity with his songs, I'll try to pick a distinctive song, one that I'm confident I'll be able to recognize again when I hear it. Perhaps three times in half a minute I'll hear it, and then he'll switch, when I'll count "2." Every time he switches to a new song, I'll count again, stopping when I hear my distinctive song again. How many switches will it be? If he runs through his entire repertoire before returning to my chosen song, perhaps I'll number somewhere between 30 and 40. Or perhaps it'll be in the 20s, or maybe the 40s. This kind of listening satisfies an immediate curiosity but is also important to help me decide when I have enough recordings from him so that I can thoroughly know his repertoire when I analyze the tape back home.

If he does sing during the dawn chorus, beginning in the hour before sunrise, will he then speed through his repertoire? If later in the day he sings 3 to 4 songs a minute and three renditions of a song before switching, will he sing more rapidly at dawn, perhaps 6 to 10 songs a minute, perhaps not repeating songs at all, instead singing with immediate variety? That's what I might expect of him, based on how other songbirds behave at dawn, because it is at dawn that they pull out all stops, singing with the greatest speed and variety. A chipping sparrow, for example, has only a single song that he sings a lethargic four or so times a minute during midday, but before sunrise he sputters as many as 60 of them a minute. An eastern bluebird has dozens of different songs; during a daytime minute he may sing 10 times, alternating two or three different songs; but before sunrise he'll easily double that singing rate, using 10 or more different songs in a minute. Warblers and wrens and flycatchers—on and on I could go, reveling in the intensity of singing at dawn. If these Bachman's sparrows do greet the dawn, just how will they sing?

When I hear neighbors singing, how will they interact? Males countersing, I have read, throughout much of the day, sometimes half an hour or more nonstop. Perhaps 50 or so yards apart, one sings, then the other, alternating their songs, each listening to what the other has sung before taking his turn again. Just what do they sing to each other? It seems that no one has listened to these birds, but I can find out. Every three or so songs, perhaps every 30 seconds, a male must choose which song he will switch to next. Does his choice depend on what the neighbor is singing? Do they match each other, song for song, each pulling from his large repertoire the identical song that the neighbor is singing? If so, I'll be able to hear it, as it's easy to compare two back-to-back songs and declare whether they are the same or different. If they match each other, then I will also know that they have learned their songs from each other, much as the Bewick's wrens did that I studied long ago.

How might all this change as they approach each other at their territorial boundary? Do they sing faster and switch to new song themes more quickly? I'll be listening for what has been called the "excited song," too, which is often given in flight when he seems agitated. He may rise up to 50 yards in the air, flying slowly with fluttering wings, giving an exuberant, bubbling combination of slurs, whistles, and trills, ending with one of his typical songs. Sometimes, after a squabble at a territory boundary, he'll give this excited song as he climbs from the ground to a higher perch, where he'll launch into an exhilarating series of his more typical songs.

These are the types of questions that have intrigued me about many species for more than 30 years, but they alone would not have brought me here. No, it is one other unknown, one that 10 years ago I couldn't have admitted. I simply need to hear these Bachman's sparrows sing. It is said that their songs are unforgettable, the most beautiful of sparrow songs by far, the most beautiful of birdsongs throughout North America, others would say, even outranking the hermit thrush. Words cannot begin to describe them, nor can any tape recording capture the essence of the performance. One must stand in the wiregrass and broomsedge among the scrubby oaks or saw palmettos in the open piney woods of the Deep South, smell the scent of those long-needled pines, and hear the song in the warmth of the morning or in the heat of the day or by the light of the moon. The songs themselves are incomplete without the accompanying chorus of pine warblers and eastern wood-pewees and brown-headed nuthatches and red-cockaded woodpeckers and summer tanagers. So I have been told.

Out of their natural context, perhaps it is futile to dissect the songs, as if a mad scientist could actually understand an alien being by probing its innards. But I needed to know the basics before encountering these songs in nature, so I have read about them and what to expect. I know I'll hear a relatively simple two-part song. He'll most likely start with a pure whistle lasting about a half-second, but sometimes the first note has a buzzy quality. The second part will be a trill, a series of perhaps a dozen identical phrases over a second and a half, usually delivered slowly enough that I'll be able to count them. Two seconds of bliss and ecstasy, it is said, but one must hear it there, among the pines, because no words are sufficient.

Whether he sings each of his songs only once or three times before switching, I am told the effect is striking. As he introduces each new song theme, I'll grasp its quality the best I can. Will the new introductory note be a pure whistle or a buzz, low- or medium- or high-pitched, higher or lower or about the same pitch as the one before? How will that introduction contrast with the quality and pitch of the trill that follows, or the one that has preceded it? If I had a better musical ear, perhaps I could confirm what one pioneering listener, Aretas A. Saunders, heard, that the pitch intervals between the introductory note and the trill are "quite perfect, being minor or major thirds, fourths, fifths, or even octaves." It is the music of nature, and of these sparrows in particular, that has brought me to the pines and palmettos, to try to understand why these songs strike us humans as so beautiful.

For all of these unknowns about this sparrow, I can't help but be reminded of one more: how to pronounce its very name. It's not BACHman, as Johann Sebastian would have pronounced his last name, but BACKman, the way Audubon's clergyman friend in Charleston, South Carolina, preferred to pronounce his name back in 1834 when Audubon named this bird after him.

🐦

There, 6:37 A.M., 40 minutes *before* sunrise, from halfway up the pine, about 50 yards to the west. I swing the parabola toward him, instinctively slipping my headphones on, the tape recorder already running since 6:15 so as not to miss his first song. That first one was a surprise, as I could hear no introduc-

Figure 43. What a diversity of songs the Bachman's sparrow sings, as illustrated by sonagrams of the six different songs that I first heard that April morning in south Florida (track 65). A few songs launch directly into the trill of repeated phrases (1), but most songs are introduced with either pure whistles (2, 3, 4) or buzzy notes (5, 6). Most songs have two parts (2, 3, 4, 5), but some have three (6) or only one (1). Feel, too, the differences in pitch and rhythm and the contrasts in overall sound quality as you listen to these songs.

tory whistle (track 65, figure 43). The headphones over my ears now, the world is muted except for one voice, his voice, now beaming into my ears.

As I hear his second song, I realize why listeners have raved about him. It's a pure, unwavering whistle that I first hear, drawn out for half a second, about three octaves above middle C. In ordinary contexts, a half-second is a split second, but not in the rapid-fire delivery of birdsongs, where a note held so long seems to go on forever. Following that whistle are nine bold whistles slurred

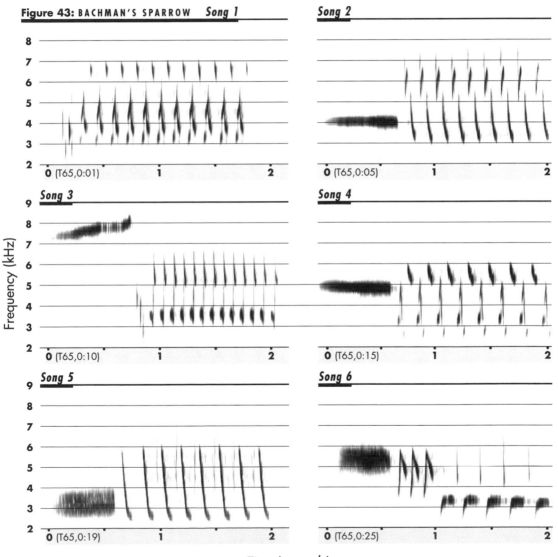

Figure 43: BACHMAN'S SPARROW *Song 1* *Song 2* *Song 3* *Song 4* *Song 5* *Song 6*

Frequency (kHz)

Time (seconds)

downward, repeated so rapidly I can just barely count them, the entire song almost two seconds long, as if he inhales on the introductory whistle and exhales on the trill. This second song is clearly different from his first of the morning, and in my mind I think of it as song type #2.

As I wait for the next song, I let that second song echo in my brain, slowing it, processing it, dissecting it, drawing it in my mind. I see the spectrogram form as he sings, the pure whistle growing from left to right at the appropriate pitch, the trill following, the slurred whistles slowly sliding down the scale, starting higher and stopping much lower than the introductory whistle. In my mental notebook, I scribble my best attempt at a picture of the song, knowing that both hearing and seeing the song will help me better remember it. Next to my mental sonagram, I will write how many times he repeats the song.

He gives me five seconds to savor that second song, and he's on to his third song, different from the first two. The introductory whistle seems an octave higher still, the air waves pulsing my eardrum 8,000 times a second, a sound so high and thin that I can barely hear it. Following that whistle is a microsecond *sli-ck,* as if he smacks his lips (though he has none, of course), and then he delivers a lower-pitched trill so rapidly I cannot count the syllables. It's #3.

And the fourth song is different, too—four different songs to start his morning, with no repeats so far. The whistle is an octave lower again, and I count seven syllables that follow, not the boldly slurred whistles of two songs ago, as these whistles feel much higher-pitched, their energy seeming to be above the introductory whistle, not below. Two times he delivers this song, encouraging me to memorize its details—finally, he has repeated himself, as I expect him to do more often as the morning progresses. That's the fourth song from his repertoire, sung twice.

The next song is strikingly different, beginning with a low, buzzy introduction, not grating and harsh, but pleasantly sibilant. Contrasting sharply with his introduction are the following eight boldly slurred whistles, sweeping down the scale. A striking song, one hard to forget. Twice he sings it. That's #5.

I'm caught off-guard by the next song, consisting of three parts—I don't remember anything in my reading about such songs. The opening note is buzzy, in a midrange pitch, followed by three pure notes at about the same pitch and then five whistles on a much lower pitch. I find myself begging him to repeat it, to burn #6 into my memory, but no, he's on to another.

I take note so far of what he has sung: 1 2 3 4 4 5 5 6. The first four songs were all different, and then he repeated song #4, as he did #5, but #6 occurred only once.

On and on he continues (track 66). I listen to each song, focusing first on the pitch and quality of the introductory note, then on the following trill or two, listening to their qualities, the individual units slowly or rapidly repeated, raspy or pure in quality, low- or mid- or high-pitched.

I'm eager to learn his vocabulary, eager to understand how he puts his song program together, and I gradually realize how to crack him. About one in five songs has a buzzy introduction, and about one in 10 songs consists of three parts—so the most distinctive song is a three-parted song with the buzzy introductory note, the one I labeled #6 earlier this morning. I can easily recognize that one whenever I hear it, and I now listen intently for him to deliver it again. I focus on other three-parted songs, too, all of which begin with whistles but then have a unique combination of trills that follow.

Some two-parted songs seem distinctive, too, like songs #2 and #5 that I heard first thing this morning. Another begins with an ultrahigh whistled introduction, followed by six or seven whistles slurred downward, repeated slowly, about four per second. Another song seems out of character for this sparrow, as the trill notes are raspy, not the slurred whistles.

Until 10 minutes past sunrise I record, capturing more than 200 songs in 50 minutes, many of them now sounding familiar to my ears. He's just repeating himself now, I am confident, revealing no new songs. He's told me all that he knows. That first three-parted song (#6), for example, has been used on four or five occasions already, and when he repeats himself like that, I have most likely thoroughly sampled his song repertoire.

I have time to ask him one quick question before he takes what will almost certainly be a post-sunrise singing break. Already this morning I have heard him respond to a neighboring male with what sounded like a perfect match of the neighbor's song. I can ask him more directly, though, by playing some of his own songs to him to see how he responds to the songs of a simulated intruder. Quickly I lay on the ground a small tape recorder with some songs recorded from him earlier in the morning.

I take note of how many songs come from the speaker, this time using letters to denote the switches from one song type to another. From the speaker is broadcast A, then B, and another B, and from the pine tree to the west comes the echo, another B; the recorder advances to C, and the bird follows to C; then to D, and the bird follows to D. Within three broadcast songs he is entrained on the songs from the recorder, and three times in a row this sparrow switches his songs to match exactly what this simulated intruder sings. He *does* pay careful attention to what other birds sing, and he can respond in kind to them. Thank you, I find myself saying, for telling me one small bit more

about how you hear your world, about how your mind listens and responds to "other" singing sparrows.

He now flutters down from the pine, landing in the needle-free branches of a fallen pine bough, just a yard above the plastic intruder. Wrenlike, he jerks his body this way, then that, flexing and then extending his legs, bouncing up and down and sideways, his wings quivering, crown feathers rising and falling, tail cocked. Bill open, he sings; closed again, he continues his dance. I take my mental video of him, preserving in my mind his dance, his good looks. His crown is a dull reddish brown, the sides of his head a smoky gray bisected by the reddish line extending behind his eye; delicate markings on his back and wings, much gray streaked and spotted with chestnut brown and black, give way to his buffy flanks and to light gray below. The tail he waves about is largely gray and dusky.

The intruder no longer singing, off into the grass he flies. Mouselike, he runs along the ground, flying the short distance up to another perch, but he seems to fly weakly, pumping his tail as if to stay aloft, then dropping to the ground again and running some more.

I lay the equipment down and step back, realizing that his singing has transformed the landscape. Mars and the stars are long gone, and the sun is above the horizon, casting long pine-trunk shadows on a sea of golden palmettos. The wiregrass glistens with dew droplets, as do the tiny white flowers about my feet. The nightjars and owls and frogs are silent, replaced by nearby songbirds and flycatchers and woodpeckers and even distant cranes.

The sparrow has ascended a nearby pine and now resumes his singing. For me, unfortunately, duty calls, as I have an 8:00 A.M. meeting in Fort Myers. I pack up and leave, driving to the interstate and heading south, reflecting on what I have learned.

❧

To the accompaniment of the chuck-will's-widow, well before sunrise, the Bachman's sparrow was first, not last, to be heard among the day's birds. This sparrow is no exception to the songbird rule, as it joins the dawn chorus like all the others. Barney's report probably tells more of his own rising time than that of the birds, a conclusion I've drawn about some other professional ornithologists before, though it's possible that the time of first song varies in some interesting way from place to place, or season to season. I'll keep an open mind on that.

I confirmed, too, that neighboring males answer each other with identical songs, at least some of the time. They are no doubt resident here in these pine woods, staying here the entire year. Like other resident songbirds, they undoubtedly learn their songs from each other, much as Bewick's wrens and marsh wrens and titmice and cardinals and Carolina wrens do.

How often did he sing each song before going on to another? Only once on many occasions, but mostly it was twice. Perhaps only one in five or six times did he sing three renditions of a song before switching to another, so he did sing with much greater variety at dawn than has been reported for later in the day.

How many different songs did he sing? As I listened, I heard some recognizable songs several times, and had I been taking written notes, I'd have a decent estimate. For now, I guess that he has at least 25 different songs that he can sing. I'll determine his repertoire later as I study the sonagrams back on my home computer.

As for the beauty in the songs, yes, I confirmed that, too, but not in any rigorous fashion, nor could I have. I took them in, one at a time, marveling at the purity of the whistles, the pleasant buzzes, the contrast among them all. I need no one to confirm my reaction, though I will seek out the opinions of those who know music, those who might hear and be able to describe better what it is about these songs that makes them so satisfying to some, perhaps all human ears.

As I drive, I realize how I had tuned the world out as the sparrow began to sing, but I now recall the background sounds. I heard no tanager or pewee or nuthatch or red-cockaded woodpecker; maybe the tanager and pewee were still in South America, but the nuthatch and woodpecker should have been there. The chuck-will's-widows stopped about 10 minutes after the sparrow began, and pine warblers soon sang, as did distant meadowlarks, a kingbird, a mockingbird, bobwhite, and some great crested flycatchers. After sunrise the flicker and red-bellied woodpeckers weighed in, typical late-arising woodpeckers. Sandhill cranes trumpeted in the distance. All this in the "open" pine woods, the walking easy through the grass among the pines and the saw palmettos.

Back home, I eagerly graph the songs in my prized 50-minute recording, and I soon see what I had heard, the whistles, the buzzes, the trills, the one- and two- and three-parted songs. Playing the tape over and over, I follow along on the computer screen, breathing in the details of each song (see "How to See Bird Sounds" in Appendix II).

I now start printing examples of each of the different songs he sings so that I can study them in more detail, to learn more about this singing maestro. The first four songs of the morning I print, because they are all different; then I print the sixth song, the eighth, the ninth, the eleventh, the thirteenth, the sixteenth . . . until I get to the sixty-fifth song in the sequence, in the thirteenth minute. I now have a catalog of 33 different songs, and he starts to repeat his repertoire in earnest. He drops down to song #23 again, then to song #2, then jumps up to #9, and then he delivers the next series of songs in exactly the same sequence that he had presented them earlier: #10, 11, 12, 13, 14, 15, 16, 17, 18, 19, 20, and 21. Then he drops to #5, then #1, and then to #25, 26, 27, 28, 29, 30, and 31, again singing the same sequence that he had delivered before. It is now clear that the song he chooses to sing next often depends on the one he just sang, as if pairs or strings of songs are somehow linked in his mind. Such is the case with many other songbirds, too, as has been shown for marsh wrens and northern cardinals. I continue studying the songs through all 229 of them, printing just one more unique song, in the 35th minute, at position 169, when he sings song #34.

I need to plot this pattern in a graph, to see how he organizes his singing. Using the spreadsheet on my computer, I type from 1 to 229 in the first column for each of the songs that he sang during my 50-minute recording. Then in the second column I type the number for the song type, from #1 to #34, that

Figure 44. A 50-minute window on the mind of my Bachman's sparrow on that April morning in south Florida. Beginning 40 minutes before sunrise (at -40; read the time scale across the top of the figure), the sparrow sang 229 songs (the scale across the bottom of the figure), consisting of 34 different types (the vertical axis on the left). Each of the 229 songs is represented by a small diamond and placed on the graph to indicate which of the 34 song types was used at each position in the 229-song sequence. Constructing the graph in this way allows us to read the figure from left to right, exploring how often and when he sings each song type, how he sings his different songs in favorite sequences, how he changes his singing rate through the morning, and more, all described in the text. The more I explore this simple figure, the more I see and hear this Bachman's sparrow sing, and the more I can identify with how his singing mind greets the dawn.

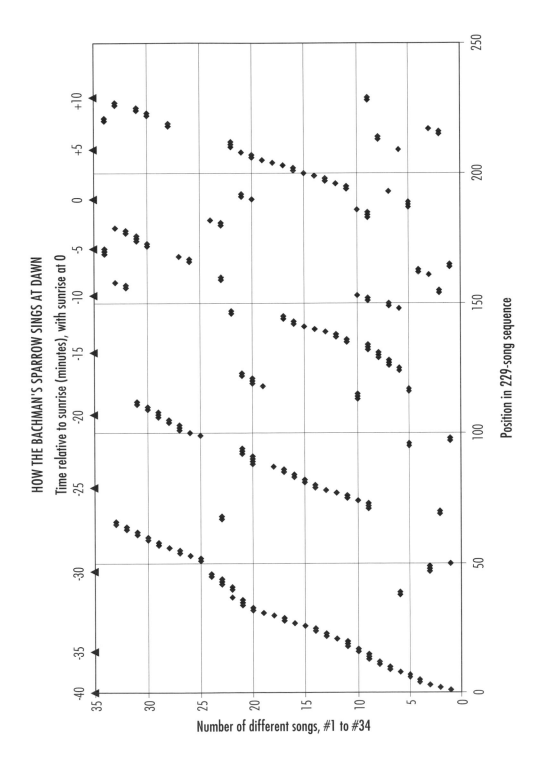

HOW THE BACHMAN'S SPARROW SINGS AT DAWN

Time relative to sunrise (minutes), with sunrise at 0

Number of different songs, #1 to #34

Position in 229-song sequence

I have identified at each of the 229 positions. I go to the software's menu, select the type of graph I want, make a few critical choices, and I now *see* what he's up to (figure 44).

I read my graph from left to right. Across the bottom are listed the 229 songs in the sequence, and across the top the 50-minute period is divided into 10 five-minute segments, with sunrise in the 40th minute, at 0. On the vertical axis is the number for each of the 34 songs. In the lower left, I look at song type #1 in position 1, the first song of the morning, and then scan across to the right, seeing that song type #1 occurs on four separate occasions: at position 1, at 50, at about 100 (where it occurs twice, as indicated by the two diamonds side by side), and at about 165 (twice again). Song type #2 also occurs on four occasions: at position 2, and then roughly at 70, 155, and 215. Beginning in the lower left and scanning up and to the right, I see the sequence with which he begins the morning: one, two, or three renditions of each song type, from song type #1 to #22, and on up to #33 (with brief interruptions to repeat songs #6, #3, and #1). My eyes wander over this simple graph of his dawn effort as I search for other patterns in his behavior. I see other unbroken strings of songs trailing to the upper right, showing his favored sequences: #11 to #17, which he does four times; #11 to #22, two times; #25 to #31, two times; and #30 to #33, two times. The neurons that control these different songs must somehow be connected in his brain, playing out these favored sequences.

From this graph I can also see how his singing rate changes during the 50 minutes. Each song occupies the same amount of horizontal space on the graph, so that the spacing of the five-minute periods across the top reveals how many songs he sang in each of those periods. He begins slowly, just 16 songs in the first five minutes, averaging 3 songs a minute. In the next five minutes (5 to 10) he nearly doubles that pace, singing 31 songs, about 6 songs a minute. The next five minutes (10 to 15) are equally intense, with another 32 songs, more than 6 songs a minute. After 30 minutes he slows considerably, singing only about 4 songs a minute. Perhaps I need to listen to more songbirds sing, but I don't know of many that sing at a slower pace than these Bachman's sparrows.

In the graph I also see how many times he sings a given song type before going on to the next. Most of the time (63 times) he sings two renditions; less common are one rendition (42 times), three renditions (19 times), and four renditions (1 time). That's an average of less than two renditions each time he introduces a new song. How odd, I continue to think, as I know of no other bird that sings quite like this.

In just 50 minutes of singing this Bachman's sparrow has taught me much, erasing most of those unknowns that have brought me to these pine woods in southern Florida. He does begin singing well before sunrise, just like other songbirds. His repertoire is sizable, at 34 different songs, and he often matches the songs of his neighbors, just as he matched my playback tape, showing that neighboring males learn their songs from each other and address each other by choosing the appropriate matching song from their repertoire. As he introduces each of his different songs during the dawn hour, he sings one to four renditions of each, averaging less than two, a unique singing behavior among birds that I know.

Yes, that last unknown is erased, too, as I have confirmed that to my ears these are among the most beautiful birdsongs in North America. Confirming that unknown alone will bring me back to these open pine woods, to stand among the wiregrass and the broomsedge, to hear and see them at dawn, and in the heat of the day, and by the light of the moon. Because no words or tape recordings can suffice, and once is not enough.

The Wood Thrush

It is in those semiconscious minutes just before the alarm that I first hear him: *ee-oo-lay . . . ah-ee-oo-lay . . .* a wood thrush. I hear the song in two parts, the loud, whistled prelude and the softer, fluty flourish that follows, and by habit I concentrate on the loud preludes. His next song is a four-whistle prelude, the first note held for an instant, then dropping to a lower pitch, then this two-note medley is transposed to a higher pitch. Store it, I tell myself, remember it and listen for him to sing it again. Next is a three-note prelude, beginning a little above where the other left off, rising higher still, then dropping back down, on only three pitches. Fix it in memory. Next is . . . no way! It's the four-whistle prelude again. Next is, yes, there's no doubt, it's the three-note prelude again.

Propped up on my elbows now, I'm fully alert. Outside my bedroom window this late April morning are the rain-soaked New England oaks and

WOOD THRUSH

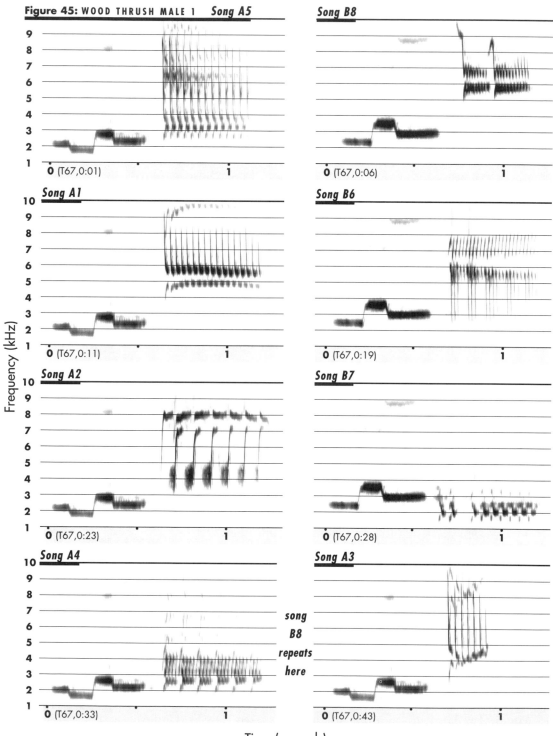

Figure 45: WOOD THRUSH MALE 1   *Song A5*

Song B8

Song A1

Song B6

Song A2

Song B7

Song A4

song B8 repeats here

Song A3

Frequency (kHz)

Time (seconds)

O (T67,0:01)
O (T67,0:06)
O (T67,0:11)
O (T67,0:19)
O (T67,0:23)
O (T67,0:28)
O (T67,0:33)
O (T67,0:43)

maples, their buds bulging, showing signs of life after a long winter, and here is the first wood thrush of the year. He continues to alternate one prelude with the other in combination with a variety of flourishes. How odd, I realize, as I've never heard a wood thrush with just two of those whistled preludes. He seems early this year, too, on April 28, a Sunday.

Dressing quickly, I'm soon on the wooded path down to the kettle pond, pausing at the north end of the clearing where he sings. Song after song, 10, 50, 100, he continues high in the trees, almost always alternating those two preludes, though with a confusing variety of terminal flourishes (track 67, figure 45). I'm close enough now that I can also hear the soft *bup bup bup* at the song's beginning, one to seven soft, low notes that introduce each song. I check him out through the binoculars, too: a little smaller than a robin, cinnamon brown on the head, grading to olive brown on the tail, with deliciously large dark spots on his white underside, perhaps colored that way so he's well camouflaged whether he's foraging on these New England forest floors or in some tropical forest, where he spends more than half his year. He's the "wood thrush," but he could just as well have been called the "wood nightingale-thrush," I reason—whoever named these birds decided for some arbitrary reason that his seven close relatives that live in the tropics year-round would be called "nightingale-thrushes," but that those species that visit us in North America would just be "thrushes." All are extraordinary singers.

I recognize these two preludes. I've heard and seen them before from other wood thrushes, because rangewide there are only 25 or so such preludes. As he now sings, I see the stick-figure sonagrams form in my mind. The first is just four brief whistles, a two-note medley transposed and immediately repeated, the entire prelude less than half a second. The three-note prelude begins just above where the other prelude left off, rises higher still, and then ends at about the high point of the first prelude; the first two whistles are about half as long as the last, giving it a pleasing tempo.

On Monday I hear him again through my bedroom window, but by Tuesday, the last day of April, the rain has stopped, and he lures me with my recording equipment down to the pond. Parabola aimed at him, headphones over my ears, I capture song after song. The two preludes are familiar, but I struggle with the flourishes. How many are there? Their pitch is so high,

Figure 45. The relatively small repertoire of the first wood thrush who sang to me in early spring. Here are the 8 different songs from a natural sequence of 9 songs (track 67): A5 B8 A1 B6 A2 B7 A4 B8 A3 (the second example of song B8 is omitted from the figure). Two preludes (A and B) combine with 8 different flourishes (1–8) to create a diverse array of songs.

almost always well above the prelude, climbing to four octaves above middle C, and so complex, too, that I cannot grasp their details.

I must know, so I head to my computer, studying the details in these songs. I inspect 50, then 100, then 150 songs on the monitor, and soon I realize that he has just 8 different flourishes to accompany his 2 preludes (figure 45). Each flourish I now identify with a number, from 1 to 8. I now realize, too, why I could not track him while listening down at the pond. In my brief recording, the prelude with four whistles (for simplicity, I'll call that "A") occurred with 7 different flourishes, songs that in shorthand I can write as A1, A2, A3, A4, A5, A6, and A8. The three-whistle (B) prelude occurred with 5 flourishes (B1, B2, B6, B7, B8), so that he produced 12 of the possible 16 different combinations (never occurring in these 150 songs were A7, B3, B4, and B5). He clearly had his favorites in these 150 songs, such as B6, which occurred 27 times, and B2 (23), A1 (22), and A5 (21).

I need to see the bigger picture. How does he choose the next song he will sing, I wonder? For starters, I construct a 12 × 12 table, called a transition matrix (table 1). At the beginning of each row and the top of each column I write the 12 combinations of prelude and flourish that he sings, from A1 to B8, and I read the table from left to right, from a particular row heading to a particular column heading, with each of the 144 cells in the table representing a sequence of two particular songs. Starting at the beginning of my 150-song sequence, I see the sequence A1 → B2 → A5. There are two transitions in that sequence, A1 → B2 and B2 → A5. To enter a tally into the table for the A1 → B2 transition, I find A1 at a row head (the preceding song), go over to the column headed by B2 (the following song), and mark one tally in that cell. To enter the tally for the B2 → A5 transition, I find B2 in the row headings, move over to the A5 column, and mark a tally in that cell. I continue through the entire record, song by song, finally adding all of the numbers in each row and column. To help organize the table, I block off in a heavy border the groups of cells that represent songs beginning with the A and B preludes. I also darkly shade the empty diagonal cells that would indicate he sings two identical songs back-to-back.

I now see one reason why I had difficulty identifying his songs as I listened: I could never know which song would come next. The song with prelude B and flourish 8 (B8), for example, was followed by 9 different songs, B6 by 7 different songs, so that about 50 different two-song sequences (or transitions) occurred in the 150 I studied, and 20 of those sequences occurred only once (for example, the sequence from A2 to B6). He did have his favorite

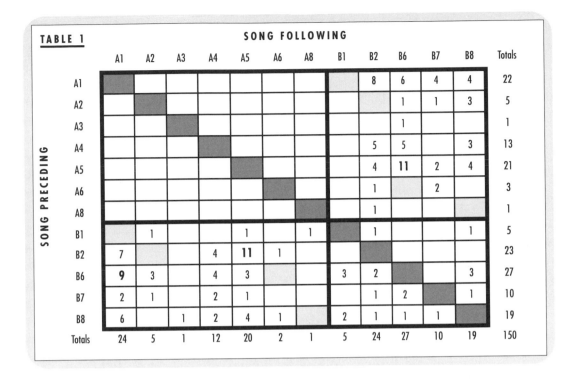

TABLE 1 — SONG FOLLOWING

SONG PRECEDING	A1	A2	A3	A4	A5	A6	A8	B1	B2	B6	B7	B8	Totals
A1									8	6	4	4	22
A2										1	1	3	5
A3										1			1
A4									5	5		3	13
A5									4	11	2	4	21
A6									1		2		3
A8									1				1
B1		1			1		1		1			1	5
B2	7			4	11	1							23
B6	9	3		4	3			3	2			3	27
B7	2	1		2	1				1	2		1	10
B8	6		1	2	4	1		2	1	1	1		19
Totals	24	5	1	12	20	2	1	5	24	27	10	19	150

sequences, such as B2 → A5 → B6 → A1, as emphasized by the bold-faced numbers in those three cells, but the only absolute rule he seemed to follow was that he'd never sing the same song back-to-back (such as A1 followed by A1, along the darkly-shaded diagonal). In fact, I now see that a song with the A prelude was always followed by a song with the B prelude (all 66 times, calculated by adding the row totals for all A preludes), and most of the time (65 of 84) the B prelude was followed by an A prelude (the other 19 times he sang back-to-back B preludes). Never did the same flourish occur in back-to-back songs, such as A1 → B1, or B2 → A2, as indicated by the lightly shaded cells in the matrix.

What have I learned from this thrush who sings for me each morning now? What is the big picture that I hear and can now see more clearly? He has 2 loud, whistled preludes (A and B) and 8 fluty flourishes (1 through 8). He sings 12 different combinations of prelude and flourish (as listed in the row and column headings), not all 16 possible combinations (but he might have sung more if I had recorded more than 150 songs). He *never* sings the same song back-to-back (darkly shaded cells in upper left to lower right diagonal). And *never* does he sing the same flourish in back-to-back songs (8 lightly shaded cells in lower left and upper right quadrants). *Rarely* does he sing the same prelude back-to-back: the A prelude is always followed by the B prelude, the B prelude usually by the A, so about 9 out of 10 times the next prelude is also different. The overall effect is a highly diverse, unpredictable, and, yes, exhilarating performance.

Three days later, on Friday, May 3, I wake to a different world. No longer do I hear the alternating A and B preludes. I still hear A, but no B, and he now sings several other preludes, too. I lie down again, window open, listening to the variety of preludes, blocking for the moment all of the flourishes (track 68, figure 46). I first listen for A, and hear it roughly every six songs. Then I pick another prelude, and another, mastering each in turn, learning to recognize it when I hear it again. Finally, a few minutes later, I have it: 6 preludes, each distinctive, each recognizable. Fifteen minutes later I'm there, beneath him, realizing that here is a new male who has arrived overnight and has already pushed the two-prelude male to the south end of the pond, where he now sings.

For 30 minutes I record, then head to my computer. I study 150 songs from this male, too, verifying the 6 preludes, but discovering 13 different flourishes. Of 78 possible combinations of preludes and flourishes (6 × 13), he sings 22. I also discover that this male has two songs that are almost identical to those of the two-prelude male, so I adjust my letters and numbers to call them A1 and A2 also (all of the other preludes and flourishes are different,

Figure 46. A portion of the larger repertoire of the second wood thrush, which consisted of 6 preludes (A–F) and 13 flourishes (only 8 of which are illustrated here). If you compare these preludes and flourishes to those of the first male (figure 45), you'll find that only prelude A and flourishes 1 and 2 are shared by the two birds (you'll have to take my word for it that the five non-illustrated flourishes of the second male are unique). When singing (listen to track 68), this wood thrush combines his preludes and flourishes in unpredictable ways. Try to match up the preludes and flourishes in this figure during the two-minute, 43-song sequence on the CD. Here are the prelude-flourish combinations that the thrush sings (read across), the first 8 of which are illustrated in the figure:

E6	D10	C5	B8	A2	F13	E1	C7	D6	B9
A4	F12	E11	C5	B8	A1	F13	E2	C7	D10
B8	A5	F12	E11	C7	B9	A1	F12	E6	B8
A5	C2	E1	F13	B8	A4	E11	C7	D10	B9
F12	E2	A5.							

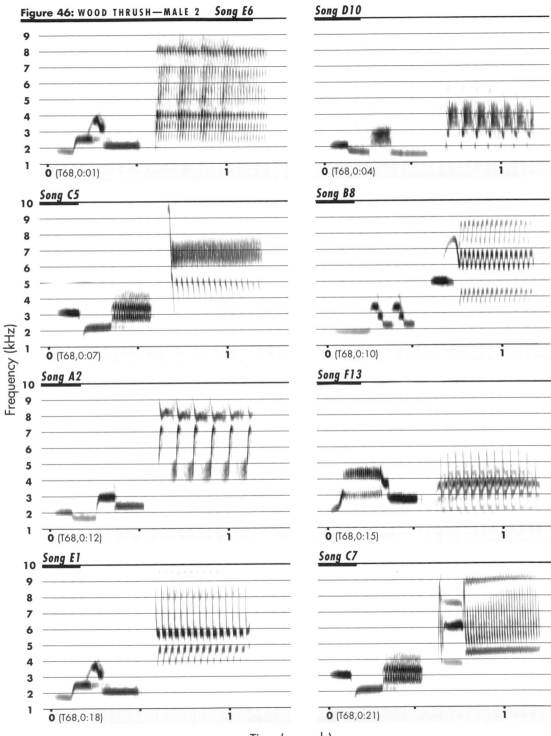

Figure 46: WOOD THRUSH—MALE 2 *Song E6*

Song D10

Song C5

Song B8

Song A2

Song F13

Song E1

Song C7

Frequency (kHz)

Time (seconds)

despite their similar labels, which I use for convenience). Again needing to see the bigger picture, I construct my transition matrix (table 2), this time a whopping 22 rows and 22 columns, filling out the row and column headings with the prelude-flourish combinations that he uses. I organize the table in much the same way that I did for the first male, boxing off areas in the matrix that demarcate cells for a given prelude, and darkly shading the upper left to lower right diagonal to mark those cells that would be transitions between identical songs. Last, I lightly shade all cells throughout the matrix that would represent a transition between songs with either identical preludes or identical flourishes.

Wow! In a quick look at the numbers, I see that six of the prelude-flourish combinations are fairly common, used 10 or more times. I read all the way across from A4, for example, and see that prelude A and flourish 4 (song A4) were used together 12 times. The other commonly used songs were B8, B9, C5, E11, and F12. The rarest four, however, are used only once or twice in the sample (A3, A6, E3, E5). The rare ones suggest that he has far more combinations that he could sing if I gave him time. In the 150 transitions from one song to the next, I find 87 different sequences (87 cells with a number in them), 50 of which are used only once. Clearly, the next song that he chooses to sing is highly unpredictable.

Before wallowing in the details of this matrix, I feel a need to distill the matrix to what I can keep track of as I listen, to a matrix with information only on the preludes. I total the tallies in key groups of cells and simplify the matrix considerably (table 3). Now I see better what I can easily hear, that two preludes of the same type never follow each other, as there are no entries on the darkly shaded diagonal. There is also great uncertainty in which prelude will come next, as each prelude is followed by three to five other preludes. I eye two of the empty cells, those showing that D and A never follow or precede each other. Is it a coincidence that A and D start with the same two notes and are therefore the most similar to each other? I bet not. I bet that this wood thrush's rule of "like never follows like" extends to situations like this, too, with "almost-alike never follows almost-alike."

I now study the two matrices for this second wood thrush and soon realize that although he has a larger repertoire than does the first male, his rules for singing are largely the same. *Never* sing the same combination of prelude and flourish back-to-back (darkly shaded diagonal in table 2). *Never* sing the same flourish back-to-back, even with different preludes (lightly shaded individual cells scattered throughout table 2). And perhaps because his repertoire of preludes is larger, his third rule becomes more absolute: *never* sing a song

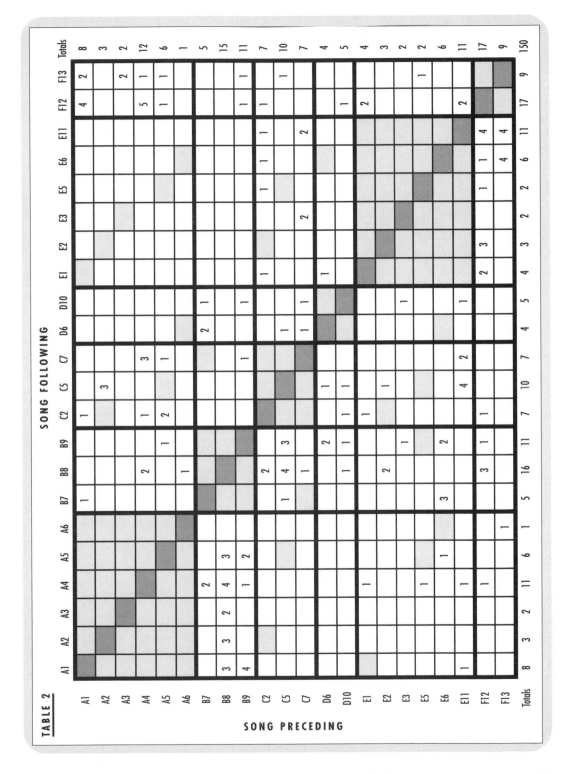

EXTREMES OF MALE SONG: Songbirds with Especially Beautiful Songs

with the same prelude back-to-back (shaded cells in table 3; or, in table 2, the darkly and lightly shaded blocks of cells along the diagonal). This male has four more preludes and five more flourishes than the first, resulting in an even more exhilarating performance.

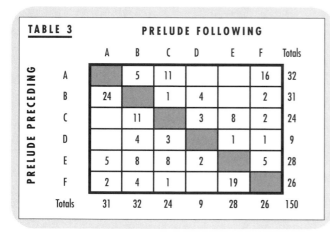

TABLE 3			PRELUDE FOLLOWING				
PRELUDE PRECEDING		A	B	C	D	E	F	Totals
	A		5	11			16	32
	B	24		1	4		2	31
	C		11		3	8	2	24
	D		4	3		1	1	9
	E	5	8	8	2		5	28
	F	2	4	1		19		26
	Totals	31	32	24	9	28	26	150

Increasingly I appreciate why these wood thrushes so captivate me and others who listen. Each song is a microcosm of musical contrasts, the bold, low-pitched whistled prelude so different from the softer, often high-pitched fluty flourish. Although this male has only 6 preludes and 13 flourishes, he recombines them, enhancing the contrasts, creating a large repertoire of unique songs. Adding to the overall effect is how he chooses to use his songs, with successive songs being especially different variations on the same theme, the next song unpredictable, as if he wants to keep every listener guessing as to what will come next.

In the bold prelude he whistles slowly enough and low enough that I can begin to hear his music, but it is as if he is just humoring me, just playing with me. He lets me barely grasp these simple preludes, but then delivers in the flourish some of the ultimate in avian music, all unappreciated by my unaided ear.

But I do have aids, and it is to these aids that I now turn. Using my Raven software (see Appendix II), I slow these songs down and lower them to a pitch where I can begin to fathom the details. I try half speed, then quarter speed, the preludes now so slowly given that I can linger on each note (track 69). What music I now hear!

Quarter speed doesn't do much for the flourishes, however. Slower, slower, there, at one-tenth speed I can hear the separate contributions of his two voice boxes. I need to see these two voices, too, so I use my computer software to stretch out some of the flourishes (figure 47). As I now look and listen to these flourishes at one-tenth speed, I find myself spellbound by the music, spellbound by the sight and sound of his two voices. I now clearly see in these flourishes that two voices prevail, as the wood thrush sings a duet with himself, both my ears and my eyes now astonished at his artistry.

The Singing Life of Birds

Not yet satisfied, I experiment with a flourish on my computer. Using Raven, I make three copies of flourish 2. In the first copy, I erase ("filter") the contributions of the upper voice and put this lower voice on the left track; in the second copy I erase the lower voice, putting the upper voice on the right track; the third copy I leave intact, just as the thrush sang it, the two voices playing together on both tracks. I now listen to these three versions as I watch the sonagram. First is the contribution from the lower voice in my left ear — a low buzz ending with a loud whistle sweeping upward, this phrase repeated several times. Next is the upper voice in my right ear — a high, shrill whistle with a little vibrato between the whistles, the vibrato probably in synchrony with that in the lower voice. Then I hear the maestro sing them together. I listen again and again, following along in the sonagram (figure 47). Absolutely extraordinary! Now that I have separated out his two voices and slowed him down ten times, I can both hear and see exactly what he is doing (track 70).

I try the same with flourish 4. In the sonagram, I see what look like two voices, but they look much alike, just on a different frequency, as each begins with a low note and then rises to a higher note. This sonagram requires a little study, as I want to be sure it is two separate voices, not just one voice with harmonics above it. Take any key on the piano, for example, such as middle A; the wire vibrates at the fundamental frequency of 440 Hz, but this vibrating wire also produces harmonics at exact multiples of 440 Hz, too, as at 880 Hz and 1,320 Hz. It is only one wire, only one "sound source," that produces these harmonically related sounds. In contrast, any two sounds that occur simultaneously and are not harmonically related must be from two different sound sources. For a bird, of course, these are his two voice boxes singing at the same time. So I quickly measure the frequency of these look-alike notes in flourish 4 — two voices, no doubt. The lower voice has its fundamental notes between 3.5 and 4.5 kHz, the harmonic between 7 and 9; the S-shaped notes of the second voice are between 5 and 6.5 kHz, perfectly sandwiched between the contributions of the lower voice. I now listen, the lower voice in my left ear and the upper voice in my right sounding alike but in a different key, and what astonishing harmony the two produce together (again, track 70).

Quick, flourish 5. Study the sonagram. The two voices are different here, the lower voice singing one down-slurred note for every four mini-sweeps from the upper voice. Listen. Again. Again. I've never heard anything like this.

Wow, flourish 7 looks even more remarkable. From his lower voice I see a low whistle at 3.8 kHz with a harmonic at 7.6 kHz ($3.8 \times 2 = 7.6$); after a brief pause, this voice resumes with a pulsing hum that, together with its upper harmonic, nicely frames the contribution of the upper voice. The upper voice initially sweeps boldly over the entire frequency spectrum and then holds on a whistle at 6 kHz for about a tenth of a second (a full second at the slow pace I'm going to listen); this voice then sweeps rapidly up and down, ending with a series of down-slurs at the rate of about 75 a second. For each bold downward sweep with his upper voice, he wavers his lower voice ever so slightly, the two voices now tightly coordinated as he finishes this flourish. I now listen at one-tenth speed . . . words fail me. No superlatives can do this thrush justice. I listen again . . . and look again, trying to imagine how this thrush controls his two voices boxes with such precision to produce such harmony.

Flourish 8 beckons. I first measure the frequency of the sounds in the sonagram, finding that the lower voice produces a bold whistle at 5 kHz, and it then continues after a brief pause with a fundamental centered on 4 kHz and a harmonic centered on 8 kHz. The upper voice is louder; it consists of a beautifully modulated whistle, beginning while the first voice whistles at 5 kHz, slowly (by thrush standards) sweeping up and then down, then resuming as a sine wave sweeping between 6 and 7 kHz. I listen, first to the lower voice, then to the upper voice, then to both, hearing the upper voice begin halfway through the prolonged whistle of the lower voice, the two voices then modulating in perfect synchrony for the remainder of the flourish.

One more, flourish 9. The artwork in the sonagram is superb (figure 47). How visually appealing is this tight coordination of two voice boxes. The lower voice has its fundamental between 3 and 4 kHz, a harmonic between 6 and 8 kHz; the fundamental of the upper voice is a continuous wave between 4 and 6 kHz, the harmonic faintly visible up above 8 kHz. I listen . . . again, and again, dumbfounded by the music I hear from this wood thrush.

I've been listening and looking piecemeal, one flourish at a time, but now I play all six one more time, feasting on the sights and sounds of these flourishes. Each time I hear and see them I am no less captivated than when I began. Questions abound. How does he do this? How does the brain control the neurons that in turn control the host of tiny muscles in the voice boxes to

Figure 47. The solo duets of this second wood thrush, showing how he uses his two voice boxes in six of his flourishes (track 70; only the first third of a second of each flourish is illustrated here). In each sonagram, the lower-pitched voice is labeled "1" and the higher-pitched voice labeled "2"; based on how other songbirds sing, voices 1 and 2 are most likely the left and the right voice boxes, respectively. Although most preludes use only a single voice at a given time, the flourishes typically use both voices simultaneously. See the text and CD for how to listen to these flourishes at one-tenth normal speed.

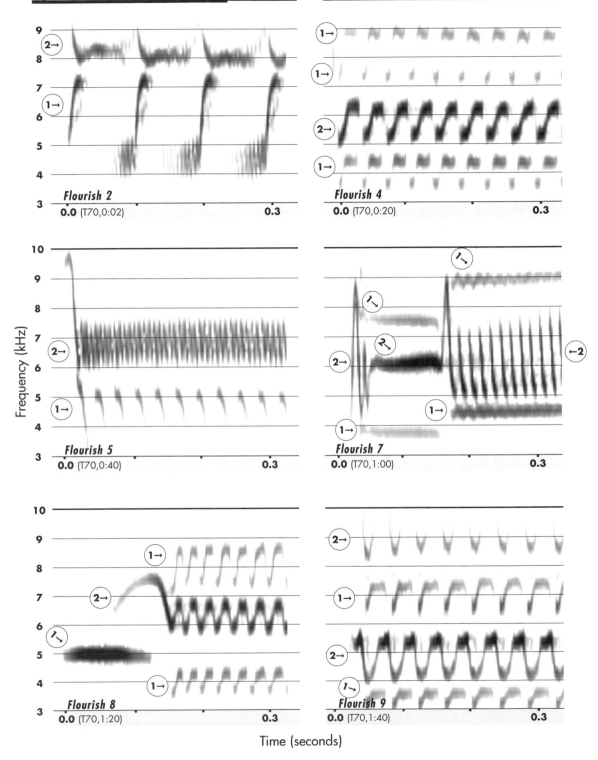

Frequency (kHz)

Time (seconds)

gate the air in just the right ways to produce something so exquisite? Who are you? I wonder. Why? Why are you? Why this kind of music? Why preludes with one kind of music, flourishes with another? I'm left with questions and a giddy sense of the unknown.

Back to earth, I think some more about those two voice boxes. In figure 47, I've labeled the lower voice 1 and the higher voice 2; it is likely that they're the left and right voice boxes, respectively, because in a number of songbirds it has now been shown that the left voice box specializes in low sounds, the right one in high sounds. That's the way it is with brown thrashers and northern cardinals, for example, and even for mockingbirds who mimic the cardinals. Ditto for gray catbirds, canaries, brown-headed cowbirds, and zebra finches. Why they're all "left low" and "right high" is unknown. Perhaps that's the scheme that the ancestral songbird worked out for some reason, and there's been no need to change it. Or perhaps there's something inherent in how songbirds produce songs that dictates this pattern.

No matter which voice is which, never will I hear a wood thrush singing in the same way again. I'll continue to grasp the whistled preludes, usually only one voice box operating at a time and at a low enough pitch for me to just barely appreciate. I'll know now that he's exercising all options in the flourishes, independently controlling the tension of the membranes in each of his two voice boxes, precisely gating the air through the passageways to vibrate the membranes so that the coordinated effort produces some of the most exquisite patterns imaginable for both eye and ear.

🐦

Two wood thrushes now singing back and forth, all morning long, all day long, first one, then the other, over and over, each on his own territory and each trying to impress the first female to arrive in the neighborhood. As I listen, I remember what I read about wood thrushes several years ago. They are apparently unlike all other songbirds that have been studied, because if neighbors have the same songs in their repertoires, they avoid answering each other with those identical songs. This conclusion was reached by playing various preludes to males and discovering that they avoided singing that particular prelude in their own next song. In other words, the singing wood thrush avoided "matching" the prelude broadcast from the loudspeaker. It would seem that the "back-to-back songs must be different" rule applies not only to a bird's own songs but also to those just heard from his neighbor as well. That's just the opposite of what other songbirds do, as males of most songbirds typically respond to each other with identical songs (as do marsh wrens, tufted titmice, northern cardinals). I find it difficult to believe that wood thrushes could be so different, but given what each male has told me so far about his own singing, I'm beginning to be convinced.

I now realize that I have the perfect opportunity to test this idea about how two singers interact. In these two countersinging males I can test whether the "back-to-back songs must be different" rule is extended to the neighbor's song. Only these two males are here, as no others have yet returned from migration, and they both sing A1 and A2. If one bird sings A1, I wonder, does the other avoid it in his next song? And the same for A2. But A2 is used far less frequently than A1, so I'm going to focus on A1.

Two days later, Sunday, I'm back, this time to record both males simultaneously. 4:40 A.M., rubber knee boots on, I wade partway into the pond so that I am roughly equidistant from where I expect the two to begin singing. On the tripod I mount my directional microphone (see "How to record birdsongs" in Appendix II), pointed south to capture the two-prelude male (male #1), and in my hand is the parabola, which I'll aim to the north to capture the six-prelude bird (male #2). The south male is recorded on the right track of my stereo recorder, the north male on the left track.

4:51 A.M., to the north he begins, awaking as do all wood thrushes, with a series of sharp *whit whit whit* notes, as if just a bit cranky, having emerged from the wrong side of the roost. Songs soon follow, the male to the south soon chiming in, too. At first the songs are barely audible over the din of spring peepers calling throughout the pond, and I kick and splash about in the water to quiet the peepers, to no avail. I continue recording, however, accepting that my recordings will not be the pristine ones I had hoped for, but will be good enough to study later, to determine exactly which songs are used when. On the first tape I record 45 minutes, then 45 minutes on another, and a final 30 minutes for good measure. Two hours of song from these two males, both of them ardently singing, as still no females have arrived.

To my computer I again go for the answers. Each song dances across my monitor, and I mark in my notes when each occurs. I choose to focus on the 50 minutes when the two birds were closest and therefore most likely to hear the details of the neighbor's songs. For these 50 minutes, I determine how many songs each male sings, how many are of the A1 variety, and exactly where in the record those A1 songs occur. I'm simply collecting numbers at this point, recalling what I once read, that "science is the art of collecting interesting numbers."

Having finished identifying all of the songs, I now tabulate the results. In these 50 minutes, male #2 sings 809 songs, 50 of which are A1. Male #1 pauses longer between songs, singing more slowly, only 548 songs, 76 of which are A1. Only six times during these 50 minutes did one male match the other, with one male singing A1 and the other following immediately. Using some relatively simple math, I calculate that those males would have matched each other twice as often if each male were simply ignoring the other and singing his own program. They seem to avoid matching each other.

The math is pretty simple, though it requires some concentrating, and the key is how often each male normally sings his A1 song. For each of the times that male #1 sings his A1 song, there is a 6.2 percent chance that the next song from male #2 will be the A1 (simply because 50 of male 2's 809 songs were A1, or 6.2 percent); so, after 76 A1 songs by male #1, I would expect by chance alone 76 × 6.2 percent = 4.7 immediate matches from male #2. The math for male #2 is similar. He sings 50 A1 songs, and it's a 13.9 percent chance that male #1's next song will be an A1 (because 76 of 548 songs from male #1 were A1, or 13.9 percent), so 50 × 13.9 percent = 7, which means that by chance alone male #1 would have sung A1 seven times immediately after male #2 sang A1. I add the two chance results together, and get twelve (4.7 + 7.0 is almost 12). By chance alone, then, if these two males ignore what the other has just sung, they would have matched each other twelve times in my recorded sample. My recordings have only six matches, however. It seems that they didn't just ignore each other, but that they also avoided singing the A1 song that the neighbor had just sung.

I'm amazed. I now realize that I need another few hours of recordings to be truly satisfied, but it looks as if my results agree with that earlier study. One thing is clear: these birds certainly don't try to match each other, or else I would have found far more than the 12 matches I had expected by chance. They don't avoid each other all of the time, either, or else I would have found zero matches. It wouldn't surprise me if these males have some complex rules by which they sing; perhaps most of the time they avoid matching each other, and sometimes they ignore each other, and sometimes, under some particular conditions, they match each other, but only when a strong message needs to be sent to the singer next door (as with song sparrows). I could record these males for many hours more and still not be able to disentangle these choices made in the mind of each wood thrush.

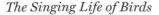

The Singing Life of Birds

This early spring frenzy with these two wood thrushes is only a prelude to our summer together. Throughout May and June they sing, both audible from my opened bedroom window. They are joined by other wood thrushes, too, another one claiming a territory on the southwest corner of the pond, and a fourth deeper into the woods to the north of the pond, northeast of our house. Each of the four thrushes has his unique combination of preludes, the voice of each bird easily identifiable. The two-prelude voice from the southeast corner of the pond continues all day long, too, revealing that he has failed to attract a mate. Perhaps it is his relatively small song repertoire that proves unimpressive to females, or maybe his slower singing rate, somehow revealing that he is young, or inexperienced, or inept in the ways of wood thrushes.

I hear sometimes, how in the heat of their territorial squabbles, the natural order of the songs breaks down. As each male becomes more agitated, I hear loud, low *bup bup bup* notes, one to seven of them, and the more agitated he becomes the faster he calls, and at increasingly higher pitches, too, sounding now more like *whit whit whit,* the same calls he awakes with in the morning. The *ee-oh-lay* preludes and the trilled flourishes are now given separately, and sometimes he abandons altogether the *ee-oh-lay* phrases and intersperses only the flourishes with loud *bup bup bup* notes. The range of expression that he can accomplish with his calls, his preludes, and his flourishes is impressive.

I have come to especially relish the evening routine, just as I cherish the evening performance of other thrushes and nightingale-thrushes that I have met throughout the New World. Winds die, and other songbirds prepare to roost, but the wood thrush now holds center stage. The male who owns our house typically perches about 5 yards up in a tree at the edge of the clearing where our house sits. With what seems like little effort, he sits erect, leisurely serenading all who will listen, the qualities of his ethereal *ee-oh-lay*s and trilled flourishes starkly contrasting with each other and with the silence of the evening.

Perhaps half an hour after sunset, he concludes his performance, flying deeper into the forest, a series of emphatic *whit whit whit* notes announcing that he is retiring for the day.

EPILOGUE

MAY 2, 2003. 6 A.M.

Time to get up. Tomorrow we leave for the big bike trip—David and I will drive to Virginia, then hop on our bikes and work our way from the Atlantic to the Pacific. It's the ultimate celebration of birdsong, listening to every chirp in our 4,500-mile route across the entire continent. So much to hear, but there's so much to do today to get ready . . . Wait! A wood thrush. He's the first of the year, arriving overnight. I lie back down, opening the window farther to hear him better. I begin my usual game. Pick out a prelude and listen for it to recur, and then another, and another, counting from the first to the next occurrence of each. All numbers converge on six. Six preludes. Six *familiar* preludes! Can it be? I sit up, pressing my ear to the screen. Listen to those flourishes, too — oh, so familiar, especially that double flourish that he occasionally sings. That's prelude F and flourishes 12 and 7 — I'd know them anywhere. I've never heard any other wood thrush do that. It must be! With those six preludes and the familiar flourishes, it must be Bird 2 from last year, because no two wood thrushes sing alike. He's made the trip to the tropics and returned here, to this very patch of New England woods that he claimed on May 3 last year. He's a day earlier this year.

I dress quickly, grab a recorder and microphone, and rush down to the pond. For 20 minutes he sings from the very same branch in the oak where I recorded him last year. Minutes later, his songs dance across my computer screen, and there is no doubt. I focus first on the preludes: there they are, E, F, B, A, C in the first five songs . . . and finally prelude D at the thirty-second song. They're all there. For good measure I scan 200 songs. Nope, just those six and no more. Now the flourishes: 11, 13, 8, 4, 5, 2, 7, 1, 12, 6, ten different flourishes in the first ten songs, and all the same as last year! Flourish 9 I find at the fourteenth song, flourish 10 at the thirty-second song. Where's flourish 3? I scan 50, 100, 150 songs . . . and there, at song 177, after 12 minutes of singing, is flourish 3. Yes, I see that unique combination, too, F12-7, the same as last year. All six preludes, all 13 flourishes, and even the unique F12-7 accounted for!

A world-traveler, a friend, he needs a name . . . Woody. I listened to Woody last summer as he phased out his singing; by mid-August he called *whit whit whit* when he awoke and when he went to roost. He was done singing for the year. He fell silent in early September; I took that to mean that he was headed south, and I wished him well. Little did I know that we would meet again. He took his songs with him, secured in his memory, and eight months later Woody returned with pinpoint accuracy to his home of the year before, bringing his songs back with him. With the window in my study open, I listen to him, a smile creeping over my face, a simple celebration of all that he is.

The Hermit Thrush

Widely hailed as the most gifted songster in all of
North America, the inspiration of countless poets
— "the grand climax of all bird music . . . our gifted Thrush sings . . . of the glory of life, . . . of the
joy of heaven."

Perhaps John Burroughs said it best:
"Mounting toward the upland again, I pause
reverently as the hush and stillness of twilight
come upon the woods. It is the sweetest, ripest
hour of the day. And as the hermit's evening
hymn goes up from the deep solitude below
me, I experience that serene exaltation of sen-
timent of which music, literature, and religion
are but faint types and symbols."

It was as if Burroughs had been with us on
that late July evening in 1997. My son David was
about to head cross-country to begin his freshman
year in college. Rolf, his Norwegian "brother" and
my "son" (an exchange student who had joined our
family for a year), had just returned from a summer
exploring the Arctic by canoe. Late that afternoon we had
climbed Monadnock Mountain in southern New Hampshire.
We then descended the western flank, where we would linger on a rock ledge
to prepare our dinner. What we planned was a feast: a gourmet meal shared
with each other at sunset, seasoned with hermit thrush songs. In the hush of
that July evening, when other birds had stopped singing for the year, first one
hermit sang, then another, and another, until the entire mountainside flamed
with the glow of the sun and the hermits' songs.

Years later, I can close my eyes and instantly recreate that Monadnock
scene, complete with smells, tastes, indeed all sensations, song after song playing in my mind. I hear a rich, haunting melody, what has come to be accepted as *Ooooooooh, holy holy, ah, purity purity, eeh, sweetly sweetly*. The *Ooooooooh*
is a pure whistle a little over a quarter-second long. Then come one or two
brief but noticeable whistles *(holy holy)*, almost always higher pitched than the
Ooooooooh, each *holy* cascading down the scale. Last are the down-slurred, ventriloquial, organlike flourishes *(ah, purity purity, eeh, sweetly sweetly)*. I say it:

HERMIT
THRUSH

Oooooooh, holy holy, ah, purity purity, eeh, sweetly sweetly, lingering on the introductory *Oooooooh* whistle, then distinctly saying *holy holy* before rushing through the *ah, purity purity, eeh, sweetly sweetly.* There it is, a two-second slice of heaven.

I find it difficult to understand why no one has studied the songs of this bird. Why has no one tried to analyze exactly what they sing, or how many different songs each male has, or how a male chooses his next song to create such a striking performance? Why have we not progressed beyond *Oooooooh, holy holy, ah, purity purity, eeh, sweetly sweetly?* It is as if these songs were sacred, unapproachable.

It was the perfect project just waiting for Jim Rivers, an undergraduate student who was seeking an honors thesis. To Arizona he went, recording birds in the Coconino and Apache-Sitgreaves National Forests, then returning to New England to record closer to home.

What did he find? Each male has 6 to 12 different songs in Arizona, 9 to 10 in New England. Successive songs from a male are always different, but some males in Arizona sang their songs in a highly predictable order, such as A B C D E F G H I A B C D E F G H I, over and over. Neighboring males have dissimilar songs, which means that they don't learn them from each other (though they could learn them someplace else and then shuffle themselves and their songs over the landscape). The introductory whistle, what I have come to think of as the prelude, is typically lower-pitched than the terminal flourish, but the whistle in New England is lower than in Arizona, so the overall song feels as if it rises more in New England than in Arizona. These are the known facts, as summarized from Jim's paper in the summer 2000 issue of the *Journal of Field Ornithology.*

3:30 A.M. I'm out the door, knowing where to find him at dawn, knowing that I must hear him firsthand to try to understand him better. I walk the quarter mile to the end of the street, crossing Pelham Road and heading into the Amethyst Brook Conservation Area. By flashlight I hike the Robert Frost trail up to the ridge, and after 40 easy minutes I stand on the rocky ledges of Mount Orient. The Holyoke Mountain Range is silhouetted against the southern sky, the lights of the Connecticut River valley spreading out to the right. To the left, above the Pelham hills, the eastern sky begins to brighten. The Swan flies overhead to the southwest, toward the Eagle. I think that the hermit thrush deserves a constellation, too—someday I'll reconfigure the constellations so they better reflect what I see and hear in the heavens. For now, though, I wait, knowing that it won't be long, knowing that for some reason he, too, favors perching here to begin his day.

Zhreeee . . . zhreeee, come the calls with a rising inflection, almost towhee-like, and I know he's awake, a good hour before the sun will rise. Songs soon follow. I start the tape recorder, drop the headphones to my ears, and aim my parabolic microphone at him. Perched atop my rocky lookout, I have a commanding view of his favorite singing perches.

For 30 minutes I record, a song almost every three seconds, catching each the best I can with the parabola (track 71, figure 48). I track him in my mind, too, trying to crack his song repertoire, trying to identify as many of his 9 or 10 different songs as I can. My first handle on him is the song that seems most distinctive, the one with a whistle at least four octaves above middle C, much higher-pitched than the others. I listen for it again, and again, and begin counting after I hear it, 6 songs to the next repetition, then 4, then 5, then 5 again. Something is wrong, I realize. I expected to count to 9 or 10 different songs before hearing him repeat any particular one, because that's how large I expect his repertoire to be. Does this male have a repertoire that is about half the normal size? Or does he have an especially favorite song?

Both are unlikely, I reason, and as I listen more I realize my mistake. I have been confusing two of his songs. The whistled prelude sounds the same, as does the brief "*holy*" that follows. It is the remaining flourish that differs. In one, which I call A, I hear three distinctive, evenly spaced notes, like *sweet sweet sweet*. "*Oooooooh holy sweet sweet sweet,*" a simple song, so high-pitched it's hard for me to appreciate the details. He's consistent, over and over, every 8 to 10 songs. The terminal flourish on the other song always consists of two phrases, each richer and sounding more complex than the first song, a little lower-pitched in overall effect (later identified as song F, with both A and F illustrated in figure 48). I now feel this difference, noting that each of these songs occurs every 8 to 10 songs, and that they alternate in the delivery, one or the other of them occurring every 4 or 5 songs.

I pick out another song and listen for it. The whistled prelude is low, perhaps only two octaves above middle C. To begin his flourish, he reaches up another octave, with three or four notes cascading down to the pitch of the prelude, this phrase then repeated several times, successive renditions of the medley seeming to be both fainter and lower in pitch (E in figure 48). What an extraordinary effect—here, in the pitch range that I can best appreciate, is the inspiration of the poets. I count, too, wanting to hear how often he uses

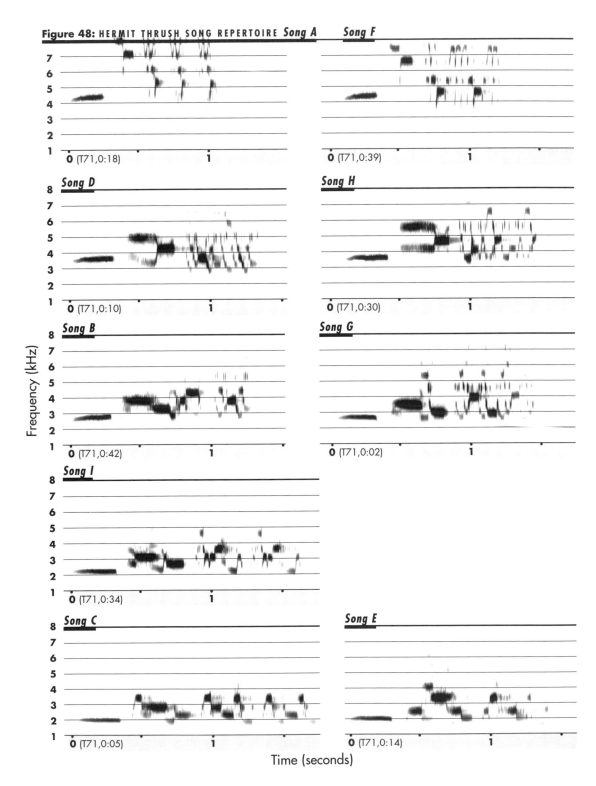

Figure 48: HERMIT THRUSH SONG REPERTOIRE *Song A*   *Song F*

Song D   Song H

Song B   Song G

Song I

Song C   Song E

Frequency (kHz)

Time (seconds)

(T71,0:18)   (T71,0:39)
(T71,0:10)   (T71,0:30)
(T71,0:42)   (T71,0:02)
(T71,0:34)
(T71,0:05)   (T71,0:14)

this song and wanting to make sure I am not confusing two highly similar songs: 6, 9, 7, 10, 9, 5, 12, in a little over three minutes. The middle value is 9, meaning this song occurs on average every 9 songs, which is about right for a male who's expected to have 9 or 10 songs.

Three loops now play in my head. As one of these three songs passes, roughly every 30 seconds and every 7 to 11 songs, I reset that loop and then listen for the other two. As each plays, I see in my mind the stick figure that I hear, and that loop resets.

I hear other songs, too, and start those loops, but know that my time is about up. I finish 30 minutes on one cassette tape, then start another, getting perhaps only 10 minutes more before he takes a lengthy pause. He now sings about 12 songs a minute, too, slower than the 18 to 20 he sang earlier. All this is only the beginning, I tell myself, as I have captured him on tape and will take him home with me where I'll get to know him better.

Back home I start my computer (see "How to see birdsongs" in Appendix II) and soon relive this dawn, over and over. I search for that A song and now see what I had heard back on Mount Orient (figure 48). The next song he delivers I label B, then C. It seems almost sacrilegious, but I must know, and I continue lettering each of the distinctive songs until I have nine: A B C D E F G H I. The repertoire is 9, typical of New England birds, as Jim had shown in his thesis. To make sure, I graph and identify just a little over 150 of his songs, in two long sequences.

SEQUENCE 1:

DCFGHIBEDIGCDFGHIABCDEFGCHIABEGCDEFGCHIBAGED-
CFGEHIABCDEFGHIBCAGDEFBCHIAGEFG (pause)

SEQUENCE 2:

CFBEDCAGHIFBEDAGCHIFBEAGDCFBEHIAGCDEFGCHIABED-
CFGEHIABCDEFGHIABHEFGCDEABCFGEHI (pause)

Staring now at the sequence of letters before me, I can't help but feel I've destroyed the essence of the hermit. What have I done, reducing his ethereal music to a series of black letters on a white page? Ashes, I think, but from ashes things grow, too. I begin to explore what is there.

I first try a transition matrix, as I did with the wood thrush, to try to determine if he delivers his 9 songs in any favorite sequences (table 4). In the

Figure 48. My hermit thrush has a repertoire of nine different songs. See how each begins with a whistled prelude followed by a flourish that is mostly higher in frequency. As I learned each particular song, I assigned it a letter; the songs have been arranged in this figure, however, so that songs with whistled preludes on the same frequency are in the same row.

row and column headings I write the letters designating his 9 songs. Into the 81 cells of the table I now tally the numbers that show how many times A was followed by B, B was followed by C, and so on, until I have tallied 150 sequences.

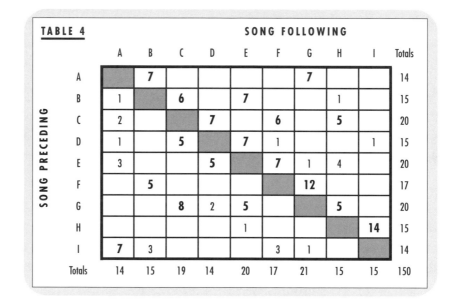

TABLE 4					SONG FOLLOWING					
	A	B	C	D	E	F	G	H	I	Totals
A		7					7			14
B	1		6		7			1		15
C	2			7		6		5		20
D	1		5		7	1			1	15
E	3			5		7	1	4		20
F		5					12			17
G			8	2	5			5		20
H					1				14	15
I	7	3				3	1			14
Totals	14	15	19	14	20	17	21	15	15	150

(SONG PRECEDING, rows A–I)

Totaling rows and columns, making sure that both add to 150 (one way to check for errors in my entries), I now begin to see the overall picture. The totals tell me that he has no really favorite songs, as he uses each 14 to 20 times (see row totals). To emphasize that he never repeats himself, I can't resist shading the diagonal cells: an A is *never* followed by another A, or B by B, and so on.

Next I study the sequences he does use. I boldface and enlarge the numbers for the 18 that he favors, the sequences that occur five or more times in the sample of 150. The H → I sequence is the most predictable, occurring 14 out of 15 possible times when he sings an H (93 percent of the time). Also highly predictable is F → G (12 out of 17 times, 71 percent), but with none of the other songs can one predict with greater than 50 percent probability which song will come next. This transition matrix suggests that one favored route through his repertoire of 9 songs is indicated by the cells just above the diagonal: A → B → C → D → E → F → G → H → I → A. But I check the raw sequences and see that he actually does that complete A → I sequence only twice. There must be far more to his singing than this crude matrix reveals.

I see now how the matrix is misleading in another way. From the matrix,

I can see that C → D and D → C are both favored sequences, so I'd expect him at times to sing C → D → C or D → C → D, just as I'd expect D → E → D or E → D → E. But *never* does he sing those sequences. It's clear to me now that this matrix tells me about pairs of songs and how often they're associated, but to predict the next song he will sing I need to know the three or four that have preceded it, not just one.

I struggle to understand what he is doing. Let me try a flow diagram, I reason (figure 49). In a circle, I write the nine letters representing his repertoire, starting with A at the top and sweeping around the clock. Now I draw the arrows for his favored transitions and start to follow him as he sings. From A he can go to either B or G. If he goes to B, he could sing the sequence along

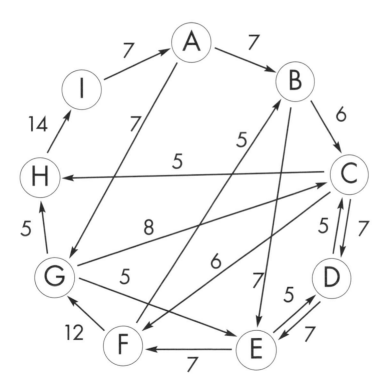

Figure 49. How my hermit thrush moves through his song repertoire is revealed in this flow diagram. After singing song A, for example, his most common choices are B (seven times) and G (also seven times). From B he has two favored directions in which to go (to C or to E), from C he has three (D, F, and H), and so on.

the outside of the circle, A → B → C → D → E → F → G → H → I. But if from A he goes to G, he can take a reverse route, such as A → G → E → D → C.

Why does he favor some sequences and avoid others? Why are C → D and D → C equally good in his mind, but never in succession? I think back to my first experience with him at Mount Orient: Is it only a coincidence that the two high-pitched songs (now labeled A and F) that I initially confused never occur back-to-back (see transition matrix)? I wonder. If he's trying to create a highly contrasting series of songs, so that successive songs are especially different, then he would space the A and F songs out in his performance, which is exactly what he does.

Could this be a general rule by which he sings, that he chooses the next song so that it is especially different from the one he just sang? Perhaps his performance is based on some rule of contrasts, such that not only are successive songs never the same, but they are *especially different* from each other. I can answer that question by studying the pitch of successive songs, and then determining if they are more different than they would be if he simply chose his next song at random. For song A, I measure the frequency of the whistle at 4,580 Hz, for B 2,780 Hz, through to song I at 2,300 Hz. I then subtract all the numbers from each other, to calculate the pitch change that would occur between each pair of songs. I can now compare the pitch changes in all of these possible sequences to those that he actually uses.

The numbers astound me. When the next song has a higher-pitched whistle than the one before, he raises the frequency on average by 1,780 Hz. If he had chosen the next song by chance alone, the difference would have been only 820 Hz. It's the same story for when he lowers the frequency. If he had chosen his next song at random, he would have dropped 960 Hz, but his songs drop 1,660 Hz. These simple numbers reveal that he does not choose his next song at random when he establishes his favored sequences, but rather that he follows some rule so that the introductory whistle of the next song is especially different from the one he has just sung.

I need to *see* this pattern, and I sketch figure after figure to try to capture what I think he is doing. After considerable fussing, I finally settle on a graph that I think shows what I hear (figure 50). Along the bottom of the graph are the positions for the 75 songs in the first sequence that I documented (see above). On the vertical I plot each song by its whistle frequency, with song C plotted at 2.0 kHz, E at 2.1, and so on, with A all the way up at 4.6 kHz. I can scan across the graph and see that song C, for example, occurs 10 times, fairly well spaced out at positions 2, 12, 20, 25, 32, 37, 45, 53, 61, and 68. Last, I connect successive songs in the 75-song sequence with a line, so that I can see more easily which songs follow which.

Many stories now jump out at me from this graph. The most noticeable pattern is the sawtooth nature of his singing, as first he goes down, then up, then down, then up, then down in frequency, on and on. And the lines between successive songs are especially long, meaning that his pitch change from one song to the next is considerable.

It is in the details of this sawtooth that I delight. I look first at the most similar pairs of songs: A and F at about 4,500 Hz, D and H at 3,700 Hz, B and G about 2,600 Hz, and C and E about 2,000 Hz. *Never* does he sing any of these especially similar songs back-to-back, as if to do so would violate one of his most important rules, that successive songs be especially different. In fact, from any given song I can see in this graph that he almost always skips over the next two most similar songs, so that the whistle of his next song is especially high or especially low in pitch compared to the one he just sang.

I see, too, that the two songs most similar to each other seem to be used interchangeably, as if there's nothing special about the song itself, but rather where it is located on the pitch spectrum. I look back at the transition matrix (table 4), and only now do I see this same pattern there, too. The two highest-frequency songs A and F, for example, can be followed by either B or G, the pair of songs in the mid-frequency range. B and G in turn are routinely followed by either C or E, the two lowest songs, which in turn routinely rise to either D or H, the pair of songs at the higher frequency. (Interestingly, of that pair, only D then drops to C or E, as H is used to incorporate lonely song I into the scheme, which in turn then tends to take the cycle back to either A or F.)

Just look at the jagged nature of the graph. It looks that way because almost always when he rises to sing the four highest-pitched songs (D, H, F, or A), he then immediately drops back down again. And when he drops to sing any one of the three lowest-pitched songs (C, E, or I), he *always* rises again. I study the 150 pitch changes in the entire sample some more and determine whether pitch changes in successive songs go up or down. Only 4 times do I find two up's in a row (an up-up sequence), 22 times a down-down, and 98 of the sequences are either up-down or down-up. Every time the whistle rises on two successive songs, he *always* rises to sing one of his two especially high-pitched whistles (song A or F; for example, C → D → F, songs 12 to 14 in figure 50). And every time the whistle descends twice in a row, he is *always* descending from one of these two high songs (for example, A → B → C, songs 18 to 20 in figure 50). When those two high-pitched songs aren't involved, he always alternates raising and lowering the pitch of successive whistles. *Always.*

All this feels so abstract. I need to feel what this thrush is doing, so I look again at figure 48. The songs there are arranged so that the pair of songs with the highest-pitched prelude is at the top (A, F), the lowest pair at the bottom (C, E), and others in between. I place my finger on song A and then have my fingers "sing" the sequence A B C D E F G H I, physically pointing to each song as I sing it. Yes, that helps. I choose another of his song sequences, A G D C F B E H I, and "sing" that — yes, I feel the up-down-up nature of what he is singing and I feel how my fingers leap from one song to the next, as there are no small steps from one frequency level to the next. I next look at his favored sequences in figure 49 and "sing" those with my fingers. From A my fingers in figure 48 spring to B and G, the paired songs at mid-frequency; from B my fingers spring to C and E, the lowest pair of songs; from C my fingers leap to D, H, and F. Wow! This thrush not only leaps from one pitch to another, but now I also feel how the two songs with the whistled preludes at any given frequency are equally viable options (B and G, C and E, D and H in these examples). And never do I move horizontally in this figure, as *never* does he sing A and F back to back, or B and G, or C and E, or D and H.

What do I make of all this? I'm not sure, as I've never encountered such striking rules like this among singing birds. In another thrush, the varied thrush of the Northwest, my friend Carl Whitney was convinced that successive songs were especially different, too, but this hermit thrush is a master at this game of contrasts. What is he thinking, or what guides his behavior? I don't know, but whatever it is, the result is an exquisite performance of contrasts in whistle pitches. They constantly rise and fall, up-down-up-down-up-down-up-down, unless he reaches for the very highest song, and then back-to-back rises or falls are allowed, perhaps because with the extreme pitch

Figure 50. The best window on the mind of my hermit thrush is revealed here, showing how he chooses successive songs that are especially different. From left to right is a sequence of 75 songs, and on the vertical axis can be read the frequency of the whistled prelude for each of those 75 songs. Begin with the leftmost song (read across to the far right and see that this is song D), then drop down to song C, then all the way up to F, down to G, up to H, and so on. As you sing your way across this graph from left to right, your eyes and fingers leap from one song to the next, following lines that are far longer than they would be if the next song were simply chosen at random. Never are successive songs the same; *never*, in fact, are successive songs even similar, as C and E never follow each other, nor do B and G, nor D and H, nor A and F. See the text for a detailed explanation.

HOW THE HERMIT THRUSH LEAPS FROM ONE SONG TO THE NEXT

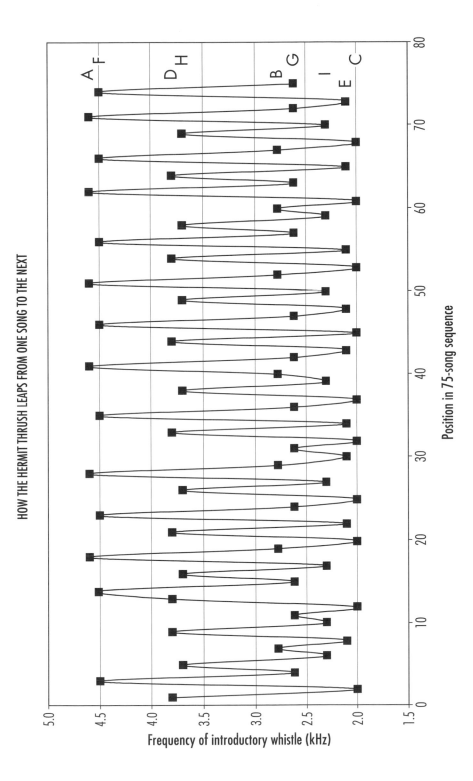

Frequency of introductory whistle (kHz)

Position in 75-song sequence

changes the successive songs can still be especially different as he works the entire scale.

I now listen to my 30-minute tape again and hear what apparently no one has ever described before. Briefly memorizing the pitch of the first whistle, I listen for the second. Clearly down. Memorize, then up. The pattern continues, down, up, down, up, down, up, down, as he alternately raises and lowers the pitch of his introductory whistles. As he spans the entire scale, I hear an occasional "up, way up" and a more frequent "down, way down," and those brief up-up or down-down runs always involve one of the two highest songs and one of the three lowest songs.

I'm convinced that I've just begun to understand how this hermit sings. How I wish I could get a handle on the flourishes that follow the whistle. What is he doing there? Unfortunately, all of the whirling and twirling there is far too complex for me to characterize. I slow the flourishes down on my computer, hoping to grasp them better, but each element feels so dainty and indistinct, each sliding into the next element in a cascading effect, that I don't feel I gain much. I can say that the pitch always rises from the whistle to the flourish, but that's about all—though it wouldn't surprise me if he follows other rules there that enhance his performance, perhaps in some way contrasting the pitch of the whistle with that of the flourish.

Just a few small insights lead to many more questions. Is this male unique among all hermit thrushes? I bet not. From Jim's thesis I know that neighboring hermits have different songs, but do they follow the same kinds of rules, each with his own unique repertoire? In the first hermits back next year, I'll be listening for this pattern, so easily heard. I'll record a few birds, too, checking the details of their songs on my computer. And I wonder how two neighboring hermit thrushes interact when they sing. Does what one has just sung influence what his neighbor chooses next, as it seems to in the wood thrush? Are successive songs of countersinging neighbors especially different, too?

Why, I puzzle again, is this hermit, this "swamp angel," so little studied? It's a common bird in North America, found in surprising places all over the continent. From Nova Scotia to Manitoba and down the Appalachian chain, the mixed forest of northern hardwoods and conifers rings with hermits. The hermit also sings in pine barrens from Cape Cod to New Jersey, and to the west in the aspen parklands from Manitoba across Saskatchewan to Alberta. The hermit also thrives in the high mountain conifers from British Columbia down to the Mexican border, as well as the lowland rain forests along the northwest Pacific coast. So many places to go and listen. Do they follow the same rules everywhere? Perhaps other rules will be discovered, rules that are simple to see in a few minutes of tape viewed on a home computer. Once the word on these hermits is out, the world will flock to their haunts, to hear them, to record them, to marvel at their music. How will anyone be able to resist?

🐦

Which was the better performance, I wonder, the sunset at Monadnock or the sunrise at Orient? I can't decide. The dawn performance is longer, as the hermit is one of the first birds to sing in the morning, beginning almost an hour before sunrise. Does he sing with more brilliance at dawn, as some have thought? Did Thoreau listen in the morning, when the hermit's song reminded him of the highest principles of freedom?

All of the other birds are singing at dawn, too, and at dusk the hermit often sings alone, until a half hour after sunset, a solo performance in the hushed, gathering twilight. It's as if he savors each song himself, proclaiming some loudly with bill opened wide, just barely whispering others from his closed bill. He seems to sing his own tune, ignoring other males around, as if a little solitary performance before going to roost were the proper way to end the day. Perhaps he sings with more tenderness at dusk, and it was then that Whitman heard him, as the songs expressed to him the grief he felt at the loss of Lincoln. Maybe there is something very different about dawn and dusk singing, but, then, it could just be me, too, and the mood I'm in at sunrise and sunset. I wonder. I must go listen some more.

Music to Our Ears

Birdsong *is* music to my ears. With that truism in mind, I read with delight "The Music of Nature and the Nature of Music," a January 2001 article in the prestigious American journal *Science*. The authors are well-known experts in music or biology, and after showing how birdsong and human music are similar in a number of ways, their concluding speculation seems inevitable: Perhaps "there is a universal music awaiting discovery," universal because the music of birds and humans (and whales) has its roots in the brains of our common ancestors, the reptiles.

With my heart I say "right on," but I read the article again, and again, my head now leading. As the always-skeptical scientist, I must dissect every one of those perceived similarities between birdsong and human music, and then see if head and heart converge.

"Some birds pitch their songs to the same scale as Western music . . . notes in the song of the wood thrush . . . are pitched such that they follow our musical scale very accurately," says the *Science* article. The authors refer to a 1956 article by Donald Borror, a pioneer in describing birdsong. I know that article, and I pull a reprint of it from my shelf, resonating especially with the title: "Vocal Gymnastics in Wood Thrush Songs." Borror measures the frequency of various notes in the thrush's song and then decides which notes on our human scale are most similar, as when he says that "notes . . . are pitched at C, A, and F sharp in the top octave of the piano range." He speaks in musical terms, describing the frequency range of the song as "1825–4025 cycles per second . . . from the third A sharp above middle C to the fourth C above middle C . . . or a range of about 14 musical intervals." He concludes that "Many notes . . . are so pitched that they follow our musical scale very accurately, thus giving a musical character to the song." My heart says "yes," because I hear the beauty in the wood thrush preludes. He doesn't take small steps from one note to the next, as from C to C-sharp; instead, he leaps from note to note, as from D up to A and then down to C-sharp, thereby creating more interesting intervals that are pleasing to my ears. My head is troubled about these notes matching our musical scales, however, as I realize that any randomly chosen tones will be near to a tone on our musical scale. The thrush isn't really *using* the Western music scale, but we can match its notes, like *any* note produced by *any* means, to notes used in Western scales. That's a subtle but important distinction to make.

I read on: "the hermit thrush [sings] . . . in the pentatonic scale (which consists of five different tones within the octave)." In the university library, I track down the original article on this thrush, in a 1951 issue of the *Auk*. The author listened to a bird with five different songs, which she identified by the pitch of the opening whistle: B, D, F, G sharp, and A sharp. By ear she "found the pitch and tone relationships satisfactory" within and among songs. Song B "is on the whole *major,* or *cheering* in its effect upon the listener. Songs F and G sharp, on the other hand, produce upon the hearer nothing but a *sad* or *minor* effect. . . . In the Hermit's songs are included a majority of the intervals used by human musicians: diminished second, major second, minor third, major third, major fourth, diminished fifth, major fifth, major sixth, and minor seventh." What this author has done is to match each of the hermit's whistled notes to notes that we have named and ordered into musical scales.

That's a fun exercise, but it remains important to realize that one could do this with any series of notes and conclude that the intervals are also found in our music.

I read on, equally troubled by some of the other statements in the *Science* article. "The canyon wren sings in the chromatic scale (which divides the octave into 12 semitones)." That's the keyboard that I know on the piano, 12 black or white keys over an octave, or one doubling of frequency, as from the 440 Hz of middle A to the 880 Hz of the A above. But has anyone bothered to measure the actual frequencies within a song of this wren? Does anyone realize that each individual has a number of different songs, so they should all be measured before one declares the scale in which this wren sings (track 72, figure 51)? I don't think so. I want these songs measured, to test in a rigorous way whether they match the claim about the chromatic scale. When this kind of tough-minded approach was taken with the white-throated sparrow, whose songs are typically a series of whistles on two pitches, the authors debunked previous claims about how similar these sparrow songs were to human music.

I love the *Science* article comparison between a modern-day orchestra and a chorus of birds: "The ambient sound of an environment mimics a modern-day orchestra: the voice of each creature has its own frequency, amplitude, timbre, and duration, and occupies a unique niche among the other musicians . . . This 'animal orchestra' or biophony represents a unique sound grouping for any given biome and sends a clear acoustical message." But I then recall my summer at Hart & Cooley Manufacturing Company in Holland, Michigan, where a room full of noisy metal presses stamped sheet metal into furnace ducts; there were all types of presses making a great variety of the noisiest sounds imaginable. Using the *Science* article definition, those machines, too, were an orchestra.

The *Science* article also points out that both learned birdsongs and our human music are cultural traditions, and they are both passed from one generation to the next in the same three ways. Parents can "teach" their offspring (vertical transmission of the tradition), nonparental adults can teach the next generation (oblique transmission), or peers can teach each other (horizontal transmission). But those are the only ways that any tradition can be passed, whether the tradition be birdsong, human music, or the art of sand sculpture.

My unease is reinforced in a telephone call. I mention to one of the authors that the whistles of the three-wattled bellbirds I study have dropped between 1974 and 2000, from 5,500 Hz to 3,700 Hz. That's an interval of a perfect fifth, I'm told, as 5,500 is almost exactly 1.5 × 3,700. But wait, I say.

Every year the whistle drops another 50 to 70 Hz, so inevitably it would pass not only this perfect fifth interval but all kinds of other intervals as well. And besides, for any particular interval to be meaningful, it would have to be sung by the same bird, either in the same or successive years, not by birds a quarter century apart. For this bellbird example and for the others that the authors offer, I can't help thinking of the maxim "I wouldn't have seen it if I hadn't believed it."

By now I am saddened, thinking that my birdsongs do not measure up. I'm the humbug, the dull scientist, the skeptic able to douse any parade. But I *know* these songs measure up, and the heart screams it. These birdsongs are as musical to me as are the best of human compositions, and far better than many. So what is it about them that I find so attractive? Why could I listen for hours on end to an avian orchestra, far longer than to a human one?

Perhaps it's some of the simple effects in birdsong, effects that are, of course, also found in human music. There's the accelerando, the bouncing ball song of the field sparrow; or the ritardando, such as the gradual slowing of the canyon wren's song. There are crescendos and diminuendos, songs that become increasingly louder and those that fade away. A melody can be retained with a change of key, such as with the *hey-sweetie* song of the black-capped chickadee; as the song is transposed up or down in frequency, the ratio of the frequency for the *hey* and the *sweetie* remain the same.

Consider themes and variations. I think of the opening of Beethoven's Fifth, and how the rhythm of those four notes recurs throughout the symphony. I think, too, of Bachman's sparrows, a perfect example of a theme varied in what seems endless ways during a performance. The theme is a sustained note followed by a trill, and what a delightful variety of variations occur. The sustained note can be a pure whistle or buzzy, and the opening note of successive songs can go up or down in pitch, or remain the same. The pitch of trills can be higher than, lower than, or about the same as the sustained note; the trill can be musical or noisy, in one part or two, the pitch of the two parts varying relative to each other, too. And the same song can be repeated once, twice, or not at all before going on to another. The many variations on

Figure 51. No visit to canyon country in the West is complete without the songs of the canyon wren (track 72). See and hear the whistled notes cascade down the scale. The four different songs illustrated here are no doubt only a small part of this male's song repertoire.

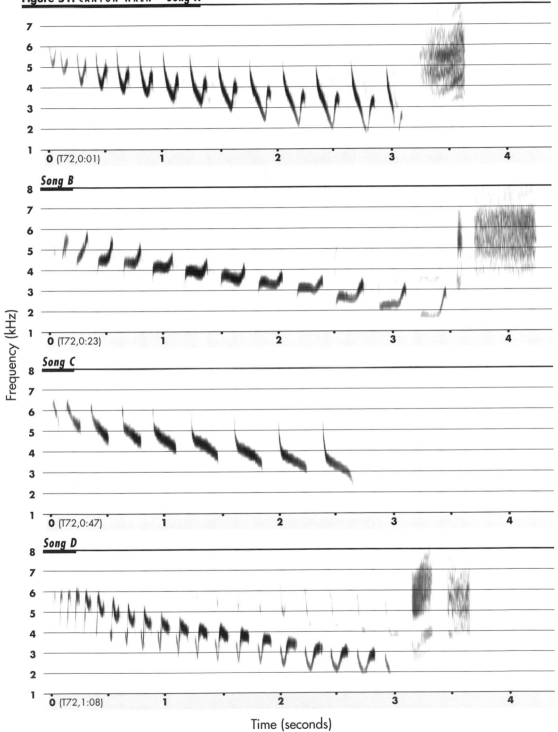

Figure 51: CANYON WREN *Song A*

Song B

Song C

Song D

Time (seconds)

this single theme and how it is delivered undoubtedly make the Bachman's sparrow one of the most revered singers in North America.

In fact, every songster could be said to have a basic theme. It is the theme by which we identify an individual as a member of a particular species, the theme being the constant features of the song that help to distinguish the songs of one species from those of another. The hermit thrush's theme is a sustained whistle followed by a flourish, and each male has 9 or 10 of those variations; the brown thrasher's theme is to sing in couplets, of which he has 2,000 or more variations.

I think of creativity, or the ability to improvise different tunes, and the range of this ability among birds. Eastern phoebes are limited to uttering the songs encoded in their genes, just as, incidentally, are chimpanzees, other apes, and monkeys, our closest living relatives. In marked contrast, some songbirds are enormously creative, this creativity being the essence of human music, too. A young sedge wren improvises hundreds of his songs, as does a young gray catbird. This type of creativity may continue into adulthood for some other species, such as northern mockingbirds.

There's another element of creativity, too, beyond the songs that the bird has acquired in its lifetime: how the songs are arranged during a performance. Just what will he sing next, I wonder, as I listen to a wood thrush? I know it's going to be different, but that's all I can know until he actually sings it. And the sage thrasher: the song can be sustained over a minute at a time, and the pace is extraordinary, exhilarating even, almost every half-second the bird choosing which of his hundreds of possibilities he will sing next. No one, perhaps not even the singer himself, can guess more than a half-second ahead as to what will follow. I delight in the unpredictability of the eastern phoebe's simple songs, too, not knowing whether the *fee-bee* or the *fee-b-be-be* will come next, or how soon it will come, as the rhythm changes depending on which song it will be; equally enjoyable is the simple *hey-sweetie* of the black-capped chickadee, as I cannot know if the next song will be on the same pitch or another.

There's the group effect, too. A bird does not sing in isolation, but in a community of singers, especially at dawn. As the tufted titmouse sings, what is he thinking as he listens to his neighbors, and when will he switch to his next song? Just listen to the magic of western marsh wrens as neighboring males match each other song for song. It's perhaps no coincidence that these kinds of "call-response" patterns also occur in human music.

Birds seem to appreciate variety and monotony in much the same way that I do, as suggested by the fact that the more continuous singers have more variations. Where, for example, is the songbird that sings as continuously as does a sage thrasher or brown thrasher or catbird or mockingbird and has just one song to sing? The general rule seems to be that the faster the pace of singing, the more variety must be presented, as if listeners (and maybe singers) would get bored with the monotony of a simple song repeated so frequently. This trend holds not only among species but also within species, as each individual seems to follow this rule, too. When singing at a leisurely pace, for example, the sedge wren sings one of its songs many times over; but get him excited and the singing rate picks up, and invariably the next song will then be different.

Monotony is also avoided by enhancing contrasts between successive songs. The wood thrush never sings the same song back-to-back—he won't even sing parts of his songs in succession. The hermit thrush follows the same rule, and clearly adds one more: Make successive songs not only different, but make them *especially* different.

Contrasts are also often enhanced by the juxtaposition of pure tones and noisy sounds, more so than in human music, which is typically far more tonal. A song sparrow song, for example, has pure tones and buzzes, as do marsh wrens and most songbirds. The tonal sounds are rarely held at a given pitch, but slurred up or down, or both in rapid succession.

I love the different paces of birdsong, too. Some, such as the *hey-sweetie* of a chickadee, are slow enough that I can savor all of the notes. Some songs are so fast, though, such as those of the western winter wren, that I know my human ears cannot begin to appreciate the details. I need to slow the tape down four or more times, lowering the pitch into my range of best hearing, too, and only then can I hear the itty-bitty elements that this male not only sings but has learned from another singing wren. Only by slowing such a song can I begin to hear the details that the bird itself can hear, and my ears undoubtedly underappreciate many aesthetic qualities that such songs have as they tickle my eardrums in real time.

The range of song complexity among birds is astounding. There are the relatively simple songs of flycatchers and nightjars, as well as of some songbirds, such as the black-capped chickadee. At the other extreme are the western winter wren and the continuously singing mockingbirds and thrashers and catbirds. No two species sound alike, and they vary along multiple dimensions, such as song duration, tonal quality, frequency range, tempo, and more.

It is the combined, unadulterated, prolonged concert that pleases me the most. As the earth continuously turns, dawn's first light sweeps relentlessly around our globe, evoking a continuous dawn chorus of birdsong. Just being a part of that millions-of-years-old process for a brief hour each spring and summer morning is an extraordinary privilege. Just as noises like ringing cell phones can destroy the moment in the orchestral hall, so do artificial, human-made noises intrude now almost everywhere on this globe, taking away a bit of the pleasure in listening.

Nor is it just the adults who please. Some of the sweetest sounds I have heard have been from young birds, just a few weeks old. In the "bird nursery" of our house, we'd stuff the babies full of food, and in their satiated state, the males in the group would often fluff up their feathers, doze lightly, and practice their singing. From young sparrows and blackbirds and wrens and towhees and warblers would pour a continuous stream of babbling-like sounds. I realize that I, too, sing best when the stomach is taken care of.

As I listen to birds singing, I enjoy knowing that perhaps the way they and I hear the world isn't all that different. Consider four Java sparrows (actually not really sparrows, but "estrildids" of the family Estrildidae, related to zebra finches) who were given a choice of sitting on perches that played music of either Bach or Schoenberg, a representative baroque and modern composer. Two clearly chose Bach (the other two apparently not caring), and those two continued to choose Bach over Schoenberg when other pieces by these two composers were played. Those two discerning sparrows also preferred Vivaldi to Carter, suggesting that they may prefer baroque music over modern music. The experiment was taken one step further when other sparrows were trained extensively with either a Bach or a Schoenberg composition. Those sparrows then favored other pieces by the same composer they were trained with; furthermore, when these sparrows were offered a choice of Vivaldi or Carter, the Bach-trained birds chose Vivaldi (another baroque composer) and the Schoenberg-trained birds chose Carter (both modern). These abilities to classify human music apparently are not limited to the song-learning songbirds, as even the non-song-learning pigeons have similar capabilities.

In one way our musical abilities are different from those of at least some birds. Starlings, for example, are good at knowing the absolute pitch of sounds, far better than we humans are, but starlings have difficulty transposing a simple melody, or even recognizing a transposed tune, as they are restricted to knowing the tune over a fairly narrow range of pitches in which they have some experience. In contrast, only a few humans have "perfect pitch," but most of us can readily recognize a tune that is transposed from one key to another, as it is the relative pitch of the notes that is important to our ears.

Given the remarkable sounds that birds make, it is no surprise to me that those who know human music best often appreciate these birds, too, even incorporating the music of nature into their own compositions. As early as 1240, the cuckoo's *cuckoo* song appears in human music, in minor thirds. The songs of skylarks, song thrushes, and nightingales debut in the early 1400s. The French composer Olivier Messiaen is my hero, as he championed bird-songs in his pieces. I love Respigghi's *Pines of Rome,* too, as the songs of a nightingale accompany the orchestra (except in the version I have, in which a canary's song has sadly been substituted). I learned recently, too, why I have always especially enjoyed the "Spring" concerto from Vivaldi's *Four Seasons:* It is the birds and their songs that celebrate the return of spring in this concer-to, and now I clearly hear the birdsongs in the brief, virtuoso flourishes by the solo violinist.

Can I know why I and others like me are so affected by the music of nature? It doesn't surprise me that human music can improve moods and test scores and reduce blood pressure and pain, or that premature infants in intensive care units do better with the right music; I would be surprised if my birdsongs could not be shown to have the same general effects. Although mothers play Mozart to babies in the womb, I think thrushes and wrens and sparrows and a more natural chorus would be at least as effective. Perhaps my appreciation of birdsong is due to my early exposure to nature, growing up in the Michigan countryside, but I think it lies deeper than that. I think that within each of us resides an innate love of nature, and especially birdsongs, perhaps in part because our ancestors emerged from their primate origins to the accompani-ment of these birdsongs. Our ancestors were no doubt good "birders," know-ing, for example, how to identify food or danger based on bird sounds, an almost lost art now being revived by naturalists who call themselves "trackers." And our earliest, halting attempts at some form of protomusic most likely included imitations of the accomplished virtuosos all about us.

All of this leads me to what seems an inescapable truism: my aesthetic tastes and those of many birds must overlap. Those of us who study birdsong believe it is the female who, over eons of time, has played a major role in shap-ing the songs of the males. The process is quite simple, in that males with cer-tain singing characteristics are chosen to be the fathers of the next generation, and those singing behaviors are then perpetuated, gradually evolving over time. So the female's tastes and mine converge, especially among the thrushes and wrens and mockingbirds and thrashers and other songsters that I and my human friends consider superior.

Isn't it also likely that the male could experience some pleasure, however primitive, at performing his skills? That pleasure need not be conscious, of course, just as much of our pleasure can be traced to simple chemical reactions in our bodies, but it does seem that there must be some measure of "joy" in how he sings. That they and I are alike in so many ways seems inescapably true, or else she wouldn't be choosing as she does, he wouldn't be singing as he does, and I wouldn't be listening as I am.

"The earth has music for those who listen," wrote the astute Shakespeare. It is *their* music, enhanced by its originality, diminished in no way by failing to match the rules of our human music. All one has to do is listen, and the music is everywhere, the original "surround-sound."

Songs on the Wing

The American Woodcock

Twice a year they pass us by: plovers, golden-plovers, yellowlegs, whimbrels, curlews, godwits, turnstones, tattlers, knots, sanderlings, dunlins, dowitchers, sandpipers. In their drabber plumages they head south, as early as July, some all the way to the tip of South America. Come spring, some nine months later, they pass again, this time bedecked in their finest dress, many of them heading almost as far north as land allows. As they pass, we might hear a *peep* from the littlest ones, or sharp notes of protest from others as we flush them on the beach. With these simplest of sounds, they're vocally uninspiring, and for good reason I had passed them by . . . until I realized who they truly are.

The best of the bird guides provide just a few hints. Songs in flight are "a melodious, ringing *kudiloo* or *trillii* repeated" (black-bellied plover); "soaring; begins with about five *wiiteew* notes, then repeated, complex *pidl WHIDyooooo*" (bristle-thighed curlew); "complex: short bursts of churring and trilling with croaking or hissing sounds" (sanderling); "chatter followed by harsh two-note phrase ending with several clear, rising *whaaay* notes" (curlew sandpiper); "low flight a remarkable, rapid, foghornlike hooting *ooah ooah . . .* continuing 10 to 15 seconds" (pectoral sandpiper); "*gididi drreee drrooo,* each phrase slightly rising but the series falling" (short-billed dowitcher).

More convincing is the enthusiasm of my friend Ted Miller who has pursued these shorebirds throughout the Arctic. Take his Baird's sandpiper, for example. During its migration up the heart of the continent, we hear a rough *kreep* at best; but follow this bird to its breeding grounds, to the very northern reaches of the continent, and hear it in full song. He arrives unpaired in his nesting area and soon begins his butterfly-flight; slow and deep are his wing strokes as he flies for minutes on end, uttering *tooowee-tooowee-tooowee-tooowee,* one of these hoarse, three-quarter second, buzzy rising notes every second, 60 a minute, over and over and over. Hear him then encounter another bird in flight, or hear him descend, and he now continuously alternates two other buzzy sounds, each about half a second, each also rising slightly in pitch, the first one over a narrower pitch range than the second, the contrast between the two striking. Ending it all is a lengthy chatter, perhaps three or more seconds. The field guide's "Flight song a series of buzzy, rising notes and long, level rattling" doesn't begin to do it justice.

Nor does any prose do these shorebirds justice. I must hear them, and to do so I turn to a kind gift given by Boris Veprintsev when I visited him in Moscow during the 1982 International Ornithological Congress. Three records, yes, the old 33-rpm type, capture nearly two hours of the best of Siberia's treeless landscapes. Eyes closed and ears wide open, I am almost there, in the land of the midnight sun, standing on the tundra, rocks and rubble and puddles extending to the horizon. It's early in the season, the males having just arrived, and they circle endlessly overhead and all around, strutting all the vocal stuff they can muster after their epic journey from the south.

Someday I must go to the Arctic, to hear and see these birds for myself, but for now, the best I can do is get a taste of them by sampling one closer to home. It is with that growing passion for this entire group that I now find myself standing beside my friend Bill's house, just up above Lawrence Swamp in South Amherst, on the evening of April 7, a Sunday. The woodcock are back.

Sunset is in five minutes, at 7:23 P.M., and the local birds are preparing to roost. A mockingbird still sings in the distance to the west, as does a robin, though more *piik piik* and *quiquiqui* notes tell me he's about done for the evening. In the hedgerow nearby are the sounds of the north country, fox and white-crowned and tree sparrows all practicing their songs, all migrants heading north to be among the woodcocks' Arctic cousins. The fox sparrow's mellow whistles are striking, but they're wavering and unstable, not quite ready for the task; it sounds as if he could develop a great variety of songs from this jumble I hear, but I know that eventually he will settle down, choosing just one, that one just like those of his neighbors where he will claim his territory. Three wood ducks fly overhead toward the east, to spend the night in the swamp, no doubt, where geese now honk.

The western sky has turned from pink to gray, but the willows lining the drive still glow, their golden catkins and branches lighting the way. The swamp a quarter mile to the east is now a reddish blur, the red maple buds and flowers casting a reddish haze to the entire bottomland forest, each individual tree a fluffy ball, enveloped in a reddish blurry halo.

Peent! In the thickets to my right he announces he is ready, and so am I. For the next hour or so that he puts on his show, I want to hear every *peent*, to dance with him in the sky, to sense his every move. *Peent! . . . Peent!* (track 73, figure 52). There is nothing now but him and me. I begin counting: 5 *peent*s in the first minute, then 9, then 10, 7, 8, all still in what must be a small clearing in the thicket out of sight. He continues: 9, 11, 10, 11, 14, 13, 11 . . . and silence, the last 11 in just 45 seconds, 118 overall, his pace picking up the last three minutes. Silence now for 10, 20, 30, 40 seconds . . . PEENT! He calls, from just behind me, in the stubble of last year's garden. How did he get there so silently? Did he sneak by me, walking to his display arena? Or did he fly, ever so ghostlike?

Just five *peent*s in 20 seconds and he launches skyward, flying off to the southwest. I try to get my bearings, to watch and listen, but I'm quickly confused. I hear his wings whistling immediately upon takeoff, but within 15 seconds he seems to be calling, and he's not supposed to do that. He's supposed

Figure 52. A single *peent* of the American woodcock, followed by brief excerpts from his flight display. The time scale is continuous, beginning in the first row at 0 and ending at 52.5 seconds in the last row, with each row displaying a 3.5-second window. **Top row:** The *peent* is a raspy, buzzy, noisy sound, followed seconds later by the whistles of his wings as he launches skyward. Count the whistles per second and you know how rapidly he beats his wings. **Second row:** See how the wingstrokes are rhythmic now, a burst of about a dozen strokes each second followed by a brief pause. It is during these pauses that he now begins to vocalize, softly at first, gradually becoming louder. **Third row:** Just ten seconds later the pace has accelerated considerably, each half-second now with a burst of wing whistles punctuated by unmistakable, lower-frequency vocalizations. **Bottom row:** Here's the culmination of his display, the loud chirping interspersed among his wingbeats. Feel the rhythm of the chirps, six of them in a series; I've numbered them the way I hear them, the third chirp the highest, the sixth the lowest. He ends his flight display now, just four seconds later swooshing past the microphone to the ground, where he begins *peent*ing again. (See track 70.)

The Singing Life of Birds

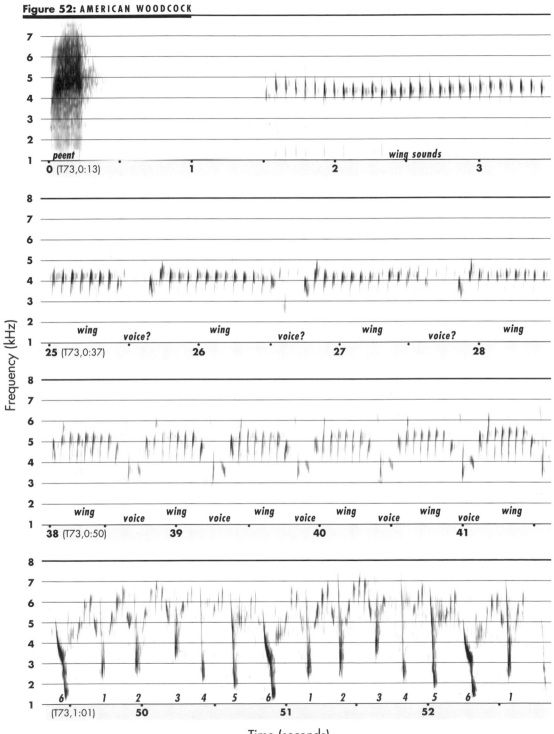

Frequency (kHz)

peent   wing sounds

0 (T73,0:13)

wing   voice?   wing   voice?   wing   voice?   wing

25 (T73,0:37)   **26**   **27**   **28**

wing   voice   wing   voice   wing   voice   wing   voice   wing   voice   wing

38 (T73,0:50)   **39**   **40**   **41**

(T73,1:01)   **50**   **51**   **52**

Time (seconds)

to twitter with his wings for about 30 seconds, then add the vocal chirping for another 15 seconds, and almost a minute after it all began, plummet back to earth and resume the *peent* calls. But I hear the chirping 15 seconds too early . . . and after 30 seconds I hear a ground *peent* from the south. Has he moved? He's supposed to return here, to this very spot, as it is his display arena, or so I thought. Then the chirping resumes from the air again, and after a total of 60 seconds since his departure, he does return, fluttering to the garden, *peent!*

How? . . . and then I realize. While I had been focusing on the male before me, as if he were the only bird here, he had been focusing on a male *peent*ing to the south. When the neighbor launched into the air, my male no longer heard the southern *peent*, and he almost certainly then heard the neighbor's wing-twitters high to the south, too, though I was oblivious to his world. Within seconds of hearing the neighbor's move, he, too, was airborne, his circling flight overlapping his neighbor's by half a minute. So when I thought my male was chirping 15 seconds too early, I was in fact hearing the neighbor, who had started his flight 15 seconds before my male. The neighbor would end earlier, too, of course, resuming his ground *peent*ing to the south.

On the ground again, the bird before me delivers 12 *peent*s in a little over half a minute, the pace much faster than before, and he's up again. I concentrate, just barely able to follow him with my binoculars in the waning light. He ascends gradually at first, quietly, off to the southwest, and after a few seconds begins his wing-twittering. I wish I could see those outer three feathers on the wing in slow motion; they're short, narrow, and stiff, and vibrate in the airflow as he beats his wings about 15 times a second, so that each wingbeat is marked by a brief whistle. Straining to keep my eyes on the bird, I watch as he continues to climb and twitter for about 10 seconds.

I then hear a subtle change in the twittering, as it becomes more melodious. He climbs more rapidly now, loops and spirals, covering roughly the area of a football field. How high is he now, 100 yards? Rhythmic bursts of soft wing-twittering now combine with the loud vocal chirping, about four chirps a second, a delightful coordination of sounds from wing and bill. After about 15 seconds of that, he begins his descent. He dives, zigs and zags, banks and plummets, as he heads back toward his display site on the ground. The last 5 seconds or so are silent, ending as he flutters gently into the garden again.

It's only 5 *peent*s this time and he's skyward again. I take advantage of the minute that he'll be gone and work my way closer to his display arena, soon standing as inconspicuously as possible only 10 yards away, behind a bush. I want to see this odd creature.

Peent! He announces his return to earth again. Binoculars raised, I check him out. He's about the size of a blue jay but probably twice the weight, downright plump. His rich buff and brown must provide great camouflage against the forest floor. But what a strange-looking creature! Protruding from his largish head is an impressively long bill, used to probe for earthworms in sandy or loamy soils. His large black eyes are perched so high and so far back on his head that he has binocular vision to his backside, no doubt enabling him to watch for

predators while working the soil with his bill. Inside that skull I know that even his brain is odd, an upside-down brain with regions all out of order compared to the standard bird brain. This woodcock is certainly an odd "shorebird," somehow so turned around that he breeds and nests in the forests, not the ancestral Arctic tundra and marshes.

After 10 *peent*s he's back in the air, and I check my watch. He again heads to the southwest, then circles to the west, his wing-twitters announcing his every move. At 39 seconds he's overhead, chirping and twittering, silent at 49, landing in front of me at 53 seconds, and 57 seconds after he took off he delivers his next *peent*. I watch again, *peent*, and he shuffles a quarter turn, *peent,* shuffles again, *peent,* shuffle, *peent,* shuffle, as if addressing an encircling audience.

It's 10 *peent*s again and he's skyward for 50 seconds. I continue to track him: 11 earthly *peent*s and 55 sky-dancing seconds; 42 *peent*s, 54 seconds in the air; 22 *peent*s, 51 seconds; 16 *peent*s, 52 seconds; 11 *peent*s, 53 seconds; 36 *peent*s, 56 seconds; 12 *peent*s, 56 seconds; 33 *peent*s, and skyward again.

It's 8:00 P.M. now, and he continues, but I am distracted by the southern male, wanting to find him, to learn more of the relationship between these two birds. I sense that their aerial maneuvers are coordinated in some way, but I don't recall reading anything about that. So I try to station myself between them, but I find the terrain difficult, and I learn little more before these two woodcock call it quits for the evening.

Count. Count. More counts. Numbers. Numbers. More numbers. Why do I obsess so with this counting game? I ask myself. I recall that "science is the art of collecting interesting numbers," but science is just organized curiosity, too. I am curious about who this male woodcock is, and it is the numbers that tell of his life, painting the picture of his evening's activities. The number of *peents* per minute tell of his mood, the *peents* between flights of his nightly rhythm, the time of his flight relative to his neighbor a clue to some relationship with him.

All of the numbers are of his choosing, his woodcock mind expressing itself, and as I count I do the best that I can to crawl inside his mind and sense the world from his perspective. What goes on in his mind? How has it come to be the way it is? He largely inherited it, of course, from his parents, who had parents of their own, and so on, back into time. If I could trace this lineage back far enough, I'd come to the ancestral woodcock, some million or more years ago. From that ancestor arose not only the lineage I know but also five others, in distant parts of the world (Eurasia; New Guinea; and three groups of islands in the western Pacific, the Moluccas, Sulawesi, and the Ryukyu Islands). To understand why my woodcock displays as he does, I would love to count a few evenings away with his woodcock relatives. The ways in which the counts are similar would tell me about the mind of the ancestral woodcock, the ancestral ways that have been preserved among all descendents; the ways in which the counts are different would tell me about how each lineage has changed since they parted, as each species evolved to become as it is now.

I could also count a few evenings with the local snipe. If I travel even farther back in time than the ancestral woodcock, I encounter the woodcock-snipe, the ancestor that gave rise to both snipe and woodcock. By listening to snipe I could better understand the broader picture of how flight and ground songs have evolved within this entire group. What little I know of these two groups already intrigues me. Both the snipe and the woodcock call from the ground, and both then fly, making mechanical noises with their feathers as they circle over their domain. The woodcock's special noisemaking feathers are in its wing, those of the snipe in its tail. As the snipe dives in his flight overhead, the wings direct the rushing wind over the two stiffened outer tail feathers, and we hear what is called the snipe's "winnow" (track 74, figure 53).

Why my male woodcock chooses to express himself as he does must be all about impressing the female woodcock. His only role in life is to impress females and mate with as many as will choose him; he supplies only sperm, nothing more, because it is the female who builds the nest and raises her young unassisted.

As I count, I imagine a parallel audience of woodcock females watching and listening to the males display. They almost certainly don't count as I do, but they compare the males in their own way, no doubt. To which talent or trait does she attend? Perhaps the male's endurance proves his good health, and the more times he sky-dances during an evening or morning performance

AMERICAN
WOODCOCK

COMMON
SNIPE

Figure 53. The American woodcock "sings" with its wings, the common snipe with both wings and tail. The woodcock uses three stiffened outer feathers on each wing to make its mechanical noises during its aerial flight displays; each wingbeat is then heard as a brief whistle. The snipe directs air from its flapping wings over a single outer feather on each side of its tail; each of the snipe's wingbeats during a display dive is then heard as a single *wu*.

the more likely she will be impressed. Or perhaps she focuses on the quality of the wing-twittering or chirping, which could demonstrate how clumsy or well coordinated a potential mate may be. Maybe his sky dances are all a prelude to the true test, how fast and consistently he can *peent* when she visits him on his strutting ground. She can no doubt detect the young males, who perhaps are still perfecting their aerial maneuvers, or who cannot *peent* with the gusto or persistence of an older male. Those young males will most likely be avoided—let them prove themselves by surviving for another year, might be the female's "reasoning." Her task is made easier because several males are within earshot of each other, and certainly several could be visited more intimately on each's ground stage for a more critical appraisal during a dusk or dawn performance.

No one knows what makes a male champion. Only the female knows, and it is she over eons of time who has shaped the males into the *peent*ers and sky dancers that they are. By choosing a male where she can compare several at a time, she has probably even orchestrated where and when males display in relation to each other. When picking the best and most impressive males, females often agree, so just a few males in one area accomplish the majority of the mating. The genes of those supermales are then passed on to the woodcocks of the next generation. Because the male displays are determined largely by instructions in the genes, sons will tend to display like their successful fathers, and daughters will tend to have the same fine tastes as their mothers. Success thus begets success, and the male antics are perpetuated and accentuated.

Yes, that's why I count. To count is to know them, and I want to know.

MONDAY, APRIL 8. Early the next morning, at 4:30 A.M., I'm back. It's pitch-black still, as official sunrise is at 6:02, an hour and a half from now, but I'm eager to hear more, as I know that he will display at dawn, too. Just 13 minutes after I arrive, at 4:43, I hear him, again in the brambles where he first began last night. I settle into a clearing in the brambles myself, on my camp chair, taking notes. Minute by *peent*ing minute goes by, 5 o'clock, 5:10, 5:20. An occasional cardinal song explodes from the thickets, as if he can't wait until dawn, and a song sparrow, too, accompanied by an occasional distant *you-alllllll* from the barred owls in the swamp.

AT 5:22 A.M., after 360 *peent*s in 39 minutes, a rate of about 9 a minute, one every 7 seconds, he's silent, 10, 20, 30 seconds, and I suspect he's moving to the garden. Yes, after 55 seconds, he *peent*s from the garden. Slowly at first, one every 8 seconds, then 7 seconds, down to 6, and abruptly it seems that he throws the switch, now one every 3 seconds. Something important has happened, I'm convinced. I check my watch, and continue counting . . . 3 . . . 6 . . . 9 . . . 11 *peent*s and 35 seconds later, I hear the neighbor's airborne chirping to the south, and I instantly know what was on my male's mind when he increased his *peent* rate. The neighbor's chirping began about 40 seconds into his flight, so within seconds of his neighbor's ascent, my male knew, either because he no longer heard the neighbor's ground *peent*ing or because he heard the airborne wing-twitters. In response, my male immediately accelerated his *peent*ing pace. Now, 4 more *peent*s and my male is into the air, too, climbing, twittering, and he begins his chirping just after his neighbor has landed again, as if the two are sky-dancing and singing their twitter-chirps in rounds.

My male lands again, *peent*. It's 5:25 now, and I choose to count *peent*s between flights, listening especially for how my male interacts with his neighbor: 30 *peent*s and a flight from my male, then 15 *peent*s, then 24, 19, 10, 12, 32, 46, 52, 19, 18, 44, 22, 14, and 12, all given at the rate of about one *peent* every 3 seconds, flights between each series of *peent*s being about a minute long. On all 17 flights he launches to the southwest, off toward where the neighbor calls, and for 6 of the flights (including the first 5 of the morning) I hear him respond to his neighbor, following him into the air by 25 to 30 seconds.

His last flight ends at 5:57. For five more minutes he cools down, *peent*ing 82 more times before lifting silently out of the garden and flying to the southwest again, this time to drop into the thickets.

The scorecard for the morning's effort: 851 *peent*s, including 385 warm-ups and 82 cool-downs; 17 flights of about a minute each, separated by an average of 24 *peent*s over about 70 seconds; 80 total minutes of effort, ending in the very minute of the official sunrise, at 6:02 A.M.

❧

MONDAY, APRIL 8, 7:00 P.M. One more time, I tell myself, as I'm determined to capture an entire evening record for this male, too, for a complete 24-hour portrait. I need to know more about how he reacts to his neighbor, too. Barely do I have time to reflect on the warmer weather than he starts calling, at 7:06, at least 15 minutes earlier than last night. *Peent, peent* . . . from the same brushy area where he started last night and early this morning. I start the hand-counter, resetting it after each minute: 3 *peent*s in the first minute, then 7, 9, 8, 5, 10, 8, 11, 9, 6, 0, 2, 4, 7, 12, 14, 11, 13, and 2 . . . and it's 50 seconds before he resumes, not in the thicket but in the garden, his special display arena. I again missed his arrival, but I'm certain he flew in, ever so silently.

Peent, he resumes: 10 *peent*s in the first minute, then 8, 10, 10, 5, 10, and suddenly the pace picks up, from one every 5 to one every 3 seconds, just like last night. I hear 6 *peent*s at the more rapid pace and mark the instant, 7:32:21 P.M., when I first hear the southern male chirping in the air. He has been airborne for 30 to 40 seconds already, his lead no doubt the catalyst that intensified my male's calling. One more *peent* from my male and he launches, too, just as he had responded to his neighbor this morning and last night. I follow him, seeing him at 40 seconds overhead during his twittering and chirping, amazed at his rapid zigzag, his erratic flight, and how quickly he flutters to earth nearby. *Peent,* exactly 60 seconds between the last *peent* of the previous series and the first of this next one.

On the eleventh *peent* he is airborne again, squeezing out a distorted *peent* while exerting all systems on takeoff. After 61 seconds, he's back. I begin the routine, counting *peent*s and seconds: 48 *peent*s, 60 seconds for the display flight; 9, 56; 9, 58; 24, and takeoff . . .

IT'S 7:41 P.M. NOW, and I'm disappointed that I've not heard the male to the south again. Is he still there? So far I have just been listening with unaided ears, but I now try the parabola, reasoning that it would help me hear the neighbor better. Recorder turned on, headphones down over the ears, I aim the parabola to the southwest, the direction that my male has just flown— and there is my answer. I hear airborne chirping within 20 seconds of my male's launch, too early for my male, and I know it is the neighbor. And 20 seconds later my male chirps overhead, landing after a 54-second flight. He resumes his ground *peent*s about 20 seconds after his neighbor. I now realize that my human senses have simply failed to hear this neighboring woodcock, though the woodcock on the ground before me missed nothing.

I now tally *peent*s and seconds aloft again, this time using the parabola to listen for the neighbor, too. When the neighbor chirps early in my male's flight, I mark the sequence with an asterisk: 18 peents, 53 seconds*; 13, 53; 36, 56*; 18, 51; 45, 56*; 25, 56*; 57, 57*; 19, 57; 34, 58*; 26, 60*; 26 . . . but no flight. His pace has slowed, to one every four seconds, then one every six seconds. And he slips away into the night as mysteriously as he had arrived.

IT'S NOW 8:06, and I survey the raw numbers that tell of his evening's activities. He warms up offstage for 20 minutes with 151 *peent*s, roughly one *peent* every 8 seconds; and in the official minute of sunset, at 7:24 P.M., he moves to his garden arena. He continues his warmup for another 6½ minutes, giving 60 *peent*s, one every 6 to 7 seconds. At the first sound of his neighbor in the air, he picks up the pace, now a *peent* every 3 seconds. He soon launches, too, his round in the air beginning about 20 seconds after his neighbor's. From 7:32 to 8:04 P.M., he launches skyward 16 times, 9 times following his neighbor, never his neighbor following him. Between display flights, he *peent*s 392 times, at a rate of about one every 3 seconds. And to end the evening, he slows the pace, to one every 4 seconds, then 5, and he's gone, 42 minutes after sunset.

Questions abound. Who is this male who displays from Bill's garden? Is he a yearling displaying for the first time, or an older, more accomplished bird? Why on all three of my vigils did he take his cue from the neighbor, not only on the first flight but on successive ones, too? Does the older, dominant bird fly first, the submissive younger bird following? Or perhaps my bird is the older, more dominant bird, eager to strut his stuff immediately after the pathetic attempts by the young bird to the south? Mine is just a 36-hour portrait, a snapshot in the life of this male woodcock. How successful will he be? Is he the top woodcock in the neighborhood, or is it possible that he'll never mate? For this mating game, he must always be ready, always "on," because he never knows when *she* might be listening; just one visit by a female during all of April or May could spell success, his genes then chosen to be represented in the next generation of sky dancers. His success is no doubt determined by the intensity and quality of his *peent*ing and sky-dancing, as females watch and listen and compare, just as I count and compare.

I must listen to the snipe next, the closest relatives of the woodcocks. How intriguing that their specialized feathers for flight sounds are in the tail rather than the wing, their tremulous *wu-wu-wu-wu-wu-wu-wu-wu-wu-wu* dive sounds created by air directed from the wings over stiffened outer tail feathers. My few hours with the woodcock have also made an Arctic trip inevitable. To know these shorebirds better, I must go to northern Canada or Alaska, to see and hear for myself these curlews and whimbrels and dunlins and dowitchers . . . but especially the sanderlings. I hear their simple calls on my favorite winter beaches, but I must hear their flight songs on the Arctic Circle north of Hudson's Bay, their froglike songs and their chatter that follows. Do they also "laugh," like some other shorebirds up there? They've sent me a standing invitation—all I have to do is clear the calendar. Perhaps next year, during June.

Tireless Singers

The Whip-poor-will

Among songbirds, there seems to be a general rule: If you've got it, flaunt it. Which came first is the old chicken-and-egg argument, of course—the getting and the flaunting had to evolve together. As the ancestors of our mockingbirds acquired a greater variety of songs, for example, they presumably sang more and more continuously, to the point where they now sing their 100 to 200 different songs nonstop for minutes on end, as if eager to tell all that they know. It's the same for their close relatives, as male catbirds and thrashers have hundreds or even thousands of songs and sing feverishly. Why have such a large repertoire of songs, after all, if they aren't delivered in such a way that listeners can appreciate them?

Less versatile singers typically perform more slowly, more deliberately. A male chipping sparrow or white-crowned sparrow with only one song to his credit typically delivers five or so brief songs a minute, the pause between songs being five or six times the duration of the song itself. A song sparrow with eight different songs does much the same, perhaps singing six or seven songs a minute. But get that song sparrow excited, as when he's courting a female or defending his territory, and he then sings faster; as one might expect, successive songs are more likely to be different, too, so speed of singing and song variety increase together. For these sparrows and other songbirds, it's as if a single song presented at high rates would bore a listener with a highly monotonous performance, so the faster he sings, the higher the likelihood that his next song will be different.

It's been speculated, too, that singing the same song rapidly over and over would fatigue the muscles of the syringes, the two avian voice boxes. Successive songs might become increasingly sloppy, or the avian analogue of repetitive stress syndrome might cripple the lusty singer. As a result, birds that sing with great variety in their songs also sing more continuously, or birds that must, for whatever reason, sing continuously do so with great variety.

So what is it with these nightjars? Their very name suggests that they jar the night, endlessly, relentlessly, with a never-ending song performance, and it's just a simple song that they use, over and over. They would seem to violate the songbird trend, to the extreme. As I pore over the literature on these nightjars, however, I soon realize that stories of their fabled singing abound, but facts are few. How much does a male really sing throughout the night? Having now asked the question, I am committed.

The sun is now six minutes below the western horizon, the full moon six minutes beneath the eastern. It's 8:03 P.M., May 7, 2001, and I'm ready, poised for the night's vigil at the Montague Plain near my home in western Massachusetts. An hour ago I parked my car at the northern end of these pine barrens, then biked to the south, scouting where I might find the whip-poor-wills, familiarizing myself with the trails in the daylight so I could move efficiently by night. My wide and knobby tires often mired in the loose sand laid down thousands of years ago in this ancient river delta, back when meltwater streams from the retreating glaciers dumped their grindings here.

From a glacial river delta to a nuclear power–generating facility in just a few thousand years—at least that was the plan until recently. Power lines still bisect the barrens, but the signs at the entrance now declare this unique area a state wildlife refuge. Biking beneath the pitch pines and among the still-leafless, stunted scrub oak, I heard the ascending *zee-zee-zee-zee-zee-zee-zee-zee* songs of prairie warblers, the *drink-your-tea* of eastern towhees, and the wheezes of blue-gray gnatcatchers. I followed the sandy path called Plains Road to the west, then at the abandoned gravel pit took a left, riding beneath the high-tension lines to the southeast, down to Old Northfield Road, where I now straddle my bike, waiting. The supposed shakers of the night still slumber, but soon the day birds will retire, and my marathon will begin.

In my mind the whip-poor-will tape now plays (track 75, figure 54), over and over, *tuck-WHIP-poor-WILL tuck-WHIP-poor-WILL tuck-WHIP-poor-WILL*, as I listen, eager to match my inner tape with sounds arriving by ear. I savor the details: the soft introductory *tuck* heard only at close distance, followed by the loud *WHIP-poor-WILL*, the *WHIP* intermediate in loudness and pitch, dropping to the *poor,* and finishing strongest and highest, on the *WILL.*

There, in the distance, far to the north. Parabola and tape recorder dangling from my shoulder, a pack of supplies on my back, I pedal the distance as fast as I can. He's opposite the gravel pit, across the power-line swath to the west. I count . . . 55 songs the first minute, 54 the next, then 56, from a phantom in the scrub oaks . . . an avian metronome, so regular, so consistent. He

Figure 54: WHIP-POOR-WILL

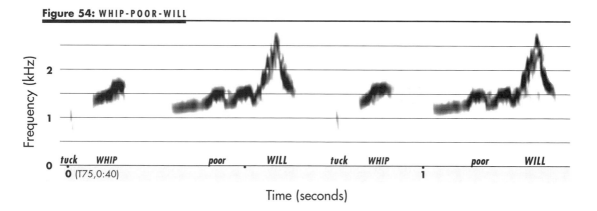

Figure 54. Seen one, seen 'em all, as it's the same tune all night long: *tuck-WHIP-poor-WILL* (track 75). Two songs are shown for good measure, to show how continuously he sings during one of his flourishes.

pauses briefly now and then but always resumes again within seconds; he averages 50 songs a minute and by 8:30 has already sung 1,000 songs.

I hear another whip-poor-will to the east, at the south end of the gravel pit — an even more insistent singer. His pace is frenetic . . . 61, 63, 60 songs a minute, as I click off each song on my hand-counter . . . 10 percent faster than the bird to the west. I'm torn. How should I sample these whip-poor-wills? Obtain an average from these two males, or get to know just one, but know him well? I choose intimacy with one, my decision swayed by the trails that I already know around the gravel pit, convinced I will be able to shadow this male throughout the night. I walk the bike over, sitting in the northwest end of the gravel pit, looking and listening across to the southeast. The moon is now up above the horizon, beaming across the brilliant white sand of the pit, the whip-poor-will's songs also beaming across this natural amphitheater to me. Although he sings more rapidly than his neighbor to the west, his pauses are more frequent, and he, too, averages about 50 songs a minute. From 8:30 to 9:00 he sings about 1,500 songs.

My plan for the night now seems clear. Here is the male I will follow. Each hour I'll tally how many songs he sings. In some hours I'll count every song, but in others I'll only sample, perhaps counting only 30 of the 60 minutes and then doubling my count to estimate what he did during that entire hour. My tally for the first hour, an abbreviated one that began at 8:10, is 2,500 songs.

He pauses more frequently during the next half hour, from 9 to 9:30. When he does sing, he does so at a clip of 55 to 60 songs a minute, but he's silent about half of the time. Perhaps he's hungry, foraging for a few moths, catching them on the wing in his cavernous mouth opening. How energetically expensive it is to sing remains controversial among those who study birdsong, but one thing is clear, that time spent singing is time spent fasting. So he must be taking time off to eat, but I can only guess, as I cannot see him. By 9:30 he has sung 840 songs, at a rate of 1,680 songs an hour.

During that half hour I also learn how to follow him without seeing him (figure 55). I listen attentively to the four neighboring whip-poor-wills, learning where they sing and trying to calibrate how softly I hear them with how distant they are. When my bird falls silent, the others usually continue in the distance, providing a reference for me to identify my bird when he resumes singing in a different place within his territory. I can follow him more easily if he moves only short distances and sings from each location, but as I gain my bearings that's less important. I soon hear this entire community of whip-poor-wills singing, enabling me to follow the movement of my bird as he flies in the four compass directions to contest territorial boundaries with each of his four neighbors.

The night is still young, and again I'm torn. Should I stay with this male or sample other whip-poor-wills at the barrens? If I stay here, I fear missing the bigger picture. It's the classic dilemma of how to sample—to know one or a few well, or many poorly. I reason that I already have a good sample for the 9:00 to 10:00 hour from my bird, and if I'm back by 10:30, I'll get a good sample for the 10:00 to 11:00 hour, too. That gives me from 9:30 to 10:30 to prowl the barrens, listening to what other birds are doing. By 10:30 I'll decide whether to resume with this male or sample other birds.

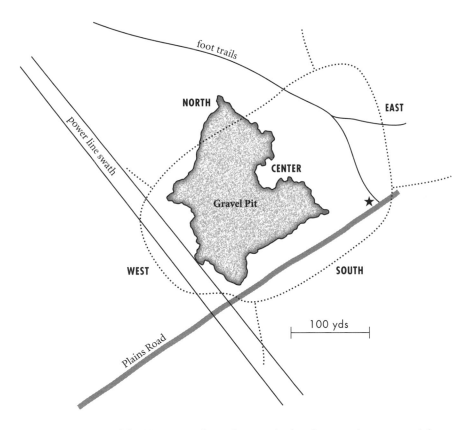

Figure 55. A map of the Montague Plains showing the key features during my nightlong vigil of the whip-poor-will. Approximate territory boundaries of the five whip-poor-wills (labeled north, east, south, west, and center) are indicated by dotted lines. The center male was my focus, but in the distance I could also monitor the singing of the other four. When the center male allowed, I sat in my easy chair at the position marked by a star.

I mount my bike again, heading northeast toward the car, listening as I go. The moon is now bright, and I hear all five whip-poor-wills as I depart the gravel pit. Then silence, except for the sound of tires in the sand. A short burst of song from a thrasher off to the left, then a cardinal up ahead, both finding the full moon irresistible. In the distance, a barred owl hoots: *Who cooks for you? Who cooks for you-alllll?* The owl repeats itself, but this time I hear *Where are the wills? Where are the whip-poor-wills?*, as I hear only three more, all concentrated to the far east on Plains Road. That's disappointing, as I'd hoped to find far more, based on accounts of birders from years past; the local population trend apparently mirrors the general decline of these birds elsewhere. Having now scouted the entire area, I know my night is back at the gravel pit, where I return, with the car, by 10:30.

10:30 TO 11:00. He continues relentlessly, pounding out song after song. He's now in the woods to the east of the gravel pit, matching song for song another male from the next territory. I aim my parabola his way, press "record," and don the headphones to hear his distant songs better. A song a second he sings, over and over, but now comes a flourish, as he squeezes five songs into the time it would normally take to sing only four. It's frenzy piled on frenzy, as if to say "take *that* and *that* and *that* and *that* and *that!*" He then takes a brief breather, resuming in the same place a minute or so later. After only 25 minutes, I count 1,090 songs, an average of 44 songs a minute.

Along Plains Road, I pace the distance from the gravel pit to this eastern border, finding that the span of his territory is about 300 yards. WHIP-*poor*-WILL WHIP-*poor*-WILL I now hear both near and far, all five males within earshot, all five males engaging in the moonlit fray. In this 30-minute period I count 1,285 songs from my companion, and double that to estimate the number that he sang from 10:00 to 11:00: 2,570 songs.

My head spins. How many songs so far? In the three hours I've followed this bird, I estimated 2,500, 1,680, and now 2,570, for a total of 6,750. With about six hours to go, my quick math tells me he's on pace to sing more than 20,000 songs in a nine-hour night. Can he keep up this pace? I'll find out, as I settle in now for my all-night vigil. I'll follow him as best I can, trying to live his life for the next six hours, until the songbirds again claim the day.

11:00 TO MIDNIGHT. He first moves to the south end of his territory, apparently discussing border issues with another male there. Again, I hear the rapid pace of about a song a second and another flourish before a pause, perhaps proving how impressively he can sing if pushed to the test. Then to the far north he flies, almost out of earshot. I walk the trail to the north, slowly, quietly, cupping my hands to my ears to continue the count. And five minutes before midnight, my watch clearly readable by the light of the moon, he makes the long flight to the far south again. For this hour, 2,112 songs.

MIDNIGHT TO 1:00. A few more songs from the southern border, just south of Plains Road, and at one minute past midnight he stops, soon to be heard again far to the north. He moves about unseen in the moonlight, a phantom creature tracked only by his incessant *whip-poor-WILL whip-poor-WILL whip-poor-WILL whip-poor-WILL*. And within six minutes he's back again on the southern border.

What calls him now to these northern and southern outposts I cannot know, but his incessant singing reveals some purpose. Perhaps he is simply defending his territory against the neighbor, his singing vigor sufficient to ward off potential intrusions. But perhaps this is the way to win a female over, too, a female who may be eager to compare two males, the more vigorous singer impressing her more. These one-on-one male contests may function as a miniature "lek," though that term is typically reserved to describe group contests among several males who display in an arena that a female then visits and chooses the male with whom she'll mate (as in sage grouse).

AT 12:25 he retreats from the southern border to sing in the heart of his territory, along Plains Road, just about 15 yards from where I now settle into my lawn chair, strategically deployed at his territorial center.

He's so close now I can easily hear the popping sound just before each *whip-poor-WILL*. All night long it has probably been *tuck-whip-poor-WILL*, but only now am I close enough to hear his full song. Slowly raising my parabola and lowering the headphones to my ears, I turn the recorder on. He now sings in my face, the subtlest of details booming into my ears: *tuck-whip-poor-WILL tuck-whip-poor-WILL tuck-whip-poor-WILL*. He speeds up, and then abruptly stops, but listen: he purrs, ever so softly. Gently lifting the headphones from my ears, I hear nothing, though he sits just yards away; headphones back on, he continues purring, catlike, as if he's decompressing from the intense performance. A full minute he purrs, the purr softly receding into the quiet of the night, and then some odd thumping sounds, whatever they are and however he makes them a mystery. At 12:30, he is silent.

In the next half hour we get our first good look at each other. He had flown to the west some, so I walked the road and moved with him, not wanting to miss anything. It is here, in the middle of the road, where we meet. He flies toward me, encountering an obstacle where none had been just minutes before. This mothlike creature stops in midair, hovering in my face for what seems an eternity. His white necklace and the white patches on the corners of the fanned tail glow in the moonlight. He seems all wings, beating rapidly, softly, quietly; he's all head, too, like a miniature owl hovering in place. Perhaps I only imagine the moon-gleams in those large owlish eyes. I want to reach out and touch him, but I freeze, respecting his space. He then swings to my left, hovering again for another eternity. *Pink . . . pink* he calls, as if unhappy with what he sees. Within what is probably only a few seconds it is all over, and he flies on, perhaps a mental note made that he must alter his flight route on darker nights when he might not have seen me, when he might have trusted his memory as to the flight paths about his territory. The half hour was rounded out with yet another trip to his northern boundary.

The hour after midnight: 2,344 songs.

1:00 TO 2:00. Back to the southern border, where the neighbor sings just beyond my male's claimed space. The two birds race through a full half hour, pausing now and then as if listening to each other, perhaps grabbing a bite to eat.

As the temperature plummets, I now retire to my chair, adding my warmest of winter clothing, wrapping myself in a heavy wool blanket. Nearby he continues to sing: *tuck-WHIP-poor-WILL tuck-WHIP-poor-WILL tuck-WHIP-poor-WILL.* The moon looms in the southern sky, the pitch pines and red oaks starkly silhouetted overhead. A woodcock has resumed his *peent*ing and sky-dancing just to the south. Then silence, and seconds later I hear six rapid *WHIP-poor-WILL*s in the gravel pit far to the west. He's on the move.

A quick tally for the hour: 2,007 songs. For the past three hours: 6,463. For the six hours so far: 13,213. Projected total for the night: just a little under 20,000 songs.

2:00 TO 3:00. The first half hour is difficult, as I hear him far to the west, on the west side of the gravel pit, and then even beyond the power lines. He disappears, only to be located after some frantic searching on my part, far to the north again. He then returns to the center of his territory, and I find my chair, counting . . . until 2:55, when after a minute's silence he is heard in the far north again. Tally for the hour: 2,440 songs.

3:00 TO 4:00. Two hours to go. Still to the north, he sings at a blistering clip of 62 to 66 songs a minute, once with an even faster flourish before a pause. As he makes his way to the south again, he stops a few times to sing at various locations en route. Smiling, I nod to him, find myself talking to him, thanking him for the short flights that make it easier for me to follow him at this hour. By 3:25 he's along the road again, in the center of his territory, and I regain my chair.

The next half hour is intense: *tuck-WHIP-poor-WILL tuck-WHIP-poor-*

WILL tuck-WHIP-poor-WILL, 60 or more a minute, pausing only occasionally. He sings about 25 of the 30 minutes, all from the center of his territory, all within 15 yards of me. Louder and louder he sounds as the night progresses. I know from physics that sound travels better in the cool, calm morning air, and perhaps that's why the neighboring whip-poor-wills seem to be closing in

WHIP-POOR-WILL

on me, too. But perhaps there's more to it than that. My weary brain is mush, the *WHIP-poor-WILL* sensors overloaded, overwhelmed, continuing to fire even when the bird itself stops, so that at times it's hard to distinguish what is real from what is imagined. The hour's total, to the best of my counting ability, is 2,466 songs . . . and only an hour to go.

4:00 TO 5:00. My eyes grow heavy, my body aches, but on and on he sings, and he's so close: *tuck-WHIP-poor-WILL tuck-WHIP-poor-WILL tuck-WHIP-poor-WILL*. By 4:12 a robin sings continuously just to the east, already heralding the sunrise he knows will come; the towhees *chewink* just eight minutes later.

THE LAST FULL HALF-HOUR. Concentrate. Focus. He makes the rounds one more time before daybreak. He flies into the woods to the east, singing there, then heads far to the north, and before the half hour is up he's back on the southern border. Throughout the night, the western border has been less contested, the wide power line perhaps serving as a natural buffer there.

Tally for what will almost certainly be the last full hour: 2,590 songs.

For just four more minutes he sings, another 189 songs, before flying west along the road, presumably to roost for the day, perhaps low on a branch within the scrubby oaks on the south side of Plains Road, just across from the gravel pit.

I add up my hourly tallies: 2,500 (from 8:10 to 9:00 p.m.), 1,680, 2,570, 2,112, 2,344, 2,007, 2,440, 2,466, 2,590, + 189 for the few minutes after 5:00 a.m. equals 20,898 songs. Two-zero-eight-nine-eight. Twenty thousand, eight hundred ninety-eight.

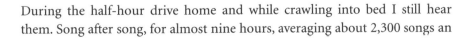

During the half-hour drive home and while crawling into bed I still hear them. Song after song, for almost nine hours, averaging about 2,300 songs an hour, 40 songs a minute, a song every second and a half in the 30-some thousand seconds from 13 minutes after sunset until 33 minutes before sunrise. *tuck-whip-poor-WILL tuck-whip-poor-WILL tuck-whip-poor-WILL tuck-whip-poor-WILL* . . . each one just the same, they still reverberate within my skull, unable to escape.

Drifting off to sleep, I whisper *tuck-whip-poor-WILL,* once every second and a half, two times every three seconds, at a clip of 40 times a minute. I imagine keeping up that average pace for the next 9 hours. But he doesn't sing quite like that. He sings much faster, about one song a second, and sings on average only 40 minutes of the hour. So I try again, *tuck-whip-poor-WILL* once a second, thinking I need to keep this up for 10 minutes straight, then take a 5-minute break before resuming. I need to repeat that cycle four times an hour, 35 times in a night. Whoever thought of counting sheep never knew the whip-poor-will.

It's a world record, as best I can tell, the fastest singing rate sustained over one entire waking period. One song every second and a half, eclipsing the old record of a song every two and a quarter seconds by a red-eyed vireo. The vireo has 20 to 50 different songs, too, successive ones always different — the whip-poor-will has only one song, successive songs always the same.

Well, okay, I admit that mine is a world record with an asterisk, as I've selected which number is important so that my whip-poor-will would win. The red-eyed vireo sang more songs in one 24-hour period (22,197) than did my whip-poor-will (estimated at 20,898), but the vireo had a 14-hour day, my whip-poor-will only a 9-hour night. Had my whip-poor-will had another 5 hours, he could have eclipsed the vireo record by 10,000 songs.

Why so much song? The weather was relatively warm and cooperative, but two other factors conspired that night to prod him on. Most important, the whip-poor-wills had just returned from migration, and my best guess is that only the males had returned. So each was still a bachelor, and each was staking out his claim for a territory, while simultaneously proclaiming his availability to any female within earshot. Once paired with a female, the singing most likely declines dramatically, as it does with most other birds; he sings to attract her and convince her he is the one, but after that is accomplished, domestic duties largely prevail.

The second important factor was no doubt the full moon, but just why I can't be sure. Other birds are known to sing more under a well-lit night sky, such as the (unpaired) mockingbird singing all night by street light. Perhaps it's easier to find food to sustain the singing under the light of a full moon. Perhaps a whip-poor-will male "knows" that females are more likely to migrate under a full moon, so he should sing more then. Whatever the reason, the next night this same whip-poor-will sang far less in the darkening hour after sunset, the time that the moon was delayed in rising. The weather was much the same, and it seems unlikely that a female would have arrived by daytime, so the difference in the two nights was most likely the light of the moon.

As for fatigue or monotony, well, neither seems to apply. The first songs a little after 8:00 P.M. seemed no more robust than those coming 20,000 songs later, after 5:00 A.M. With aesthetics, of course, one must consider the ears of the beholder. Perhaps a prospecting female demands rapid repetition of the *tuck-WHIP-poor-WILL,* so that she can listen carefully to the quality of each, to hear how perfectly he can repeat his song hour after hour. The quantity of song no doubt reflects a male's stamina, perhaps an indication of a genetically superior male, perhaps an indication of a good territory with lots of food, or perhaps both. In how well and how often he sings his simple song she may find most of the information she needs to choose her partner for the season.

I've answered my question, the simple one about how much a male nightjar sings in the night. It was just one male, and just one night—a small start to understanding these mysterious birds. How little we know of these birds is reflected in another of their names, the goatsuckers. It was once thought that these birds made a living by drinking the milk of goats by night. How absurd, one might think; no bird does that. The name, however, is a continuing reminder of our ignorance of even the simplest facts about these elusive birds.

The Red-eyed Vireo

Louise de Kiriline Lawrence is my hero. A half century ago she accepted the challenge of a Big Day event proposed by a British friend Noble Rollin. She could have chosen any birding adventure, such as seeing as many bird species as possible within 24 hours, but she chose to get to know one bird, just one individual, by following it from dawn to dusk. He was a male red-eyed vireo, just recently arrived and without a mate on his territory some 180 miles north of Toronto. The big day was May 27, 1952, and she was out at 3:00 in the predawn, "the most enchanting and mysterious moment in the 24 hours." By 4:00 it was light enough to take notes without her flashlight, and by 4:22, 20 other species had already announced their awakening.

And then, nine minutes before sunrise, from high in the crown of a quaking aspen, the vireo began, dropping his songs one by one into the dawn chorus. By 5:00 A.M., at 40 to 50 songs each minute, he had already delivered nearly 1,700 songs, and by 6:00 A.M. he'd sung another 2,155, at times reaching a clip of 70 songs a minute, more than one a second. He paused to preen or forage at times, occasionally singing with his mouth full, and almost 14 hours after first singing he dropped to roost in a thick stand of young evergreens. He had been singing for 10 of those hours, a total of 22,197 songs. Never monotonous or repetitious or "preacherlike" did she hear him, but always lovely and clear, simple and eloquent.

Lawrence's vireo had spent the northern winter somewhere in Amazonia, that vast lowland region east of the Andes in South America. He probably left his tropical home by mid April, working his way up through Panama, Costa Rica, and the rest of Central America, then reaching the United States either by land or by sea, either moving up eastern Mexico or flying directly across the Gulf from the Yucátan to the Gulf states. By now he'd be singing, and at night he'd fly north, over other vireos who had already settled in the southern part of their range, finally arriving at this far northern outpost. By the time he arrives and claims his two acres or so, he's ready, his songs now perfect red-eyed vireo songs. Over the next week or two, his neighbors will arrive; the later ones will most likely be yearlings, some of whom will still be practicing to get their songs right.

And sing he does. "The preacher" this vireo has been called by some listeners (though not by Lawrence), apparently for droning on hour after hour, delivering a short phrase and then pausing for reflection, over and over again from half an hour before sunrise to dusk, and throughout some of the hottest of summer days: *Listen now, do you hear me, believe me, that's right* . . . Each song is only a third of a second, the following pause usually a little over a second. Those who have studied these songs have found that each male can sing up to 30 or 40 different songs, a sizeable repertoire, and neighboring males have different songs.

Determined to know this vireo better, I accept the next invitation offered. In the Berkshire hills of western Massachusetts, I have finished my early morning listening with chestnut-sided warblers, and there he sings, above the car, as I am packing away the morning's gear. I pause, listening, smiling. Song after song he drops from the canopy onto my ears, just as Lawrence's bird had onto her ears, each song a split-second slur of whistles, then a second or so pause. I hear the nuances of each song, how each is different from the next, and within five minutes have already heard 200 songs.

To understand him better, I know to listen for an odd song, an especially peculiar one that I'll easily recognize again. I've heard these vireos sing a mimicked jay call of a blue jay, for example, and other borrowed sounds. But not this vireo. He's more of a challenge, as I hear no mimicry from him, and only one song stands out at first. It sounds like two pure whistles, each held for an instant, the second higher than the first (song A in track 76, figure 56). I play this "bell song" over and over in my mind, two times a second, comparing his songs to my looped memory, and, yes, there it is, about 20 of his songs later. Again, and again, roughly every half minute I hear this particular song.

I start to recognize other songs and play the same game with them, soon realizing that he must be presenting all that he knows every 30 or so seconds. I need to capture him, to take him home with me, so I unpack the recorder and parabola from the car and tape-record him, first for 15 minutes, and then another 15 for good measure (track 77).

At home, I listen to the tape recording as I had first listened to him in the field. I pick the bell song (A) and hear that it occurs two times in the first 50 songs on the tape. I choose another recognizable song (B, track 76, figure 56), this one a doubled note, *blip-blip* to my ears, rewind the tape, and hear it three times in the 50 songs. A third song (C) that I can recognize occurs five times. So the "typical" song occurs three times (simply the middle number of two, three, and five), and my rough estimate of how many different songs occur in these 50 songs is 50 divided by 3, or 17 songs. Curious as to how accurate my estimate is, I graph each of the 50 songs on my computer and then sort them. The sorting process is easy, because he clearly has a limited number of distinct, repeatable songs. And how many? I tally 18, pretty close to the 17 that I had estimated with my unaided ear.

What if I listen to more songs, say 200? What will I learn then? I use songs A, B, and C again and rewind the tape three more times, finding that A occurs 7 times, B 10 times, and C 16 times. If I take the middle value (10), divide it into 200, I come up with an estimate of 20 different songs in the 200. To determine how accurate I am, I make sonagrams of the 200 songs and sort them, finding exactly 20 different songs in the sample of 200.

It's the simplest of field-testing exercises I have completed. After reading that male red-eyed vireos can sing 30 to 40 songs, I go to the field to determine if I can hear it. To make sure, I record enough so I can listen repeatedly at home and graph the songs, too. With just a few hours of sleuthing, I can return and listen to these red-eyed vireos with far more confidence, and with more curiosity.

I return to my male in the Berkshires, listening to him again. I hear the bell song and the other two songs I now know so well. Checking out his two neighbors, I hear none of these three familiar songs. Each male does have his own unique set of songs, just as I have read. It's nice to confirm that, to hear it firsthand.

I also heard the loud, catlike *myaah* that punctuates the social lives of these red-eyes. Two of the males were fighting at their territorial boundary, screaming *myaah myaah*. As they fought and screamed, I know their crown feathers were raised, as if in anger, as that is how I have seen these vireos before, calling in the same way as I approached a nest. Both the male and female swooped at me then, snapping their bills, their crests raised, loudly scolding *myaah myaah myaah* . . .

I return to their songs, to puzzle over them. Males have different songs, but how does that come to be? They're songbirds, most of which imitate, and as young birds imitate, they acquire the same songs as the adult singers around them. Based on some of the mimicry that I hear from these vireos, I know that they are capable of imitating. So how do I explain the unique songs of each vireo? One possible explanation is that a young male learns his songs, but not at the place where he establishes his territory; his songs might then be exactly

Figure 56. Illustrated here are the first 24 songs from the 100-song sequence in track 77. "Read" the figure through from beginning to end, starting with the 1st song and continuing to the 24th, and see how successive songs are always different. The variety of songs seems endless and overwhelming until one begins to visually dissect this vireo's performance. Look at that distinctive song in position 4, for example, and see how it recurs two rows down in position 16; see how the song in position 8 recurs in position 23. Look at how identical these matches are and you appreciate what fine control this vireo has over his song repertoire. The control is so fine that you wouldn't mistake the somewhat similar songs in positions 2 and 10 as the same, and with a little searching you will find a perfect match for each elsewhere in the 24 songs. Go ahead—see how you do in matching up the songs in this figure; I find eight identical pairs (4 and 16, 8 and 23, and six others) and one particular song even occurs three times, leaving 5 songs without matches in these 24 songs. The 3 particular songs I thought especially distinctive are labeled A (position 7), B (position 21—not to be confused with the similar song at position 12), and C (positions 8 and 23). As you familiarize yourself with these 3 songs on track 76 and then listen for them on track 77, you will not only see but also hear how this red-eyed vireo uses his limited repertoire of different songs in an extended performance.

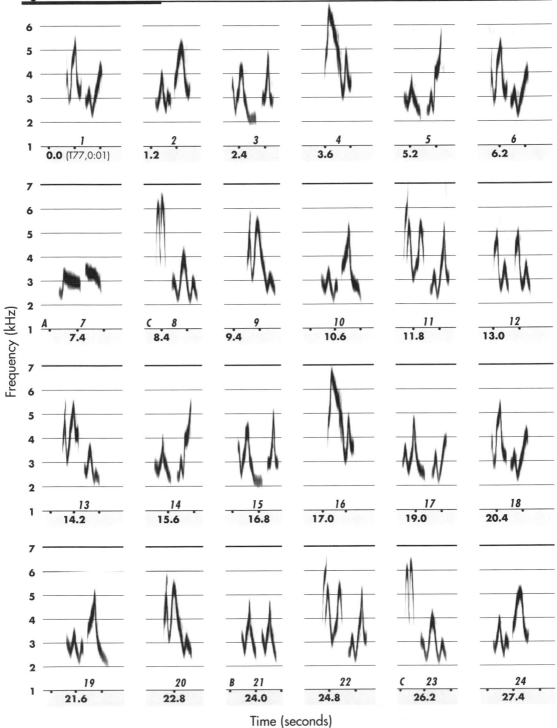

Frequency (kHz)

Time (seconds)

like the songs of another male some distance away, but neighbors would never have identical repertoires. That's possible, and although seemingly rare among songbirds, it is believed to happen in a close relative, the white-eyed vireo.

I think another explanation is more likely, that a young male largely makes his songs up, inventing and improvising his songs early in life (perhaps like the sedge wren), occasionally mimicking the songs of another bird. No one knows, but I know how I could find out, by raising a few babies in my home and studying how they acquire their songs when I control exactly what they hear. Yes, I could do that, but for now I'll be content to just wonder.

I wonder . . . are red-eyed vireos the same everywhere? I check the range map, seeing it colored in from the maritime provinces to Florida, and then west to Texas, northwest to the Yukon. I realize, too, that my planned coast-to-coast bike trip, from Virginia to Oregon, will be almost continuously in red-eye country. I will be listening and counting as I go.

I also eye the northwest part of the vireo's range up in the Yukon. Far to the southeast of there, Lawrence had 22,197 songs in one 14-hour day. A world record, but breakable? Checking my sunrise and sunset Web site, I find that day length at Yellowknife, on Great Slave Lake in the Northwest Territories, is about 19 hours during early June when the red-eyes would arrive. I'd have at least five more hours than Lawrence had—to see if I could break her Big Day record. One of these years . . .

It's mid July now, early afternoon, a hot and humid day. I sit in the shade of my umbrella on the back deck at my Amherst home, sipping iced tea and listening . . . blue jays call, distant crows caw, but all else is silent, *except* for the singing red-eyed vireo. Why? Why does he sing when all others are silent? I can understand Lawrence's all-day singer in late May, as he was a bachelor, eagerly searching for a mate at the beginning of the season. But my red-eye is paired, as are the others in the neighborhood.

Why, then, does he continue to sing so much? Can he never let up? Is he always trying to impress, either his own mate or the females on neighboring territories? Given the effort he makes, the amount of song must be an index as to what is at stake; perhaps females are always listening and making decisions about choices they will make when laying their next eggs. That's what a 1998 study suggests, because most of the babies (11 out of 19) in that study were fathered by a male other than the one who seemed to be paired to the female with the nest. Maybe the most persistent singers father far more than their share of young in the neighborhood? Maybe.

And just when will the males stop singing? When the females are no longer interested in sex, I bet. The females need sex (whether she "enjoys" it or not is irrelevant, of course) to obtain sperm so they can fertilize their eggs, but if no female in a neighborhood "plans" to lay any more eggs in a season, there's no reason for the males to continue singing, either. I'd love to try an experiment, using three forested areas. In early July, I'd catch the females in one area and give each a dose of "anti-estrogen," a hormone that turns off her reproductive system so that there would be no chance that she'd lay another clutch of eggs. The second forested plot would be a control, in which the females would go about their business as usual. In the third plot, each of the females would receive an estrogen boost, thereby prolonging her sexual activity through August. By mid-July, I'd predict dead silence from the male vireos in the forest plot where the females were turned "off"; males in the control area would probably stop singing during early August, the normal time when females stop breeding; those males with energized females in plot three, however, would continue to sing through August. I am confident that the males would adjust their singing according to the opportunities offered by the females, because it is a male's lifelong business to know these things.

Overhead, he continues, closer now. High in the canopy, he hops along the red oak branches, feeding, then pausing to sing every few seconds, flying a yard or so perhaps every 10 seconds. Raising the binoculars, I see his crimson red eye; the crown is blue gray, its fine black lateral edges contrasting sharply with the white line just above the eyes, which contrasts again with a dusky eyeline itself, the overall effect making him look cross. Below he is a soft olive green and bright white, and I can clearly see his vireo bill, wide at the base and slightly hooked at the tip.

I hear him running through the familiar songs in his repertoire. Slower now, every few seconds . . . There's the goldfinch imitation again, the "question," the whistle with rising inflection that the goldfinch uses to punctuate his song. Instinctively, wanting to know when I'll next hear it, I start counting, 1 . . . 2 . . . 3 . . .

5

The Hour Before the Dawn

AS DAWN'S FIRST LIGHT sweeps the globe, so too does a wave of birdsong sweep from east to west, endlessly, day after day, millennium after millennium. Commonly known as the "dawn chorus," this period of intense singing remains largely an enigma, partly because few people thrive on getting up early enough to study this remarkable phenomenon.

Listening to how birds sing at dawn is key to understanding them, as illustrated in many accounts in this book. Miss a chestnut-sided warbler's dawn chorus, for example, and you'll fail to realize the context in which his special dawn song undoubtedly evolved. Hear a black-capped chickadee at dawn and realize the intensity with which he cycles through a broad range of frequencies for his *hey-sweetie* song. Hear any singing bird at dawn, and you'll likely hear something special, perhaps even undescribed in all of the written literature about that species.

Of the vast array of species or groups I would have loved to include in this chapter, I finally settled on three groups: 1) certain flycatchers, for the uniqueness of their dawn efforts, including especially the eastern wood-pewee for the beauty in its dawn singing; 2) two sparrows, the chipping sparrow and Brewer's sparrow, to show their dual personalities, the fierce singers at dawn replaced by more placid singers later in the day; and 3) the eastern bluebird, a most beloved ultrablue bird whose songs have been largely ignored.

The Eastern Wood-Pewee

By late May the spring chorus that I hear from my bedroom window is almost complete. First to sing in the spring were the resident chickadees and titmice and cardinals, followed by the migrant phoebes, robins, ovenbirds, tanagers, and so many others. They're all accounted for now, except the last one, the plaintive *pee-ah-wee* signature to mark his arrival.

Where is he now, I wonder? Somewhere between my small forested plot in New England and his winter home in Venezuela or Colombia, or maybe even in Brazil—I enjoy thinking of him in mid January foraging in the treetops along the Amazon, thriving midwinter in South America, the ancestral home of all our northern flycatchers. He knows where to return each winter—so sure is he that not a single one of his kind has ever been caught lingering in North America over the winter. Now the northern winter is past, and I know that by mid-April his kind have already returned to the southern states, filling in the eastern half of the continent from south to north; any day now the wave will sweep over me in western Massachusetts as the birds settle into the northern part of their range. The arrival of these smudges of drab grays and greens in the forest canopy would go largely unnoticed were it not for their song.

MAY 28. *Pee-ah-wee,* from high in the oaks above our deck he announces his return. It's over breakfast, not at dawn, when I first hear him (track 78, figure 57). He's arrived overnight, and it'll perhaps take him a day or more before he sings at dawn. This slurred whistle, this *pee-ah-wee,* is his unmistakable trademark. A pure whistle, only a second long, it begins about three octaves above middle A, first rising in pitch during the *pee,* then falling to the *ah,* then rising and finishing strong on the *wee,* the peewee gliding smoothly through his namesake. *Pee-ah-wee.* I feel the rhythm of the song. I see the *pee-ah-wee* pattern form in my mind, a simple sonagram I can easily draw by hand.

One, two, three, four times *pee-ah-wee,* and then a *wee-ooo.* The *pee-ah-wee* is incomplete without it, as if the pewee needs to answer his own question: *Pee-ah-wee? . . . wee-ooo.* He begins strong on the *wee,* rising just slightly, and then drops to the *ooo.* He sounds mournful, a full 10 seconds from one mini-dirge to the next.

JUNE 5, 9:40 A.M. For an hour I will sit on our deck and just listen to him. It's the first of two steps in a summer promise I have made to myself, to understand him better, both during the day and at dawn. I settle into my deck chair now, on the table beside me an ink pen and 4 sheets of paper on a clipboard. Each sheet of paper has room for 15 minutes of songs: 15 rows of 60 periods, the dots broken into groups of 10, so that as he sings I can consult my watch and mark to the nearest second when each song occurs. When he sings, I'll mark from the dot up to the right if it's a *pee-ah-wee,* and down to the right if it's a *wee-ooo.*

The first minute: *pee-ah-wee . . . pee-ah-wee . . . pee-ah-wee . . . wee-ooo . . . pee-ah-wee . . . pee-ah-wee . . . wee-ooo.*

I could have stopped there, as I would learn little more over the next 59 minutes. A song every 9 to 10 seconds, 381 of them overall, two or three *pee-ah-wee*s followed by a single *wee-ooo*. Nine times he sang as many as four to six *pee-ah-wee*s in a row, but mostly it was just three *pee-ah-wee*s (34 times), two (59 times), or only one (9 times), followed by a single *wee-ooo*, never more. Never during his metronomic performance did I tire of listening, never did I feel called to move on to anything more important.

He must still be unpaired, I surmise, or else he wouldn't sing so. With a mate and a nest to think about, he'd sing only occasionally, nothing like this kind of marathon performance.

Over the next week I bike my forested route, up Buffam Brook Road to the top of Pelham hill, then to the top of Shutesbury on West Pelham Road, then to Lake Wyola, through Wendell State Forest, and hear other peewees, too. Those who sing tell largely the same story, though they differ in whether to use two, three, or four *pee-ah-wee* songs before answering with a *wee-ooo*. I wonder why. It is known that fewer *pee-ah-wee* songs are used when a male

Figure 57: EASTERN WOOD-PEWEE

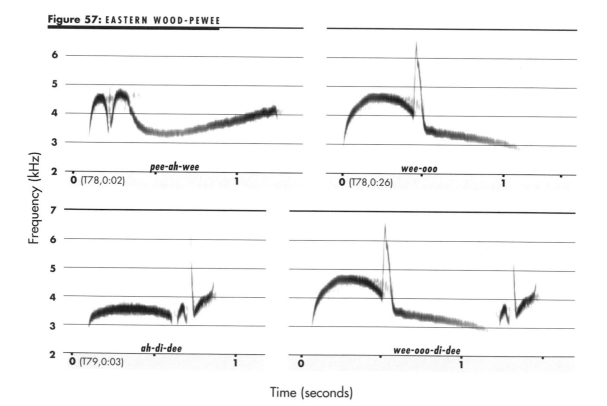

Time (seconds)

The Singing Life of Birds

interacts with other pewees. Perhaps those males who sing more *pee-ah-wee* songs are singing all alone, and those with fewer are singing near another male. Maybe yearlings are more easily agitated and use fewer *pee-ah-wee* songs than older birds? Or perhaps males simply differ in their personalities, regardless of age. Perhaps all of the above.

The second part of my summer's promise is to be with him at dawn, as he awakes. From a thorough 1943 monograph on pewees, I know what to expect. I must be in place at the special tree, waiting, more than an hour before sunrise. The prelude will be in the distance, the full treatment overhead, followed by the postlude, either overhead or in the distance.

I scouted him a few days ago and know the tree. It's a towering silver maple on the north edge of the clearing down by Kettle Pond, just a hundred yards from my home. Why that tree, I don't know. Perhaps being at the edge of the clearing is important, as the songs might carry farther. I must be waiting there tomorrow morning, a full hour before sunrise.

JUNE 17. Sunrise will be at 5:12 A.M. Rats! Here it is, 4:21, and I'm late. I missed it, missed the beginning. Already in the distance, to the south, I hear him in his leisurely prelude: two or three *pee-ah-wee* songs followed by a single *wee-ooo,* just like his daytime singing, though the tempo is a little faster, perhaps 10 to 12 songs a minute. I put the parabola on the tripod, aim the parabola up into his favorite maple tree, and turn the tape recorder on, making sure that I capture him as soon as he arrives. Walking south toward him, I hear him better, jotting down on my clipboard the strings of *pee-ah-wee* songs followed by a single *wee-ooo*—still the prelude. Silent for 10 seconds, he resumes behind me, between me and his tree. I walk back, hearing above me three *pee-ah-wee* songs in a row, then a *wee-ooo.* Now beneath his tree, I hear him twitter overhead, announcing that he's here, and ready; it's 4:25 A.M., and I know that I've heard my last two *pee-ah-wee* songs in a row for some time.

Following the twitter is a single *pee-ah-wee,* then an *ah-di-dee,* and he's under way (track 79, figure 57). Here is his *ah-di-dee,* his third song type, used mostly at dawn, the song that signals the end of the prelude. He now launches into a frenzy of singing, and I capture the next 10 seconds on my clipboard:

Figure 57. Songs of the eastern wood-pewee (tracks 78 and 79). For the eastern wood-pewee, the *pee-ah-wee* and the *wee-ooo* are his standard daytime songs, the *ah-di-dee* the additional song heard at dawn and dusk. The particular pewee I listened to had a special "hybrid" song that he also used at dawn, a *wee-ooo-di-dee* (not on the CD).

∴⌐ ⋯⌐ ., or written out as *wee-ooo . . . pee-ah-wee . . . ah-di-dee . . . wee-ooo . . . ah-di-dee . . .*

And the next 10: / ⋯⌐ ./⌐ written out as *pee-ah-wee . . . wee-ooo . . . ah-di-dee . . . pee-ah-wee . . . wee-ooo-di-dee . . .*

In 20 seconds alone he delivers 10 songs, at a rate of one every two seconds, 30 a minute. Already he teaches me one of his combination songs, the *wee-ooo-di-dee.* On my clipboard I have kept pace, glancing at my illuminated stopwatch and from the dot on the page marking up and to the right for a *pee-ah-wee,* down and to the right for a *wee-ooo,* a vertical mark through the dot for an *ah-di-dee,* a combination of the last two for the *wee-ooo-di-dee.* I can keep up, I know, as dozens of other listeners have succeeded, all reported in Wallace Craig's survey back in 1943.

I soon hear some of his favorite sequences. One is *pee-ah-wee . . . wee-ooo . . . ah-di-dee . . . ,* and I soon realize that most *wee-ooo-di-dee*s are followed by an *ah-di-dee.*

Knowing that all of these songs are being automatically recorded by my setup beneath the tree, and knowing that I can study them later, I slack off on the note-taking. Beyond the pewee, I now hear the halting dawn songs of the scarlet tanager, his hoarse notes delivered almost one by one, more like a red-eyed vireo than the well-packaged two-second song that I know from later in the morning. A wood thrush sings to my left, another behind me, the two taking turns as if answering each other.

EASTERN
WOOD-PEWEE

I find the pewee irresistible. I tiptoe to the recording setup and slip the headphones over my ears, listening to what the tape recorder is capturing. The *pee* of the *pee-ah-wee* first explodes into my ears, then the song ends high, as if he asks a question. He answers, *wee-ooo.* He inquires in a different way, *ah-di-dee?* He answers the same, *wee-ooo.*

At 22 minutes into his performance, I raise the binoculars, wondering if it's light enough now to see him. Scanning the canopy, I spot him, sitting on a stub of a dead branch perhaps 10 feet below the top of the tree. He sings, scans quickly left and right, then sings again, scans again, as if alert for a hawk who would make him a meal. He then hops into the air and alights facing the other direction, perhaps eager to broadcast to listening pewees in all directions.

After 25 minutes, at 4:50 A.M., 22 minutes before sunrise, he ends as he began: *pee-ah-wee . . . wee-ooo-di-dee . . . ah-di-dee . . . pee-ah-wee . . .* in

The Singing Life of Birds

rapid fire, then a twitter, and off he flies, back to the south from where he had come. Twenty seconds later I hear him in the distance, strings of two or three *pee-ah-wee* songs followed by a single *wee-ooo*. He continues this postlude for almost two minutes, and at 4:52, 20 minutes before sunrise, is silent.

🐦

Months later, in October, I listen to the peewees again, this time in my home. Headphones on, I first hear those distant *pee-ah-wee* and *wee-ooo* songs of the prelude, the songs becoming louder as he approaches the tree where my parabola is aimed. He twitters, then launches into his 25-minute performance; this time I capture each song on my clipboard. The sights and smells seem to play back, too, as I relive those few minutes spent with this pewee at dawn. The frustration plays back, too, as I realize that I probably missed about 10 minutes of his prelude, the first minutes of which were only an occasional *wee-ooo,* the first one uttered from his roosting place.

I now focus on those 25 minutes of his most intense effort. In my notes, the *pee-ah-wee* becomes a 1, the *wee-ooo* a 2, the *ah-di-dee* a 3, the *wee-ooo-di-dee* a 4. I can't resist looking at what he does in each minute (table 5):

TABLE 5

MINUTE	SONG SEQUENCE
1	21323 12314 31231 23123 14312 31231
2	21321 41321 42312 31231 43123 123
3	12321 23123 21413 21321 23123 12312
4	31231 23123 14312 31231 23143 12312
5	31231 23213 21321 32132 13413 21321 32
6	31231 23123 21231 23123 13231 23143 141
7	32143 21321 32132 31231 43123 12312 31
8	32132 31231 23123 12312 31231 21321 3213
9	23123 12312 31231 23123 12431 23123 13
10	23123 12312 31231 23143 12312 31231 4
11	31231 23123 12413 21323 12123 1231
12	32143 12314 31231 23141 43123 12
13	31321 32131 23143 12312 31421 23
14	31231 43123 12312 31231 23123 12312
15	31231 23123 14312 31231 23123 1231
16	23123 12312 31231 23123 14312 312
17	31321 32132 13213 21321 23132 314
18	31231 23123 12312 31231 32143 14
19	31231 41323 12314 31231 41321 2
20	31431 21321 32123 13214 3141
21	21231 23123 12314 12314 132
22	12314 31231 23231 23143 1231
23	41321 41231 21112
24	12131 41341 43143 141
25	31412 14121 14121
Number of songs each minute	5 10 15 20 25 30 35

The simple list of 682 numbers itself becomes a figure when I add the scale at the bottom, the scale that tells me how many songs he sang in each minute. The shape of this list of numbers bulges to the right when he was singing most intensely during minutes 5 through 10, reaching a peak of 34 songs in minute 8. I see, too, how his rate tapers off toward minute 25, when the postlude began.

I yearn for yet another way to think of how he sings. Given that he sings a *pee-a-wee*, for example, what is the probability that the next song will be a *wee-ooo*, or an *ah-di-dee*, or a *wee-ooo-di-dee*? I study all of the transitions, chart them all (just as I did with the wood thrushes and hermit thrushes), so that I can see which song will follow which (table 6). Rather than study the information for all 682 songs, I want to summarize, so I convert the numbers to percentages (by dividing the number in each cell by 682 and multiplying by 100). I now look at a transition matrix for a "typical" 100 songs.

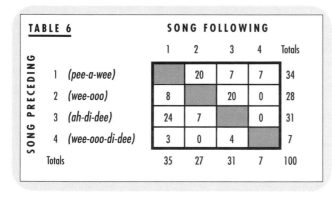

TABLE 6	SONG FOLLOWING				
SONG PRECEDING		1	2	3	4	Totals
1 (pee-a-wee)		20	7	7	34
2 (wee-ooo)	8		20	0	28
3 (ah-di-dee)	24	7		0	31
4 (wee-ooo-di-dee)	3	0	4		7
Totals	35	27	31	7	100

I begin to feel I understand a little better what he is doing. I first look at the far right column for the total number of times he uses each song, noting that the *wee-ooo-di-dee* is rather rare, occurring only 7 times in 100 songs; the other three songs are about equally common. Next I look at the sequences he favors. When he sings a *pee-a-wee*, which he does 34 times in 100 songs, the song that follows is most likely going to be a *wee-ooo* (20 out of 34 times), less likely an *ah-di-dee* or a *wee-ooo-di-dee* (only 7 out of the 34 times for each). The *wee-ooo* is typically followed by an *ah-di-dee*, which in turn is followed by *pee-a-wee*, so that his favorite sequence is the 1 2 3, the *pee-a-wee* to *wee-ooo* to *ah-di-dee*. I study table 5 again, finding that the 1 2 3 sequence occurs a total of 116 times. Never during this dawn singing does a *pee-a-wee* immediately follow another *pee-a-wee*; nor, for that matter, does he repeat any of his four songs immediately (see darkly shaded cells on the diagonal of table 6).

I wonder if there's some meaning to the particular sequences he chose that morning. Would he choose the same sequences on the following day? How might he change his singing during different phases of the breeding cycle? If I studied neighbors, would they be doing the same things? If I knew the ages of the birds, might young birds sing differently from older birds? All are intriguing questions, and all are answerable, most of them by anyone willing to arise early enough and simply listen.

Each summer day, in my mind I hear these pewees and their songs over the entire eastern half of the continent, sweeping west during a two-hour period from Nova Scotia and northern Florida to southern Manitoba and eastern Texas, stopping abruptly halfway into Oklahoma, Kansas, Nebraska, and the Dakotas. No regional learned dialects occur in this pewee's songs, because the genes have all the instructions for these songs, so that young birds do not need to learn their songs from adults. As a result, pewees everywhere agree on their songs because it seems that they, as eastern wood-pewees, all share the same song genes.

The genes change midcontinent, just across the Great Plains. From there west to the Pacific and up to Alaska is another pewee, the western wood-pewee. The plaintive whistles of the East give way to a harsher *peeer*, slightly descending in pitch, heard throughout the day in the West. At dawn, the three-song performance of the East gives way to a two-song performance, the *peeer* alternated with a three-noted *tswee-tee-teet: Peeer . . . tswee-tee-teet . . . peeer . . . tswee-tee-teet . . .* (track 80, figure 58). The sounds of these two wood-pewees are distinctive, but their looks are not. By just looking, one could hardly know that the pewee divide had been crossed mid-continent, as pewees

Figure 58: WESTERN WOOD-PEWEE

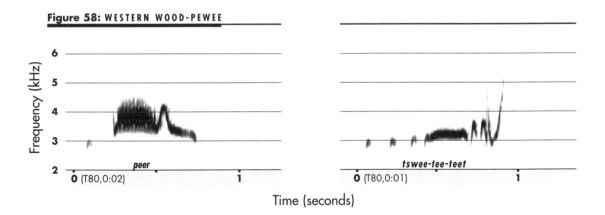

Time (seconds)

Figure 58. Songs of the western wood-pewee (track 80). Each male has only two songs; the *peeer* is his standard daytime song, and at dawn he adds the *tswee-tee-teet*. Look at that stuttered ending of the *tswee-tee-teet*. Is it only a coincidence that there is also a stuttered ending to the *ah-di-dee* dawn song of the eastern wood-pewee? Perhaps the *ah-di-dee* and *tswee-tee-teet* reveal two slightly different versions of a dawn song that was used by the ancestral wood-pewee that gave rise to these two sibling species.

everywhere are grayish olive above and more grayish below, with two whitish bars on a darker wing. No, it's not the appearance, but rather the songs, or more specifically the song genes, that inform of the great midcontinent shift.

I wish I knew more about this western bird, that I had paid more attention to him when I lived in Oregon. When he first arrives on his territory in the spring, how does he sing throughout the day as he tries to attract his female? Does he use the simple, harsh *peeer* instead of the eastern's *pee-ah-wee* and *wee-ooo?* How does he greet the new day? Does he begin a prelude from his overnight roost, and if so, which song does he use first? Does he have a *peer* prelude before he flies to a favorite singing perch, and does he then alternate the *peeer* and the *tswee-tee-teet,* singing each an equal number of times, or does he favor one over the other, or does it depend on the individual? My lack of attention years ago means that I must travel to the West again, to understand better how the song genes of eastern and western wood-pewees differ and how they're the same.

Why, I wonder, do these two pewees differ in their singing? They are sibling species, closest of relatives, derived from a common ancestor. What was that ancestor like? How did it sing? Because both of its descendents now have a three-noted song at dawn, the eastern *ah-di-dee* and the western *tswee-tee-teet,* the ancestor perhaps had such a three-parted song, too. Perhaps the slurred *wee-ooo* of the East and the *peer* of the West are homologous, each derived from a particular song of their ancestor. If the ancestral pewee had two songs, the eastern descendent somehow and for some reason derived an extra song, the *pee-a-wee.* I know I can learn more about the ancestral pewee by studying the songs of the other members of this genus *Contopus,* too. No fewer than 10 other pewees occur in the Americas, and a survey of their singing should tell me far more of their collective song history.

Because Europeans settled our North American continent from east to west, the eastern bird was described first, hence the name "pewee" after its *pee-ah-wee* song. Had the continent been explored from west to east, I wonder what they would now be called. The eastern and western wood-peeers?

My inspiration for listening to pewees comes from Wallace Craig, whose 1943 treatise was entitled "The song of the wood-pewee . . . a study of bird music." Its 186 pages tell us most of what we know today about how the eastern wood-pewee sings. Craig and his small army of volunteer listeners had only their well-trained ears and notepads, coupled with an eagerness to explore, the only ingredients needed to study most of nature's music.

Chipping and Brewer's Sparrows

Over the third of a century that I've been listening to birds, two events especially stand out. Both occurred in the predawn darkness, and in both the actors were unseen. One event was along a roadside in Michigan, where four chipping sparrows sang at my feet, the other in the sagebrush of central Oregon, where countless Brewer's sparrows sang, also, it seemed, within arm's reach. As a new millennium resolution, I vowed to reexperience these two events, perhaps to understand them better.

THE CHIPPING SPARROW

JUNE 13. Quabbin Cemetery, Ware, Massachusetts. By 6:00 A.M. it's all over, but I'll be back tomorrow, as this morning is only a rehearsal. I'll stand here, beneath this lone ash tree, looking across the gravel lane called Pine Ridge Road. There the land rises from the lane, the gravestones thronging up the bank and spilling over the top and beyond, out of sight.

Two of the stones on the bank are the favorite dawn singing posts of the chippy who owns that territory:

EMILENE
Daughter of
Henry & Eunice
Haskins
died Aug. 9, 1815
At 10 Months

MONTAGUE
son of Henry and
Wealthy Haskins
died Jan. 21, 1817.
At 7 weeks.
"Dust thou art and unto dust
shalt thou return. Genesis 3:19."

At such tender ages, Emilene and Montague died and were buried, only to be uprooted more than a hundred years later and moved, like the other residents here, to this new home, to what is now chipping sparrow heaven. Emilene and Montague's old home now lies beneath the huge Quabbin Reservoir to the north, or perhaps in the watershed that feeds the reservoir that in turn feeds Boston. Their final resting places had become semifinal when Boston took the land for its water, though some combination of good manners and water-purity standards demanded that the hundreds of remains scattered throughout the "discontinued" towns of Dana, Enfield, Greenwich, and Prescott be exhumed and moved here, consolidated, hundreds of years' worth of scattered remains now all neatly contained in this one cemetery.

I check my bearings, knowing I'll need them in the dark early tomorrow morning (figure 59). Up the lane to my right is the cul-de-sac, bounded by forest—only two chipping sparrows with territories up there. Pine Ridge Road and Oak Way intersect just to my left, a fourth sparrow singing from just beyond, often near the street sign. The bulk of the cemetery lies beyond that sign, to the southwest and west, as I'm off in the far northeast corner, biting off a mere four birds from the two dozen or more who make this cemetery their summer home.

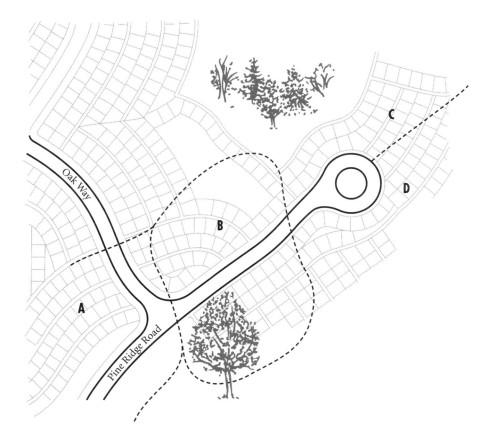

Figure 59. A map of the northeast portion of the Quabbin Cemetery, Ware, Massachusetts, showing the territories of the four chipping sparrows there. The ash tree in Bird B's territory was my base; from there, Bird B would sing among the gravestones on the bank across Pine Ridge Road, Bird A would be to the left, and Birds C and D to my right.

It didn't take long this morning before I knew these four by their songs alone. They all have a typical chipping sparrow song consisting of a simple rattle or trill, a single split-second phrase repeated many times over (examples in figure 60). A young chipping sparrow has perhaps 30 different versions of this song from which to choose his one, and luckily, the songs of my four birds are all different. The simplest song is owned by Rattles, up on the left side of the cul-de-sac; his song is the driest of mechanical rattles, almost insectlike, as if produced by a rattle shaken 20 to 30 times a second. In front of me, above the bank across Pine Ridge Road, is Raspy, his song more deliberate, perhaps only a dozen pulses a second, each pulse consisting of a raspy, harsh sound.

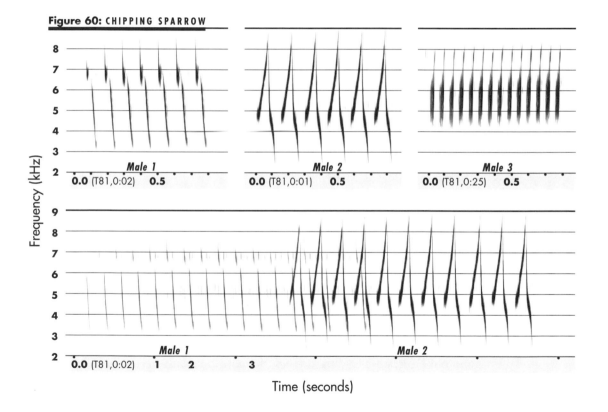

Figure 60: CHIPPING SPARROW

Figure 60. Top row: Brief songs of three male chipping sparrows, showing just three out of the great diversity of songs among males of this species (track times in parentheses tell where these three individuals can first be heard on the CD). **Bottom row:** A typical dawn exchange by two males, with the song of Male 2 in the foreground overlapping the end of Male 1's song in the background.

The songs of the other two males are equally distinctive. They're less mechanical and more pleasant, musical even, sounding like brief whistles that rapidly rise or fall in pitch; the songs are slower-paced, too, perhaps only eight phrases a second, just about slow enough for me to count them. The two differ in their overall effect. To my left, at the intersection of Pine Ridge and Oak Way, the energy in each of the syllables seems to fall, the whistles slurred downward, most of the energy feeling to come about three octaves above middle C. In contrast, to my right, on my side of Pine Ridge and up to the right side of the cul-de-sac, the energy in the syllable rises, the whistles in each syllable slurred upward, each syllable sounding loudest about four octaves above middle C. Once tuned to this difference, I can easily identify the two birds, as they no doubt can easily identify each other (for examples of such distinctive chipping sparrow songs—but not the four males described here, see figure 60 and listen to tracks 81, 82).

I'm tempted to name these two also, but names will be far harder to keep track of than something simpler, such as letters. The down-slurring whistler to my left I will call A, Raspy in front of me is B, Rattles is C, and the sweet whistler to my far right is D. Left to right, all in their places, A, B, C, and D. Our time together will feel less personal this way, but keeping track of everyone will be easier come morning.

I listen a little more. From high in the trees across the lane, I hear Raspy —no, B—each song typically three to four seconds long. Beyond him to the west, a most persistent male sings about four songs a minute; he is no doubt unpaired, advertising for a mate, as he has been singing for some time now. B now twitters from the ground just across the lane, accompanied by his mate. C (aka Rattles) sputters his song from the cul-de-sac.

I'm ready now for the real thing. I take one last look at my bearings, read the stories on a few more gravestones, and leave for the day.

JUNE 14, 4:00 A.M. I'm back. I don't expect them to begin for at least half an hour, but I'm ready, standing in the dark beneath the ash tree, waiting for the first birds. Accompanied by a chorus of nearby crickets, a distant robin sings, probably by the streetlight on the road to the west. At 4:31 a robin sings perhaps 100 yards to the left, a minute later a hermit thrush in the woods behind me. Otherwise, it remains eerily quiet.

4:34. A few territories to the west a single chipping sparrow begins, his songs no longer than a second apiece. For two minutes he owns the cemetery, the only chipping sparrow announcing his residence.

4:36. To my left, on the gravel in the intersection or in the grass just beyond it, Bird A begins. His first song is about two seconds long, but the next just a fraction of a second, perhaps only three of those down-sweeping whistles. A split second later another short song follows, and within seconds I hear the raspy song of Bird B on the bank opposite me. The dawn fusillade has begun.

My head spins as I try to follow these birds. Bird D now sings from the cul-de-sac, also sputtering brief songs from the ground, but then I hear him just to my right, the bird in the cul-de-sac now silent. He's moved. A is to my left, B in front of me, and D to my right, all three singing phantoms within five yards of me, all unseen, all on the ground or a gravestone, each sputtering his distinctive song. B delivers, but he's cut off by D, whose song in turn is overlapped by A. Sometimes they alternate, sometimes overlap, but I cannot keep track of who plays what role in this game.

CHIPPING
SPARROW

The whir of wings, a twitter, and I no longer hear B in front of me but to my right, once, twice, his spitfire song coming one a second. Bird D is initially silent, but then resumes his ground threats toward the cul-de-sac, showing that his first advance has been repulsed. For perhaps two minutes they hold their lines, but Bird A has now advanced from the left, as his songs now come from the bank, near B's favorite stone, where I soon hear B, too. They sing as if one bird, from one location, but I know it must be two, because one song often overlaps the other, and no one bird can sing two such different songs, let alone two at once. In my mind I see them, just a few feet apart, facing each other, perhaps B on his stone and A below him on the ground. Half a minute passes, these two so engaged, with Bird B often seeming to sing first and then being cut off by A. And then there is only B, with A soon singing off to the left again, from the intersection.

B's raspy songs then stop. He must be over the bank to the west, challenging a neighbor there just as his neighbors come to challenge him. Within a minute he returns, Birds A and D soon advancing, each within 5 yards of him; A then retreats left to the intersection as D leapfrogs over Bird B. For a minute Bird D stays, jousting with B, and then D is back toward the cul-de-sac, just past the small American flag I can now see there. In the growing light, I can see these forms moving about, but I easily lose track, still relying on my ears.

4:59. They carry on, sparring, but I hear a fifth bird beyond A who intrigues me. Walking toward the intersection, I hear A, but just beyond I hear what sounds like A again, as if this bird sings back and forth from two locations. It's two birds, of course, but with identical songs, immediate neighbors. Back and forth they sing, mostly alternating, as if taking turns, but often Bird A overlaps the song of his neighbor, seemingly interrupting him. I smile and say a small thank-you, not only to these two birds but also to Wan-chun Liu, the student who taught me how to interpret what is happening here.

Back to the ash tree I walk, listening for the continuing battles, as I want to stick with the entire group of four sparrows until they are done. I hear Bird C rattling from the cul-de-sac, he not once having joined the fray where I stand. I wonder why. Is he shy, bashful, or insecure? Or is he so dominant over the others that he doesn't need to do battle, and everyone knows it? Birds B and D still sing nearby, though from opposite sides of the road, their songs now longer, some of them two to even three seconds long. I now clearly see B, too, perched atop a gravestone.

5:06. Here is the beginning of the end, as Bird A now sings from five yards up in the tree, up above the sign at the intersection of Pine Ridge and Oak Way (in track 82, hear how songs gradually lengthen during the dawn chorus, becoming much longer as the bird sings from the trees). One thousand one, one thousand two . . . his first song more than five seconds long, as if all the sputtering this morning had prepared him for this longer song. That's the longest one, as those that follow are only three or four seconds long. At 5:06, exactly 30 minutes after Bird A began it all, still 6 minutes before sunrise, he seems to have raised the white flag, calling an end to the ground battles. The other males soon follow, each singing from high in a tree in what is now clearly his own territory. Bird B is in a red oak across Pine Ridge, and D is in the pines at the cul-de-sac, where Rattles also sings.

Thanks to years of persistence in the early morning hours by a dedicated graduate student, I can now understand much of what I heard this morning. Before sunrise males sputter brief songs from the ground, up to 60 a minute. Over the next half-hour or so the singing rate slows and song length gradually increases, until the ground singing is over and males rise to sing from the trees. Paired males then sing little for the rest of the day, but a male still seek-ing a mate continues to sing these longer songs all day.

The what and why of the dawn skirmishes are more of a mystery. If terri-tories are widely dispersed, it seems that the males still convene at a tradition-al location, sparring there even if some of the males don't own territories that border that place. The older, dominant males begin the dawn singing on any given morning, and an older bird more often overlaps the songs of a submis-sive or younger neighbor, rather than the other way around. To interrupt a singer, to cut him off, is a strong, aggressive message.

Are these males jockeying for position in a dominance hierarchy, with the winners having some advantage in holding real estate or impressing the females? What else could they be doing? If a female chooses to have a fling with a male other than her partner, and much evidence shows that females of many songbird species have young in their nest fathered by more than one male, then perhaps she will choose as an extra-pair father the male who in some way wins these dawn skirmishes. Perhaps.

What about the two males with the same song, Bird A and his neighbor to the south? There is a simple and most satisfying answer. One almost cer-tainly learned his song from the other, either this spring or late last summer. Given how Bird A often overlaps the songs of this neighbor, I bet that Bird A is the older male. Most likely the young bird had dispersed some distance (a mile or more not being unlikely) from his hatch territory and settled next to Bird A, and during their battles over space, the young bird learned the adult's song. If the battles and learning occurred last summer, then both birds migrated south last fall and returned this spring to this very place, at the inter-section of Pine Ridge and Oak Way in Quabbin Cemetery. If the learning occurred this spring, the yearling migrated back here after the adult and then learned his song as he fought for a territory.

Why don't more neighbors have the same songs? Even though every young bird seems to learn his one song from an immediate neighbor, why in any given year at Quabbin Cemetery do only three or four pairs of neighbor-ing males share songs and thus reveal this learning process? Part of the answer is that these birds lead too short a life, roughly half of them dying each year. Suppose that a young bird learns the song of his adult neighbor during late summer; there's only a 1 in 4 chance that both will survive until the next spring. Even if they do both survive, they may part for reasons other than death, as males often move from one territory to another, breaking up these tutor-pupil pairs. Also, males have many different songs from which to choose, 20 to 30 of them, so among the males at the cemetery there is a great diversity of songs. Because a young male imitates the songs of just one adult, the youngsters perpetuate the diverse song lineages. If a young male learned his song in other ways, such as by learning the most common song he heard, then the diversity in chipping sparrow songs would be lost, and all chipping sparrows would come to sing the same song, as black-capped chickadees do.

THE BREWER'S SPARROW

JUNE 6. Dyson Lane, locally known as Marble Hot Springs Road, Sierra Valley, Plumas County, California. A flight into Reno, the drive down interstate 80 to Truckee, then north on 89 to Sierraville, north again toward Beckworth, right onto Dyson Lane, and I stand in a different world.

A sea of waist-high sagebrush extends in all directions, the light green clumps nearby already giving way to a liquefied, distant blur in the midmorning heat, merging with the darker hills in the distance, the hills merging in turn with the brilliant blue sky. Hidden in the blur to the east and west, I know, are the marshes where I hear the noisy blackbirds, the red-wings and the yellow-heads. A line of white pelicans floats over the hills to the south. A pair of sandhill cranes trumpet to the north.

I listen closer, waiting, wanting to be sure this is the place. One by one they assure me, as over the next hour I hear perhaps a dozen of them. *Zreeeee zrrr-zrrr-zrrr* one sings, followed by a *tir-tir-tir-tir deee-deee-deee* from his neighbor. These two sing again, *zreeeee zrrr-zrrr-zrrr, tir-tir-tir-tir deee-deee-deee,* each male from his own territory. Simple two-parted songs they are, two to three seconds long, each of these males consistently singing his particular version (track 83, figure 61). One of the dozen males has a three-parted song, *Cheeeeee zre-zre-zre-zre chp-chp-chp-chp-chp,* another a one-parted song, a simple raspy sound repeated rapidly many times, *z-z-z-z-z-z-z-z-z-z,* almost insectlike. Yes, here is where I'll return tomorrow morning, well before sunrise, to hear these Brewer's sparrows at dawn.

JUNE 7. Sunrise will be at 5:40, but I can't resist, and I arrive at Dyson Lane by 3:00. The nearly full moon to the southwest sets the whole valley aglow, and the entire world seems awake. A western marsh wren sings from the ditch along the road as I drive in, and snipe winnow overhead, others calling *kit kit kit kit* from the marsh. To the north a bittern pumps, coots squawk and flail about in the water, and a single Virginia rail cuts loose: *kik kik kik kidik-kidik-kidik-kidik-kidik-kidik-kidik-kidik.* From the sagebrush in all directions arise a thousand tinkling bells, horned larks singing by moonlight.

At 3:35, with Venus just over the eastern horizon, two ruddy ducks display in the pool just north of the bridge. Each one pumps his bill against his chest in turn, each pumping out a muffled *jif jif jif jif ji ji ji ji jijijijiijiwirrrrrr.* The bells continue, as do the winnows, the pumps, and other sounds of those already or still about. But the sparrows so far are silent.

When they will begin I do not know, but I must be ready. Tape recorder slung over my shoulder, headphones perched atop my cap, parabolic microphone in hand, I walk out into the sagebrush to the north, pausing at as likely a spot as any. I hope to find a place where I can simply stand and listen, swinging my parabolic ear 360 degrees as I listen and record these Brewer's sparrows. At 4:00 they're still quiet, not a single one to be heard.

There, to the east. I walk slowly toward the lightening horizon, eager to get in position, but then one begins to my left, and then to my right, and behind me. All around the sparrows have come alive, the sagebrush in all directions bubbling with their songs. How do I choose where, and whom, and . . .? I lose minutes, how many I don't know, before I catch myself, planting my feet, dropping the headphones over my ears, and turning the tape recorder on, at 4:22.

I swing my parabola to the left and right, the signal strong in my ears when I'm aiming at a singer, weaker as I pass to either side. I home in on one

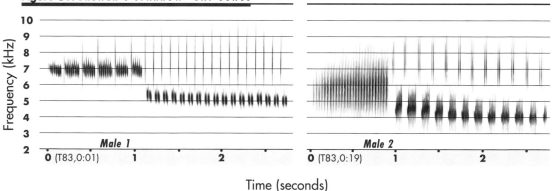

Figure 61: BREWER'S SPARROW—DAY SONGS

Figure 61. Daytime songs of two Brewer's sparrows. These daytime songs are relatively simple, typically consisting of just two trills (track 83), the first higher than the second. Each male tends to have a unique song or "songprint" that distinguishes him from others in the neighborhood.

just in front of me, to the east (track 84, figure 62). The first is a four-parted song, a canary-like ramble over almost five seconds, but curses! A loud insect calls between the bird and me, destroying my recording. *Zeeet zeeet zeeet zeeet zeeet zeeet zeeet zeeet* it calls, continuous and high-pitched, perhaps four octaves above middle C. I maneuver to the left, but the insect follows, and the sparrow delivers a five-parted song. To the right I move, *zeeet zeeet zeeet zeeet zeeet*, and the buzzing insect moves, too, more *zeeet*s followed by a seven-parted song. But wait! The insect always stops when the bird sings. Now 18 *zeeet*s, then a 13-parted song.

It's clear now. There can be no other explanation. It is the sparrow who *zeeet*s that high-pitched insect buzz a dozen or more times, and then he sings his canary-like ramble, filling in every possible second with sound. How easily I was duped, I chuckle—I probably shouldn't admit this to anyone.

I listen more closely now and sense a pattern. Perhaps 20 *zeeet*s, but the two trills that follow are also high-pitched; more *zeeet*s, and then the pitch of the following trills cascades down, the pitch dropping to half of what it was before, feeling now like only three octaves above middle C. More *zeeet*s and only three high-pitched trills, then *zeeet*s followed by an eight-parted series of canary-like trills that again drops to the lower pitch. The next series of trills is also low, then high, then low, low, high, low, high, high, low, high, low, low, and high over the next several minutes. It feels like the high trills are merely variants of his *zeeet*s, excitedly staying high in pitch, but the canary-like ramble is so low-pitched that it sounds like a different bird. On and on he goes, rarely a second's pause, *zeeet*s followed by a few high-pitched trills, then *zeeet*s typically followed by the lower canary ramble.

Searching for other dawn singers, I swing the parabola around to the north and then west, locking on a male who is a little farther away there. I boost the gain on the recorder, bringing him closer. Wow, 18 trills in his first canary ramble, well over half a minute, then more *zeeet*s, and then his high-pitched trills, singing in the same pattern as the closer male to the east. He continues, 16 canary trills, *zeeet*s, then three high trills, 19 lower canary trills, *zeeet*s, and 4 high trills (track 85).

Figure 62. Dawn song of the Brewer's sparrow, the east male. See and hear (on track 84) the energy in this singing male, from the high-pitched buzzes and trills to the cascading series of lower-pitched trills. No male sings alone at dawn, and as this particular male buzzes above 7 kHz during the first four seconds in this figure, a male in the background descends to his lower trills; the songs of background sparrows are again visible beginning at about 0:18.

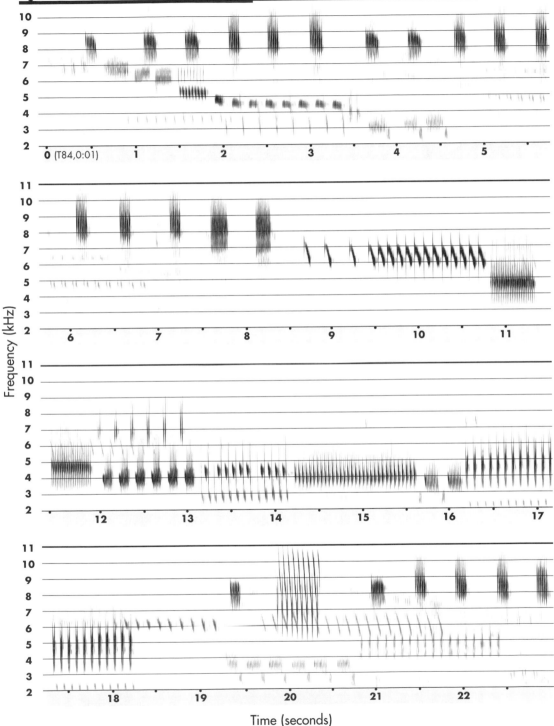

Frequency (kHz)

Time (seconds)

I swing the parabola again, confirming that the eastern male is still there, then focus on a bird to the southeast. He also tends to alternate series of high- and low-pitched trills, and he also fills every available second with either *zeeet*s or trills.

Finding my bearings, I swing to the east again, then to the southeast, confirming that these are two different birds, perhaps only 5 to 10 yards apart. To the west again: yes, he's still there. So far, he's the champion singer, with the longest canary rambles. I glance at my watch and count: 25 low-pitched trills over as many seconds, then 28, 25, and then the longest so far, 36 trills in about 40 seconds, typically alternating these series of low trills with just a few high-pitched ones, and all the while *zeeet*ing in between.

It's 4:51 now, and I must hurry to check all points of the compass. How many more birds are singing here? I swing to my reference point, the eastern bird singing close by. South I swing, stopping to the southeast, verifying that he's still there. That's two. Continuing, I hear a male directly south, another to the southwest, listening to and recording each new male for about two minutes. I then swing back through south to southeast again, just to double-check, to make sure that no one has moved. No, the count is fine. Directly to the western male I go next: he's number 5. Swinging around slowly, I pick up another at north-northwest, then north, then northeast, and I swing back around to the west again, verifying the count at eight. Another is singing at east-northeast, and I finally return to my reference bird again, the eastern male, completing the circle at 5:02 A.M. Nine birds are within reach of my parabolic microphone, all *zeeet*ing, all alternating a short series of high-pitched trills with the longer and lower-pitched canary ramble. Nine birds, I again say to myself. Nine!

I complete the survey just in time, as within a few minutes, it's all over. I swing to the west again, eager to hear more from the most impressive singer in the bunch, but he now sounds much farther away, as if he's moved off into the distance. The bird to the southwest seems more distant, too. Swinging east again, to my most reliable singer, I find nothing. It's 5:09 A.M., about 50 minutes after it began, and still half an hour before sunrise.

To the east I now hear a *zreeeee zrrr-zrrr-zrrr,* a two-parted song, the shorter song used throughout the day. The others soon follow suit, as I now listen with my headphones off my ears, my parabola lowered. They all seem so far away now, as if they had gathered at dawn but have now dispersed to their own territories. Or was that only an illusion, the parabola so deceptive, so effective at bringing in distant sounds to make them sound at arm's reach? Or was it the darkness that deceived me, making it feel that the world was closing in on me, the birds all singing from close by? Or maybe it was the calm of the hour before the dawn, a cold dawn just above freezing, that amplified the songs, booming them into my ears. I cannot be sure, but I like to think that they may have behaved just like the chipping sparrows, the males gathering in their vocal contest in the predawn darkness. And I would bet that every female in residence is paying attention, as it seems likely that she depends on these male contests to help her choose who will be the father of her offspring.

I catch my first glimpse, the bird just to the east now perched atop the sagebrush, *zreeeee zrrr-zrrr-zrrr*, and he darts down, out of view, as if taking all of the answers to my questions with him. I must return another day, I promise myself, to know these little sparrows of the sagebrush better.

The Eastern Bluebird

Her e-mail address is MaBlue. She runs a "bluebird trail" here in Amherst, Massachusetts, 35 nest boxes in a figure eight, two loops centered on her house, and she loves checking the boxes to see how her birds are doing. When are the boxes first claimed in the spring? Is the nest done yet? Has she laid her first egg, the last? How soon will the babies hatch? And watching the babies depart the nest cannot be missed. Such a sparkle in her eye, a glow to MaBlue's face, such a passion for bluebirds.

In MaBlue the bluebirds have a friend, and thanks to hundreds like her the bluebirds have made a dramatic comeback from what seemed like the brink of extinction in the late 1960s and 1970s. Perhaps it was just the severe winters and snowy spring storms that caused the decline, or the loss of beaver swamps that produced good habitat, or pesticides, or perhaps it was those two introduced varmints, the house sparrow and European starling, who aggressively stole the bluebird nesting cavities. Whatever the reason, in the 1970s Lawrence Zeleny rallied bluebird lovers everywhere, founded the North American Bluebird Society, and the rest is history. You can look them up on the Internet: in the year 2000 alone, for example, more than 17,000 nest boxes on hundreds of trails produced 7,097 eastern bluebird babies (and 2,160 mountain bluebirds and 342 western bluebirds). Many states and provinces have their own associations, and, as one might have guessed, MaBlue is president of the Massachusetts Bluebird Association.

What is it about bluebirds that commands such devotion? Well, they *are* blue, the most vivid of blues, claim their devotees, especially on the male's back and head, the blue there contrasting sharply with the red orange throat, breast, and flanks and with the sparkling white lower belly and undertail feathers. They don't hide in the treetops, either, but live out in the open, in places with little cover, so we can watch them; they typically sit on a perch and scan for insects on the ground, then drop down to nab their prey. They also readily accept nest boxes we provide for them, and before our very eyes the mother and father raise their family. They're tame, too, some would even say friendly. Those are the reasons, I think.

It's certainly not the song that inspires. "No great singer; he cannot begin to compete with the greater songsters of the famous thrush family" is the way the naturalist Bent put it, even though by bloodlines the bluebird belongs to the thrush family (Turdidae). I must confess that, until recently, I'd heard the bluebird songs a few times, thought them curiously uninspiring, and then went on to listen to what I thought were more interesting songsters. My professional friends had done the same, so that I could not find a single study of bluebird songs in the scientific literature. No one had cared enough to record them and to try to understand their singing better. I reminded myself that first impressions are often deceiving and resolved to learn more.

So I read what I could about the sounds of this eastern bluebird. "Most charming," say those who love this bird. "Full of richness and sweetness, and even expressing affection," wrote Bent. In his book *A Guide to Bird Songs,* Aretas Saunders tried a more objective approach: the song is "a series of short single notes, slurs, or two-note phrases, which, though not actually connected, are sung so rapidly as to suggest a warble. The quality is sweet, melodious, and pleasing, but the voice soft and not carrying far." Saunders also heard the male alternate two songs, perhaps the first rising in pitch, the other falling, as if the bird asks a question and then gives the answer: *Ayo ala looee? . . . alee ay lalo leeo.*

I learned a little more in my reading. The males sing from the highest perches around, but also from the nest box and nearby perches. The loudness of the song varies considerably, from so soft one can't hear it unless near, to so loud it carries 100 yards. Sometimes males "chatter" before the song, especially when "angry," such as when predators threaten the nest. Unpaired males sing up to 20 songs a minutes. Males in a New York study had two different songs that they sometimes alternated. And females sometimes sing.

But I was impressed more by what was not known. The 1998 everything-you-ever-wanted-to-know account of eastern bluebirds said it rather bluntly. "The vocal behavior . . . is poorly known." Many questions had no answers: How does a male awake in the morning? Where, when, and how does he sing, or doesn't he sing at all at dawn? Given that nothing seems to be known about this topic, perhaps he's a late riser. Do males really have just two songs apiece? How unthrush-like. "Repertoires, if they exist, are not obvious," said the expert account, and males are "never" observed to countersing (that is, sing back and forth to each other, as if taking turns in some singing game). The more I read, the more curious I became.

EASTERN BLUEBIRD

I must discover for myself what these bluebirds are all about. This is when I meet MaBlue, who eagerly shows me her 35-box trail. The best place to listen will be the Cherry Hill Golf Course, she concludes, given that several pairs are already there and that the traffic noise won't be too bad. Nest box #22 is where I'll begin—a male and female are courting there, and the female has already placed a few threads of nest material into the box. It's April 11, 2000, a Wednesday.

I BEGIN ON SATURDAY. Sunrise is at 6:11 A.M., so I am here at 5:00. A quarter-moon to the south obscures all but the brightest stars—still, the two Dippers and the polestar are obvious, and the Dragon's head is almost directly over mine. The Swan flies overhead, too, and Cassiopeia is well up in the east. The north wind is chilly, but I am here, ready, waiting for Mr. Bluebird. I know his nest box is just 30 yards to the south, out in the open from where I hide in the trees, but it is far too dark to see. I'll hear him when he awakes, I am confident.

It is 5:09 when a woodcock begins *peent*ing. At 5:24 a cardinal utters a single song, and at 5:25 a song sparrow offers one of his own; each begins singing in earnest in a few minutes, as robins already are. But no bluebird. By 5:45 all the local birds are singing, so I leave the area and walk the golf course, searching and listening near other nest boxes. Not a bluebird to be seen or heard. By 6:05 I return to box 22, and there he is, in the nearby trees. He beat the sunrise, but just barely. His lady friend is there, too.

I am ready to listen. On Wednesday, when we had first scouted this bird, he sang so softly, so unlike any other songbird I had ever listened to that I was sure I missed a lot of what he was doing. So today I have my "big ear," my parabola with its microphone, my tape recorder, and my headphones. From about 50 yards away I train my parabola's sight on this male and turn up the recorder's gain, at first to midlevel, and then as far as the dial can go. He sings, and I listen, and listen some more, to song after song coming through my headphones. I take the headphones off and hear nothing. He is singing softly, sometimes only to himself it seems, or maybe to the female who is nearby.

Headphones on again, what a variety of songs I hear! Yes, I hear him alternate two songs, and then he plays with three different songs, switching among them in unpredictable ways (track 86, figure 63). Then I hear what sounds like a string of at least five different songs in a row. Now he rises from his perch in the sumac tree, singing on the wing, up and over his nest box, intercepting another bird, presumably a male, who is flying over. The invader is escorted back to where he had come from, and in the distant tree line to the northwest I hear that "song melee" I had read about. It must be only the two males, though it sounds like a dozen, each singing so rapidly, no pauses between songs, singing continuously and simultaneously. What a racket! Just as suddenly it is over, and he reappears, flying back to his nest box. Thanks to my "big ear," I had heard it all, but MaBlue, who stood listening nearby, had heard nothing.

Figure 63: EASTERN BLUEBIRD—3 SONGS

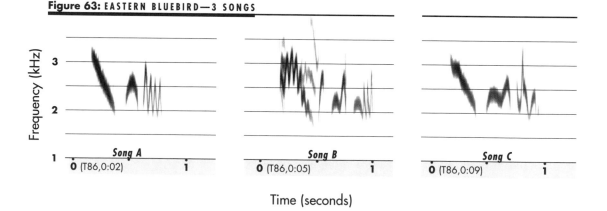

Figure 63. Three different songs from the eastern bluebird. See how distinctive each song is and listen to how reliably the male repeats them in track 86, in the sequence A B C C B A B C B A C.

How could I have overlooked bluebirds all these years? Such variety to their songs, so expressive by how loudly and rapidly they sing that I need to know more, like where he is when his cousins the robins are singing 45 minutes before sunrise. I find it unthinkable that he'd sleep in, the only late-arising songbirds I know being in the dreams of those who study them, those who themselves find it difficult to get out so early. And *when* he sings well before the sunrise, with what kind of variety will he sing, and in what contexts?

SUNDAY, THE NEXT DAY, I'm back, again at 5:00. The woodcock is here again, the cardinals, too, and the nearby robin awakes at 5:12 in what sounds like the typical feisty-robin mood. Then, at 5:25, a few bluebird songs just east of the nest box area, and then nothing more. Is that it? Is he done? No, a few minutes later I hear a singing male much farther to the east, but nothing back at the nest box. It must be him, over toward the housing development. In the darkness I hustle as best I can the 50 yards over there. He seems to be perched on the fence posts in the garden just west of the driveway, but I can't make him out, even though he's in the open just a few yards in front of me.

Three minutes later and he's gone again, this time apparently another 50 yards to the east, where I faintly hear a song melee. Like yesterday, it's probably just two males having a frank and candid discussion, but it sounds like far more have convened there. I lose track of time — perhaps it lasts only a minute — and soon this warrior is back singing in the garden from where he had just departed. It's not long until the male from the east visits, the two now singing rapidly back and forth to each other across the driveway.

At 5:45 the dawn frenzy seems to be all over, only 20 minutes after it began. The male I am watching returns to the nest box area, and eventually his female shows up. I don't know where the other male is — someplace off to the east, to an area I feel I can't easily explore because of all of the houses there.

Okay, *now* I am ready. I know what to expect in the predawn darkness, and I'll return, on Monday, again with my big ear and tape recorder. I'll catch him on tape and then listen again more thoroughly at home, making graphs of his songs so that I'll understand better exactly how he sings.

MONDAY MORNING. I have been waiting for him, and at 5:29 he begins, in the garden beside the driveway, just like yesterday. Fifteen songs a minute. He's playing with three or four different songs here, maybe five, alternating them in unexpected ways, the next song almost always startlingly different from the one before. I am just beginning to get the feel for each of those songs, recognizing each when it is delivered, and then he's gone.

At 5:33 he's off to the east again. Six minutes of confusion follow, at least on my part. I can see nothing in the darkness, but I hear them in the same battleground as yesterday. Another song melee, each male singing rapidly, overlapping the other's songs.

Six minutes is all it lasts, and he then returns to his garden by the driveway. It seems he's all charged up now, a song every three seconds, and he often chatters between songs. There's the so-called "anger" that I've read about, this same chatter apparently used to mob predators that threaten the nest. A second male now sings from the rooftop of the blue green building to the south —he's right at the apex, where he delivers a few songs and then drops down the other side of the roof, out of sight, his songs muffled. For 14 minutes, until 5:53, these two males duke it out. First one sings from the rooftop, then the other, then both sing within yards of each other down in the garden, then they square off, one on each side of the driveway, each "leaning" toward the security of his own territory.

Just that quickly it's over. Within three minutes, by 5:56, the male I am intent on watching is working his way back to his nest box, to assume his more domestic duties for the day. He first sings from the sumac to the east of his nest box, then from the tall trees to the south and north, and finally from the nest box itself. With my big ear, I hear all that he sings, even those soft, sweet songs from the box. His female eventually shows up, and the day's routine will now be rather predictable. They'll spend a lot of time foraging together, some time at the nest box, with him whispering sweet nothings that only she can hear. Maybe she'll begin building her nest in earnest today, maybe not.

TUESDAY, APRIL 17. I'm back. I want another morning with them, one more time to hear how they sing at dawn. I know where and when to be ready, in the small garden just to the west of the driveway. He catches me by surprise. He's eight minutes earlier today, beginning at 5:21 A.M., and he now sings from the roof support of the yellow house just east of the driveway, not from the garden. My days of listening pay off, as I can now readily hear how he sings, switching among three different songs. I give each of the songs a letter: the first one I call A, the next one B, the next C. Minute by minute I listen and take mental notes as I tape-record (table 7).

I couldn't identify a couple of songs. No problem—I don't have to be perfect in this game. I'm not sure what the first two songs were, as it took me just a few seconds to catch on. Those songs in the last minute were of a different kind, but he flew off, not letting me hear them often enough to appreciate how they would fit into the new sequence.

Figure 64: EASTERN BLUEBIRD—DAWN SONGS AND CHATTER

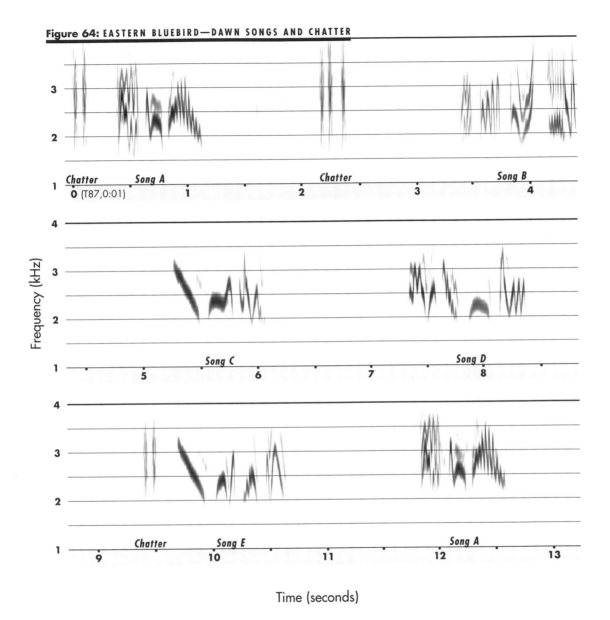

Figure 64. Intense dawn singing and chatter, part of an intense dawn effort during which the male bluebird used 10 different songs among 24 songs in one minute (track 87). Here are the first 14 seconds and 6 songs of those 24 songs that were sung in the sequence A B C D E A F C C C A D C C F A C G H I F C A J. (These songs were given letters independently of the songs in figure 63; by chance, song C is the same in both figures, but A and B are not.)

TABLE 7

MINUTE	SONG SEQUENCE
1	? ? A A B B B A B B
2	A B C A B A B
3	B C A B A C C A B A C
4	C A C A C B C B C
5	B A C C B A C C B C C C A C A B
6	A C A ? C A C C C ? ?

and after 40 seconds in minute 6 he flies

Where does he go? Yes, of course, it is off to the east again, to do battle with his neighbor there. From 5:28 to 5:47, for 20 frenzied minutes I do my best to keep up with them. First far to the east, then to the rooftops, then to the garden, with lots of chatter accompanying the songs. My male then finally returns to his garden to sing a blistering 24 songs in one minute (track 87, figure 64); with my big ear I tape-record that minute, discovering later why my heart is pounding almost loud enough to be recorded. Each song is about a second long, so the pauses between them aren't much longer, and among those 24 songs are 10 different ones, in the following sequence:

A B C D E A F C C C A D C C F A C G H I F C A J

By coincidence, song C here is the same as song C in the first sequence that he gave at dawn (but songs A and B are not — each time I listen, I start with A again, because he has so many songs that I can't keep track of which is which from one listening session to the next). It seems that this particular song is his favorite. I wonder what to make of that. Do his neighbors share that song?

Twenty minutes after the confrontation between these two males started, the dawn rush is all over. It had been a 20-minute battle yesterday, too. My male now returns to his nest area and doesn't bother to respond to the male from the east who now boldly sings from just east of the driveway. Enough is enough. My male has retired from battle, to eat some of last year's sumac fruit and to sing in the tall trees north and south of his nest box.

He sings more slowly now, a song every six seconds, about 10 times a minute, and I can again detect his pattern (table 8). I start listening intently at 6:10, about sunrise, and until 6:30 hear only four different songs. One reminds me of a bobolink song, bubbling and unbluebird-like (that's song type C in table 8), but sometimes he gives only the first few notes of that song (which I identify with C').

In minute 20 he's moving on to new songs, so I stop my listening there. Four different songs were used over the 20 minutes, with perhaps some rare odd ones thrown in here and there. Interestingly, song D here is the same song as the common song (C) in the other two sessions. It does seem to be his favorite. At the end of minute 5 in this sequence he flew from the treetops above his garden just east of the driveway to the treetops north of his nest box. In minute 13 he flew to the nest box, delivering the rest of his songs from there, but without the female near. Some songs were muted again, but my trusty parabola enabled me to hear everything. Is it just a coincidence that during both flights he sang the bobolink-like song, the one that the bobolink also gives in flight? In minute 21 it was the same bobolink-like song that he sang in a nonstop fashion as he flew to the distant trees. Intriguing. Is it possible that this male bluebird learned both this song and how to use it from a bobolink somewhere?

Each morning a gripping drama unfolds among these bluebirds, beginning in the dark hour before sunrise. Little did I know, or I'd have been here years ago. Little does anyone know, it seems, including the occupants of this housing complex, whose yard and garden and rooftops are a bluebird battleground each morning. In the parking lot on Monday were 53 cars, one pickup, and one motorcycle, but over the days that I watched not one owner emerged during that dawn hour when the bluebirds were at their finest.

There's much more I need to hear and see from these birds. I'd love to watch a male when he first arrives on his territory, to see him fly rapidly from place to place, singing and chattering as he claims his territory. To watch an unpaired male first encounter a female in his territory, to see him as he shows off all of his blueness, to hear him sing persuasively that he is the one. To watch his butterfly routine that I've read about, wings fully extended but beating deeply and slowly, tail spread, singing continuously as he slowly flies to the nest box. To hear how family members communicate with each other through the seasons with their simple whistle, the *tu-a-wee*.

TABLE 8

MINUTE	SONG SEQUENCE									
1	A	B	A	C	B	A	C'	B	A	C'
2	A	B	C	A	C'	A	?	C	C	A
3	A	A	C'	A	A	A	A	A		
4	C'	A	C	A	?	A	A	C'		
5	A	A	B	C'	A	A	C'	A	C	A
6	C'	A	A	A	C'	A	A	A	C'	C'	A
7	A	A	A	A	A	A				
8	?	A	A	A	A					
9	A	A	A	A						
10	A	A	A	A						
11	C'	A	A	A	A					
12	A	A	C'	A	C	C				
13	C	C'	C	D	D	D	D	D	D	
14	D	D	D	D	D	D	D			
15	D	D	D	D	D	D	A			
16	D	D	A	D	A	D	A			
17	D	D	A	D	D	D				
18	D	D	D	D	D	C	D			
19	D	A	D	D	D	D	D			
20	D	D	?	?	?	?	D	?	?	?

Mostly, I need to know what this dawn singing is all about. What do these males accomplish during the dawn hour? It must have to do with who is where in the local pecking order, I reason. The top bird may have first choice of territory, but there's more to it than that. Although bluebirds appear to be a model of domestic tranquility, with mother and father rearing a family, DNA fingerprinting has revealed that the female doesn't mate exclusively with her social partner. Her broods are often mixed, with some babies fathered by her social partner but others by males on neighboring territories. If I could in some way know who wins these dawn song contests, could I predict which males would be the most desirable fathers for the babies of the local females? I wonder how and where she listens in the dark. I wonder . . .

6
She Also Sings

T HOSE WHO STUDY birdsong have largely overlooked the female, but in a number of species she sings, too. Such songs may be only occasional, as in white-crowned sparrows, or regular, as in their close relative the white-throated sparrow, in which males and females can be either tan- or white-striped on the crown, the white-striped females preferentially pairing with tan-striped males and singing more than their mates. Male and female wren-tits of the Pacific coast both sing, his song an accelerating series of clear, popping whistles *(pwip pwip pwipwipdrpdrdrdr),* her song slower, shorter, and nonaccelerating. Among blackbirds, the female red-wing often answers her mate's *konk-a-ree* with a harsh, songlike rattle; and early in the season, male and female common grackles often perch together in a treetop flock, the female and her mate often answering each other with their raspy song, a hissing unmusical *kh-sheee.* The list goes on, especially in the tropics where female song is much more common, probably because most species are permanent residents and a female sings to defend not only her territory but also her mate.

In this section, I focus on three species. Barred owls have their familiar *who-cooks-for-you, who-cooks-for-you-all,* together with a variety of other calls, and just a few night hours and a visit to the world's most remarkable sound archive reveals how a female's sounds can be readily distinguished from her mate's. The Carolina wren is a tropical wren in the north temperate zone, her buzzy chatter accompanying his rich *tea-kettle tea-kettle tea-kettle* song only a small hint of the remarkable, coordinated duetting among their tropical relatives. The northern cardinal duets, too, the male and female answering each other with a sizable repertoire of identical, rich, whistled songs.

The Barred Owl

In early spring I often hear them from my bedroom window. It's almost always distant, and always muffled, but the rhythm gives them away. *Who-cooks-for-you, who-cooks-for-you-all* he hoots, she responding in kind but on a slightly higher pitch. I imagine them on opposite sides of Kettle Pond, just 100 or so yards away through the woods, calling from the oaks and maples bordering its swampy edges.

For 20-some years now, the invitation has been there, ever since we moved into our Amherst home, and for all those years I have been too busy. *Come-check-us-out, come-check-us-out-now* they increasingly seemed to call. Finally, in our twenty-first year together, I reply, curious as to where these barred owls would take me.

For starters, I assemble all of my field guides and the authoritative *Birds of North America* account for this owl. I want to begin by standing on the shoulders of the experts, taking advantage of the pooled knowledge of all those who have listened to these owls before me. According to these sources, I can expect to hear four types of sounds.

The *cook* call is the best known, the *who-cooks-for-you, who-cooks-for-you-all,* with an accent on the *you* (track 88, figure 65). The three notes of the *who-cooks-for* are all evenly spaced, occurring over roughly a second, with the *for* note slightly lower pitched and not quite as loud. Quickly following the second *for* is the emphasized *you-all* note, rising in pitch and loudness on the *you* and then dropping on the *all* note. Instead of *you-all,* some of my sources hear *hooaw* or *hoo-ah,* but I'll stick with *you-all.*

BARRED
OWL

The "legato" call is an ascending series of *who* notes followed by the familiar *you-all: who-who-who-who-who-who-who-you-all* (tracks 88, 89, figure 65). The six to nine *who* notes are all evenly spaced, rising gradually in pitch and perhaps increasing slightly in loudness. "Legato," according to my dictionary, means "smooth and connected; without breaks between successive tones," which nicely describes the series of *who* calls.

Third is the raucous hooting and caterwauling, a "maniacal laughter" lasting up to two minutes at a time. It's "a raucous jumble of cackles, hoots, caws, and gurgles," "an extremely loud chorus of howls, hoots, shrieks, and tremulous wailings" (tracks 88–90). These sounds are "most spectacular and thrilling, loud, emphatic, and quite varied. The antiphonal hooting of a pair of these owls . . . will hold the hearer spellbound . . . [It is] startling, as if a pair of demons were fighting." Were it not for an occasional *you-all* giving away the source, I am cautioned, I could easily mistake these owls for courting mountain lions.

A fourth sound is a drawn-out *youuuuuuu-all,* given all by itself (track 91, figure 65).

In the *Birds of North America* account I confirm two other crucial pieces of information. Both the male and female make these sounds, and the pitch of the female's voice is higher. That pitch difference is intriguing, because she actually weighs about a third more than he does, a typical size difference for owls, and still he has the lower voice. It is probably the male hormones that make his voice box or resonating cavities bigger, giving him the lower voice.

Now knowing what to listen for, I pull a Peterson CD set from my shelf. Disc 1, track 39: Barred Owl (see track 88). For 25 seconds my office reverberates with the hooting of a pair of owls, one seeming to call from the wall itself, the other a little softer, just beyond in the background. They both give a combination of the *cook* and legato calls, with just a few seconds of caterwauling at the end. The pitch difference is striking, the female clearly in the foreground, the more mellow, resonant hooting from the male in the background.

I play the sequence again . . . and again, now intrigued at what I hear. I reach for the headphones, wanting to block out all extraneous noise, to concentrate with an owl perched at each ear. Not only is the female higher-pitched, but she has more of a drawl, a *you-allllll,* with an extended vibrato on the end. Four times in the foreground I hear her give the *you-allllll,* with the male's simpler *you-all* in the background. Especially telling is the last five seconds, when she caterwauls with an extended *you-allllll,* he following immediately with a caterwaul ending with an abbreviated *you-all.* She has both the first and last word in this 25-second sequence, as she begins with the *cook* call and, after the caterwauling exchange, offers a muted *you-allllll,* at her characteristically higher pitch.

Could it be that here is a fundamental difference between male and

Figure 65: BARRED OWL *Female cook, Male legato*

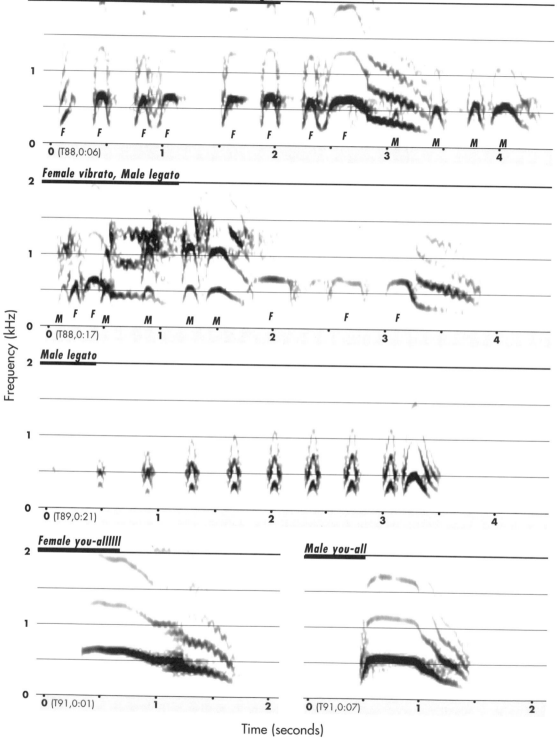

female, that her hoots always contain the extended vibrato? It seems unlikely that no one would have noticed this difference before. Alternatively, perhaps it's just an individual difference, with some individuals having more vibrato than others, and in this first pair it was only by chance that the female had more vibrato than the male.

Two possible explanations. Which is it?, I wonder, as I go to my shelf again, this time grabbing the *Stokes Field Guide*, Disc 2, track 14 (track 89). Over and over I listen to the 40 seconds of hooting. Five times, 10 times, perhaps 15, concentrating on the variety of sounds and how to interpret them, finally confirming what I hear by displaying their songs on my computer screen. Four different recordings have been used by my bicycling and birding friend Lang Elliott to put this sequence together. In the first, a higher-pitched female in the foreground exchanges the *cook* call with a male in the background—she has the extended vibrato in the *you-allllll*, he a simple *you-all*. The second is a single *youuuuuuu-all* from two birds, the male in the foreground, the female in the background—again, she has the more vibrato, though just barely. The third is a single call, a legato, low-pitched like that of a male, *who-who-who-who-who-who-who-you-all*—with no vibrato.

Before I listen again to the fourth recording in the Stokes guide, I do the simple math in my head. It's like a coin flip, I reason, a simple probability problem. If I call "heads" and then flip a coin, I know that I have a 1 in 2 chance of the coin showing heads, because there are only two possible sides of the coin *and* each side is equally probable. If I call "heads" on each of three coin flips, I know that there are 8 possible combinations: 3 heads (1 chance), 2 heads and 1 tail (3 chances), 2 tails and 1 head (3 chances), and 3 tails (1 chance). I can simply multiply the probabilities for each correct "head" flip by each other: $\frac{1}{2} \times \frac{1}{2} \times \frac{1}{2} = \frac{1}{8}$. When I know that the chance of getting heads is

Figure 65. Not only does the larger female barred owl sing at a higher pitch, but she also has more vibrato in her *you-allllll*. **Top two rows:** Exchanges by a male and female (track 88), the notes of the female marked with an F, those of the male by an M. The top row begins with a female *cook* call, *who-cooks-for-you, who-cooks-for-you-allllll*, all eight notes clearly visible; the *you-allllll* has lots of vibrato in the *allllll* (especially evident in the upper harmonics), and the fundamental frequency of the highest portion of the *you* is about 600 Hz. The top row ends with a male legato; there is little vibrato in his *all*, and the frequency of his *you* is lower than hers, about 550 Hz. **The second row** reveals these same female-male differences, showing another male legato and two of the female's *you-allllll* calls. **Third row:** Another example of a male legato, from track 89. **Fourth row:** Wonderful examples of a female *you-allllll* and male *you-all*, again showing vibrato and pitch differences (track 91).

50:50, actually calling heads correctly three times in a row is a fairly rare event, happening roughly only 1 in 8 times. If a coin consistently comes up heads more often than 50:50, I must conclude that my original expectations for this coin were wrong.

It's much the same with the owls. I begin by assuming no sex difference, that with each pair of owls there's a 50:50 chance that the female will have more vibrato in the *you-all* call than the male. I got this idea by listening to the Peterson CD and begin testing it with the Stokes CD. I call "female" three times in a row, and each time it is the female with more vibrato. If males and females are equally likely to have a lot of vibrato in their *you-all*, then only 1 in 8 times would I expect such biased results. I begin to suspect a sex difference in the vibrato of the *you-all*.

The fourth recording in the Stokes CD is the most fascinating, "the alternation and overlap of excited monkey-like hoots when two owls greet one another in the dark." What an extraordinary combination of sounds! Seven times the foreground bird without the vibrato hoots its odd cackling and laughing sounds, five times the bird in the background accompanies with a restrained legato, *who-who-who-you-alllllllllll*, with the extended vibrato. Because the sounds of the two birds are so different, I cannot rely on pitch differences to sex them—but if I am right about the female having the vibrato, then this sequence takes on far more meaning. It is he with the seven maniacal sequences in the foreground, she humming her five legato accompaniments in the background. The roles of male and female in this frenzied caterwauling, apparently never before having been disentangled, are suddenly clear . . . but only if I am right about the sex difference.

Enough armchair biology—I must field-test this idea. I go to Lawrence Swamp in South Amherst, knowing that two or three pairs of owls own territories in the bottomland forests there. 2:30 A.M. the fourth of May I'm out the door, playing the CD sounds over and over in my head as I drive the 10 minutes, preparing myself for what I might hear. I'll try a passive vigil first, setting my lawn chair in the grass beside the parking lot on Station Road.

Now ready, I close the car door, and instantly, across the road, from the stand of old white pines comes an immediate reply: *youuuuuuu-alllllllllll.* Another, and another; four in all, over about a minute's time. Frozen, I stand there, waiting for more . . . silence, save for a few peeps of the peepers and the occasional mutterings of the bullfrogs.

My CDs left me ill-prepared for this moment. The purity of the extended *youuuuuuu* and the 7 to 10 tremolos in the *alllllllllll* lingered in the night air.

In the dead stillness every leaf, twig, branch, and trunk seemed to reverberate and amplify all of the details in this *youuuuuuu-alllllllllll.* At the sound of the closing door, the owl had seemed to inquire *whooooooo's-therrrrrrre?* Was it the male or female? If I had perfect pitch, perhaps I could have known, but to use the pitch cue I need to hear the male and female together, to hear one higher than the other. If it is the female with the extended vibrato, then it is she who greeted me. Again I sense the power in using the vibrato to sex the birds.

The gibbous moon hangs on the western horizon, slowly sinking, the landscape darkening before the sunrise. Four songbirds find the night air irresistible, and every 10 to 15 minutes a single song is blurted out, from a song sparrow, swamp sparrow, cardinal, or mockingbird. Beavers are active in the pond just to the northeast, too, a small tree falling, the slap of a tail. No more owls, until 4:38, in the distance to the south. Distance with the owls can be a problem, as the territory of a pair of owls is often a mile across. I quickly work my way south along the trail, only to hear them next far to the west. There seems to be no good way to get close.

I cup my hands to my ears and listen. *Who-cooks-for-you, who-cooks-for-you-all . . . who-cooks-for-you, who-cooks-for-you-alllll,* the male and female responding to each other. The pitch difference is obvious when they're calling together, and it is she who sings the *you-alllll* with the extended vibrato.

At 4:59 A.M., 42 minutes before sunrise, the catbirds are singing everywhere around me, and the owls have now switched to their legato call. *Who-who-who-who-who-who-who-you-all . . . who-who-who-who-who-who-who-you-alllll.* The pitch of the second bird is again higher, and her vibrato is still there. I can now be sure—it was she who greeted me in the parking lot more than two hours ago.

Twenty-four hours later I'm back. I wait for an hour, until 5:00 A.M., when the songbirds are in full swing, but I hear nothing from the owls. Eager to learn just a little more this morning, I inquire briefly of them with a *cook* sound, so easily imitated. Briefly, I emphasize—I don't want to harass them. It feels as if I'm cheating, simulating an intrusion by another owl to get the male and female to duet with each other, but this ruse works well. Five minutes later they respond with a burst of legato calls, from perhaps 100 yards down the path. I rush toward them, hoping to hear them more clearly as they continue their 30-second exchange.

A 15-second pause, and they duet again, now only about 20 yards away, the male with five legato calls in rapid succession, the female simultaneously with three of her own. Another 15-second pause and they respond again, this time the male with eight calls, she with five, all during a 25-second span. Six more times they call over the next three minutes, but their response wanes, as each time the male and female give only one or two calls.

Like yesterday, the higher-pitched bird always sang the *you-allllll* with the extended vibrato. Also, during each duet, the male typically sang one to three more legato phrases than did the female. And I heard just a trace of the caterwauling in two of his legato calls, the last two *who* notes becoming more of a *haa*, almost a cackle. Walking back to the car, I hoot softly with my lips puckered and then continue hooting as I open my mouth wide; the *who*s resonate into *haa*s in the enlarged oral cavity, my voice box straining to cackle more than hoot. How the owls produce these odd sounds is anyone's guess, but as I reshape my mouth I can begin to imagine the possibilities for cackles, gargles, shrieks, and all manner of otherworldly sounds.

For nine days I savor these experiences and—perhaps just as important —let these owls rest. I need one more visit to confirm that these owls are consistent in how they call, to confirm that the lower-pitched male never sings a vibrato, that the higher-pitched female always does. In the hours before midnight on May 14, I get my answers. Using the pitch difference to sex the two birds, I confirm that she has the extended vibrato in her *you-allllll,* whether that sound ends her *cook* or her legato call or whether it is her isolated *youu-uuuu-allllll.* The male's *you-all* lacks the vibrato and is a simple rise and fall in pitch. In their legato duets, he typically calls one or two more times than she does (track 90).

I learn something new, too. Both male and female occasionally replace the *who* with the cackling *haa* in the legato sound. Furthermore, the female occasionally gives a very odd version of the *cook* call. It is still two-parted, with four notes in the first part and five in the second, but the tempo and quality of the sounds in the *who-cooks-for-you, who-cooks-for* portion is strange. She consistently uses these unique sounds over a period of at least 10 minutes, so they must be a standard part of her vocal repertoire. But how odd that no one seems to have ever described them before. Increasingly I realize how little we know of the lives of these night owls.

I am almost tempted to drop my other projects and study these owls. I'd love to live with them over an annual cycle. I'd start with the babies just out of the nest, listening to their *ksssssshhip,* the rising hiss of a young begging bird. Perhaps I could even attach a small microphone transmitter to the young owl, to monitor how he or she eventually comes to hoot like an adult. Do the young practice hooting during their hatching summer? What do their earliest attempts sound like? Is it possible that a young owl must learn its hoots, just like a songbird? It's possible, yes, given how little we know of them. I've talked to bird rehabilitators, who occasionally take in an orphaned owlet, and some of them are convinced that their barred owls must learn to hoot, but so far I find the evidence inconclusive. Conclusive evidence for learning would be a barred owl who learned to hoot like a great horned owl, for example, or a barred owl who, in the absence of adult "tutor" owls, never learned to hoot properly.

I'd also like to know when during the annual cycle the adult birds call the most, and what kinds of calls they use then, as that information might tell me the functions of all these sounds. A pair is on the same territory throughout the year, year after year, until death do them part, and perhaps it is especially in spring when their "grotesque love-making" lightens up the night. What if a widow or widower must court anew, to invite a bird of either sex to the territory? Such a situation would inform me aplenty. Many questions, but no one knows the answers.

For now, though, I find myself absorbed by one small question: Does a female always have more vibrato in her *you-all* call than does her mate? To know for sure would give me insight into how to listen to barred owls. I update my math to include the Lawrence Swamp pair in my data: $(\frac{1}{2})^4 = \frac{1}{16}$. If there is no sex difference, there's only a 1 in 16 chance that the female in all four of the pairs I've studied (three pairs on the Stokes CD and the Lawrence Swamp pair) would have more vibrato. That's not yet good enough—I want to be more certain.

I need more data. I could go back to Lawrence Swamp to find another pair or two, or I could go anywhere in the surrounding hills, but I know where else I can go for some ready answers: to the Library of Natural Sounds (LNS) at Cornell University's Laboratory of Ornithology, in Ithaca, New York, and I'm soon on my way. At the end of my five-hour drive, I pull off Sapsucker Woods Road into the parking lot next to "the lab." Entering the building, I pause briefly at the large viewing window over the pond, then take the hallways back to LNS. Adorning the walls are paintings by Louis Aggasiz Fuertes—falcons, goshawks, ducks, woodpeckers, meadowlarks, and many more. Through the door into LNS, and after a warm welcome from the staff there, I walk down the hallway to the first door on the left.

When no one else is working in the archive, I step inside and close the door, momentarily leaving the lights out. With no sights to distract me, I can hear the birds better. Directly in front of me I visualize one of the six two-sided, floor-to-ceiling shelving units that run the length of the room. Nine shelves on a side, each with 350 7-inch open-reel tapes, over 3,000 in all. Another 3,000 are on the other side of this unit, and another 6,000 on the next shelving unit, and so on. The four walls, too, have floor-to-ceiling shelves, and stacked in available spaces here and there are the boxed safety copies, ready to be shipped off to some nearby cave to insure that these voices will forever be preserved.

Throughout the room are hundreds of thousands of bird voices, all captured in the wild and taken here, to live on forever. I know the names of the recordists on the tape boxes: Ted Parker, one of the greatest Neotropical ornithologists of all time, renowned for his ability to recognize thousands upon thousands of different bird species by their sounds alone, sadly killed in a 1993 plane crash while on a bird-research trip in Ecuador; Arthur A. Allen, founder of the Laboratory of Ornithology, and his partner Peter Paul Kellogg, the sound engineer who made the early equipment work; Paul Schwartz, who contributed a large collection of Venezuelan bird sounds; Greg Budney, current curator of the library and ardent recordist; Linda Macaulay, worldwide recordist and philanthropist, for whom the LNS is now named; and many others, among them Myles North, George Reynard, Irby Davis, Bret Whitney, Tom Schulenberg, Mark Robbins, and Rob Bierregaard. The lights still out, I see them all in the aisles, mingling with each other, pulling their tapes from the shelves, just holding them, smiling, as if they, too, hear the birds on them. So many of the world's best and most dedicated sound recordists, so many of the world's finest bird sounds, all here, in this one room.

The two light switches now flipped on, the recordists vanish and the avian clamor wanes, the noise of the climate-control system rumbling throughout the room. I walk along the length of the first aisle to where I find the five boxes marked *Strix varia*, the Latin name of the barred owl. Inside are 19 "cuts," the first one made in 1953 by Arthur A. Allen and Peter Paul Kellogg, the last by the legendary Ted Parker in 1990.

In one of the recording studios I sit and listen. From Florida to Georgia, Louisiana, New York, Oregon, and even to El Salvador I travel, to hear the voices of owls long since deceased, escorted by the voices of the recordists themselves. I focus on those seven recordings in which two duetting birds were recorded, undoubtedly a male and female of a pair.

Recording number six, Georgia, 2 May 1963, by Robert Carrington Stein and William W. H. Gunn, both pioneers in sound recording, both now deceased. The owls are caterwauling, as in the third example on the Stokes CD. The higher-pitched bird has lots of vibrato in the *you-all*, and "she" seems to hum in the background as "he" cackles and gobbles loudly in the foreground.

The same pattern occurs in another Georgia recording from 1964 and two Florida recordings, in 1984 and 1989. A priceless Florida recording by Bill Evans has a lower-pitched *youuuuuuu-all* and a higher pitched *youuuuuuu-alllllllllll* in the same recording (track 91). The last example was recorded by Ted Parker in Louisiana: again, more vibrato in the higher pitched *you-all*.

The seventh recording, one from Oregon, is a problem. I can't detect much of a pitch difference between the two birds — it's a tossup, a tie, more or less. But again the humming bird has the extended vibrato, the cackling, gobbling, laughing bird hardly any vibrato. By now, I'll wager a hefty sum that the accompaniment in this particular recording is provided by the female, the cackling by the male, even though I can hear no pitch difference.

How much would I be willing to wager? A lot, given the rather low probability that I am wrong. I can calculate that probability: All three examples from the Stokes CD, the pair from Lawrence Swamp, and all six examples from Cornell's LNS have had the higher-pitched female with more vibrato. If I assume that males and females do not differ, just as if I assume that heads and tails on the coin are equally likely, the probability of calling either "female" or "heads" correctly 10 times in a row is $(\frac{1}{2})^{10} = 0.001$, or 1 in 1,000. When I declare that females have more vibrato in their *you-all*, I have a 99.9 percent chance of being right. Those are odds I'll take any day.

🐦

For more than 20 years the invitation had been there. What took me so long to accept it? Was I really all that busy? Once I accepted, it seemed as if these owls had much to teach about themselves.

I now have a handle on how to listen in the night. I have already learned that he is the more likely to gobble and cackle and produce all kinds of unimaginable sounds, she the more likely to "hum" an accompaniment of muted legato sounds. I can learn much more. I can know whether it is he or she who calls, who instigates the duets, how often each calls within the duet, who has the last word. I can hear whether these patterns change from summer to winter, or differ from one pair to the next. I can now dissect their "courting antics . . . [in which they utter] the most weird and uncouth sounds imaginable . . . [some] given with the full power of their lungs . . . [others] soft and cooing and more expressive of the tender emotions; sounds resembling maniacal laughter and others like mere chuckles . . . interspersed here and there between loud *wha wha*s and *hoo-hoo-aw*s." I am a small step closer to understanding what it means to be a barred owl.

The Carolina Wren

OCTOBER 17, 6:30 A.M. Naples, Florida, at Audubon's Corkscrew Swamp Sanctuary, standing on the boardwalk just outside the visitor's center. Sunrise will be at 7:26. I am ready for them, ready to hear that burst of energy as they stir from their sleeping places and announce to the world that they made it through the night, that they live another day, that they still defend this small patch of pine and palmetto.

It's October. Families were raised during spring and early summer, during the primary singing season, and the young birds left home months ago. Most have by now found a territory of their own, but some have not, and it is the constant pressure from these young unpaired and nonterritorial birds that forces each territorial pair to be on guard.

I'm early, perhaps half an hour early, but I didn't want to chance missing them. I need to just stand here, too, silently, listening, smelling, absorbing all that these wrens experience during these waking minutes. In the distance to the west, no doubt from the very top of a cypress, a limpkin wails its anguished screams and mournful rattles. A silent shadow floats by, the slow wing beats those of a barred owl, punctuated by the asthmatic scream of a young one nearby; another hoots in the distant cypress swamp, an abbreviated *who cooks, who cooks for you-all,* the bird too distant for me to distinguish male from female.

In the waterway beneath the boardwalk I hear tiny splashes and ripples from unknown creatures moving about in the gathering light. Insects tick and hum in the dense undergrowth, the stillness then fractured by an explosion of mockingbird chats and song, but it's just one bird and ever so briefly, jumping the gun, a false start. That same start at the right time, in just a few minutes, will sweep contagiously through these pine flatwoods, 10 or more mockingbirds almost immediately weighing in, bursts of their harsh *chat chat chat* everywhere around me.

LIB-er-ty! LIB-er-ty! LIB-er-ty! LIB! There's the first wren of the morning, a hundred yards to the east, a single song, a bold phrase repeated three and a half times on what must be the next territory over. The emphatic, powerful waves of his song radiate out, to be heard by all, everyone put on notice. Every leaf, twig, and trunk, every being within a quarter mile reverberates with each *LIB-er-ty!*, rousing every molecule and bone in my body, too, I warming to the sound from the inside out as if I were in some giant outdoor oven that uses this wren's sound waves rather than microwaves. I brace myself, ready for action, wondering if this is a false start among the wrens or the beginning of the wren day. Within seconds comes another song from the same bird, and then another, each one a rousing *LIB-er-ty! LIB-er-ty! LIB-er-ty! LIB!*

Four seconds later, just 10 yards to my left, in the wax myrtle beside the boardwalk, comes the two-second reply from the male I've been waiting for: *CHE-wortel! CHE-wortel! CHE-wortel! CHE-wortel! CHE-wortel!* He is not alone, she is quick to point out; her strident, buzzy chatter from just to my right is imposed on the five phrases of his song within a second of his start and then extends a second and a half beyond his last *CHE-wortel!*, thus ensuring that she is heard, too (track 92, figure 66). Only 15 yards separate them when they first sound off, and almost certainly they roosted nearby, too, perhaps even together in the same roosting nest, as my friend Gene Morton tells me they do in Maryland.

Ten seconds later they repeat the proclamation, he with another five-phrase *CHE-wortel!*, she now beginning her extended rattle on his first phrase, within half a second of his beginning. Ten times during two and a half minutes they duet, he with his *CHE-wortel!* song, she with her buzzy rattle. After three songs he shortens his song by one phrase, to *CHE-wortel! CHE-wortel! CHE-wortel! CHE-wortel!*, and her effort wanes, too, sometimes to just a brief hiccup during the male's song, to be heard by no one except me (thanks to my parabola and headphones), as if she means well, but doesn't think it important enough for a full-blown response . . . Until he pauses for more than 30 seconds, then sings again, her response now as emphatic as ever; 8 seconds later he sings again, her response again emphatic and extending well beyond his song.

Then silence, 10 seconds, 20, 30, a minute. I'm distracted, by the wailing limpkin, the chatting mockingbirds, the chirping yellowthroats, the wheezing gnatcatchers and chucking thrashers and meowing catbirds and wheeping great crested flycatchers and screaming red-shouldered hawks and . . . there he is! Or, I catch myself, there a wren is, as I cannot know whether it is he or she. It perches in the open, above where the female was singing, in the leafless branches of a small red maple tree along the waterway. It preens, the head pivoting and extending on the neck, the bill reaching high onto the breast and shoulder and back, then straightening feathers under the left wing, then under the right. What must be a morning ritual continues, the feathers being straightened after a night's rest, two minutes, three, four, five . . .

Cho-WE Cho-WE Cho-WE Cho-WE Cho-WE Cho-WE Cho-WE Cho-WE Cho-WE Cho-WE Cho-WE Cho-WE Cho-WE!!, a rapid-fire three-second song, 13 phrases in all, a song strikingly different from his first series of the morning. And it was *he* who was preening, he who had flown from the place of his first song over to hers. What had moved him? Was it something she said, or how emphatic her last two replies were that told him it was time? To this song she replies, too, her strident chatter revealing that she remains low in the bush where she first called this morning. Seconds later he sings again, now only 10 *Cho-WE* phrases, and then a third song, with only nine phrases. Her response remains strong on the second song, but weakens on the third, not extending beyond his.

Still 10 minutes before sunrise, he now drops down into the tangle at the base of the maple, and thanks to the ability of the parabola to gather in the softest of sounds and bring them to the headphones over my ears, I hear them

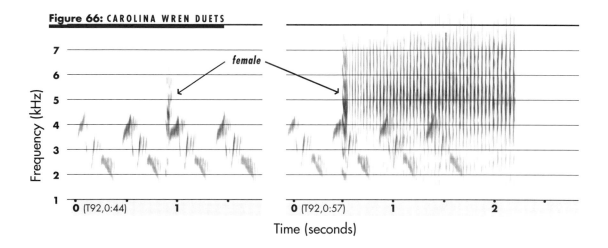

Figure 66: CAROLINA WREN DUETS

Frequency (kHz)

7
6
5
4
3
2
1

female

0 (T92,0:44)   1   0 (T92,0:57)   1   2

Time (seconds)

Figure 66. Two duets by the male and female Carolina wren, the eighth and tenth songs in track 92. The parabola is focused on the female, so her chatter is sharp and crisp in the sonagram; off to the left is the male, well out of the parabola's focus, so his song is faintly recorded and more blurred. In the duet on the left, the female offers only a brief hiccup at the beginning of the male's third phrase; on the right, however, she starts earlier in the male's song and chatters well beyond the end of his song.

twittering, greeting each other face to face. A minute later they depart together to make the rounds, to search for food and repair whatever boundary fences need mending.

I remain, to listen in as they move about. The woodpeckers are finally awake, the whinny of the downy and coarse rattle of the hairy giving them away, the *chig-chig* from red-bellies everywhere. A pileated laughs *kuk-kuk-kuk-kuk-kuk-kuk* to the west, toward the cypress swamp. Slipping by me on the boardwalk is a bobcat, who five yards away turns to stare, and for ten seconds we eye each other, I admiring every inch of him, or her, from the tip of that tiny tail to the abundant whiskers. High overhead a rattle, my wren sensors saying female Carolina wren, but I quickly realize it's a belted kingfisher, the quality of its rattle at a distance not all that dissimilar to the chatter of a female wren.

Perhaps 20 minutes after they depart the maple, I hear him singing to the south. It's just two songs, different from his other two series this morning, and she is silent, for the first time this morning not singing with him. For another hour or so I listen, hearing a couple of other songs from him, and once she chimes in, but only halfheartedly. The business of singing seems over for the most part, and this October day will be spent largely searching for food, just maintaining the status quo until next spring, when it will once again be time to raise a family.

Hiking the boardwalk through the pine flatwoods community and out to the cypress swamp, I warm even more to these wrens as I reflect on their tropical origins. South of the border, through Mexico, Central America, and into South America, I can hear another two dozen of their closest relatives, the other species in the genus *Thryothorus;* they are distinguished singers, loud and emphatic, with pure tones, not a strident note among them. Named largely by their looks, they are black-throated or black-bellied or black-crowned or black-capped, or whiskered or moustached, or rufous-throated or stripe-throated, or rufous- or stripe- or speckle- or buff- or fawn-breasted, or gray, or even plain. Or they're named by where I'd find them, the bay or riverside wren, or the Sinaloa, or Inca, or our particular one, the Carolina wren. My favorite, in name, is the happy wren. Some of them I have heard firsthand, the rest only from recordings made by others.

Had more of these wrens been named as they were experienced alive in nature rather than dead in the hand of the gun-toting taxonomist, I might know them as the whistler or the flutist or the musician, or as the melodious or warbling or mellow wrens. The sweet wren. The pleasant wren. The harmonious wren. Or the superb wren. All names in superlative form, all reflecting their status as world-class songsters.

The Carolina one, thankfully, has escaped its tropical homeland. I know these wrens from throughout the eastern states, and over the last century they have pressed on, finding New England, upstate New York, and Michigan. They're tropical songsters in temperate climes, and I see them in my mind's eye, rusty above, cinnamon below, and with a strikingly white throat and eyeline. They could well have been named the rusty-backed wren, or the cinnamon-breasted or white-throated wren, had they not been named for where they were first described. Personally, I'd go for re-sounding wren, a tribute to one of the loudest singers I know in North America. Or the res-onating wren, or the rhapsodical wren, or . . .

I replay this morning's tape in my head. *LIB-er-ty! . . . CHE-wortel! . . . Cho-WE . . .* and others, my two- or three-syllable attempts at capturing his songs, all variations on the unmistakable stop-dead-in-your-tracks-and-listen Carolina wren theme, all ren-ditions from the large song repertoire that each male Carolina wren has. Shadow a male for a day or two and hear the variety (track 93, figure 67). He repeats each variation several times, some-times well over 200 times if he is unpaired and it's midday and nothing all that exciting is happening, and then he abruptly switches to another, and eventu-ally to another, and another. He has 20 to 50 different songs, each one having been learned from neighboring males so that neighbors share almost identi-cal repertoires. They often respond to each other with identical songs, too, no doubt playing the same kind of song-matching games that so many other songbirds also play (for examples, see the sections on song sparrow, tufted tit-mouse, Bachman's sparrow).

Then there's her chatter. I puzzle over its simplicity, an insectlike buzz of

Figure 67. Sonagrams of eight different songs used by the male Carolina wren at Corkscrew Swamp Sanctuary near Naples, Florida. Watch the sonagrams as you listen to the songs (track 93) and you can begin to appreciate the great variety of songs that each male Carolina wren can sing. Look carefully at songs F and H, seeing how the shape and emphasis of the two lower notes differs in the two sonagrams; listen in track 93 for what you see here.

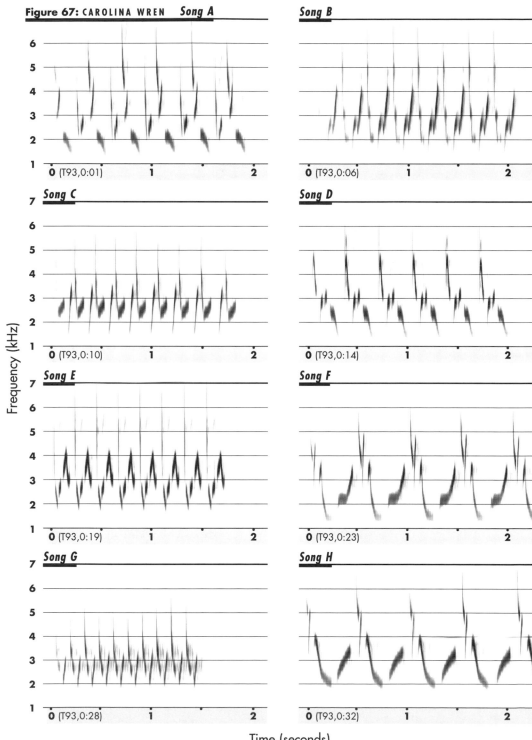

Figure 67: CAROLINA WREN *Song A*

Song B

Song C

Song D

Song E

Song F

Song G

Song H

Frequency (kHz)

0 (T93,0:01)   1   2
0 (T93,0:06)   1   2
0 (T93,0:10)   1   2
0 (T93,0:14)   1   2
0 (T93,0:19)   1   2
0 (T93,0:23)   1   2
0 (T93,0:28)   1   2
0 (T93,0:32)   1   2

Time (seconds)

about 30 notes a second, not unlike what I would expect from a cicada her size. What a contrast her chatter is to the music in his songs, and what a contrast to the songs of her tropical cousins in Central America. There, the songs of a female are often as impressive as those of her mate, and in some species she is even the lead singer in the duo. Their duets can be so well coordinated, too, that unless I stand between the male and female I can't even tell that two birds are involved. From the stripe-breasted wren I hear *who's to SEE/me, little me/who's to SEE/me, little me,* she slipping her softer, whistled *me, little me* precisely into the gaps between his louder *who's to SEE.* Whoever named the "plain wren" could never have heard them duet in perfect synchrony, the *chinchiri/gwee/ chinchiri/gwee/ chinchiri/gwee* consisting of his *chinchiri* and her *gwee.* If our Carolina wren were more typical of its southern relatives, its loud *LIB-er-ty! LIB-er-ty! LIB-er-ty! LIB!* song would be delivered by two birds, the male perhaps producing the *LIB-er,* the female the *-ty,* their timing flawless. Instead, the lady Carolina wren beats her own drum, her "song" a simple chatter. I'll take her as she is. (But *what if* she were more typical? See track 94.)

Tropical birds, these Carolina wrens. Even in October the males still sing, and pairs stay together throughout the year, actively maintaining their territory. How different these male wrens are from the local towhees, some of whom are also resident but so quiet now, so quiet that no one knows what they do over the winter months. And how different the wrens are from the local mockingbirds, who are also still paired but who awake with their loud calls, the "chatbursts," as the mockingbirds rely more on these harsh calls than on songs to defend their winter territory. And how different from the local cardinals who chip but do not sing. Yes, how different these singing tropical wrens are from the other songbirds that spend their winter here, too, as most are relatively silent, often using simple calls to defend territories.

It's as if each of these species, in its own way, provides an answer to the age-old question, "Why do birds sing?" The routine answer is "To defend a territory and attract or impress a mate for breeding," because it's difficult to disentangle these two possible functions. It seems to me, however, that these wrens provide a partial answer for us. The relatively little singing they do throughout the winter seems to be for defending the territory and maintaining the pair bond, because the wrens are not nesting and mating then; the abundant song during the spring and summer seems to be more about breeding and sex and who mates with whom. It might be claimed that territories become more important to defend in the spring, and that's why the wrens sing more then. Yes, but I would argue that the male-male singing contests in spring are less about territorial rights than about impressing females; the abundant spring song is more about sex than territory, and if there were no sex, there would be no song.

The mockingbirds seem to have an answer for why birds sing, too. During the winter, song is minimal, and calls are more important for territorial defense; the exuberant spring song, then, must also be about mating, about who will be the father of whose offspring. The same for the cardinals. And all of those migrants who defend their winter territory with simple calls seem to be declaring that their complex spring song is not so much about defending a territory either, but mostly about sex, about impressing one's own mate or the mate next door.

Continuing on the boardwalk, I'm past the lettuce pond, where the night herons are roosting, and now among the old-growth cypress towering overhead; below them, linear arrays of luxuriant ferns smother massive fallen logs, the dense growth here a wren haven, the prime territories often hotly contested. I pause to look, to listen, to revel in the vocal brawl I was part of here last April. I was watching a pair to the left of the boardwalk, catching a glimpse of them now and then in the dense cover. He then perched in the open a few yards over the water, singing *tea-kettle tea-kettle tea-kettle tea-kettle,* several times over a minute or so, she remaining silent nearby. This tranquil domestic scene was shattered by the *CHE-wortel CHE-wortel CHE-wortel CHE-wortel* just behind me, to the right of the boardwalk. The *tea-kettle* and the *CHE-wortel* songs were hurled back and forth across the boardwalk, both females now involved, too, every second or third song from the first female's mate punctuated with her buzzy chatter, as if to say to the other female *I'm here, too; this is my territory; keep out;* and as if to remind her mate that *I'm here, a female, your mate, don't take your aggression out on me.*

The male behind me then switched to a new song, *WHEE-del WHEE-del WHEE-del,* echoed almost instantly by the male before me, *WHEE-del WHEE-del WHEE-del.* Back and forth they sang, their mates chiming in, too. After four or five songs they both switched to another, *willy-way willy-way willy-way.* Back and forth again they took turns singing, but now I heard the asymmetry in their exchanges. When the male behind me sang, he was followed instantly—and sometimes even overlapped—by the male in front of me, and then there was silence, though perhaps for only two seconds. *Túrtree túrtree túrtree* now rings behind me, followed instantly by *túrtree túrtree túrtree* in front of me, the female's buzzy chatter accompanying each, this frenzied foursome battling across an unseen line drawn in the swamp.

Over the next few minutes, the intruding pair behind me retreated from the boardwalk, back into the swamp, he switching to a new song on the way, *jo-ree jo-ree jo-ree jo-ree*. My male continued his old song, *túrtree túrtree túrtree*. They continued to counter each other, back and forth, but now just a twosome, the females silent. No longer did the males match songs, and their responses were more measured, the silent pauses after each's songs now about equal.

I remember glancing at the blank pages in my notebook, chuckling, realizing that I was as caught up in that border skirmish as they were, as I have no record, other than my memory, of what happened there. I queried that memory, trying to understand this exchange better. How long had that male behind me been singing by the time I heard him? If I had been listening, would I have heard that pair approach gradually, or did they come out of nowhere, perhaps flying to the border just for this skirmish? How many songs of each type did the two males sing before they switched? Less than 10, I think, perhaps less than a minute's time? Exactly when did the females chime in? Did a female chatter especially when her mate switched to a new song, or did the females respond more to each other than to what their mates were doing? Did her chatter influence his singing, with him perhaps singing fewer renditions of a song before switching if she sang, too? Perhaps his next song was shorter if she also sang, just a *tea-kettle tea-kettle*, or maybe longer, a *tea-kettle tea-kettle tea-kettle tea-kettle*. Did the males play games with the duration of their song, a short one followed by a long one, or vice versa, or short by short, long by long? When did the song of my male no longer perfectly bisect the silent space between the songs of the other, the interaction then becoming asymmetrical, the nearby male signaling his aggressiveness by overlapping the song of the intruder? What rules of disengagement did they follow as the pair behind me retreated? Many questions and few answers, but the next time I'm caught up in a skirmish like this, I'll try to keep my senses, capturing some of those answers in my notebook.

Whatever the game is, the young males enter it much as did my Bewick's wrens that I studied over three decades ago. Late each summer, in August and September when most birds are quiet, I hear the young Carolina wren males practicing. Their babbling contrasts with the precision of the adult song, in which each syllable is precisely enunciated, over and over. I hear the uncertainty in the youngster's voice, no two attempts at the same sound alike, his future songs all mixed up in his brain: *Too-kottle ti-piddle CHEtle-chi ket-WHEE del-jo ree-ree, wor-choo-WEE* he drunkenly blurts out in a loud, rambling monologue, nothing in its proper place. He babbles and babbles, working on all the phrases of his adult songs; his *too-kottle ti-piddle* eventually becomes a precise *tea-kettle tea-kettle,* as he perfects 20 or 30 or even 50 different songs, so that when he is only three months old he is already a formidable singer and can match the songs of the older neighbors where he has chosen to settle. In the meantime, though, he comes up with hilarious combinations every bit as comical as our own children attempting to get our spoken language right (track 9).

He eventually gets it right, of course, as all Carolina wren songs that I've ever heard have been a variation on the familiar theme. What if he didn't get it right? What if he perfected a very different song, of the kind that he first started practicing in which each phrase is different? Using my computer software, I pluck a syllable from each of several songs and try them in various combinations (track 95). How about a song that begins slowly and speeds up? Or begins rapidly and slows down? Or how about a random sequence of brief and long syllables? I love the effects, love imagining the possibilities for a Carolina wren of a different sort.

The female Carolina wren enters the game differently. While the complex songs of a male are learned from adult singers, her simple chatter is inborn. He takes about three months to get his songs just right, as he must memorize and practice, practice, practice, but she's in good form shortly after leaving the nest, when only a few weeks old. She is different, too, from all of her tropical relatives. Those tropical females in all the other *Thryothorus* species have complex songs, much like those of the males, and therefore must also learn their songs.

These singing differences are reflected in how their brains are wired, too. The male Carolina wren has perhaps the largest song repertoire among all *Thryothorus* wrens, and he also has especially large groups of specialized, song-learning neurons in his forebrain. It's a simple matter of more brain space needed to control his larger, learned vocabulary. Search for these song-learning centers in the female Carolina wren, though, and you'll find nothing. Her simple rattle is not learned and is more likely controlled not in the forebrain but in some more primitive part of the brain.

Further support for this idea that more brain space is needed to learn larger vocabularies comes from other *Thryothorus* wrens. The female rufous-and-white wren, for example, has about half as many learned songs as her mate, and she sings relatively little, too; her song-control centers are also about half the size of his. In the duetting bay wren and buff-breasted wren, however, males and females have equally complex song repertoires, and their brains are alike, too, with about the same amount of brain space devoted to learning and controlling their songs.

Because the female Carolina wren has no obvious song-learning centers in her brain, and because her chatter isn't learned, some experts might argue that she doesn't actually "sing." After all, all songbirds have "learned songs" that require some kind of experience to get the songs right; that experience might require memorizing the songs of other adults (as in the Bewick's wren) or it might involve just being able to hear oneself practice as songs are improvised (as in the sedge wren). Those imitated or improvised songs are controlled by the forebrain's song-control centers, the cascading series of nerve centers that collect information from the ear, integrate it in the brain, and then send commands to the two voice boxes. No, the female Carolina wren doesn't sing, it might be argued; her chatter is just a simple, innate call note that she uses in combination with the male's song.

Carry this idea one step further and one could claim that flycatchers don't sing, either. Flycatchers are not true "songbirds"; furthermore, their "songs" are innate, and no song-learning centers have been found in their brains either. Then, do their relatives the bellbirds sing because their sounds are learned? Do we need to inspect their brains before we decide this matter?

I'm amused by the tangle we often create for ourselves by trying to shoehorn the world into the simple vocabulary that we use. Does she "sing"? Or does she only "call"? Using the words "song" and "call," we will never satisfy all of the people all of the time, because these are words that we impose on the diverse array of sounds that birds make. Whatever the neural basis of her simple chatter, and no matter whether it is innate or learned, she plays a game every bit as important to her as his is to him; it makes no difference to her what word we use.

Her chatter imposed on his song informs neighboring pairs and perhaps especially single females that here is a pair, that this male and his territory are occupied. Her chatter also reminds her mate that she is female—without that reminder, the consequences could be fatal, so aggressive is the male toward other males. It's a delicate balance here in the pine and palmetto. She needs him and he needs her, and together they have teamed up to claim this space and each other. It's a partnership confirmed by their duets, a pact that together they will give it their best shot to use this space and each other to raise a family and leave their mark on future Carolina wren generations.

The Northern Cardinal

The beloved cardinal. It's the state bird of seven states, more than any other bird: North Carolina, Virginia, West Virginia, Kentucky, Ohio, Illinois, and Iowa all claim this bird as their own. What more striking picture is there than the brilliant red, crested male with his black facemask sitting on the greenest of evergreen branches in the whitest of a winter scene? In my mind he's one of the "big three," because he was pictured with the scarlet tanager and rose-breasted grosbeak on the front of the Peterson's field guide that I learned birds with; he's also the mascot of St. Louis sports teams. He's a rare combination, with both good looks and great sounds, a rich variety of flutelike whistles that enthrall anyone who listens. The cardinal was once called the Virginia nightingale, perhaps for its habit of occasionally singing during the night, but perhaps just for the sheer beauty of its song.

The cardinal is my quarry for this early morning, as I've convinced myself I must hear them up close, both male and female, to know them better. It's a little before 5:00 A.M., April 25, with sunrise about an hour from now, and I stand waiting patiently beside Eliza and Arthur Bourne, or at least their earthly remains and the tombstone marking the spot here in Wildwood Cemetery. If Eliza and Arthur could talk, they'd tell of a bird haven, of frequent visits by local birders, especially in May when the warblers move through. They'd tell of the cardinals, too, I'm sure, residents of the cemetery now just as permanent as they are.

I have read much about these cardinals, these "northern" cardinals (to distinguish them from the vermilion cardinal in South America and the pyrrhuloxia in the Southwest), and I try to recall some of the facts. Come spring, he's red, it's true, but some males are more cardinal than others, depending in part on how rich in carotenoid pigments his food was when he grew his feathers last fall. Oh, the pain when pinched by that massive, conical bill, as I've felt many times when removing these birds from my mist nets. They mate for life, or, well, perhaps I should say that their "divorce rate" is far lower than it is among humans. During late spring and all summer I see them in pairs as they defend their breeding territories of roughly 2 to 4 acres against all comers, but I know that each pair is part of a larger community, too, and that when territories break down during harsh winter weather a dozen or more birds may flock, all coming to feeders at once. They're responsible for a fair number of my bird-related telephone calls in spring, too: "There's a cardinal at my window (or the side mirror of my car in the driveway), throwing himself into the window for hours on end. What's his problem?" I explain how the territorial cardinal sees his reflection and attacks the apparent intruder in his territory. She does the same, as it's male against male, female against female when defending a territory against another pair.

And, oh, how he sings (for examples of cardinal songs, though not these particular birds, see track 96, figure 68)! In my mind's play-center I hear his *what cheer, cheer, cheer,* his whistles as brilliant as he is handsome. The short *what* may slur briefly up, each *cheer* then taking most of a second to slur smoothly down the scale. *What cheer, cheer, cheer, birdie-birdie-birdie* follows, as he adds a little flourish on the end, then another *what cheer, cheer, cheer.*

I hear other songs, too, of a clearly different pattern. Perhaps it's *pichew pichew tiw tiw tiw tiw tiw tiw tiw,* over and over. I count them as he sings: 10, 15, 20 or so times and then it's another song, perhaps a *wooiit wooiit wooiit wooiit chew chew chew chew.* All consist of pure whistles, some slurred up, some down; some are almost a second long and repeated slowly, others just a

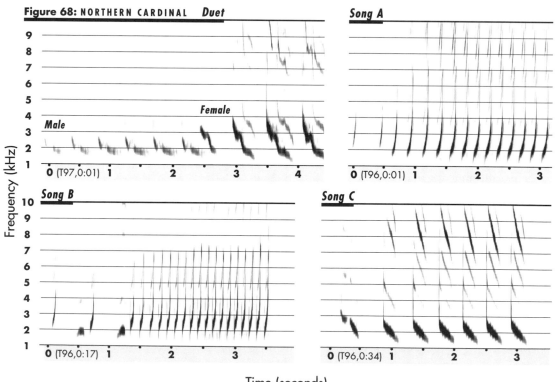

Figure 68: NORTHERN CARDINAL *Duet*

Song A

Song B

Song C

Frequency (kHz)

Time (seconds)

The Singing Life of Birds

fraction of a second and delivered rapidly. It is fairly easy to hear the 8 to 10 different songs as he sings—he repeats each one enough times that I can get to know it, and then he goes on to another, each so different from the others. I soon hear his favored sequences, too, as I can often predict the next song based on his current song.

Like many other songbirds, the males engage in community conversations. I've heard them here in the cemetery, the resident male and two of his neighbors hurling identical songs back and forth at one another, as their repertoires are much the same. In heated debates the songs become longer and more complex, with extra whistled phrases and perhaps even a red squirrel-like *chirr* added to the end of the song. In these vocal skirmishes they switch to new songs more frequently, too, and match each other more often than not, typically repeating each song just a few times before introducing another, as if the war will be won by who switches to a new song first, or by he who refuses to follow the leader, or in some other conversational convention that only cardinals know. Yes, I've heard them here in the cemetery, and elsewhere, too, on Cape Cod, and in almost every state down to Florida, west to Texas and north to Minnesota, as they play the same games everywhere.

And she also sings. It is *she* who has brought me here, to know her and her singing role better. By March or April, perhaps a month after he's been in full song, she chimes in, at least according to the expert accounts I have read. She sings far less than he does; it seems that her songs are not repeated as precisely as his, and they seem not to be as loud, either. She often sings from under cover, too, while the showy male is perched in the open. There's nothing second-rate about her songs, though, as her repertoire is essentially identical to his. She sometimes uses her songs to defend her territory against an intruding female, but mostly she duets with her mate, and usually when they are rather close by. And when she duets with her mate, she almost always matches him,

FEMALE
NORTHERN
CARDINAL

Figure 68. Songs of the northern cardinal. In the duet, see the faintly recorded song of the male in the background and how the female responds immediately after his song with four whistled phrases of her own (track 97). Songs A, B, and C are three different songs in the repertoire of a male cardinal (track 96).

his *pichew pichew tiw tiw tiw tiw tiw tiw tiw* followed quickly by hers, his *what cheer, cheer, cheer* by hers (for sample duet of another pair of cardinals, listen to track 97).

What my friend Sylvia Halkin tells me about these duets, after she studied them for several years in Wisconsin, is rather remarkable. As the female cardinal sits on the nest, she occasionally sings, and she seems able to control whether her mate will bring food to the nest by when she sings and by whether she matches the song he is singing. How appropriate, I think—with male song used to impress (some would say "manipulate" or "control") females, here is a female who controls the male directly through her songs.

I want to know more about these cardinals, so I wait patiently here in Wildwood Cemetery, as I must hear this female for myself, to try to understand how she uses her songs, to hear how she might control him. The pair would have no nest yet this early in the year, but I expect to hear an exchange of songs early in the morning as they awake. Just where will they awake? That's the puzzle for the moment. After surveying the cemetery, I've taken my best guess, standing here beside Eliza and Arthur and beside the wild tangle of bushes near their plot, thinking that the safety of this tangle is where I'd choose to roost for the night if I were a cardinal. I expect them to awake just as they go to roost, their sharp *tik tik* notes giving them away, the first and last thoughts of the day often expressed in their "alarm" or aggressive notes, just like so many other songbirds go to roost (for example, the American robin, northern mockingbird, and wood thrush).

Cheer cheer! Right beside me, deep in the safety of this tangled thicket! How satisfying, to have pretended to be the cardinal and chosen the same roosting place he did. It must be him, not her, given how loud the song, but I will need to see him to be sure. That first song was an early one, blurted into the quiet of the coming dawn, a brief promise of more to come, but only when he's ready. A minute passes . . . *cheer cheer!* Again he sings, and again only a partial song, just two whistles, and then silence. Soon a third song, a fourth, and he's under way, though still unseen in the darkness.

It's a full song now, containing two different phrases: *cheer cheer wit wit wit wit wit wit wit.* I close my eyes, concentrating, listening to this virtuoso, and I try to imagine all that is involved in producing such a song. The next song begins deep in the song-control centers of his forebrain, from symmetrical nerve centers on the left and the right sides of the brain, nerves firing, commands sent throughout the body. Every nerve and every muscle in his body has memorized its role, thanks to half a year of practice during the months after he hatched and well into the following spring as he repeated the same songs over and over and over, perfecting each little detail. His entire being seems to tense as lungs and air sacs pressurize, the left voice box now largely closing down as the right opens; a small army of tiny muscles flexes, tensioning membranes that now vibrate 7,000 times a second in the passing airstream. Ever so smoothly the muscles relax, as does the tension of the membranes they control, the whistled air from the open beak slurring smoothly down the scale. After sweeping the whistle through a full octave, to 3,500 vibrations a second, nerve impulses from the brain close down the right voice box and continue whistling down nearly another octave with the left, the specialist at the lower pitches. Two voices produce this one whistled *cheer*, the two voice boxes so expertly coordinated that no one would ever know were it not for some meddling scientists prying into the inner workings of the syringes of a singing cardinal. Young birds must practice this coordination to get it right: early efforts clearly show two separate whistles produced by separate voice boxes, but the two whistles slowly merge over time as the adult song is perfected.

All that for the opening *cheer*, and here comes the second *cheer*. He inhales, leisurely, over half a second, and repeats the entire process, *cheer*, the song so well practiced that he could sing it in his sleep. Two *cheers*, and then the pace picks up: *wit wit wit wit wit wit wit wit wit wit*, 10 brief phrases over two seconds, each phrase with two notes, a low one produced by the left voice box, a higher one produced by the right. He inhales briefly after the second *cheer*, then exhales in a perfectly timed sequence through the left and then the right voice boxes, quickly inhales as he prepares himself for the next *wit*, exhales left and then right, and then inhales, throughout the entire sequence the muscles and membranes tensing and relaxing on schedule, yielding an exquisite series of paired whistles, each one just like the others. *Cheer cheer wit wit wit wit wit wit wit wit wit wit*. After months of practice, he has four seconds of perfection, requiring 11 minibreaths and 12 expertly timed coordinations of his left and right voice boxes, a masterpiece.

I try to appreciate his next song with the awe it is due. *Cheer cheer wit wit wit wit*, and he stops short. As each song emerges from the tangle, I know his entire body is quivering, from the tip of his crest to the tip of his tail—he breathes rapidly, up to five times a second, alternating control of left and right voice boxes, his song a precise routine. *Cheer . . . cheer cheer . . . cheer cheer wit wit wit wit wit wit wit wit . . .* Sometimes it is a single *cheer*, sometimes a pair of them, sometimes combined with only a few *wit* syllables, sometimes with as many as 16. Some songs are muted, some deafeningly loud. Nearby a robin begins calling, soon launching into his dawn songs. A mourning dove laments, a nearby chickadee begins his *hey-sweetie* chorus, the crescent moon hanging over the eastern horizon. Robins all at once seem to be singing everywhere.

Well into his fifth minute of singing, he is in peak form, delivering a 5-second song, *cheer cheer wit wit wit wit wit wit wit wit wit wit wit wit wit wit wit*. He pauses 5 seconds, then repeats it, another 5 seconds of perfection, now singing at a clip when songs are as long as the pauses between them. Then nothing, 10 seconds, 20 seconds, and the tangles whistle a new tune. This one begins low, rising up the scale, a pleasant contrast to his first song, as if he must show he is equally adept in the left-to-right voice box transition. Softly at first, and just one whistle, then two, four, and up to seven whistles in a song, a total of 11 songs in two minutes.

As the chickadee shifts his *hey-sweetie* to a higher pitch, the cardinal switches songs again, too, now another right-to-left transition, much like the *cheer* of his first song, boldly slurred whistles starting high and sweeping low. The transition to this new song is again gradual, first just two whistles, then four, then five, each song also accelerating, the pause between the first two slurred whistles twice that between the last two.

Churrr churrr, a brown thrasher stirs within the bushes, followed by a brief commotion and a blur of departing cardinal. In a flash I confirm it was him, not her, and to the top of a nearby oak he now flies, within seconds resuming his singing, but with a different song, his fourth of the morning. He now starts low again and sweeps up, *wooiit*. Another single *wooiit*, then a *wooiit wooiit chew,* the *chew* a brief down-slurred note. His pattern of singing is fascinating. As he switches from one song form to another, not only does he alternate between down-slurs and up-slurs at the beginning of the songs, but he also maintains good contrast within the song, too, so that a few long down-slurs at the beginning are balanced by many brief up-slurs at the end *(cheer cheer wit wit wit wit)*, or long up-slurs at the beginning are balanced by many rapid down-slurs at the end *(wooiit wooiit chew chew chew chew)*.

As I log this new version into my notes, my mind wanders . . . to the chickadee, who continues his *hey-sweetie* serenade, every minute or two shifting his song to a new pitch . . . to the nearest robin, who oddly now seems stuck on singing *hisselly* notes . . . to the titmice, three males within earshot, each singing the same song, *peter peter peter* . . . to the bluebird, his grating chatter between songs showing he now really means business . . . to the blue jays, who cannot agree on whether to use their grating *jay* or the less strident squeaky-gate call . . . to the chipping sparrow who still sputters his songs from the gravestone to my right . . . and the mourning doves . . . and the crows . . . and the wavering *poor sam peabody peabody peabody* song, the song of this lingering, northbound white-throated sparrow still imperfect.

Among all those demanding my attention, I barely notice her first song. Glancing at my watch and my check sheet, I realize he's been carrying on from the very top of the leafless oak for four minutes and has just belted out his twenty-fifth song in the series, a *wooiit wooiit chew chew chew chew chew chew chew chew chew chew chew chew*. From low in the cluster of rhododendrons and yew, just 20 yards to the northeast of him, and within a split second of the end of his song, comes her muted echo, *wooiit wooiit chew*. She must have caught his attention, for he pauses, 8, 10, 12 seconds, and she repeats herself, another muted *wooiit wooiit chew*, just enough of the song for both him and me to know that she is matching his exact song. He waits, another 5 seconds, then responds with an abbreviated song himself, *wooiit wooiit chew chew chew*.

The conversation continues . . . Over the next minute he sings only four songs, all abbreviated, as if he sings and then listens, wondering what message will arise from the rhododendron below. Then silence, 30, 40, 50 seconds, and she sings again, so softly I can barely hear her, *wooiit wooiit chew chew chew chew*. Within two seconds he replies, and seconds later again, *wooiit wooiit chew chew chew chew chew chew chew chew chew chew chew chew chew*, one of his longest songs yet, well over four seconds of his finest, she then responding within a fraction of a second of his finish, *wooiit wooiit chew*, again softly from the rhododendron. For two more minutes they carry on, she always brief and soft, and "polite," too, her songs never overlapping his, instead coming either immediately after his or after a lengthy silence. Two more minutes pass, his songs often muted, sometimes reduced to a single soft *wooiit*, then surging in both length and loudness, seemingly emboldened, until she responds quickly with two songs, the last her longest and loudest effort, *wooiit wooiit chew chew chew chew chew chew chew*.

More silence, for 10, 20, 30 seconds . . . The songs of the robin and chickadee in the nearby maple seem deafeningly loud, as if they are exploiting the unclaimed airspace, though it is more likely they are just exploiting my unclaimed attention.

He begins anew, with a single *wooiit*, followed by another, and another, a tentative beginning, and then a full song, though still muted. Six seconds later he introduces another song type, his fifth of the morning, perhaps to match the male who now sings this tune from the north. Following the contrasting pattern he has established this morning, this new song begins high and sweeps low, from the right voice box to the left, the opposite of the song he has just abandoned. Three songs of this type, and she responds, but with the old type, as she has not switched with him. Half a minute passes, and he resumes, ever so softly, one song, then a second, and a third, becoming louder, until she responds again, this time with just a snippet of the old song, *wooiit*. He sings again, then again, and then, nearly 90 seconds after he switched song types, she does so, too, matching him.

Nearly a minute passes, and he resumes, softly, then louder, but she doesn't let him finish, as she overlaps the last second of his song with hers. Among males of some species, this is believed to be the strongest, the most threatening reply — a reply that overlaps. She sings again, this time louder, her longest song yet.

Tik tik tik from the bushes, her sharp call notes commanding his attention, he now flutters in the treetops to turn and face her. Half a minute later he mutes a brief song, as she does in reply, *cheer cheer cheer*. She quickly follows with another, somewhat louder *cheer cheer cheer cheer cheer cheer,* and another, louder still, CHEER CHEER CHEER CHEER CHEER CHEER CHEER, culminating in her loudest and longest, an emphatic no-holds-barred CHEER CHEER CHEER CHEER CHEER CHEER CHEER CHEER.

I know that tone of voice, I find myself thinking, as I've heard it countless times in my own home. Don . . . Doonn . . . DOONNAALLDD . . . DOONNAALLDD!! Is this some universal "language," recognizable by "guys" anywhere? No, I shouldn't anthropomorphize, I caution myself. Just tell the facts (but in this loose thinking, I remind myself, are the germs of ideas that could be tested in a rigorous, scientific way).

Four songs from her in rapid succession, escalating from three to six to seven to eight *cheers,* and each song progressively louder. Within seconds he floats from the treetop down to the rhododendron, where she awaits. Still a quarter of an hour before sunrise, quietly they greet, the beginning of a new day that will be spent largely together, foraging throughout their cemetery as they prepare for the upcoming nesting season.

Wow. What have I witnessed here? What games are these two cardinals playing? What's she thinking? How about him? There is extraordinary potential for complex conversations in these exchanges, in how loud or complete the song, or how rapidly he or she sings, or whether one waits for the other to reply, or how quickly one replies, or whether one overlaps or alternates with the partner's songs, or whether she matches his songs, or he hers. To complicate matters, all of these exchanges between a male and female must take place in the context of a larger cardinal community in which other pairs are also singing, in which the exchanges between countersinging males on neighboring territories must have their own sets of rules, perhaps with many of the same conventions that a male and female use with each other.

In less than half an hour, on just one morning in late April, I have heard and seen enough to know that I'll be back. I want to see and hear more, to see how the male courts his female, how he struts and sways and twists and rotates, showing off his brightest reds, to hear how he sings in flight over her, his breast feathers all fluffed, his crest raised, beating his wings in rapid, shallow strokes, slowly fluttering down toward her. I need to find their nest, to hear the female sing there, to watch and listen to how her mate responds. I want to see the babies leave the nest, too, to listen to the young males and females practicing their songs as they find their places in the local cardinal community.

More early mornings are a must, too. I must hear them awake and greet each other as I heard them this morning, to understand better what it means to be paired "for life," through summer and through winter. It's more likely to be death, too, not brief flings with the neighbor's mate, that would separate them, as a fair number of nests have babies fathered by a male on a neighboring territory, not by the attending male. These song exchanges between male and female and among neighboring males must help each female form her opinions. How does he measure up? I can almost hear her asking. How does he attend to me? How does he compare to the males next door? I can listen, she says, and hear who sings when, who switches to the next song, and whether the neighbors alternate or overlap songs with my mate. I can listen for that rapid *chirr* on the ends of songs, too, the elements of the *chirr* given so rapidly that he cannot take minibreaths between them, the quality and duration of his *chirr* perhaps a good indication of how healthy he is. Yes, just by listening I can know much.

Among these cardinals, it is *she* who is in charge, *she* who controls the success of her mate and the other singing males around her. And this morning, it was *she* who had last say, *she* who ended the conversation in four songs that became increasingly emphatic. How fitting that, in the world of birdsong, where much of the noise is designed to impress her, she would have the last word.

Bird Sounds on the Compact Disc

THE 98 TRACKS ON THIS CD illustrate sounds that are discussed in the book's text and are often illustrated in figures with sonagrams, and I encourage you to listen to these sounds and follow along in the sonagrams when the tracks are referenced in the book. For those readers who wish to read all of the text first and listen to the CD later, however, I provide enough information here so that the contents of the CD can be appreciated without reference back to the book's text.

Only the sounds of birds (and one babbling child) are on the CD; no voice commentary announces the contents of the tracks. Without a voice announcement, you can practice listening to a particular track by playing it repeatedly, as if listening to a longer recording of a particular individual than is actually on the CD. This technique is especially helpful for listening to birds such as the American robin (tracks 12 and 13), the northern mockingbird (tracks 18 and 19), the winter wren (track 61), the wood thrush (tracks 67 and 68), the hermit thrush (track 71), the red-eyed vireo (track 77), and, well, quite a few others, in fact.

When accumulating the sounds for this CD, I soon realized a great irony: in trying to make the listening experiences as enjoyable as possible, my friends at the Macaulay Library of Natural Sounds and I often attempted to create conditions that didn't exist in nature. The titmice (track 52), for example, were recorded in my backyard, and I recorded them early in the morning before traffic noise of nearby roads became too loud; nevertheless, the dull roar of distant traffic is always present, so we electronically filtered out the lower frequency sounds, leaving as best we could only the bird sounds on the CD. As we listen in nature, we accomplish much the same effect by listening attentively to a particular sound (such as a titmouse) and by ignoring extraneous noises (such as distant traffic). Thus, although the sounds on the CD are not always unaltered recordings of nature, the presentation on the CD is designed to simulate what one might experience in nature.

Most recordings on the CD are monaural, as a single shotgun microphone or parabolic microphone records the bird and that one recorded sound track is then put onto both the left and right tracks of the compact disc. More recently, however, sound recordists are using two or more microphones that capture a more realistic, stereo listening experience. Two microphones in a parabola, for example, record the target bird equally loudly on both the left and right tracks of a stereo recorder, but birds to the left and right of the parabola's focus are heard faintly in the background on the left and right tracks, respectively. Listen to the chestnut-sided warblers in stereo, for example, and hear this effect (tracks 45 and 47), or listen to the gentle waves on the seashore as a male northern cardinal sings in the sea oats (track 96). You can read more about how stereo parabolic microphones capture sounds at the Telinga Microphone Web site: http://www.bahnhof.se/~telinga/.

The sounds on this CD come from a variety of sources. Some are my own, either pulled from my collection or recorded specifically for this book (unless otherwise noted, the sounds were recorded in Massachusetts by me). Other sounds have generously been provided by other recordists, and they are gratefully acknowledged with each track.

HEARING AND SEEING BIRD SOUNDS

As an introduction to appreciating sonagrams and to "seeing" bird sounds, listen to tracks 1 through 8 while viewing the sonagrams in figures 1 through 5.

TRACK 1: Downy woodpecker (figure 1, page 3). Drumming, the bill striking the tree at the constant rate of about 15 times a second. *Recorded in Oregon by Geoffrey A. Keller (Macaulay Library of Natural Sounds Recording 44905).*

TRACK 2: Hairy woodpecker (figure 1, page 3). Drumming, the bill striking the tree more rapidly, at the constant rate of about 25 times a second. *Recorded in California by Geoffrey A. Keller (MLNS 50166).*

TRACK 3: Yellow-bellied sapsucker (figure 1, page 3). Drumming, with a halting rhythm, rapidly at first, then slower, trailing off at the end. A second bird drums in the background. *Recorded in Ontario by William W. H. Gunn (MLNS 42983B).*

TRACK 4: White-throated sparrow (figure 2, page 4). Song, the *poor-sam-peabody* song, three roughly half-second whistles followed by four *peabody* triplets, the first two prolonged whistles at a higher pitch than the remainder of the song. This particular song is more accurately rendered *poor-poor-sam-peabody-peabody-peabody-peabody;* each bird (females also sing) has only one version of this song that is sung over and over (as the songs from one bird on this track indicate), but visit the north woods and hear how birds differ, especially in the relative frequency of the song's introductory whistles and the *peabody* ending. *Recorded in Ontario by William W. H. Gunn (MLNS 66771).*

TRACK 5: Common yellowthroat (figure 2, page 4). The *witchity-witchity* song, each *witchity* consisting of three rapidly repeated notes, the entire song consisting of four *witchity* phrases. Listen to two songs at normal speed, then one song at one-half and then one-quarter speed, the slower speeds revealing to our human ears many of the details that can be seen in the sonagram. As with white-throated sparrows, there is a great diversity of songs among individual yellowthroats, with no two individuals seeming to agree on the exact form of the *witchity. Recorded in New York by Steven R. Pantle (MLNS 53174).*

TRACK 6: Field sparrow (figure 3, page 7). Two of the "bouncing-ball" daytime songs of the field sparrow followed by two of his more complex dawn songs. Feel the acceleration in the first two songs, how they begin slowly and speed up toward the end. Feel how the last two songs are more complex, consisting of four parts, but how they accelerate, too, in their own way (see figure 3). Normally, a male awakens and sings his complex songs for half an hour or so before sunrise, and then throughout the day he sings his simpler bouncing-ball song. The sequence in this recording is reversed from the transition that one would normally hear about sunrise. *Recorded in West Virginia by Will Hershberger (MLNS 94480).*

TRACK 7: Songs of the "red" fox sparrow (first two songs) and the "large-billed" fox sparrow (last four songs; figure 4, page 8). Hear the sweet whistles of the first two songs, the bold pattern identical in the two songs here. Each male red fox sparrow has only one song that he sings over and over, successive songs differing from each other in only minor ways. Songs of this sparrow vary from place to place, too, in the form of dialects, with songs of some localities so beautiful that they can bring tears to the eyes. *Recorded in Ontario by William W. H. Gunn (MLNS 64273).*

The songs of the large-billed fox sparrow from the California Sierras begin slowly, much like those of the red fox sparrow, but then the pace picks up. Successive songs of these birds are always different, and the four songs here (the first two illustrated in figure 4, page 8) each have their own distinctive pattern, as do the other three songs that this particular male sang. Try playing these four songs repeatedly, seeing and hearing and feeling the differences among them; you'll soon recognize each of these distinctive songs by ear alone. *Recorded in California.*

TRACK 8. Common loon (figure 5, page 11). Fantastic sounds, among the favorites of many bird listeners. These sounds instantly transport a listener to the north country, to paddling a canoe in tranquil boreal lakes, the yodels and wails and tremolos of loons heard throughout the day and night. In this track, three recordings are spliced together to give a brief sequence of typical loon sounds. Watch the sonagrams in figure 5 as you listen here.

The yodel (0:01–0:05) is the male's territorial proclamation; see him crouching low in the water, his neck outstretched, the lower bill just above the water's surface, swinging his head from side to side as he calls. So loud is the yodel that it can carry for a mile or two under the calmest of conditions, each of the territorial loons on adjacent lakes announcing his presence. Dominating the yodel are the paired notes (three pairs in this recording), each one rising to a sustained pitch and then falling, the second note of the pair longer than the first. *Recorded in British Columbia by Robert C. Stein and Martin C. Michener (MLNS 922).*

The wail (0:06–0:22) can sound like a wolf howl, *oo-oo-oo*, shifting abruptly from one frequency to another. Male and female often call to each other, as in this recording, answering each other as if trying to establish or maintain contact. *Recorded in New York by Steven R. Pantle (MLNS 107963).*

The tremolo (0:25–0:30) is considered a "distress call," often heard as boaters (or recordists) approach loons too closely. Male and female often call back and forth rapidly, as in this recording, using a "warble" that rapidly rises and falls in pitch. *Recorded in New York by Ted Mack.*

THE BEWICK'S WREN

Songbirds learn to sing much like we humans learn to speak. Listen first to the babbling of a child and compare it to what you know a good English-speaking adult says. Then listen to an adult Bewick's wren, comparing the adult to the babbling of the young wren that follows.

TRACK 9: Babbling of a 1½-year-old child, showing how the young child takes bits of sounds out of context and strings them together in a nonsensical sequence. My daughter was sitting in her high chair and looking out the large picture window to the garden, and from around the corner I held the microphone, capturing what sounded to me like "bow wow wow wow va wa . . . wee wee wee . . . m hi daddy ba ma ba wow wa wa . . . den da daddy daddy!

Da daddy bow wow wow wow . . . dere da ditty . . . hey didit-ty . . . hey daddy . . . nyeh . . . na no . . . down." Clearly evident here are simple syllables and entire words that will eventually be incorporated into her adult English. The "bow wow" refers to the dog, "ditty" to the kitty, and "daddy" to me, although neither the dog, cat, nor I am in the room. The "wee wee wee" is the little piggy's homeward cry, recalled from the "this little piggy went to market" toe-pulling game. *Recorded in Corvallis, Oregon, in 1972.*

TRACK 10: Bewick's wren, four different songs of one adult male (figure 6, page 16). Listen to how sharp and crisp each song is, how precisely this adult male sings each of the repeated elements within a song. A male sings one of these songs many times over before switching to another, each rendition unwavering and unmistakable (to save time on the CD, only one rendition of each song is given). Play the track several times while watching the sonagrams and you'll soon realize how distinctive each of these songs is and how it might not be all that difficult to learn to recognize all 16 to 20 different songs that this individual might sing (as I did when I first started listening to birds). *Recorded in Oregon.*

TRACK 11: Bewick's wren (figure 7, page 19). The babbling of a young male, showing how he takes bits of sounds out of context and strings them together in a continuous, nonsensical sequence, much the way a human child does. This young wren is about three months old; he has left his parents and has moved about a mile away to a territory that he will defend for the rest of his life. Hear the scratchy, inconsistent nature of his voice, how he doesn't practice one song over and over but rather jumbles all of his thoughts together. *Recorded in Oregon.*

A SECOND BEGINNING—THE AMERICAN ROBIN

It is the all-American robin, common almost everywhere throughout North America, who has so much to teach us about listening to birdsong.

TRACK 12: American robin, daytime singing with "liquid, caroled phrases, rising and falling" (figure 8, page 26). At first, simply listen to this minute of robin song and absorb the overall pattern: Rob sings 5 phrases and pauses briefly, then 5 more and another pause, then 6, then 5, 9, 7, 6, 8, 6, and 5. Listen again, and again, eventually following along in figure 8 as you listen to the first 20 seconds. Rob uses 9 different phrases in these 60 seconds, in the following sequence (the spaces represent silent intervals): ABCDD ABCEC CFFCGH FCHGC FCHC<u>G</u>DGHC CH<u>G</u>DGH<u>G</u> HAGAG<u>I</u> ABGABHGA ABHBGA BHABH (underlining explained on page 371). Listen again as you follow these letters and feel his overall pattern of singing. Perhaps watch in figure 8 and listen for phrase A to repeat itself during this minute, then phrase B (the rising *weep*), then phrase C (the three-noted buzzy *ze-oo-ze*), and so on. You'll soon know Rob well enough to recognize him anywhere. (Note: Rob sometimes doesn't complete his phrases. Phrase G, for example, sometimes occurs without the last note; I've underlined three such examples (G) in the above sequence and two examples in the sequence on the next track.)

TRACK 13: American robin, Rob's liquid carols plus a new feature, the *hisselly* (see figure 9, page 31). As with track 12, listen first to the entire track, simply absorbing the overall pattern. Hear how Rob now sings several liquid carols followed by a single, high-pitched *hisselly* phrase; he then pauses briefly and repeats this pattern. Here are the details of exactly what Rob is doing in this minute, with the usual letters for the caroled phrases (see figure 8) and with numbers now representing the different *hisselly* phrases: ABHGHA1 ABH1 ABHC HAGD2 ABH3 ABHCGD2 HAG4 AGD5 ABH6 ABHGI D7 HAG8 ABHG I FCG8 FCH8 FCH9 CHC10 HAGI HAG11. See how *hisselly* #1 occurs twice, as does #2 (though not after back-to-back series of caroled phrases); #8 appears three times in a row. Listen again to this minute, now attending to the details of both the caroled phrases and the *hisselly* phrases. Or, for an uninterrupted two minutes of robin song, try listening to tracks 12 and 13 back to back, reveling in the details of all that you now hear.

(By now some readers will be wondering, so it must be mentioned. As you listen to tracks 12 and 13, notice the four times that Rob uses the relatively rare phrase "I" (double underlined in the song sequence for both tracks). In track 12 and in the third example of track 13, he uses the I phrase at the end of a caroled sequence, much like a *hisselly* phrase would be used. In track 13, he pauses ever so briefly after the first I phrase and he hesitates both before and after the second. Hear, too, how phrase I sounds higher-pitched than the other caroled phrases. I think Rob himself is confused as to whether phrase I is a caroled phrase or a *hisselly* phrase, and when I listened to him so early in the season, I think he was still working things out. I have called this phrase a caroled phrase because Rob used it during extensive daytime singing when he used no obvious *hisselly* phrases.)

GOOD LISTENING, GOOD QUESTIONS, THIS BOOK

Listening to a singing American robin prompts questions about its evolutionary history and how it has come to sing the way it does. Compare the American robin with two robins from Costa Rica, one a superb songster, the other not (at least according to our ears).

TRACK 14: White-throated robin (see figure 10, page 40). Listen to this bird race through his repertoire; hear how he delivers a series of low-pitched phrases followed by an occasional high-pitched phrase, just as the American robin does. Learn to recognize phrases A through F in figure 10 and then hear how he sings those phrases throughout this track, in the following sequence: A B C D E F A 1 2 C A 1 B A 2 C A, where phrases 1 and 2 are high-pitched phrases like the *hisselly* phrases of the American robin. "A superb songster with a large repertory of contrasting phrases, frequently delivered in doublets, the rich, melodious, robinlike caroling phrases often interspersed with thin, rather chaffy chatters and trills," say Stiles and Skutch in their field guide to Costa Rican birds. *Recorded in Monteverde, Costa Rica.*

TRACK 15: Mountain robin, a robin with not quite the reputation of some of its close relatives. "Song an almost endless, mechanical succession of weak, unmelodious notes with little variation in pitch, most unthrush-like," according to Stiles and Skutch. In this particular recording from Monteverde, Costa Rica, we listen to the last 26 seconds of a 54-second song. How different this mountain robin is from the robin in North America.

THE WHITE-CROWNED SPARROW

Adult male white-crowned sparrows learn to sing the proper dialect, but a young bird who never hears an adult develops nonsensical songs.

TRACK 16. Here are five songs (figure 12, page 47): one song of the *Clear* dialect and one song of the *Buzzy* dialect at normal speed; those same two songs at half speed; and a song of an unschooled young bird at normal speed. For the songs of the Clear and Buzzy dialects, hear the two introductory whistles, the second higher than the first. The rest of the Clear song is a series of rapidly down-slurred whistles, but the rest of the Buzzy song begins with a pair of raspy notes. These raspy notes are especially noticeable at half speed. The songs of the unschooled young bird are truly strange. He was taken from a nest and then not allowed to hear songs of adults. Having never heard a normal white-crowned sparrow song, this young bird did the best he could on his own. Based on his best effort, one would never know he was a white-crowned sparrow. *Songs of Clear and Buzzy dialect recorded in California by Myron C. Baker; song of unschooled bird in the laboratory by Mark Konishi.*

THE SONG SPARROW

Here's another sparrow who has taught us much about how songbirds learn to sing. Each male has a repertoire of eight or so songs, as illustrated here.

TRACK 17: Song sparrow. This male has a repertoire of eight different songs (figure 13, pages 59, 60). So that you know what to expect as you listen, I suggest that you first study the sonagrams in figure 13. Then, with that figure before you, listen to the 10 songs on this track, given in the following sequence: A A A B C D E F G H. The first three songs are heard in the normal singing cadence, with about 10 seconds between songs. Then, with about three seconds between the songs, the rest of the male's repertoire follows quickly. As you listen for the distinguishing features that you have seen in figure 13, hear how precisely the male delivers song A the three times, and then hear how different each of the other songs is.

In this song sparrow is a wonderful opportunity for sharpening your listening skills. Listen to this track several times as you follow along in figure 13, but then close your eyes as you listen, visualizing what the sounds look like in the sonagrams. Next, sketch your own sonagrams on a pad of paper as you listen to the songs. Last, if you live in song sparrow country (and most of us in North America do), take your skills to the field: find a live singing bird and get to know it, song by song.

The songs on this track are extracted from a longer sequence that I recorded over 38 minutes from a male at Claytor Lake State Park, Virginia. In the longer sequence, the male sang 3 renditions of A (he most likely sang several more before I began recording him), then 17 of B, 20C, 22D, 8E, 21F, 27G, 26H, 38A, and then 4B before he flew away. That's 186 songs at the rate of about five a minute.

THE NORTHERN MOCKINGBIRD

The mockingbird, the ultimate song-learner, the ultimate mimic. Compare here how the pace of night singing (track 18) by this bachelor male is far more measured and less frantic than is his dawn singing (track 19). Also, use these tracks to train your ears how to listen to mockingbirds: Set your CD player to play track 18 over and over and then track 19 over and over as you learn to recognize the different songs. Pretend you're listening to a never-ending performance from a mockingbird with an abnormally small repertoire, and as you listen, count the number of songs he introduces before you hear a particularly recognizable song again. Or play tracks 18 and 19 back to back, perhaps making the game a little more challenging. Listen then for the cardinal song that begins each track, the "machine gun" at 0:25 in track 18 and at 2:19 in track 19, or the soft *jrrrt jrrrt jrrrt jrrrt* calls of the blue jay at 0:25 and 1:30 in track 19. Pick any sound that you think is unique and then listen for it to recur as the two tracks repeat themselves. Then find a live mockingbird in all his glory and apply these same skills—you'll be amazed at what you now hear.

TRACK 18: Northern mockingbird, a full minute of night singing, sonagrams for the first 32 seconds illustrated in figure 15, page 72. This sequence begins with a northern cardinal imitation (A). *Recorded in Naples, Florida.*

TRACK 19: Northern mockingbird, dawn singing, sonagrams for the first 32 seconds illustrated in figure 16, page 77. The two minutes and 30 seconds here begin with the same cardinal imitation that begins track 18 (compare figures 15 and 16). At 1:12 and 1:38 he utters the high-pitched call note of a young mockingbird. At 1:45 he begins his longest pause, almost two and a half seconds; in the distance he no doubt also hears a male reply with the identical song that he has just sung, an exchange that launches him into another frenzy of singing. *Recorded in Naples, Florida.*

TYRANT FLYCATCHERS—ALDER AND WILLOW FLYCATCHERS, EASTERN PHOEBE

Unlike songbirds, these flycatchers don't learn their songs. When all instructions for songs are somehow encoded in the genes, songs are relatively simple and repertoire sizes are fairly small (one to three for these flycatcher species).

TRACK 20: Alder flycatcher, adult male (figure 17, page 82). This adult male repeats his simple *fee-bee-o* song over and over throughout life, the five songs in 15 seconds here only a small slice of his lifetime. All alder flycatcher males have this same song, an innate *fee-bee-o*. *Recorded by Will Hershberger in Maine (MLNS 85215).*

TRACK 21: Alder flycatcher, a youngster just out of the nest (figure 17, page 82). He (or she) has been separated from his siblings, and this scratchy, feeble version of the adult *fee-bee-o* song seems to be used as a "contact call" in an attempt to reestablish contact with the other siblings. Finally, at the very end of this track, another youngster returns the call, a weak *fee-bee-o* heard in the distance. Hear how unstable the eight calls of this bird are, with no two renditions alike. Appreciate, too, that a songbird at this age is just beginning to memorize what it should learn and could never at such a tender age produce a sound recognizable as the adult song.

TRACK 22: Willow flycatcher, adult male (figure 17, page 82). Here is a more varied singing performance from a flycatcher, a relative so close to the alder flycatcher that the two were considered the same species until the 1970s. The male willow flycatcher uses three songs, *fitz-bew*, *fizz-bew*, and *creet*. In the first song on this track, hear the sharp *fitz* followed by the buzzy *bew*, the *fitz-bew* song; the second song begins with the buzzy *fizz* followed by the buzzy *bew*, the *fizz-bew* song; the third is the rolling, rising *creet*. The first nine songs in this 45-second performance are as follows: *fitz-bew, fizz-bew, fitz-bew, creet, fitz-bew, fizz-bew, fitz-bew, fizz-bew, creet* . . . I leave the last four songs up to you. Enjoy the background songs of a common yellowthroat, song sparrow, American robin, Canada geese, and others. *Recorded in Indiana by Geoffrey A. Keller (MLNS 105603).*

TRACK 23: Eastern phoebe (figure 18, page 85). Hear the DNA of this fly-catcher speak in this phoebe's two songs, the raspy *fee-bee* (songs 1, 3, 5, 6, 7) and stuttered *fee-b-be-be* (songs 2, 4, 8). Feel the rhythm in how the phoebe delivers his songs, too. He rushes to deliver his *fee-b-be-be* soon after the *fee-bee*, but he takes his time to deliver the next *fee-bee*. *Recorded in Alberta by William W. H. Gunn (MLNS 61886).*

THE THREE-WATTLED BELLBIRD

The bellbird is a close relative of the suboscine flycatchers and was thought not to learn its songs. They do learn, however, and in the following eight tracks is proof: Bellbirds have song dialects (that even change from one year to the next, though not illustrated in these tracks), young birds learn the songs of both dialects, and a young bellbird raised in captivity was found to imitate a blackbird.

TRACK 24: Three-wattled bellbird, adult male (chestnut and white), *Monteverde* dialect (figure 19, page 91). In this sequence are the four sounds typically heard from a male on his displaying perch: 1) a loud, isolated *bonk* (at 0:01); 2) a song dominated by four loud whistles (0:06–0:12; figure 19, song A); 3) a song with a loud *bonk* and whistle (0:17–0:23; figure 19, song B), accompanied by a young male squawking in the background (at 0:15, 0:25, and 0:27); and 4) a song beginning with a loud *bonk* (0:32–0:36; males don't sing this rapidly — silent intervals between songs have been reduced to save time on the CD). All songs except the isolated *bonk* have softer notes that can't be heard unless one is close to the bird, as I am with this male, who is just 10 yards away from me in the understory of the Monteverde cloud forest. *Recorded in Costa Rica.*

TRACK 25: Three-wattled bellbird, a young, all-green male practicing his Monteverde dialect. Listen to the Monteverde adult in track 24 again and then listen here to this youngster attempting his *bonks*, whistles, and softer swishing sounds. Various squawks will eventually become finely controlled *bonks*; the series beginning at 0:12 is especially interesting, because it begins with an attempted *bonk* and has a rudimentary whistle just 2 seconds later, with softer swishing attempts before and after the whistle, the overall sequence just like adult song B in figure 19. The quality is laughable and at times he sounds more like a squawking parrot than a regal bellbird—but eventually his songs will transform into perfect songs of the local dialect, just as his all-green body will transform to the immaculate chestnut and white plumage of the adult. *Recorded in Costa Rica.*

TRACK 26: Three-wattled bellbird, adult male, *Panama* dialect. The dominant sounds of this dialect are harsh and grating *quacks*, a sharp contrast to the whistled notes and the *bonks* of the Monteverde dialect. Here are the typical sounds of a displaying adult of the Panamanian dialect: 1) a song with two harsh *quacks* followed by a series of swishing notes that end with the characteristic three rising notes, after which the male flutters into the air and lands again on the same perch (song C; 0:01–0:10); 2) a single *quack* (0:15); and 3) a song with three harsh *quacks* followed by a shorter series of swishing notes, again ending with those three characteristic rising notes (song D; 0:21–0:27). Given how different these songs are from those of the Monteverde singers, is it any wonder that I initially thought these "Panamanian singers" were not even bellbirds? *Recorded in Costa Rica.*

TRACK 27: Three-wattled bellbird, a young greenish bilingual bird at Monteverde, Costa Rica, who has learned the songs of both the Monteverde and Panama dialects. Here are six of this youngster's songs: 1) Monteverde dialect song B, the *bonk* and whistle song, like that in figure 19 (0:01–0:07), page 91. The overall rhythm of the song is remarkably good, and most of the soft swishing elements seem to be in place; the whistle is there, too, though it is just barely audible. 2) Monteverde dialect song A, a whistle song (0:09–0:13; see upper sonagram in figure 19). He sings only three of the four loud whistles and has the appropriate softer swishing notes before each whistle, but after a brief pause he concludes the song with several swishing sounds from the end of song B (0:14–0:15; see top of figure 19). This kind of disjointed performance is typical of young birds. 3) A hybrid song, with elements of both Monteverde and Panama dialects. A Monteverde *bonk* (at 0:18) is followed by the terminal swishing notes of Panamanian songs C and D, with the characteristic three rising notes (0:22–0:24). 4) An isolated, strained Panamanian quack (at 0:26). 5) Panamanian song D (0:32–0:38), its three loud *quacks* and softer components all present, though the softer elements are presented with uneven emphasis and tempo. 6) Panamanian song C (0:40–0:47), its two *quacks* and softer components present (again with uneven emphasis and tempo), although the softer elements are not always easily detected with other birds calling loudly in the background. In these songs are the almost unequivocal proof that these birds learn their songs (see text for explanation). *Recorded at Monteverde, Costa Rica.*

TRACK 28: Three-wattled bellbird, adult male, Nicaraguan dialect. Yet another dialect of the three-wattled bellbird occurs to the north of Costa Rica; listen to the male in the background, too, as he sings the same songs. These Nicaraguan songs are so different from the other two dialects that it seems difficult to believe that these Nicaraguan birds are the same species. They can be the same species only, of course, if they learn their songs. *Recorded in Nicaragua by Julio Sánchez.*

TRACK 29: Bare-throated bellbird, adult song. Ah, here in tracks 29, 30, and 31 comes the absolute proof that bellbirds learn. We travel to Brazil to listen to another bellbird species, the bare-throated bellbird. The repertoire of the bare-throated bellbird is simpler than that of the three-wattled bellbird and consists mostly of a series of loud *pong* notes, each sounding much like a hammer striking an anvil and then ringing momentarily afterward. *Recorded in the courtyard of a home in Arapongas, Brazil, by Hernán Fandiño.*

TRACK 30: Bare-throated bellbird, a caged bird with the wrong songs. How strange the sounds of this bare-throated bellbird found in another courtyard in Arapongas, Brazil. When this bellbird attempts a *pong* (first nine seconds), the hammer strikes the anvil but there is no ring afterward. Then hear his loud purr followed by a series of whistles, sounds that no bare-throated bellbird has ever before been heard to produce, sounds that the birdsong experts quickly identify as those of a Chopi blackbird. This bellbird clearly has it all wrong. *Recorded in Brazil by Hernán Fandiño.*

TRACK 31: Chopi blackbird. The strange sounds of the odd bare-throated bellbird in track 30 make sense only when one learns that he was in fact raised with Chopi blackbirds whose purrs and whistles he learned. Leading off this track is the blackbird's loud purr, the purr that was learned by the caged bellbird. Following that purr is a series of whistles, sounds that the caged bellbird also learned. Go ahead—play the purr and whistles of the odd bellbird on track 30 again and then the purr and whistles of the blackbird here. What do you think? You know what I think: *bellbirds learn!* They SHOUT it from the treetops with every *bonk* and whistle and *quack* and *pong* and every one of those subtle whispered swishing sounds in between. There is *absolutely no doubt.* What remarkable creatures—what an exciting turn of evolutionary events, to have a close relative of the flycatcher learn its songs. (Sorry—I get carried away. I'll stop now.) *Recorded in Brazil by Hernán Fandiño.*

THE SEDGE WREN

The sedge wren occurs from the tip of South America north into Canada. The differences in songs from place to place as illustrated on the following tracks are consistent with what has long been suspected of the sedge wren, that it is actually several different species improperly lumped into one. The North American birds largely improvise their songs, but Central and South American birds imitate.

TRACK 32: Sedge wren, North America (figure 21, page 106). In this relatively uninspired performance by a male singing in a field near Ithaca, New York, the bird repeats each song several times before switching to another (if he were more energized, successive songs would all be different). In this track are three different songs that the male sings in the following sequence: C C C C C D D D D D D E D E E E E, abbreviated to 5C 6D E D 4E. The transition from D to E is typical, as he sings a new song (E), then the old one (D), and then continues with the new one (E), as if he at first can't make up his mind that he really wants to switch to the new song. The songs in this track are part of a longer sequence recorded from this male: A B A 9B 9C 6D E D 10E 10F 5G 8H I H. This male and his singing neighbor (heard in the background) arrived in this Ithaca field during July, most likely after they had already raised a family elsewhere. *Recorded in New York by Gregory F. Budney (MLNS 43928).*

TRACK 33: Sedge wren, North America, at one-fifth speed (figure 21, page 106). Songs of North American sedge wrens consist of a couple of introductory notes and then a trill of repeated elements. In this track, four of the repeated elements are extracted from each of the nine different songs (A-I) mentioned in track 32. The repeated elements of the third, fourth, and fifth songs (C, D, and E) are illustrated in figure 21. Hear the snowflakes under the microscope, how each is strikingly different from the others when we hear them slowed down.

TRACK 34: Sedge wren, Brazil (figure 22, page 117). A 23-second countersinging duel by two Brazilian sedge wrens. We join the action with a single song (A), followed by six quick exchanges with songs B, C, B, A, B, and C, ending with a single B; the interaction than escalates, becoming too intense for the birds to sing, as the birds call and then engage in physical combat. Here is the most convincing evidence that resident sedge wrens in Central and South America learn their songs; if they didn't learn songs from each other, they wouldn't have identical songs to hurl back and forth in countersinging exchanges like this. *Recorded in Brasilia National Park, Brazil.*

TRACK 35: Sedge wren, Costa Rica. In a half-minute, accompanied by his mate (heard as a single buzzy note), this male sings four different songs in the following sequence: A B A B A C B D (note: song B sometimes has an extended buzzy note on the end, sometimes not). Listen to this track several times until you hear the pattern. This sequence is part of a longer sequence: A X Y X A B A B <u>A B A B A C B D</u> A C D B D D E F D F D E D E G (where X and Y songs are part of a song series just being concluded; songs in track 35 on the CD are underlined). Notice how a particular song is introduced, such as A, used several times (7 for A) while alternated with other songs, and then abandoned while he moves on to play with another of his hundreds of other songs. *Recorded near Cartago, Costa Rica.*

TRACK 36: Sedge wren, in the always windy Falkland Islands. In a half-minute of singing this male also uses four different songs, in the following sequence: AB C BD C A BC. He continues this sequence (not in this track) with the following songs: A BC A BC A B C A C A. Note how he also alternates songs and how some songs are doubled up, such as AB, a habit of these southern hemisphere sedge wrens. The careful listener will hear a jackass penguin (more properly called a Magellanic penguin) accompanying the wren. *Recorded on Kidney Island, Falkland Islands.*

THE GREAT MARSH WREN DIVIDE

As surely as I know that birds have feathers, I know there are two species of marsh wren in North America, not one as the field guides declare. Contrast the songs of these eastern and western wrens and then you make the call.

TRACK 37: Marsh wren, eastern (figure 23, page 124). These ten songs in 55 seconds unequivocally declare "eastern marsh wren." Listen to all ten songs for the first time, just absorbing their general nature. They seem like a homogeneous lot, with none of them especially different from the others; that's a typically eastern characteristic (wait until you hear the western birds in track 38 to fully appreciate this feature). Now listen again and hear that nasal buzz in the introduction of the first and tenth song—that's a dead giveaway, as no western birds give that call. That's the call that a male gives when he's especially excited, and when he escorts a female through one of his courting centers he's all "abuzz." Depending on how intensely he's singing, too, relatively few or all of his songs might be preceded by this buzz. Last, listen to the overall pattern of singing in this ten-song sequence; the sequence of songs is A B C D E C F G H I. Listen for how song C occurs in both the third and sixth positions. This male has given just a hint of how most eastern males sing, as most males sing a sequence in which there is more repetition, such as A B C A C B D C E D. *This bird was recorded shortly after midnight in a Delaware marsh* *by Lang Elliott.* (Note: Eastern marsh wrens along the Atlantic coast often have more of a rambling introduction to the song, as in song A, than do interior eastern wrens.)

TRACK 38: Marsh wren, western (figure 24, page 129). A series of songs from this male and his neighbors in the background reveals so much about these western birds. Listen to the variety of buzzes and rattles the foreground male sings, such variety never to be heard among eastern marsh wrens (nor are any of those introductory eastern nasal buzzes heard in this western singer). Focus on the first song and then concentrate, listening for the bird to repeat it. Try the second, or the third. Hear how distinctive each song is, but choose any of the songs and you'll find no repeats within this series, as the male is racing through his repertoire of over 100 songs, singing in this brief sequence A B C D E F GH I J K L MN O P Q R S T, a total of 20 songs (GH and MN are "double songs").

Now listen some more, this time paying attention to what the wren in the background is doing. Do you hear the two wrens matching each other with identical songs? This kind of matching almost never occurs among eastern birds, yet among western birds it is routine. Listen especially from 0:26 to 0:31, as the background bird sings a double song that is then matched exactly by the foreground bird (songs GH). That's an obvious match, but if you listen carefully during the following times you'll hear other examples of the foreground bird matching what the background bird has just sung: 0:00 to 0:03, 0:21 to 0:25, 0:41 to 0:45, 0:45 to 0:49, 1:18 to 1:22. Only once does the foreground bird obviously sing a song that is then followed by a background bird, during seconds 0:34 to 0:37. Based on what I can hear, I can now rewrite that earlier song sequence, inserting what I hear from the background birds as lowercase letters: aA B C D E fF ghGH Ii J kK lL MN O P Q R S tT (try listening to track 38 as you follow along in this lettered sequence, and I think you'll hear the interactions).

And there's more! There are actually two background birds, and when one of them isn't matching the foreground bird, the two are matching each other, as from 0:49 to 0:51 and from 0:58 to 1:01 (confirmed on my Raven software —see Appendix II). Wow! All that is packed into just 85 seconds, and I'm sure there's a lot more going on in this recording than I've listed above—imagine a full morning or a lifetime with these frenzied, hyper-energetic western marsh wrens. These wrens are in a different time zone, both literally and figuratively, from the eastern birds. *Recorded in Montana (a monaural recording, unfortunately).*

TRACK 39: The intricate details of eight eastern and eight western marsh wren songs revealed at a slower speed (figures 23, page 124; 24, page 129). For each song, I have selected about 0.4 seconds from the repeated elements in the trill; when slowed to one-fifth speed, each selection then is about two seconds long. The first eight selections are from the eastern marsh wren: A B C D E F G H (as in track 37 and illustrated in figure 23). The last eight are from the western marsh wren: A D GH L MN O (as in track 38 and illustrated in figure 24). I suggest that you first just listen to this entire track and savor the variety among the eight eastern songs and the variety among the eight western songs. Listen again and concentrate on how different the eight eastern songs are from the eight western songs. Last, watch along in figure 23 as you listen to the first four eastern songs on this track and in figure 24 as you listen to the first four western songs. Contrast those often dainty elements of the eastern birds with the harsh, often angry-sounding, and certainly more diverse songs of the western wrens. What different beasts these two wrens are! If the plumages of the eastern and western marsh wrens were as different as their songs, they would have been classified as two species long ago.

THE BLACK-CAPPED CHICKADEE

The simplest of songsters poses one of the greatest mysteries. Named for its *chick-a-dee-dee-dee* call, how does the chickadee maintain such a consistent learned *hey-sweetie* song across much of the North American continent, and why does this pattern break down in the East on Martha's Vineyard and in the West from the Cascade Mountains to the Pacific?

TRACK 40: Black-capped chickadee, *chick-a-dee-dee-dee* call. *Recorded in New York by Robert C. Stein (MLNS 14655).*

TRACK 41: Black-capped chickadee, the *hey-sweetie* song (figure 26, page 138). Hear this male chickadee transpose his simple song to a lower key in the fifth and seventh songs of this nine-song series. A male usually sings a series of songs on one frequency and then a series on another frequency, eventually shifting the pitch of the song throughout a broad frequency range, but here he is caught alternating high and low songs during a transition from a high series to a low series.

TRACK 42: Black-capped chickadee, odd songs of a bird raised away from adult singers (figure 26, page 138). Take a baby chickadee away from the *hey-sweetie* adults who can teach him, and he sings the strangest songs, thus confirming that he must learn his *hey-sweetie* song from other chickadees.

TRACK 43: Black-capped chickadee, strange eastern songs (figure 26, page 138). At Gay Head on the western end of Martha's Vineyard, that small island off the coast of Massachusetts, a male chickadee sings a low-pitched and a high-pitched *sweetie-hey* and nothing in between. During the dawn chorus, this male alternates his low- and high-pitched songs, but during less energized singing later in the day he'd deliver a series on one pitch and then a series on the other. Unlike the *hey-sweetie* birds on the mainland only a few miles away, these island birds 1) have songs that are monotonal, with both whistles on the same pitch; 2) have a break in the first whistle instead of the second; and 3) sing at only two pitches instead of shifting the pitch over a range of frequencies.

TRACK 44: Black-capped chickadee, strange western songs (figure 26, page 138). From Cape Cod west to the Cascade Mountains one hears the familiar two-toned *hey-sweetie*, but beyond the crest of the Cascades are several dialects with different songs. The male who sings here has two different songs. One is a monotonal *hey-sweetie*, all on one pitch with a break in the second whistle. The other song is my favorite, a descending series of whistles, each whistle successively longer. *Recorded in Oregon by Geoffrey A. Keller (MLNS 105761, 105762).*

THE CHESTNUT-SIDED WARBLER

Like many other warbler species, these chestnut-sided warblers use one group of songs at dawn and in highly aggressive contexts and another group during the daytime in pursuit of females.

TRACK 45: Chestnut-sided warbler, aggressive singing before sunrise. Come with me to my favorite power-line swath in the Berkshire hills, high in the town of Florida, Massachusetts. Wait in the pre-dawn hours, and soon after 4:30 A.M., after the overnight thunderstorms and continuing showers, the wind still whistling in the treetops, mosquitoes buzzing around our ears . . . come listen to these warblers. This male sings from the branches at the very top of a cherry tree overhanging the power-line swath from the north. He delivers a series of notes, then another, and another, followed immediately by a song from the male to the right (hear him faintly at 0:06 in the right speaker or earphone, as this is a stereo recording), and only then does this male sing his aggressive song (at 0:08), one that is noticeably different from his neighbor's; he calls some more, the male to the right sings again (at 0:14), and our male delivers another song (at 0:16); a male to the left now sings (faintly in the left earphone at 0:21) before the male above us chips and sings again (at 0:24); after the male to the left sings again, our male calls some more and then delivers another song (at 0:33) . . . overall only a half-minute of energized action in the lifetime of these warblers.

TRACK 46: Chestnut-sided warbler. Feast on the diversity of aggressive songs among the males, with eight different songs from eight different males (the first four illustrated in figure 28, page 146). A given male sings his favorite song hundreds of times during each dawn chorus, but neighbors almost always sing markedly different songs.

TRACK 47: Chestnut-sided warbler, the more placid singing of the *meetcha* songs later in the morning. The male in track 45 has now descended from the treetops and sings from the mountain laurel low in the power-line swath. In this (stereo) recording, he sings three renditions of his *meetcha* songs, but listen, too, to the identical *meetcha* songs of the males to the left and right in the background. The emphasized endings to these *meetcha* songs always sound the same, the songs of the males now far more similar to each other than they were during the aggressive singing before sunrise.

TRACK 48: Chestnut-sided warbler. Listen to the similarity of the *meetcha* songs, again eight songs from eight different males (the first, second, fifth, and seventh songs illustrated in figure 30, page 153). Hear the strikingly similar, emphatic endings to these eight songs, but hear also the subtle differences in how they begin. In this track are the following: a *wheedle* song, three *see* songs, two *che* songs, and two *swee* songs (see figure 30). The *wheedle* song is perhaps easiest to distinguish from the others, with its characteristic beginning and single *MEETCHA* ending; the other songs all have at least two bold upstrokes, as in *MEETMEETCHA*. Each male chooses one of these four variations as his favored daytime song, though he may also be able to sing all four. (Note: the *wheedle* song was fairly common in the Berkshires during the 1980s and early 1990s, but since then seems to have gone extinct. I now recall that I couldn't find it along the Skyline Drive in Virginia's Shenandoah National Park during 1987 either, nor along the Blue Ridge Parkway in 2003 or 2004. Once common, has it gone extinct elsewhere in the range of these warblers, too?)

TRAVELS WITH TOWHEES, EASTERN AND SPOTTED

Each male towhee has a small repertoire of several different songs; during rapid singing before sunrise, males typically alternate songs, in an A B A B type pattern, but during more relaxed singing later in the day, a given song is repeated several times before another is introduced (as in A A A A B B B B). As you listen to each towhee in the following three tracks, realize that neighboring males in the migratory populations of Massachusetts have dissimilar repertoires but neighboring males in the resident populations of Oregon and Florida have nearly identical repertoires. Hear the differences in the call notes from these locations, too, as each track begins with representative calls for that region.

TRACK 49: Eastern towhee, Massachusetts (figure 31, page 160). *Chewink* call, followed by nine songs in the pattern A A A B C B C B C. Play this track several times and the three commonly used songs in the repertoire of this male become easily recognizable. These three songs were used throughout a 35-minute pre-sunrise performance by this male, from 4:32 to 5:06 A.M., with sunrise at 5:12. Having said that, how can I resist showing what he did during the entire 35 minutes? In the following table, read down, so that the first 10 minutes are in the first column, minutes 11 through 20 in the second column, and so on (the actual performance is more complicated than presented here, because all *chewinks* and other calls are omitted from this series).

AAAA	BBBCCBCBAA	BAABBABABAB	BBBBBBBBBABA
AAAAAAA	CACBCBABAAB	BABBBBAABA	BABAAAAAAAA
AAAAAAA	AABCBBBB	BABABAAABAABCB	AAAAAAAABABA
AAAAA	CBCBCABBABB	CBCBABABCABABA	BABBBABABBBB
BBBBBBB	ABABABABABBC	CAAACACACAACAC	BBBAB
BBBBBB	CBCBCBCBA	ACBCBABABABAB	
BBBBBBA	BABABABAABABAB	ABABABABAAABA	
BABAABBB	BABABABABABAB	ABABABABABAAB	
BBABABBBAB	ABABABADBCB	ACACACACCCAAA	
BBCBCBCBC	CBCBCBCBCBABAB	CACACACACAAB	

See how he begins slowly, singing only four to seven songs a minute and repeating one song over and over. The pace then picks up, reaching a peak of 14 songs a minute; as he sings faster, he tends to alternate songs, too, so that successive songs are different. Toward the end of his performance, especially in minute 31, he reverts to what will be his daytime pattern of singing in which he repeats a song many times before switching to another. (Why he uses his rare song D only once in minute 19 must remain a mystery.)

TRACK 50: Spotted towhee, Oregon. Two *zhreeee* calls followed by one example of six different songs. Each of these songs is extracted from a longer singing performance in which the selected song is repeated up to 30 times. These songs typically lack the introductory *drink-your* of the eastern towhee, and the *teeeee* is often much faster, sometimes sounding like a simple buzz, as with the first song. *Recorded in California and Oregon by Geoffrey A. Keller (MLNS 118843, 119455, 44871, 44870).*

TRACK 51: Eastern towhee, Florida. Hear the unique *sweee* call of these Florida towhees and how a male alternates three of his songs during a pre-sunrise singing performance. The eight songs here, in the sequence A B C B C

B C A, are part of an 18-minute recording from a male at Audubon's Corkscrew Swamp Sanctuary, during which the male sang his seven different songs (A–G) in the following sequence (the underlined part is on track 51):

```
ABABCBCBCBCBCB       FGFGFGFGFGFEFEBEBE
BCBCBCBCBCB          BEBEBEBEBEBEBEEBE
CBBCBCBBBBBB         BEFBAFABAFAFCBC
BCBBCBCB             AABCACFCFABCFCBC
CBBCBCBBCBCBC        BCABCBCBCBCBABAB
CBCDDADADEDED        FCBFAFGFGFGFGFG
EDEEDEDEDEDEDED      FGFGFGBGFGAGAFC
EDEDEEDEDEDE         BABCBCBCACBCB
FGFGFGFGFGGFGF
GFGFGFGFGFGFGFGFG
```

That sequence began at 6:27 A.M. and ended at 6:45 A.M., about a half-hour before sunrise. Singing rates are high, and successive songs are almost always different. Later, when I returned to this male at 7:52 A.M., 40 minutes after sunrise, he was consistently repeating his songs ten or more times before switching to a new song. *Recorded in Florida.*

THE TUFTED TITMOUSE

Titmice have small repertoires of distinctive songs, and a male is usually singing the same song that his neighbors are singing. A number of songbirds engage in this "matched countersinging," but this behavior is especially striking among titmice.

TRACK 52: Tufted titmouse (figure 32, page 168). In this track are four segments, each about 15 seconds long and each containing a brief series of one of the four songs commonly used by the males around my home in Amherst, Massachusetts (songs A, B, C, D in figure 32). I emphasize "a brief series," because a natural series of one of these songs could last tens of minutes, not tens of seconds, before the male switches to a new song. Listen to the entire track, concentrating on each song as it is delivered and comparing it to the next; you'll no doubt soon appreciate how distinctive each of these four songs is. Perhaps it is most challenging to distinguish the first two series (songs A and B in figure 32), as they are both down-slurred whistles, but the tempo of A is much faster than the tempo of B. Listen closely to the first segment (with song A) and you'll hear two birds answering each other, a bird in the foreground and the background hurling this song back and forth. With "F" and

"B" designating Foreground and Background birds and a number from 2 to 4 indicating how many down-slurred whistles are in each song, the sequence is as follows: F3 B2 F2 B2 F4 B2 F2. Listen also to the second section with song B; in it you'll hear a bird in the background also singing song B.

THE BLUE JAY

The jays may not sing like typical songbirds, but what a remarkable variety of calls they use. Consider the following as only a brief introduction to the sounds you can hear from blue jays (see figures 34–36).

TRACK 53: Blue jay (figure 34, page 182). Here are examples of the three types of sounds most commonly heard. These calls were recorded on different occasions from the jays near the nest that I watched.

The jay call. These three brief selections illustrate the variety of qualities that the *jay* call can have.

0:01–0:07. Three calls.

0:09–0:14. Seven calls.

0:15–0:20. Four calls by a bird in the foreground, different from the *jay* call of the bird in the background.

The squeaky-gate call. 0:22–0:33. Here is one sequence with seven calls uttered by two birds. The first three calls are a rapid exchange by the two birds, with each bird uttering the same variant of the squeaky-gate. One of the birds calls again, followed three seconds later by another rapid exchange. The seventh and last call is a squeaky-gate that sounds more strained. Throughout this sequence, a third bird "whines" continuously in the background (see "Whine," next track).

The bell call. Two brief examples.

0:34–0:37. Two bell calls from a single bird.

0:39–0:42. Two bell calls from one bird and several *jay* calls from what sound like two other birds.

TRACK 54: Blue jay. Here are some of the less audacious sounds made by jays.

The rattle. Two examples of the call given exclusively by the female.

0:01–0:04. Just one rattle, accompanied by one *jay* call (and a northern flicker singing in the background).

0:05–0:08. Another rattle, immediately answered by a rapid exchange of squeaky-gate calls by two birds, and a fourth bird accompanies them by "whining" softly.

The jrrrt call. 0:10–0:17. A rapidly repeated, softly given call. I think of the birds as "contented" when they use this call.

Whine. 0:19–0:29. A little more feverish pitch than for the *jrrrt* call. What I call the *jrrrt* and the "whine" calls are almost certainly not discrete categories that the jays would recognize; rather, these calls are probably examples on a continuum along which the jays can vary these softer sounds.

Hawk alarm. (figure 34). 0:31–0:32. Unmistakable. These jays can fool the best of us most of the time with this call.

A variety of calls. 0:34–0:50. This example begins with a bell call, followed immediately by a squeaky-gate. About three seconds later, another squeaky-gate, a bell call, and a *jay* call. More bell calls, a few more *jay* calls, the softer *jrrrt* calls, and this brief sample ends with bell calls fading into the distance.

TRACK 55: Blue jay. Here are four different calls used by one jay over just a few seconds (figure 35, page 187): Squeaky-gate version 1, bell, squeaky-gate version 2, and, as he flies into the distance away from the nest area, *jay-jay*. What was this jay "thinking" as he used all of these sounds? What did listeners think? It's a puzzle what all these sounds mean.

TRACK 56: Blue jay. Songbirds with songs often engage in "matched countersinging," in which they hurl identical learned songs back and forth (marsh wrens and tufted titmice, for example); blue jays match each other not with songs but with their calls. Listen as the blue jay roosting in the hemlock outside my bedroom window awakes with a somewhat tonal, pleasing form of the *jay* call (figure 36, page 190). For the first 20 seconds of this recording, jays in the distant background use squeaky-gate and *jay* calls. At 0:23, at least two jays invade the yard, calling loudly with a harsher version of the *jay* call. The bird in the hemlock pauses for 17 seconds, her longest pause of the morning, no doubt processing all that is going on, and then she responds in kind, with harsh *jay* calls. At 1:03, hear one of the invaders switch back to the tonal call; by 1:15 the invaders are both using the tonal *jay* sound, and a second later my hemlock bird switches to the tonal *jay* sound, too. This track is a condensed version of the full interaction described in the text of the book. This CD track picks up the action just before the neighboring jays invade the yard; at 0:55, a 76-second section is omitted during which the hemlock bird calls harshly 19 more times (and the background birds call harshly, too); track 56 then resumes to capture the group of jays switching back to the tonal *jay* call.

THE BROWN THRASHER

The champion singer of all birds, the bird with the enormous song repertoire that numbers into the thousands.

TRACK 57: Brown thrasher (figure 37, page 194). At his measured pace, the brown thrasher delivers song after song, each separated from the others by about a second. Songs tend to be couplets with a particular sound delivered twice in rapid succession, but some sounds occur only once, others three times. Pick a song, memorize it, and try to find another example. Pick another, and another—you're doomed to failure as this thrasher repeats nothing, instead revealing more and more of all he knows. *Recorded in South Carolina by Gregory F. Budney (MLNS 43536-15).*

THE SAGE THRASHER

The incomparable sage thrasher, the great mimic, he who stitches sage to sky in his song flights, he who races through his repertoire deciding every split second what he will offer next. Just listen!

TRACK 58: Sage thrasher (figure 39, page 205). Hear this bird come bounding in from a distance, singing on the wing and landing in the sagebrush just above the microphone, where he delivers two lengthy songs. In his second song, follow along in figure 39, identifying the imitation of the sora rail's descending whinny that is repeated three times. Feel the energy in the songs, the extraordinary speed with which this bird races through his repertoire of hundreds of song bits. *Recorded in California by Gregory F. Budney (MLNS 01-CA).*

TRACK 59: Sage thrasher. You simply must hear the song sparrow imitations that he sang for the first time in the eighth hour that I listened to him. He begins this song with a series of imitations of California quail (though no quail occur here), and at 0:22.5, after a series of very rapid notes, he delivers his first song sparrow imitation, a trill of four musical phrases. As if to confirm his thievery, as if to verify that he is indeed singing song sparrow and no one should doubt it, just a little later (at 0:24.6) he delivers what sounds like a common introduction to a song sparrow song, a pair of buzzy notes followed by a single high-pitched, tonal note and then a lower buzzy note. Those who know song sparrow songs recognize these song sparrow imitations instantly and without doubt. *Recorded in California.*

TRACK 60: Sage thrasher—just how good is this sage thrasher's mimicry? You make the call by listening to the five sounds on this track (see also figure 40, page 209).

1) 0:01–0:05. Here is a real sora, a four-second descending whinny. *Recorded in North Dakota by Lang Elliot.*

2) 0:07–0:10. Next are what sound to me like the sora imitations extracted from the thrasher's second song in track 58. Similar, you might say, but not identical. The thrasher seems to have pilfered the sora's song, but the thrash-

er's imitation is much too brief and is sung three times in rapid succession. Consider this maestro's dilemma, however, as he contemplates the sora's song. The sora's lengthy song doesn't fit his program; he's in too much of a hurry to repeat a four-second song in its entirety, because he needs a new sound every split second. So he compromises. He identifies the essence of sora, chops up the sora's call to his liking, and then sings only the first three-quarters of a second three times in succession.

3) 0:12–0:15. Here I play an electronic version of the sage thrasher's game myself, using the computer to extract three-quarters of a second from the sora's call and then repeating it three times. Now compare the thrasher's rendition (part 2 of this track) with this computer-generated sound based on the sora's call and ask yourself, just how good is this sage thrasher? Not bad, I would submit. One more thing: the sora didn't even learn this call, as the thrasher had to, because the sora's calls are believed to be innate!

4) 0:18–0:21. A song sparrow song. This is song G from the Virginia song sparrow illustrated in figure 13 (ninth song on track 17). It's a universal song sparrow pattern, sung by song sparrows everywhere: two low introductory notes, followed by a high then low note, a trill of repeated elements, ending with another buzzy note.

5) 0:25–0:26. The sage thrasher's imitations of song sparrow, arranged to match the universal song sparrow pattern in part 4 of this track. From track 59, I've extracted what I hear as two song sparrow pieces and then reversed the order. What a remarkable resemblance this thrasher's song has to the song of a random song sparrow from more than 2,000 miles away, although again the thrasher seems to hustle through this song sparrow song at twice the speed that a sparrow would. An unmistakable mimic, this sage thrasher.

THE WINTER WREN

The longest, most precisely repeatable song that I know among birds, the only wren song heard around the world, the song of the winter wren. Listen to the tiny details of each song as the notes tumble from the wren's opened bill; what is a blur to our ears must be crystal clear to the birds, each note highly defined, as each young bird must learn the microdetails of his songs from adult singers. Listen, too, to how different the eastern and western wrens in North America are; almost certainly they are two different species. The wrens of the Old World, as in Japan, sing much like the wrens in eastern North America, but the Old World wrens likely deserve to be a third species. Last, at one-sixth speed, listen to the exquisite detail in the songs of the North American birds.

TRACK 61: Winter wren, eastern North America (figure 41, page 218). This eastern winter wren has two different songs, easily told apart by the position of the high-pitched and low-pitched trills within the song. Listen to the first song (song A in figure 41) and hear a trill of rapidly repeated high notes almost two seconds into the song; then start counting, one thousand one, one thousand two, and after those two seconds you'll hear a much slower trill at a lower pitch; and two seconds after that the song ends on another rapid, high trill. Ditto for the second song. Try your counting on the third song and you'll realize the wren is telling you something new (song B in figure 41). At about two seconds into the song you hear a high trill, as expected, but the low trill is only a half-second later. This new song has a late high trill, too, but it doesn't end the song; instead, the end is a distinctive down-slurred whistle. The fourth song is the same as the third, so the four songs here are in the sequence A A B B. You can pretend that you are listening to a long series of early morning songs from this bird if you set your CD player to play this track over and over; listen then for other details that distinguish these two songs.

TRACK 62: Winter wren, western North America. The three songs here are chosen to illustrate what you might be able to hear in the field (see figure 42, page 221). First just listen to the entire track, marveling at how different these songs are from those of the eastern winter wren; our ears can appreciate the tonal notes of the eastern bird better than the more percussive, rapidly delivered notes of the western bird. So often the western wren stops short, not completing his full song, but all three of these songs are seven or eight seconds long and end with a high-pitched, rapid trill, typical of a normal song ending. Listen to the track again, and again, concentrating on all of the nuances of each song. Feel the pattern of notes in the first two seconds of each song, and perhaps you'll eventually hear that the first two songs have the same two-second introduction but the third is different (see figure 42). If you've mastered the introductions, try hearing how the first two songs diverge after two seconds. As you struggle to hear the details, realize that these western winter wrens learn their songs from each other, a feat that reveals how acute their hearing must be. *Recorded in Oregon by Geoffrey A. Keller (MLNS 42192, 109126).*

TRACK 63: Winter wren, eastern and western North America, at one-sixth normal speed. Go back to figures 41 (page 218) and 42 (page 221) and look at the details, and now hear song A of the eastern male and song 3 of the western male at a speed that our human ears can begin to manage. For the eastern bird, hear each dainty whistle and the relatively narrow frequency range over which it is slowly slurred; feel how slowly the eastern song unravels when compared to the breakneck speed of the western song. Play this track again and again, appreciating the difference between East and West.

TRACK 64: Winter wren, Japan. One song of a winter wren from the Old World, revealing that the quality of the whistled notes is much like that in the songs from eastern North America. To create this relatively long song (10 seconds), the wren doubles back in his song and repeats a 3.5-second portion. With repeated listening, you can hear that. Try listening carefully to the last five notes of the song, the four high notes followed by a single down-slurred note; listen to the song again and you'll hear those same notes about four seconds into the song. With repeated listening, an ultra-fine ear, and a good memory for sounds, you might hear the song in four parts: A (1.7 seconds), B (3.3 seconds), C (1.3 seconds), B (3.5 seconds), showing that he creates his long song by singing the B part over again. *Recorded in Japan by Hiroshi Momose.*

THE BACHMAN'S SPARROW

One of the most beautiful singers in North America. This sparrow's theme is an introductory whistle or buzz followed by one or two trills, and he varies that theme in ways that delight the ear.

TRACK 65: Bachman's sparrow, examples of the six different songs I first heard that morning when I went exploring in south Florida (figure 43, page 229). Realize that these songs are taken out of context here, with only one rendition of each song, and realize, too, that they are presented at a faster pace than a sparrow would normally sing them. Watch the sonagrams in figure 43 as you listen, appreciating just a few of the many variations on the Bachman's sparrow theme. *Recorded in Florida.*

TRACK 66: Bachman's sparrow, a natural series of songs from another Florida male. In these 12 songs are nine different types, in the sequence A B B C C D D E F G H I. As you listen to each song, savor all of its qualities, and then compare it to the next. Is the next song the same or different, and if different, in what ways? And the next song, and the next. Play the sequence again, and again; try sketching your own sonagrams as you listen, seeing on paper the contrasts that you hear as you revel in this sparrow's performance. *Recorded in Florida by Geoffrey A. Keller (MLNS 73891).*

THE WOOD THRUSH

Together with the hermit thrush, the wood thrush is one of the premier singers in North America, a first cousin of the famed "nightingale-thrushes" of Central and South America, a favorite of all who hear him. Not all males are equally accomplished, however, as revealed by the two males featured here. Just listen to the artisan at work as you hear and see what he accomplishes with his two voice boxes.

TRACK 67: Wood thrush, male #1, as discussed in the text. In 45 seconds, he sings nine songs, as illustrated in figure 45, page 238. Listen carefully, hearing the soft *bup bup bup* at the beginning of the songs. Hear the contrast between the whistled preludes and the more percussive flourishes. Hear, too, how the prelude in the next song is always different from the one he just sang, as he alternates his two preludes in the sequence A B A B A B A B A. To hear this pattern, pick one prelude and listen for it to recur in every other song; then listen for the other prelude, as learning the preludes one by one is the easiest approach. The A prelude is followed by five different flourishes (1–5), the B prelude by three (6–8); only the second and eighth songs in this series are the same (prelude B, flourish 8). Play this track repeatedly until you can easily recognize the two preludes, and perhaps then try the greater challenge, recognizing the different flourishes.

TRACK 68: Wood thrush, male #2 (figure 46, page 243). Hear the more diverse singing performance of this second wood thrush, his six preludes (A–F) combined with 13 different flourishes. Savor the beauty in these 43 songs and all of the contrasts within and among songs. While viewing figure 46, pick out one prelude and listen for it to recur; when you've mastered that one, pick another, and then another, until you can identify each of the six preludes. If you're up to the challenge, try to recognize one or more of the flourishes. Play the track repeatedly, as listening to such a cooperative bird singing continuously is a great way to build confidence for when you are out listening to a real bird in nature.

TRACK 69: Wood thrush, preludes of male #2 at quarter speed. Listen to the music of these preludes at a slowed-down speed. Follow along in figure 46, as these preludes play in the same sequence that they are illustrated there: E D C B A F.

TRACK 70: Wood thrush, six flourishes at one-tenth speed, revealing to our ears the two voices at work (figure 47, page 249). For each flourish, I have isolated the contributions from the two voice boxes so that the left plays first on the left track of the CD, then the right voice plays on the right track, and then the two voices play together, as the wood thrush sang them. As you listen to this track, read the text, pages 246–248, and follow along in figure 47 for a full description of the magic in these flourishes.

THE HERMIT THRUSH

The swamp angel he's called, and listening to his songs reveals why. The hermit is hailed by many as the finest songster in North America.

TRACK 71: Hermit thrush, a 28-song sequence from my hermit, G C D E <u>A G C</u> H I <u>F B E</u> D <u>C G H</u> I A B C <u>F G E</u> D C <u>A B E</u>, the letters here matching the songs in figure 48, page 258 (underlining explained below). There's so much to hear from this male. On your first pass, just savor the quality of these songs, the pure whistle followed by the lusty flourish. Hear it as the essence of hermit thrush. Then listen to how flourishes tend to rise from the introductory whistle. Hear, too, how successive songs are always different. Try playing this track repeatedly as if you were listening to an extended sequence of songs from this male. Then pick out one song that sounds especially distinctive to you and start counting as other songs pass by, trying to contain the smile on your face as you hear your chosen song again. Try that again with another song. Listen, too, to how the whistle changes in successive songs; there is an overall tendency for the whistle to rise and fall in successive songs (figure 50), but this particular sequence has six song trios where the frequency rises or falls twice in succession (those song trios are underlined in the above sequence).

MUSIC TO OUR EARS

Songs of many birds strike us as especially beautiful (or musical), stopping us in our tracks when we hear them. Such is the song of the canyon wren, as much a part of the canyonlands of the American west as the rock walls themselves.

TRACK 72: Canyon wren (figure 51, page 271). Each male has a variety of whistled songs, each song cascading down the scale, but exactly how many different songs a wren can sing no one seems to have discovered. He sings one particular song several times before switching to another, and in this track are two examples of each of four different songs extracted from a longer sequence of 36 songs (A A . . . B B . . . C C . . . D D . . .). Listen to the first song, and compare its overall quality to the second — it's the same, you'll no doubt conclude. Then hear the abrupt change to the third song, which is the same as the fourth, and so on. *Recorded in Oregon by Geoffrey A. Keller (MLNS 120251).*

THE AMERICAN WOODCOCK

Many birds in open habitats sing on the wing, as getting high off the ground is the best way to get one's message heard. Not only do the woodcock and snipe sing on the wing, but the woodcock sings *with* its wings, and the snipe *with* its wings and tail.

TRACK 73: American woodcock (figure 52, page 279). Put your headphones on or sit in the "sweet spot" between the two speakers of your stereo set, close your eyes, and pretend you are sitting in an easy chair near this displaying woodcock in the Adirondacks of upstate New York. Spring peepers call in the distant wetlands, but nearby the woodcock struts on the ground. He *peents* repeatedly, then up he flies, whistling with his wings, soon circling high overhead. Feel the changing rhythms of his wingbeats and hear how the whistling of his wings gradually combines with his vocalizations (illustrated in figure 52); he finally plummets to earth, fluttering past you to his display arena again where he resumes *peent*ing. Listen to the woodcock in the background, too: After our male has taken to the air, a single *peent* is heard in the distance at 0:17, and for 10 seconds after our male has ended his aerial calling another male can be heard calling overhead in the distance. In this particular recording, our nearby male was first to the air, followed by his neighbor about ten seconds later. *Recorded in New York by Gregory F. Budney (14 May 1994).*

TRACK 74: Common snipe. The snipe also calls from the ground, giving a series of *chipa chipa chipa* calls. Before long, he's into the air and soon high overhead, circling above his territory; as he dives toward earth, the outer tail feathers sing *wuwuwuwuwuwuwuwuwuwuwu*, each *wu* one wingbeat of air directed past the specialized feathers in the tail. He pulls out of his dive only to climb again, singing *wuwuwuwuwuwuwuwuwuwuwu* over and over until he plummets back to earth to resume his *chipa chipa chipa* calls. Ground and flight sounds in this track are not part of a continuous display but are spliced together here. Note that the snipe's winnow was recorded with a parabola, so it is heard as if the listener were riding the back of the snipe itself; in contrast, the woodcock's aerial display (track 73) was recorded with directional (stereo) microphones on the ground near his display arena, and as a result the aerial display is heard more faintly, as one would hear it from the ground. Chipa *calls recorded in Manitoba by Arthur A. Allen and Peter Paul Kellogg (MLNS 3135), flight sounds in Alberta by William W. H. Gunn (MLNS 64217).*

THE WHIP-POOR-WILL

They are called nightjars for their extreme performances, jarring the night from dusk to dawn with their incessant singing. Imagine a nine-hour vigil with this bird, counting each time he hurls out his namesake, totaling over 20,000 songs.

TRACK 75: An avian metronome, this nightjar sings *tuck-WHIP-poor-WILL tuck-WHIP-poor-WILL tuck-WHIP-poor-WILL* over and over (figure 54, page 289); he then speeds up (at about 0:39 on the track) as he ends his singing with a brief flourish. After these songs is a purring sound, the entire performance ending with mysterious thumping sounds and a few more odd purrs. This male is part of a whip-poor-will community, and one other male can be heard singing in the background. With some careful listening, a third whip-poor-will can be heard, too: listen again to the male's purring from 0:48 to 0:52 and you'll hear the purrs of a second bird, no doubt his mate who is nearby. *Recorded in Indiana by Geoffrey A. Keller (MLNS 109253).*

THE RED-EYED VIREO

Another extreme performer, this vireo has been dubbed the "preacher bird" for droning on and on from his treetop pulpit, throughout even the warmest of summer afternoons. Because he sings incessantly and because each male has a few especially distinctive songs, the red-eyed vireo offers a wonderful opportunity to sit and listen to how an avian mind plays out all of the songs that it knows.

TRACK 76: Red-eyed vireo. To prepare you for listening to the songs of a particular vireo (in track 77), I've selected three of his most distinctive songs and play them repeatedly here, three examples of A, three of B, and three of C. Play this track several times while you look at these particular songs in figure 56; when you're confident you've got them down, proceed to the next track.

TRACK 77: Red-eyed vireo (figure 56, page 301). A vireo has not three but a dozen or more different songs, of course; listen now to this two-minute, 100-song performance by Mr. Vireo, first appreciating the great variety of songs that he sings, as successive songs are always different, and then trying to identify those three distinctive songs that you've memorized from track 76. On a piece of paper make three columns, headed by A, B, and C, and now count from 1 to 100 as the vireo sings, identifying which songs are A, which B, and which C. Perhaps start with song A, the most distinctive song, and listen for it first. Then try B and C. Do your numbers match mine? A: 7, 39, 66. B: 21, 33, 42, 63, 69, 79, 98. C: 8, 23, 29, 37, 43, 54, 86, 93. These numbers can be used to estimate how many different songs he sang in the 100 songs. If three of his songs are used a total of 18 times (go ahead, count them), that's an average of 6 times apiece (18/3 = 6). If we assume each of his different songs is used about 6 times, we can divide 100 by 6 to give an estimate of 17 different songs in this performance. (If you have difficulty identifying all three songs in this long performance, don't despair; many vireos have far more distinctive songs than does this particular vireo. Choose your own vireo, one with a few especially distinctive songs, and play your games with him.)

THE EASTERN WOOD-PEWEE

In the hour before sunrise, the eastern wood-pewee is at its best, pulling out all the stops. He then uses all three of his songs, *pee-ah-wee, wee-ooo,* and *ah-di-dee,* and he delivers them at a blistering pace. Later in the day, he sings only *pee-ah-wee* and *wee-ooo,* now at a far more leisurely pace. His western counterpart makes for a fascinating comparison, as the western wood-pewee has just two songs that he uses at dawn, the *peeer* and the *tswee-tee-teet,* only the *peeer* being used during daytime singing.

    TRACK 78: Eastern wood-pewee, daytime singing (figure 57, page 306): *pee-ah-wee pee-ah-wee pee-ah-wee wee-ooo.* The pace is a song every 7 to 10 seconds, with several *pee-ah-wee* songs followed by a single *wee-ooo.*

    TRACK 79: Eastern wood-pewee, dawn singing (figure 57, page 306). Feel the energy in his singing as you identify each of his three whistled songs. Practice writing down your own notation as he sings, perhaps P for *pee-ah-wee,* W for *wee-ooo,* and A for *ah-di-dee,* preparing yourself for your own encounters with pewees at dawn. The first five songs are *pee-ah-wee, ah-di-dee, ah-di-dee, wee-ooo,* and *ah-di-dee* (P A A W A, if you like the letters). I leave the rest of the songs to you—grab a pencil and write down the sequence of the remaining songs, and then find a live pewee at dawn and capture him on paper.

    TRACK 80: Western wood-pewee, dawn singing (figure 58, page 311). He alternates his *tswee-tee-teet* and *peer* at dawn, as illustrated here, but during the daytime he sings only the *peer. Recorded in California by Randy Little (MLNS 61838).*

CHIPPING AND BREWER'S SPARROWS

Given their placid, uninspiring daytime singing, one would never predict the energy and style with which these sparrows sing in the dark before sunrise.

    TRACK 81: Chipping sparrows (figure 60, page 315). Before sunrise, these sparrows often spar with neighbors, sometimes four of them gathered in a small cluster on the ground, all hurling staccato bursts of brief songs at each other. In the first 24 seconds of this track, two males (1 and 2 in figure 60) sing from nearby gravestones in one of my favorite cemeteries; they mostly alternate their songs, taking turns singing, although the foreground bird on three occasions overlaps the song of the background bird (the bird who sings solo on track 82). The last five songs on this track are from a different male, a male who was singing by himself about 30 yards from the other two; his dawn songs are relatively long, but he leaves little time between songs, so that he is singing most of the available time.

TRACK 82: A chipping sparrow, showing how the songs of an individual become progressively longer during the dawn chorus. When a male first starts singing, he sings from the ground; his songs are often only a fraction of a second and consist of just a few elements, as in the eight song-bursts that begin this track (0:01–0:12). With this male, 15 to 20 minutes later his songs were 1 to 2 seconds long (four examples, 0:14–0:27). After the dawn chorus, he flew up to the nearby tree, delivering a much longer four-second song (0:31–0:35).

TRACK 83: Brewer's sparrow, two daytime songs from each of two individuals (figure 61, page 321). These songs typically consist of two trills, the first higher-pitched than the second. As with chipping sparrows, each male has a single song that he repeats over and over, and neighboring males routinely have identifiably different songs. At 0:08 hear the daytime *peer* of a western wood-pewee. *Recorded in California by Randy Little (MLNS 99358) and in Oregon by Geoffrey A. Keller (MLNS 109255).*

TRACK 84: Brewer's sparrow. Before sunrise this sparrow is transformed into one of the most remarkable singers of North America (figure 62, page 323). Listen to this male who sang beside me in the sagebrush of Sierra Valley, eastern California. He begins with his insectlike buzzes, continuing for about ten seconds before he descends to a series of trills at a much lower pitch. Back up he goes, buzzing again, then giving a high-pitched trill, then buzzing and descending again to his lower trills, this pattern repeating itself over and over during his dawn performance. In the background can be heard other sparrows, each of them doing the same. On and on they sing, stopping well before the sun's first rays sneak over the distant hills and strike their sagebrush home.

TRACK 85: Brewer's sparrow. Here is the champion dawn singer in my group of sparrows. He sings to the west of me, perhaps 50 yards away, but how far I cannot be sure, as I have yet to see any birds in this darkness. I aim my parabola at him and turn up the gain of my tape recorder, boosting not only his songs but also the sounds of all the other birds now singing here in the sagebrush and the nearby marshes; snipe call and winnow overhead, ducks quack, and other species chime in, too. The sparrow begins this particular effort with four seconds of buzzy notes before descending to his lower trills; over the next 37 seconds, he sings trill after trill, about one a second, until he concludes with two punctuating *bzeet bzeet* notes on a higher pitch . . . and seconds later he is at it again.

THE EASTERN BLUEBIRD

Well-known and loved as the blue bird who nests in the house next door, the eastern bluebird is also a remarkable singer, though one wouldn't know the intensity with which it sings unless one rises well before sunrise.

TRACK 86: Hear the bluebird use three different songs in this relatively "tame" performance (figure 63, page 328), in the sequence A B C C B A B C B A C. Play the track over and over, gradually coming to identify each of the songs as you hear it.

TRACK 87: Wow! Just back from a distant border skirmish, the bluebird lands beside me and blisters through a full minute of singing, 24 songs in all, 10 different ones in the sequence <u>A B C D E A F C C C A D C C</u> F A C G H I F C A J (only the underlined songs are on this track; see figure 64, page 331). And then off he flies again, energized and intense, battling yet again with the neighbor. (On tracks 86 and 87, song C is the same, but A and B are different.)

THE BARRED OWL

Yes, she also sings. It has long been known that the female's hooting is higher-pitched than his, but some sleuthing now reveals that her hoots also end with more vibrato than his. Knowing this difference allows one to hear what role the male and female play in duets when there are few or no pitch-cues available, as in their remarkable caterwauling exchanges.

TRACK 88: From the *Peterson Field Guide to Western Bird Songs*. Listen to these owls and hear how the higher-pitched bird has more vibrato in its *you-allllll* (figure 65, page 338). It was here that I first wondered if the female always has more vibrato in her *you-allllll* than does her mate. (Scientists would call such wondering a "hypothesis.") *Recorded in New York by Gregory F. Budney and James L. Gulledge (14 June 1983).*

TRACK 89: From *Stokes Field Guide to Bird Song; Eastern Region* (figure 65, page 338). Four different recordings are used to illustrate the range of sounds produced by these owls (0:00–0:16, 0:17–0:20, 0:21–0:25; 0:25–0:38), each recording further confirming my suspicion that females have more vibrato in their *you-allllll* than do males. See text, pages 339–340, for how to listen to the details of this track. *Recorded in Florida and Louisiana by Lang Elliott and William R. Evans.*

TRACK 90: Listen to "my" owls in Lawrence Swamp, Amherst, Massachusetts. Hear how the lower-pitched bird, the male, has a simple *you-all* that rises and falls in pitch; the higher-pitched bird has more of a *you-allllll*, with an extended vibrato section on the end. Play the track over and over until you can identify the roles that male and female play in these exchanges.

TRACK 91: One of my favorite recordings of barred owls, a lovely *youuuuuuu-allllllllll* by the female followed by a simple *youuuuuuu-all* by the male, the birds now confidently sexed not only by the differences in pitch but also by the differences in the vibrato ending (figure 65, page 338). *Recorded in Florida by William R. Evans (MLNS 49701).*

THE CAROLINA WREN

The male Carolina wren has a resounding song, much like other wrens in the largely tropical genus *Thryothorus*. The female Carolina wren uses a simple chatter to duet with her mate; she appears unique among all *Thryothorus* females, because her "song" is so simple and apparently not learned.

TRACK 92: Ten male-female duets given over two and a half minutes (see figure 66, page 348), condensed here to about a minute by removing silent intervals between the exchanges (actual times between the duets are 11, 10, 10, 24, 15, 10, 9, 35, and 8 seconds). Stand with me on the boardwalk at Audubon's Corkscrew Swamp Sanctuary near Naples, Florida, parabola in my hand, a separate set of headphones for you and me, waiting for the first sounds from the local pair of Carolina wrens. To the left, he sings *CHE-wortel! CHE-wortel! CHE-wortel! CHE-wortel! CHE-wortel!*, five phrases, she chattering almost immediately to our right; the male initially sings in the direction the parabola is pointing, so his songs are fairly clear, but she is well off to the side, her chatter poorly recorded. I swing the parabola toward her, getting a better aim on her for the second duet. By the third duet, I am well focused, the parabola pointing directly at her, every little hiccup now recorded as he sings off to the side. Listen to these first ten exchanges on this October morning, following along with the description in the text on pages 347–348.

TRACK 93: Each male Carolina wren has a sizable repertoire of 30 to 40 different songs, and one example of each of eight songs is illustrated here from the male at Corkscrew Swamp (figure 67, page 351). Realize that when the male sings, he repeats one song many times before switching to another, so you would never hear a Carolina wren singing like this. Hear and see (in figure 67, songs A–H) the striking differences in the eight songs, how rapidly the elements are repeated in some, how slowly in others, the percussive quality of some, the sweet tonal quality of others. Concentrate especially on distinguishing songs F and H, two highly similar yet consistently different songs.

TRACK 94: If our north-temperate Carolina wren were typical of the tropical wrens in this genus, what might they sound like? I wonder. Let me play a little, taking two songs of the male Carolina wren and putting one on the left track and the other on the right track. Now I space out the repeated elements on each track just enough so that I have what sounds like a "male" and a "female" perfectly synchronized in their "duet." Beautiful. I do the same with another pair of songs. Yes, that is perhaps how the male and female Carolina wrens would duet if they were still tropical.

TRACK 95: A young male Carolina wren must learn his songs, and like a male Bewick's wren (track 11), he initially gets it all wrong, singing nonsensical sequences of phrases that belong in different songs. In spite of how disjointedly a young male sings, all Carolina wrens I have heard always get the song "right," always repeating the same element several times within a song. What if a young male got it wrong, I wondered, perfecting instead the jumbled nature of his practice songs? Again I experiment, this time taking an element from several different adult male songs in track 93 and combining them into one song. I create three songs like this. Egads—what odd songs! I like the real Carolina wren better.

THE NORTHERN CARDINAL

The female cardinal and her mate learn the songs of the local dialect, so they have essentially identical repertoires. She sings less often than he does and her songs often aren't quite as sharp as his, but that may simply be a consequence of less testosterone in her blood. What the male and female cardinal are saying as they respond to each other with matching songs remains largely a mystery.

TRACK 96: This male cardinal sings from the sea oats along the beach in Naples, Florida (figure 68, page 358). Three different songs are included here, in an A A B B C C pattern, those six songs extracted from a longer series of 27 songs (5A, 5B, and 17C). Overall, during 32 minutes before sunrise on this early July morning, this male sang a total of ten different songs (A–J). At 0:40, a heron squawks, the only other significant background sounds in this stereo recording being the gentle washing of waves on the beach.

TRACK 97: A male-female exchange, or duet (figure 68). The longer song of the male is in the background, the briefer song of the female in the foreground. In this exchange, he leads off, followed immediately by her (from 0:00 to 0:06); he sings, she sings, and he sings again (from 0:10 to 0:22); she utters a single element from her song but then stops (at 0:25); he then sings again, and she responds immediately (from 0:27 to 0:32). Hear the *hey-sweetie* of the black-capped chickadee in the background? *Recorded in New York by Gregory F. Budney (MLNS 49063).*

THE SOOTY SHEARWATER

TRACK 98: Sooty shearwater (a CD bonus, not discussed in the book's text). We see silent shearwaters off the coast of the northern hemisphere, but visit them on their nesting grounds far to the south, as I did with this pair on Kidney Island in the Falkland Islands. One of the birds has been at sea all day and at dusk has, like thousands of others on this tiny island, returned to its mate in the nesting burrow. The entire island now resounds with the *ooooooh*ing and *aaoaah*ing of sooty shearwaters. There's something universal in the quality of these sounds, and it seems fitting that the birds themselves have the final comment about the sheer wonder and joy of birdsong.

Techniques

Anyone can enjoy listening to bird sounds without ever tape recording them or seeing pictures of them, but the recording and seeing can add so much to the enjoyment and appreciation that I include information here on how one could proceed.

How to Record Bird Sounds

I must begin with a warning: Tape recording birdsong can become addictive. Oh, it begins harmlessly enough, with the intention of just capturing a few bird sounds in the backyard, and using the simplest of equipment. "I just want to hear the spring thrush this winter, just to remind me in those darkest hours, that's all." First the thrush, then the ovenbird, the robin, and then the inevitable. One after the other "needs" to be captured, better equipment is needed, a tape library is started, and then the traveling begins. Don't tell me I didn't warn you. Read on only if you dare.

I know that you think this warning doesn't apply to you, but here's what happened to the first person who read a rough draft of this book, a draft without the CD and the beautiful sonagrams to match. On February 22, 2004, I received this e-mail message from Marie Alice (name changed to protect the guilty): "I feel I should warn you about the power of your book. Within a few weeks of finishing it, I found myself on the phone ordering the Raven software . . . and then there was the call to Marice Stith . . . and then I was signing up for the summer workshop in the Sierras . . ." Then, late June, I received a postcard from Yuba Pass in the California Sierras: "I am *so* glad that I took the sound recording workshop . . ." Marie Alice bought the tape-recording gear, bought the Raven software from Cornell so that she could see her songs, *and* took the sound recording workshop from the experts. Then, a few months later, she confessed to ordering a parabola, because the shotgun mike she bought first wasn't good enough. Birdsong has taken over her life. Last warning: read on at your own risk, though this warning is perhaps already too late.

Getting started is almost too easy. Perhaps try this system that I used for a couple of years: a cheap cassette tape recorder with an external microphone input, a microphone, and a plastic funnel, all still available for under $50. Slit the narrow end of the funnel enough to insert the microphone so that the head of the mike is at the base of the funnel. Connect the mike to the recorder, and you're ready to go. Get as close to your singing bird as you can without disturbing it, point the funnel at the bird so that the sounds collected by the funnel are reflected toward the head of the microphone, and punch "record." If you have some headphones you might try listening as you record (if your recorder will let you), but otherwise you can rewind the tape when you're done recording and listen to it afterward. It's that simple.

Just a couple of comments on that simple system. My hand-held microphone worked better than the microphone built into the recorder, because I could mount it in the funnel and point it at the bird, and because the noise of the recorder made it difficult for the internal microphone to pick up the relatively soft, distant sounds of birds. The "automatic gain control" of the recorder's electronic circuitry automatically boosted recorded sounds to some preset level, so I didn't have to worry about adjusting the recording level. If you upgrade, however, and get serious about recording bird sounds, you'll probably want the manual controls, not the automatic controls (see below).

There are many uses such a simple system could be put to. Record the singing robin, for example, and then listen to the songs over and over in the comfort of your easy chair as you learn how to dissect what he is doing; listen again in late winter as you train your ears for a new season; or listen at your computer as you watch the songs dance by on the monitor (see next section, How to See Bird Sounds). Or record the eastern phoebe at dawn, later listening at your leisure to how he uses his *fee-bee* and *fee-b-be-be* songs. Oh, and how about the eastern wood-pewee, to hear those plaintive *pee-a-wee* and *wee-ooo* and *ah-di-dee* dawn songs from your very own bird in the dead of winter, when he is basking in the Amazon forests? Capture 15 minutes of a mockingbird on tape and then listen to your recording several times as you get to know him better, and estimate how many different songs he can sing. Is that the same wood thrush in my wood lot who was there last year? Quick, compare last year's recordings with this year's . . . yes, same preludes, same favored sequences, same bird! He left last fall, flew those thousands of miles to the tropics, and then returned to this very place. The possibilities are endless.

Soon you'll be eyeing those equipment catalogs, and well before Christmas. How about a little better tape recorder? A better microphone? If you had better headphones, you'd be able to concentrate better on what you're recording. And perhaps you should take some lessons on how to tape-record better.

Let me tell you about the system that I now use, the system I can't imagine going to the field without. I want to tell you of its advantages (and disadvantages), and once you understand them, you can look at the components of my system and make some intelligent decisions for the system you put together for yourself.

THE MICROPHONE. It's the mike that catches the bird sounds and converts the sounds to electrical impulses, so it's the logical place to start. Basically, two types of microphones are used by people who record birds. One is a hand-held, highly directional "shotgun" mike, so named because it looks like a gun barrel (and is sometimes mistaken for one). It's convenient, packs easily for trips, and is as easy to use as pointing your own finger at the singing bird.

The other microphone system uses a parabolic reflector, or dish, as it is sometimes called. The dish comes in various sizes, from a foot in diameter to three or more feet. When the parabola is pointed at a singing bird, all of the sound that strikes the parabola is reflected to a focal point, which is where the microphone is placed, of course.

Here's why I wouldn't be caught dead in the field with only a shotgun mike. On a remote hillside in Costa Rica, Julio Sánchez and I were standing side by side, he with his shotgun mike, me with my parabola. A good 100 yards up on the hillside was a singing black-thighed grosbeak, one of the finest and most melodious of singers I have ever heard anywhere. Julio dropped his headphones to his ears, pointed his shotgun mike, and with a serious look on his face began to record. I did the same, but with a smile on my face. (Normally, mind you, I am far more serious than Julio.) Eyeing Julio, I knew what had to be done. "Here, Julio, try my headphones." I kept the sights of my parabola aimed at the distant bird, and, unaware of the power of a parabola, Julio slipped my headphones on. It took just one song from the finch to transform this shotgun user to a lifelong convert of the parabola. Into his ears were now streaming songs that were loud and pure, and his beaming face and hanging jaw made me realize how expensive this moment was. I lost my parabola on that hillside in 1995, and to this day the parabola and Julio's smile travel together in Costa Rica. It was a small price to pay for the joy it put into Julio's life.

Or take the unsuspecting tourists who walk the trails of the Monteverde cloud forests in Costa Rica. They round a corner in the trail and encounter me, standing there in my camouflage clothes with all of my gear, parabola aimed up into the canopy. They hear the three-wattled bellbird up there, but they usually can't see it. If the group lingers, searching for this mysterious singer, I offer my headphones to one of them and wait for the reaction. *BONK!* The listener is typically blown back a step on the trail, the mouth wide open, the eyes bulging, the knees buckling, so effective is the parabola at bringing a sound up close. (Well, okay, sometimes I turn the volume up a little on the headphones, just for the effect.)

The professional side of me says I should objectively weigh the advantages and disadvantages of the two systems. Okay. The shotgun mike is more convenient to use, the parabola rather cumbersome; but that's not so much of a problem with a parabola that rolls up and fits in my sleeve (such as the Telinga parabola—see page 407). A good shotgun mike treats all frequencies of the bird's sound almost equally (that is, it has a "flat frequency response"), but the parabola distorts the sound a little, amplifying some frequencies more than others (a trivial matter for most purposes, I feel—I'm just trying to be fair and thorough). The flat frequency response of the shotgun mike is important for low frequency sounds, because parabolas are ineffective below frequencies at which the wavelength of the sound is equal to the diameter of the reflector. A 24-inch parabola, for example, is ineffective below 565 Hz. Fortunately, most bird sounds are above 1,000 Hz, the point at which a relatively small 13-inch parabolic reflector can become effective. Both the parabola and shotgun make you look suspicious, but the only time I've been chased by police was when I was biking and terrorizing Martha's Vineyard and its chickadees with my "shotgun."

The main reason I favor the parabola is because it is far more effective at capturing distant or soft sounds. The reason is simple: the amount of sound captured by the area at the opening of the parabola is much greater than that captured by the area of the shotgun microphone's head. If the radius of a "two-foot" parabola is 30 centimeters and that of the shotgun's head only 1 centimeter, for example, the parabola will capture 900 times more sound energy than will the shotgun ($3.14 \, r^2$ is the formula for area, with r being the radius, so $3.14 \times 30^2 \div 3.14 \times 1^2 = 900$). It is this 900x factor that produced Julio's smile on that Costa Rican hillside, the factor that makes an enormous difference in the quality of sound recorded from any distance. This reason for preferring a parabola is less important with loud, close sounds, conditions under which the choice between the shotgun microphone and the parabola would, for me, become more of a tossup.

For one more reason I give the nod to the parabola. The shotgun is said to capture bird sounds more like we hear them, whereas the parabola produces a much shriller sound. That may sound like a vote for a shotgun, but for me it's not. Take a black-capped chickadee singing *hey-sweetie* up in the tree, for example. The sound leaves the birds' bill and radiates out in all directions; some of the song reaches our ears directly, but this song takes other paths to our ears, too, bouncing off leaves and then arriving at our ears slightly delayed, so that the sharp, crisp *hey-sweetie* that left the bird's bill is now somewhat blurred. It is that blurring that distresses me. With the shotgun, the blurring can be enough to obscure that amplitude drop in the middle of the *sweetie* portion of the song. Because the parabola is much more directional than the shotgun, it can eliminate those echoes (and other background sounds) from the recording, thereby recording the sound that comes on a direct path from the bird's bill. These differences are readily seen in sonagrams: A "shotgun sonagram" shows the trailing echoes and smudges after the bird's song, but the "parabola sonagram" is much sharper and crisper (almost all sonagrams in this book are parabola sonagrams). So a shotgun mike may record sounds as we hear them, with lots of natural reverberation and echo, but the parabola captures the songs more like the bird sang them, as if reaching out and grabbing the sound directly from the bird's bill. I want the parabola.

HEADPHONES. I like the heavy, padded headphones that fit snugly over my ears and block out everything except what I am recording. Such headphones let me focus and concentrate better on what is going to the recorder. Other recordists who want to hear more of what is going on around them prefer the "open-air" headphones, which have foam pads that fit lightly over the ears, but with them I never know for sure what is on the tape and what I'm hearing from the environment around me.

TAPE RECORDER. Recording technology changes rapidly. In the late 1960s I started with open-reel tape recorders, and only in the mid 1990s did I finally convert to the standard analog cassette recorder. Until 2002, I was using a stereo, analog cassette recorder, a Sony TCD5ProII. Somewhat to the chagrin of professional purists, I bought an HHB minidisc recorder mid-2002, because it has some advantages over the analog cassette (better speed control was crucial for recording bellbirds—see page 89). These minidisc recorders are convenient and relatively inexpensive and are becoming increasingly popular.

The problem with minidisc technology is that it has been based on how we humans hear sounds, not on how birds hear them. If our ears can't detect certain features of a sound, the minidisc is programmed to omit that part of the sound from the recording (the sound is "compressed"). As a result, the signal recorded from a bird is not the same as what the bird sang. That's fine for most purposes, but not for all. I would not want to use a minidisc recording that distorted sounds, for example, if I wanted to analyze the fine structure of a song, because I'd be studying some unknown mix of what the bird sang and how the recorder modified the song. Nor would I want to use minidisc recordings to study how birds respond to the fine details of their own songs, if I were doing an experiment that required me to ask them in a "playback" experiment, because the birds most likely can detect some of the odd things that the minidisc recorder does to the songs. New minidisc models introduced in 2004, however, promise to avoid these distortions and allow high-quality recordings. They're called HiMD recorders, made by Sony. Discussions and arguments about these matters are favorite topics among bioacousticians, and you can read all about it on the appropriate Web sites (such as http://cetus. pmel.noaa.gov/Bioacoustics.html). For all practical, nonprofessional purposes, even the minidisc recorders that compress sounds are terrific recorders, because the convenience and ease of use make having fun easier—and that's what this is all about, just in case you forgot.

THE RECORDING SYSTEM FOR YOU? When (not "if") you get hooked on recording and are ready to upgrade that very simple funnel system, you have lots of choices, perhaps too many. Here's what I'd recommend doing. Go to the Web site of the Macaulay Library of Natural Sounds at Cornell University's Laboratory of Ornithology (www.birds.cornell.edu/macaulaylibrary). They have lots of good advice about equipment and about how to record, including a full-length article about how to record birds in the tropics, which is pretty much how you'd record them in the temperate zone, too. Then go to one of my favorite catalogs, that of Marice Stith Recording Services (www.stithrecording.com), where you can read all about recorders and microphones and headphones. Or check out what is available at Mineroff Electronics (www.mineroff.com).

Then ask yourself how serious you want to be. When I'm most serious, I use my Telinga parabola with a Sennheiser ME62 microphone, AKG K-240DF tight-fitting headphones, and an HHB minidisc recorder—total cost as of winter 2004 about $2,400. The parabola is clear plastic, lightweight and easy to hold up for hours on end, and it can be rolled up into a coat sleeve for traveling. But when I'm out for capturing some memories and taking them home with me, just for fun, I take my tiny Sony minidisc recorder (models change rapidly, but my latest is the MZ-NF810), which fits in the palm of my hand; a "short shotgun" microphone (Sennheiser ME66); and no headphones. Using this less expensive system (perhaps $700) enabled me to capture hours upon hours of good sounds during a recent cross-country bicycle trip.

Improvise and come up with your own system, on your own budget. Try whittling back on the cost of my systems, if you wish. Go to Edmund Scientific (www.scientificsonline.com), for example, and purchase a parabola for tens rather than hundreds of dollars. Get an inexpensive microphone from Radio Shack and rig up some way to hold the microphone at the focal point of the parabola. Consider a lower-end analog cassette recorder, perhaps the Sony TCM-5000EV (a favorite of many birders and tour guides), for a little under $500, or try the cheapest possible cassette recorder you can find at Radio Shack and see what results you get. Remember, you don't have to make professional-quality recordings, and you don't need the best of all possible equipment. Don't forget why you're doing this: you're simply out to have some fun.

Should you take lessons in how to record? Why not. Join others for the weeklong recording course taught by the Cornell group, and you will forever be hooked. During 2001 I spent a week with this course in the California Sierras, feasting on Brewer's sparrows and sage thrashers, among others, and had the time of my life. I found that I still had a lot to learn from this group.

Pretty soon you'll be on e-mail lists with others like you. You'll frequent Web sites that tell about the study of bioacoustics (such as www.birds.cornell.edu/brp; or a site "dedicated to the recording of bird vocalizations with simple, inexpensive equipment," at ourworld.compuserve.com/homepages/ G_Kunkel). You may join the Nature Sounds Association (www.nature-sounds.org) or a group of nature recordists on-line (http://groups.yahoo. com/group/naturerecordists). Perhaps you'll upgrade your gear and begin contributing to the sound archives at places like Cornell University or Ohio State University (blb.biosci.ohio-state.edu/), or perhaps to the National Sound Archive in the British Library in London (www.bl.uk/collections/ sound-archive/wild.html). Recording in your backyard will no longer satisfy you, and you'll be off to Costa Rica, Brazil, or even Africa. And all that started with a simple 50-cent funnel that you pulled from your garage shelf. I warned you.

How to See Bird Sounds

By the time you read these words in this appendix, I hope you are a convert to the power of seeing birdsongs in the form of sonagrams. Personally, I can't imagine a world without sonagrams, as I can't imagine listening without also seeing. I have combined the listening and seeing throughout this book, and I hope that you will continue this practice on your own. Take a CD of bird sounds off your shelf and play it into your computer, now seeing the songs come to life, appreciating the details and the differences among them. Make your own recordings, bringing them home to gorge yourself on the details of how a robin or thrush or warbler sings. Or try the ultimate in techie birding —get the appropriate software program (see below), a laptop computer, and a microphone, and you can watch the songs dance across your computer monitor in the great out-of-doors as you listen to birds there. Listen as you see, and you will hear a different world singing to you.

Although graphing a bird's sound not too long ago required equipment costing thousands of dollars, most of us already have all that we need in our personal computers. These computers routinely have sound cards, and with the appropriate software our home computers can come alive with sights and sounds that change the way we experience singing birds.

What software is right for you? Because the availability of software can change rapidly, I can make no guarantee that what is available as I write this will be available by the time these words are in print. So let me begin with the surest of bets, that the software now available from the venerable Bioacoustics Research Program at the Cornell Laboratory of Ornithology will remain available long into the future.

The software from Cornell University is called "Raven." This marvelous program runs on both Macs and PCs and was designed by researchers who have spent decades devising new ways to record and analyze animal sounds for their work. I love this advanced program that is designed for professional use by researchers, and I used it to produce all of the sonagrams in this book. Even better news, however, is that most readers of this book will be thoroughly happy with the simplified and far less expensive version of Raven that is now available. The cost of the simpler version is a small price to pay for Raven's ease of use and the world of joy that this program can bring. You can visit the

Raven Web site (www.birds.cornell.edu/Raven) and download a free trial version of either the advanced or simplified Raven. Go ahead, give Raven a try.

It's always nice to get a full working version of something for free, too, and there will always be free software programs available for graphing birdsongs. For the PC, one free yet powerful program called Sound Analysis Pro is designed for researchers (http://ofer.sci.ccny.cuny.edu/html/body_sound_analysis.html). A simpler PC program is Syrinx (www.syrinxpc.com). One for the Mac is WildSpectra, available from a professor at the University of North Carolina (www.unc.edu/~rhwiley/wildspectra). A host of other "freeware" is available, too (for example, see http://cetus.pmel.noaa.gov/Bioacoustics.html). Some of this software is excellent and easy to use, but most of it will not have the institutional backing and support that Cornell supplies for Raven. As a result, using some of this other software might be cash-free but somewhat more expensive in time, and perhaps exasperation. "You get what you pay for," says the adage.

There's not much more I can tell you. Take your recording and put it into the player, or put the CD into the CD player. Use a standard audio cable to run from the "line-out" of the player to the "line-in" of the sound card on the computer. Or use the CD player built into your computer. Start your software program. Start your player. And watch the world of birdsong dance before your eyes.

Many questions that you hadn't even thought of asking before reading this book are now not only "askable," but answerable. Is that the same robin or thrush or ovenbird that was singing from those bushes in your backyard last year? Use your simple tape-recording setup to capture some songs in successive years and then compare the songs — for many songbirds (though not all), different songs mean different individuals. How many different songs does that song sparrow or cardinal or titmouse have? Tape-record him or her for a little while and then start printing out a few sonagrams until he seems to have nothing new to say — you now know his song repertoire.

It was in using these simple techniques that I learned how to distinguish male and female barred owls, how to hear the magic in the songs of hermit thrushes and wood thrushes. Indeed, every account in this book contains answers that were found by the simple processes of tape-recording and then studying the sonagrams.

I can't help but feel a bit exposed at this point, now that all of my secrets are revealed. There's no longer any mystique to what I have done all these years. Anyone can do this kind of stuff. And anyone should.

Taxonomic List of Species Names

THIS LIST GROUPS THE SPECIES that are a focus in the book according to their scientific classification — order, family, genus, and species. Knowing relationships among these birds is important for appreciating how similar or different they are to each other. The eastern and western wood-pewees are in the same genus, for example, and within the last few million years they evolved from a common ancestor; knowing their relationship causes one to reflect on how little their appearance has changed since their common ancestor and also on how much their songs have changed. The chipping and Brewer's sparrows are also closely related in the same genus, and not surprisingly both do remarkable things at dawn; that makes one wonder what the field sparrow, also in the same genus, does at dawn (also amazing things, I assure you, worth going out and listening to them). The snipe and woodcock are not in the same genus but are in the same family, meaning that these two birds had a common ancestor farther back in time, perhaps ten million years ago; knowing their relationship makes it interesting to reflect on how one came to sing with its tail and the other with its wings.

Class Aves

Order Gaviiformes

FAMILY GAVIIDAE
>Common loon, *Gavia immer*

Order Procellariiformes

FAMILY PROCELLARIIDAE
>Sooty shearwater, *Puffinus griseus*

Order Charadriiformes

FAMILY SCOLOPACIDAE

Common snipe, *Gallinago gallinago*
American woodcock, *Scolopax minor*

Order Strigiformes

FAMILY STRIGIDAE

Barred owl, *Strix varia*

Order Caprimulgiformes

FAMILY CAPRIMULGIDAE

Whip-poor-will, *Caprimulgus vociferus*

Order Piciformes

FAMILY PICIDAE

Yellow-bellied sapsucker, *Sphyrapicus varius*
Downy woodpecker, *Picoides pubescens*
Hairy woodpecker, *Picoides villosus*

Order Passeriformes — the Suboscines

FAMILY TYRANNIDAE

Western wood-pewee, *Contopus sordidulus*
Eastern wood-pewee, *Contopus virens*
Alder flycatcher, *Empidonax alnorum*
Willow flycatcher, *Empidonax traillii*
Eastern phoebe, *Sayornis phoebe*

FAMILY COTINGIDAE

Three-wattled bellbird, *Procnias tricarunculata*
Bare-throated bellbird, *Procnias nudicollis*

Order Passeriformes — the "Songbirds"

FAMILY VIREONIDAE

Red-eyed vireo, *Vireo olivaceus*

FAMILY CORVIDAE

Blue jay, *Cyanocitta cristata*

FAMILY PARIDAE

Black-capped chickadee, *Poecile atricapillus*

Tufted titmouse, *Baeolophus bicolor*

FAMILY TROGLODYTIDAE

Canyon wren, *Catherpes mexicanus*

Carolina wren, *Thryothorus ludovicianus*

Bewick's wren, *Thryomanes bewickii*

Winter wren, *Troglodytes troglodytes*

Sedge wren, *Cistothorus platensis*

Marsh wren, *Cistothorus palustris*

FAMILY TURDIDAE

Eastern bluebird, *Sialia sialis*

Hermit thrush, *Catharus guttatus*

Wood thrush, *Hylocichla mustelina*

Mountain robin, *Turdus plebejus*

White-throated robin, *Turdus assimilis*

American robin, *Turdus migratorius*

FAMILY MIMIDAE

Northern mockingbird, *Mimus polyglottos*

Sage thrasher, *Oreoscoptes montanus*

Brown thrasher, *Toxostoma rufum*

FAMILY PARULIDAE

Chestnut-sided warbler, *Dendroica pensylvanica*

Common yellowthroat, *Geothlypis trichas*

FAMILY EMBERIZIDAE

Spotted towhee, *Pipilo maculatus*

Eastern towhee, *Pipilo erythrophthalmus*

Bachman's sparrow, *Aimophila aestivalis*

Chipping sparrow, *Spizella passerina*

Brewer's sparrow, *Spizella breweri*

Field sparrow, *Spizella pusilla*

Fox sparrow, *Passerella iliaca*

Song sparrow, *Melospiza melodia*
White-throated sparrow, *Zonotrichia albicollis*
White-crowned sparrow, *Zonotrichia leucophrys*

FAMILY CARDINALIDAE

Northern cardinal, *Cardinalis cardinalis*

FAMILY ICTERIDAE

Chopi blackbird, *Gnorimospar chopi*

Notes and Bibliography

YEARNING TO KNOW HOW ANIMALS, and especially birds, communicate has been a passion for many, and their studies fill volumes. Some general treatises on how animals communicate are those by Sebeok (1977), Smith (1977) —a favorite of mine, Hauser (1996), Bradbury and Vehrencamp (1998), Hopp, Owen, and Evans (1998), Owings and Morton (1998), and Hauser and Konishi (1999). But there's nothing quite like an entire book on birds themselves. Of these, some are written more for a general audience, such as those by Armstrong (1963), Hartshorne (1973), and Jellis (1977), and especially the recent ones by Catchpole and Slater (1995) and by Marler and Slabberkorn (2004). More technical are the volumes by Greenewalt (1968), Hinde (1969), and Thorpe (1961) in the 1960s; by Thielcke (1970) in the 1970s; and two volumes I helped edit in the 1980s (Kroodsma and Miller, 1982). Two more edited volumes were published in the 1990s, summarizing the latest thinking by specialists, one by McGregor (1992) and one that I again helped with (Kroodsma and Miller, 1996). Particularly intriguing is a recent book by Pepperberg (1999), in which she chronicles her studies with Alex, an African gray parrot, showing how intelligent this creature is.

To learn more about birdsongs, where in this heap of books should a beginner go? If I were starting out, I think the two most useful, general reference books would be the relatively recent book by Catchpole and Slater and the most up-to-date volume by Marler and Slabberkorn. For the sheer joy of listening to birds, and for a perspective that makes many scientists squirm, consult my favorite philosopher-naturalist, Charles Hartshorne. For lots of good solid natural history, see Armstrong or Thorpe. For the most technical of details, see the edited volumes, where each expert has his or her say. For anything that you ever wanted to know about a particular species in North America, whether it be about song or molt or migration or *anything*, consult the *Birds of North America* series published by the Academy of Natural

Sciences and the American Ornithologists' Union, a series that I consulted for each species mentioned in the text. Finally, all modesty aside, if you want a "good read" about birdsongs and the people who are obsessed with them, see the recent book by Don Stap (2005).

Notes

PAGE

1. BEGINNINGS

HEARING AND SEEING BIRD SONGS
9 **four different fox sparrows** R. M. Zink and J. D. Weckstein. 2003.

THE BEWICK'S WREN
12 **songbirds and their songs** Most influential were R. A. Hinde, ed. 1969; P. Marler and M. Tamura. 1962, 1964.
13 **parabolic reflector** For shorthand, I use the term "parabola" to mean "a parabolic reflector equipped with a microphone." Technically, the reflector is shaped like a parabola so that all incoming sound is reflected back to the reflector's focal point, where the microphone is placed. More fully, I'd use "parabola" to refer to the shape of the reflector's curve, "parabolic reflector" to refer to the reflecting dish itself, and "parabolic microphone" to refer to reflector plus microphone.
bands on their legs As a scientist, I need federal and state permits for many of my activities, because these birds are protected by law. Permits are required for catching birds in nets and banding them, for example, and for taking baby birds and raising them for serious study in the laboratory. In addition, a code of ethics guides not only birders but scientists, and the code is promoted by the American Birding Association (see http://www.americanbirding.org/abaethics.htm).
21 **almost identical song repertoires** D. E. Kroodsma. 1974.
across their geographic range D. E. Kroodsma. 1985b.
that of the Bewick's wren contracted E. D. Kennedy and D. W. White. 1996.

THE AMERICAN ROBIN
23 **Yes, the robin** Bird names can be confusing. When I say "robin," I clearly refer to the American robin, whose scientific name is *Turdus migratorius*. There is a "robin" in the Old World, too, the European robin (*Erithacus*

rubecula), but the close relative of our American robin in Europe is the Eurasian blackbird (*Turdus merula*), not the European robin. How about those "four-and-twenty blackbirds baked in a pie"? Those aren't "true" blackbirds, as in the New World family Icteridae (e.g., the red-winged blackbird, *Agelaius phoeniceus*), but instead the same all-dark robin the British call a blackbird. How about "Morning has broken like the first morning, blackbird has spoken like the first bird"? You guessed it— British. The Eurasian blackbird of the Old World is one of the first singers in the morning, just like its relative the American robin is in the New World. The word "flycatcher" can also confuse. In the New World there are "tyrant flycatchers," family Tyrannidae, members of the "non-songbird" (suboscine) group of the order Passeriformes; there are flycatchers in the Old World, too, but they're songbirds, closely related to thrushes, and they learn their songs. How about "ovenbirds"? The ovenbird that breeds in North America is a "wood-warbler," a songbird in the family Parulidae; the many ovenbird species that occur throughout South America are not songbirds, but instead are suboscines, close relatives of flycatchers.

23 **"loud, liquid song"** National Geographic Society. 1987.
"a clear caroling" R. T. Peterson. 1991.

24 **expert accounts about robin song** R. Sallabanks and F. C. James. 1999; C. M. Sousa. 1999.

25 **Sibley's guide** D. A. Sibley. 2000.

28 **A. C. Bent's classic** A. C. Bent. 1949.
both voice boxes How the two voice boxes coordinate to produce birdsong is remarkable, as reviewed in a series of articles by Rod Suthers, such as R. A. Suthers. 1999. See also accounts in this book on brown thrashers (p. 191) and northern cardinals (p. 357).

34 **computer-assisted analyses** C. M. Sousa. 1999.
infamous "hawk alarm" P. Marler. 1955.

35 **so high-pitched** G. M. Klump, E. Kretzschmar, and E. Curio. 1986.

GOOD LISTENING, GOOD QUESTIONS, THIS BOOK

37 **inborn, as in most birds** P. Marler and S. Hope. 2004.
raising some baby robins Steve Johnson, a graduate student at the University of Massachusetts, has now done this very project. He finds that robins seem to invent (or improvise) most of their caroled phrases but that they imitate perhaps a quarter of them or so from other birds around them.
lengthy discourses D. A. Spector. 1994.

39 **songbirds in forests** E. Morton. 1975; R. H. Wiley. 1991.

40 **whether or not the birds migrate** For example, D. E. Kroodsma. 1977a.

2. HOW SONGS DEVELOP

THE WHITE-CROWNED SPARROW

46 **read so much about** For example, M. C. Baker. 1975; M. C. Baker, D. B. Thompson, G. L. Sherman, M. A. Cunningham, and D. F. Tomback. 1982.

48 **"relationship between song 'dialects'"** P. Marler and M. Tamura. 1962. See also P. Marler and M. Tamura. 1964.

a simple speculation Discussed by F. Nottebohm. 1969.

50 **To sing properly** P. Marler. 1970.

The ability to learn Ibid.; M. A. Cunningham and M. C. Baker. 1983.

Field studies had shown B. D. Blanchard. 1941.

Marler summed it this way P. Marler. 1970.

Luis Baptista concurred L. F. Baptista. 1975.

young birds can learn after 50 days M. A. Cunningham and M. C. Baker. 1983; L. F. Baptista and L. Petrinovich. 1984.

anecdotes from wild birds L. F. Baptista and L. Petrinovich. 1984.

51 **Some evidence supported these ideas** For example, M. C. Baker. 1983.

Hints at the answer For example, L. F. Baptista and M. L. Morton. 1982.

The needed field work M. C. Baker and L. R. Mewaldt. 1978.

52 **counterreply by Baker and Mewaldt** The original paper: ibid. A counter-charge was filed by L. Petrinovich, T. Patterson, and L. F. Baptista. 1981, which in turn was responded to by M. C. Baker and L. R. Mewaldt. 1981.

53 **beginning new song dialects** M. C. Baker. 1975.

Yes, according to Baker M. C. Baker, D. B. Thompson, G. L. Sherman, M. A. Cunningham, and D. F. Tomback. 1982.

No they don't R. M. Zink and G. F. Barrowclough. 1984.

Yes they do! M. C. Baker, A. E. M. Baker, M. A. Cunningham, D. B. Thompson, and D. F. Tomback. 1984.

and yet another pair of scientists D. J. Hafner and K. E. Petersen. 1985.

a summary paper I wrote for *Current Ornithology* D. E. Kroodsma, M. C. Baker, L. F. Baptista, and L. Petrinovich. 1985. In the same year a major debate on this issue was published in M. C. Baker and M. A. Cunningham. 1985.

new study of white-crown genetics E. A. MacDougall-Shackleton and S. A. MacDougall-Shackleton. 2001.

a different race of the white-crown The full Latin name of the Nuttall race is *Zonotrichia leucophrys nuttalli*, that of the mountain white-crown

Zonotrichia leucophrys oriantha. They are two of the four subspecies of white-crowned sparrows found in North America, the other two being *Z. l. gambeli* from Oregon north to Alaska, and *Z. l. leucophrys* across boreal Canada to the Atlantic. These other races are equally fascinating, but the northern two lack the small dialects.

54 **it is answers we want** Still another study deserves mention but not major focus. In Alberta, a population of white-crowns exists in which males sing one of two different songs, i.e., the dialect consists of two songs, not one. Females in this population appear to choose males irrespective of their songs: a father's song appears not to influence which type of singer a young female chooses, and females often choose males with different songs in successive years. G. Chilton, M. R. Lein, and L. F. Baptista. 1990.

THE SONG SPARROW

56 **Margaret Morse Nice** M. M. Nice. 1943.

vesper sparrows D. E. Kroodsma. 1972.

house wrens D. E. Kroodsma. 1973.

the conclusion for the song sparrow The evidence we accumulated for the song sparrows lies in a box somewhere in my office, and we never published our findings.

57 **I'd find a singing male song sparrow** Again, I want to remind the reader that this kind of work requires both federal and state permits.

by their songs alone (yes) D. E. Kroodsma. 1976. See also M. A. Harris and R. E. Lemon. 1976; P. K. Stoddard, M. D. Beecher, C. L. Horning, and M. S. Willis. 1990.

learn their songs (again yes) D. E. Kroodsma. 1977b.

work of Mike Beecher M. D. Beecher, S. E. Campbell, and P. K. Stoddard. 1994.

62 **Here he ranges** P. A. Arcese. 1987, 1989.

learns his final songs As determined in captive-reared sparrows: J. C. Nordby, S. E. Campbell, and M. D. Beecher. 2001.

fixed for life J. C. Nordby, S. E. Campbell, and M. D. Beecher. 2002.

63 **Overall, those adult tutors** Actual numbers are 3.01 versus 1.21.

memorizes more than the eight or nine songs As a young male practices his songs, it is clear that he "overproduces," that is, practices more songs than he will eventually retain in his repertoire. Up until the last minute, then, he has choices and can choose to retain songs that best match those being used by his neighbors. See P. Marler and S. Peters. 1982; P. Marler and D. Nelson. 1992.

64 **first set of such experiments** M. D. Beecher, P. K. Stoddard, S. E. Campbell, and C. L. Horning. 1996.

65 **choices started to make sense** M. D. Beecher, S. E. Campbell, J. M. Burt, C. E. Hill, and J. C. Nordby. 2000.

further playback experiments J. M. Burt, S. E. Campbell, and M. D. Beecher. 2001.

66 **reason for the song-learning strategies** M. D. Beecher, J. C. Nordby, S. E. Campbell, J. M. Burt, C. E. Hill, and A. L. O'Loghlen. 1997.

males impress females when they share songs Idea originally developed by S. I. Rothstein and R. C. Fleischer. 1987.

Those who share songs live longer M. D. Beecher, S. E. Campbell, and J. C. Nordby. 2000.

67 **those that we know in the East** M. M. Nice. 1943; D. J. Borror. 1965; M. A. Harris and R. E. Lemon. 1972.

These west-east differences D. E. Kroodsma. 1999.

THE NORTHERN MOCKINGBIRD

73 **a quarter of a male's songs** K. C. Derrickson. 1987.

Peter Merritt found P. G. Merritt. 1985.

according to Joyce Wildenthal J. L. Wildenthal. 1965.

Kim Derrickson found J. L. Wildenthal. 1965; K. C. Derrickson. 1987.

74 **only a bachelor** K. C. Derrickson and R. Breitwisch. 1992.

75 **A friend has speculated** F. Nottebohm. 1972.

the mocker's contentious spirit J. R. Baylis. 1982.

TYRANT FLYCATCHERS—ALDER AND WILLOW FLYCATCHERS, EASTERN PHOEBE

80 **dialects among suboscines** W. E. Lanyon. 1978; R. B. Payne and P. Budde. 1979.

work in the 1960s R. C. Stein. 1963.

officially recognized among ornithologists The official decisions are made by a committee of the American Ornithologists' Union, the premier professional organization for ornithologists in North America. See their conclusion about these two flycatchers in American Ornithologists' Union. 1973.

If songs of suboscines W. E. Lanyon. 1969; R. B. Payne. 1986.

81 **1,100 suboscine species** B. L. Monroe, Jr., and C. G. Sibley. 1993.

I envision a simple experiment This story published in D. E. Kroodsma. 1984.

respond in one of two ways A third possibility, highly unusual among song-birds, is for the isolated bird to "improvise," or make up, a large repertoire of songs that are surprisingly "normal." For a detailed account of this style of song development, see the account on the sedge wren (p. 102).

85 **a little hormone boost** How hormones affect singing is an extensive field of study. Briefly, lengthening days in the spring increase the secretion of testosterone in male birds, which then causes them to sing. If a female songbird is given testosterone, she will attempt to sing, too, perhaps after a week to 10 days. What she "sings" is often unrecognizable, however, but not in these female phoebes, which sang perfectly normal songs.

more to this phoebe story D. E. Kroodsma. 1985a.

86 **songs inborn and not influenced** D. E. Kroodsma. 1989a.

87 **removing the cochlea from the inner ear** D. E. Kroodsma and M. Konishi. 1991.

88 **1997 monograph** M. L. Isler, P. R. Isler, and B. M. Whitney. 1997.

songs of those populations differ J. A. Sedgwick. 2001.

Several new suboscine and non-songbird species For example, K. J. Zimmer, A. Whittaker, and D. C. Oren. 2001.

Ridgely and Tudor's Volume II R. S. Ridgely and G. Tudor. 1994.

89 **We need to know about them** D. E. Kroodsma, J. M. E. Vielliard, and F. G. Stiles. 1996.

THE THREE-WATTLED BELLBIRD

89 **the CD Greg Budney has given us** D. L. Ross, Jr., and B. M. Whitney. 1995.

field guide to birds of Costa Rica F. G. Stiles and A. F. Skutch. 1989.

Barbara and David Snow had written D. W. Snow. 1973; B. K. Snow. 1977.

92 **the Traill's flycatcher into the willow and alder** R. C. Stein. 1963.

the western flycatcher into the Pacific coast and cordilleran American Ornithologists' Union. 1998.

98 **as with indigo buntings** R. B. Payne. 1996.

102 **Among hummingbirds** D. Snow. 1968; S. L. L. Gaunt, L. F. Baptista, J. E. Sánchez, and D. Hernandez. 1994.

Or consider the humpback whale K. Payne, P. Tyack, and R. Payne. 1983.

forcing the youngsters to play catchup Not unlike the explanation proposed by K. Aoki. 1989.

the way dialects change in humans W. Labov. 1994.

What next? For further reading on bellbirds, see D. Stap. 2000.

103 **Jerry's marsh wren work** J. Verner. 1976.

105 **"short-billed marsh wren"** The name change was made official in American Ornithologists' Union. 1983.

106 **It is my job to analyze** For research on sedge and marsh wrens, Roberta Pickert was an invaluable assistant, the "my" and "I" in the text more accurately being "our" and "we."

109 **I'm home free** Those were the "olden days." Such an approach would now be impossible, especially given the heightened security after 9/11.

110 **A friend bands 10 adults** J. T. Burns. 1982.

In Michigan, too References provided in J. Herkert, D. E. Kroodsma, and J. P. Gibbs. 2001.

111 **Each song is a snowflake** These field and laboratory studies published in D. E. Kroodsma and J. Verner. 1978.

114 **The results confirm what we had found** D. E. Kroodsma, W.-c. Liu, E. Goodwin, and P. A. Bedell. 1999.

I soon fly to Brazil Costa Rica and Brazil studies published in D. E. Kroodsma, J. Sánchez, D. W. Stemple, E. Goodwin, M. L. da Silva, and J. M. E. Vielliard. 1999.

then to the Falkland Islands D. E. Kroodsma, R. W. Woods, and E. A. Goodwin. 2002.

For the Mérida wren D. E. Kroodsma, K. Wilda, V. Salas, and R. Muradian. 2001.

116 **"the comparative method"** J. Felsenstein. 1985.

3. DIALECTS: HOW AND WHY SONGS VARY FROM PLACE TO PLACE

THE GREAT MARSH WREN DIVIDE

121 **in isolation they slowly transformed** The process of species formation may have begun well before the Pleistocene, but it is believed that the Pleistocene completed the speciation process. See J. Klicka and R. M. Zink. 1999.

123 **What he described for his marsh wrens** See J. Verner. 1976.

125 **how these eastern wrens learn their songs** For example, D. E. Kroodsma. 1979; D. E. Kroodsma and R. Pickert. 1980, 1984.

127 **and impressing his listeners** Survey of marsh wren singing from Illinois, North Carolina, New York, Washington, and California published in D. E. Kroodsma and J. Verner. 1987.

128 **Lots.** R. A. Canady, D. E. Kroodsma, and F. Nottebohm. 1984; D. E. Kroodsma and R. A. Canady. 1985.

132 **The analyses soon confirm** D. E. Kroodsma. 1989b.

133 **western male's courting center** In an attempt to attract a female, a male marsh wren builds a number of nests in a relatively small area of the marsh; he spends most of his time in that "courting center," singing and inviting females to nest there.

134 **American Ornithologists' Union checklist committee** American Ornithologists' Union. 1998.

THE BLACK-CAPPED CHICKADEE

136 **the scales they play** A. G. Horn, M. L. Leonard, L. Ratcliffe, S. A. Shackleton, and R. G. Weisman. 1992.

137 **the strangest assortment of whistled songs** You can read all the gory details of this experiment in D. E. Kroodsma, D. J. Albano, P. W. Houlihan, and J. A. Wells. 1995.

a most remarkable article A. M. Bagg. 1958.

140 **terrorizing Vineyard citizens** As told in D. E. Kroodsma. 1996.

141 **invaded the island in force** D. Stap. 1995.

143 **"a level, desolate moor"** P. W. Dunwiddie. 1994.

Such movements are well known As summarized in the source of all knowledge about chickadees: S. M. Smith. 1993; also S. M. Smith. 1991.

144 **Does the female somehow enforce** Females listen to the males and make mating decisions based on what they hear, and males signal their aggression by whether they match the pitch or timing of neighbors, as detailed in K. A. Otter, L. Ratcliffe, M. Njegovan, and J. Fotheringham. 2002; D. J. Mennill, L. M. Ratcliffe, and P. T. Boag. 2002.

THE CHESTNUT-SIDED WARBLER

151 **a friend published a paper** M. R. Lein. 1978.

like several other species M. S. Ficken and R. W. Ficken. 1967; D. H. Morse. 1967, 1970.

152 **all the recordings for these two species** Results of this initial study: D. E. Kroodsma. 1981.

played songs to territorial males D. E. Kroodsma, W. R. Meservey, A. L. Whitlock, and W. M. Vander Haegen. 1984.

raised baby warblers D. E. Kroodsma. 1988; D. A. Spector, L. K. McKim, and D. E. Kroodsma. 1989.

152 **the Grace's warbler** C. A. Staicer. 1989.

the Caribbean Adelaide's warbler C. A. Staicer. 1996a, 1996b.

the golden-winged warbler R. T. Highsmith. 1989.

the yellow warbler D. A. Spector. 1991, 1992.

the prairie warbler P. W. Houlihan. 2000.

endangered golden-cheeked warbler J. S. Bolsinger. 2000.

year of the chestnut-sided warbler D. E. Kroodsma, R. C. Bereson, B. E. Byers, and E. Minear. 1989.

learning far more about these birds B. E. Byers and D. E. Kroodsma. 1992; B. E. Byers. 1995, 1996a, 1996b.

155 **our banded birds** Each bird in our studies is usually banded with an aluminum band and two colored bands, these bands combined in such a way that we can uniquely band hundreds of different warblers and later identify them by simply studying their legs through the binoculars.

156 **Bruce's latest surprise** B. E. Byers, H. L. Mays, I. R. K. Stewart, and D. F. Westneat. 2004.

TRAVELS WITH TOWHEES, EASTERN AND SPOTTED

158 **in 1969, a paper appeared** J. B. Roberts. 1969.

160 **sufficient to warrant a scientific publication** D. E. Kroodsma. 1971.

161 **similar, though far more thorough, study** Some of Dave's thesis would be published years later, in a joint publication with me: D. N. Ewert and D. E. Kroodsma. 1994.

164 **producing hybrids** J. D. Rising. 1983.

two species in North America American Ornithologists' Union. 1998.

THE TUFTED TITMOUSE

166 **what I know about them** Based primarily on two papers I've studied: D. J. Schroeder and R. H. Wiley. 1983a, 1983b.

"A whistled chant" R. T. Peterson. 1980.

167 **each male . . . has a history** Information on life history gleaned from T. C. Grubb, Jr., and V. V. Pravosudov. 1994.

174 **Do they all sing by the same rules** Here's a great place to start reading: P. K. Gaddis. 1983.

he has only three different songs Ibid.

175 **that's a different story** D. E. Kroodsma. 1999.

176 **my quest to find the titmice rules** I'll start by checking out an unpublished thesis: C. L. Coldren. 1992.

177 **"simplest and shortest of all our bird songs"** A. A. Saunders. 1951.

"one of the poorest of vocal efforts" R. T. Peterson. 1947.

THE BLUE JAY

179 **the most intelligent of birds** For example, see B. Heinrich. 1995, 2000.

blue jay sounds have been studied The two theses I found most useful were S. Conant. 1972; and S. M. Cohen. 1976.

***Birds of North America* account** K. A. Tarvin and G. E. Woolfenden. 1999.

183 **she on the nest, he perched nearby** Only when she is on the nest and he attending her can I know who is who in this pair.

185 **He'll do more of this** J. W. Hardy. 1961.

186 **April is a time of transition** K. A. Tarvin and G. E. Woolfenden. 1999.

the infamous hawk calls J. P. Hailman. 1990.

Some have heard the jay "sing" W. M. Tyler. 1946.

189 **I can hardly wait to get started** Much of what I would do is harmless and would not intrude on the life of the jays, and it is those activities that can provide much free fun for anyone who wants it. Other activities, however, such as using radio transmitters and raising baby jays, are regulated by state and federal law, and require permits. Still other activities, such as playing recorded calls to birds, may not be regulated by law, but a code of ethics guides anyone who would engage in these kinds of activities (see the code of the American Birding Association at http://www.american birding.org/abaethics.htm).

THE BROWN THRASHER

191 **Each male chipping sparrow** D. J. Borror. 1959a.

white-crowned sparrows P. Marler. 1970.

common yellowthroats D. J. Borror. 1967.

rufous-sided towhee D. J. Borror. 1959b.

song sparrows J. A. Mulligan. 1966.

A Bewick's wren D. E. Kroodsma. 1974.

a Carolina wren D. J. Borror. 1964.

northern mockingbirds J. L. Wildenthal. 1965.

193 **a new sound analyzer** C. D. Hopkins, M. Rossetto, and A. Lutjen. 1974.

I would eventually show D. E. Kroodsma. 1975.

196 **we did know a little more about this thrasher** Our results were published in D. E. Kroodsma and L. D. Parker. 1977.

196 **By some simple math** Using a statistical estimating procedure, I estimate that this male was capable of singing 2,992 different songs. This approach assumes, though, that the male has a stable repertoire of songs from which he draws, and that assumption almost certainly is violated, because the singing brown thrasher is probably improvising as he goes. Details of statistical method in Kroodsma, Woods, and Goodwin. 2002.

198 **The Methuselah of brown thrashers** J. F. Cavitt and C. A. Haas. 2000.

I was not alone in my fascination M. J. Boughey and N. S. Thompson. 1981.

199 **a team of researchers at Indiana University** R. A. Suthers. 1999.

THE SAGE THRASHER

206 **filling half of the night air** Later analyses of this four-hour record would show the following: For the first 30 minutes of the morning, average song length was 5 seconds, the time between songs 24 seconds. For the next seven half-hour periods, song length averaged 10, 13, 13, 14, 13, 15, and 16 seconds. Average time between songs for those seven half-hour periods was 13, 14, 15, 28, 18, 18, and 18 seconds. With song length approaching the length of time between songs, this sage thrasher was singing almost half of the time.

210 **as with European marsh warblers** F. Dowsett-Lemaire. 1979.

birds are more likely to move A. A. Dhondt and F. Adriaensen. 1994.

211 **new software program for my computer** K. Beeman. 1996.

213 **unmatched by anything I have ever heard** How does the sage thrasher compare to some other species? In 10 minutes, a sage thrasher makes over 1,000 decisions about what he will sing next. In 10 minutes, a tufted titmouse might change songs only once, thereby making only one decision. A Bachman's sparrow might make 25 decisions, a marsh wren at most 200, a northern mockingbird 250, a brown thrasher 400.

THE WINTER WREN

215 **"trying to burst [his] lungs"** S. Cramp, ed. 1988.

"Wonderful . . . charming . . ." A. C. Bent. 1948.

several males I have studied D. E. Kroodsma. 1980.

217 **Those details differ from place to place** As documented in England, too: C. K. Catchpole and A. Rowell. 1993.

my studies in the West D. E. Kroodsma. 1980.

223 **Birds throughout Asia and Europe** M. Kreutzer. 1974; D. E. Kroodsma and H. Momose. 1991.

224 **more about this wren** Good places to learn more about the private lives of this wren are in E. A. Armstrong. 1955; and S. J. Hejl, J. A. Holmes, and D. E. Kroodsma. 2002.

all wrens originated in the New World My hunch is now supported by some genetic data: S. V. Drovetski, R. M. Zink, S. Rohwer, I. V. Fadeev, E. V. Nesterov, I. Karagodin, E. A. Koblik, and Y. A. Red'kin. 2004.

also their call notes K. L. Garrett and J. L. Dunn. 1998; Hejl, Holmes, and Kroodsma. 2002.

THE BACHMAN'S SPARROW

225 **"everything you ever wanted to know" account** J. B. Dunning. 1993.

two birds recorded by Donald Borror D. J. Borror. 1971.

Another bird in Texas L. L. Wolf. 1977.

227 **Words cannot begin to describe or capture the essence of the performance** G. A. Dorsey. 1976.

228 **so I have read about them** J. B. Dunning. 1993.

one pioneering listener A. A. Saunders. 1951.

234 **Such is the case with many other songbirds** Studying the sequence with which males deliver their repertoire of songs has been a favorite topic of study. C. W. Dobson and R. E. Lemon. 1977b; R. E. Lemon, C. W. Dobson, and P. G. Clifton. 1993.

THE WOOD THRUSH

237 **on only three pitches** For the musically inclined: My musician friend Carrie Jones-Birch tells me that, in the first prelude, she hears an interval of a minor third between both the first pair (notes B and G#) and the second pair (notes E and C#) of whistles; as with the black-capped chickadee's *hey-sweetie,* the tune is truly transposed, with the musical interval remaining the same as the notes are sung on a different frequency. Carrie hears the three notes of the second prelude as notes D, A, and F#; again, the interval between the last two notes (A and F#) is a minor third.

239 **only 25 or so such preludes** C. L. Whitney. 1989.

242 **The overall effect** Much as I would have expected based on C. L. Whitney. 1985.

244 **used together 12 times** The astute reader may realize that the same information could be gleaned from the column totals. That's true, but because 151 songs are needed to get 150 transitions, the row and column totals will differ slightly. In a long sequence of 151 songs that begins with A4

and ends with B8, for example, A4 will occur as a preceding song (row totals) one more time than as a following song (column totals), and B8 will occur as a following song one more time than as a preceding song. This discrepancy does not occur with the other 149 songs in the sequence because each of them has both a preceding and following song.

250 **even for mockingbirds who mimic the cardinals** S. A. Zollinger and R. A. Suthers. 2004.

what I read about the wood thrushes C. L. Whitney. 1990.

THE HERMIT THRUSH

255 **"the grand climax of bird music"** Pages 235, 236 in F. S. Mathews. 1967.

John Burroughs said it best A. C. Bent. 1938.

Ooooooooh, holy holy P. Jones and T. M. Donovan. 1996.

256 **as summarized from the summer 2000 issue** J. W. Rivers and D. E. Kroodsma. 2000.

260 **The totals tell me** Row and column totals for a given song won't always add to the same number, because some songs begin a sequence and others end it. As a result, some songs will have no song preceding and some no song following. To chart 150 song sequences in two segments of my recordings, I actually had to identify 152 songs.

262 **all of these possible sequences** For his nonfavored sequences, I don't include the A → A, B → B types of sequences, that is, the sequences that he never sings. I'm more interested in which song he chooses from among the other eight that are available.

he raises the frequency on average Technically, these values are "medians," the middle values of a series of numbers. When I statistically compare the frequency changes in favored and nonfavored sequences, I find that the difference between 1780 Hz and 820 Hz is highly significant, far more different than I'd expect by chance (for the technically inclined: 2-tailed Mann-Whitney U-test, $p < 0.05$).

264 **my friend Carl Whitney was convinced** C. L. Whitney. 1981a, 1981b.

MUSIC TO OUR EARS

267 **"The Music of Nature and the Nature of Music"** P. M. Gray, B. Krause, J. Atema, R. Payne, C. Krumhansl, and L. Baptista. 2001.

268 **a 1956 article by Donald Borror** D. J. Borror and C. R. Reese. 1956.

the original article on this thrush A. H. Wing. 1951.

269 **one could do this with any series of notes** Also the opinion of T. Hold. 1970.

the authors debunked previous claims C. W. Dobson and R. E. Lemon. 1977a.

269 **the art of sand sculpture** L. B. Hunter. 1998.

270 **the simple effects in bird song** My favorite reading on this topic is in C. Hartshorne. 1973.

A melody can be retained R. Weisman, L. Ratcliffe, I. Johnsrude, and T. A. Hurly. 1990.

what a delightful variety of variations Example from C. Hartshorne. 1973.

272 **the essence of human music, too** P. Marler. 2000.

273 **bored with the monotony of a simple song** This is Charles Hartshorne's "monotony threshold principle." Although many scientists object to the freethinking, philosophical, anthropomorphic approach that Hartshorne took, he knew his bird songs worldwide far better than most scientists. C. Hartshorne. 1956.

274 **human-made noises intrude now almost everywhere** The pastor and naturalist Edward A. Armstrong felt deeply about this issue: "The preservation of areas where those yet unborn may be able to hear, study and enjoy natural sounds secure from interruption by machine noises is of vital importance but presents such difficulties, because amenity is subordinated to profit, that conservationists, in a world with its priorities astray, appear too daunted even to contemplate its possibility. Man's desecration of his environment by noise is the most pervasive and gratuitous of his many outrages against nature." E. A. Armstrong. 1969.

Consider four Java sparrows S. Watanabe and M. Nemoto. 1998; S. Watanabe and K. Sato. 1999.

even the non-song-learning pigeons D. Porter and A. Neuringer. 1984.

starlings have difficulty transposing S. H. Hulse and S. C. Page. 1988.

275 **even incorporating the music of nature** T. Hold. 1970.

It doesn't surprise me that human music J. J. Tramo. 2001.

naturalists who call themselves "trackers" J. Young. 2001.

THE AMERICAN WOODCOCK

276 **guides provide just a few hints** Quotes here taken from D. A. Sibley. 2000.

277 **kind gift given by Boris Veprintsev** Pioneering recordist in the former Soviet Union who built an impressive archive of Eurasian bird sounds, a copy of which now resides at Cornell's Library of Natural Sounds.

281 **don't recall reading anything about that** D. M. Keppie and R. M. J. Whiting. 1994.

THE WHIP-POOR-WILL

288 **would bore a listener with a highly monotonous performance** C. Hartshorne. 1956.

288 **fatigue the muscles of the syringes** M. M. Lambrechts. 1996.

290 **he must be taking time off to eat** If I had had an infrared night scope, I would no doubt have seen him sallying from his perch, catching moths from the air. C. L. Cink 2002.

296 **eclipsing the old record** L. d. K. Lawrence. 1954.

297 **most likely the light of the moon** Others have found that nightjars sing more in bright moonlight, too, as summarized by C. L. Cink 2002.
   the information she needs to choose her partner W. A. Searcy and K. Yasukawa. 1996.

THE RED-EYED VIREO

she chose to get to know one bird Read all about this adventure in L. d. K. Lawrence. 1954.

298 **Those who have studied these songs** R. E. Lemon. 1971; D. J. Borror. 1981.

299 **male red-eyed vireos can sing 30 to 40 songs** Ibid.

302 **believed to happen in a close relative** R. A. Bradley. 1981.
   a 1998 study E. S. Morton, J. Stutchbury, J. Howlett, and W. Piper. 1998.

303 **I'd catch the females** S. Runfeldt and J. C. Wingfield. 1985.

5. THE HOUR BEFORE THE DAWN

304 **remains largely an enigma** C. A. Staicer, D. A. Spector, and A. G. Horn. 1996.

THE EASTERN WOOD-PEWEE

305 **not a single one of his kind** J. P. McCarty. 1996.

306 **fewer *pee-ah-wee* songs are used** W. J. Smith. 1988.

307 **1943 monograph on pewees** W. Craig. 1943.

308 **Wallace Craig's survey** Ibid.

309 **the first one uttered from his roosting place** Ibid.

CHIPPING AND BREWER'S SPARROWS

318 **a dedicated graduate student** W.-c. Liu. 2001.

321 **jif jif jif jif . . .** Said no better than by D. A. Sibley. 2000.

325 **on these male contests that she depends** D. J. Mennill, L. M. Ratcliffe, and P. T. Boag. 2002.

THE EASTERN BLUEBIRD

Lawrence Zeleny rallied bluebird lovers L. Zeleny. 1977.

on the Internet As of 2004, the Web address is www.nabluebirdsociety.org.

326 **the way the naturalist Bent put it** A. C. Bent. 1949.

"Full of richness and sweetness" Ibid. p. 250.

A Guide to Bird Songs A. A. Saunders. 1951.

learned a little more in my reading Two very useful sources were D. C. Krieg. 1971; P. A. Gowaty and J. H. Plissner. 1998.

327 **"The vocal behavior . . . is poorly known"** P. A. Gowaty and J. H. Plissner.1998.

331 **Do his neighbors share that song?** After my bluebird experiences, I discovered an unpublished manuscript that had the answer to my question. In central Kentucky, neighboring males share very few songs out of their large song repertoires (up to 81 total songs documented for one male, but the sample was deemed incomplete). B. O. Huntsman and G. Ritchison. 2002.

333 **much more I need to hear and see** P. A. Gowaty and J. H. Plissner. 1998.

334 **DNA fingerprinting has revealed** History of these studies provided ibid.

6. SHE ALSO SINGS

THE BARRED OWL

336 ***Birds of North America* account for this owl** K. M. Mazur and P. C. James. 2000.

337 **"a raucous jumble of cackles"** C. F. Smith. 1975.

"an extremely loud chorus of howls" T. Bosakowski, R. Spelser, and J. Benzinger. 1987.

"most spectacular and thrilling" A. C. Bent. 1938.

probably the male hormones For example, see A. H. Miller. 1934.

a Peterson CD set R. T. Peterson. 1991.

339 ***Stokes Field Guide*** L. Elliott, D. Stokes, and L. Stokes. 1997.

343 **their "grotesque love-making"** E. H. Forbush. 1927.

the Library of Natural Sounds R. Dickinson. 1996. The Web site for the LNS is a must-visit, as it provides a wealth of information on bird sounds (http://birds.cornell.edu/macauleylibrary/).

Entering the building My fond memories describe the old building in which the collection was housed until 2002, not the spacious new building where the collection is now.

345 **"the most weird and uncouth sounds imaginable"** E. H. Forbush. 1927.

THE CAROLINA WREN

346 ***LIB-er-ty! LIB-er-ty! LIB-er-ty! LIB!*** is the patriotic American rendition. The British version lingers in some field guides: *tea-kettle tea-kettle tea-kettle.* Thanks to David Spector for this explanation.

350 **world-class songsters** The philosopher Charles Hartshorne ranked songsters from round the world, giving world-class status to many wrens in this genus. C. Hartshorne. 1973.

352 **more about breeding and sex** The amount of singing depends to some extent, too, on how much food is available. A male in Maryland who is supplied extra food during January will sing far more than his neighbors. E. S. Morton. 1982.

353 **To remind her mate that I'm here** A female who doesn't chatter is dead, Gene Morton tells me, because the male will attack and kill her. To a male, a bird who doesn't chatter is another male, his competitor and enemy. D. H. Owings and E. S. Morton. 1998.

355 **a Carolina wren of a different sort** Other listeners have heard what seems to be mimicry from the Carolina wren, to the extent that it has been called the "mocking wren." A. C. Bent. 1948.

she's in good form shortly after leaving the nest My friend Gene Morton raised a young female once, naming her "Peanut Butter." Peanut Butter never heard male song until she was 52 days old, when Gene played her one from a tape recorder; she immediately and perfectly responded with her female chatter. For other juicy tidbits on Carolina wren singing and biology, see T. M. Haggerty and E. S. Morton. 1995.

song-learning centers in the female P. M. Nealen and D. J. Perkel. 2000.

Further support for this idea E. A. Brenowitz and A. P. Arnold. 1985, 1986.

356 **Carry this idea one step further** D. E. Kroodsma and M. Konishi. 1991.

makes no difference to her Though which word we use does make a big difference to those of us who study birdsong, because the words guide our thoughts, and we become entangled in them. D. A. Spector. 1994.

THE NORTHERN CARDINAL

357 **mascot of the St. Louis sports teams** Yes, I know, the football team has now moved to Arizona, and the Rams have moved to St. Louis. Reality aside, my sports teams in St. Louis are still the Cardinals.

I try to recall some of the facts Lots of details and references in S. L. Halkin and S. U. Linville. 1999.

how rich in carotenoid pigments his food was K. J. McGraw, G. E. Hill, R. Stradi, and R. S. Parker. 2001.

361 **meddling scientists prying into the inner workings** For the details of how a number of species use their two voice boxes to produce songs, see R. A. Suthers. 1999.

364 **Among males of some species** D. Todt and H. Hultsch. 1996.

APPENDIX I: BIRD SOUNDS ON THE COMPACT DISC

372 **A superb songster** F. G. Stiles and A. F. Skutch. 1989.

398 **Listen to these owls** Cornell Laboratory of Ornithology and Interactive Media. 1991.

   Four different recordings L. Elliott, D. Stokes, and L. Stokes. 1997.

APPENDIX II: TECHNIQUES

403 **Perhaps try this system** I was working with swamp sparrows in a New York marsh and needed a simple system to get adequate recordings without the high risk of losing expensive equipment when I (all too routinely) took a dunking. This "disposable" system captured the songs well.

404 **the system I now use** All of the equipment mentioned here is available through my favorite distributor, Stith Recording Services, in Ithaca, New York. Located near the Cornell Laboratory of Ornithology, it works closely with the Library of Natural Sounds to offer the best and most reliable gear for people like us. Their Web site, as of 2004, is www .stith-recording.com.

405 **parabolas are ineffective below frequencies** D. C. Wickstrom. 1982.

Bibliography

American Ornithologists' Union. 1973. Thirty-second supplement to the American Ornithologists' Union check-list of North American birds. *Auk* 90: 411–419.

———. 1983. *Check-list of North American Birds,* 6th ed. Washington, D.C.: American Ornithologists' Union.

———. 1998. *Check-list of North American Birds,* 7th ed. Washington, D.C.: American Ornithologists' Union.

Aoki, K. 1989. A sexual-selection model for the evolution of imitative learning of song in polygynous birds. *American Naturalist* 134: 599–612.

Arcese, P. A. 1987. Age, intrusion pressure and defence against floaters by territorial male song sparrows. *Animal Behaviour* 35: 773–784.

———. 1989. Intrasexual competition, mating system and natal dispersal in song sparrows. *Animal Behaviour* 38: 958–979.

Armstrong, E. A. 1955. *The Wren.* London: Collins.

———. 1963. *A Study of Bird Song.* London: Oxford University Press.

———. 1969. Aspects of the evolution of man's appreciation of bird song. In

Bird Vocalizations (ed. by Hinde, R. A.), pp. 343–381. Cambridge: Cambridge University Press.

Bagg, A. M. 1958. A variant form of the chickadee's "fee-bee" call. *Bulletin of the Massachusetts Audubon Society* 43: 9.

Baker, M. C. 1975. Song dialects and genetic differences in white-crowned sparrows (*Zonotrichia leucophrys*). *Evolution* 29: 226–241.

———. 1983. The behavioral response of female Nuttall's white-crowned sparrows to male song of natal and alien dialects. *Behavioral Ecology and Sociobiology* 12: 309–315.

Baker, M. C., A. E. M. Baker, M. A. Cunningham, D. B. Thompson, and D. F. Tomback. 1984. Reply to "Allozymes and song dialects: a reassessment." *Evolution* 38: 449–451.

Baker, M. C., and M. A. Cunningham. 1985. The biology of bird-song dialects. *The Behavioral and Brain Sciences* 8: 85–133.

Baker, M. C., and L. R. Mewaldt. 1978. Song dialects as barriers to dispersal in white-crowned sparrows (*Zonotrichia leucophrys nuttalli*). *Evolution* 32: 712–722.

———. 1981. Response to "Song dialects as barriers to dispersal: a re-evaluation." *Evolution* 35: 189–190.

Baker, M. C., D. B. Thompson, G. L. Sherman, M. A. Cunningham, and D. F. Tomback. 1982. Allozyme frequencies in a linear series of song dialect populations. *Evolution* 36: 1020–1029.

Baptista, L. F. 1975. Song dialects and demes in sedentary populations of the white-crowned sparrow (*Zonotrichia leucophrys nuttalli*). *University of California Publications in Zoology* 105: 1–52.

Baptista, L. F., and M. L. Morton. 1982. Song dialects and mate selection in montane white-crowned sparrows. *Auk* 99: 537–547.

Baptista, L. F., and L. Petrinovich. 1984. Social interaction, sensitive phases and the song template hypothesis in the white-crowned sparrow. *Animal Behaviour* 32: 172–181.

Baylis, J. R. 1982. Avian vocal mimicry: its function and evolution. In *Acoustic Communication in Birds. Vol. 2* (ed. by Kroodsma, D. E., and E. H. Miller), pp. 51–83. New York: Academic Press.

Beecher, M. D., S. E. Campbell, J. M. Burt, C. E. Hill, and J. C. Nordby. 2000. Song-type matching between neighbouring song sparrows. *Animal Behaviour* 59: 29–37.

Beecher, M. D., S. E. Campbell, and J. C. Nordby. 2000. Territory tenure in song sparrows is related to song sharing with neighbours, but not to repertoire size. *Animal Behaviour* 59: 29–37.

Beecher, M. D., S. E. Campbell, and P. K. Stoddard. 1994. Correlation of song learning and territory establishment strategies in the song sparrow. *Proceedings of the National Academy of Sciences, USA* 91: 1450–1454.

Beecher, M. D., J. C. Nordby, S. E. Campbell, J. M. Burt, C. E. Hill, and A. L. O'Loghlen. 1997. What is the function of song learning in songbirds? In *Perspectives in Ethology* (ed. by Owings, D. H., M. D. Beecher, and N. S. Thompson), pp. 77–97. New York: Plenum Press.

Beecher, M. D., P. K. Stoddard, S. E. Campbell, and C. L. Horning. 1996. Repertoire matching between neighbouring song sparrows. *Animal Behaviour* 51: 917–923.

Beeman, K. 1996. *SIGNAL V3.0 User's Guide (IBM PC)*. Belmont, Massachusetts: Engineering Design.

Bent, A. C. 1938. Life histories of North American birds of prey. Washington, D.C.: *Smithsonian Institution United States National Bulletin* 170.

———. 1948. Life histories of North American nuthatches, wrens, thrashers, and their allies. Washington, D.C.: *Smithsonian Institution United States National Bulletin* 175.

———. 1949. Life histories of North American thrushes, kinglets, and their allies. Washington, D.C.: *Smithsonian Institution United States National Museum Bulletin* 196.

Blanchard, B. D. 1941. The white-crowned sparrows (*Zonotrichia leucophrys*) of the Pacific seaboard: environment and annual cycle. *University of California Publications in Zoology* 46: 1–178.

Bolsinger, J. S. 2000. Use of two song categories by golden-cheeked warblers. *Condor* 102: 539–552.

Borror, D. J. 1959a. Songs of the chipping sparrow. *Ohio Journal of Science* 59: 347–356.

———. 1959b. Variation in the songs of the rufous-sided towhee. *Wilson Bulletin* 71: 54–72.

———. 1964. Songs of the thrushes (Turdidae), wrens (Troglodytidae), and mockingbirds (Mimidae) of eastern North America. *Ohio Journal of Science* 64: 195–207.

———. 1965. Song variation in Maine song sparrows. *Wilson Bulletin* 77: 5–37.

———. 1967. Song of the yellowthroat. *The Living Bird* 6: 141–161.

———. 1971. Songs of *Aimophila* sparrows occurring in the United States. *Wilson Bulletin* 83: 132–151.

———. 1981. The songs and singing behavior of the red-eyed vireo. *Condor* 83: 217–228.

Borror, D. J., and C. R. Reese. 1956. Vocal gymnastics in wood thrush songs. *Ohio Journal of Science* 56: 177–182.

Bosakowski, T., R. Spelser, and J. Benzinger. 1987. Distribution, density, and habitat relationships of the barred owl in northern New Jersey. In *Biology and Conservation of Northern Forest Owls: Symposium Proceedings, 1987 Feb. 3–7, Winnipeg, Manitoba* (ed. by Nero, R. W., R. J. Clark, R. J. Knapton, and R. H. Hamre), pp. 135–143. Fort Collins, Colorado: General Technical Report RM-142, U.S. Department of Agriculture, Forest Service, Rocky Mountain Forest and Range Experiment Station.

Boughey, M. J., and N. S. Thompson. 1981. Song variety in the brown thrasher (*Toxostoma rufum*). *Zeitschrift für Tierpsychologie* 56: 47–58.

Bradbury, J. W., and S. L. Vehrencamp. 1998. *Principles of Animal Communication.* Sunderland, Massachusetts: Sinauer Associates, Inc.

Bradley, R. A. 1981. Song variation within a population of white-eyed vireos (*Vireo griseus*). *Auk* 98: 80–87.

Brenowitz, E. A., and A. P. Arnold. 1985. Lack of sexual dimorphism in steroid accumulation in vocal control brain regions of duetting song birds. *Brain Research* 344: 172–175.

———. 1986. Interspecific comparisons of the size of neural song control regions and song complexity in duetting birds: evolutionary implications. *Journal of Neuroscience* 6: 2875–2879.

Burns, J. T. 1982. Nests, territories, and reproduction of sedge wrens (*Cistothorus platensis*). *Wilson Bulletin* 94: 338–349.

Burt, J. M., S. E. Campbell, and M. D. Beecher. 2001. Song type matching as threat: a test using interactive playback. *Animal Behaviour* 62: 1163–1170.

Byers, B. E. 1995. Song types, repertoires and song variability in a population of chestnut-sided warblers. *Condor* 97: 390–401.

———. 1996a. Geographic variation of song form within and among chestnut-sided warbler populations. *Auk* 113: 288–299.

———. 1996b. Messages encoded in the songs of chestnut-sided warblers. *Animal Behaviour* 52: 691–705.

Byers, B. E., and D. E. Kroodsma. 1992. Development of two song categories by chestnut-sided warblers. *Animal Behaviour* 44: 799–810.

Byers, B. E., H. L. Mays, I. R. K. Stewart, and D. F. Westneat. 2004. Extra-pair paternity increases variability in male reproductive success in the chestnut-sided warbler, a socially monogamous songbird (*Dendroica pensylvanica*). *Auk* 121: 788–795.

Canady, R. A., D. E. Kroodsma, and F. Nottebohm. 1984. Population differences in complexity of a learned skill are correlated with the brain space involved. *Proceedings of the National Academy of Sciences, USA* 81: 6232–6234.

Catchpole, C. K., and A. Rowell. 1993. Song sharing and local dialects in a population of the European wren *Troglodytes troglodytes*. *Behaviour* 125: 67–78.

Catchpole, C. K., and P. J. B. Slater. 1995. *Bird Song: Biological Themes and Variations*. Cambridge, England: Cambridge University Press.

Cavitt, J. F., and C. A. Haas. 2000. Brown thrasher (*Toxostoma rufum*). In *The Birds of North America*, no. 557 (ed. by Poole, A., and F. Gill), pp. 1–28. Philadelphia: The Birds of North America, Inc.

Chamberlin, T. C. 1965. The method of multiple working hypotheses; with this method the dangers of parental affection for a favorite theory can be circumvented. *Science* 148: 754–759.

Chilton, G., M. R. Lein, and L. F. Baptista. 1990. Mate choice by female white-crowned sparrows in a mixed-dialect population. *Behavioral Ecology and Sociobiology* 27: 223–227.

Cink, C. L. 2002. Calling and foraging behavior of whip-poor-wills during a lunar eclipse. *Kansas Ornithological Society Bulletin* 53: 39–40.

Cohen, S. M. 1976. Blue jay vocal behavior. Ph.D. thesis, University of Michigan.

Coldren, C. L. 1992. A comparison of the songs of the tufted and black-crested titmice in Texas. M.Sc. thesis, Texas A&M University.

Conant, S. 1972. Visual and acoustic communication in the blue jay, *Cyanocitta cristata* (Aves, Corvidae). Ph.D. thesis, University of Oklahoma.

Cornell Laboratory of Ornithology and Interactive Media. 1991. *Peterson Field Guide to Western Bird Songs*. Boston: Houghton Mifflin.

Craig, W. 1943. The song of the wood pewee *Myiochanes virens* Linnaeus: a study of bird music. *New York State Museum Bulletin* 334: 1–186.

Cramp, S., Ed. 1988. *Handbook of Birds of Europe, the Middle East and North Africa: The Birds of the Western Palearctic*. Oxford: Oxford University Press.

Cunningham, M. A., and M. C. Baker. 1983. Vocal learning in white-crowned sparrows: sensitive phase and song dialects. *Behavioral Ecology and Sociobiology* 13: 256–269.

Derrickson, K. C. 1987. Yearly and situational changes in the estimate of repertoire size in northern mockingbirds (*Mimus polyglottos*). *Auk* 104: 198–207.

Derrickson, K. C., and R. Breitwisch. 1992. Northern mockingbird (*Mimus polyglottos*). In *The Birds of North America,* no. 7 (ed. by Poole, A., P. Stettenheim, and F. Gill), pp. 1–32. Philadelphia and Washington, D.C.: The Academy of Natural Sciences, The American Ornithologists' Union.

Dhondt, A. A., and F. Adriaensen. 1994. Causes and effects of divorce in the blue tit *Parus caeruleus* Linnaeus. *Journal of Animal Ecology* 63: 979–987.

Dickinson, R. 1996. A library of sound. *Living Bird* 15: 16–19.

Dobson, C. W., and R. E. Lemon. 1977a. Bird song as music. *Journal of the Acoustical Society of America* 61: 888–890.

———. 1977b. Markovian versus rhomboidal patterning in the song of Swainson's thrush. *Behaviour* 62: 277–297.

Dorsey, G. A. 1976. Bachman's sparrow: songs and behavior. *The Oriole* 41: 52–58.

Dowsett-Lemaire, F. 1979. The imitative range of the song of the marsh warbler *Acrocephalus palustris,* with special reference to imitations of African birds. *Ibis* 121: 453–468.

Drovetski, S. V., R. M. Zink, S. Rohwer, I. V. Fadeev, E. V. Nesterov, I. Karagodin, E. A. Koblik, and Y. A. Red'kin. 2004. Complex biogeographic history of a Holarctic passerine. *Proceedings of the Royal Society of London Series B—Biological Sciences* 271: 545–551.

Dunning, J. B. 1993. Bachman's sparrow. In *The Birds of North America,* no. 38 (ed. by Poole, A., P. Stettenheim, and F. Gill), pp. 1–16. Philadelphia and Washington, D.C.: The Academy of Natural Sciences, The American Ornithologists' Union.

Dunwiddie, P. W. 1994. *Martha's Vineyard Landscapes: The Nature of Change.* Martha's Vineyard, Massachusetts: The Vineyard Conservation Society and Peter W. Dunwiddie.

Elliott, L., D. Stokes, and L. Stokes. 1997. *Stokes Field Guide to Bird Song: Eastern Region.* Ithaca, New York: Nature Sound Studio.

Ewert, D. N., and D. E. Kroodsma. 1994. Song sharing and repertoires among migratory and resident rufous-sided towhees. *Condor* 96: 190–196.

Felsenstein, J. 1985. Phylogenies and the comparative method. *The American Naturalist* 125: 1–15.

Ficken, M. S., and R. W. Ficken. 1967. Singing behaviour of blue-winged and golden-winged warblers and their hybrids. *Behaviour* 28: 149–181.

Forbush, E. H. 1927. *Birds of Massachusetts and Other New England States.* Boston: Massachusetts Department of Agriculture.

Gaddis, P. K. 1983. Differential usage of song types by plain, bridled and tufted titmice. *Ornis Scandinavica* 14: 16–23.

Garrett, K. L., and J. L. Dunn. 1998. Passerine call notes: an underappreciated character in the study of geographic variation of North American birds? Abstract. St. Louis: North American Ornithological Conference.

Gaunt, S. L. L., L. F. Baptista, J. E. Sánchez, and D. Hernandez. 1994. Song learning as evidenced from song sharing in two hummingbird species (*Colibri coruscans* and *C. thalassinus*). *Auk* 111: 87–103.

Gowaty, P. A., and J. H. Plissner. 1998. Eastern bluebird (*Sialia sialis*). In *The Birds of North America,* no. 381 (ed. by Poole, A., and F. Gill), pp. 1–32. Philadelphia: The Birds of North America, Inc.

Gray, P. M., B. Krause, J. Atema, R. Payne, C. Krumhansl, and L. Baptista. 2001. The music of nature and the nature of music. *Science* 291: 52–56.

Greenewalt, C. H. 1968. *Bird Song: Acoustics and Physiology.* Washington, D.C.: Smithsonian Institution Press.

Grubb, T. C., Jr., and V. V. Pravosudov. 1994. Tufted titmouse (*Parus bicolor*). In *The Birds of North America,* no. 86 (ed. by Poole, A., and F. Gill), pp. 1–16. Philadelphia and Washington, D.C. The Academy of Natural Sciences, The American Ornithologists' Union.

Hafner, D. J., and K. E. Petersen. 1985. Song dialects and gene flow in the white-crowned sparrow (*Zonotrichia leucophrys nuttalli*). *Evolution* 39: 687–694.

Haggerty, T. M., and E. S. Morton. 1995. Carolina wren (*Thryothorus ludovicianus*). In *The Birds of North America,* no. 188 (ed. by Poole, A., and F. Gill), pp. 1–20. Philadelphia and Washington, D.C.: The Academy of Natural Sciences, The American Ornithologists' Union.

Hailman, J. P. 1990. Blue jay mimics osprey. *Florida Field Naturalist* 18: 81–82.

Halkin, S. L., and S. U. Linville. 1999. Northern cardinal (*Cardinalis cardinalis*). In *The Birds of North America,* no. 440 (ed. by Poole, A., and F. Gill), pp. 1–32. Philadelphia: The Birds of North America, Inc.

Hardy, J. W. 1961. Studies in behavior and phylogeny of certain New World jays (Garrulinae). *University of Kansas Science Bulletin* 42: 13–149.

Harris, M. A., and R. E. Lemon. 1972. Songs of song sparrows (*Melospiza melodia*): individual variation and dialects. *Canadian Journal of Zoology* 50: 301–309.

———. 1976. Responses of male song sparrows (*Melospiza melodia*) to neighbouring and non-neighbouring individuals. *Ibis* 118: 421–424.

Hartshorne, C. 1956. The monotony-threshold in singing birds. *Auk* 73: 176–192.

———. 1973. *Born to Sing. An Interpretation and World Survey of Bird Song.* Bloomington: Indiana University Press.

Hauser, M. D. 1996. *The Evolution of Communication.* Cambridge, Massachusetts: MIT Press.

Hauser, M. D., and M. Konishi, eds. 1999. *The Design of Animal Communication.* Cambridge, Massachusetts: MIT Press.

Heinrich, B. 1995. An experimental investigation of insight in common ravens (*Corvus corax*). *Auk* 112: 994–1003.

———. 2000. *Mind of the Raven: Investigations and Adventures with Wolfbirds.* New York: Harper Collins.

Hejl, S. J., J. A. Holmes, and D. E. Kroodsma. 2002. Winter wren (*Troglodytes troglodytes*). In *The Birds of North America,* no. 623 (ed. by Poole, A., and F. Gill), pp. 1–32. Philadelphia: The Birds of North America, Inc.

Herkert, J., D. E. Kroodsma, and J. P. Gibbs. 2001. Sedge wren (*Cistothorus platensis*). In *The Birds of North America,* no. 582 (ed. by Poole, A., and F. Gill). Philadelphia: The Birds of North America, Inc.

Highsmith, R. T. 1989. The singing behavior of golden-winged warblers. *Wilson Bulletin* 101: 36–50.

Hinde, R. A., ed. 1969. *Bird Vocalizations.* London: Cambridge University Press.

Hold, T. 1970. The notation of bird-song: a review and a recommendation. *Ibis* 112: 151–172.

Hopkins, C. D., M. Rossetto, and A. Lutjen. 1974. A continuous sound spectrum analyzer for animal sounds. *Zeitschrift für Tierpsychologie* 34: 313–320.

Hopp, S. L., M. J. Owren, and C. S. Evans, eds. 1998. *Animal Acoustic Communication: Sound Analysis and Research Methods.* New York: Springer-Verlag New York, Inc.

Horn, A. G., M. L. Leonard, L. Ratcliffe, S. A. Shackleton, and R. G. Weisman. 1992. Frequency variation in the songs of black-capped chickadees (*Parus atricapillus*). *Auk* 109: 847–852.

Houlihan, P. W. 2000. The singing behavior of prairie warblers (*Dendroica discolor*). Ph.D. thesis, University of Massachusetts.

Hulse, S. H., and S. C. Page. 1988. Toward a comparative psychology of music perception. *Music Perception* 5: 427–452.

Hunter, L. B. 1998. *Images of Resiliency: Troubled Children Create Healing Stories in the Language of Sandplay.* Palm Beach, Florida: Behavioral Communications Institute.

Huntsman, B. O., and G. Ritchison. 2002. Use and possible functions of large song repertoires by male eastern bluebirds. *Journal of Field Ornithology* 73: 372–378.

Isler, M. L., P. R. Isler, and B. M. Whitney. 1997. Biogeography and systematics of the *Thamnophilus punctatus* (Thamnophilidae) complex. In *Studies in Neotropical Ornithology Honoring Ted Parker* (ed. by Remsen, J. V., Jr.), pp. 355–382. Washington, D.C.: American Ornithologists' Union.

Jellis, R. 1977. *Bird Sounds and their Meaning.* London: British Broadcasting Corporation.

Jones, P., and T. M. Donovan. 1996. Hermit thrush (*Catharus guttatus*). In *The Birds of North America*, no. 261 (ed. by Poole, A., and F. Gill), pp. 1–32. Philadelphia and Washington, D.C.: The Academy of Natural Sciences, The American Ornithologists' Union.

Kennedy, E. D., and D. W. White. 1996. Interference competition from house wrens as a factor in the decline of Bewick's wrens. *Conservation Biology* 10: 281–284.

Keppie, D. M., and R. M. J. Whiting. 1994. American woodcock (*Scolopax minor*). In *The Birds of North America*, no. 100 (ed. by Poole, A., and F. Gill), pp. 1–28. Philadelphia and Washington, D.C.: The Academy of Natural Sciences, The American Ornithologists' Union.

Klicka, J., and R. M. Zink. 1999. Pleistocene effects on North American songbird evolution. *Proceedings of the Royal Society of London,* Series B—*Biological Sciences* 266: 695–700.

Klump, G. M., E. Kretzschmar, and E. Curio. 1986. The hearing of an avian predator and its avian prey. *Behavioral Ecology and Sociobiology* 18: 317–323.

Kreutzer, M. 1974. Stereotypie et variations dans les chants de proclamation territoriale chez le troglodyte (*Troglodytes troglodytes*). *Revue du Comportement Animal* 8: 270–286.

Krieg, D. C. 1971. The behavioral patterns of the eastern bluebird (*Sialia sialis*). *New York State Museum and Science Service Bulletin* 415: 1–139.

Kroodsma, D. E. 1971. Song variations and singing behavior in the rufous-sided towhee, *Pipilo erythrophthalmus oregonus. Condor* 73: 303–308.

———. 1972. Variations in the songs of vesper sparrows in Oregon. *Wilson Bulletin* 84: 173–178.

———. 1973. Coexistence of Bewick's wrens and house wrens in Oregon. *Auk* 90: 341–352.

———. 1974. Song learning, dialects, and dispersal in the Bewick's wren. *Zeitschrift für Tierpsychologie* 35: 352–380.

———. 1975. Song patterning in the rock wren. *Condor* 77: 294–303.

———. 1976. The effect of large song repertoires on neighbor recognition in male song sparrows. *Condor* 78: 97–99.

————. 1977a. Correlates of song organization among North American wrens. *American Naturalist* 111: 995–1008.

————. 1977b. A re-evaluation of song development in the song sparrow. *Animal Behaviour* 25: 390–399.

————. 1979. Vocal dueling among male marsh wrens: evidence for ritualized expressions of dominance/subordinance. *Auk* 96: 506–515.

————. 1980. Winter wren singing behavior: a pinnacle of song complexity. *Condor* 82: 356–365.

————. 1981. Geographical variation and functions of song types in warblers (Parulidae). *Auk* 98: 743–751.

————. 1984. Songs of the alder flycatcher (*Empidonax alnorum*) and willow flycatcher (*Empidonax traillii*) are innate. *Auk* 101: 13–24.

————. 1985a. Development and use of two song forms by the eastern phoebe. *Wilson Bulletin* 97: 21–29.

————. 1985b. Geographic variation in songs of the Bewick's wren (*Thryomanes bewickii*): a search for correlations with avifaunal complexity. *Behavioral Ecology and Sociobiology* 16: 143–150.

————. 1988. Song types and their use: developmental flexibility of the male blue-winged warbler. *Ethology* 79: 235–247.

————. 1989a. Male eastern phoebes (Tyrannidae, Passeriformes) fail to imitate songs. *Journal of Comparative Psychology* 103: 227–232.

————. 1989b. Two North American song populations of the marsh wren reach distributional limits in the central Great Plains. *Condor* 91: 332–340.

————. 1996. A song of their own. *Living Bird Quarterly* 15: 10–17.

————. 1999. Making ecological sense of song development by songbirds. In *The Design of Animal Communication* (ed. by Hauser, M. D., and M. Konishi), pp. 319–342. Cambridge, Massachusetts: MIP Press.

Kroodsma, D. E., D. J. Albano, P. W. Houlihan, and J. A. Wells. 1995. Song development by black-capped chickadees (*Parus atricapillus*) and Carolina chickadees (*P. carolinensis*). *Auk* 112: 29–43.

Kroodsma, D. E., M. C. Baker, L. F. Baptista, and L. Petrinovich. 1985. Vocal "dialects" in Nuttall's white-crowned sparrow. *Current Ornithology* 2: 103–133.

Kroodsma, D. E., R. C. Bereson, B. E. Byers, and E. Minear. 1989. Use of song types by the chestnut-sided warbler: evidence for both intra- and inter-sexual functions. *Canadian Journal of Zoology* 67: 447–456.

Kroodsma, D. E., and R. A. Canady. 1985. Differences in repertoire size, singing behavior, and associated neuroanatomy among marsh wren populations have a genetic basis. *Auk* 102: 439–446.

Kroodsma, D. E., and M. Konishi. 1991. A suboscine bird (eastern phoebe, *Sayornis phoebe*) develops normal song without auditory feedback. *Animal Behaviour* 42: 477–488.

Kroodsma, D. E., W.-c. Liu, E. Goodwin, and P. A. Bedell. 1999. The ecology of song improvisation as illustrated by North American sedge wrens. *Auk* 116: 373–386.

Kroodsma, D. E., W. R. Meservey, A. L. Whitlock, and W. M. Vander Haegen. 1984. Blue-winged warblers (*Vermivora pinus*) "recognize" dialects in type II but not type I songs. *Behavioral Ecology and Sociobiology* 15: 127–131.

Kroodsma, D. E., and E. H. Miller, eds. 1982. *Acoustic Communication in Birds,* 2 volumes. New York: Academic Press.

———. 1996. *Ecology and Evolution of Acoustic Communication in Birds.* Ithaca, New York: Cornell University Press.

Kroodsma, D. E., and H. Momose. 1991. Songs of the Japanese population of the winter wren (*Troglodytes troglodytes*). *Condor* 93: 424–432.

Kroodsma, D. E., and L. D. Parker. 1977. Vocal virtuosity in the brown thrasher. *Auk* 94: 783–785.

Kroodsma, D. E., and R. Pickert. 1980. Environmentally dependent sensitive periods for avian vocal learning. *Nature* 288: 477–479.

———. 1984. Sensitive phases for song learning: effects of social interaction and individual variation. *Animal Behaviour* 32: 389–394.

Kroodsma, D. E., J. Sánchez, D. W. Stemple, E. Goodwin, M. L. da Silva, and J. M. E. Vielliard. 1999. Sedentary life style of neotropical sedge wrens promotes song imitation. *Animal Behaviour* 57: 855–863.

Kroodsma, D. E., and J. Verner. 1978. Complex singing behaviors among *Cistothorus* wrens. *Auk* 95: 703–716.

———. 1987. Use of song repertoires among marsh wren populations. *Auk* 104: 63–72.

Kroodsma, D. E., J. M. E. Vielliard, and F. G. Stiles. 1996. Study of bird sounds in the Neotropics: urgency and opportunity. In *Ecology and Evolution of Acoustic Communication in Birds* (ed. by Kroodsma, D. E., and E. H. Miller), pp. 269–281. Ithaca, New York: Cornell University Press.

Kroodsma, D. E., K. Wilda, V. Salas, and R. Muradian. 2001. Song variation among *Cistothorus* wrens, with a focus on the Mérida wren. *Condor* 103: 855–861.

Kroodsma, D. E., R. W. Woods, and E. A. Goodwin. 2002. Falkland Island sedge wrens (*Cistothorus platensis*) imitate rather than improvise large song repertoires. *Auk* 119: 523–528.

Labov, W. 1994. *Principles of Linguistic Change*. Cambridge, Massachusetts: Blackwell.

Lambrechts, M. M. 1996. Organization of birdsong and constraints on performance. In *Ecology and Evolution of Acoustic Communication in Birds* (ed. by Kroodsma, D. E., and E. H. Miller), pp. 305–320. Ithaca, New York: Cornell University Press.

Lanyon, W. E. 1969. Vocal characters and avian systematics. In *Bird Vocalizations* (ed. by Hinde, R. A.), pp. 291–310. London: Cambridge University Press.

―――. 1978. Revision of the *Myiarchus* flycatchers of South America. *Bulletin of the American Museum of Natural History* 161: 427–628.

Lawrence, L. d. K. 1954. The voluble singer of the tree-tops. *Audubon Magazine* 56: 109–111.

Lein, M. R. 1978. Song variation in a population of chestnut-sided warblers (*Dendroica pensylvanica*): its nature and suggested significance. *Canadian Journal of Zoology* 56: 1266–1283.

Lemon, R. E. 1971. Analysis of song of red-eyed vireos. *Canadian Journal of Zoology* 49: 847–854.

Lemon, R. E., C. W. Dobson, and P. G. Clifton. 1993. Songs of American redstarts (*Setophaga ruticilla*): sequencing rules and their relationship to repertoire size. *Ethology* 93: 198–210.

Liu, W.-c. 2001. Song development and singing behavior of the chipping sparrow (*Spizella passerina*) in western Massachusetts. Ph.D. thesis, University of Massachusetts.

MacDougall-Shackleton, E. A., and S. A. MacDougall-Shackleton. 2001. Cultural and genetic evolution in mountain white-crowned sparrows: song dialects are associated with population structure. *Evolution* 55: 2568–2575.

Marler, P. 1955. Characteristics of some animal calls. *Nature* 176: 6–7.

―――. A comparative approach to vocal learning: song development in white-crowned sparrows. *Journal of Comparative and Physiological Psychology* 71: 1–25.

―――. 2000. Origins of music and speech: insights from animals. In *The Origins of Music* (ed. by Wallin, N., B. Merker, and S. Brown), pp. 31–48. Cambridge, Massachusetts: The MIT Press.

Marler, P., and S. Hope. 2004. The structure and function of bird calls. In *Nature's Music* (ed. by Marler, P., and H. Slabberkorn). New York: Academic Press.

Marler, P., and D. Nelson. 1992. Neuroselection and song learning in birds: species universals in a culturally transmitted behavior. *Seminars in Neuroscience* 4: 415–423.

Marler, P., and S. Peters. 1982. Developmental overproduction and selective attrition: new processes in the epigenesis of birdsong. *Developmental Psychology* 15: 369–378.

Marler, P., and H. Slabberkorn, eds. 2004. *Nature's Music.* New York: Academic Press.

Marler, P., and M. Tamura. 1962. Song dialects in three populations of the white-crowned sparrow. *Condor* 64: 368–377.

———. 1964. Culturally transmitted patterns of vocal behavior in sparrows. *Science* 146: 1483–1486.

Mathews, F. S. 1967. *Field Book of Wild Birds and Their Music.* New York: Dover Publications, Inc.

Mazur, K. M., and P. C. James. 2000. Barred owl (*Strix varia*). In *The Birds of North America,* no. 508 (ed. by Poole, A., and F. Gill), pp. 1–32. Philadelphia: The Birds of North America, Inc.

McCarty, J. P. 1996. Eastern wood-pewee (*Contopus virens*). In *The Birds of North America,* no. 245 (ed. by Poole, A., and F. Gill), pp. 1–20. Philadelphia and Washington, D.C.: The Academy of Natural Sciences, The American Ornithologists' Union.

McGraw, K. J., G. E. Hill, R. Stradi, and R. S. Parker. 2001. The influence of carotenoid acquisition and utilization on the maintenance of species-typical plumage pigmentation in male American goldfinches (*Carduelis tristis*) and northern cardinals (*Cardinalis cardinalis*). *Physiological and Biochemical Zoology* 74: 843–852.

McGregor, P. K., Ed. 1992. *Playback and Studies of Animal Communication.* New York: Plenum Press.

Mennill, D. J., L. M. Ratcliffe, and P. T. Boag. 2002. Female eavesdropping on male song contests in songbirds. *Science* 296: 873.

Merritt, P. G. 1985. Song function and the evolution of song repertoires in the northern mockingbird, *Mimus polyglottos.* Ph.D. thesis, University of Miami.

Miller, A. H. 1934. The vocal apparatus of some North American owls. *Condor* 36: 201–213.

Monroe, B. L., Jr., and C. G. Sibley. 1993. *A World Checklist of Birds*. New Haven, Connecticut: Yale University Press.

Morse, D. H. 1967. The contexts of songs in black-throated green and Blackburnian warblers. *Wilson Bulletin* 79: 64–74.

———. 1970. Territorial and courtship songs of birds. *Nature (London)* 226: 659–661.

Morton, E. 1975. Ecological sources of selection on avian sounds. *American Naturalist* 108: 17–34.

———. 1982. Grading, discreteness, redundancy, and motivation-structural rules. In *Acoustic Communication in Birds*. Vol. 1 (ed. by Kroodsma, D. E., and E. H. Miller), pp. 183–212. New York: Academic Press.

Morton, E. S., B. J. M. Stutchbury, J. S. Howlett, and W. H. Piper. 1998. Genetic monogamy in blue-headed vireos and a comparison with a sympatric vireo with extrapair paternity. *Behavioral Ecology* 9: 515–524.

Mulligan, J. A. 1966. Singing behavior and its development in the song sparrow, *Melospiza melodia*. *University of California Publications in Zoology* 81: 1–76.

National Geographic Society. 1987. *Field Guide to the Birds of North America*. Washington, D.C.: National Geographic Society.

Nealen, P. M., and D. J. Perkel. 2000. Sexual dimorphism in the song system of the Carolina wren *Thryothorus ludovicianus*. *Journal of Comparative Neurology* 418: 346–360.

Nice, M. M. 1943. Studies in the life history of the song sparrow. II. The behavior of the song sparrow and other passerines. *Transactions of the Linnaean Society of New York* 6: 1–328.

Nordby, J. C., S. E. Campbell, and M. D. Beecher. 2001. Late song learning in song sparrows. *Animal Behaviour* 61: 835–846.

———. 2002. Adult song sparrows do not alter their song repertoires. *Ethology* 108: 39–50.

Nottebohm, F. 1969. The song of the Chingolo, *Zonotrichia capensis*, in Argentina: description and evaluation of a system of dialects. *Condor* 71: 299–315.

———. 1972. The origins of vocal learning. *American Naturalist* 106: 116–140.

Otter, K. A., L. Ratcliffe, M. Njegovan, and J. Fotheringham. 2002. Importance of frequency and temporal song matching in black-capped chickadees: evidence from interactive playback. *Ethology* 108: 181–191.

Owings, D. H., and E. S. Morton. 1998. *Animal Vocal Communication: A New Approach*. Cambridge: Cambridge University Press.

Payne, K., P. Tyack, and R. Payne. 1983. Progressive changes in the songs of humpback whales (*Megaptera novaeangliae*): a detailed analysis of two seasons in Hawaii. In *Communication and Behavior of Whales. AAAS Selected Symposia Series* (ed. by Payne, R.), pp. 9–57. Boulder, Colorado: Westview Press.

Payne, R. B. 1986. Bird songs and avian systematics. In *Current Ornithology* (ed. by Johnston, R. J.), pp. 87–126. New York: Plenum Publishing Corporation.

———. 1996. Song traditions in indigo buntings: origin, improvisation, dispersal, and extinction in cultural evolution. In *Ecology and Evolution of Acoustic Communication in Birds* (ed. by Kroodsma, D. E., and E. H. Miller), pp. 198–200. Ithaca, New York: Cornell University Press.

Payne, R. B., and P. Budde. 1979. Song differences and map distances in a population of Acadian flycatchers. *Wilson Bulletin* 91: 29–41.

Pepperberg, I. M. 1999. *The Alex Studies. Cognitive and Communicative Abilities of Grey Parrots.* Cambridge, Massachusetts: Harvard University Press.

Peterson, R. T. 1947. *A Field Guide to the Birds: Giving Field Marks of all Species Found East of the Rockies.* Boston: Houghton Mifflin Co.

———. 1980. *A Field Guide to the Birds East of the Rockies.* Boston: Houghton Mifflin.

Petrinovich, L., T. Patterson, and L. F. Baptista. 1981. Song dialects as barriers to dispersal: a re-evaluation. *Evolution* 35: 180–188.

Porter, D., and A. Neuringer. 1984. Music discrimination by pigeons. *Journal of Experimental Psychology: Animal Behavior Processes* 10: 138–148.

Ridgely, R. S., and G. Tudor. 1994. *The Birds of South America.* Vol. 2, *The Suboscine Passerines.* Austin, Texas: University of Texas Press.

Rising, J. D. 1983. The Great Plains hybrid zones. *Current Ornithology* 1: 131–157.

Rivers, J. W., and D. E. Kroodsma. 2000. Singing behavior of the hermit thrush. *Journal of Field Ornithology* 71: 467–471.

Roberts, J. B. 1969. Vocalizations of the rufous-sided towhee, *Pipilo erythrophthalmus oregonus. Condor* 71: 257–266.

Ross, D. L., Jr., and B. M. Whitney. 1995. *Voices of Costa Rican Birds. Caribbean Slope.* Ithaca, New York: Library of Natural Sounds, Cornell Laboratory of Ornithology.

Rothstein, S. I., and R. C. Fleischer. 1987. Vocal dialects and their possible relation to honest status signaling in the brown-headed cowbird. *Condor* 89: 1–23.

Runfeldt, S., and J. C. Wingfield. 1985. Experimentally prolonged sexual activity in female sparrows delays termination of reproductive activity in their untreated mates. *Animal Behaviour* 33: 403–410.

Sallabanks, R., and F. C. James. 1999. American robin (*Turdus migratorius*). In *The Birds of North America,* no. 462 (ed. by Poole, A., and F. Gill), pp. 1–28. Philadelphia: The Birds of North America, Inc.

Saunders, A. A. 1951. *A Guide to Bird Songs.* Garden City, New York: Doubleday & Company, Inc.

Schroeder, D. J., and R. H. Wiley. 1983a. Communication with repertoires of song themes in tufted titmice. *Animal Behaviour* 31: 1128–1138.

———. 1983b. Communication with shared song themes in tufted titmice. *Auk* 100: 414–424.

Searcy, W. A., and K. Yasukawa. 1996. Song and female choice. In *Ecology and Evolution of Acoustic Communication in Birds* (ed. by Kroodsma, D. E., and E. H. Miller), pp. 454–473. Ithaca, New York: Cornell University Press.

Sebeok, T. A., Ed. 1977. *How Animals Communicate.* Bloomington, Indiana: Indiana University Press.

Sedgwick, J. A. 2001. Geographic variation in the song of willow flycatchers: differentiation between *Empidonax traillii adastus* and *E. t. extimus. Auk* 118: 366–379.

Sibley, C. G., and J. E. Ahlquist. 1990. *Phylogeny and Classification of Birds of the World.* New Haven: Yale University Press.

Sibley, C. G., J. E. Ahlquist, and B. L. Monroe, Jr. 1988. A classification of the living birds of the world based on DNA-DNA hybridization studies. *Auk* 105: 409–423.

Sibley, D. A. 2000. *The Sibley Guide to Birds.* New York: Alfred A. Knopf.

Smith, C. F. 1975. Distribution ecology of barred and great horned owls in relation to human distribution. M.Sc. thesis, University of Connecticut.

Smith, S. M. 1991. *The Black-capped Chickadee: Behavioral Ecology and Natural History.* Ithaca, New York: Cornell University Press.

———. 1993. Black-capped chickadee. In *The Birds of North America,* no. 39 (ed. by Poole, A., P. Stettenheim, and F. Gill), pp. 1–20. Philadelphia and Washington, D.C.: The Academy of Natural Sciences, The American Ornithologists' Union.

Smith, W. J. 1977. *The Behavior of Communicating.* Cambridge, Massachusetts: Harvard University Press.

———. 1988. Patterned daytime singing of the eastern wood-pewee (*Contopus virens*). *Animal Behaviour* 36: 1111–1123.

Snow, B. K. 1977. Territorial behavior and courtship of the male three-wattled bellbird. *Auk* 94: 623–645.

Snow, D. 1968. The singing assemblies of little hermits. *The Living Bird* 7: 47–55.

Snow, D. W. 1973. Distribution, ecology and evolution of the bellbirds (*Procnias*, Cotingidae). *Bulletin of the British Museum of Natural History* 25: 369–391.

Sousa, C. M. 1999. How male singing behaviors affect extra-pair copulations in a population of American robins. Senior honors thesis, University of Massachusetts.

Spector, D. A. 1991. The singing behavior of yellow warblers. *Behaviour* 117: 29–52.

———. 1992. Wood-warbler song systems: a review of paruline singing behaviors. *Current Ornithology* 9: 199–238.

———. 1994. Definition in biology: the case of "bird song." *Journal of Theoretical Biology* 168: 373–381.

Spector, D. A., L. K. McKim, and D. E. Kroodsma. 1989. Yellow warblers are able to learn songs and situations in which to use them. *Animal Behaviour* 38: 723–725.

Staicer, C. A. 1989. Characteristics, use and significance of two singing behaviors in Grace's warbler, *Dendroica graciae. Auk* 106: 49–63.

———. 1996a. Acoustical features of song categories of the Adelaide's warbler (*Dendroica adelaidae*). *Auk* 113: 771–783.

———. 1996b. Honest advertisement of pairing status: evidence from a tropical resident wood-warbler. *Animal Behaviour* 51: 375–390.

Staicer, C. A., D. A. Spector, and A. G. Horn. 1996. The dawn chorus and other diel patterns in acoustic signaling. In *Ecology and Evolution of Acoustic Communication in Birds* (ed. by Kroodsma, D. E., and E. H. Miller), pp. 426–453. Ithaca, New York: Cornell University Press.

Stap, D. 1995. The bird sessions. *Audubon* 97: 56–63, 117.

———. 2000. The bell of the rainforest. *Living Bird Quarterly* 19: 20–24.

———. 2005. *Birdsong*. New York: Charles Scribner's Sons.

Stein, R. C. 1963. Isolating mechanisms between populations of Traill's flycatchers. *Proceedings of the American Philosophical Society* 107: 22–50.

Stiles, F. G., and A. F. Skutch. 1989. *A Guide to the Birds of Costa Rica*. Ithaca, New York: Cornell University Press.

Stoddard, P. K., M. D. Beecher, C. L. Horning, and M. S. Willis. 1990. Strong neighbor-stranger discrimination in song sparrows. *Condor* 92: 1051–1056.

Suthers, R. A. 1999. The motor basis of vocal performance in songbirds. In *The Design of Animal Communication* (ed. by Hauser, M. D., and M. Konishi), pp. 37–62. Cambridge, Massachusetts: MIT Press.

Tarvin, K. A., and G. E. Woolfenden. 1999. Blue jay (*Cyanocitta cristata*). In *The Birds of North America,* no. 469 (ed. by Poole, A., and F. Gill), pp. 1–32. Philadelphia: The Birds of North America, Inc.

Thielcke, G. 1970. *Vogelstimmen.* Berlin: Springer-Verlag.

Thorpe, W. H. 1961. *Bird Song: The Biology of Vocal Communication and Expression in Birds.* London: Cambridge University Press.

Todt, D., and H. Hultsch. 1996. Acquisition and performance of song repertoires: ways of coping with diversity and versatility. In *Ecology and Evolution of Acoustic Communication in Birds* (ed. by Kroodsma, D. E., and E. H. Miller), pp. 79–96. Ithaca, New York: Cornell University Press.

Tramo, J. J. 2001. Music of the hemispheres. *Science* 291: 54–56.

Tyler, W. M. 1946. Northern blue jay. In Life histories of North American jays, crows, and titmice (ed. by Bent, A. C.), pp. 32–52. Washington, D.C.: *Smithsonian Institution United States National Museum Bulletin* 191.

Verner, J. 1976. Complex song repertoire of male long-billed marsh wrens in eastern Washington. *Living Bird* 14: 263–300.

Watanabe, S., and M. Nemoto. 1998. Reinforcing property of music in Java sparrows (*Padda oryzivora*). *Behavioural Processes* 43: 211–218.

Watanabe, S., and K. Sato. 1999. Discriminative stimulus properties of music in Java sparrows. *Behavioural Processes* 47: 53–57.

Weisman, R., L. Ratcliffe, I. Johnsrude, and T. A. Hurly. 1990. Absolute and relative pitch production in the song of the black-capped chickadee. *Condor* 92: 118–124.

Whitney, C. L. 1981a. Patterns of singing in the varied thrush: I. The similarity of songs within individual repertoires. *Zeitschrift für Tierpsychologie* 57: 131–140.

———. 1981b. Patterns of singing in the varied thrush II. A model of control. *Zeitschrift für Tierpsychologie* 57: 141–162.

———. 1985. Serial order in wood thrush song. *Animal Behaviour* 33: 1250–1265.

———. 1989. Geographical variation in wood thrush song: a comparison of samples recorded in New York and South Carolina. *Behaviour* 111: 49–60.

———. 1990. Avoidance of song matching in the wood thrush: a field experiment. *Wilson Bulletin* 103: 96–101.

Wickstrom, D. C. 1982. Factors to consider in recording avian sounds. In

Acoustic Communication in Birds. Vol. 2 (ed. by Kroodsma, D. E., and E. H. Miller), pp. 1–52. New York: Academic Press.

Wildenthal, J. L. 1965. Structure in primary song of the mockingbird (*Mimus polyglottos*). *Auk* 82: 161–189.

Wiley, R. H. 1991. Associations of song properties with habitats for territorial oscine birds of eastern North America. *American Naturalist* 138: 973–993.

Wing, A. H. 1951. Notes on the song series of a hermit thrush in the Yukon. *Auk* 68: 189–193.

Wolf, L. L. 1977. Species relationships in the avian genus *Aimophila*. *Ornithological Monographs* 23.

Young, J. 2001. *Exploring Natural Mystery: Kamana One (Kamana Naturalist Training Program).* Shelton, Washington: Owlink Media.

Zeleny, L. 1977. Song of hope for the bluebird. *National Geographic* 151: 855–865.

Zimmer, K. J., A. Whittaker, and D. C. Oren. 2001. A cryptic new species of flycatcher (Tyrannidae: *Suiriri*) from the cerrado region of central South America. *Auk* 118: 56–78.

Zink, R. M., and G. F. Barrowclough. 1984. Allozymes and song dialects: a reassessment. *Evolution* 38: 444–448.

Zink, R. M., and J. D. Weckstein. 2003. Recent evolutionary history of the fox sparrows (genus: *Passerella*). *Auk* 120: 522–527.

Zollinger, S. A., and R. A. Suthers. 2004. Motor mechanisms of a vocal mimic: implications for birdsong production. *Proceedings of the Royal Society of London Series B-Biological Sciences* 271: 483–491.

Index

NOTE: In **bold** type is the most important information for key species in the book: the track number(s) where that particular species can be heard on the CD, the range of pages for the section that focuses on that particular species, and the text that describes the CD track(s). In *italics* is the page number for sonagrams.

jay, blue, 182–84, 387
  robin, American, 35–36
Alaska, 7, 9, 217, 222, 224, 287, 311
Alauda arvensis. See skylark, Eurasian
Alberta, 134, 217, 222, 224, 266
Albright, Darilyn, 134
Aleutian Islands, Alaska, 222
Allen, Arthur A., 344
Alps, 222
Amazon River, 39, 81, 298, 305
American Ornithologists' Union, 134, 416
Amethyst Brook Conservation Area (Amherst,
    Mass.), 256
Amherst, Mass., 132, 136, 152, 168, 180, 277,
    302, 325, 336, 340
Ammodramus
  henslowii. See sparrow, Henslow's
  savannarum. See sparrow, grasshopper
amplitude, 4, 269, 406
Andes, 103, 114, 115, 130, 133, 298
Antarctica, 39
antbirds, 80, 88–90
Anthus spragueii. See pipit, Sprague's
antshrike, slaty (*Thamnophilus punctatus*),
    88
antthrushes, 88
antwrens, 88
apes, great, 44, 80, 272
Aphelocoma coerulescens. See scrub-jay,
    Florida
Appalachian Mountains, 21, 153, 217, 222,
    266
Arapongas, Brazil, 94, 95
Archbold Biological Station (Fla.), 162
Arctic, 120, 178, 281, 255, 277, 287
Argentina, 114, 115
Arguedas, Mario, 98
Arizona, 21, 152, 165, 174, 176, 256
Arkansas, 110
arrangements of songs. *See* singing patterns
    and styles
Asia, 39, 179, 220, 223, 224
Atlantic Ocean, 81, 120, 133, 137, 143, 222

Australia, 39, 179
awaking calls. *See* calls, call notes

babbling (subsong, practice song)
  bellbird, three-wattled, **tracks 25, 27,** 96,
    101
  cardinal, northern, 361, 365
  flycatcher, alder, **track 21,** *82,* 83
  flycatcher, willow, 84
  human, **track 9,** 15, 369–70
  jay, blue, 187
  musicality of, 274
  owl, barred, 343
  role in song learning, 87
  by songbirds, 274
  sparrow, song, 58, 63
  sparrows, migrant, 277
  titmouse, tufted, 167, 174
  vireo, red-eyed, 298
  warbler, chestnut-sided, 154
  wren, Bewick's, **track 11,** 15, 18, *19,* 369–70
  wren, Carolina, **track 95,** 354–55
  wren, marsh, 110
  wren, sedge, 110, 356
  wren, winter, 223
babies, juveniles. *See also* babbling (subsong,
    practice song); lab-reared birds;
    learned song; yearlings, behavior of
  bellbird, three-wattled, 93, 96, 101
  chickadee, 137–39, 143–44
  learning processes, 87
  musicality of songs, 274
  practice by. *See* babbling (subsong, practice
    song)
  wren, Bewick's, 15, 18–20
  wren, marsh, 127–28, 109–10
Bach, Johann Sebastian, 274
bachelor songs
  mockingbird, northern, 74, 78, 373–74
  vireo, red-eyed, 302
  warbler, chestnut-sided, 153, 156
  whip-poor-will, 296
Bae, Rolf, 255

Borror Laboratory of Bioacoustics, Ohio State University (Columbus, Ohio), 152, 225

Borror, Donald, 225, 268

borrowed songs. *See* mimicry (borrowed songs)

Bosques, Pedro, 92

Boston, Mass., 136, 313

Botaurus lentiginosus. See bittern, American

Boughey, Michael, 198

brains. *See* physiology of song

Branta canadensis. See goose, Canada

Brasilia, Brazil, 114, 115, 378

Braulio Carillo National Park (Costa Rica), 90–93

Braun, Mike, 134

Brazil, 88, 94, 95, 101, 114, 115, 116, 117, 118, 305

breathing. *See* physiology of song

Brewster, William, 137

British Columbia, 136, 142, 217, 222, 223, 224, 266

British National Sound Archives (London, U.K.), 98

Bryce Canyon National Park (Utah), 10

Bubo virginianus. See owl, great horned

Budney, Greg, 89, 98, 99, 139, 207, 208, 344

Bullfrog, **track 38** (in background), 340

bunting
    indigo (*Passerina cyanea*), 98, 121, 134
    lazuli (*Passerina amoena*), 121, 134

Burma, 222

Burroughs, John, 255

Busby Swamp (Savoy, Mass.), 145–51

Buteo
    jamaicensis. See hawk, red-tailed
    lineatus. See hawk, red-shouldered
    platypterus. See hawk, broad-winged

Buzzy dialect (white-crowned sparrow), **track 16**, 45–47, *47*, 51–52, 54–55, 372

Byers, Bruce, 90, 93, 141, 142, 152, 155, 156

Cabin Lake, Ore., 202

Calidris
    alba. See sanderling
    bairdii. See sandpiper, Baird's
    ferruginea. See sandpiper, curlew
    melanotos. See sandpiper, pectoral

California, 7, 21, 42, 44, 48, 52, 53, 96, 127, 128, 130, 165, 174, 202, 203, 217, 222, 320

California Institute of Technology (Pasadena, Calif.), 87

Callipepla californica. See quail, California

calls, call notes, awaking and roosting
    cardinal, northern, 360
    mockingbird, northern, 172, 360
    robin, American, 29–30, 32, 360
    thrush, wood, 172, 360
    chickadee, black-capped, 135, 381
    defined, 37–38
    mockingbird juvenile, 375
    as song, 35, 356
    towhee, eastern, **tracks 49, 51**, 157, *160*, 162
    towhee, western, **track 50**, 158
    use of, in mimicry, 43
    vireo, red-eyed, 300
    wren species, 224
    wren, Carolina, 356

Campbell, Liz, 64

Canada, 7, 9, 278, 287

Canady, Rick, 127

canary, island (*Serinus canaria*), 57, 248, 275, 322, 324

canasteros, 88

Caprimulgidae, 412

Caprimulgiformes, 412

Caprimulgus
    carolinensis. See chuck-will's-widow
    vociferus. See whip-poor-will

Caracas, Venezuela, 114

cardinal, northern (*Cardinalis cardinalis*), **tracks 96–97**, 24, 32, 41, 68, 70, 71, 73, 75, 76, 78, 79, 120, 168, 233, 234, 248, 251, 284, 292, 304, 327, 329, 335, 341, 352, 353, **357–65**, *358*, **400**, 414

Craig, Wallace, 308, 310, 312

crakes, 89

Crane Lake, Sask., 133

crane, sandhill (*Grus canadensis*), 232, 320

creeper, brown (*Certhia americana*), 180

crickets, 316

crow, American (*Corvus brachyrhynchos*), 130, 169, 177, 179, 191, 302, 363

Cuculus canorus. See cuckoo, common

cuckoo, common (*Cuculus canorus*), 275

curlew, 276, 287

    bristle-thighed (*Numenius tahitiensis*), 276

Cyanocitta

    cristata. See jay, blue

    stelleri. See jay, Steller's

cycles per second, 3–4. *See also* pitch

"Cycle Utah," 10–11

Dana, Mass., 313

da Silva, Maria Luisa, 114

Davis, Irby, 344

dawn songs. *See also* daytime songs; evening songs; night songs

    bluebird, eastern, **track 87**, 329–34, *331*

    cardinal, northern, 360–64

    community singing, 272–73

    intensity of, 226

    jay, blue "calls," **track 56**, 189–90, *190*

    mockingbird, northern, **track 19**, 76–78, *77*

    robin, American, **track 13**, 30–33, *31*

    sparrow, Bachman's, 228–31

    sparrow, Brewer's, **tracks 84–85**, 321–24, *323*

    sparrow, chipping, **tracks 81–82**, 316–20, *315*

    sparrow, field, **track 6**, 6–7, *7*

    thrasher, sage, 204–7

    thrush, hermit, 267

    towhee, eastern, 384

    towhee, spotted, 159

    ubiquity of, 232–33

warbler, chestnut-sided, **tracks 45–46**, 146–50, *146*

woodcock flight song, **track 73**, 284–85, *279*

wood-pewee, eastern, **track 79**, 306–10, *306*

wood-pewee, western, **track 80**, *311*

wren, Carolina, **track 92**, 346–48, *348*

wren, eastern winter, 216

wren, sedge, 113

daytime songs. *See also* dawn songs; evening songs; night songs

    bluebird, eastern, **track 86**, 332–33, *328*

    chickadee, black-capped, 136

    robin, American, **track 12**, 24–27, *26*

    sparrow, Bachman's, 226, 236

    sparrow, Brewer's, **track 83**, 320, *321*, 324–25

    sparrow, chipping, **track 82**, 316, 318

    sparrow, field, **track 6**, 6–7, *7*

    towhee, eastern, 384

    towhee, spotted, 159

    warbler, chestnut-sided, **tracks 47–48**, 150–51, *153*

    wood-pewee, eastern, **track 78**, 305–6, *306*

    wood-pewee, western, *311*

    wren, sedge, **track 32,** 112

    wren, winter, 215–16

Dendroica

    adelaidae. See warbler, Adelaide's

    chrysoparia. See warbler, golden-cheeked

    coronata. See warbler, yellow-rumped

    discolor. See warbler, prairie

    graciae. See warbler, Grace's

    nigrescens. See warbler, black-throated gray

    pensylvanica. See warbler, chestnut-sided

    petechia. See warbler, yellow

    pinus. See warbler, pine

    virens. See warbler, black-throated green

Derrickson, Kim, 73

dialects. *See also* geographical song variation; matched countersinging; territories, territorial defense

    bellbird, three-wattled, 90–94, 100

boundary limits, 51–55
chickadee, black-capped, 120, 136–44
and dispersal from next, 48–55
formation of, 52–53
gender differences, 120, 153–55
human, 119–20
minidialects, microdialects, 61–63, 67, 318–19
reasons for studying, 119–20
sparrow, song, 67
sparrow, white-crowned, 42–55
titmouse, tufted, 173
towhee, spotted, 159
ubiquity of among songbirds, 80
uniform songs over large areas, 136–37, 143–44
warbler, chestnut-sided, 120, 153–55
wren, eastern winter, 216–17
wren, marsh, 119–20, 120–35
Discovery Park (Seattle, Wash.), 43, 57, 64, 67, 142
dispersal from nest
impacts of dialect boundaries, 48–55, 97, 143
and song-learning behaviors, 15, 18, 20–21, 48–55, 62, 67, 143, 161, 174, 319
DNA analysis
bluebird, eastern, 334
corvids, 179
sparrow, white-crowned, 53–54
warbler, chestnut-sided, 156
wren, marsh, 134
DNA-encoded songs. *See* inborn (innate, DNA-encoded) song
dog, 181
Dolichonyx oryzivorus. See bobolink
Doolittle Lake, Neb., 131, 133
doraditos, 88
dove, mourning (*Zenada macroura*), 35, 36, 362, 363
dowitcher, 287
short-billed (*Limnodromus griseus*), 276

Drakes dialect (white-crowned sparrow), 48
Dryocopus pileatus. See woodpecker, pileated
duck, 43, 343
ruddy (*Oxyura jamaicensis*), 321
wood (*Aix sponsa*), 278
duet. *See also* female birdsong
barbet, prong-billed, 93
cardinal, northern, **track 97,** 356–65, *358*
owl, barred, **tracks 88–90,** 336–46, *338*
thrush, wood, **track 70,** 246, *249*
Thryothorus wrens, **track 94,** 335
wren, Carolina, **track 92,** 346–56, *348*
Dumetella carolinensis. See catbird, gray
dunlins, 276, 287
Dunning, Barney, 225, 233
duration of sound (sonagrams), 3

earthcreepers, 88
Ecuador, 88, 114, 344
Edberg, Dawn, 210
Edgartown, Martha's Vineyard, Mass., 140, 141
El Salvador, 344
elaenias, 88
Elanoides forficatus. See kite, swallow-tailed
Elliott, Lang, 339
Emberizidae, 413
Empidonax
alnorum. See flycatcher, alder
difficilis. See flycatcher, Pacific coast
occidentalis. See flycatcher, cordilleran
traillii. See flycatcher, willow
energetics. *See* fasting
Enfield, Mass., 313
England, 193, 223
Eremophila alpestris. See lark, horned
Ericson Lake, Neb., 132, 133
Erithacus rubecula. See robin, European
Estrildidae, 274
Eurasia, 223, 224, 282
Europe, 39, 220, 222, 223, 224
Evans, Bill, 345

flourishes
- thrush, hermit, **track 71,** 257–59, *258*, 268
- thrush, wood, **track 70,** 239–50, *238, 243, 249*

flycatcher species. *See also* bellbird, three-wat-tled; phoebe, eastern
- absence of dialects, 80
- innate (DNA-encoded) songs, 43, 80–89, 116
- Old World (songbirds), 417
- songs as reliable species indicators, 88–89

flycatcher, 22, 23, 24, 37, 41, 43, **79–89,** 116, 226, 273, 304, 305, 356, 417
- alder (*Empidonax alnorum*), **tracks 20–21,** 43, **79–89,** *82,* 92, 95, 145, **374,** 412
  - adult and fledgling songs, 82–84
  - babbling, practice song, 83
  - inborn songs, 43, 84
  - lab-reared birds, 81–84
- cordilleran (*Empidonax occidentalis*), 92
- great crested (*Myiarchus crinitus*), 233, 347
- Pacific coast (*Empidonax difficilis*), 92
- western, 92. *See* flycatcher, Pacific coast; fly-catcher, cordilleran
- willow (*Empidonax traillii*), **track 22,** 43, **79–89,** *82,* 92, **374–75,** 412
  - adult songs, 82–84
  - inborn songs, 43, 84
  - lab-reared birds, 81–84

foliage-gleaners, 88

Fort Lawton (Seattle, Wash.), 57

France, 223

frequency (hertz; Hz). *See also* aesthetics of birdsong, musicality; pitch
- annual drop in, among bellbirds, 97–99, 101
- chickadee dialects, 139–42
- harmonic relationships, 199
- jay, blue, fundamental note, 183
- octaves, 4–5
- owl, barred, 336, 337–39, *338,* 342, 345
- representation for, 3–5
- of sound produced by two voice boxes, 200, 201, 248–50, 337, 360–61
- thrush, hermit, pitch changes, 262–66
- thrush, wood, flourishes, 247–49
- viewing on sonagrams, 2–11

frogs, 145, 232, 287

Frost, Robert, 256

Fuertes, Louis Aggasiz, 343

Fulica americana. See coot, American

Furnariidae, 80

Gabelli, Fabian, 114

Gallinago delicata. See snipe, Wilson's

Gaviidae, 411

Gaviiformes, 411

Gay Head, Martha's Vineyard, Mass., 139, 140, 141, 143

geese, 43

genetic differences. *See also* DNA analysis
- and dialect boundary limits, 52–54
- studying using nonlearned songs, 80–81, 88–89, 311–12
- wrens, eastern and western marsh, 127–34

geographical distribution. *See also* dialects; dispersal from nest
- cardinal, northern, 357
- and song dialects, 21, 119–20
- thrush, hermit, 266–67
- vireo, red-eyed, 302
- warbler, chestnut-sided, 155
- wood-pewee, eastern, 305, 311
- wren, Carolina, 350
- wren, winter, 222–23

geographical song variation. *See also* dialects; Great Plains fracture zones
- east-west continental differences
  - sparrow, song, 57, 67
  - wren, marsh, 130–35
  - wren, winter, 217, 223
- relative absence of
  - chickadee, black-capped, 136–37
  - sparrow, chipping, 315

hermit (hummingbird), 89

Hertz, H. R., 4

hertz (Hz). *See* frequency; pitch

Highsmith, Tod, 152

Hill, Chris, 142

Himalaya Mountains, 39, 222, 223

Hirundo rustica. See swallow, barn

hisselly songs (American robin), **track 13**, 28–31, *31*

Holland, Mich., 122, 125, 269

Holyoke Mountain Range, Mass., 256

hooting sound (barred owl), 336–46

Hope College (Holland, Mich.), 122, 130

hormones, 41, 85, 303, 337

horneros, 88

Houlihan, Peter, 152

Houston, Stuart, 133

Hudson Bay, Canada, 222

Hudson River, N.Y., 109, 123, 128

humans
    audible sound, 4
    babbling, 15, 369–70
    dialects, 119–20

hummingbirds and song learning, 43, 102

Hylocichla mustelina. See thrush, wood

hypothesis
    "bellbirds learn," 100–101
    "dialects limit dispersal," 51–54
    as an educated guess, 142–43
    other guesses, 21, 37, 66, 75, 78, 143, 144, 154, 156, 161, 164, 184, 233, 290, 296, 342, 360

Hz (hertz). *See* frequency; pitch

Iceland, 222, 224

Icterus
    bullockii. See oriole, Bullock's
    galbula. See oriole, Baltimore

Idaho, 217

Illinois, 103, 111, 114, 123, 125, 127, 128, 179, 357

immediate variety singing style, 225–26

improvised song. *See also* inborn song; invented song; learned song
    and musicality of birdsong, 272
    possible reasons for, 118, 161
    robin, American, 37
    snowflake strategy, 111
    wren, North American sedge, 54, 67–68, 109–11, 114–16

inborn (innate, DNA-encoded) song. *See also* improvised song; invented song; learned song
    acquisition of, 80–88
    flycatcher species, 43, 78–79, 116
    learning by suboscines, 89–102
    phoebe, eastern, 43, 84–88
    as "real" songs, 356

innate song. *See* inborn song

India, 222

Indiana, 116

Indiana University (Bloomington, Ind.), 199

individuals, recognized by human ear
    owl, barred, 336–46
    robin, American, 35–36
    sparrow, chipping, 315–16
    thrush, wood, 242, 254
    vireo, red-eyed, 300
    warbler, chestnut-sided, 146–50

individuals recognizing each other, song sparrow, 57

Innis, Doug, 142

insect, 116, 156, 169, 315, 320, 322, 326, 346, 350

International Ornithological Congress, 277

introductory passages (Bachman's sparrow), 228

invented song. *See also* improvised song; inborn song; learned song
    thrasher, brown, 196, 199
    vireo, red-eyed, 302
    wren, sedge, 114

Iowa, 110, 132, 136, 357

Iran, 222

"chatbursts," 352
dawn singing, 76–78
estimating repertoire size, 71–73
impressing females, 74–75
mimicry by, 68–79
night listeners, 73–74
night singing, 68–71
repertoire variety, 69–70
why mimic?, 75
Molothrus ater. See cowbird, brown-headed
monotony, avoidance of, by songbirds, 273
Montague, Mass., 152, 288, 313
Montana, 136, 217
Monteverde dialect (three-wattled bellbird),
    track 24, 90–93, *91,* 96–99
moonlight, and singing rates, 296–97
Morehead City, N.C., 125
Moriarty, Mike, 211
Morocco, 222
Morse code, 29, 33
Morse, Doug, 152
Morton, Gene, 21, 100, 152, 347
Moscow, Russia, 222, 277
Mount Monadnock, N.H., 255, 267
Mount Orient (Amherst, Mass.), 256–59, 262,
    267
movies, with wrong sounds, 9
Muradian, Roldan, 114
music and birdsong, impact on mood and
    health, 275
musicality, beauty of birdsong. *See* aesthetics
    of birdsong, musicality
mute birds (vultures), 39, 177
Myiarchus crinitus. See flycatcher, great crested

Nantucket, Mass., 142
Naples, Fla., 68, 70, 346
Nebraska, 111, 114, 116, 121, 130–34, 136, 311
    marsh wren geographical divide, 130–32
neighbors. *See also* dialects; learned song;
        matched countersinging; territories,
        territorial defense

learning songs from, 43
type versus repertoire song matches,
    65–66
nesting cycles, blue jay, 186
neurons. *See* physiology of song
Nevada, 53, 174
New England, 84, 120, 136, 145, 153, 161, 163,
    164, 170, 214, 237, 239, 256, 259, 305,
    350
New Guinea, 39, 282
New Hampshire, 136, 255
New World, 39, 43, 114, 179, 220, 223, 224,
    253
New York, 56, 92, 109, 123, 125, 127, 128, 136,
    161, 179, 193, 198, 326, 343, 344, 350
New Zealand, 39
Newfoundland, 7, 9, 220, 222
Nicaraguan dialect (three-wattled bellbird),
    track 28, 100, 101
Nice, Margaret Morse, 56
Nicolle Flats, Sask., 133, 134
night heron, 353
night songs. *See also* dawn songs; daytime
        songs; evening songs
    impact of moonlight, 296–97
    mockingbird, northern, **track 18,** 69–73, *72*
    thrasher, sage, 203, 204–6, 210
    whip-poor-will, **track 75,** 289–95, *289*
nighthawk, common (*Chordeiles minor*)
    sage thrasher, mimicry of, 203, 206, 207, 211,
        214
nightingale
    common (*Luscinia megarhynchos*), 275
    Virginia, 357. *See* cardinal, northern
nightingale-thrush (*Catharus* spp.), 90, 239
    evening songs, 253
nightjars, 178, 225, 232, 273, 288, 297
    persistence and stamina of, 178, 287–97
nomadic species, 55, 67–68, 110–11, 115. *See
    also* migration
nonlearned (innate) song. *See* inborn (innate,
        DNA-encoded) song

reptiles, 267
resident populations. *See also* nonmigratory
    species
    and development of song dialects, 144
    and repertoire size, 161, 163
    and song-learning behaviors, 118, 161
Respighi, Ottorino, 274
Reynard, George, 344
Rhode Island, 136
rhythm
    bellbird, three-wattled, 94, 376
    mockingbird, northern, 75
    and musicality, 272
    owl, barred, 336
    phoebe, eastern, 86, 375
    robin, American, 25
    sapsucker, yellow-bellied, 367
    on sonagrams, 2, 5–6, 8–9
    sparrow, Bachman's, 228
    thrasher, brown, 193
    warbler, chestnut-sided, 146–48
    woodcock, American, 278–81, 394
    wren, Bewick's, 22
    wren, eastern winter, 216
    wren, winter, 215–17
Rivers, Jim, 256
Robbins, Mark, 344
robin
    American (*Turdus migratorius*), **tracks
        12–13**, 1, 3, 22, **23–36**, *26, 31*, **37–41**,
        145, 166, 168, 180, 187, 239, 277, 295,
        304, 316, 327, 329, 360, 362, 363,
        370–71, 413, 416
        ancestry and song, 39–41
        caroled songs, 24–28
        detailed listening, 23–36
        estimating repertoire size, 33–34
        functions of songs and calls, 38–39
        hawk alarm, 35–36
        hisselly songs, 28 35
        individuality, 35–36
        mechanisms of singing, 25, 41

song development, 37–38
    clay-colored (*Turdus grayi*), 39
    European (*Erithacus rubecula*), 416–17
    evolutionary history of, 39–40
    mountain (*Turdus plebejus*), **track 15**, 39,
        372, 413
    pale-vented (*Turdus obsoletus*), 39
    sooty (*Turdus nigrescens*), 39
    white-throated (*Turdus assimilis*), **track 14**,
        39, *40*, 41, **371–72**, 413
Rockefeller University Field Research
    Center (Millbrook, N.Y.), 57, 106, 127,
    193
Rocky Mountains, 145, 222
Rollin, Noble, 297
rooftop sound recordings, 165–71
roosting calls. *See* calls, call notes
Ryukyu Islands (Japan), 282

Salas, Viviana, 114
Salpinctes obsoletus. See wren, rock
San Francisco Bay, Calif., 22, 46
Sánchez, Julio, 90, 93, 99, 114, 404
sanderling (*Calidris alba*), 276, 287
sandpiper
    Baird's (*Calidris bairdii*), flight song, 277
    curlew (*Calidris ferruginea*), 276
    pectoral (*Calidris melanotos*), 276
Santa Cruz Island, Calif., 21
sapsucker, yellow-bellied (*Sphyrapicus varius*),
    track 3, 2, *3*, 5, 6, **367**, 412
Saskatchewan, 81, 115, 121, 133, 134, 216, 217,
    222, 224, 266
Saskatoon, Sask., 133
Saunders, Aretas A., 228, 326
Sauvie Island, Ore., 21
Sayornis phoebe. See phoebe, eastern
scales, linear versus logarithmic, 4–5
Scandinavia, 222
Schoenberg, Arnold, 274
Schulenberg, Tom, 344
Schwartz, Paul, 344

song playback
jay, blue, 189
owl, barred, 341
sparrow, Bachman's, 231, 237
sparrow, song, 64–65, 67
thrasher, brown, 199
thrush, wood, 250
wren, marsh, 123
song-sharing (song sparrow), 66
song type matches, behavioral responses,
65–66
sora (*Porzana carolina*), sage thrasher
mimicry of, 203–7, *205, 209*
Sorenson, Eric, 210
sound. *See also* physiology of song; song
calls versus songs, 37–38, 356
components of, 3–4
evolutionary factors, 39–40
functional analysis, 38–39
Sound Analysis Pro software, 410
sound analyzer, continuous spectrum, 106,
193
sound recording
equipment, 13, 68, 104, 165, 402–9
software for, 409–10
sound transmission, 10–11, 25, 39, 73–74,
136, 178, 295
and sharp recordings, 406
Souris River, N.D., 112
South America, 39, 79, 80, 81, 88, 89, 114, 115,
179, 224, 233, 276, 298, 305, 349, 357
suboscine species, 79–80, 81, 88
South Carolina, 225, 228
South Dakota, 121, 136, 163, 164, 311
South Sioux City, Neb., 132
sparrow, 22, 275
American tree (*Spizella arborea*), 277
Bachman's (*Aimophila aestivalis*), **tracks
65–66**, 9, 178, **225–37**, *229*, 270, 272,
350, **391**, 413
beautiful songs of, 4–9, 227
dawn singing, 225, 228

diversity of songs, 228–31
favored song sequences, 235–36
graphical analysis, 234–36
matched countersinging, 226–27, 231–33
musicality of, 178, 227–28, 237, 270, 272
repertoire size, 225, 234–35
singing rate, 235–36
two-part songs, 231
unique singing style, 225–26
the unknowns, 225–28
Brewer's (*Spizella breweri*), **tracks 83–85**, 7,
10, 202, 313, **320–25**, *321, 323*, **397**,
411, 413
daytime songs, 320–21
feverish dawn singing, 321–25
chipping (*Spizella passerina*), **tracks 81–82**,
7, 42, 54, 119, 144, 162, 168, 177, 191,
192, 226, 288, **313–20**, *315*, 325, 363,
396–97, 411, 413
dawn singing, 226, 317–18
daytime singing, 318
individuality of songs, 315–16
repertoire size, 191, 226
singing competitions, 317–19
singing rate, 288
song learning behaviors and "microdialects," 42, 54, 162, 319
English. *See* sparrow, house
field (*Spizella pusilla*), **track 6**, 6, *7*, 193,
270, **368**, 411, 413
fox (*Passerella iliaca*), **track 7**, 7–9, *8*, 277,
368–69, 413
large-billed and red, **track 7**, 7–9, *8*,
368–69, 413
grasshopper (*Ammodramus savannarum*),
175
Henslow's (*Ammodramus savannarum*), 175
house (*Passer domesticus*), 325
Java (*Padda oryzivora*), 274
mountain white-crowned (*Zonotrichia leucophrys*), 53
song (*Melospiza melodia*), **track 17**, 43,

55–68, *59*, *60*, 108, 155, 173, 191, 192, 207, 211, 212, 213, 224, 226, 252, 273, 284, 288, 303, 327, 341, 350, **372–73**, 414
   dispersal, 62, 67
   early studies, 56–57
   microdialects, 67
   repertoire size, 58–61
   sage thrasher mimicry of, 207, 211–13
   song-learning behaviors, 61–63
   song-sharing behaviors, 61–68
   type versus repertoire song matches, 65–66
  swamp (*Melospiza georgiana*), 57, 109, 123, 145, 341
  vesper (*Pooecetes gramineus*), 56
  white-crowned (*Zonotrichia leucophrys*), **track 16**, 42, 43, **44–55**, *47*, 67, 96, 97, 119, 177, 191, 192, 193, 277, 288, 335, **372**, 414
   controversy, 52–54
   dialect regions, 44–48
   dialects, 45–54
   dialects and dispersal, 48–52
   females, song preferences, 51
   female songs, 335
   repertoire size, 192
   singing rate, 288
   song-learning behaviors, 48–50
  white-throated (*Zonotrichia albicollis*), **track 4**, 4–6, *4*, 145, 269, 335, 363, **367**, 414
   female songs, 335
   repertoire size, 4–7
species differences. *See also* DNA analysis
  impact on song development, 109–11, 163–65
  sister species, 79–80
  wrens, eastern and western marsh, 127–34
  wrens, winter, 223–24
Spector, David, 152
speech, **track 9**, 15, 42, 119, 188, 335, **369–70**

Spencer, Iowa, 132
Sphyrapicus varius. See sapsucker, yellow-bellied
spinetails, 88
Spizella
  arborea. See sparrow, American tree
  breweri. See sparrow, Brewer's
  passerina. See sparrow, chipping
  pusilla. See sparrow, field
squirrel, red, 216, 359
stamina
  nightjar species, 178, 287–97
  whip-poor-will, 292–95
Staicer, Cindy, 152
Stanton, Neb., 132, 133
starling, European (*Sturnus vulgaris*), 24, 55, 325
  mimicry by, 43
  perfect pitch, 274
Stein, Robert Carrington, 344
Stemple, Dave, 82, 83, 89, 90, 92, 93, 96, 99, 114
Stiles, Gary, 89
Strigidae, 412
Strigiformes, 412
Stokes CD, 339–40
Strix varia. See owl, barred
"Studies in the Life History of Song Sparrows" (Nice), 56
Sturnella
  magna. See meadowlark, eastern
  neglecta. See meadowlark, western
Sturnus vulgaris. See starling, European
suboscines, 79–81, 84, 87–90, 97, 101, 412
  bellbird, three-wattled, 89–102
  flycatchers, 79–89
  inborn songs, 79–89
  learned songs, 89–102
  song acquisition, 80–89, 89–102, 311
  species of, 79–80, 88
subsong. *See* babbling (subsong, practice song)